THIRD EDITION

Designing Effective *Mathematics Instruction*

A Direct Instruction Approach

MARCY STEIN
University of Washington, Tacoma

JERRY SILBERT
National Center to Improve the Tools of Educators (NCITE)

DOUGLAS CARNINE
University of Oregon

Merrill
Prentice Hall

Merrill, an Imprint of Prentice Hall
Upper Saddle River, New Jersey   Columbus, Ohio

Library of Congress Cataloging-in-Publication Data

Stein, Marcy,
    Designing effective mathematics instruction : a direct instruction
approach / Marcy Stein, Jerry Silbert, Douglas Carnine. — [3rd ed.]
      p.   cm.
    Rev. ed. of: Direct instruction mathematics / Jerry Silbert,
Douglas Carnine, Marcy Stein. 2nd ed. ©1990.
    Includes bibliographical references and index.
    ISBN 0-13-596651-5
    1. Mathematics—Study and teaching (Elementary)   I. Silbert,
Jerry.   II. Carnine, Douglas.   III. Silbert, Jerry.   Direct
instruction mathematics.   IV. Title.
QA135.5.S54   1997
372.7'2—dc21   96-39673
                                          CIP

Cover photo: Marjory Dressler
Editor: Ann C. Davis
Production Editor: Julie Peters
Production Coordination: Betsy Keefer
Design Coordinator: Julia Zonneveld Van Hook
Cover Designer: Proof Positive/Farrowlyne Associates, Inc.
Production Manager: Laura Messerly
Illustrations: The Clarinda Company
Director of Marketing: Kevin Flanagan
Advertising/Marketing Coordinator: Julie Shough

This book was set in Optima by The Clarinda Company and was printed and bound by Courier/Kendallville,
Inc. The cover was printed by Phoenix Color Corp.

 © 1997 by Prentice-Hall, Inc.
Upper Saddle River, New Jersey 07458

Earlier editions, entitled *Direct Instruction Mathematics* © 1990, 1981 by Prentice-Hall, Inc.

Printed in the United States of America

10 9

ISBN: 0-13-596651-5

PRENTICE-HALL INTERNATIONAL (UK) LIMITED, *LONDON*
PRENTICE-HALL OF AUSTRALIA PTY. LIMITED, *SYDNEY*
PRENTICE-HALL CANADA INC., *TORONTO*
PRENTICE-HALL HISPANOAMERICANA, S.A., *MEXICO*
PRENTICE-HALL OF INDIA PRIVATE LIMITED, *NEW DELHI*
PRENTICE-HALL OF JAPAN, INC., *TOKYO*
PEARSON EDUCATION ASIA PTE. LTD., *SINGAPORE*
EDITORA PRENTICE-HALL DO BRASIL, LTDA., *RIO DE JANEIRO*

Preface

Mathematics instruction is becoming increasingly holistic in nature, stressing the application of mathematics in a variety of contexts. Although the goals of current approaches to mathematics instruction are reasonable, often the methods for achieving those goals are lacking. The need for improvement in mathematics instruction has been well documented by national, even international, evaluations. Moreover, research has also suggested that many teachers are ill-prepared to meet the needs of a diverse student population. We have received numerous requests from teachers who found their preparation to teach mathematics to be inadequate. Teachers were particularly vocal about the lack of specific guidance in how to support students who have difficulty learning mathematics. This text explains the inadequacies of some instructional programs and provides teachers with the information needed to modify the programs.

Although we have found the procedures suggested in this book to be effective, we do not claim they are panaceas. Implementing our suggestions requires hard work on the part of the teacher. It is our hope that the systematic procedures and teaching strategies recommended here will stimulate the development of even better techniques.

FEATURES OF THIS BOOK

Designing Effective Mathematics Instruction: A Direct Instruction Approach includes these features:

- A description of essential skills and procedures for teaching these skills
- Procedures for evaluating, selecting, and modi-

fying mathematics programs to meet the needs of all students

- Techniques for effectively presenting lessons, including techniques for pacing tasks, motivating students, and diagnosing and correcting errors
- Suggestions for classroom organization that maximize the amount of time students spend engaged in math instruction
- A Topics of Interest table that summarizes how the book might be used by primary, intermediate, and remedial teachers.

STRUCTURE OF THIS BOOK

The book is organized into two parts: Part I, Perspective, and Part II, Skills and Concepts. Chapter 1 in the Perspective section discusses the philosophy and techniques of direct instruction in general; Chapter 2 examines how these direct instruction techniques can be integrated into a school mathematics program; and Chapter 3 provides a brief review of relevant research on effective mathematics instruction.

The Skills and Concepts chapters in Part II are the heart of the book. Each chapter covers a specific skill area: counting skills, symbol identification and place value, basic facts, addition, subtraction, multiplication, division, problem solving, fractions, decimals, percent, telling time, money, measurement, study skills, and geometry. These chapters include suggestions for introducing each skill or concept, procedures for teaching specific strategies, and analyses of the major problem types within each skill area. Each chapter also contains an Instructional Sequence and Assessment Chart. The sequence is designed to minimize student failure and to provide the practice and review necessary for student mastery. The assessment items can serve as a diagnostic test, and as a basis for constructing short-term goals for Individual Education Plans (IEPs).

Also included in some skills and concepts chapters are descriptions of the ways in which various skills are presented in commercial programs and discussions of how and why these procedures must often be modified in order to meet the needs of diverse students. (These discussions will be particularly useful to the increasing number of classroom teachers who teach students with disabilities in the general education classroom.)

REVISIONS IN THE THIRD EDITION

One of the most obvious changes in this edition is the research sections in the individual chapters have been replaced by an entire chapter on relevant research in mathematics instruction. This chapter includes research on instructional design, teacher effectiveness research, and research on direct instruction. In addition to the research chapter, readers are encouraged to read the article in Appendix A that describes a comprehensive national study. This article documents the effectiveness of many of the direct instruction mathematics strategies presented in this text. Appendix B has been added to this edition to address questions that are frequently asked about the implementation of direct instruction.

Since the publication of the second edition, a new elementary (SRA) direct instruction mathematics program, *Connecting Math Concepts,* has been published. *Designing Effective Mathematics Instruction* was edited to include some of the strategies from that program. The chapter on basic facts, as well as the chapters on problem solving, fractions, and multiplication were reorganized to include some of the strategies designed for that program. Other less extensive revisions were made throughout the book to incorporate feedback from various instructors and students. Finally, a comprehensive Instructor's Manual that includes answers to the application items is available.

ACKNOWLEDGMENTS

Foremost among the many people to whom we are grateful are the direct instruction teachers who prove that math failure is not inevitable. We are also grateful to Zig Engelmann, whose melding of logical analysis and empiricism has resulted in the development of numerous highly effective mathematics programs. Many of the procedures described in this book were derived from the *DISTAR Arithmetic, Corrective Mathematics, Core Concepts in Mathematics,* and the new *Connecting Math Concepts* series authored by Engelmann and his colleagues. Special thanks go to Ronda Simmons, Mary Godwin Austen, Russell Batten, and Betsy Keefer who worked diligently on the third edition. Additional ideas have been contributed by our colleagues and students, including Randy Williams, Kathy Jungjohahn, Linda Carnine, Bernadette Kelly, Linda Olen, Frank Falco, and Wes Becker. We are particularly indebted to our reviewers, Dan Fennerty, Central Washington University; Harry L. Fullwood, East Texas State University; Eric D. Jones, Bowling Green State University; Ann L. Lee, Bloomsburg University; and Dorothy Spethmann, Dakota State University, who provided us with invaluable feedback and suggestions. We also appreciate the efforts of Lori McGinty, Kathy Thomas, Debbie Evans, Janet Thomas, Mardi Klotz, Marciana Liquid, Mary Grannon, and Susan Wayne.

Topics of Interest

Contents

7 Addition 99

8 Subtraction 128

9   *Multiplication*   *152*

10   *Division*   *179*

11   *Problem Solving*   *216*

12 Fractions   255

Formats for Teaching Major Skills

PART ONE

Perspective

CHAPTER 1

Direct Instruction

Many mathematics texts discuss the philosophy and theory of mathematics instruction. Most methods texts provide activities and games involving mathematics. Few, however, deal extensively with the instructional specifics. *Direct Instruction Mathematics* focuses on what teachers can do to maximize the likelihood that students will learn. The learning theory underlying this book is elaborated in detail elsewhere (Engelmann & Carnine, 1982) and cannot be adequately summarized here. A theoretical framework, often referred to as *constructionist,* does provide a general notion about our assumptions. The term *constructionist* implies that students seek meaning from learning situations. The learner tries continually to "make sense" out of what a teacher says and does. The way in which teachers organize the learning environment determines how successful learners will be in constructing the meaning that teachers intend to convey. Direct instruction provides a comprehensive set of prescriptions for organizing instruction so that students acquire, retain, and generalize new learning in as humane, efficient, and effective a manner as possible.

The need for effective instruction is growing rapidly. While many variables influence students' acquisition of mathematics, these variables are certainly central: (1) instructional design, (2) presentation techniques, and (3) organization of instruction. These three variables are *all* essential ingredients of a successful mathematics program. A well-designed program and a good teacher will not produce significant gains if instructional time is too limited. Similarly, a well-designed program and adequate instructional time will not lead to success if the teacher is not skilled. Finally, adequate time and a skilled teacher will not adequately serve students if the materials are poorly designed.

As will become apparent later in this book, no single type of instructional program, presentation technique, or classroom organization is appropriate at all times. Direct instruction, therefore, takes on different characteristics, depending on the students being taught and the objective. Direct instruction, when used with intermediate-grade-level students at average or above average skill levels, is characterized by a heavy emphasis on student-directed independent work. On the other hand, the use of direct instruction with primary-level students or with intermediate-level students who have encountered difficulty in earlier grades is characterized by a more structured, more teacher-directed environment. For these students, teachers need to ask many questions, provide immediate feedback and corrections, and praise frequently.

Before describing direct instruction procedures in more detail, we need to consider their application to instructionally sophisticated students. Direct instruction procedures are intended to make learning mathematics easier by breaking down complex tasks into their component skills, teaching these components, and demonstrating to students how the components are combined. This simplification of complex tasks is particularly important for instructionally naive students, but can also accelerate the learning of instructionally sophisticated students if used appropriately. A potential misuse of direct instruction with instructionally sophisticated students results from unnecessarily slowing their speed of learning. Unnecessary practice and redundant explanations waste valuable teaching time. This situation can be avoided by giving students an initial assessment. The teacher should provide instruction for only those exercises that students cannot do. In short, instructionally sophisticated students benefit from direct instruction if they are moved through a mathematics program at an optimal rate and are provided no more structure than is necessary.

INSTRUCTIONAL DESIGN

To effectively teach mathematics, teachers need to construct the kinds of lessons and to develop the specific teaching procedures that will best meet their students' needs. In addition, teachers often need to be able to modify or supplement certain aspects of commercial programs. This book assists teachers in acquiring these skills. We assume that almost all children can learn mathematics if lessons are designed so that students can readily understand the concepts that are being presented. The following nine steps outline what is necessary to design an effective instructional program.

1. Specify long- and short-term objectives.
2. Devise procedural strategies.
3. Determine necessary preskills.
4. Sequence skills.
5. Select a teaching procedure.
6. Design teaching formats.
7. Select examples.
8. Specify practice and review.
9. Design progress-monitoring procedures.

The following discussion outlines the critical aspects of instructional design that are the basis for the procedures outlined in this text.

Specify Long- and Short-term Objectives

The first step in designing an instructional program is to specify long-term objectives, i.e., what students are supposed to be able to do when they have completed the program. Based on the long-term objec-

tives, the short-term objectives can be written. These are needed to identify smaller "chunks" of content that must be taught and to provide guidance in constructing progress indicators. In order for teachers to determine when these objectives have been met, performance indicators must be stated as specific, observable behaviors. In a performance indicator, the type of task is specified, along with accuracy and rate criteria. For example, a performance indicator for single-digit addition might be worded as: Given 25 single-digit addition problems, a first grade student will correctly solve at least 22 in one minute with no more than one error. In contrast, an objective stating that students will understand the concept of addition is nonspecific, nonobservable, and, therefore, unacceptable.

Devise Procedural Strategies

Whenever possible, instructional programs should teach explicit strategies designed to enable students to work a broad set of examples. The strategies need to be generalizable as well as explicit. Devising explicit strategies, also called cognitive routines, is fairly simple for computation problems, but very difficult for application problems, as illustrated by word problems. (See Chapter 11 for examples of such strategies.) This text, while by no means comprehensive, contains procedural strategies for a range of basic mathematics skills that teachers can incorporate into their daily mathematics instruction.

Determine Necessary Preskills

Instruction should be sequenced so that the component skills of a strategy are taught before the strategy itself is introduced. The component skills, therefore, can be referred to as preskills. For example, in order to solve a percent problem (What is 23% of 67?), the student must be able to (1) convert percent to a decimal (23% = .23), (2) work multiplication problems with multi-digit factors (.23 × 67), and (3) place the decimal point correctly in the product (15.41).

$$
\begin{array}{r}
67 \\
\times.23 \\
\hline
201 \\
134 \\
\hline
15.41
\end{array}
$$

Sequence Skills

The order in which information and skills are introduced affects the difficulty students have in learning them. Sequencing involves determining the optimum order for introducing new information and strategies. Three sequencing guidelines are (1) preskills of a strategy are taught before the strategy; (2) easy skills are taught before more difficult ones; and (3) strategies and information that are likely to be confused are not introduced consecutively.

Within any given area of mathematics, one can predict which problem types will cause students the most difficulty. Generally, the more steps in a strategy and the greater the similarity of the strategy to other previously taught strategies, the more difficult the problem will be. Teachers should carefully analyze various problem types for their relative difficulty. The need for a careful analysis of problem types can be illustrated by looking at column subtraction. Obviously, problems that require renaming (borrowing) are more difficult than problems that do not require renaming. However, not all problems that require renaming are of equal difficulty. A problem such as $3,002 - 89$ is significantly more difficult than a problem such as $364 - 128$ because of the difficulty students demonstrate in renaming numbers with zeroes.

Another example of the need for careful analysis occurs when teaching teen numerals. Primary grade teachers are well aware of the problems low-performing students have identifying 11, 12, 13, and 15. What is not as obvious is why students have these problems. Two possible causes are irregularity and the direction of reading (beginning with the digit on the right). Students usually read numerals from left to right (21 is read by starting with the tens number—"twenty-one"), but they must read teen numerals from right to left. For example, when identifying 16, students start with the number represented by 6 on the right before saying the suffix "teen." Similarly, students read 14 as **four**teen" not "teen four." In addition to this general problem, the numerals 11, 12, 13, and 15 are irregular. While the numeral 16 is read "sixteen," and 14 is read "fourteen," 15 is not read "fiveteen" nor is 13 read "threeteen." Our sequencing recommendation for symbol identification (not for counting exercises) is to introduce the regular, thus easier, teens (14, 16, 17, 18, and 19) before the more difficult ones (11, 12, 13, and 15). Sequencing from easy to difficult reduces student errors and frustration, which is a major goal of direct instruction.

The third sequencing guideline is to separate the introduction of information and/or strategies that are likely to be confused. The more similar two tasks or symbols are, the more likely students are to confuse them. For example, students are likely to confuse the numerals 6 and 9. Thus, 6 and 9 should not be introduced consecutively. Likewise, the skip counting series for 6s and 4s are quite similar in that they both contain 12, 24, and 36 (6, **12,** 18, **24,** 30, **36** and 4, 8, **12,** 16, 20, **24,** 28, 32, **36**). Introducing these series consecutively would be likely to cause confusion on the part of some students.

Sometimes potential areas of confusion are hard to predict. For example, in an earlier edition of *DISTAR Arithmetic 1** the authors introduced the symbol 5 immediately after the symbol 4. They noted that a significant number of low-performing students confused 4 and 5. Upon analysis, they realized the reason for the confusion was that the names of the two numerals begin with the same sound— *four* and *five*. In revising the program, the authors separated the introduction of 4 and 5, thereby reducing student errors.

Select a Teaching Procedure

There are three basic types of tasks in mathematics instruction: motor tasks, labeling tasks, and strategy tasks. The majority of tasks for young children are motor and labeling tasks; tasks introduced to older students consist primarily of strategy tasks.

MOTOR TASKS In a motor task, students must memorize and articulate a rule ("You must end up with the same number on this side AND the other side" or a series of numbers (skip counting by 6), or they must execute a precise movement (writing numerals). A four-step procedure is used to teach motor tasks: model, lead, test, delayed test. A *model* is simply a demonstration by the teacher. For example, the teacher models skip counting by saying, "My turn to count by 6s: 6, 12, 18, 24, 30." In a *lead* the teacher helps students make the desired response, saying, "Count by 6s with me. Get ready, 6, 12, 18, 24, 30." Teachers continue to lead the students until the students appear able to make the response independently. (The lead may also consist of a physical prompt. For example, the teacher guides the student's hand as the student writes numerals.)

The *test* consists of the teacher asking the students to make the response without any assistance.

DISTAR Arithmetic I is an instructional program based on a direct instruction approach. The *DISTAR Math Program* was co-authored by Siegfried Engelmann and Doug Carnine (Chicago: Science Research Associates, 1969, 1975). A new six-level basal mathematics series also based on direct instruction theory is called *Connecting Math Concepts* (Engelmann, Carnine, Engelmann, and Kelly, 1991–1995).

The *delayed test* occurs several minutes later, after "interference" in the form of a different task. For example, after teaching students to say the first part of a 6 series (6, 12, 18, 24, 30), the teacher might present an exercise on fractions and then retest the students on the 6 series. If the students are able to respond correctly, the teacher goes on to the next task in the lesson. If the students do not respond correctly, the teacher repeats the model-lead-test steps. Thus, instruction is individualized; lower-performing students receive extra practice, while higher-performing students move on to other tasks.

LABELING TASKS Labeling tasks are those in which the student must say the word that correctly labels an object (e.g., saying "four" when shown the symbol 4, saying "triangle" when shown that form, and saying "dime" when shown that coin). In labeling tasks, students are assumed to have the motor skill needed to produce the response. They must just learn when to make the response—say "four" when they see a 4 but not when they see a 5. The procedure for teaching labeling tasks involves three steps: (1) model, (2) alternating test, and (3) delayed test. The *model* involves the teacher pointing to the symbol, telling the students what it is called, and having the students repeat the label. The teacher then proceeds to the *alternating test* pattern, alternating between the new example and other previously taught examples. In the alternating pattern, the number of previously taught examples between presentations of the new example gradually increases. The teacher might present the new example, a review example, the new example, two review examples, the new example, and then three review examples. For instance, if x is the new example and a, b, and c are review examples, the sequence of an alternating test might look like this: x a x b a x a c b x. (Note that the review examples should not be presented in the same order each time.) The teacher follows the alternating pattern until the students respond correctly to the new example after three or four previously introduced examples are presented. This alternating pattern is very important because it requires the students to remember the response to the new example and to discriminate the new example from other examples. Gradually increasing the intervals for which students are required to remember the new response builds student retention of the new examples and at the same time minimizes the probability of failure. If a student makes an error, the teacher returns to the beginning of the pattern. The *delayed test* simply consists of the teacher asking the students to identify the new example later in the lesson. If the students respond incorrectly, as with motor tasks, the teacher returns to earlier steps, in this case, the model and alternating test pattern.

STRATEGY TASKS Strategy tasks are those that require the integration of a series of sequential steps to form a generalizable strategy. Strategies are taught by using a model, guided practice, and a test procedure.

The *model* consists of a demonstration to the students of how to work the problem. This model step differs from those used in teaching motor or labeling tasks because, in this case, the teacher asks questions to prompt each step.

In the *guided practice* step, the teacher prompts the students less, although she still asks them strategy-based questions as they work the problem. The structured guidance is gradually faded until the students are eventually working problems on their own, the *test*. This step includes supervised independent work, in which students work problems independently while the teacher carefully monitors their work.

Design Formats

Once the appropriate teaching procedure (motor, labeling, or strategy task) has been selected, formats should be written. A format translates a general teaching procedure into the specifics of what a teacher says and does. A format also should include correction procedures for errors and examples to be presented to the students. Formats must be designed so that teacher explanations are clear and unambiguous; teachers must take care not to use language students do not understand.

This text is unique in that it contains formats for teaching major mathematical skills and concepts. The formats have been carefully designed so that instruction is clear as well as concise and directs student attention to the important features of a strategy. In designing the formats, a major consideration was the use of consistent language throughout the format. Consistency in teacher wording and explanations fosters student understanding. As mentioned in the preface, we do not suggest that our formats represent the ideal teaching procedures. It is our hope that the systematic procedures recommended here will encourage the development of even better techniques. If teachers modify the formats in this book or create their own, however, they should be careful to maintain consistency and clarity throughout the format.

Some educators may object to the idea of memorizing what are, in essence, scripts. Our response is that preparing and rehearsing formats in advance allows the teacher, during instruction, to focus full attention on the students. Rather than being distracted by thinking of additional examples or the next steps to present, the teacher can concentrate on monitoring student answers, correcting mistakes, and keeping motivation high.

Select Examples

Selecting examples refers to constructing problems that will be presented along with the teaching formats. The first guideline for selecting examples is to include only problems that students can solve by using the current or a previously taught strategy. For example, if students had just been taught a renaming strategy for solving subtraction problems, the teacher would not give students a problem such as 304 - 87. Because of the zero in the tens column, this type of problem is more difficult, and new steps need to be taught before this problem type is introduced.

The second guideline is to include not only examples of the currently introduced type (introductory examples) but also examples of previously introduced problem types that are similar (discrimination). The purpose of including these previously introduced problem types is to provide students with practice in determining when to use the new strategy and when to use previously taught strategies. The importance of including this mixture of problem types cannot be overemphasized. Unless previously taught problem types are included, students will forget or misapply earlier taught strategies.

Specify Practice and Review

A critical instructional goal is to teach skills in a manner that facilitates skill retention over time. Providing practice and review sufficient for skill mastery is an essential aspect of instructional design. Research has suggested a strong relationship between student achievement and sufficient practice and review. If adequate time is not spent teaching and reviewing mathematics skills and concepts, either students will fail to learn them initially, or they will not retain them.

Questions concerning the amount of practice and appropriate mastery levels require further research. We can, however, provide these general guidelines:

1. Provide massed practice until mastery is reached. Mastery is attained when the student is able to work problems accurately and fluently. Specify-

ing exact fluency criteria for advancement is difficult since the speed at which students work problems is contingent in early grades on their motor skills, and in later grades on their knowledge of basic mathematics facts. Therefore, the only area for which we will suggest fluency criteria is fact learning (see Chapter 6).

2. Provide systematic review. Once students have reached a certain specified level of mastery, the teacher can gradually decrease the number of problems of that type that appear on daily worksheets. The problem type should, however, never entirely disappear but should be systematically reviewed. In some cases, this will require deliberate planning in order to ensure that the problem type appears in future practice activities. In other cases, built-in review is naturally provided as the problem type becomes a component skill for a more advanced problem type. For example, as subtraction problems with renaming (borrowing) are mastered, they would be integrated into story problems. Practice in the higher-level skill (solving word problems requiring subtraction with renaming) would then naturally review the earlier skill (subtraction with renaming).

Design Progress-Monitoring Procedures

Items selected to monitor student progress should be similar to those selected for instruction, since the assessment should focus on what is taught. The initial assessment is needed to establish which long- and short-term objectives the student has already met. As much as possible, instruction should target those objectives from the assessment that have not yet been mastered.

Student progress should be assessed at regular intervals to determine if students are learning at an acceptable rate. New methods of assessment, such as curriculum-based measurement (CBM), represent alternative approaches to measuring student progress.

CURRICULUM-BASED MEASUREMENT Curriculum-based measurement (CBM) refers to a specific set of systematic procedures developed to help teachers determine whether their students are progressing at an optimal rate. CBM offers an alternative both to informal observations, which tend to be inconsistent, and to achievement tests, which are administered too infrequently to help teachers make instructional decisions. According to Deno (1985), CBM has two distinctive features that separate it from other curriculum-based assessments. First, the recommended procedures possess reliability and validity commensurate with standardized achievement tests; second, the procedures are designed to be administered frequently enough to provide teachers with ongoing performance data.

Ideally, CBM materials are derived from the local school curriculum, and peer sampling is conducted to establish local norms. A norm sample is helpful for teachers in determining how close an individual's performance is to that of her classmates. The development of CBM procedures generally involves a four-step process (Fuchs, Fuchs, Hamlett, Stecker, 1990):

1. Identifying a long-range goal, e.g., given a set of computational problems representing a fifth grade math curriculum, the student will work a specified number of problems and write a specified number of symbols correctly in two minutes.
2. Creating a pool of test items from the local curriculum.
3. Frequently measuring student performance.
4. Evaluating the results—this is the means for determining if instructional changes need to be made.

CBM currently is being used both in regular and special education settings in a variety of ways. The procedures have been used to make decisions regarding initial screening, identification for special services, program planning, progress monitoring, and program evaluation. Since it is not within the scope of this book to elaborate on these procedures, we refer the reader to work currently being done by Drs. Lynn and Doug Fuchs at Vanderbilt University on computer applications of CBM.

PRESENTATION TECHNIQUES

The second major aspect of direct instruction involves teacher presentation techniques. How a teacher presents skills significantly affects both the student's rate of learning and the student's self-concept. The need to be concerned with developing student self-image while teaching academic subjects has been discussed by Engelmann (1969):

> The sphere of self-confidence that can be programmed in the classroom has to do with the child's ability to stick to his guns, to have confidence in what he has learned, and to approach school tasks with the understanding that he is smart and will succeed. For a child to maintain such an impression of himself, he must receive demonstrations that these descriptions of himself are valid. If he finds himself failing in school, displeasing the teacher, feeling unsure about what he has learned, he must reevaluate himself and perhaps conclude that he is not a complete success. (p. 68)

As mentioned earlier, different presentation techniques are appropriate for different stages of mathematics instruction. For example, during math instruction in the early grades, direct instruction typically involves more teacher-directed group instruction than independent work. In the upper grades the amount of group instruction decreases, and the amount of independent work increases. Another example of how different techniques are used at different times involves diagnosis. The diagnosis of student skill deficits during early math instruction is done by evaluating students' oral responses; in later grades, a diagnosis is often based on an analysis of students' written answers to worksheet exercises.

In general, early primary grade (K through second grade) teachers must be proficient in the variety of presentation techniques needed to maintain student participation in oral question-answer exchanges. On the other hand, intermediate grade teachers must be more skilled in managing students who are working independently. In both cases, however, teachers must provide a secure instructional environment where students are not afraid of taking risks.

Teacher presentation techniques may be divided into two main areas. The first area involves *maintaining student attention* during group instruction. The second area includes those teacher behaviors that ensure students master all skills being presented. We call this second area *teaching to criterion*.

Maintaining Student Attention

The more attentive the student is during instruction, the higher the probability that the teaching demonstration will be successful. Attentiveness is maintained by structuring tasks to keep students actively involved and by establishing a learning environment that contributes to student motivation. A discussion of how to foster student motivation would require many pages. Instead of giving a simplified overview, we will refer to several books that discuss this critical topic in depth (Jones and Jones, 1995; Sprick and Howard, 1995; Paine et. al., 1988). The following is a discussion of ways in which the teacher can structure tasks to keep students involved.

The length of a teacher's explanation or demonstration affects the likelihood that students will be attentive. Teachers should make explanations brief and concise. The more time the teacher spends talking, the fewer opportunities there are for student involvement. Teachers working with primary grade and lower-performing, intermediate grade students should structure their presentation so that students are required to answer frequent questions. Teachers presenting beginning skills might structure lessons that require students to answer questions every ten to fifteen seconds. Since a teacher cannot call on every individual student at that rate, we recommend, whenever possible, that the teacher use some unison responses in daily lessons to ensure student engagement in the lesson.

Mathematics instruction, especially at the lower levels, involves many tasks for which there is just one correct answer and, thus, lends itself quite well to unison responding. The advantage of unison responding is that it increases student attention. Some educators consider unison responding to be an inhumane practice that discourages creative thinking. Our reply to this criticism also addresses the issue of humane practice. Since resources allocated to schools are limited, the humane question before us is how to use the resources available to meet the needs of the students. By incorporating unison responding into lessons, a teacher is attempting to provide sufficient learning and practice opportunities to *all* of the students in the classroom. We realize the dangers inherent in unison responding if it is misused. If used properly, however, unison responding is an effective tool for engaging students in learning, as well as for monitoring students' progress.

Some very specific presentation skills are required of the teacher who incorporates unison responses into instruction. These skills include: (1) appropriate use of signals, (2) pacing, and (3) seating arrangements.

SIGNALS A signal is a cue given by the teacher that tells students when to make a unison response. The effective use of signals allows participation by all students, not just the higher performers who, if allowed, tend to dominate the lower-performing students. For example, if a teacher neglects to use a signal when presenting a story problem, higher-performing students are likely to respond long before lower performers have had a chance to organize and produce their responses. As a result, the lower-performing students may learn to copy responses from the other students, or they may just give up. Either result leads to a reduction in the amount of practice these lower-performing students receive. A signaling procedure can avoid this problem.

To signal a unison response, the teacher (1) gives directions, (2) provides a thinking pause, and (3) cues the response. In giving directions, the teacher tells the students the type of response they are to make and asks the question. For example, if presenting an addition fact task, the teacher might say, "Listen. Get ready to tell me the answer to this problem: 4 + 6."

After the directions comes the thinking pause. The duration of the thinking pause is determined by the length of time the lowest-performing student needs to figure out the answer. (If one student takes significantly longer to answer than the other students in the group, the teacher should consider providing extra individual practice for that student or placing him in a lower-performing group.) For easier questions (simple tasks involving review of previously taught skills), the thinking pause may be just a split second, while for more complex questions, the thinking pause may last 5 to 10 seconds. Carefully controlling the duration of the thinking pause is a very important factor in maintaining student attentiveness and providing students with a successful learning experience.

The final step in the signaling procedure is the actual cue to respond. A cue or signal to respond may be a clap, finger snap, hand drop, touching the board, or any similar type of action. This procedure can be modified for use with most tasks. On tasks calling for a long thinking pause, the teacher would say, "Get ready" an instant before signaling. The purpose of the get-ready prompt is to let the students know when to expect the signal to respond. Since the length of thinking pauses varies with the difficulty of the question, students do not know when to respond following a pause. Therefore, in order to elicit a group response in which each student has the opportunity to *initiate* his answer independently of the students next to him, the cue "Get ready" is given. This cue is particularly useful for teacher-directed worksheet tasks, since students are looking at their worksheets and cannot see a hand signal from the teacher.

The essential characteristic of any good signal is its clarity. The signal must be given so that students know exactly when they are expected to respond. If a signal is not clear, students will not be able to respond together. The teacher should use the students' behavior to evaluate the clarity of her signals. A repeated failure to respond together usually indicates that the signals are unclear or that the teacher has not provided adequate thinking time.

PACING Anyone who has observed young children watching TV shows such as *Sesame Street* can attest to the value of lively pacing in keeping students attentive. Teachers need not put on an elaborate show to foster attention but should be familiar enough with their material to present it in a lively, animated manner and without hesitation. Teachers who are well versed in their materials will not only be able to teach at a more lively pace, but will also be able to focus their attention more fully on the students' performance.

Another aspect of good pacing involves the efficient organization of materials. Just as a teacher should be well prepared to present tasks, she should also have clearly thought out the most efficient ways of handling teacher and student materials. Simply being able to locate the appropriate instructional materials easily and quickly might well save several minutes daily. Arranging student materials so that the teacher can quickly hand them out will also save minutes each day. This may seem trivial, but several minutes saved each day add up, by the end of the school year, to a significant amount of instructional time.

SEATING ARRANGEMENT   Lower-performing students should be seated at the front of the room so their responses can be monitored more easily. Teachers can better hear and see responses of students seated near the front of the room. The teacher is then more able to assist and, when appropriate, praise those students who are attending and working hard.

Although most math instruction is delivered to an entire class of students, lower-performing students learn better when they receive instruction in small groups. For small-group instruction in primary grades, we recommend seating the students in chairs, without desks, in a semicircle. The students face into a wall or corner, with their backs to the rest of the room. The teacher sits facing the group and looking out at the classroom so that he can monitor the rest of the class. Since the students in the group have their backs to the rest of the class, they are less likely to be distracted. Students should be seated close enough to the teacher so that he is able to easily monitor their performance. Lower-performing or

distractible students should sit toward the center of the group, since they require the most careful monitoring. Figure 1.1 shows a sample seating arrangement. Students instructed in small groups like the one pictured in Figure 1.1 are often given lapboards to assist them in their written work during the lesson.

Criterion Teaching

Teaching to criterion occurs in two stages. First, teachers need to present a particular format until the students are able to answer every question in the format correctly. Second, teachers should present a set of examples until students can respond correctly to all of the examples in the set. Criterion teaching, then, is a composite skill that involves appropriate monitoring, correcting, diagnosing, and remedying of problems. Only by teaching to a high criterion can teachers ensure student mastery and retention of the material.

MONITORING   Monitoring student performance (determining whether or not the student responds correctly) is rarely a problem when a teacher is working on a one-to-one basis with a student. Monitoring the performance of a group of students, however, requires a great deal of skill, especially when utilizing unison responding. It can be very difficult for the teacher to hear mistakes made by one or two students in a group. In addition to listening to student responses, the teacher also must watch the students' faces. The positions of the students' eyes and mouths can give the teacher much information. For example, the teacher can watch the students' mouths to see if they are responding on signal and giving the correct response. The teacher can also watch the students' eyes to see whether they are looking at the appropriate example on their worksheets or at the teacher's visual display. If a student is not looking at

FIGURE 1.1   Suggested seating arrangement. An open circle (**O**) indicates lower-performing or distractible students. Note that these students are not placed next to each other.

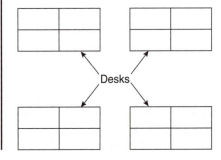
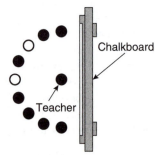

the appropriate place, the student may simply be mimicking other students' responses rather than initiating her own answer. Simultaneously monitoring every student on every unison response is impossible. Consequently, a teacher must systematically switch her attention from student to student, focusing primarily on lower-performing students.

Individual tests (calling on individuals) are a very important monitoring tool because they provide more accurate information than unison responses. With unison responses, a teacher can never be absolutely certain whether or not the student has been copying the responses of other students. An individual test, therefore, indicates much more clearly whether or not the student knows the correct answer. If the student makes a mistake when responding individually, the teacher should provide additional group practice and repeat the individual test later.

The teacher should give individual tests only after all the students in the group appear to be answering correctly during unison practice. Calling on a student who has not had enough practice to master the task may needlessly embarrass the student in front of his peers.

Since individual tests are time-consuming, they should not be given to every student after every task. As a general rule, turns should be given to all lower-performing students each time a new or difficult task is presented. Higher-performing students, on the other hand, would be tested less often. Note, though, that any student who has had difficulty on a task should receive more frequent individual turns on that task during the next several lessons.

When presenting tasks that call for written responses the teacher should devise systems for giving immediate feedback to the students. For example, when working with younger students on tasks such as numeral writing, the teacher should monitor lower-performing students after every response and higher-performing students after at least each third or fourth response. When working with older students, the teacher can either tell students the correct answer or have a higher-performing student write the answer on the board while the other students mark their own papers. She should also walk around the room looking at the students' work so that she can adjust her presentation to their performance and provide immediate corrections when needed.

Students' independent work should be checked daily. Older, more responsible students can often check their own papers using an answer key. With less responsible or younger students, the teacher, a paraprofessional, or volunteer should mark the papers. Note also that, ideally, all errors on papers should be corrected by students before the papers are sent home. Requiring students to go back and correct errors helps teachers determine if errors were caused by lack of knowledge or lack of concentration.

The importance of careful monitoring cannot be overemphasized. The sooner the teacher detects a student's skill deficit, the easier it will be to remedy. For each day that a student error goes undetected, the student is, in essence, receiving practice in doing something the wrong way. To ameliorate a skill deficit, the teacher should plan to spend a couple of days reteaching for every day the student's errors go undetected. Thus, careful monitoring is a critical component of efficient instruction.

CORRECTING   The first step in correcting errors made by students during group instruction is to determine the cause of the error. The teacher must decide if the error resulted from inattentiveness or from a lack of knowledge.

The cues a teacher uses in judging whether inattentiveness is the cause of the problem are these: (1) where the student is looking when the question is asked and (2) what the student was doing before the question was asked. A student looking away from the board before responding is not likely to be attending.

Teachers must be quite careful in responding to errors that appear to stem from inattentiveness. Negative teacher attention may result in reinforcing the undesired student behavior. To eliminate the possibility of inadvertently encouraging nonattending, the teacher should praise another student who attends and responds correctly. Later, when the previously inattentive student is paying close attention, the teacher must be sure to praise him. Letting the student know that he will get attention when he follows directions is essential. If a student makes many errors because of inattentiveness, the teacher must systematically work on increasing the student's motivation to attend. Once again, we refer the reader to the classroom management texts mentioned earlier. Working with the unmotivated student requires a good deal of teacher skill and understanding. There is no simple formula that will work in all instances.

The correction procedure for errors that result from lack of knowledge depends on the nature of the task. Correction procedures differ for motor, labeling, and problem-solving tasks.

To correct errors that stem from a motor deficit (e.g., writing a symbol or counting), the teacher models the correct response, leads the students until they appear able to respond correctly, and then tests them. The teacher continues the correction until students can make the correct responses several times in a row. The extra practice needed to produce several consecutive correct responses in a motor task is very important in facilitating retention. If students respond ten times incorrectly and then just once correctly, they are not likely to remember the correct response. Therefore, having students repeat the correct response several times is essential to increasing the probability of retention. Note that students should repeat the correct response several times consecutively only in motor tasks.

When presenting a labeling task, the teacher follows the three-step procedure of model, alternating pattern, and delayed test. In labeling tasks the alternating pattern provides for adequate repetition of the correct response. For example, if a student does not respond when asked to identify the numeral 4, the teacher first models the correct response: "This is 4." After modeling, the teacher would alternate between 4 and the other numbers in the task: 3, 8, 6, and 5. The teacher might follow this pattern: 4, 3, 4, 8, 6, 4, 5, 6, 3, 4. The delayed test is given later, possibly at the end of the lesson. The purpose of the delayed test is to help diagnose the severity of the confusion. If the error persists on the delayed test, the teacher knows that more practice must be provided before introducing new information.

If an error occurs when the teacher is presenting a strategy, the teacher usually follows a two-step correction. First, the teacher corrects the specific error, modeling the correct response if necessary, or, preferably, prompting the students by asking questions from the strategy. In the second step, the teacher returns to the beginning of the strategy and presents the entire strategy again. The purpose of returning to the beginning of the strategy after correcting an error is to ensure that the students do not lose track of how all of the steps in the strategy are integrated. Returning to the beginning of the strategy is very important when introducing strategies. For example, a student answers the problem:

$$\tfrac{3}{4} = \square/20 \quad \text{by writing} \quad \tfrac{3}{4} = \tfrac{8}{20}$$

The correction procedure for this error involves pointing out to the student that to rewrite a fraction without changing its value, the student must multiply it by a fraction that equals one whole (multiplying a number by 1 does not change its value). The teacher then guides the student through critical steps to figure out the fraction that equals one: Four times what number equals 20? . . . That means the denominator of the fraction we multiply $\tfrac{3}{4}$ by is 5. So what must the numerator be? . . . Why? . . . "

These questions prompt students to derive the answer without actually being told the answer.

Correction procedures for errors resulting from inattentiveness and lack of knowledge have been discussed. Two further kinds of errors, both relative to unison responding tasks, can also occur: late responses and failure to respond at all. When a student gives the correct response but answers after the other students have responded, the teacher cannot be sure if the student knew the answer or was simply copying the responses of other students. Similarly, if a student does not respond, the teacher does not know whether the student knows the answer.

Teachers should be careful in handling these situations to avoid making negative comments to the late or nonresponding student. Also, it is important that the teacher attempt to identify the reason for the inadequate response. If there is a reasonable probability that the student needed more time to figure out the response, the teacher should simply repeat the task later, providing the student with a longer thinking pause. However, if the inadequate response appears to be caused by a lack of cooperation, the teacher should reward students who do respond through praise or physical contact (handshake, pat on back). The reward is designed to make clear to the students that answering correctly is important and will result in teacher attention. Some students give wrong answers to elicit attention from the teacher. Rewarding students who respond correctly will help buttress against students deliberately making incorrect responses for attention and will provide an appropriate model for gaining teacher attention.

A final note on corrections. Teachers must always be careful when correcting student errors not to inadvertently humiliate a student. As mentioned earlier, the teacher needs to create a warm, accepting environment in which students feel safe to take risks with their learning.

DIAGNOSING AND REMEDYING   Diagnosis involves determining the cause of a set of errors; remediation is the procedure of reteaching a skill, based on the diagnosis. Note that a correction is quite different from a remediation in that a correction *immediately* follows an error to a teacher question and requires minimal diagnosis, since the teacher knows exactly what question the student missed.

A diagnosis, on the other hand, consists primarily of an error analysis teachers make when evaluating student independent work. The first decision to make in diagnosing errors is determining whether they are "can't do" versus "won't do" problems. "Won't do" problems occur when students have the necessary skills but are careless, do not complete their work, or are inattentive. A diagnosis of "won't do" errors requires a remediation that focuses on increasing student motivation. A diagnosis of "can't do" problems requires a remediation that focuses on the student's confusion or skill deficit.

The teacher diagnoses errors by examining the missed problems on worksheets and/or by interviewing the students about how they worked problems they missed.

The following basic steps apply to diagnosing and remedying errors on any type of problem:

1. The teacher analyzes worksheet errors and hypothesizes what the cause of the errors might be.
2. The teacher interviews the student to determine the cause of the errors, if it is not obvious.
3. The teacher provides reteaching through board and/or worksheet presentations.
4. The teacher tests the student on a set of problems similar to the ones on which the original errors were made.

An error can be one of three basic types: a fact error, a component skill error, or a strategy error. Basic facts are the one hundred addition and multiplication facts formed by adding or multiplying any two single-digit numbers and their subtraction and division corollaries. Sometimes students miss problems solely because of a fact error. Here are examples of such problems:

$$
\begin{array}{ccc}
\begin{array}{r} 8 \\ 7\overline{)65} \\ \underline{63} \\ 2 \end{array}
&
\begin{array}{r} 44 \\ 379 \\ \times\ 6 \\ \hline 2268 \end{array}
&
\begin{array}{r} 8 \\ 2\cancel{9}3 \\ -\ 58 \\ \hline 234 \end{array}
\end{array}
$$

Note that in each problem, the student followed the correct sequence of steps for working the problem but missed the problem because of a basic fact error ($8 \times 7 = 63$, $6 \times 9 = 48$, $13 - 8 = 4$).

Component skills are previously taught skills that are integrated as steps in a problem-solving strategy. Component-skill errors in the lower grades usually involve a counting or symbol identification error. In the later grades, a much wider range of component-skill errors may occur. Below is an example of a fraction problem missed because of a component-skill error:

$$
\frac{3}{4} + \frac{2}{5} =
$$

$$
\textit{incorrect:}\ \frac{3}{20} + \frac{2}{20} = \frac{5}{20} \qquad \textit{correct:}\ \frac{15}{20} + \frac{8}{20} = \frac{23}{20}
$$

Note that in the incorrectly solved problem, the student knew to convert both fractions to a common denominator but did not know the component skill of rewriting a fraction as an equivalent fraction.

A strategy error occurs when the student demonstrates that he does not know the sequence of steps required to solve the particular problem type. For example, in the following example, the student merely subtracts the denominator from the numerator when instructed to convert an improper fraction to a mixed number.

$$
\frac{13}{6} = 7 \qquad\qquad \frac{15}{2} = 13
$$

This student's performance indicates he does not know the strategy for rewriting improper fractions. Being able to determine the cause of an error is very important, since the choice of a remediation procedure is determined by the cause. If a student misses problems because of basic fact errors, the remediation procedure consists of either providing practice on specific facts or increasing student motivation to perform accurately. If the student misses a certain fact consistently, the remediation must involve practice on that fact. If, however, the student does not consistently miss any one fact but gets the same fact correct in one problem and not in another, the remediation would involve increasing incentives for accurate work. As mentioned earlier, if not motivated, students will often rush through problems, not carefully applying their knowledge.

A component-skill error may also result from inattentiveness. Therefore, teachers should not remedy a component skill unless the student makes an error on the component skill several times on the assignment. The remediation procedure initially involves reteaching that particular component skill. When the student is consistently able to perform the component skill, the teacher reintroduces examples of the problem type that was originally missed. For example, when given the following story problem, the student makes the mistake indicated:

Lisa wants to run 515 miles.
If she runs 5 miles a day, how many days must she run?

incorrect: $5\overline{)515}$ 13
               $\underline{5}$ days
               15

correct: $5\overline{)515}$ 103
             $\underline{5}$ days
             01
             $\underline{00}$
             15

In solving the problem the student was able to translate the words into the correct equation but made a division error when solving the equation. The remediation procedure for this error would involve presenting the format for solving division problems that have a zero in the quotient. The teacher would present the format for two consecutive days, or longer if more practice was needed to generate consistently accurate responses from the student. After the student is able to work the component skill correctly, he would again be given division story problems with a zero in the quotient, which is the type of problem in which the component skill was initially missed. Note that the remediation focuses solely on the component skill missed; the teacher does not have to reteach the skill of translating story problems.

If a student misses a problem because of a strategy error, the teacher reteaches the strategy for that particular skill, beginning with the initial, highly structured presentation. Again, a strategy remediation is not called for unless the student misses that strategy several times in the assignment.

Unfortunately, diagnosis and remediation are not as simple as outlined above. Sometimes students will perform inconsistently, making different types of errors in one example and not in other similar examples. For example, when given a worksheet including a variety of subtraction problems, with and without renaming, the student may perform as in the example below:

a.
$$\begin{array}{r} 35 \\ -14 \\ \hline 21 \end{array}$$

b.
$$\begin{array}{r} 26 \\ -18 \\ \hline 8 \end{array}$$

c.
$$\begin{array}{r} 45 \\ -32 \\ \hline 13 \end{array}$$

d.
$$\begin{array}{r} 57 \\ -19 \\ \hline 42 \end{array}$$

e.
$$\begin{array}{r} 34 \\ -18 \\ \hline 16 \end{array}$$

f.
$$\begin{array}{r} 26 \\ -12 \\ \hline 14 \end{array}$$

g.
$$\begin{array}{r} 40 \\ -32 \\ \hline 12 \end{array}$$

h.
$$\begin{array}{r} 54 \\ -30 \\ \hline 24 \end{array}$$

i.
$$\begin{array}{r} 20 \\ -12 \\ \hline 8 \end{array}$$

j.
$$\begin{array}{r} 42 \\ -24 \\ \hline 18 \end{array}$$

Note that the student missed two problems (d and g) because of strategy errors but solved other problems of the same type correctly (b, e, i, and j). When inconsistency results in student performance below 85% to 90% accuracy level, the remediation procedure should involve close supervision to determine the cause of the errors. If there is no apparent pattern to the errors, increasing incentives for accurate work (increasing motivation) is essential.

A final note on diagnosis and remediation concerns examining student worksheets. Teachers should pay special attention to student performance on review worksheets containing just one or two examples of previously introduced problem types. If a student makes a strategy or component-skill error when there are just a couple of problems of that type, the teacher should test the student on several more problems of that type to determine if remediation is necessary. For example, if a worksheet contained two subtraction problems requiring renaming and the student failed to rename in one problem, the teacher would test the student on a larger set of subtraction problems to determine if extensive remediation is necessary. The test would involve a worksheet containing a mixture of problems including the problem type missed and similar, but earlier introduced problem types. Teachers might prepare a series of worksheets, each focusing on a particular problem type, at the beginning of the school year and put them in files for easy accessibility.

ORGANIZATION OF INSTRUCTION

The final aspect of direct instruction, organization of instruction, involves organizing instruction in the classroom and throughout the school to ensure effective use of resources, particularly the use of time. These topics are discussed in depth in the next chapter.

CHAPTER 2

Organizing Mathematics Instruction

This chapter outlines specific procedures for organizing mathematics instruction and integrating direct instruction program design and presentation techniques into the classroom. The chapter is divided into four sections. The first section discusses how to select materials. The second outlines specific procedures for modifying a commercial program to make it more effective for a more diverse group of students. The third section specifies procedures for initial assessment, including information on placing and grouping students for instruction. The fourth section outlines the important aspects of presenting a unit. These four sections are intended to create a context in which the application of the information in the remaining chapters can be better understood. Finally, at the end of this chapter are two skill hierarchies, one for beginning mathematics instruction and one for elementary mathematics instruction. These skill hierarchies provide a graphic overview of how instruction in individual skills can be sequenced and integrated throughout several grade levels.

SELECTING INSTRUCTIONAL MATERIALS

The quality of mathematics instructional materials is an important factor in determining not only how quickly some students will learn new skills but also whether some students learn certain skills at all. High-performing students can learn mathematics from a variety of approaches; many middle ability students also will learn from many different types of materials, but perhaps at a slower rate. Lower-performing students, on the other hand, may not master many important mathematics skills unless carefully designed materials are used.

Types of Mathematics Programs

Three basic types of instructional programs are most frequently used in the schools: the developmental basals, the specific-skill programs, and those programs designed especially for low-performing students.

DEVELOPMENTAL BASALS At the core of mathematics instruction in most classrooms is the developmental basal mathematics program, which includes sequentially planned student and teacher materials for grades K–6. These programs are developmental in that they are designed for students who are learning mathematics for the first time. There are about a dozen major developmental basal programs on the market.

Basal programs are usually divided into between 10 to 20 topical units to be presented in a school year. Each unit focuses on a particular set of related skills such as addition, subtraction, multiplication, division, etc. Table 2.1, which contains the contents of three first-grade basal workbooks (Programs A, B, and C), illustrates this topical organization. The advantage to the teacher in using the basal programs is their comprehensiveness. The typical basal program includes, in one form or another, nearly all of the skills in the scope and sequence of elementary mathematics instruction. However, major weaknesses can be found in most basal programs. First, many programs lack specific instructions for the teacher. The teacher's guides that accompany most basal programs contain general directions for the teacher, using terms such as *explain* or *discuss,* rather than providing the teacher with carefully crafted directions on how to present skills and correct student errors.

Second, the programs often fail to include an adequate amount of practice and review for students to develop mastery.

This weakness is partly the result of the spiral curriculum design employed in the basals' construction. In the spiral curriculum, one or two units devoted to a particular topic are presented each year. For example, a unit on fractions is usually included in each math book from the first grade to the sixth. Each year the concepts introduced become more complex. In the first grade book, simple fraction drawings might be introduced; in the third grade, adding fractions; in the fourth, equivalent fractions. The problem with the spiral design has been that relatively little review of a skill is provided once the unit is completed. Although recent editions of the basal programs have given more emphasis to review, they often still do not provide adequate practice. Several practice examples of a new skill may appear for just three or four lessons, even though many students may require weeks of practice to develop mastery. Because of the lack of specific strategies and adequate practice and review, basal series require substantial modifications to become effective tools for teaching instructionally naive students. The problems with basal programs result in part from the publishers' failure, despite the money invested in production, to systematically test program components for their effectiveness.

SPECIFIC-SKILL PROGRAMS Specific-skill programs focus on one related group of skills (e.g., addition, subtraction, fractions, division, multiplication).

Table 2.1   Scope and Sequence for First Grade Programs

Unit	Program A	Program B	Program C
1.	Sets	Numbers through 5	Numbers through 6
2.	Numbers through 9	Sums through 5	Numbers through 10
3.	Subtraction (first number 5 or less) & addition (sums of 5 or less)	Subtraction, first number through 5	Geometry (circles & squares, rectangles & triangles, paths, segments, curves, closed figures)
4.	Numbers through 50	Geometry (ball, can, box, circle, rectangle, square)	Subtraction & addition of numbers to 6
5.	Subtraction & addition through 6	Numbers through 10	Place value (numbers to 100)
6.	Subtraction & addition through 8	Sums through 10 (three addends)	Subtraction & addition (through 10)
7.	Numbers through 100	Measurement & geometry	Measurement
8.	Fractions (1/2, 1/3, 1/4), time (half-hour & hour), money (through quarter)	Subtraction, first number through 10	Subtraction & addition (through 12)
9.	Subtraction & addition through 10	Addition & subtraction	Fractions (1/2, 1/3, 1/4 of a set and region)
10.	Geometry (sphere, cylinder, cone, cube, square, triangle) & measurement (centimeter, inch, liter, cup, kilogram, pound)	Numbers through 99	Subtraction & addition (two-digit numbers—no regrouping)
11.	Subtraction & addition through 12	Sums through 99 (no sequencing)	Subtraction & addition (through 18)
12.	Subtraction & addition through 18	Measurement	
13.		Subtraction, first number through 99 (no regrouping)	
14.		Addition & subtraction (sums through 18)	

Some of these programs are carefully sequenced and planned. Others are simply a collection of worksheets designed to provide extra practice. The advantage of specific-skill programs is that they are more likely to provide adequate practice to facilitate mastery of the skill. A disadvantage of such programs is their lack of comprehensiveness. A teacher using only specific-skill series would have to provide systematic review of skills from previously taught areas and would have to ensure that students were taught all of the skills in the scope and sequence of instruction required by the school district.

PROGRAMS FOR LOW-PERFORMING STUDENTS The third type of mathematics program is developed especially for the student who is having difficulty or is likely to have difficulty in school. These programs may be marketed as remedial programs or as programs for students with disabilities. Teachers must be very cautious when examining these programs, for while some are constructed very well, others are not.

We conducted an informal analysis to determine the extent to which basal programs and programs for low-performing students utilize direct instruction principles, using three mathematics programs: a traditional basal, a program for students at risk for school failure, and a program for students with disabilities. The analysis looked at single-digit addition. Each program was evaluated on each of the subskills of addition: equality, symbol identification, various counting skills, relationship between numerals and lines, etc. Each subskill was rated positive, neutral, or negative along several dimensions: whether it was included in the program, whether the teaching procedure was adequate, whether sequencing was appropriate, and whether practice was adequate. The ratings for each program were summarized as a percentage, which was calculated by dividing the number of neutral and positive ratings by the total number of ratings. The percentages reflected how well the program was designed and therefore could be used to predict how effective the program might be for low-performing students. The percentages were 48 for the traditional basal, 16 for the program for students at risk and 11 for the program designed for students with disabilities. Note that the programs designed for the lowest-performing students were judged to be the worst designed.

Program Evaluation

When evaluating commercially developed programs, four main areas should be critically examined, based on the instructional design principles discussed in the previous chapter: (1) instructional strategies, (2) sequence of skills, (3) example selection, and (4) amount of practice and review.

INSTRUCTIONAL STRATEGIES Whenever possible, a commercially developed program should teach strategies in a clear, concise manner. For example, explicit strategies for word problems are illustrated in Chapter 11. Except for the direct instruction mathematics programs (published by Science Research Associates), these types of strategies for word problems seldom appear in textbooks. In contrast, the recommendations in many commercial programs tend to be vague and somewhat confusing. For example, many recently published mathematics programs suggest that teachers have students *read, analyze, plan, and solve* word problems. The suggestions are helpful only if the students *already* know how to work the problems.

Once a strategy is taught, the program should provide a step-by-step transition from explicit teacher-directed instruction to completely independent work. The transition is best accomplished through guided practice, where the teacher asks only a few important questions to prompt the next steps in a strategy and is available to answer students' questions when they need help.

A good strategy teaches only the skill intended without leading to misinterpretations. In teaching beginning addition, for example, most programs use pictures to introduce the skill. Students are usually shown two groups of objects and asked to identify the number of objects in each group. The teacher then "joins" the groups and asks "how many in all?" Next, the students are shown pictures of two groups with the appropriate symbols written above. Note that in this specific demonstration, the students can work the problem without ever attending to the symbols; they can merely count the objects under the box and write the answer. The difficulty for low-performing students occurs when they are subsequently given problems with symbols only: $4 + 2 = 6$. The program assumes that students will either draw objects and then count them or they will remember the answer to the problem. In our experience, this assumption does not hold for instructionally naive students. These students need to be guided through a strategy. If students had been taught to draw pictures to represent the numerals, then count the pictures, the strategy would have been useful for low-performing students, since it would have given them an explicit procedure they could apply to a variety of problems (See Figure 2.1).

FIGURE 2.1 Addition problem with pictorial representation.

Finally, in well-designed instruction only one strategy is taught for a given skill. For example, in some programs two or more algorithms may be presented for working multiplication problems with multi-digit factors. Students are first shown the long form algorithm (example a), then several days later the short form algorithm (example b).

$$
\begin{array}{ll}
 & \overset{2\;2}{} \\
\text{a.}\quad 234 & \text{b.}\quad 234 \\
\underline{\times\;\;7} & \underline{\times\;\;7} \\
28 & 1638 \\
210 & \\
1400 & \\
\overline{1638} &
\end{array}
$$

Teaching more than one strategy for a skill is a common characteristic of many commercial programs. A related trend in mathematics instruction is to encourage students to generate their own strategies for solving problems. The underlying assumption is that the students will better understand the process by generating their own strategies and/or by exposure to multiple strategies. However, in our experience, multiple strategies often confuse instructionally naive students and compromise teaching time with the result that no strategy is mastered.

Modification of strategies is a time-consuming task for teachers, especially when the worksheets or practice activities in a program all correspond to the strategy suggested in the teacher's guide. Teaching students a strategy different from that in the text often involves writing new worksheets. Examining teaching strategies is particularly critical when evaluating first grade programs, since many tasks involve illustrations or manipulatives. In later grades, a teacher can often use the examples in the student textbook and workbook even after modifying the strategy. In later chapters, we present strategies that can be incorporated into most programs.

SEQUENCE OF SKILLS The sequence in which skills are presented contributes in part to the amount of difficulty students will have in learning strategies. Skills that are likely to be confused should not be introduced consecutively. Also, preskills should be taught prior to the introduction of strategies that require their application. Many programs do not teach all the necessary preskills. For example, most beginning-level programs assume all students can rote count and have students count objects on the very first lesson. However, some students will need to learn to rote count before they are able to count objects. A program should allow ample time for the students to master the preskills. Most commercial programs that do provide for the teaching of preskills, however, often fail to provide enough practice on the preskill before it is integrated into a strategy.

EXAMPLE SELECTION Problems that appear in student assignments should be carefully controlled. Only problems that can be solved through application of previously taught strategies should be included in independent work. Also, a variety of problem types should be included to teach students to discriminate *when* previously taught problem-solving strategies should be applied. After a new problem type is introduced, worksheet exercises should include a mixture of problems, including the newly introduced problem type and similar problem types that have been taught previously. For example, after subtracting with renaming (borrowing) is introduced, worksheets should contain problems that do and do not require renaming. On that worksheet, then, students not only practice renaming, but they also practice the skill of discriminating *when* renaming is appropriate.

Commercial programs often fail to include adequate discrimination practice. For example, in one widely used program we examined, when renaming is introduced in subtraction, 125 of the 127 problems require renaming. This lack of discrimination practice may cause some students to rename every subtraction problem they encounter.

PRACTICE AND REVIEW Adequate practice of new skills should be provided to enable students to develop mastery; adequate review of earlier taught skills should be provided to facilitate retention. Programs should specifically indicate the problems designated for review. Furthermore, in evaluating a program, the teacher should note the degree to which massed practice is provided immediately after a new problem type is introduced. The more complex the strategy, the longer massed practice should be continued. Teachers should note also the degree to which a systematic review of problem types is provided. After massed practice has enabled students to develop mastery, problems of that particular type should be reviewed periodically.

EVALUATION SCALE The four areas of evaluation are summarized in the Instructional Materials Rating Scale in Figure 2.2. This scale was designed to provide guidance to teachers in evaluating commercial programs in areas related to student achievement. When inspecting a commercial program, the teacher using the scale may inspect several major skill areas: counting, symbol identification, and vocabulary teaching in beginning level programs; addition, subtraction, story problems, and basic facts in first to second grade programs; multiplication, division, fractions, basic facts, story problems, and decimals in intermediate grade materials. Specific factors to consider in relation to each skill area are discussed in each of the subsequent chapters in this text. When examining the way a particular skill area is presented in a commercial program, we recommend that the teacher first read the corresponding chapter in this text, noting relevant instructional variables specific to that skill area. Then the teacher can look for those variables when rating the program with the Instructional Materials Rating Scale.

In some instances, teachers will have to choose among several programs, none of which the teacher may feel is designed satisfactorily. When teachers have limited options regarding which programs they may select, they should choose the program that

provides the best systematic practice and review of problem types.

This recommendation is based on the fact that the area of practice and review is probably the most time-consuming area to modify. Modifications often involve the construction of daily student worksheets, a task similar to writing a complete program. On the other hand, if a program provides adequate practice on various types of problems, a teacher could replace complex or confusing strategies suggested in the program with clearer, more explicit strategies that generalize to a wide range of problems.

Modifying Commercial Programs

Many commercial programs will need some degree of modification to make them suitable for low-performing students. This section provides specific guidance in making these modifications. The modifications should be made *before* the teacher uses the program, ideally during a summer workshop.

As mentioned earlier, most basal programs are divided into 10–20 units, each focusing on a particular skill area. A specific-skill program can be considered one unit since it focuses on one skill area. The five steps outlined below are designed to help teachers closely examine a unit and make appropriate modifications. Teachers should keep in mind that the performance levels of their students determine the need for making the modifications. Extensive modifications are usually needed for low-performing students, who require careful teaching and adequate practice for successful learning.

Five Steps in Modifying an Instructional Unit
1. Set priority objectives and levels of mastery.
2. Select problem-solving strategies.

FIGURE 2.2 Instructional Materials Rating Scale

Program	Year	Area Examined	Poor	Excellent
I. Strategy				
A. Presentation of the strategy by the teacher is carefully specified to ensure clarity and maintain consistency for related problem types.			1 2 3 4 5	
B. Presentation of the strategy is designed for systematic transition from a highly structured presentation to a less structured one.			1 2 3 4 5	
II. Sequence				
A. All preskills are taught sufficiently prior to introduction of the strategy to allow for development of mastery of the preskill.			1 2 3 4 5	
B. A problem type is not introduced until students have been taught a strategy to solve problems of that type.			1 2 3 4 5	
III. Example Selection				
A. A mix of the current and previous types of problems is provided.			1 2 3 4 5	
IV. Practice and Review				
A. Sufficient numbers of examples are presented to enable students to master new skills.			1 2 3 4 5	
B. Sufficient review of skills is included to facilitate retention.			1 2 3 4 5	

3. Construct teaching formats for the major skills (and for preskills when necessary).
4. Select practice examples.
5. Design worksheets or select pages of the text to provide review of previously taught skills.

SET PRIORITY OBJECTIVES AND LEVELS OF MASTERY If the program has not already done so, the teacher must determine the objectives of the unit by examining the problem types that are presented in the unit. To do this, the teacher first examines each page in the student textbook and workbook and lists the specific problem types found in the unit. Teachers can use the Instructional Sequence and Assessment Charts found at the beginning of most chapters in this book as guides in identifying problem types. Identifying specific problem types is very important. Teachers should take care not to assume (as do some instructional programs) that because students have learned a problem-solving strategy for a specific problem type, they will always be able to generalize the strategy to related problem types. For example, students who have been taught a strategy in column addition for renaming in the ones column and tens column will not necessarily be able to apply the strategy to examples that require renaming in the tens and hundreds columns. Likewise, students may be able to work a problem when it is vertically aligned but not be able to work the same problem when it is rewritten horizontally.

After determining the problem types presented in the unit, the teacher must then decide which problem types to delete, delay teaching, or add to the unit. Our general recommendation for teachers of low-performing students is to initially concentrate instruction on the most essential grade-level skills. Only when students have mastered all the essential skills should the teacher present instruction in less essential skill areas. In evaluating the degree to which a skill is essential, the teacher must consider both how often the student will apply or use the skill and whether the skill is a prerequisite for more advanced problem solving.

Once the teacher has determined the problem types students should be able to work at the conclusion of the unit, the teacher must decide on appropriate levels of mastery for the various problem types. Both accuracy and fluency must be considered when specifying levels of mastery.

The minimally acceptable accuracy level depends on the nature of the skill. Relatively simple tasks that are components of more advanced problems should be practiced until students develop 95–100% accuracy. For example, a teacher should provide practice on basic addition facts such as 6 + 3, 8 + 5, and 9 + 2 until the student can accurately respond to any basic fact question. On problem types that require the application of a multi-step strategy, the minimum accuracy level may be somewhat lower than 95%. Unfortunately, we have no experimental data on which to base recommendations. However, we recommend that teachers provide supervised practice until students reach an 85–90% accuracy level for worksheet assignments containing a mixture of problem types that require the application of multi-step strategies.

A fluency criterion depends also on the relative complexity of the problem type and the students' motor skills. As a general rule, we recommend that for each fact computation in a problem, the teacher allow about 2–3 seconds. For example, in working the problem 7×243, a teacher would set a fluency goal of 10–15 seconds, since five fact computations (7×3, 7×4, $28 + 2$, 7×2, and $14 + 3$) are needed to work the problem. The exact fluency criterion will depend on the student knowledge of basic facts. The criterion is faster for students who have mastered basic facts and slower for those who have not.

Presently, experimental data on appropriate fluency criteria are not readily available. However, there is little doubt that fluency is important. Students who work problems with relative fluency are more likely to retain strategies over a longer period of time.

SELECT STRATEGIES As mentioned earlier, developmental basals, in an apparent attempt to develop conceptual understanding, often simultaneously introduce two or more alternative problem-solving strategies for the same skill. Rather than developing a conceptual foundation, the introduction of alternative problem-solving strategies often confuses many instructionally naive students. Therefore, we recommend that, when using a program that presents several alternatives, teachers select just one of the strategies to teach students.

In deciding which strategy to select, teachers should consider two important factors: (1) the relative efficiency of the strategy and (2) the degree to which the strategy is similar to strategies taught by other teachers in the school. The notion of efficiency is central to a direct instruction philosophy. Students should be taught strategies they can learn easily and can apply to a range of related problems. The second factor calls attention to the need for continuity from grade level to grade level in teaching procedures. Many students will have difficulty in mathematics if they are taught a different strategy each year. Each chapter in this book outlines recommended strategies for major skill areas. The strategies sometimes represent a compromise between what we consider to be ideal and what is likely to be used by a majority of teachers.

CONSTRUCT FORMATS   A format translates a general teaching procedure into specific teacher and student behaviors. Formats should reflect a carefully designed progression, beginning with a teacher demonstration of the strategy and followed by teacher-guided worksheet practice, worksheet practice with less teacher direction, supervised worksheet practice, and, finally, independent work. Chapters 4–19 contain teaching formats to teach various math skills. Formats can illustrate the first four stages: Part A, the Structured Board Presentation; Part B, the Structured Worksheet; Part C, the Less Structured Worksheet; and Part D, Supervised Practice. In teaching addition, the teacher uses a chalkboard demonstration to introduce students to the steps in adding two numbers. In the structured worksheet presentation, the teacher guides students in applying the strategy to problems on their worksheets. In the less structured worksheet presentation, the teacher provides systematically less guidance. During supervised practice, the teacher closely monitors students as they work problems on their own, providing only corrective feedback. Supervised practice is continued until students develop accuracy. As mentioned earlier, accuracy is reflected by the low rate of student errors. Attaining a high level of accuracy does not, however, guarantee fluency. Therefore, once students attain accuracy, massed independent practice on the specific skills should be maintained until students are fluent as well as accurate in their worksheet performance.

The number of days it takes to make a transition from the structured stage to the independent stage is dependent on the relative complexity of the problem type. If a new problem type involves a simple extension of a previously taught strategy, the stages can be covered in approximately two days. If a new, complex strategy is being taught, approximately six to ten days may be required for the transition. For example, column addition with a two-digit and a one-digit number is introduced after problems containing two-digit numbers have been taught. The absence of a tens number in a problem such as

$$\begin{array}{r} 34 \\ + 9 \\ \hline \end{array}$$

can be confusing for some students. However, if they know the strategy for adding two-digit numbers, most students can progress through all four stages of the format for introducing the new problem type in two days. In contrast, most students would not be able to master division with double-digit divisors in such a short time.

As mentioned earlier, although a well-constructed format is critical in teaching low-performing students, how the teacher presents the format also is essential to its effectiveness as a teaching tool. Teachers should practice the instructional formats prior to teaching students so that, while teaching, the teacher can concentrate on student performance. Teachers should become familiar enough with a format so that they are able to present the format using any relevant examples. The preparation required for an effective presentation is time-consuming. However, the improved student performance that results from preparation time is apparent.

SELECT EXAMPLES   Many commercial programs do not include sufficient numbers of examples in their initial teaching presentations to enable students to develop mastery. Also, the programs rarely provide an adequate mixture of problem types to enable students to practice discriminating *when* to apply the appropriate strategy. Teachers, therefore, must be prepared to construct worksheets or other practice activities to supplement the practice provided by the program.

The Less Structured Worksheet and Supervised Practice parts of a format always include practice with a mixture of the currently introduced problem types and previously introduced types. The purpose of presenting students with a variety of problems is twofold. First, after students learn the steps in a given problem-solving strategy, they must learn to discriminate when it is appropriate to apply the strategy. Without carefully designed worksheet practice, low-performing students tend to apply the last strategy they have learned to all related problems on a worksheet. For example, after some students learn a subtraction strategy for double borrowing in problems with the zero in the tens column,

$$\begin{array}{r} 2\,9 \\ 3\!\!\!/0\!\!\!/4 \\ -\ 19 \\ \hline 285 \end{array}$$

they might apply the strategy inappropriately to all subtraction problems containing zeroes in the tens column, whether renaming is necessary or not.

$$\begin{array}{r} 2\,9 \\ 3\!\!\!/0\!\!\!/4 \\ -\ 24 \\ \hline 270 \end{array} \qquad \begin{array}{r} 2\,9 \\ 3\!\!\!/0\!\!\!/4 \\ -\ 13 \\ \hline 281 \end{array}$$

The second reason for including various problem types in practice activities is to provide the review necessary for students to maintain mastery of the previously taught skills. Without systematic review, low-performing students, in particular, will forget and/or confuse earlier taught strategies. A discussion of example selection guidelines is provided for each format in the book. The guidelines will enable teachers to generate examples over the course of time the format is being presented.

PROVIDE REVIEW Many commercial programs do not provide adequate review to facilitate retention of skills. Intensive practice on a new problem type should be provided so that students develop both accuracy and fluency. After mastery is achieved, problems of that type need no longer appear in mass on every worksheet. However, systematic review of skills should be provided. Teachers can provide this review by selecting problems from various pages in the basal text and workbook, by selecting worksheets from supplementary programs, or by preparing their own worksheets. An example of a teacher-made worksheet to provide review on previously introduced skills appears in Figure 2.3. The worksheet is one made by a fourth grade teacher late in the school year. The problems in the worksheet are numbered to facilitate workchecks in which students mark their own papers.

Initial Assessment

Following the selection, evaluation, and modification of a program, teachers should prepare to assess their students to help determine appropriate instructional goals. The following discussion covers recommendations for testing and for placing students in programs. Two types of tests help teachers determine the skill level of their students: placement tests and diagnostic tests.

PLACEMENT TESTING The placement tests should contain a representative sample of problems from the mathematics program being used. The purpose of the test is to determine whether the teacher needs to design remediation activities for any students prior to placing students in the grade-level program. Although many programs contain their own placement tests, some programs do not. Also, some programs may contain tests that are inappropriate because they omit essential skills and assess too many nonessential skills. We recommend that teachers examine the program tests carefully and evaluate the relative importance of the items tested. If program tests do not exist, the teacher may want to construct a test of sample prob-

FIGURE 2.3 Student Review Worksheet

Name _____ Date _____

1. $7\overline{)2135}$

2. $\begin{array}{r} 204 \\ \times\ 37 \\ \hline \end{array}$

3. $\begin{array}{r} 4002 \\ -\ 86 \\ \hline \end{array}$

4. $\begin{array}{r} 3742 \\ 1856 \\ +3928 \\ \hline \end{array}$

5. $5/9 + 2/3$

6. $3/4 \times 8$

7. $3\tfrac{2}{5} - 2$

8. $3/4 = \square/20$

9. 5×135

10. $9010 - 328$

11. 52×87

12. $314 - 9$

13. Jill earned 1,085 points in May.
Ann earned 1,036 points in May.
How many points did they earn altogether? _____

14. Sarah scored 184 points this season.
If she scored 8 points each game, how many games did she play? _____

15. Dina ran $3\tfrac{2}{5}$ miles on Monday and $5\tfrac{4}{5}$ miles on Tuesday. How many more miles did she run on Tuesday than on Monday? _____

16. Jack reads $3/4$ of an hour each night.
How many hours will he read in 12 days? _____

17. a. What is the sum of 5 and 3? _____
b. What is the difference of 5 and 3? _____
c. What is the product of 5 and 3? _____

18. How many inches in 4 feet? _____ _____

19. Three pounds equal how many ounces? _____ _____

20. Jane has 2 quarters, 3 dimes and 2 nickels.
How many cents does she have altogether? _____ _____

lems representing the skills students are expected to have mastered the previous year.

DIAGNOSTIC TESTING Teachers who work exclusively with students with disabilities will have to write Individual Education Programs (IEPs) for each student they serve. Therefore, these teachers often need to conduct more thorough initial testing. Chapters 4–19 contain instructional sequence and assessment charts arranged by grade level for the critical skills covered in each chapter. The sample items in these sequences can be used to construct a more thorough test that can be used in setting up IEPs for students with disabilities.

Grouping Students

Teachers are consistently faced with issues of grouping for instruction. Teachers may elect whole-class instruction or small-group instruction. If teachers elect to group students, they should decide on the number of instructional groups they are able to teach per day. In the primary grades, since all students (even high-performing students) require a significant amount of teacher-directed, closely supervised instruction, a class should be divided into two or three instructional groups. On the other hand, in the intermediate grades, students performing at grade level can be placed in relatively large groups (20–25 students) since they are more instructionally sophisticated and do not need as much constant monitoring and immediate feedback. An exception, of course, is made for students performing below grade level.

If the teacher decides to group her students for instruction, she needs to place the lowest-performing students in an instructional group first. If one or two students score significantly lower or higher than the rest of the class (see students 1, 29, and 30 in Figure 2.4), the teacher should explore the possibility of grouping those students with students from another class who are performing at a comparable level, or she should provide additional instruction. Also, in constructing groups, the teacher should remember that, if possible, the group of low performers should be the smallest group in the class. This group is kept small so that each student can receive more individual attention from the teacher.

After constructing the group comprised of the low-performing students, the teacher looks for cut-off scores that would result in homogeneous grouping for the remaining students. For example, in Figure 2.4 students 17–28 would form a group. Next, the teacher needs to make decisions about "borderline" students, those students whose test scores place them between a higher and lower group (see

FIGURE 2.4 Sample List of Placement Test Scores

Teacher <u>Smith</u>   Grade <u>5</u>   Test Form Given <u>E</u>

Student	Number Correct	Student	Number Correct
1	0	16	12
2	3	17	16
3	4	18	16
4	4	19	16
5	4	20	17
6	6	21	18
7	6	22	18
8	7	23	18
9	7	24	19
10	7	25	19
11	7	26	19
12	8	27	19
13	8	28	19
14	8	29	25
15	8	30	25

student 16 in Figure 2.4). Before grouping these students, the teacher should examine their placement tests more closely to determine the types of errors they made. If several errors on a student's test were caused by mistakes in basic facts, the teacher should consider placing the student in the higher group, If, on the other hand, the student's errors indicated a lack of problem-solving strategies, he should be placed in the lower group. Examples of the two types of errors are illustrated below:

Fact Errors

$$
\begin{array}{cccc}
\overset{1}{46} & \overset{1}{69} & 24 & 5\overline{)372}^{\ 64} \\
+27 & +35 & \times37 & \underline{35} \\
\hline
74 & 103 & 161 & 22 \\
& & 720 & \underline{20} \\
& & \hline & \\
& & 881 & \\
\end{array}
$$

Strategy Errors

$$
\begin{array}{cccc}
46 & 69 & 24 & 5\overline{)372}^{\ 10} \\
+27 & +35 & \times37 & \underline{5} \\
\hline
613 & 914 & 72168 & 2 \\
\end{array}
$$

A final, but still very important, topic involves regrouping. In grouping students, it is important to keep in mind that a student's initial test performance should never be the sole determinant for the student's group placement for the entire school year. The other major determining factor is the student's performance in the group. If the teacher discovers that a student learns new skills more quickly than the rest of her group, the teacher should consider moving the student into a higher-performing group. Similarly, if the teacher discovers that one student consistently makes more errors than the other students in his group, the teacher would consider placing that student in a lower-performing group. Regrouping should be done during the first week or two of instruction. The earlier the regrouping, the easier it is for students to transition from one group to another.

Placing Students in a Program

A student should be placed in an instructional program at a point as close to his ideal instructional level as possible. That is, a student must have previously mastered all skills introduced up to that point in the program and not have mastered the majority of skills introduced after that point. Placing students appropriately in a program is very important. Placing students at a level too high may result in failure; placing students at a level too low is inefficient and may lead to discipline problems as students become bored. Teachers working with students on a one-to-one basis can determine a starting lesson by testing skills in the order in which they are introduced in an instructional program. Teachers would continue testing until a skill deficit appears, and then teach the student this skill. Teachers working with groups of students or the entire class will find that placing a group of students at a starting lesson is more difficult, since no two students, especially in the immediate grades, are likely to have mastered an identical set of skills. Teachers must select a starting lesson that will not be too low for the higher performers in the group, nor too high for the lower performers.

Groups with many students who score below 60% on the program placement test for their grade level may need to be placed in a lower-grade-level book, or in special remedial materials. Again, caution must be exercised. Some students may perform quite poorly the first day or two of school, but with minimal practice improve significantly. Therefore, for students scoring poorly on the placement test, the teacher should spend about a week or two attempting to reteach how to work problems similar to those missed on the initial test. Following the tutoring, the teacher should give the test again. If, after this time, students can get 60% or more of the items on the placement test correct, they can be placed in their grade-level text. The group, though, would require very careful instruction and close monitoring throughout the school year.

Students who, after a week or so of tutoring, are still unable to perform at a 60% level on the placement test may need to be placed in material from a lower grade level or in remedial material.

Presenting a Unit

Once teachers have prepared materials and grouped and placed students, they can begin presenting units from the program. Presenting a unit from a basal series or a specific-skill program involves (1) a pretest of the skills in that unit, (2) presenting the daily lessons that make up the units, and (3) progressing at an optimal rate.

PRETESTING   Before teaching a specific unit, the teacher will need to construct and administer a pretest. Administering a pretest is helpful in several ways. Pretesting prevents the teacher from either overlooking a prerequisite skill that needs to be taught or spending instructional time on skills students have already mastered. In addition, the pretest can be used as a posttest to measure skill acquisition after the unit has been completed.

The pretest for a specific unit should include the following:

1. problem types in that skill area that had been taught in the preceding grades,
2. preskills required to solve the new problem types taught in the unit, and
3. examples of the new problem types presented in the unit.

Problem types taught in earlier grades are included so that the teacher can identify any deficits that should be remedied before more difficult problems are introduced. Generally, items should be drawn from the two previous grades. The preskills and problem types from the current unit are included so that the teacher can determine where instruction should begin, i.e., whether the teacher needs to teach the preskills and/or what problem types require direct instruction.

Two or three problems of each type should be tested. The Instructional Sequence and Assessment Charts at the beginning of Chapters 4–19 provide a bank of pretest items the teacher can draw from. These charts include a sequential list of problem types with several illustrative problems listed for each type. A fifth-grade teacher about to teach a multiplication unit, for example, would construct a test that included all the multiplication problem types listed on the Instructional Sequence and Assessment Chart as being introduced in grades three through five. Note that these charts do not include every problem type students will encounter. Any problem types not listed on the charts, but to be included in the unit, should be added to the test.

A record form that can be used to record student performance on pretests appears in Figure 2.5. Students' names would be listed in the first column. Across the top of the form are spaces for the problem types. Each box is divided into two parts, one to record student performance on the pretest and one to record student performance on the posttest. The teacher would record student performance by writing a+ if the student got all the problems of a particular type correct and a− if the student missed any of the problems of that type.

After testing the students, the teacher must decide which problem type to teach first. As a general guideline, we recommend beginning instruction with the earliest problem type failed by more than one-fourth of the students in the group. Starting at this point would allow the teacher to make efficient use of group instructional time, since the teacher would be presenting material that is new to a significant proportion of the students in the group. However, teachers must be extremely cautious in following this procedure. A teacher must remember that he is responsible for seeing that each student receives the instruction necessary for mastering important skills. Therefore, when first presenting a unit, he needs to plan on working individually with the students who missed earlier problem types. The extra instruction should continue until those students have caught up with the rest of the group.

Presenting Daily Lessons

A daily mathematics lesson includes three basic parts: (1) teacher-directed instruction, (2) independent seatwork, and (3) a workcheck.

TEACHER-DIRECTED INSTRUCTION   Time allocated for the teacher-directed instruction is generally from 15 to 30 minutes. Less time is required by intermediate students functioning at grade level; more time with younger students and intermediate students functioning below grade level. Instructional time is filled with one or both of the following activities:

1. *Remediation of previously taught skills.* The teacher should remedy any of the previously taught skills or problem types with which several of the students had difficulty. If only one or two students experience difficulty, the teacher should

work with these students individually, independent of group instructional time. Student performance on the independent worksheets should serve as a basis for planning remediation exercises. Remember, whenever a student's performance is below 85–90% on two consecutive review worksheets, or the student misses several examples of a specific problem type, a remediation procedure is called for. The remediation procedure usually requires the teacher to reteach one of the worksheet exercises with the relevant format (i.e., structured worksheet presentation, less-structured worksheet, etc.).

2. *Introduction of new skills.* The teacher introduces new skills to students by demonstrating the conceptual basis for the skill and modeling how to apply the skill. Following the introduction, that teacher may direct students to work several similar problems on the board, guide students through worksheet activities, supervise cooperative activities, or a combination of the above.

INDEPENDENT SEATWORK   Independent seatwork refers to the exercises that students complete without assistance at a designated time other than the teacher-directed instructional time. Exercises for independent seatwork can include those found in workbooks or textbooks, problems written on the board, or cooperative activities designed to be accomplished in groups. Part of independent seatwork should include massed practice on the most recently introduced problem types. The other part of the seatwork exercises should include a variety of earlier introduced problem types. As a general rule, we recommend that students be assigned exercises that require 20–30 minutes to complete. Teachers working with older intermediate grade students can assign these worksheets as homework.

WORKCHECK   A workcheck is an activity specifically designed for correcting the work students complete independently. Workchecks allow teachers to examine worksheets to determine skills that might require remediation during instructional time. Student work must be checked daily in order to provide useful feedback to students. The sooner a student's weakness or deficit can be identified, the easier it is to remedy. At the same time, the longer a student practices doing something the wrong way, the more difficult it is to correct.

Teachers of younger students will find it most efficient to mark papers themselves. Teachers of older students have several alternatives. Higher-perform-

Figure 2.5 Pretest Record Form

Unit _____

Pretest Date _____

Post-test Date _____

Student Names	Problem Type																				
	Pre	Post	Pre	Post	Pre	Post	Pre	Post	Pre	Post	Pre	Post	Pre	Post	Pre	Post	Pre	Post	Pre	Post

ing students may mark papers, students can mark their own papers, or the teacher can conduct a group workcheck, in which he reads the answers and the students mark their own papers.

An important part of any workcheck is having students rework the problems they missed on the completed independent assignment. Watching students rework problems helps teachers determine the cause of the student errors. If a student is consistently able to correctly rework problems that he missed, the teacher can assume that lack of motivation is a likely cause of the errors. If, on the other hand, the student is not able to rework the missed problems, the teacher knows that there is a specific-skill deficit that requires a remedy.

Progressing at an Optimal Rate

A critical teaching skill is the ability to ensure that a group of students progresses at an optimal rate. A rate is optimal when a teacher spends no more instructional time on a skill than is necessary for students to develop accuracy. As mentioned earlier, generally, students can be said to have developed accuracy when they can answer correctly 85–90% or more of the problems on a worksheet containing examples both of the currently introduced type and previously introduced types, with no assistance from the teacher.

Ideally, a teacher should work on a problem type until all students in a group have achieved this accuracy criterion. However, a teacher should not significantly delay the progress of the majority of students because just one or two students are having difficulty. Various alternatives exist for students who consistently require additional time to master new skills. For example, teachers may choose to preteach the lesson to a small group of students before teaching the entire class. Through preteaching, students will be receiving the instruction twice. Other alternatives for meeting the needs of low-performing students include peer tutoring, cooperative learning, or homework clubs.

Skill Hierarchy for Beginning Mathematics Instruction (Kindergarten and First Grade)

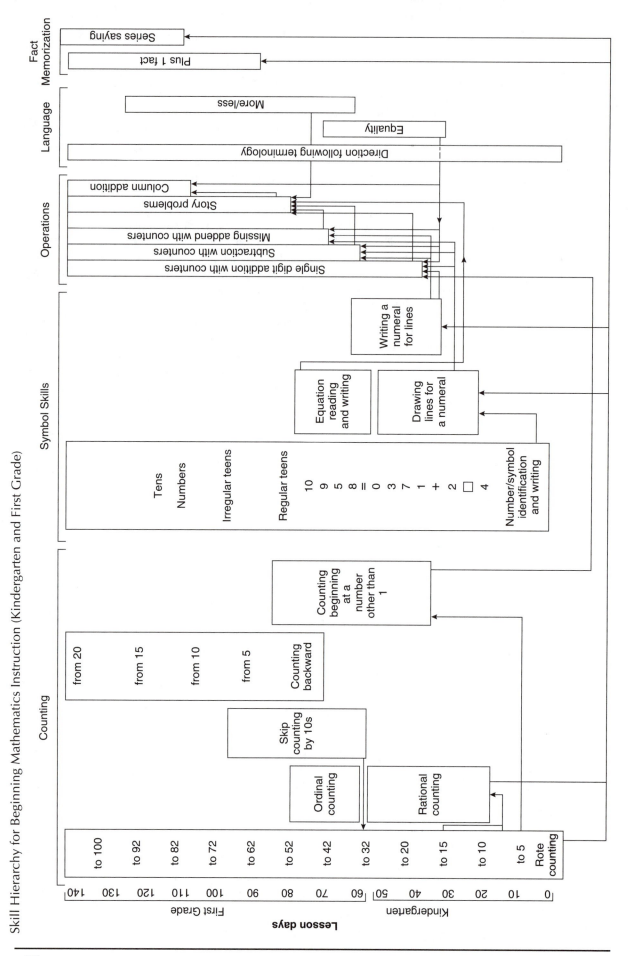

Skill Hierarchy for Elementary Mathematics Instruction

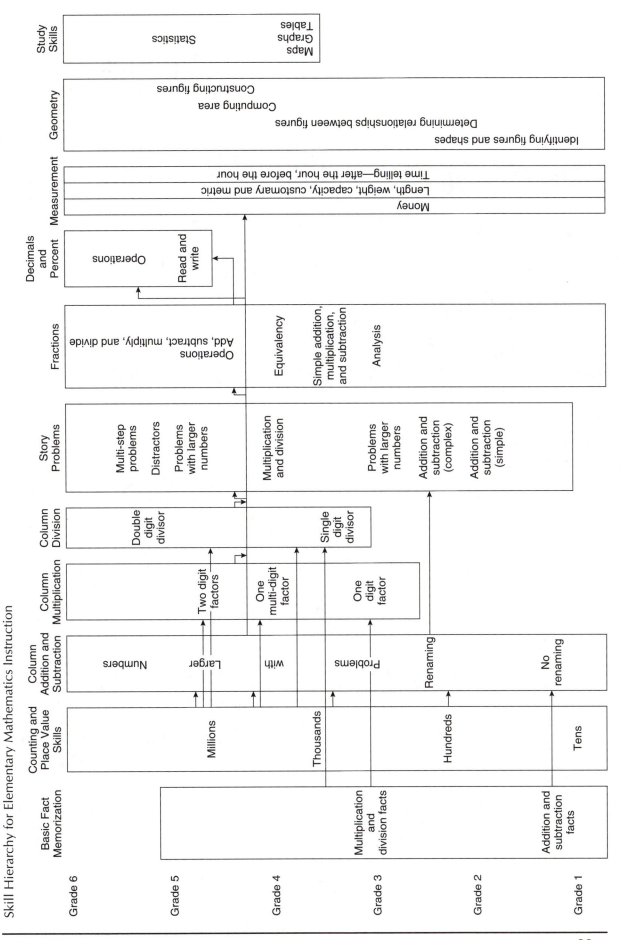

CHAPTER 3

Relevant Research in Mathematics Instruction

WITH ROBERT C. DIXON

MISCONCEPTIONS IN MATHEMATICS

Much research in mathematics education over the past 10 to 15 years has focused upon the kinds of errors students make in mathematics, possible causes of such errors, and possible remediation. Mathematical errors are referenced in the literature as inaccurate generalizations, misconceptions, misrules, cognitive bugs, and even what Resnick and Omanson (1987) call *malrules*. Although these labels are not always used to indicate identical phenomena, in one way or another, they refer to instances wherein students "do math" incorrectly.

The specific errors students make in mathematics are no doubt endless. However, many common, systematic, or typical error types have been identified in the literature, including but not limited to the following:

Trafton (1984) identifies the following as common errors: subtracting with regrouping when there are zeros in the subtrahend, dividing with zeros in the quotient, confusing the algorithms for adding and multiplying fractions, and confusing the formulas for computing perimeters and areas.

Zawojewski (1983) identifies specific areas of decimal work to be particularly error prone.

For example, students frequently count 12.08, 12.09, *13.00* or 20.97, 20.98, 20.99, *30.00*.

Offner (1978) points out that many students confuse the various formulas for computing volume.

Peck and Jenks (1981) show that students who could represent individual fractions (by drawing pies, for example) did not understand those fractions well enough to use them in operations.

Baroody and Ginsburg (1983) find that many elementary students treat the equal sign (=) as signifying an operation, rather than as an indicator of equality.

Lewis and Mayer (1987) cite several sources identifying the solution of word problems as a major difficulty for students.

Hamann and Ashcraft (1986) identify large addition and multiplication facts as being particularly difficult for students from first grade through college.

Lindvall and Ibarra (1980) point out the many difficulties students have in attempting to solve open sentence addition and subtraction problems, such as $3 + \square = 7$ or $7 - \square = 4$.

Despite the generally poor mathematics performance in American general education (Rothman,

30

1988) and in special education (Algozzine, O'Shea, Crews, & Stoddard, 1987), the research documenting the difficulties experienced by students in mathematics is largely descriptive, leaving open for interpretation the *causes* of these difficulties. We suggest that the possible causes of mathematics misconceptions may be categorized as follows:

1) Some important facts, algorithms, principles, linkages, etc., may simply not be taught. Students, then, quite reasonably appear to "not understand" such untaught material, when the problem is primarily a lack of background knowledge. This lack of prerequisite, or background, knowledge may be characterized as a problem with "opportunity to learn." The simple solution is to provide instruction. For example, if students have difficulty with large math facts, those facts should be practiced more. What complicates this apparently simple solution considerably is disagreement among researchers on *what* is important to teach. The "interference from everyday knowledge" to which Leinhardt, Zaslavsky, and Stein (1990) refer is an instance of the role that prior knowledge plays in the development of new mathematical understanding. Complex algorithms, for example, comprise fundamental subskills that students may have learned inadequately, may have "invented" or may have never learned at all.

2) Some important mathematical knowledge may be taught and learned, but not adequately retained. This, too, may largely be an "opportunity to learn" issue, since our analysis of mathematics instructional materials indicates that students often receive little opportunity to apply and retain the information that has been taught. Once a particular domain or area of mathematics has been targeted for instruction, then it seems reasonable that students be provided with an adequate opportunity to practice the skill in order to retain the knowledge within that domain.

3) Although no one would *intentionally* set out to teach a faulty algorithm or other faulty information, it is entirely possible that some misconceptions derive from instruction that is inadvertently unclear to students. In short, initial explanations that are inadequately explicit may be communicated to learners.

4) Finally, a category suggested most strongly by the research on mathematical misconceptions pertains to the types of examples presented to learners. For instance, we would not be surprised to see the kinds of decimal fraction misunderstandings indicated above by Zawojewski (1983) if instruction failed to include many of the practice examples representing those types.

The following section outlines research whose ideas have been incorporated into the direct instruction approach in order to help prevent the types of misconceptions articulated above.

INSTRUCTIONAL RESEARCH

One classification system for reviewing research in mathematics learning is suggested by Rosenshine and Stevens (1984) in their well-recognized review of effective schools research. Their taxonomy of *teaching functions* is useful in that it derives from a review of empirical studies of instructional effectiveness, and it is supported by other similar research (Brophy & Good, 1986), some of which was conducted on math instruction in particular (e.g., Good & Grouws, 1979). The instructional functions identified by Rosenshine and Stevens are:

1. Daily review, checking previous day's work, and reteaching (if necessary)
2. Presentation of new content/skills through high frequency of questions and overt student practice
4. Corrective feedback
5. Independent practice until students achieve mastery
6. Consistent and cumulative review

This system of instructional functions strongly implies three rather straightforward and intuitive stages for instruction: initial presentation of new material, guided practice or application, and independent practice. We have organized the remainder of the review of research around these broad stages.

Initial Instruction

The bulk of the experimental research we have located on instruction focuses on the initial stage of instruction, referred to as the "development phase" by Good and Grouws (1979). This phase of instruction is considered by some to be the most important part of mathematics lessons (Good, Grouws, & Ebmeier, 1983). Trafton (1984) found research studies that illustrated the benefit of devoting a majority of the total instructional time to development. (The term *development* appears at times to refer to initial instruction *and* to the guided practice that immediately follows initial instruction.) In this section, we review research on instructional design features that are relevant to the initial phase of instruction. Topics to be discussed include discovery versus expository instruction, explicitness, prior knowledge, examples, rate of introduction, sequencing, and efficiency.

DISCOVERY VERSUS EXPOSITORY INSTRUC-TION   One of the most widely debated controversies in instructional research lies in this stage of initial instruction. At its simplest, discovery instruction may be characterized as inductive (examples leading to a particular generalization), while expository instruction is deductive (wherein a generalization is first stated explicitly, followed by examples). In many of the early studies of expository versus discovery learning, a highly directed discovery approach was compared with a simplistic expository approach in which students were told a rule and then expected to immediately apply it independently: the method referred to by Romiszowski (1981) as "traditional." In these studies, the discovery approach, of course, appeared more effective. However, these early studies did not recognize the ranges of either discovery or expository learning articulated by Romiszowski.

Several large-scale studies of basic skills instruction for elementary-level at-risk students have tended to confirm the effectiveness of more direct, expository approaches over discovery, inquiry-oriented approaches (Fisher, Berliner, Filby, Marliave, Cahen, & Dishaw, 1980; Stallings, 1975; Stebbins, St. Pierre, Proper, Anderson, & Cerua, 1977). A group of studies directed specifically at elementary mathematics showed that a direct expository introduction of new material was superior to less direct methods across mathematics skills of differing cognitive levels and among students of differing grade and ability levels (Kameenui, Carnine, Darch, & Stein, 1986).

The notion that explicit expository instruction shows positive effects at strategic levels of cognition finds further support in a comprehensive review of effective mathematics instruction by Lloyd and Keller (1989). They conclude:

> Teach students explicit algorithms for solving problems, making sure that those algorithms are integrated with related algorithms and that students are taught to use them flexibly. (p. 9)

Additional support for expository teaching also has been provided by McDaniel and Schlager (1990), who investigated expository and discovery approaches to teaching problem-solving with the goal of transfer to new problem-solving situations. They found that discovery learning did not produce better skills at applying the discovered strategy during transfer. They did, however, find discovery useful when the transfer task required discovering the same kind of information that had to be discovered during instruction.

EXPLICITNESS   Explicitness of initial instruction is closely related to the issue of discovery versus expository approaches to initial instruction. Generally, expository approaches are the more explicit approaches, but there are varying degrees of explicitness within each expository approach. We refer to explicit instruction as clear, accurate, and unambiguous; therefore, the clearer the instruction, the more efficient it tends to be as well.

Several researchers have pointed out the need for explicitness in the initial/development stage of mathematics instruction. Leinhardt (1987) suggests that the explanation is a critical component of instruction and identifies three elements of a clear mathematics explanation: stating a goal, using parallel representations, and connecting old and new information. Resnick and Omanson (1987) contend that for many children who have difficulty learning or remembering the rules for written arithmetic, providing instruction that explicitly links the principles to the symbols is helpful. For example, in algebra, Resnick, Cauzinille-Marmeche, and Mathier (1987) advocate making instruction more explicit as a means of clarifying for students the kinds of constraints that are inherent in algebraic rules.

Carnine and Stein (1981) found that explicitly teaching students a counting strategy for learning basic arithmetic facts resulted in greater accuracy in the use of those facts and better retention, supporting an earlier finding by Thornton (1978).

Several related studies have found similar support for the use of explicit instruction in mathematics problem-solving. In one study of problem-solving, Gleason, Carnine, and Boriero (in press) compared the use of computer-assisted and teacher-directed instruction in teaching students with mild disabilities to solve story problems. Both treatments utilized explicit instruction for problem-solving, and both treatments resulted in more accurate problem-solving, greater understanding of the concepts underlying the problems, and transfer.

Darch, Carnine, and Gersten (1989) specifically examined the effects of teaching a highly explicit, step-by-step method for translating story problems into mathematical equations. In this study, explicit instruction was compared to a traditional approach to problem-solving found in many basal mathematics programs, in which teachers are directed to relate problems to students' experiences but are not directed to teach any explicit strategy to solve the problem. Students who were taught explicit strategies outperformed the students taught using the traditional approach, in spite of the fact that the students taught with the traditional approach received over three additional hours of instruction. These two basic approaches to initial mathematics instruction, the explicit and the open-ended or implicit, were studied by Kameenui et al. (1986), who found, in their analysis of three different mathematic skill areas, that the explicit approach appeared to be more effective in terms of acquisition, maintenance, and transfer.

PRIOR KNOWLEDGE   There is widespread recognition of the importance of preskills and preknowledge (which we will refer to collectively as prior knowledge) in the research literature (Carnine 1980). Jackson and Phillips (1983) found that vocabulary-oriented preknowledge instruction significantly enhanced the achievement of seventh grade students in solving ratio and proportion problems. Barron, Bransford, Kulewicz, and Hasselbring (1989) pointed out that basic math facts are a critical prerequisite for solving even simple word problems. Darch et al. (1989) have found the preteaching of problem-solving skills to be significantly effective, particularly in conjunction with explicit initial instruction on those skills. Case and Bereiter (1984) argue that instruction should build upon previously learned skills and concepts and that it should explicitly move students through the development of those skills and concepts.

The fundamental solution to the problem of lack of prior knowledge is to provide students with the opportunity to either learn or correct prerequisite knowledge or skills prior to instruction that requires that knowledge. Behr, Wachsmuth, and Post (1985) recommend that middle- and low-performing students in particular receive more initial and continuous practice on prerequisite skills. We call this cumulative practice and review.

EXAMPLES   In 1990, Leinhardt, Zaslavsky, and Stein, wrote, "The selection of examples is the art of teaching mathematics." Support for this statement can be found in the instructional design literature, as well as in the research literature. For example, instructional design theorists Markle and Tiemann (1970) propose that four different learning outcomes are predictable solely on the basis of relationships among examples: accurate generalization, undergeneralization, overgeneralization, and misconceptions. We will refer to some of these types of problems on the following pages, as well as throughout the text.

Several problems identified by Trafton (1984) relate specifically to instructional examples. For example, Trafton points out that it is quite common for students to have problems subtracting when there are zeros in the subtrahend, and to have prob-

lems with division when there are zeros in the quotient. Assuming that accurate, explicit algorithms have been taught, problems with zeros could occur if the selection of examples used in the initial instruction did not adequately represent problems with zeros. The finding of Hamann and Ashcraft (1986) that students receive relatively little practice with even simple addition facts involving zero adds to the plausibility of this explanation.

Another common problem identified by Trafton (1984) was confusing the algorithms for adding and multiplying fractions. It is conceivable that confusing the fraction algorithms may be due to a lack of opportunity to discriminate among them. For example, in an examination of a commercially developed mathematics program, Kelly, Carnine, Gersten, and Grossen (1986) found that both adding and subtracting fractions were taught within a single 14-day unit. Strategies for multiplying and dividing fractions were then taught in the following unit, but with no opportunity to discriminate the new strategies from those taught earlier.

The source of other common confusions, such as the one over the various formulas for computing volumes pointed out by Offner (1978), also may be attributed to a lack of opportunity to discriminate among several similar formulas.

Based on this research, we recommend using two example selection guidelines for analyzing and/or designing mathematics instruction. First, teachers need to pay careful attention to the range of example types presented during instruction so that learners will be able to generalize to new examples (and avoid undergeneralization). Second, teachers need to carefully examine the relationships among examples and nonexamples to prevent overgeneralizations and misconceptions. For example, teachers cannot assume students will be able to solve problems with zeros without a careful introduction to these types of examples. In addition, after initial instruction in these problem types, students must be given adequate opportunities to practice discriminating problems with zeros from those that do not have zeros.

RATE OF INTRODUCTION   Once concepts have been targeted for instruction, the question arises regarding the optimal rate at which those concepts should be introduced to learners. Porter (1989) makes a strong case for the need to carefully plan the rate at which mathematical concepts are introduced. He found that approximately 70% of the topics covered within a school year are given less than 30 minutes of instructional time each across the entire school year. Only 10 to 20 topics received as much as two hours of instructional time. Porter refers to this situation as *teaching for exposure.* In basal mathematics programs, many of the same topics are taught for exposure, year after year, in a spiral curriculum design, rarely giving students who have not mastered the concepts adequate instruction or opportunity to be successful. In addition, teachers and textbooks are highly consistent in focusing the majority of practice exercises—65–80%—on skills, as opposed to conceptual understanding. Porter concluded his review with an argument for teaching less content more thoroughly. One way he suggested doing that is to better coordinate the mathematics curriculum across grade levels in ways that decrease the instructional overlap from year to year.

Perhaps the strongest evidence that rate of introduction is an important *instructional* consideration comes from the mastery-learning model (Bloom, 1968; Carroll, 1963) and the research in support of that model (Slavin, 1990; Kulik, Kulik, & Bangert-Drowns, 1990). The rate of instruction in that model is determined wholly on the basis of individual student performance. Well-designed computer-based instruction also can adjust the rate of introduction of new material based upon the performance of individuals.

SEQUENCING Another major question related to the introduction of new material is the sequence in which that material is introduced. Van Patten, Chao, and Reigeluth (1986) have identified two levels of sequencing strategies in their exhaustive review of the research: macro and micro strategies for sequencing. Macro sequencing strategies apply to the order in which concepts, principles, or skills are introduced to learners. Micro sequencing strategies apply to the order of definitions, examples, and practice associated with a given concept, principle, or skill.

Van Patten et al. (1986) reviewed research on both micro and macro strategies for sequencing. They outline two steps required for sequencing: 1) the identification of what element of instruction (e.g., concepts, examples) is to be sequenced and 2) the selection of some organizing principle for ordering the identified elements. In the case of micro sequencing, the first step involves a selection of examples that does, in fact, include the range of examples intended for generalization. In the case of macro sequencing, the first step would involve the selection and prioritization of instructional content.

Van Patten et al. found very few studies that addressed the second step, that of selecting an organizing principle for ordering examples (in the case of micro sequences) or concepts (in macro sequences), in part because early studies did not make clear the distinction between micro and macro sequencing.

However, Van Patten et al. did find current empirical research on micro sequencing that suggests the following sequencing principles:

1. Match examples and nonexamples in a way that highlights the critical attributes of the generalization being taught. For example, during initial instruction in identifying fractions, juxtapose proper and improper fractions in practice exercises.
2. Make successive examples divergent (either by varying noncritical attributes across examples or critical attributes between an example and nonexample). For example, in teaching regrouping in addition, provide practice discriminating problems that require regrouping from those that do not.
3. Present examples to show the range of the generalization, moving from easier to more difficult examples. For example, in teaching long division, introduce division without zeros first, followed by instruction in division with zeros.

EFFICIENCY The goal of efficiency for mathematics education is important given the performance levels of American students in relation to their peers from other highly industrialized countries. Moreover, logic suggests how crucial this goal is for students with disabilities, who are behind their general education classroom peers.

An emphasis on identifying and prioritizing key concepts in mathematics instruction is one way to make mathematics instruction more efficient. By prioritizing concepts—teaching those key concepts that contribute to the greatest mathematical understanding—increased instructional efficiency is unavoidable. There is simply inadequate empirical evidence to support an exhaustive selection of specific algorithms and strategies in a mathematics curriculum.

However, there is evidence relative to some specific instructional variables that addresses questions of efficiency. For example, Wheatley and McHugh (1977) found that a direct algorithm for teaching column addition and an indirect tens method, based on looking for combinations that add up to ten, were equally effective in terms of accuracy, but that the direct method was 17% faster in achieving accuracy. The efficiency in the direct method appears to have been the result of the *directness* of that method, in that fewer steps were required than in the alternative approach. While we must be cautious not to overgeneralize from this finding, it is consistent with other research that suggests clarity or explicitness may contribute to efficiency as well as to accurate conceptualization.

Initially, explicit-strategy instruction may be more time-consuming than some alternatives. For example, Carnine and Stein (1981) found explicit-strategy instruction more time-consuming than memorization instruction for teaching basic facts. Yet, the explicit-strategy students performed more accurately, justifying the additional instructional time.

The theoretical arguments in favor of discovery approaches to initial instruction are based upon the assumption that such approaches result in better learning. Were that the case, then the well-documented inefficiency of discovery approaches would be justified. However, McDaniel and Schlager (1990) have concluded from their research that:

> . . . the increased effort and training time associated with discovery modes of instruction will not always be beneficial. Specifically, discovery learning per se does not seem to provide subjects with more insight into the information targeted for learning (e.g., a particular strategy). Once learned, the information (e.g., a strategy) seems to be transferred with equal facility, regardless of whether or not it was discovered or explicated for the learner. (p. 154)

Much of the previous discussion on the importance of example selection for instruction related specifically to the prevention of various categories of misconception, particularly discrimination errors. The judicious selection of both positive and negative examples, however, appears to make instruction more efficient as well as more effective. Williams and Carnine (1981) found that the juxtaposition of minimally different positive and negative examples (and, it should be noted, consistent initial instruction) resulted in either greater efficiency or better transfer or both. Park and Tennyson (1980) found that an adaptive example selection strategy, in which discrimination examples were presented immediately following a student error, resulted in the overall presentation of fewer examples and less instructional time to mastery than two other treatments that were equally effective in terms of mastery alone.

In short, maximum efficiency in mathematics instruction appears to require the coordination of several instructional variables that result in efficiency when used in conjunction with one another, as well as the efficient implementation of each variable individually.

Guided Practice

Earlier, we noted that any sequence of instruction could be thought of as having up to three general phases: initial instruction, guided practice, and independent practice or application. The boundaries

between each stage—particularly the first two—are not always clear. For example, the *development* phase of instruction sometimes appears to refer to initial instruction only, and at other times to include both initial instruction and a phase of guided instruction immediately following initial instruction.

Trafton (1984) illustrates these phases by identifying the first stage as a demonstration phase, wherein students actively respond to questions posed, in order to ensure initial understanding. The second stage, according to Trafton, is a "brief tryout" in which students work under the close scrutiny of the teacher, who offers additional instruction as performance warrants it. The final phase includes work that students perform independently, which provides further opportunity for the teacher to make instructional decisions based on student performance.

Quite surprisingly, we are once again looking at an instructional variable with considerable theoretical support, but with less empirical support. In one study, Drucker, McBride, and Wilbur (1987) studied a computer-based error-analysis approach to solving basic subtraction problems. The role of the computer in the study was that of simply identifying and classifying student error types. Based upon that error analysis, teachers provided instruction in the following sequence:

1. The students were told exactly what their error was.
2. The students then demonstrated to the teacher the correct procedure.
3. Under direct teacher guidance, the students solved practice problems.
4. With a reduced level of teacher guidance, students then solved two more problems.
5. Finally, students worked additional problems independently.

The results of the study were dramatic, in that the control group showed a slight drop on the posttest, while the experimental group showed dramatic gain.

Paine, Carnine, White, and Walters (1982) conducted two related studies of the effects of fading prompts during instruction on arithmetic problem-solving skills. In one experiment, they studied the effects of gradually building student independence by moving from a stage of instruction in which every step of the procedure is prompted to a stage including only a few key prompts. In the other experiment, they studied the effects of a more rapid fading schedule. In both cases, the experimental groups outperformed the control groups, who received demonstrations and practice only, without the intervening prompted stage. The researchers concluded that all students benefited from a stage of prompted instruction, but that higher-performing students needed less prompting (or more rapid fading) than lower-achieving students.

Carnine and his colleagues have implemented a "faded prompt" component of instruction in other experiments involving effective instructional interventions (Gleason et al., in press; Woodward, Carnine, and Gersten, 1988; Kameenui et al., 1986; Kelly et al., 1986) with similar results.

Independent Practice

At some point in a given sequence of mathematics instruction, teachers provide fewer demonstrations and teacher guidance is faded. Students begin to practice what they have learned, independently, or with minimal guidance. It is unclear when such *practice* becomes *review,* and therefore, we address both practice and review in this section.

A goal for all students is to remember what they have learned in the earlier phases of an instructional sequence, whether that information is in the form of facts, algorithms, procedures, understandings, or problem-solving strategies. Moreover, retention of the material should be at a level of *automaticity,* that is, a level that allows students to perform fluently and effortlessly. Ashcraft (1985) argues that the automatic retrieval of basic arithmetic facts is necessary in order to "free up" the resources of working memory necessary for utilizing those facts within more advanced applications, such as multicolumn addition. Of course, the importance of automaticity is not limited to basic arithmetic facts. Cooper and Sweller (1987) found that "rule automation" is a critical factor in obtaining problem-solving transfer in algebra. We presume that concepts or skills important enough to be targeted in the development phase of instruction are important enough to remember.

Several researchers have confirmed the role of practice on mathematics achievement. In a discussion of an information-processing model of elementary mathematics, Pellegrino and Goldman (1987) review research that suggests students with math disabilities are often hampered in executing complex mathematical procedures because their basic fact knowledge units are weak, and because following complex procedures requires a considerable amount of practice in using the procedures. Swing and Peterson (1988) state the following in reference to the relationship between practice and the ability to learn mathematics for understanding:

> Our results provide evidence that integrative and elaborative processes such as analysis, defining, and comparing are related to better memory and understanding scores, but that supplementary instruction or alternative instructional techniques are needed to optimize effects,

especially for lower ability students. Instruction for elaboration could be incorporated into teachers' presentations (Good et al., 1983), or teachers could instruct students explicitly in elaborative and integrative thought processes via such techniques as thinking aloud. Whatever the instructional mode, extensive practice is necessary if students are expected to effectively execute elaborative and integrative thought processes on their own (p. 63).

We need to emphasize here that an emphasis on practice must be carefully integrated with a program of study that incorporates the other instructional variables known to contribute to long-term achievement. Examples of these variables discussed previously include instruction in explicit strategies that make clear the linkages between the concrete and symbolic, as well as careful example selection designed to enhance accurate generalization and key discrimination. Darch et. al. (1989) found that students who were taught explicit strategies designed to promote rich understanding performed better, and *with significantly less practice,* than students taught with approaches derived from commercially designed curriculum in which initial instruction did not adhere to principles outlined in this chapter.

CONCLUSION

In summary, our review of recent mathematics instructional research revealed an emphasis and interest in the types of mathematics misconceptions demonstrated by students. Misconceptions appear to be both widespread and systematic; significant numbers of children consistently display similar types of misconceptions. We conceive of effective mathematics instruction, therefore, as that instruction that either preempts or effectively corrects misconceptions common to many students.

Evaluation of mathematics instruction is important but difficult. Ideally, comprehensive instructional programs should be evaluated for effectiveness prior to their widespread dissemination, in part because of some of the equivocation in the literature, and in part because effective parts may not add up to an effective whole. (For an evaluation of the effectiveness of a direct instruction mathematics program with low-income students, see Appendix A.) Short of such prepublication testing, teachers, administrators, and curriculum specialists must analyze, modify, and develop mathematics instruction using the instructional features mentioned above. In the next section of this text, readers will find *specific* recommendations, based on this research literature, that will help them with their task of designing and implementing effective mathematics instruction for all learners.

PART TWO

Skills and Concepts

CHAPTER 4

Counting

TERMS AND CONCEPTS

Set A collection of concrete or abstract elements.

Cardinal Number The number that identifies the number of elements or members of a set.

Numeral The symbol representing a cardinal number.

Rote Counting Identifying number names in sequence.

Rational Counting Identifying the cardinal number of a set, i.e., object counting; sometimes called one-to-one correspondence.

Ordinal Numbers Numbers associated with position, e.g., first, second, third.

Manipulatives Concrete objects often used to facilitate instruction of mathematics concepts.

Skip Counting Identifying every nth number in the counting series, e.g., in skip counting by 2s, students say every second number: 2, 4, 6, 8; for 8s, every eighth number: 8, 16, 24.

SKILL HIERARCHY

Counting skills are not only important in and of themselves, but are also important prerequisite skills for many problem-solving strategies. The Instructional Sequence and Assessment Chart outlines a recommended instructional sequence for the major counting skills: rote counting, rational counting, counting from a number, skip counting, and ordinal counting. Note that counting instruction forms a major component of first grade instruction and should be continued in second and third grades.

Rote counting refers to identifying number names in sequence (e.g., 1, 2, 3, 4, 5, 6). During first grade, students are taught to count to 99; in second grade, through 999; in third grade, into the thousands.

Rational counting refers to coordinating counting with the touching of objects to determine the quantity of a particular set. Rote counting is a prerequisite skill for rational counting. Students should be able to say numbers in sequence before they are expected to coordinate saying numbers while touching objects. We recommend that students be able to rote count to 10 before rational counting is introduced. Initial rational counting exercises involve counting a group of objects. Later exercises involve counting two groups of objects, a prerequisite skill for early addition.

Counting from a number is also a prerequisite skill for addition. In counting-from-a-number tasks, students begin with a number other than 1; e.g., they begin with 6 and then count 7, 8, 9. In early addition problems such as 6 + 3, students would be taught to say 6 for a few seconds and then count markers for the second addend: sssiiixxx, 7, 8, 9.

Skip counting refers to counting in which the students say multiples of a base number; e.g., when

Instructional Sequence and Assessment Chart

Grade Level	Problem Type	Performance Indicator
K-1	Counting by 1s beginning at 1; counting through 20	Verbal test: teacher asks students to count to 20
K-1	Counting a group of objects	Teacher writes four lines, asks how many lines. Repeat with seven lines, five lines.
K-1	Counting two groups of objects	Teacher writes | | | | | | | | | and asks how many lines all together?
K-1	Counting by 1s, beginning at 1, counting through 30	Verbal test: teacher asks students to count to 30.
K-1	Ordinal counting first through tenth	Verbal test: teacher draws 10 lines on board, asks students to touch third line and seventh line.
K-1	Skip counting by 10s 10-100	Verbal test: teacher asks students to count by 10 to 100.
K-1	Counting backward from 10 to zero	Verbal test: teacher asks students to count backward from 10 to zero.
K-1	Counting by 1s from 1 through 100	Written test: write the number that comes next: 26, _____ , _____ , 29, _____ 46, _____ , _____ , 49, _____
K-1	Skip counting by 2, 5	Fill in the missing numerals: 2, 4, 6, __ , __ , __ , __ 5, 10, 15, __ , __ , __ , __
2a	Counting by 1s 100 to 999	Write the numeral that comes next: 349 _____ 299 _____ 599 _____ 699 _____ 499 _____ 704 _____ 889 _____ 509 _____
2b	Skip counting	Fill in the missing numerals: 9, 18, 27 __ , __ , __ , __ , __ , __ , __ , __ 4, 8, 12 __ , __ , __ , __ , __ , __ , __ , __ 7, 14, 21 __ , __ , __ , __ , __ , __ , __ , __ 3, 6, 9 __ , __ , __ , __ , __ , __ , __ , __ 8, 16, 24 __ , __ , __ , __ , __ , __ , __ , __ 6, 12, 18 __ , __ , __ , __ , __ , __ , __ , __ 100, 200, 300 __ , __ , __ , __ , __ , __ , __ , __
3a	Counting by 1s 1,000 to 9,999	Write the numeral that comes next: 3,101 _____ 2,529 _____ 5,499 _____ 7,308 _____ 3,999 _____ 7,999 _____
4a	Counting by 1s 10,000 to 999,999	Write the numeral that comes next: (Similar to above)

counting by 5s students say 5, 10, 15, 20, 25, 30. We recommend that skip counting by 10s be taught early to facilitate teaching rote counting to higher numbers. From skip counting, students learn that 40 follows 30; therefore, they more easily learn to say 40 after 39. Similarly, they learn to say 50 after 49, 60 after 59.

Skip counting by 10s is taught after students can rote count to 30. Skip counting by 2s and 5s is taught later in first grade. Other skip-counting series are taught in second and third grade. Learning the skip-counting series in early grades also facilitates learning basic multiplication facts. Skip counting by 2s three times yields 6; 3×2 also yields 6. (See Multiplication chapter)

Ordinal counting (counting associated with position) is introduced when the students have mastered rational counting. Ordinal counting is taught because of the common use of ordinal numbers. Teachers often use ordinal numbers in directions, e.g., "Touch the third problem."

INTRODUCING THE CONCEPT

The teaching procedures for the major counting skills appear in this section. The skills are listed in their relative order of introduction. Rote counting by 1s to 30 is discussed first. Rational counting is discussed next. Rational counting would be introduced when students can rote count to about 10. Thereafter, daily lessons would include both rote and rational counting exercises. After students learn to count one group of objects, they count two groups of objects and determine the total quantity. Next, procedures for teaching students to count from different numbers, to ordinal count, to rote count between 30 and 100, to rote count between 100 and 999, and to skip count are discussed.

Initial counting instruction is most efficient with pictorial representations of objects. Teachers are better able to monitor student performance during group instruction if the students are touching and counting pictures. As soon as students are proficient in counting pictures of objects, they can apply their skills to different types of manipulatives. Many low-performing students will learn to count manipulatives more easily by first receiving instruction on counting pictorial representations of objects.

Rote Counting by 1s to 30

On the first day of instruction, the teacher tests the students to determine how high they can rote count without error. The teacher tests the students individ-ually simply by asking them to count as high as they can. The teacher records the highest number each student counts. The performance of the group determines which new numbers are introduced. The teacher notes the lowest number correctly counted to by any members of the group and adds the next two or three numbers in the counting sequence. If a student counts to 11 on the pretest, the new part would be 11, 12, 13 (the last number said correctly on the pretest, 11, and the next two numbers, 12 and 13). The teacher should test several students informally at the beginning of each lesson to determine whether new numbers can be introduced. If the students count correctly, the teacher introduces several new numbers. If the students make errors, the teacher repeats the format with the previously introduced numbers.

The format for introducing new numbers in the counting sequence appears in Format 4.1. The teacher first models counting from 1 to 13, then models just the new part, 11, 12, 13 (see step 1 in Format 4.1). In step 2, the teacher leads the students in saying the new part. When introducing new numbers, during both the model and lead (steps 1 and 2), the teacher should emphasize the new numbers by saying them in a loud voice so that students are always hearing a correct answer. When the students appear able to say the new part by themselves, the teacher tests (step 3), then has them say the entire counting series from 1 through the new part (step 4). The students should repeat the counting sequence until they say it correctly several times in a row. Providing sufficient practice for students to count correctly several times is important to facilitate retention. Teachers should not forget to have individual students count by themselves. Finally, teachers should give a delayed test to ensure that students have mastered the sequence.

The teacher often will need to provide practice in teaching students to count at a lively pace. To do this, she uses a model-lead-test presentation, first modeling how fast she wants the students to count. Counting at a lively pace helps keep students attentive and facilitates learning the number sequence. Initially, the teacher should establish a counting speed that is slightly faster than one number per second. In future lessons, as the students become more proficient, rate should be increased to two numbers each second and a half.

Counting at a lively pace will be difficult for lower performers and will require lots of practice. Some students may need fifteen to twenty trials before being able to say a new part of the counting sequence correctly. If teachers provide adequate repetition during the first weeks of instruction, they will find that they save time in later weeks. When students can count familiar numbers at a lively pace, the teacher introduces new numbers in the counting sequence.

When presenting a counting task, the teacher must be quite careful not to give the students inappropriate cues. For example, some teachers have a tendency to count quietly when students are supposed to be counting alone (steps 3 and 4). Sometimes teachers just move their lips. This movement cues the students on the next number to say and precludes the students from initiating their own responses. If teachers find a number of students who have no trouble counting in groups but cannot perform the task on an individual test, the teacher might be providing extra help during group instruction.

Teachers also must be careful to correct all student errors. If students fail to stop at the appropriate number, the teacher models the correct response, emphasizing the last number in the counting sequence. "I am going to count and end with 6—**end with 6:** 1, 2, 3, 4, 5, **6.** I counted and *ended with 6.*" If students leave out a number (counting 1, 2, 3, 4, 6) they should be stopped immediately and the teacher should model the "hard part" by saying four numbers, beginning two numbers before the missed number (3, 4, 5, 6). Next the teacher would lead the students on the hard part, test them on the hard part, then have them begin counting again from 1.

The teacher should be quite careful when making this correction. If a counting error is corrected inappropriately, students may become quite confused. The mistake teachers should avoid is saying the skipped number after the student has made the error. For example, the student says "1, 2, 3, 4, 6," and the teacher says "5." What the student hears is "1, 2, 3, 4, 6, 5." The teacher can avoid this mistake by saying "stop" when a student makes an error and then by modeling the entire hard part. The teacher should

repeat a rote counting exercise until students can respond correctly to the complete series three times in a row. Sometimes students will make errors several times before responding correctly. If the teacher does not provide sufficient practice, students are less likely to remember the correct sequence the next day.

Mastering rote counting will require even more practice for lower-performing students. One way to prevent students from becoming frustrated while practicing counting is to spend only two to three minutes on rote counting tasks at any one time, but to present counting tasks several times during a lesson. This distributed practice is better than spending ten to fifteen minutes on counting all at once, because when a counting task is too grueling, students will stop trying and just respond randomly until the task is over. Also, counting practice should not be restricted to the instructional time allotted for arithmetic. The teacher can have students practice counting when they are lining up for recess, just before they go to lunch, during opening exercises in the morning, or during the last five minutes of class. These extra few minutes of practice during the day will be reflected through increased retention of newly taught numbers. Finally, the teacher should treat counting as a fun exercise. One way this can be done is to incorporate game-like activities into counting exercises. For example, having students count one time with their hands on their knees, the next time with hands on their heads, etc.

Rational Counting: One Group

Rational counting is the one-to-one correspondence of touching objects and counting. As mentioned previously, we recommend that initially teachers use pictures to teach rational counting skills for reasons of efficiency. The preskill for rational counting is rote counting. The initial exercises in rational counting can begin when the students can rote count to 10.

Summary Box 4.1   Rote Counting: Introducing New Numbers into a Counting Sequence

1. Teacher models counting sequence, emphasizing new part.

2. Teacher models and tests students on the new part of the sequence until students are able to say the new part correctly three times in a row.

3. Teacher tells students what number they will be ending with.

4. Teacher tests students from the *beginning* of the sequence through the new part.

5. Teacher practices new counting sequences frequently throughout the day.

Initially, rational counting involves coordination of touching pictures of objects and/or lines while saying a number in the counting sequence.

The format (Format 4.2) has two parts. In Part A, the teacher touches lines as the students count and then asks what number they ended with. The teacher must use very clear signals when touching the lines. In Part B, the students count illustrations of objects on their worksheets. The objects in the illustrations in Part B should be placed about a half-inch from each other so that the students won't become confused about which object they are touching. Note that the students are to begin the task by *pointing at,* not touching, the first object. The teacher signals by saying "Get ready," pausing, and then clapping. If the students are already touching the first object, they might touch the second object when they hear the clap. The teacher claps at about 1 to 1–$\frac{1}{2}$ second intervals. The teacher should not go too fast, as this might result in coordination errors. The cadence should be kept very predictable so that students do not make unnecessary errors.

Monitoring student performance is particularly critical in this format. Since coordinating touching and counting is the key behavior, listening to the students count is not sufficient. When the skill is first taught, the teacher must repeat the task enough times to enable her to watch each student touch some objects as the student counts. Monitoring at the very start of the task is also important. If students do not begin at the first picture, they will make mistakes. Note that during step 1 of Part B the teacher demonstrates that counting can be done from left to right or right to left. However, to facilitate monitoring, the students should always count from left to right.

Students may make coordination or rote counting errors. If a student makes a coordination error, i.e., saying the number before touching the picture of an object, the teacher tells the student to count *only* when the student touches an object. The teacher then repeats the task, saying "Go back to the first object and point to it." The teacher checks to make sure students are pointing and then repeats the task. As with all corrections in early counting instruction, after an error is made a student should repeat the task until she performs it correctly several times in a row. If a student has a lot of difficulty coordinating counting and pointing, the teacher can slow the cadence to a clap each 2 seconds and prompt the student by taking the student's hand, counting with her, and moving the student's index finger from object to object. The teacher might need to repeat this procedure at least three times before testing the

student by having her touch and count the objects without assistance.

If students make many rote counting errors (e.g., counting 1 2 3 5 6), the teacher should delay rational counting and provide extra practice on rote counting. Exercises in counting objects on worksheets should be done daily for several weeks. After students can quickly and accurately count lines and pictures of objects, they should be given manipulatives to count. Initially, the objects can be arranged in a row, which makes counting manipulatives easier. Counting objects in rows is like counting pictures in rows. After students can count objects in rows, objects should be placed randomly. The teacher would model, lead, and test counting random objects, if necessary.

Rational Counting: Two Groups

Counting two groups of lines is introduced when students are able to count a single group of six to eight lines. The format for counting two groups of lines teaches students the function of the word *all* and prepares them for addition. When students first add, they count two groups of lines—*all* of the lines. The format for counting two groups of lines appears in Format 4.3. In Part A the teacher draws two groups of lines on the board and has the students count and tell how many lines in the first group, in the second group, and finally in both groups. Part B is a worksheet exercise in which the students count two groups of lines on their worksheets.

The error students are likely to make in Part A occurs when they are asked to count all of the lines. After counting the lines in the first group, a student is likely to say "one" for the first line in the second group instead of continuing to count. To correct, the teacher models and tests students on that step, and then repeats all the steps. For example, if in counting the lines in this diagram | | | | | |, the student counts 1 2 3 4, 1, 2 the teacher models counting, saying "When we count *all* of the lines, we keep on counting. My turn: 1 2 3 **4** 5 6." The teacher then tests the students on counting all of the lines and then repeats the format from the beginning.

Counting from Different Numbers

Counting from numbers other than 1 saves time when teaching rote counting to higher numbers. For example, in teaching students to count 38, 39, 40, the teacher would model and test from 36 (36, 37, 38, 39, 40), rather than modeling and testing counting from 1. If students can start at numbers other than 1, teachers can focus on the relevant parts of number sequences. A second reason for teaching counting beginning at a number other than 1 is that this counting skill is a component skill of the early addition strategy. Students solve a problem such as 4 + 3 = ___ by saying 4 for the first group and then counting each line in the second group: 5, 6, 7.

Format 4.4 shows how to teach students to count beginning at a number other than 1. This format would be introduced when students can rote count to about 15. The format contains two parts. The first part teaches students the meaning of the term *get it going*. (When the teacher says "Get it going," the students say the designated number verbally, holding the number as long as the teacher signals, e.g., 4 is said "fffooourrr.") The signal used is quite different from signals used in other rote counting tasks. To prompt the students to say the number for a longer time, the teacher signals by moving her hand from side to side. The students are to begin saying the number as the teacher begins the signal (moving her finger) and to stop saying the number when the teacher stops the signal (dropping her hand). The purpose of the get-it-going signal is to better enable the students to respond in unison.

The teacher should present a set of at least three examples each time Part B is presented. Initially, the examples should all be less than 10. The exercise is repeated until students respond correctly to the entire set, which increases the likelihood that they can generalize the skill to other numbers. Responding correctly to the entire set implies that if a mistake is made on one example, the teacher repeats all of the examples until the students can respond to them consecutively with no errors. Students will need several repetitions before they will master the entire set. However, if a high criterion is maintained initially, the amount of practice needed to master subsequent sets will be reduced.

Sometimes students make the error of starting over at 1, e.g., "fffooour 1 2 3 4." The teacher corrects by modeling and then leading the students several times with an emphasis on the first counted number. However, if the students continue to have problems, the teacher can introduce a procedure where she counts quickly from 1 to the get-it-going number and then signals for the students to respond on the next number. For example, the teacher would say, "I'll start counting and when I signal, you count with me: 1 2 3 fffooourr (signal) **5** 6 7 8 9." The

teacher responds with students several times, then tests. After the students begin responding correctly to several consecutive examples, they no longer need the prompt of beginning the sequence at 1.

Ordinal Counting

Ordinal counting involves saying the number associated with relative position, i.e., first, second, third, fourth, fifth, sixth. Ordinal counting is introduced only when students can rote count to 20 and can tell the cardinal number for a group. A model-lead-test procedure is used to introduce ordinal counting. Teachers might introduce ordinal counting by having children participate in a race, after which the teacher discusses the positions of the runners. "Who came in first? Who came in second?" The teacher then models and tests ordinal counting sequences.

Counting by 1s from 30 to 100

The procedure for counting by 1s from 30 to 100 should demonstrate the relationship between each tens grouping, i.e., each decade has a sequence in which the numerals 0, 1, 2, 3, 4, 5, 6, 7, 8, 9 appear in the ones column: **40, 41, 42, 43, 44, 45, 46, 47, 48, 49.** Two preskills related to counting higher numbers are rote counting beginning at a number other than 1 (e.g., starting at 5 and counting 6, 7, 8) and skip counting by 10s (10, 20, 30, 40, 50, 60, 70, 80, 90, 100), which is discussed later in the chapter.

The format for counting numbers from 30 to 100 is basically the same as that in Format 4.1 for introducing new numbers in the early counting sequence, with these modifications. First, the new part would begin at a 10s number ending in 7 and continue through the next 10s number ending in 2 (e.g., 27, 28, 29, 30, 31, 32, or 47, 48, 49, 50, 51, 52). Starting at higher number (e.g., 8 or 9), gives students too little time to prepare for transition to the next decade. Starting at the beginning of the decade (e.g., 21, 22) makes the task too time consuming. Second, instead of testing the students on counting from 1, the teacher has them count from a number approximately 10 to 20 numbers lower than the new part.

The first exercises should teach students to count from the thirties to the forties. Counting from the forties to the fifties, and higher, should be introduced several days later or whenever students master the lower numbers. After students practice counting through a new decade for 2 days, the examples are modified daily to promote generalizability. For example, students might count from 27 to 42 one day, from 25 to 47 the next, and from 27 to 49 the next.

Counting Between 100 and 999

Students are usually taught to count from 100 through 999 during second grade. First, students are taught to count by 100s from 100 to 1,000. The 100s skip counting series is usually quite easy for students to learn, requiring only a few days of practice. Once students can count by 1s through 99 and by 100s from 100 to 1,000, the teacher can introduce counting by 1s in the 100s numbers. A three stage procedure is used. First, the teacher has students count a single decade within a single hundred (e.g., 350–359). The teacher uses a model-lead-test procedure on four to five sets of examples each day. Examples similar to the following would be presented daily until students demonstrate mastery:

350, 351, 352, 353, 354, 355, 356, 357, 358, 359
720, 721, 722, 723, 724, 725, 726, 727, 728, 729
440, 441, 442, 443, 444, 445, 446, 447, 448, 449
860, 861, 862, 863, 864, 865, 866, 867, 868, 869

The objective of the second stage is making the transition from one decade to the next (e.g., 325–335). An example set would include several series extending from a number with 5 in the ones column to the next number in the counting sequence that has 5 in the ones column. Examples similar to those below would be presented daily until students demonstrate mastery. Lower-performing students may require about two–three weeks practice.

325, 326, 327, 328, 329, 330, 331, 332, 333, 334, 335
785, 786, 787, 788, 789, 790, 791, 792, 793, 794, 795
435, 436, 437, 438, 439, 440, 441, 442, 443, 444, 445
115, 116, 117, 118, 119, 120, 121, 122, 123, 124, 125

The third stage focuses on the transition from a hundreds series to the next hundreds series (e.g., 495–505). The example set would include several series extending from a hundreds number ending with 95 to the next number in the counting series that has a 5 in the ones column. A daily lesson might include these examples:

495, 496, 497, 498, 499, 500, 501, 502, 503, 504, 505
295, 296, 297, 298, 299, 300, 301, 302, 303, 304, 305
795, 796, 797, 798, 799, 800, 801, 802, 803, 804, 805
595, 596, 597, 598, 599, 600, 601, 602, 603, 604, 605

Review can be provided through written worksheets in which the teacher writes a number on a worksheet with 10 spaces across from it. The students are to fill in the next 10 numbers.

Skip Counting

Skip counting refers to counting each number of a specified multiple. When a student skip counts by 5s, the student says "5, 10, 15, 20, 25, 30, 35, 40, 45, 50." When skip counting by 8s, the student says "8, 16, 24, 32, 40, 48, 56, 64, 72, 80." Throughout this book, we will refer to skip counting by saying the *count-by series.* Knowledge of the count-by series for multiples of 2, 3, 4, 5, 6, 7, 8, 9, and 10 serves as an important component skill for the memorization of basic multiplication and division facts. Students should learn to count ten numbers for each series (except 5s): 2 to 20, 3 to 30, 4 to 40, 6 to 60, etc. Students should learn to count by 5s to 60, since telling time requires this skill. Teachers also may want to teach counting by 25s to 100 as a prerequisite to counting money.

The first count-by series to be introduced should be the 10s, since knowledge of this series is a component skill for rote counting to 100. Counting by 10s is introduced when students can rote count by ones to about 30, usually several months into first grade. The next count-by series, the 2s, might not be introduced until several weeks later. Thereafter, a new series may be introduced when students are able to say each of the previously introduced series accurately and fluently. Students are fluent on a specific series when they can say the series within approximately eight seconds.

We suggest teaching the count-by series cumulatively in the following sequence: 10, 2, 5, 9, 4, 25, 3, 8, 7, 6. This order is designed to initially separate those count-by series that contain many of the same numbers. For example, several numbers in the 4 series also appear in the 8 series: 4, **8,** 12, **16,** 20, **24.** Therefore, the introductions of the 4 and 8 series are separated by two other dissimilar series.

Separating similar series helps prevent errors in which students switch series. Switching series, a common count-by error, involves counting by one number and then switching to another series after saying a number common to both series. For example, students may begin counting by 4s and switch to 8s when they come to 16, 24 or 32 (e.g., 4, 8, 12, 16, 24, 32, 40). The chances of making that error are reduced when the two series are not introduced consecutively. Therefore, the recommended sequence for teaching count-by series can make learning them easier.

The count-by format includes two parts (see Format 4.5). Part A demonstrates to students that they end up with the same number whether they count by 1s or count by another number. Also, the demonstration is intended to show that counting by a number other than 1 can save time. Part A would be presented just for the first lessons in which count-by 2s and 5s are taught. Part B is designed to teach students to memorize the various count-by series. Part B of the count-by format also includes a review of previously introduced count-by series. Two or three previously taught series should be reviewed daily.

The teacher uses a model-lead-test procedure, saying the numbers of the new series alone, saying the numbers of the new series with the students, and finally having the students say the numbers themselves. Teachers working with more naive students would introduce just the first three numbers of a series, while teachers working with more sophisticated students might introduce the entire series. For example, the first day the count-by 9 series is presented to a group of lower-performing students, the teacher would introduce just the first three numbers of the series: 9, 18, 27. On the other hand, a teacher working with higher-performing students might present the whole series: 9, 18, 27, 36, 45, 54, 63, 72, 81, 90. Teachers working with average students might introduce a whole series in several days, while teachers working with lower-performing students may expect the students to require about two weeks to master a series.

On the second day of instruction on a series, the teacher tests the students on the part of the series taught during the previous lesson. If the students make an error, the teacher repeats the model-lead-test procedure from step 1 of Part B. If the students know the part of the series previously taught or require just a couple of practice trials to say the previously taught part correctly, the teacher introduces the next several numbers of the count-by series. The new part includes the last two familiar numbers and the next two or three numbers in the series. For example, if students have been previously taught 9s to 36: (9, 18, 27, 36), the new part would include 27 and 36, the last two numbers from the previously taught part, plus the next two numbers in the series, 45 and 54. The teacher uses a model-lead-test procedure, first on 27–54 and then on the series from the beginning.

As with any rote counting task, adequate repetition must be provided for student mastery. A teacher may have to lead lower-performing students five to ten times through a series until they are able to say it fluently without errors. When leading students, the teacher should initially use a loud voice, particularly when saying difficult parts of a counting sequence. The purpose of using a loud voice is to ensure that all students are hearing the correct response and to prevent them from cueing on students who may be responding incorrectly. A brisk rhythm should be established by the teacher's tapping her foot or clapping her hands to make mastering the series easier. The numbers in a series should be said at a rate slightly faster than a number a second, i.e., saying 9, 18, 27 . . . 90 in about eight seconds.

Corrections for skip-counting errors follow the model-lead-test correction procedure. When the teacher hears an error, she stops all the students, models the hard part (the two numbers just before the missed number and the one number following the missed number), leads the students on the hard part several times, tests the students on the hard part, and then has them say the entire series from the beginning. For example, if students count "8, 16, 24, 32, 40, 48, 54," the teacher stops them as soon as she hears 54 instead of 56. Next she models, leads, and tests on the hard part: 40, 48, **56,** 64. After students perform acceptably on the test of the hard part, the teacher has the students begin counting with 8.

A new series is introduced only when students know all of the previously introduced series. Teach-

---

Summary Box 4.2   Skip Counting: Introducing a New Count-by Series

1. Teacher writes new count-by series on the board and models saying the series.

2. Teacher leads the students in reading the new series from the board. (The teacher determines how much of the series to introduce at once, based on previous performance of the students.)

3. Teacher gradually erases numbers in the series as students practice saying the series.

4. Teacher tests students on saying the series from memory.

5. Teacher alternates practice with previously introduced series and new series.

APPLICATION ITEMS: COUNTING

1. A student counts "5,6,7,9." Immediately after the student says "9," the teacher says "8," to correct her. What is the problem with this correction? What *should* the teacher say and do?

2. In counting from 1–10, a student makes an error at 8. The teacher models and tests the student on the hard part. The student responds correctly. Is this correction sufficient? Tell why.

3. Two days ago the teacher introduced rote counting to 16. At the beginning of the lesson, the teacher tests the students and they can all count to 16. What would the teacher do that day? What if the students had not been able to count to 16?

4. The teacher tells the students to count to 45. A child counts correctly until 39 and then says 50. What is the correction?

5. When counting this group of lines: IIIII, a student ends up with 8. What are two possible causes of the error? How would the correction procedures differ?

ers should expect students to make frequent errors when a series similar to one previously taught is presented. When the 6 series is presented, the teacher may find that students make errors on the 4s series. Both series include 24. A student might count 4, 8, 12, 16, 20, 24, 30, 36, 42, switching from the 4s to the 6 series at 24. With adequate practice, this confusion can be eliminated. Practice on previously taught series can also be provided through peer tutoring or other partner practice activities.

FORMAT 4.1   Format for Introducing New Numbers

TEACHER	STUDENTS
1. I'm going to count and end up with 13. What am I going to end up with?	13
Yes, 13, listen. 12345678910 **11, 12, 13.** *(Quickly count to 10 and then emphasize 11, 12, 13.)* Listen to the new part: 11 12 13	
2. When I drop my hand, say the new part with me. Teeeeeennnn. *(Drop hand and respond with students.)*	11, 12, 13
11, 12, 13. Again Teeeeeeennnnn. Drop hand. 11, 12, 13. *(Repeat until students respond correctly several times in a row.)*	
3. Say the new part all by yourselves: Teeenn. *(To correct: return to step 2)*	11, 12, 13
4. Now you're going to count and end up with 13. What number are you going to end up with? Starting at 1, get ready, count. 1, 2, 3, 4, 5, 6, 7, 8, 9, 10, 11, 12, 13 *(Call on individuals.)*	13

FORMAT 4.2   **Format for Rational Counting**

PART A: STRUCTURED BOARD PRESENTATION

TEACHER	**STUDENTS**

1. *(Draw four lines on the board.)*
   My turn. Every time I touch a line, I count. Watch.
   (Touch lines at 1 second intervals.) 1, 2, 3, 4.
   What number did I end with?   4
   (Repeat step 1 with seven lines.)

2. *(Draw six lines on the board.)* Every time I touch a line you count.
   (Point to left of line.) Get ready. *(Touch lines from left to right at one*   1, 2, 3, 4, 5, 6
   second intervals as students count.)
      To correct: If students make counting errors, count with them.
      Repeat task until student can respond correctly without assistance.
      If students count before you touch a line, tell them. Watch my finger.
      When I Touch a line, you count.

3. What number did we end with?   6

4. So, how many lines are there?   6

5. *(Repeat steps 2–4 with three lines, then seven lines. Give individual*
   turns to several students.)

PART B: STRUCTURED WORKSHEET PRESENTATION

TEACHER	**STUDENTS**

Sample worksheet items:

1. *(Hold up a worksheet, point to a group of objects and say)* We're going
   to count all the objects. Watch me count. *(Touch the objects from left to*
   right and count) 1, 2, 3, 4, 5. Watch me count again. *(Touch objects from*
   right to left and count) 1, 2, 3, 4, 5.

2. Everyone, hold your finger over the first picture. *(Check to see that all*
   students are pointing to but not touching the appropriate picture.)
   Each time I clap, you touch an object and say the number. Get ready.   1, 2, 3, 4, 5
   (Clap one time per second. Count with students while monitoring their
   touching.)

3. All by yourselves, you're going to count the pictures. Hold your finger
   over the first picture. *(Check)* Get ready. *(Clap one time per second.)*   1, 2, 3, 4, 5
   How many lines are there?   5

4. *(Repeat steps 2 and 3 with other examples. Give individual turns to*
   several students.)

FORMAT 4.3   **Format for Counting Two Groups of Lines**

PART A: STRUCTURED BOARD PRESENTATION

TEACHER	STUDENTS
1. (*Write on board:*) ‖‖‖ ‖‖ Here are two groups of lines. *(Touch the first group.)* Here are the lines in the **first** group. *(Touch the second group.)* Here are the lines in the second group.	
2. Let's count the lines in the **first** group. *(Touch as students count.)* How many lines in the **first** group?	1, 2, 3, 4, 5 5
3. Let's count the lines in the **second** group. *(Touch as students count.)* How many lines in the **second** group?	1, 2, 3 3

4. Now let's count all the lines. You count the lines in the **first** group and then you keep on going and count the lines in the **second** group.
(Touch as students count.)
    To correct: Watch me count all the lines. *(Point and count.)* Your turn. Count all the lines. *(Touch as students count.)*
    How many lines in all?
	1, 2, 3, 4, 5, 6, 7, 8
	
	8

5. *(Repeat steps 1–4 with* ‖‖‖ ‖‖ *then* ‖‖ ‖‖‖*)*	

PART B: STRUCTURED WORKSHEET PRESENTATION

TEACHER	STUDENTS
a. ‖‖‖ ‖‖‖‖ b. ‖‖‖‖ ‖‖ c. ‖‖ ‖‖‖‖ d. ‖‖‖‖ ‖‖‖	
1. Touch lines in a. *(Check).*	
2. Touch the lines in the first group. I'll clap. You count the lines in the first group. Put your finger over the first line. *(Pause while students place finger over first line.)* Get ready. *(Clap at 1 second intervals.)* How many lines in the first group?	3
3. *(Repeat step 2 with the second group.)*	
4. Now you're going to count all the lines. Start counting with the first group. Put your finger over the first line. *(Pause while students put finger over first line.)* Get ready. *(Clap at 1 second intervals.)* How many lines in all? *(Call on individual students.)*	7
5. *(Repeat steps 1–4 with other examples.)*	

FORMAT 4.4   **Format for Counting from Numbers Other Than 1**

PART A: PRESKILL—GET IT GOING SIGNAL

TEACHER	STUDENTS
1. Get it going means to say a number as long as I move my finger.	
2. *(Hold up hand.)* My turn. I'm going to get 4 going. *(Move hand in circular motion saying foouuurrr. After several seconds, drop hand and stop saying 4.)*	
3. *(Repeat step 2 with the numbers 6 and 9).*	

4. Let's do it together. We have 4. How many do we have? Get it going. *(Repeat step 4 with the numbers 8 and 2)*	4 fooouuurrr
5. You have five. How many do you have? Get it going. *(Repeat step 5 with the numbers 7 and 3.)*	5 fiiivvve

PART B: ORAL PRESENTATION

TEACHER	STUDENTS
1. We're going to get it going and count. My turn. We have four. Get it going. *(Signal by moving hand in circular motion. After two seconds, drop hand.)* Fooouuurr, 5, 6, 7, 8, stop. *(Count at a rate of about two numbers a second.)*	
2. Get it going and count with me. You have 4. How many do you have? Get it going. *(Begin signal.)* Foouuurr. *(After about two seconds drop hand.)* Five, six, seven, eight.	4 foouurrr
3. All by yourselves. You have 4. Get it going. *(Begin signal; after two seconds drop hand. Say stop after children say 8.)*	foouurr, 5, 6, 7, 8
4. *(Repeat steps 1–3 with the number 7 and then 3. Give individuals turns with 7, 4, or 3.)*	

FORMAT 4.5   **Format for Count-by**

PART A: INTRODUCING THE COUNT-BY

TEACHER	STUDENT
1. *(Draw lines in groups of two on the board:)* | | | | | | | | | | Let's find out how many lines we have. I'll touch and you count. How many lines are there? *(Write 10 next to the last group.)* Now I'll show you a fast way to count those lines. *(Circle each group of two lines with your finger. For each group, ask, "How many lines in this group?" After asking about all five groups, ask, "How many lines are in each group?")* When we count groups of 2, we count lines the fast way.	1, 2, 3, 4, 5, 6, 7, 8, 9, 10 10 2 2
2. Let's figure out the numbers we say when we count by 2. Count the lines in the first group. *(Point to each line as students count.)*	1, 2
Yes, there are two lines, so I write 2 above the first group. *(Write 2 above the first group.)*	
Count the lines in the first and second groups.	1, 2, 3, 4
You counted four lines so far, so I'll write 4 above the second group. *(Write it.)*	
(Continue to have the students count each successive group from the beginning, writing the appropriate numeral above each group, such as the following:	

```
2    4    6    8    10
||   ||   ||   ||   ||
```

When the students have finished, the lines should look like the above example.)

(continued on next page)

FORMAT 4.5   **(continued)**

TEACHER	STUDENTS
4. Now you know what numbers to say when you count by 2. Let's count the lines again, but this time we'll count by 2. *(Point to each numeral as students count.)*	2, 4, 6, 8, 10
5. How many did you end up with when you counted by 2? *(Point to the 10 written next to the last group.)* How many did you end up with when you counted the regular way?	10 10
See, the fast way really does work.	6, 12, 18, 24, 30, 36, 42, 48

PART B: STRUCTURED BOARD PRESENTATION

TEACHER	STUDENTS
1. *(Write on board 6, 12, 18, 24, 30, 36, 42, 48)* Today we are going to learn to count by 6. I will say the numbers in the series. 6, 12, 18, 24, 30, 36, 42, 48. Say the 6s with me as I touch each number. Get ready. *(Signal)* 6, 12, 18, 24, 30, 36, 42, 48 *(Lead students until they appear able to say series without help.)* To correct: Model, then lead the students until they can recite the series by themselves with no errors.	6, 12, 18, 24, 30, 36, 42, 48
2. Say the new part by yourselves. Get ready. *(Signal.) (Give individual turns to several students.)*	6, 12, 18, 24, 30, 36, 42, 48
3. *(Teacher erases one of the numbers in the series.)* Say the 6s this time, including the missing number.	6, 12, 18, 24, 30, 36, 42, 48
(Repeat step 3, erasing another number each time, until students appear able to say series without help.)	
4. *(Integrate previously learned count-by series with practice on new series.)*	

CHAPTER 5

Symbol Identification and Place Value

TERMS AND CONCEPTS

Number   The number that identifies quantity of elements or members of a set; a cardinal number.

Numeral   A symbol used to represent a number.

Place Value   The system by which the value of a digit is determined by the position it occupies relative to the decimal point.

Expanded Notation   A numeral written as a sum in which each digit's value is expressed as an addend, e.g., in 342, the digits 3, 4, and 2 are written as the addends 300 + 40 + 2.

Column Alignment   Writing numerals one above the other so that the units, tens, and hundreds positions are in columns: 32 + 426 is written

```
  32
+426
```

SKILL HIERARCHY

Symbol identification and place value may be divided into three major areas: (a) reading and writing numerals, (b) column alignment, and (c) expanded notation. Numeral identification (reading and writing the numerals 0 through 10) is the foundation of the skill hierarchy for these areas.

Place value concepts are introduced through the remaining instructional activities: reading and writing teen numbers, hundreds, thousands, and millions numbers; expanded notation; and column alignment. In reading multi-digit numbers, students translate each digit into a value according to its position and then identify the entire numeral. For example, in reading 58, students must note that the 5 represents five tens and that five tens is read as "fifty." Eight ones is read as "eight." The students then put the parts together and identify 58 as "fifty-eight." Writing numerals requires the reverse—breaking a number into parts rather than putting parts together. When students are told to write 58, they break the number into parts: 50 and 8. Fifty is represented by a 5 in the tens column; so students write that part. Eight is represented by an 8 in the ones column; so students write that part. In summary, to read numerals, students determine the value of each part and then put the values together. To write numerals, students break the number into parts and write the digit representing each value.

The introduction of expanded notation and place value parallels that of reading and writing numbers. For example, when teachers see that students can read and write hundreds numbers, they introduce column alignment problems with hundreds numbers:

```
342 + 8 is rewritten as 342
                        +  8
```

Instructional Sequence and Assessment Chart

Grade Level	Problem Type	Performance Indicator
K-1	Reading numerals zero through 10	Read these numerals: 4 2 6 1 7 3 0 8 5 9 10
K-1	Writing numerals zero through 10	Write these numerals: 4 2 6 1 7 3 0 8 5 9 10
K-1	Writing a numeral to represent members of a set	4 6 |||| ||||||
K-1	Writing members of set (lines) to represent a numeral	4 6 _____ _____
1a	Reading teen numbers	Read these numerals: 15 11 13 12 17 19 14 16 18
1b	Writing teen numbers	Write these numerals: 15 11 13 12 17 19 14 16 18
1c	Reading numbers from 20 to 99	Read these numerals: 64 81 44 29
1d	Writing numbers from 20 to 99	Write these numerals: 47 98 72 31
1e	Column alignment Rewriting horizontal addition and subtraction problems	$85 + 3 =$ _____ $4 + 25 =$ _____ $37 - 2 =$ _____
1f	Expanded notation	$63 =$ _____ $+$ _____ $92 =$ _____ $+$ _____
2a	Reading and writing numbers between 100 and 999 except those with a zero in the tens column	Read: 320 417 521 Write seven hundred fifteen _____ Write four hundred thirty-six _____ Write three hundred fifty _____
2b	Reading and writing numbers between 100 and 999 with zero in the tens column and zero in the ones column	Read: 300 800 200 Write four hundred _____ Write six hundred _____ Write nine hundred _____
2c	Reading and writing numbers between 100 and 999 with zero in tens column only	Read: 502 708 303 Write four hundred eight _____ Write seven hundred two _____ Write three hundred three _____
2d	Rewriting horizontal equations, one number is a hundreds number	$305 + 8 + 42 =$ _____ $428 - 21 =$ _____ $31 + 142 + 8 =$ _____
2e	Expanded notation with hundreds numbers	$382 =$ _____ $+$ _____ $+$ _____ $417 =$ _____ $+$ _____ $+$ _____ $215 =$ _____ $+$ _____ $+$ _____

Grade Level	Problem Type	Performance Indicator
3a	Reading and writing thousands numbers between 1,000 and 9,999 with no zeroes in hundreds or tens column	Read: 3,248 7,151 1,318 Write five thousand three hundred fourteen _____ Write two thousand six hundred forty-three _____ Write one thousand one hundred forty-one _____
3b	Reading and writing thousands numbers between 1,000 and 9,999 with zeroes in hundreds, tens, and ones columns	Read: 3,000 7,000 2,000 Write four thousand _____ Write eight thousand _____ Write six thousand _____
3c	Reading and writing thousands numbers between 1,000 and 9,999 with a zero in the hundreds column	Read: 7,025 8,014 2,092 Write five thousand seventy-two _____ Write one thousand forty _____ Write six thousand eight-eight _____
3d	Reading and writing thousands numbers between 1,000 and 9,999 with zeroes in the hundreds and tens columns	Read: 4,008 2,002 1,009 Write six thousand eight _____ Write nine thousand four _____ Write five thousand two _____
3e	Column alignment: Rewriting horizontal problems	$35 + 1,083 + 245 =$ _____ $4,035 - 23 =$ _____ $8 + 2,835 =$ _____
4a	Reading and writing all thousands numbers between 10,000 and 999,999	Read: 300,000 90,230 150,200 Write two hundred thousand _____ Write ninety thousand four hundred _____ Write one hundred thousand two hundred _____
4b	Reading and writing numbers between 1 million and 9 million	Read: 6,030,000 5,002,100 1,340,000 Write seven million _____ Write three million, eighty thousand _____ Write eight million, six hundred thousand _____
5a	Reading and writing numbers between 10 million and 999 million	Read: 27,400,000 302,250,000 900,300,000 Write ten million _____ Write forty million two hundred thousand _____

and then expanded notation problems with hundreds numbers:

$$342 = 300 + 40 + 2$$

The Instructional Sequence and Assessment Chart lists specific skills, indicating their relative order of introduction. Note that many of the tasks in kindergarten and first grade require teachers to test students individually. In later grades, only tasks requiring students to read numerals need be tested individually.

INTRODUCING THE CONCEPT

This section deals with skills normally taught during kindergarten and early first grade. These skills are prerequisites for the equality-based strategies that provide a conceptual understanding of addition and subtraction. The skills, listed in the order they are discussed in this section, are:

1. Numeral identification (zero through 10)
2. Numeral writing (zero through 10)
3. Symbol identification and writing (+, −, □, =)
4. Equation reading and writing
5. Numeral and line matching

Numeral Identification

Numeral identification tasks begin when students can rote count to 8. Introducing numeral identification is delayed until after students can rote count to 8 in order to avoid confusion between counting and numeral identification. Students who enter school knowing how to count can begin learning to identify numerals immediately.

The sequence in which numerals are introduced is important. A basic guideline in sequencing the introduction of numerals is to separate similar-looking and similar-sounding numerals. Students are likely to confuse 6 and 9 because they look so much alike; likewise, students may have difficulty discriminating 4 and 5 since they sound alike, both beginning with the same sound. Therefore, a good sequence of introduction would separate both pairs of numerals by several lessons. One possible sequence for introducing numerals 0–10 is: 4, 2, 6, 1, 7, 3, 0, 8, 5, 9, 10. Note the separation of 6 and 9; 1, 0, and 10; and 4 and 5. This sequence is included as an example and is certainly not the only sequence that will minimize student errors.

A second sequencing guideline is to introduce new numerals cumulatively. A new numeral is not presented until students have demonstrated mastery of the previously introduced symbols. Teachers working with students who enter school with little or no previous knowledge of numerals can generally introduce new symbols at a rate of one new symbol each three to five lessons.

The format (see Format 5.1) for introducing new numerals to students consists of a model, in which the teacher points to the numeral and tells the students the name of the numeral; a test, in which the teacher asks the students to identify the new numeral; and discrimination practice, in which the teacher asks students to identify the new numeral and previously introduced numerals.

In this format, the teacher first writes a set of numerals on the board. The new numeral is written several times. Each of the previously introduced numerals is written once. The new numeral is written several times to ensure that the student attends to the *appearance* of the numeral, rather than its position on the board. The most important part of the introduction is the discrimination practice in step 2 of the format. Note that the presentation of the numeral follows an alternating pattern: new numeral, one previously introduced numeral, new numeral, two previously introduced numerals, new numeral, three previously introduced numerals, etc. The time the student has to remember the new numeral is gradually increased by adding more familiar numerals. This pattern is designed to help students better remember a new or difficult numeral. Individual turns are given after the teacher presents the discrimination practice. If, when giving an individual turn, a student misidentifies or does not respond, the teacher identifies the numeral and uses the alternating pattern, focusing on that numeral and previously identified numerals.

A clear point-and-touch signal is essential for clear presentation of this format. The features of a good point-touch signal are illustrated in Figure 5.1 below. When signaling, the teacher points under the numeral (not touching the board), making sure that no student's vision is blocked by any part of the teacher's hand or body. After pointing under the numeral for one to two seconds, the teacher signals by moving her finger away from the board and then back toward it, touching under the numeral. The out-and-in motion is done crisply with **the finger** moving away from the board (about six inches) and then immediately back to the board. When the finger touches below the numeral, the students are to respond. The out-and-in motion should be done the same way every time it is used. Any hesitation or inconsistency makes unison responding difficult

FIGURE 5.1   Point, Out, In and Touch Signal

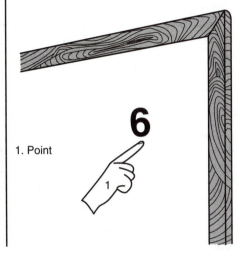

1. Point

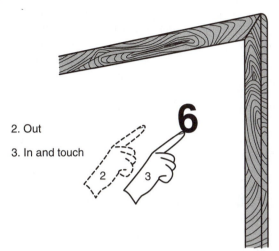

2. Out

3. In and touch

because the students cannot tell when they are supposed to respond.

Pacing is extremely important for an effective presentation. As a general rule, the teacher should point to a numeral for a second or two, then signal. After the students respond, the teacher should confirm the response ("Yes, this is a 6") or correct the error ("This is a **6**. What numeral?"). Then the teacher immediately points to the next number in the task, pauses a second or two, then signals. When pointing to numerals that have been newly introduced or ones that have caused students difficulty in the past, the teacher might initially pause three to four seconds before signaling. The primary goal of good pacing is to give students sufficient practice, with feedback, in a short amount of time.

As with rote counting, the numeral identification tasks are more efficiently taught if presented for three to five minutes at several different times during the lesson, rather than in one long session. Numeral identification can also be practiced at various times of the day. Many teachers make cardboard numerals and put them on a bulletin board or wall in the room. The teachers then ask the students to identify the symbols during early morning exercises, before going to recess or lunch, etc. The practice provided by these brief tasks, interspersed throughout the day, can make a great difference in how quickly low-performing students learn to identify symbols.

Numeral Writing

Numeral writing is an important skill in itself and also reinforces numeral identification. As a general rule, a new numeral can be introduced into numeral

writing exercises several lessons after it first appears in a numeral identification format. As noted in symbol identification, symbols are introduced cumulatively. Instructionally naive students will be ready to practice writing a new numeral every three to five lessons. There are three basic stages in teaching students to write single-digit numerals:

1. Tracing numerals written on worksheets
2. Copying numerals
3. Writing numerals from dictation

For worksheet tracing exercises, we recommend that dots be used to prompt the students where to begin writing the numeral.

• •   • •   • •   • •

During the first several lessons, the teacher leads the students through tracing, monitoring them quite carefully and, if necessary, moving the students' hands to help them make the lines. The students say the name of the numeral each time they write it. When the students are able to trace a numeral without assistance, the teacher introduces copying. In initial copying exercises, dashed lines and dots appear for the first numeral but only dots for the remaining numerals.

When students can do this exercise, a more sophisticated copying exercise is introduced in which no dots or dashed lines are used as prompts. The students should practice writing each numeral at least 10 to 20 times each day for the first week the symbol is introduced. The number of repetitions can be gradually reduced as student performance improves.

The third and final stage of numeral writing includes numeral dictation exercises in which the teacher says a number, and the students write the numeral. Some students find dictation exercises quite difficult in that they not only have to remember what a numeral looks like but also how to write it. The prerequisites for introducing a numeral in dictation exercises are being able to identify and copy the numeral.

In a numeral dictation exercise, the teacher follows the same alternating pattern used in numeral identification tasks. For example, if students have learned to write 4, 2, 6, 1 and are being introduced to 7 in a dictation exercise, the sequence of examples presented by the teacher might be: 7, 4, 7, 6, 1, 7, 4, 2, 6, 7. The worksheet on which the students are to write the numerals should have blank spaces or boxes large enough to write each symbol.

Monitoring and pacing are both important teacher presentation behaviors for numeral dictation. The teacher should check the responses of all low-performing students after each numeral is written. The responses of higher-performing students can be checked after every second or third numeral. As soon as the last student has finished writing a symbol, if no mistakes were made, the teacher should dictate the next numeral. Too much time between tasks can result in off-task behavior.

The correction procedure for errors involves a model-test-alternating test procedure. The teacher shows the students how to write the numeral, has the students copy it, and then alternates between having students write the missed numeral and other numerals.

Teachers must be careful in setting reasonable criteria for neatness. Students with little prior writing experience may require many months of practice before they consistently write numerals neatly. The teacher should gradually increase criteria for legibility and neatness. In initial exercises, writing a reasonable facsimile of a numeral is the critical student behavior. If a student writes a number backward, the teacher may respond by acknowledging that the correct numeral was written but correct the positioning: "Good. That is a 4, but here's how to write it." Note that the correction is made in a positive manner.

Symbol Identification and Writing

The symbols for plus, minus, equal sign, and empty box are taught with the same procedures as for numerals. An empty box can be introduced as "how many." Introducing a box as "how many" facilitates reading equations, e.g., $6 + 5 = \square$ is read: "Six plus five equals how many?"

Introduction of the various symbols should be interspersed throughout the lessons in which numerals are introduced. The first symbol would be introduced after several numerals; subsequent symbols would be introduced after two to three additional numerals had been introduced.

Equation Reading and Writing

Equation reading is a prerequisite skill for problem solving and learning math facts. Students must be able to read an equation fluently if they are to be able to derive the answer and see its relationship to other equations.

Children may have difficulty reading a problem such as $6 - 3 = \square$, even though they can identify each symbol in isolation. When they read a problem, they must connect the numerals and symbols together, which requires some practice.

Equation reading is introduced when the students know enough numerals and symbols for the teacher to create equations. Students should be able to identify the numerals almost instantaneously prior to equation reading. If students have not received adequate practice to quickly identify numerals when they appear in isolation, they will have much difficulty reading equations. Because the procedure for teaching the reading of equations is quite straightforward, a format is not included. The teacher would follow the model-lead-test procedure. The teacher writes several equations on the board:

$$4 + 3 = 7 \quad 7 - 3 = 4$$

The teacher models reading the first equation at a rate of about a numeral or symbol each second. (Reading at a faster rate should be avoided initially, since it may encourage guessing.) The teacher then responds with the students as they read the statement. Lower-performing students may need 10 or more trials. When the students are able to read the statement by themselves, the teacher tests the group and then individuals. The same model-lead-test procedure is used with each statement.

Equation reading would be practiced daily for several weeks. It can be discontinued when addition is introduced, since the addition formats begin with the students reading an equation. The rate at which students read statements should be increased gradually.

Equation writing requires students to write equations dictated by the teacher; e.g., "Listen: Four plus three equals how many? Say that . . . Write it." Equation writing is introduced when the students can read equations with relative ease and are somewhat fluent in writing numerals and symbols, writing most numerals within two to three seconds after the teacher says the numeral in a dictation exercise.

The format for equation writing (see Format 5.2) involves the teacher dictating a statement, the students repeating the statement at a normal rate, then repeating the statement at a slow rate (a word each two to three seconds), and finally writing the statement. The purpose of having students say the statement slowly is to help students remember the latter part of the statement as they are writing the earlier part.

A common error is writing a numeral or symbol out of order. As soon as the teacher notices an error in a written equation, she points to each symbol while saying the correct statement. For example, if a student writes 6 + □ = 2 for 6 + 2 = □, the teacher says, "6" and points to 6; says "plus" and points to +; says "2" and points to the box that the student has written. The teacher immediately says, "This is not 2; let's try the problem again." The teacher has the student cross out or erase the problem, then repeats the equation, has the student say the equation, and then has the student write the equation.

Numeration Tasks: Numeral and Line Matching

There are two types of numeration tasks. The first starts with symbols. The student identifies a symbol and then writes the appropriate number of lines; e.g., the student identifies the numeral 2 and then draws two lines under the 2. The second starts with lines. The student counts the number of lines or other objects and writes the numeral that represents the number; e.g., for the task below, the student writes a 2 in the box.

$$| \ |$$
$$□$$

Both tasks are component skills for the equality-based strategies students are taught to solve addition and subtraction; therefore, they should be taught relatively early in the instructional sequence, after students have learned to identify and write about five numerals and can count objects in a group. Both numeration skills can be introduced within a short period of time, since they are usually easy for students to learn. As soon as the students learn to identify a new numeral, teachers should incorporate it into numeration tasks.

IDENTIFYING A SYMBOL, THEN DRAWING LINES   Prior to introducing tasks in which the students draw lines to correspond to a numeral, the

teacher may need to provide practice for lower-performing students in simply drawing lines. The teacher would give students a piece of paper with a series of dots about 1/4 inch apart and 1/2 inch above a horizontal line. The teacher then would model how to draw lines. This initial exercise would be followed by an exercise in which students write a line each time the teacher claps (at a rate of about a clap each 2 seconds).

• • • • • • • • •
_____

Students may write crooked lines or crowd them together, e.g., \/\/\11. Either error may cause overlapping or crossed lines. The teacher should carefully monitor and correct by modeling and then, if necessary, guiding the student's pencil as the student makes the lines. When students can draw lines as the teacher claps, the teacher introduces an exercise in which the students also count as they draw lines. When the students can count and draw lines as the teacher claps, exercises with numerals can be introduced.

Format 5.3 includes the format for teaching students to draw lines for numerals. In the format, students first identify a numeral, state that the numeral tells them to draw a certain number of lines, and then draw the lines. Since most students readily learn this skill, presentations in two to four lessons are often sufficient before including this problem type on independent worksheets. Note that a "how many" box is included in the teacher presentation because it is easy to learn and because students must know that not every symbol tells them to draw lines.

If students make errors on independent worksheet items, the teacher should test to determine the cause of the error. Did the student identify the numeral correctly? If not, the misidentification caused the error. If the student identified the numeral correctly, the error resulted from a line drawing error, which is corrected by reviewing Format 5.2.

COUNTING THE LINES, THEN WRITING A NUMERAL   Writing a numeral to represent a set of objects is important in itself and is also an integral part of the strategy to teach a conceptual base for addition and subtraction. After students draw a set of lines for one side of an equation, they must write the numeral for that set. For example:

$$4 + 2 + □$$
$$||||\ \ ||$$

Students count six lines and write a 6 in the box. The format for writing a numeral for a set of objects (see

Format 5.4) begins with an explanation of the function of the lines under a box: "The lines under a box tell what numeral goes in the box." The students are then told to count the lines under the box and write the numeral for the number they end with. If students have mastered the necessary preskills of rational counting and numeral writing, they will have little difficulty. After presentations in two or three lessons, items of this kind can be included on worksheets as independent activities.

The two mistakes students make on this task are either miscounting the lines or writing the wrong numeral. Often it is not clear by looking at a worksheet how a student derived an answer. In such a situation, the teacher should ask the student to work several items in front of him, counting aloud so that the cause of the error can be identified and an appropriate correction provided. If the student cannot correctly count lines in several problems, the teacher should provide practice on line counting (see Chapter 4). If a student writes the wrong numeral, the teacher needs to provide practice in numeral identification and numeral dictation.

Mistakes involving mechanics such as writing a numeral backward are not critical. If the teacher can identify the numeral the student has written, the answer is acceptable. The teacher would praise a student who has written the correct numeral but has written it backward. After praising the student, however, the teacher would point out that the numeral is written backward. Some students will need months of practice writing numerals before they consistently write them in the correct form. The teacher should *not* put undue pressure on students who write numerals backward.

PLACE VALUE SKILLS

Three skills related to place value are discussed in this section: (a) reading and writing numerals, (b) column alignment, and (c) expanded notation. Teaching procedures are discussed for reading and writing each type of number: teens, tens, hundreds, thousands, and millions. The procedures are quite similar for the different number quantities. In reading numbers, the students identify the number in each column (e.g., two 10s and four 1s), their value (e.g., two 10s equal 20), and combine the values to come up with the entire number (e.g., 20 + 4 = 24). In writing numbers, students first expand the numbers into their component parts (e.g., 24 = two 10s and four 1s) and then write each component.

Variations in the teaching procedures are called for with teen numbers and numbers with zero. With teen numbers, students say the ones number first (e.g., 16 is read "sixteen," not "teensix") but write the tens number first (e.g., in writing 16, students write the 1, then the 6). Numbers with zeroes are difficult because students must omit the zeroes when reading (e.g., 306 is read "three hundred six," not "three hundred zero six") but include them when writing, even though the students don't hear them. Instructions in reading and writing should be carefully coordinated. Students should be introduced to numeral identification first and then to numeral writing for that numeral type.

Reading and Writing Teen Numbers

READING TEEN NUMBERS Reading teen numbers is introduced when the students can read all numerals between zero and 10. Regular teens are introduced before irregular teens. The numbers 14, 16, 17, 18, and 19 are regular teens. The irregular teens are 11, 12, 13, and 15. For example, 14 is pronounced **four**teen but 12 is not pronounced "**two**teen" and 15 is not pronounced "**five**teen."

The format for teaching students to read teen numbers appears in Format 5.5. The format has three parts. In part A, a structured board exercise, the teacher makes a chart on the board, with spaces for the tens and ones columns. The teacher tells the students that they read one ten as "teen" and models reading teen numerals. Then the students read them. On the first day of instruction, examples would be limited to regular teen numbers: 14, 16, 17, 18, and 19. The next day one irregular teen would be introduced. A new irregular teen would be introduced each day, unless students have difficulty with previously introduced teens. When a new irregular teen fact is introduced, the teacher alternates between the new number and previously introduced numbers (e.g., 13, 14, 13, 16, 18, 13, 17, 14, 19, 13).

Part B is a less structured exercise in which the students read teen numbers with no prompting. Part B would be presented daily for several weeks. Part C is a worksheet exercise designed to reinforce the place value concept. In Part C the students are shown pictures of counters and are instructed to circle the appropriate numeral. After the writing of teen numbers has been introduced, students can write the appropriate numeral rather than circling it.

WRITING TEEN NUMBERS Writing teen numbers is introduced when students are able to read teen numbers accurately and with a moderate degree of fluency. As in the procedure for reading teen numbers, regular teen numbers (14, 16, 17, 18, and 19) are introduced first, then irregular teen numbers (11, 12, 13, and 15). Irregular teens can be introduced about two days after regular teens. If students have no or little difficulty, a new irregular teen would be taught each day.

Format 5.6 includes the format for teaching students to write teen numbers. Part A contains a model-test procedure for teaching students to tell the component parts of a teen number: 14 = a 1 for the teen (ten) and a 4. Part B is a structured board presentation. The teacher refers to the chart on the board and writes the digits in the appropriate columns. Part C is a structured worksheet exercise in which the teacher prompts the students as they write numerals. Part D is an independent dictation exercise in which the teacher says teen numbers and the students write them. If students are able to decode (read words) adequately, the dictation exercise can be replaced with a written worksheet in which students write the numerals indicated by written words.

Practice in writing teen numbers would be continued daily for several weeks to facilitate the development of fluency. The place value chart would be included in writing exercises only for the first several weeks and then dropped.

The worksheet exercise in Figure 5.2 contains pictures of a group of 10 objects and several single objects. The students are to fill in numerals in the tens and ones columns. This exercise, which reinforces the place value concept, can be introduced after students become proficient in writing dictated numerals.

Reading and Writing Numerals 20–99

READING NUMBERS 20–99   The reading of numbers from 20 through 99 is introduced when students can read teen numbers accurately and with modest fluency (i.e., reading a group of five teen numbers within eight seconds). Students should also be able to count by 1s and skip count by 10s to 100 (10, 20, 30, 40, 50, 60, 70, 80, 90, 100). The format for teaching students to read numerals between 20 and 99 appears in Format 5.7.

Parts A and B utilize piles of 10 blocks to reinforce the place value concept for tens numbers. In Part A the teacher draws several sets of 10 blocks. The teacher then tells students various place value facts for tens numbers (nine tens equal 90) and has the students count by tens to verify the facts.

In Part B the teacher uses a model-test procedure to facilitate memorization of the various place value facts for tens numbers. Lower-performing students can be expected to have difficulty with translating two tens, three tens, and five tens, since the names for these numbers are irregular. While four tens equal forty, and eight tens equal eighty, two tens do not equal "twoty." Likewise, three tens do not equal "threety" and five 10s do not equal "fivety."

Part C and Part D actually involve reading numbers in the place value chart. In Part C, the teacher instructs students to start reading in the tens column. He asks what numeral is in the tens column and what number that group of tens equals. Finally, the teacher asks for the sum of that number and the number in the 1s column (30 + 5 = 35).

In Part D, students read numerals with no prompting from the teacher. (Note that for the last five lessons in which Part D is used, the place value chart should not be included.) About a fourth of the examples in Part D should be teen numbers.

In Part E, the student is to select the numeral that represents a group of blocks. The teacher writes diagrams with sets of 10 and individual blocks. The students determine the total by first counting the piles of 10. Then they figure out what number the groups of 10 equal (three tens equal 30). Finally, they count the single blocks, starting with the tens number they left off with (e.g., 31, 32, 33, 34), which assumes the preskill of counting from different numbers.

WRITING NUMERALS 20–99   Writing numerals for 20 through 99 is introduced after students can read these numerals. The format for teaching students to write these numerals appears in Format 5.8. Parts A and B are preskills. Part A teaches the student to say the composite parts of the number (e.g., 97 is

FIGURE 5.2   Teen Numbers Worksheet Activity

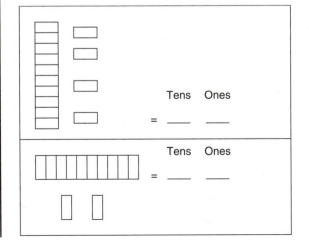

90 and 7). Part B teaches the students to tell how many tens in a tens number (e.g., 50 is five 10s). Part C introduces writing numbers from 20 through 99. The teacher says a number and has the students say its component parts. The teacher then asks how many 10s in the tens number and writes the numeral. The teacher then asks, for example, "84 equals 80 and what else?" After the student says "4," the teacher writes the 4 in the ones column. Part D has the same steps as Part C, except the students write the numerals. Part E is a dictation exercise. The teacher dictates numbers and the students write the appropriate numerals. About a third of the examples in this part should be teen numbers.

Teachers working with remedial students can expect these students to have particular reversal problems with numbers ending in 1. For example, students may write 31 as 13, 71 as 17, or 21 as 12. To remedy these reversal problems, the teacher would first present Parts B, C, and D of the writing teens format (Format 5.6) for one or two lessons. She would concurrently present the writing tens numbers format (Format 5.8), excluding all tens numbers ending with 1 (e.g., 21, 31, 41, 51). The purpose of excluding the tens numbers ending in 1 is to ensure students' mastery of easier numbers before introducing numbers students typically reverse. After the student writes teen and tens numbers without assistance for several days, the teacher begins working directly on the reversal problem. She presents Part C of the writing teens format (Format 5.6) with minimally different examples, focusing on the discrimination between tens and teen numbers like 13 and 31, 17 and 71. Part C may have to be reviewed daily for several weeks for students who are confused. Note that minimally different pairs are used only for remedial students, not for younger students learning the skill for the first time.

Reading and Writing Numbers 100–999

READING HUNDREDS NUMBERS The reading of hundreds numbers is usually taught during second grade. Students should be able to read and write numerals for numbers below 100 prior to the introduction of numbers from 100 to 999. The teaching procedure is very similar to that used for teaching students to read tens numbers. The format for reading hundreds appears in Format 5.9. In Part A, the teacher introduces the hundreds column, explaining that numerals in that column tell how many hundreds. The teacher then leads students in reading numerals. He points to the digit farthest to the left,

asks what column it is in, and then asks what number the digit represents: "What column is 5 in? . . . What do five hundreds equal?" The teacher then does the same for each remaining digit in the numeral. "What column is the 4 in? . . . What do four tens equal? . . . What column is the 8 in? What do eight ones equal?" A slight modification of the basic procedure is used for numbers with a 1 in the tens column. This modification appears at the end of Part A. In Part B, the teacher has the students say the numbers without teacher prompting.

Daily exercises in reading numbers would be continued for several weeks. Thereafter, practice in reading numbers would be incorporated into computation strategies where the first step always involves reading the problem. Practice can also be provided through worksheet exercises like that in Figure 5.3, where students read numerical words and then circle the correct numeral. Obviously, such written exercises would be appropriate only for students able to decode the words.

The sequence in which hundreds numbers are introduced is important. Hundreds numbers that do not include a zero in the tens column should be introduced first. Numbers with a zero in the tens column are difficult because the student says nothing for the zero. This more difficult type would be introduced in Part A about a week after the easier numbers. A slight modification in the format is required: In step 3 of Part A, the teacher would say "We have zero tens, so we don't say anything when I point to the numeral zero." In step 5, the students should not say anything when the teacher points to the zero. For example, for 608, students say "600" when the teacher points to 6, remain quiet when the teacher points to 0, and then say "8" when the teacher points to 8.

When presenting exercises to teach students to read hundreds numbers with a zero in the tens column, the teacher would include several sets of examples like these: 38, 308, 380; 42, 420, 402; 703, 730, 73. Note that in each set there are three minimally different numbers: a tens number and two hundreds numbers. The hundreds numbers include the same

FIGURE 5.3 Worksheet Exercise for Reading Hundreds Numbers

Circle the correct numeral:			
three hundred sixty-two	320	362	360
four hundred eighty-six	48	468	486
two hundred seventy-one	217	270	271
nine hundred thirty-two	729	932	923

numerals that appeared in the tens number, plus a zero. In one of the hundreds numbers, the zero appears in the tens column and in the other hundreds number the zero appears in the ones column.

WRITING HUNDREDS NUMBERS Students usually have more difficulty learning to write hundreds numbers than to read them. The sequence in which hundreds numbers are introduced in writing tasks is the same as for reading. We recommend that hundreds numbers be introduced in two stages. During the first stage, hundreds numbers with a zero in the tens column should be excluded; 248 would be acceptable but 208 wouldn't. Two hundred eight is troublesome because no tens number is heard. During the second stage, numbers with a zero in either the tens or the ones column may be used.

Format 5.10 includes the format for teaching students to write the first type of hundreds numbers (those without a zero in the tens column). In Part A, the teacher presents a verbal exercise in which she has the students tell the component parts of a hundreds number (e.g., 382 = 300 + 80 + 2). Note the wording in steps 3 and 4 of Part A, in which the teacher asks the students if they heard a tens number and a ones number. This wording is intended to prepare students for numbers in which there is a zero in either the tens or the ones column.

In Part B the teacher guides the students in writing numerals for numbers through 999. For example, in guiding the students through writing 486, the teacher asks students to say the first part of the number (400) and points out that since it's a hundreds number, they start writing the numeral in the hundreds column. The teacher asks how many hundreds and has the students write the numeral (4) in the hundreds column. The teacher then asks what column comes next (tens). This question is designed to remind students that they must always write a numeral in the tens column. The teacher has the students say the tens number (80), asks how many tens in that number (8), and has the students write that numeral (8) in the tens column. The ones column is completed next. The students write 6 in that column.

Part C is a supervised practice exercise in which numbers are written as words and students must write the numerals. Teachers working with students unable to decode well would read the words to the students. Daily practice would be continued for several weeks. A place value chart would be incorporated into exercises for the first several weeks and then dropped.

Note that several tens numbers are included in the exercises. The tens numbers are included to reinforce the concept of proper column alignment. The first digit in a tens number is written in the tens column, while the first digit in a hundreds number is written in the hundreds column.

Numbers with a zero in the tens column are introduced in writing exercises after students can accurately write three-digit numerals without zeroes in the tens column. For numbers with a zero in the tens or ones column, step 3 in Part B would have to be modified. For example, after the students indicate that they do not hear a tens number, the teacher asks, "So what do we write in the tens column?" "Zero." "Write a zero in the tens column." The teacher then proceeds to step 4.

Examples would be the same as for exercises focusing on reading numbers with a zero in the tens column; minimally different sets such as 902, 92, 920; 48, 480, 408; and 702, 72, 720 should be used.

Reading and Writing Numbers 1,000–999,999

READING THOUSANDS NUMBERS Thousands numbers are usually introduced during third grade. The format for introducing students to thousands numbers is fairly simple (see Format 5.11). Students are taught that the numeral in front of the comma tells how many thousands. They read that number, say "thousand" for the comma, and then read the rest of the number. In reading 3,286 they say "3," then "thousand" for the comma, and finally "286."

Students would read 8 to 10 numbers in the format. The sequence in which thousands numbers are introduced should be carefully controlled. We recommend that thousands numbers be introduced in this sequence:

1. Numbers between 1,000 and 9,999 that have any numeral other than zero in each column
2. Numbers between 1,000 and 9,999 that have zero in one or more columns
3. Numbers between 10,000 and 99,999
4. Numbers between 100,000 and 999,999

We recommend not including numbers with zeroes initially, since students may mistakenly develop the misrule that thousands have something to do with the number of zeroes in a numeral rather than the number of places. When numbers with zeroes are introduced, the teacher should pay careful attention to example selection. A fourth of the numbers would have a zero in the hundreds and a zero in the tens column, a fourth would have a zero in just the hundreds column, another fourth would have a zero in just the tens column, and a final fourth would have no zeroes at all. A sample set might include 2,000, 2,058, 2,508, 2,815; 7,002, 7,020, 7,200, 7,248; and 9,040, 9,400, 9,004, 9,246.

During fourth grade, students should be introduced to thousands numbers between 1,000 and 9,999 that do not have a comma. Some reference materials students encounter will have thousands numbers written without a comma. In presenting thousands numbers without a comma, the teacher tells the students that when a number has four digits, it is a thousands number and then presents a list that includes a mix of thousands and hundreds numbers.

WRITING THOUSANDS NUMBERS Writing thousands is taught in four stages, just as reading thousands is. During the first stage, all numbers have a digit other than zero in the hundreds column and tens column. In the second stage, numbers with a zero in the hundreds column and/or the tens column are introduced. (The example in Format 5.12 is from the second stage, numerals with a zero.) Numbers with a zero in the hundreds column are difficult because students may not write the zero. Students will often write the number four thousand-eighty-five as 4,85, leaving out the zero in the hundreds column. Often students simply write the numbers they hear: four thousand, eighty, and five. The teaching procedure for writing numbers must be designed to reinforce the place value concept that digits must be written in the thousands, hundreds, tens, and ones columns. Writing numbers with a zero in the hundreds or tens column might be introduced about a week after the easier number types are taught. Just as with reading thousands numbers, sets of minimally different examples should be presented in numeral writing exercises: 4,028, 4,208, 4,218, 4,280; 6,200, 6,002, 6,020, 6,224; 5,090, 5,900, 5,009, 5,994.

Format 5.12 shows a format for writing thousands numbers. Note that the format is very similar to the one for writing hundreds. (Format 5.10). Before students write a number, the teacher tells them to make a long line for the thousands and shorter lines for the hundreds, tens, and ones numbers. The teacher then has the students tell how many thousands and instructs them to write the appropriate numeral. The students then write a comma for the word *thousand*. Note that the comma should be started on the line with a slightly curved downward-pointing line. Many students will write the comma in the middle of the line (e.g., 4'326) so that it looks like the numeral 1. The teacher should watch for this error and immediately correct mistakes by modeling where to write the comma. After the comma is written, the teacher repeats the number, asking the students if they hear a hundreds number. If the answer is no, the student writes a zero. The same procedure is used with the tens and ones column. In Part B the students write numbers without assistance.

Practice in writing thousands numbers should be continued daily for several weeks. Practice can be provided through worksheet exercises similar to those in Figure 5.3 for writing hundreds numbers where students read number words then write the appropriate numerals.

Reading and Writing Millions

The millions numbers are usually taught during late fourth grade and fifth grade. Reading millions can be taught using a procedure similar to that used for reading thousands. The teacher instructs students to identify millions by examining the number of commas in the number. Students are taught that when two commas appear, the numbers in front of the first comma signify millions, while the numbers in front of the second comma signify thousands. The teacher initially prompts students by having them say the number a part at a time. See Summary 5.1 Box below.

Example selection for reading millions numbers should include a mix of millions numbers and thou-

---

Summary Box 5.1   Symbol Identification: Reading Millions

1. Teacher asks students to identify how many commas.

2. Teachers asks what the number in front of the first comma tells about and to identify that number.

3. Teacher asks what the numbers in front of the second comma tell about and to identify that number.

4. Teacher asks students to identify the entire number.

sands numbers so that the students receive practice in discriminating what to do when there are two commas versus one comma.

Writing millions numbers is taught by using a blank line for each figure in the number and placing the two commas correctly for students:

——, —— —— ——, —— —— ——.

The teacher leads the students through writing the numerals, using basically the same steps as in the format for writing thousands numbers (see Format 5.12): "Listen. 5 million, 203 thousand, 450. How many million? . . . Write 5 in the millions column . . . 5 million, 203 thousand. How many thousands? . . . Write 203 in the spaces before the thousands comma . . . Listen. 5 million, 203 thousand, 450. Write the rest of the number."

Numbers that will be especially difficult for students to write are those with zeroes in either the hundred-thousands, the ten-thousands, or the thousands columns, such as 3,064,800, 2,005,000, or 8,000,124. These numbers are introduced in writing exercises only after the students can write easier numbers. Again, as with thousands numbers, minimally different sets should be used (e.g., 6,024,000, 6,204,000, 6,024, 6,240,000, 6,240). The sets should include a mix of millions and thousands numbers. A great deal of practice reading and writing millions numbers will be necessary before students develop mastery. This practice should be provided through oral and worksheet exercises over a period of several months.

Column Alignment

Column alignment involves writing a series of numerals so that the appropriate digits are vertically aligned. Column alignment is an important skill because it is a prerequisite for advanced computation and story problems, in which the numbers to be computed do not appear in a column in the story: e.g., "Fred has 4,037 marbles. He gives 382 marbles to his younger brother. How many does he have left?" Column alignment exercises also test students' understanding of place value. For example, students who try to solve the problem about Fred's marbles by writing

$$\begin{array}{r} 4,037 \\ -\ 362 \\ \hline \end{array}$$

not only will arrive at the wrong answer but also have not mastered important place value skills.

Column alignment problems usually involve numerals with different numbers of digits written as row problems. The complexity of these column alignment problems increases as the number of digits increases. At first, problems would involve adding tens numbers and ones numbers (32 + 5 + 14); later, hundreds, tens, and ones (142 + 8 + 34); then thousands, hundreds, tens, and ones (3,042 + 6 + 134 + 28).

The strategy we recommend involves rearranging the order of the numbers: the number with the most digits is written first and the other numbers under that number. The purpose of writing the largest numeral first is to establish the columns. The teaching procedure would involve a simple model-test procedure in a structured worksheet format (see Format 5.13). The teacher tells the rule about the numeral with the most digits being written first and then guides the students in determining in which column to begin writing the other numerals. The structured worksheet exercise would be presented for several lessons. Thereafter, practice on about five problems daily would appear on independent worksheets for several weeks.

Expanded Notation

Expanded notation involves rewriting a number as an addition problem composed of the numerals that each digit represents. For example, the number 3,428 is rewritten as 3,000 + 400 + 20 + 8, or vertically as:

$$\begin{array}{r} 3,000 \\ 400 \\ 20 \\ +\ 8 \\ \hline \end{array}$$

The sequence in which expanded notation problems are introduced parallels the order in which students are taught to read and write numerals: teens, 20–99, 100–999, 1,000–999,999, etc.

The teaching procedure for the verbal component of expanded notation is included in the previously discussed numeral writing formats; e.g., "What makes up 16?" (see Format 5.6) and "Do you hear a tens number in 382? . . . What tens number?" (see Format 5.10). With this background, students should have relatively little trouble saying a number as an addition problem (354 = 300 + 50 + 4), which is the focus of the structured board presentation (see Format 5.14). On the structured worksheet, students say numbers as addition problems and then write the problems. Since a less-structured format is unnecessary, supervised practice can follow the structured worksheet.

APPLICATION ITEMS: SYMBOLS AND PLACE VALUE

1. The teacher is presenting a task on which the numerals 4, 2, and 5 appear. When the teacher points to 4 and asks, "What number?" a student says, "five." What is the correction procedure?

2. A child writes a 7 in an empty box over a group of five lines. Tell two possible causes of this error. How could you determine the exact cause? Describe a remediation.

3. During a test of writing numbers, a student writes a 2 as a 5. What would the teacher do?

4. Below is a worksheet item done independently by a child. The item required the student to write the appropriate number of lines to represent a numeral. Note the errors made by the student and describe the probable cause. Describe a remediation.

2	5	6	4	3	7
II	IIII	IIIIII	IIIII	III	IIIIIII

5. When presenting a format in which the students are being taught to read tens numbers, a student identifies 71 as 17. What does the teacher say in making the correction?

6. Two teachers are introducing the reading of hundreds numbers. Below are the examples each included in the lesson. Which set is more appropriate? Tell why.

> Teacher A: 306, 285, 532, 683, 504
> Teacher B: 724, 836, 564, 832, 138

7. A child writes 38 when the teacher says "three hundred eight." Specify the wording the teacher uses to correct (see appropriate format).

8. The numerals below are representative of various types. Tell the type each numeral illustrates. List the order in which the types would be introduced.

> 836; 13; 18; 305; 64; 5,024; 5,321

9. Construct a set of six to eight examples to be used in presenting the specified parts of the following formats.

   a. Format for reading hundreds numbers: the less structured board presentation used when teaching hundreds numbers with a zero in the tens column.

   b. Format for reading thousands numbers: the less structured board presentation used when teaching thousands numbers with zeroes in the hundreds and/or the tens column.

FORMAT 5.1   Format for Introducing New Numerals

Note: This format is used with each new symbol. In this example, we assume that the numerals 1, 4, 6, and 2 have been introduced and that the numeral 7 is being introduced.

TEACHER	STUDENT
1. *(Write the following numbers on the board.)*	

7 2

4 6 7

7 1

TEACHER	STUDENT
(Model and test. Point to 7 and say) This is a seven. What is this? *(Touch 7)*	7
2. *(Discrimination practice):* When I touch it, tell me what it is. *(Point to 2, pause a second, then touch 2. Repeat step 2 with these numerals: 7, 2, 7, 6, 1, 7, 2, 1, 6, 7, etc.)*	2
3. *(Individual turns: Ask individual students to identify several numerals.)*	

FORMAT 5.2   Format for Equation Writing

TEACHER	STUDENTS
1. *(Give students paper and pencil.)*	
2. You are going to write a problem. First you'll say it. Listen: Six plus two equals how many? Listen again. Six plus two equals how many? Say that.	Six plus two equals how many?
To correct: Respond with students until they can say the statement at the normal rate of speech.	
3. Now we'll say it the slow way. Every time I clap, we'll say a part of the statement. *(Respond with the students.)* Get ready. (Clap) Six. *(Pause two seconds; clap.)* Plus *(Pause two seconds; clap.)* Two. *(Pause two seconds; clap.)* Equals. *(Pause 2 seconds; clap.)* How many? *(Repeat step 3 until students appear able to respond on their own.)*	six plus two equals how many?
4. Now I'll clap and you say the statement by yourselves. *(Pause.)* Get ready. *(Clap at two-second intervals.)*	Six plus two equals how many?
To correct: Respond with students.	
5. Now write the problem.	Students write 6+2 = ☐
6. *(Repeat steps 1–5 with three more equations.)*	

FORMAT 5.3 **Format for Identifying a Symbol and then Drawing Lines:**
Structured Worksheet

4	6	☐	2

TEACHER	**STUDENTS**
1. Everybody touch the first numeral on your worksheet. *(Hold up worksheet and point to 4.)* What is it?	4
A 4 tells you to make four lines. What does a 4 tell you to do?	Make 4 lines.
Each time I clap, draw a line and count.	Students draw lines and count.
(Signal by clapping once each two seconds.)	1,2,3,4
How many did you end up with? Good.	4
2. Touch the next symbol. What is it?	6
A 6 tells you to make six lines. What does a 6 tell you to do?	Make 6 lines.
Each time I clap, draw a line and count.	Students draw lines and count.
(Signal by clapping once each two seconds.)	
How many did you end up with?	6
3. Touch the next symbol. What is it?	Box
Does a box tell you to draw lines? No. A box does not tell you to draw lines.	
Does a box tell you to draw lines?	No
So are you going to draw lines?	No
4. Touch the next symbol. What is it?	2
What does 2 tell you to do?	Draw two lines.
Do it. *(After students draw lines, say,* Get ready to count the lines. Get ready. *(Signal by clapping once each two seconds.*	1,2
How many did you end up with?	2

FORMAT 5.4 **Format for Writing a Numeral for a Set of Objects:**
Structure Worksheet

TEACHER	**STUDENTS**
1. Everybody, here's a rule: The lines under a box tell what numeral goes in the box. Get ready to count the lines	

TEACHER	STUDENTS
under this box. *(Point to the first problem on the worksheet and pause while the students point to the first line.)* Count as I clap. Get ready. *(Clap each second.)*	I, 2
How many lines are under this box?	2
So what numeral are you going to write in the box?	2
Write that numeral.	

2. *(Repeat step 1 for additional examples.)*

FORMAT 5.5   Format for Reading Teen Numbers

PART A: STRUCTURED BOARD PRESENTATION

TEACHER   **STUDENTS**

1. (Write on board)

tens	ones
1	4
1	6
1	7
1	8
1	9

1. *(Point to the tens column.)* This is the tens column. *(Point to the ones column.)* This is the ones column.

2. These numerals all start with one ten. For one ten, we say teen. Listen to me read the numerals. *(Point to 14.)* 14 *(Point to 16.)* 16 *(Point to 17.)* 17 *(Point to 18.)* 18 *(Point to 19.)* 19

3. Your turn to read these numerals. *(Point to numerals in random order as students read.)*

4. *(Give individual turns to several students to read two numerals.)*

PART B: LESS-STRUCTURED BOARD PRESENTATION

1. *(Write on board: 14. Point to 14.)* What number?   14

2. *(Repeat step 1 with 19, 17, 18, 16.)*

PART C: PLACE VALUE WORKSHEET

1. *(Give students worksheets with problems such as this one.)*

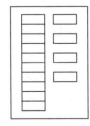   12   14   4   10

(continued on next page)

FORMAT 5.5   **(continued)**

TEACHER	STUDENTS
2. Look at the picture. The big pile has 10 blocks in it. The small pile has 4 blocks in it. I'll count: 10. *(pause),* 11, 12, 13, 14. How many blocks?	14
3. There are 14 blocks. Put a circle around the numeral 14.	

FORMAT 5.6   **Format for Writing Teen Numbers**

PART A: COMPONENTS OF TEEN NUMBERS

TEACHER	STUDENTS
1. You're going to write teen numerals. Remember, the ending "teen" tells you the numeral has one ten. Listen: 16. Write a 1 for the teen and then a 6. Listen: 19. What do I write for 19?	A 1 for the teen and a 9.
Listen: 14. What do I write for 14?	A 1 for the teen and a 4.
2. Your turn: 14. What do you write?	A 1 for the teen and a 4.
3. *(Repeat step 2 with 16, 19, 17, 18.)*	
4. *(Give individual turns to several students on step 2 or 3.)*	

PART B: STRUCTURED BOARD PRESENTATION

1. *(Write the following chart on the board.)*

tens	ones

2. *(Point to the tens column.)* This is the tens column. This is where we write a 1 for teen, for one ten.

3. What do you write for 14? *(Write 1 in tens column, 4 in ones column.)*

4. *(Repeat steps 1 and 2 with 17, 19, 16, 18.)*

5. *(Call on students.)* Read each numeral. *(Point as students read.)*   A 1 for the teen and a 4.

PART C: STRUCTURED WORKSHEET—DICTATION

(Give students a worksheet similar to the one below.)

	tens	ones
a.		
b.		
c.		
d.		

TEACHER	**STUDENTS**
1. Touch the space for problem a. You're going to write 14. What number?	14
2. What do you write for 14?	A 1 for the teen and a 4.
3. *(Write 14.)* Read the number you just wrote.	14
4. *(Repeat steps 1–4 for 16, 19, 14, 17, 18.)*	

PART D: LESS-STRUCTURED WORKSHEET—DICTATION

1. *(Give students worksheet with place value chart.)* You're going to write 14 on the first line. What are you going to write?	14
Write 14.	
To correct: use steps 1–4 from Part C.	
2. *(Repeat step 1 with 16, 18, 19, 17.)*	

FORMAT 5.7   Format for Reading Numbers 20–99

PART A (PRESKILL): INTRODUCING TENS PLACE VALUE FACTS

TEACHER	**STUDENTS**
1. *(Show students a diagram like this.)*	

TEACHER	**STUDENTS**
2. Each pile has 10 blocks. How many blocks in each pile?	10
3. Count by 10 each time I touch a pile. *(Touch piles.)*	10, 20, 30, 40, 50
4. How many blocks in all? Right, five tens equal 50. *(Repeat steps 2 and 3 with two tens and four tens.)*	50

PART B (PRESKILL): PRACTICING TENS PLACE-VALUE FACTS

1. *(Erase board. Model.)* Let's practice what groups of 10 equal. Listen. Three tens equal 30. What do three tens equal? *(Repeat with two tens and five tens.)*	30
2. *(Test.)* What do two tens equal? *(Repeat with five tens, three tens, six tens, eight tens, and four tens until students can respond correctly to all examples.)*	20
3. *(Present individual turns on step 2.)*	

(continued on next page)

FORMAT 5.7   (continued)

TEACHER	STUDENTS

PART C: STRUCTURED BOARD PRESENTATION

1. (Write the follow chart on the board.)

     tens   ones
      4   6

2. *(Point to tens column.)* What column?   tens column
   (Point to ones column.) What column?   ones column

3. How many tens?   4

   What do four tens equal?   40

4. How many ones?   6

   What is 40 and 6?   46

   So what does the whole numeral say?   46
   (Repeat steps 1–3 with 52, 38, 93, 81.)

PART D: LESS STRUCTURED BOARD PRESENTATION

1. *(Write the following chart on the board.)*
   tens   ones
    7   2

   What does this whole numeral say?   72
   (Pause 2–3 seconds, then signal.)
     To correct: Point to 7. What column is 7 in?
   What do seven tens equal? What is 70 and 2?

2. *(Repeat step 1 with 95, 20, 16, 31, 47, 50, 12.)*

3. *(Give individual turns to several students.)*

PART E: LESS-STRUCTURED BOARD PRESENTATION

                43   30   40   34

1. Let's find out how many blocks are in this picture. How many piles of tens are there?   3

2. What do three tens equal?   30

3. But we're not done. *(Point to four remaining blocks.)* We have to count these blocks. *(Point to tens group.)* We have 30 blocks here. Start counting at 30 and touch these blocks as I count. *(Touch blocks and count 31, 32, 33, 34.)*

4. How many blocks in this picture? Put a circle around the numeral 34.   34

FORMAT 5.8   **Format for Writing Numbers 20–99**

PART A: EXPANDED NOTATION PRESKILL

TEACHER	**STUDENTS**
1. Say this number: 84	84
2. Eighty-four equals 80 and 4. What does 84 equal?	80 and 4
What's the first part of 84?	80
3. Eighty-four equals 80 and what else?	4
4. *(Repeat steps 1–3 with 72, 95, 88, 43.)*	

PART B: TENS NUMBERS PLACE VALUE FACTS PRESKILL

1. Twenty has two tens. How many tens in 20?	2
2. *(Repeat step 1 with 60 and 30.)*	
3. How many tens in 40?	4
4. *(Repeat step 3 with 80, 30, 60, 20, 50.)*	
5. *(Give individual turns to several students.)*	

PART C: STRUCTURED BOARD PRESENTATION

1. *(Write the following chart on the board.)*

tens	ones

2. I want to write some big numbers. When we write big numbers, we write the tens first. Then we write the ones. What do we write first?	the tens
What do we write next?	the ones
3. Listen: 84. What is the first part of 84?	80
4. How many tens in 80? So I write 8 in the tens column. *(Write 8 in the tens column.)* Eighty equals eight 10s.	8
5. Listen: Eighty-four equals 80 and what else? So I write 4 in the 1s column. *(Write 4 in the 1s column.)*	4
6. What number did I just write?	84
7. How many tens in 84?	8
How many ones in 84?	4
8. *(Repeat steps 2–5 with several examples.)*	

(continued on next page)

FORMAT 5.8 (continued)

PART D: STRUCTURED WORKSHEET PRESENTATION

TEACHER	**STUDENTS**

(Give students the following worksheet.)

tens	ones

a.

b.

c.

d.

e.

f.

1. Touch a. Next to a you are going to write 79. What are you going to write?	79
2. What is the first part of 79?	70
How many tens in 70? Write 7 in the tens column.	7
3. Seventy-nine equals 70 and what else? Write 9 in the ones column.	9
4. What number did you write?	79
5. How many tens in 79?	7
6. How many ones in 79?	9
7. *(Repeat step 1–6 with several examples.)*	

PART E: LESS-STRUCTURED WORKSHEET (DICTATION)

(Give students worksheets labeled like the example below.)

a. _____

b. _____

c. _____

d. _____

e. _____

f. _____

1. You're going to write a numeral on each line.	
2. Touch line a.	
3. You're going to write 49. What are you going to write?	49
4. Write 49.	Students write 49.
To correct: Use steps 2–3 from Part D.	
5. *(Repeat steps 2–4 with 73, 20, 99, 14, 51, 42, 61, 17.)*	

FORMAT 5.9   **Format for Reading Numbers 100–999**

PART A: STRUCTURED BOARD PRESENTATION

TEACHER	**STUDENTS**

1. *(Write the following chart on the board.)*

hundreds	tens	ones
5	4	8

   (Point to appropriate column as you say:)
   This is the hundreds column.
   This is the tens column.
   This is the ones column.
   Tell me the names of the columns.
   (Point to the columns, starting with hundreds; repeat until students are firm.)

   Students say hundreds, tens, ones.

2. The first thing we do when we read a number is identify the column the number starts in. *(Point to 5 in 548.)*

   What column does this number start in? hundreds

   How many hundreds do we have? 5

   What do five hundreds equal? 500

3. *(Point to 4.)* What column is this? tens

   How many tens do we have? 4

   What do four tens equal? 40

4. *(Point to 8.)* What column is this? ones

   How many ones do we have? 8

   What do we say? *(Repeat steps 2–4 until firm.)* 8

5. Let's read the whole number. When I touch a numeral, you tell me what it says.
   (Point to 5, pause a second, touch 5.) 500
   (Point to 4, pause a second, touch 4.) 40
   (Point to 8, pause a second, touch 8.) 8
      To correct: If children do not respond correctly when you touch a number, say. This is the _____ column. How many _____ do we have?
      So what do we say? *Then return to the beginning of the number.*

6. Say the whole number. 548

7. *(Repeat steps 2–6 with 697, 351, 874, 932, all written in place value charts.)*
   (When presenting examples with a 1 in the tens column, the teacher presents the following steps instead of 3, 4, and 5 in the format. The following example shows how to teach the number 514.)

8. What column is this? tens

   How many tens do we have? 1

9. How many ones do we have? 4

   We have one 10 and four ones, so what do we say? 14

10. Let's read the whole number. *(Point to 5.)* What do we say for this? 500

   (Point to 14.) What do we say for these? 14

(continued on next page)

FORMAT 5.9 (continued)

PART B: LESS-STRUCTURED BOARD PRESENTATION

TEACHER   **STUDENTS**

(Write the following chart on the board.)

hundreds	tens	ones
4	4	6

1. Now we are going to read the numbers without saying the parts first. This time when I point, you are going to tell me the whole number. *(Point to 446 and then pause 2–3 seconds.)*

2. *(Repeat step 1 with 249, 713, 321, 81, 720, 740.)*

3. *(Give individual turns to several students.)*

FORMAT 5.10 Format for Writing Hundreds Numbers

PART A: EXPANDED NOTATION

TEACHER   **STUDENTS**

1. Count by hundreds. Get ready, count.   100, 200, 300, 400, 500, 600, 700, 800, 900

   Now count by tens. Get ready, count.   10, 20, 30, 40, 50, 60, 70, 80, 90

2. Listen to this number: 362. Do you hear hundreds in 362?   yes

   What hundreds number?   300

3. Listen again: 362. Do you hear a tens number in 362?   yes

   What tens number?   60
   To correct: Tell answer, return to step 2.

4. Listen again: 362. Do you hear a ones number in 362?   yes

   What ones number?   2

5. 362 = 300 + 60 + 2. Say it with me.   362 = 300 + 60 + 2

   Say it yourselves.   362 = 300 + 60 + 2

6. *(Repeat steps 2–5 with 428, 624, and 139.)*

7. *(Give individual turns on steps 2–5 to several students.)*

PART B: STRUCTURED WORKSHEET PRESENTATION (DICTATION)

1. *(Give students a worksheet in which columns and spaces are written as illustrated.)*

	hundreds	tens	ones
a.			
b.			
c.			
d.			
e.			

TEACHER	**STUDENTS**

You are going to write hundreds numbers. Touch the hundreds column. Touch the tens column. Touch the ones column. *(Monitor responses.)*

2. What's the first part of 648?	600
So what column do you start writing in?	hundreds
How many hundreds in 600? Write 6 in the hundreds column.	6
3. What column comes next?	tens
Do you hear a tens number in 648?	yes
What tens number? Write 4 in the tens column.	4
4. What column comes next?	ones
Do you hear a ones number in 648?	yes
What ones number?	8
Write 8 in the ones column.	
5. We finished. How many 100s in 648?	6
How many 10s in 648?	4
How many 1s in 648?	8
Read the number you wrote.	648

6. *(Repeat steps 2–5 with 326, 463, 825, 253, 866.)*

PART C: SUPERVISED PRACTICE

(Give students a worksheet like the one below.)
Write these numerals:

a. two hundred sixty-one
b. four hundred eighteen
c. eight
d. nine hundred sixty-two
e. forty-eight
f. four hundred eighty
g. twelve
h. nine hundred seven
i. forty-one
j. three hundred ninety-seven

hundreds	tens	ones

1. The instructions tell you to write the numerals.

2. Read the words. Write the numeral.

3. Write the numerals.
    To correct: Use steps 2–4 from Part B.

4. Repeat steps 2 and 3 with the remaining examples.

FORMAT 5.11   **Format for Reading Thousands Numbers**

PART A: STRUCTURED BOARD PRESENTATION

TEACHER	STUDENTS
1. When a big number has one comma, the comma tells about thousands. Here's the rule. The number in front of the comma tells how many thousands. What does the number in front of the comma tell? *(Write on board: 6,781.)*	how many thousands
2. What number comes in front of the comma?	6
So what is the first part of the number?	6 thousand
3. *(Point to 781.)* Get ready to read the rest of the number.	781
4. Now you are going to read the whole number. *(Point to 6, then comma, then 781.)*	6,781
5. *(Repeat steps 2–4 with these numbers: 2,145 3,150 5,820 6,423.)*	
6. *(Give individual turns to several students.)*	

PART B: LESS STRUCTURED BOARD PRESENTATION

TEACHER	STUDENTS
1. *(Write on board: 3,820.)* Get ready to tell me this number. *(Pause several seconds.)* To correct: Repeat steps 2–4 from Part A.	3,820
2. *(Repeat step 1 with 9,270 3,174 3,271 9,563 4,812.)*	
3. *(Give individual turns to several students.)*	

FORMAT 5.12   **Format for Writing Thousands Numbers**

PART A: STRUCTURED WORKSHEET

TEACHER	STUDENTS
1. (Write on the board: _____ _____ _____ _____) The big line is for thousands. The other lines are for the hundreds, tens, and ones. Write lines for the thousands, hundreds, tens, and ones on your paper.	
2. Listen to this number: 8,024. How many thousands?	8
Write 8 on the thousands line. And what do you write after the thousands number?	a comma
Write a comma.	Students write a comma.
3. Listen again: 8,024. You already wrote 8 thousand. What do you have left?	24
4. Are there any hundreds in 24?	no
So write zero in the hundreds column.	Students write zero.
5. Are there any tens in 24?	yes
What do you write in the tens column?	2
Write it. *To correct: 8,024.* What tens number do you hear? How many tens is 20?	Students write 2.

TEACHER	**STUDENTS**
6. Are there any ones in 24?	yes
What do you write in the ones column?	4
Write it.	Students write 4.

7. *(Repeat steps 1–6 with 8,204 and 8,240; then with 6,008, 6,800, 6,080.)*

PART B: SUPERVISED PRACTICE (DICTATION)

1. Now you are going to write some numerals without help.

2. Make a long line for thousands and shorter lines for hundreds, tens, and ones.

3. Listen to this number: 9,028. What number? Write 9,028. *(Monitor responses.)* *To correct:* Use steps 2–6 from structured part.	9,028

4. *(Repeat step 3 with these numbers: 9,208 and 9,280; then 8,004, 8,400, 8,040.)*

FORMAT 5.13   **Format for Teaching Column Alignment: Structured Worksheet**

TEACHER	**STUDENTS**

1. *(Write the following addition problems on the board.)*
    a. 42 + 361 + 279   361
                                279
                              + 42	

b. 79 + 604 + 324	
1. Touch problem a. I'll read it. 42 + 361 + 279. Problem a has been rewritten in a column. Touch the column problem. The largest number is on top. Touch 361. The smallest number is on the bottom. Touch 42. The 4 on 42 is in the tens column.	
2. Touch problem b.	Students touch 79 + 604 + 324.
Read the problem.	79 plus 604 plus 324
3. We're going to write the numerals in a column so we can add them. We write the largest number first. What's the largest number?	604
Write it and then cross out 604 in the row problem.	Students write 604.
4. Now get ready to write 324 under 604.	
What column does 324 start in?	hundreds
Write 324 and cross it out in the row problem.	Students write 604 324
5. Now get ready to write 79. What column will you start writing in?	tens
Write 79 and cross it out in the row problem.	604 324
79 + 604 + 324	79

(continued on next page)

FORMAT 5.13 (continued)

TEACHER	STUDENTS
6. Have you crossed out all the numerals in the row problem?	yes
What kind of problem is this?	addition
Write in the sign. You're done writing the problem. Now work it.	604 324 + 79
7. *(Repeat steps 1–5 with four more problems.)*	

FORMAT 5.14   **Format for Expanded Notation**

Part A: Structured Board Presentation

TEACHER	STUDENTS
1. Listen to this number: 624. Say the number.	624
2. Now listen to me say 624 as an addition problem: $600 + 20 + 4$	
3. Your turn. Say 624 as an addition problem.	$600 + 20 + 4$
4. *(Repeat step 3 with 29, 406, 317, 29, 871, 314.)*	

Part B: Structured Worksheet

(Give students worksheets with problems like the following.)

624 = _____ + _____ + _____

386 = _____ + _____ + _____

Write these numbers as addition problems.

CHAPTER 6

Basic Facts

There are 390 basic arithmetic facts: 100 addition, 100 subtraction, 100 multiplication, and 90 division. Basic addition facts include all possible combinations in which each of the addends is a whole number under 10. Basic subtraction facts include all possible combinations in which the subtrahend and the difference (a and b in $c - a = b$) are one-digit numbers. Tables 6.1 and 6.2 include all the basic addition and subtraction facts.

Basic multiplication facts include all possible combinations in which each of the factors is a single-digit number (i.e., in $a \times b = c$, a and b are single

digits). Basic division facts include all possible combinations in which the divisor and quotient are single-digit numbers (e.g., in $c \div a = b$, a and b are single-digit numbers and a does not equal 0). Table 6.3 includes all basic multiplication and division facts.

TEACHING PROCEDURES

Ashlock (1971) outlines three different types of instructional activities designed to teach basic facts:

Table 6.1   Basic Addition Facts

					Addends					
Addends	*0*	*1*	*2*	*3*	*4*	*5*	*⑥*	*7*	*8*	*9*
0+	0	1	2	3	4	5	6	7	8	9
1+	1	2	3	4	5	6	7	8	9	10
2+	2	3	4	5	6	7	8	9	10	11
3+	3	4	5	6	7	8	9	10	11	12
4+	4	5	6	7	8	9	10	11	12	13
5+	5	6	7	8	9	10	11	12	13	14
6+	6	7	8	9	10	11	12	13	14	15
⑦+	7	8	9	10	11	12	⑬	14	15	16
8+	8	9	10	11	12	13	14	15	16	17
9+	9	10	11	12	13	14	15	16	17	18

Note: Problems are formed by an addend from the column on the left, an addend from the row on top, and their intersection; e.g., the numerals for 7 + 6 = 13 are circled.

Table 6.2   Basic Subtraction Facts

						Subtrahends				
Minuends	*0*	*1*	*2*	*3*	*4*	*5*	*6*	(*7*)	*8*	*9*
1–	1	0								
2–	2	1	0							
3–	3	2	1	0						
4–	4	3	2	1	0					
5–	5	4	3	2	1	0				
6–	6	5	4	3	2	1	0			
7–	7	6	5	4	3	2	1	0		
8–	8	7	6	5	4	3	2	1	0	
9–	9	8	7	6	5	4	3	2	1	0
10–		9	8	7	6	5	4	3	2	1
11–			9	8	7	6	5	4	3	2
12–				9	8	7	6	5	4	3
(13–)					9	8	7	(6)	5	4
14–						9	8	7	6	5
15–							9	8	7	6
16–								9	8	7
17–									9	8
18–										9

Note: Problems are formed by a minuend from the column on the left, followed by a subtrahend from the top row, and finally, the difference, which is the intersection; e.g., the numerals for 13 − 7 = 6 are circled.

Table 6.3   Basic Multiplication/Division Facts

÷/×	*0*	*1*	*2*	*3*	*4*	*5*	*6*	(*7*)	*8*	*9*
0	0	0	0	0	0	0	0	0	0	0
1	0	1	2	3	4	5	6	7	8	9
2	0	2	4	6	8	10	12	14	16	18
3	0	3	6	9	12	15	18	21	24	27
4	0	4	8	12	16	20	24	28	32	36
5	0	5	10	15	20	25	30	35	40	45
(6)	0	6	12	18	24	30	36	(42)	48	54
7	0	7	14	21	28	35	42	49	56	63
8	0	8	16	24	32	40	48	56	64	72
9	0	9	18	27	36	45	54	63	72	81

Note: Problems are formed by a number from the column on the left, a number from the top row, and their intersection; e.g., the row and column for the numerals 6 and 7 intersect at 42; these circled numbers form 6 × 7 = 42 and 42 ÷ 6 = 7.

activities for understanding, activities for relating, and activities for mastery. The activities for understanding involve concrete demonstrations of the operations, similar to those we have included in Chapters 7–10.

Relating activities are exercises designed to teach the relationships among various facts. The primary way of teaching these relationships is through the introduction of fact families. Fact families can be constructed as a series, such as the + 1s (3 + 1, 4 + 1, 5 + 1, etc.), the + 4s (5 + 4, 6 + 4, 7 + 4, etc.), the

+ doubles (2 + 2, 3 + 3, 4 + 4, etc.), and as sets of three related numbers that generate four facts. Below are examples of fact families constructed from three related numbers:

addition / subtraction
3, 5, 8

3 + 5 = 8
5 + 3 = 8
8 − 3 = 5
8 − 5 = 3

multiplication / division
3, 5, 15

$3 \times 5 = 15$
$5 \times 3 = 15$
$3\overline{)15} = 5$
$5\overline{)15} = 3$

Note how the commutative relationship between each pair of addition facts ($3 + 5 = 8$, so $5 + 3 = 8$) and multiplication facts ($3 \times 5 = 15$, so $5 \times 3 = 15$) greatly reduces the memorization load for students. Instead of memorizing each fact individually ($5 + 3$ **and** $3 + 5$), students can be taught that if they know one fact, they also know the reverse. Instructional procedures based on the commutative principle are discussed later.

Our recommendations for how to group facts into sets of fact families appear in Figures 6.2 through 6.5. These sets form the basis for presenting facts. The relationship formats listed in these figures are discussed after the next section.

Mastery activities are designed to facilitate fact memorization. The activities we have identified for building mastery require a sequence for introducing facts, coordination of relationship activities with memorization activities, intensive and systematic review, specific performance criteria that define when new facts can be introduced, record-keeping procedures that allow the teacher to monitor each student's mastery of facts, and motivation procedures.

RELATIONSHIP ACTIVITIES

Since the understanding activities Ashlock recommends are presented in the chapters for each respective operation, this chapter focuses only on the relationship and mastery activities. The teaching procedures for the relationship activities include (1) exercises with number families based on a series (e.g., 3×1, 3×2, 3×3) and (2) exercises demonstrating inverse relationships between addition/subtraction and multiplication/division (e.g., $4 + 2 = 6$, $2 + 4 = 6$, $6 - 4 = 2$, $6 - 2 = 4$). While the teaching procedures include strategies similar to those in the other chapters, the intent of the strategies in this chapter is different. Although the relationship strategies can be used to solve problems, their purpose is to show the relationship among number families so that fact memorization will be easier. It appears that memorization of *related* bits of information, as represented by number families, is easier than memorization of random bits of information. Following a

discussion of the teaching procedures for relationship activities, mastery activities will be discussed.

Preskill

Prior to introducing basic addition facts, teachers should teach students a strategy to figure out plus 1 facts. (Students who know 30 or more facts do not need to receive instruction on this preskill.) Prior to instruction in facts, students most likely have been using picture representations or concrete objects to solve simple equations. The format for plus 1 facts (see Format 6.1) not only teaches plus 1 facts but also begins teaching students that numbers are related in systematic ways. Plus 1 facts, which should be introduced in first grade, are taught through the application of this rule: When you plus 1, you say the next number. From the rule, students learn that the first addend is systematically related to the sum:

$$6 + 1 = 7 \qquad 9 + 1 = 10$$

To prepare students for the plus 1 rule, the term *next number* is taught in Part A of the format. At first, the teacher counts several numbers, holding the last number for several seconds (e.g., "3, 4, 5, ssiix"). The students say the next number, "7." After presenting several examples in which the teacher says a series of numbers and asks students the next number (step 2), the teacher presents examples in which she says just a single number, not a series of numbers (step 3), and the students say the next number. A common error made by students is that they continue counting rather than stopping at the next number. The teacher should stop students immediately if they say more than the next number, model saying just the next number, then repeat the same example before presenting additional examples.

Part B should not be introduced until students have mastered the next number skill taught in Part A. In Part B, the teacher presents the plus 1 rule, models several examples, and then tests. As a prompt, the teacher emphasizes the first addend, stretching it out for several seconds, and de-emphasizes the words "plus 1" (e.g., in siiiixxx plus 1, the "plus 1" is said quietly so that students can make the 6, 7 counting association).

In Part C, the teacher presents the plus 1 facts without any prompting. The teacher should initially pause two to three seconds before signaling for a response, so that the students will have time to figure out the answer. After several days of practice, the teacher can decrease the pause to a second. The teacher continues to provide practice on plus 1 facts until the students can respond instantly to any plus 1 problem.

Series Saying

Series saying, one of the major relationship activities, involves teaching the students to say a consecutively ordered set of fact statements. Series saying prompts students to notice the counting relationship among facts, as indicated by the circled numerals in the following series:

$$
\begin{aligned}
6 + 2 &= 8 \\
7 + 2 &= 9 \\
8 + 2 &= 10
\end{aligned}
$$

Series saying may be incorporated into instruction for any of the four types of basic facts: addition, subtraction, multiplication, and division. Format 6.2 includes a series saying format. Although the format illustrates an addition series, the same format can be used to present other types of series.

There are four parts to the series saying format. In Part A, students read the consecutively ordered statements. In Part B, the teacher erases the answers and the students read the statements. In Part C, the teacher erases everything and requires the students to say the series from memory. Part D is a drill on randomly presented facts. The teacher writes the fact questions on the board without the answer. The facts are written in random order (e.g., 7 + 2, 5 + 2, 8 + 2, 6 + 2). The teacher points to each fact, pauses, and then signals the students to respond. He repeats the facts until the students can respond after a one-second pause. The facts are written in random order so the students will not memorize the order of the answers.

Teaching students to read statements (Part A) in a rapid, crisp fashion is critical for instructionally naive students because they often read statements slowly or inaccurately. If students cannot *read* the series of statements in a crisp, rapid fashion, they will have a great deal of difficulty saying the series from memory and remembering facts during the random drill (Part D). The teacher must provide adequate practice to enable the students to say the series of statements at a fast rate.

The teacher should set a pace for saying the statements so that each statement in the series is said in approximately two to three seconds (two seconds for older students, three seconds for younger students). There should also be a slight pause, about one second, between each statement. The pacing of the task is illustrated in Figure 6.1. The top row indicates seconds elapsed. Across the bottom row are the statements the teacher would say. The same pace should be continued in Parts B and C.

The correction for slow pacing is to keep leading (responding with the students) at a brisk pace and gradually fade the lead so that the students are saying the statements independently. The teacher must be quite careful to provide the adequate repetition in an enjoyable manner. Teachers working with lower-performing students may find that several days of practice on Parts A and B are needed before continuing on to Parts C and D. Teachers working with higher-performing students may be able to present all parts in a day or two.

The first day that Part D is presented, only the first three facts in the series should be presented. A new fact would be included in Part D each of the next two days.

Three Number Fact Families

The other major format designed to demonstrate the relationships among facts is taught through the introduction of three number fact families. These are sets of three numbers from which students can be taught to generate four statements, either addition/subtraction or multiplication/division. For example, given the numbers 3, 4, and 7, students are taught to construct the addition statements 3 + 4 = 7 and 4 + 3 = 7. Later students learn to construct the subtraction statements based on the same three numbers: 7 − 4 = 3, 7 − 3 = 4

There are two formats for teaching number families. The first teaches students to use the commutative properties of addition (if a + b = c, then b + a = c) and multiplication (if a × b = c, then b × a = c). The second teaches students to generate subtraction statements from addition statements and division statements from multiplication statements. The commutative property is extremely important in that it greatly reduces the number of facts students need to

---

FIGURE 6.1   Pacing of Series-Saying

Seconds	0 1 2	3	4 5	6	7 8	9
Statements	6 + 2= 8	pause	7 + 2 = 9	pause	8 + 2 = 10	

memorize. For every fact that students learn, they can derive the answer to the inverse fact quickly and easily by using the commutative property. For example, if students have memorized that 5 + 3 = 8, they also know the answer to 3 + 5. Note that the term *commutative property* is not explicitly taught, just the function of the property.

The first format, which consists of three parts, appears in Format 6.3. Although the example shown illustrates the commutative property with addition, the same format can also be used to teach the commutative property of multiplication. In Part A, students are taught how to construct a pair of addition statements from a set of three numbers. For example, given 2, 5, and 7, the students construct 2 + 5 = 7 and 5 + 2 = 7. One member of each pair has been previously presented in a series saying format. The second member of each pair is the reverse fact. For example, if students have been taught the plus 2 facts (e.g., 5 + 2, 6 + 2, etc.), the new facts would be the 2+ facts (2 + 5, 2 + 6, etc.). In Part B, the students are orally tested on the new "reversed" facts. Part C is a worksheet exercise in which the students are given a diagram like this:

$$\boxed{}\quad \begin{array}{c}\boxed{2}\\[4pt]\boxed{5}\end{array}$$

$$\underline{} + \underline{} = \underline{}$$
$$\underline{} + \underline{} = \underline{}$$

and are asked to fill in the sum (called the "big number") and generate two addition statements.

The second format for teaching three number families demonstrates how facts can be related across operations (see Format 6.4). It is used to generate subtraction facts from addition facts and division facts from multiplication facts. The teacher demonstrates how to generate the subtraction or division statements. For example, after constructing 3 + 4 = 7 and 4 + 3 = 7, students are taught to generate the subtraction statements of 7 − 4 = 3 and 7 − 3 = 4.

The format for subtraction and division facts includes two parts. Although examples in Figure 6.4 illustrate subtraction, the same format can be used to introduce division facts. In Part A, the teacher demonstrates how three related numbers such as 3, 5, and 8 can generate two subtraction statements. The teacher first has the students add the two smaller numbers (3 and 5), then points out that two subtraction statements can be made. The teacher introduces the rule that *when you subtract, you always start with the big number,* which helps avoid errors like

3 − 8 = 5. Part B is a worksheet exercise in which the students construct four statements, two addition and two subtraction, from three numbers.

Sequence for Introducing Facts

Basic facts should be introduced in a carefully planned sequence. New sets of facts should be introduced systematically to avoid potential confusion and to facilitate learning. Figures 6.2, 6.3, 6.4, and 6.5 suggest orders for introducing addition, subtraction, multiplication, and division facts. In each figure there are about 25 sets of facts, each set comprised of three or four facts. The sets are lettered in their order of presentation, i.e., the facts in Set A would be introduced first, followed by the facts in Sets B, C, D, etc. Across from each set of facts is the relationship format recommended for introducing the facts. For example, in Figure 6.3 for subtraction facts, the teacher would present the Set G facts (6 − 3, 8 − 4, 10 − 5, 12 − 6) using the three numbers subtraction format. For the 6 − 3 fact, the teacher would write

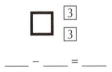

$$\underline{} - \underline{} = \underline{}$$

in Part A. The teacher writes blanks for only one statement because only one subtraction statement, 6 − 3, can be generated from the numbers 6, 3, and 3. The teacher would present Part A with all four sets of numbers and then present Part B with the four sets of numbers. While the teacher is introducing the new set of facts, memorization worksheet exercises on the previous sets continue. Each relationship exercise, as illustrated with Set G for subtraction, is presented for several days before the facts are introduced into mastery exercises.

In constructing these sequences, three guidelines were followed: (1) easier facts were introduced first, (2) related facts were introduced together, and (3) the reverse of specific series of facts was taught relatively soon after the initial series was presented. These sequences are provided to illustrate just one possible order for introducing facts and are not intended to represent the only or best sequence for teaching facts.

In developmental math programs, addition facts are introduced first, followed by subtraction, multiplication, and division facts. The question of exactly when to introduce subtraction, multiplication, and division facts is a difficult one. More specifically, it is difficult to say whether students should master all of one type of fact before the next type is introduced or whether different facts should be introduced concurrently, using the three number relationship that extends across operations. For example, should subtraction facts be introduced while students are still learning addition facts (and, if so, when?), or should subtraction facts be introduced only after students have mastered all addition facts? A similar question can be raised about multiplication and division facts.

Unfortunately, little experimental research has been done to answer the questions about when to introduce the various fact strands. In our observations of lower-performing students, we have found that students have more difficulty when a set of addition facts and the inverse subtraction facts are introduced concurrently. Consequently, we recommend introducing related subtraction or division facts for a particular set a month or more after the original addition or multiplication set has been introduced. More specifically, teachers might begin introducing subtraction facts when the students have learned about half of their addition facts. The

teacher would then alternate between introducing sets of addition and subtraction. Following this recommendation, teachers would first introduce addition sets A through M, then introduce subtraction set A. Thereafter, the teacher would alternate between addition and subtraction fact sets. Addition Set N would be followed by subtraction Set B, which would be followed by addition Set O, then subtraction Set C, etc.

The question of when to introduce multiplication facts is important. Many students will not have mastered all basic addition and subtraction facts at the time a program calls for the introduction of multiplication. We recommend that the teaching of multiplication facts begins no later than third grade, even though addition and subtraction facts have not been completely mastered. Knowledge of basic multiplication facts is a critical prerequisite for more advanced operations and, thus, should be mastered no later than fourth grade. Teachers might devote extra time to basic facts for students who have not mastered the basic addition and subtraction facts by third grade. Two practice sessions might be conducted daily, one focusing on addition and subtrac-

FIGURE 6.2   Sequence of Addition Facts

Plus 1 Format is Format 6.1.
Series Saying Format is Format 6.2.
Three Number Format is Format 6.3.

Sets of New Facts	*Relationship Formats*
A. $2 + 1, 3 + 1, 4 + 1, 5 + 1$	Plus 1, series-saying
B. $6 + 1, 7 + 1, 8 + 1, 9 + 1$	Plus 1, series-saying
C. $2 + 2, 3 + 2, 4 + 2, 5 + 2$	Series-saying
D. $6 + 2, 7 + 2, 8 + 2, 9 + 2$	Series-saying
E. $3 + 3, 4 + 4, 5 + 5, 6 + 6$	Series-saying
F. $2 + 3, 3 + 3, 4 + 3, 5 + 3$	Series-saying
G. $6 + 3, 7 + 3, 8 + 3, 9 + 3$	Series-saying
H. $1 + 2, 1 + 2, 1 + 4, 1 + 5$	Three numbers—addition (1, 3, 4) (1, 4, 5) (1, 5, 6)
I. $1 + 6, 1 + 7, 1 + 8, 1 + 9$	Three numbers—addition (1, 6, 7) (1, 7, 8) (1, 8, 9) (1, 9, 10)
J. $2 + 4, 2 + 5, 2 + 6$	Three numbers—addition (2, 3, 5) (2, 4, 6) (2, 5, 7) (2, 6, 8)
K. $2 + 7, 2 + 5, 2 + 6$	Three numbers—addition (2, 7, 9) (2, 8, 10) (2, 9, 11)
L. $3 + 4, 3 + 5, 3 + 6$	Three numbers—addition (3, 4, 7) (3, 5, 8) (3, 6, 9)
M. $3 + 7, 3 + 8, 3 + 9$	Three numbers—addition (3, 7, 10) (3, 8, 11) (3, 9, 12)
N. $7 + 7, 8 + 8, 9 + 9, 10 + 10$	Series-saying
O. $1 + 0, 2 + 0, 3 + 0 . . . 9 + 0$	Series-saying
P. $0 + 1, 0 + 2, 0 + 3 . . . 0 + 9$	Three numbers—addition (6, 0, 6) (7, 0, 7) (8, 0, 8)
Q. $5 + 4, 6 + 4, 7 + 4$	Series-saying
R. $7 + 6, 8 + 6, 9 + 6$	Series-saying
S. $4 + 5, 4 + 6, 4 + 7$	Three numbers—addition (4, 5, 9) (4, 6, 10) (4, 7, 11)
T. $6 + 7, 6 + 8, 6 + 9$	Three numbers—addition (6, 7, 13) (6, 8, 14) (6, 9, 15)
U. $7 + 4, 8 + 4, 9 + 4$	Series-saying
V. $7 + 7, 8 + 7, 9 + 7$	Series-saying
W. $9 + 8, 8 + 9, 4 + 8$	Three numbers—addition (8, 9, 17) (8, 4, 12)
X. $6 + 5, 7 + 5, 8 + 5, 9 + 5$	Series-saying
Y. $7 + 8, 7 + 9, 4 + 9$	Three numbers—addition (7, 8, 15) (7, 9, 16)
Z. $5 + 6, 5 + 7, 5 + 8, 5 + 9$	Three numbers—addition (5, 6, 11) (5, 7, 12) (5, 8, 13) (5, 9, 14)

tion facts and one focusing on multiplication and, later, division facts.

We recommend that multiplication and division facts be presented to intermediate grade remedial students before addition and subtraction. The reason for this recommendation is that these students are likely to have some type of finger strategy that allows them to compute addition and subtraction facts correctly. (More advice on the use of fingers appears at the end of the chapter.) On the other hand, these students are likely to have no viable strategy for figuring out multiplication and division facts. Teaching multiplication and division facts first will allow the teacher to present a wider range of operations during the school year. After multiplication and division facts are mastered, the teacher would go back and work on addition and subtraction facts.

COORDINATING MASTERY AND RELATIONSHIP ACTIVITIES

As a general rule, new sets of facts should be presented in relationship exercises before appearing in mastery exercises. The teacher introduces a set of facts through a relationship exercise and then provides practice to develop mastery on that set of facts. Figures 6.2–6.5 suggest the relationship format to present before introducing each new set of facts. The specific format to present is listed across from each respective set of facts. Remember, the relationship format would be presented for several days **before** including facts from that set in memorization exercises.

FIGURE 6.3   Sequence of Subtraction Facts

Series-Saying Format is Format 6.2.
Three-Number Format is Format 6.3.

Sets of New Facts	*Relationship Format*
A. 3 − 1, 4 − 1, 5 − 1, 6 − 1	Series-saying
B. 7 − 1, 8 − 1, 9 − 1, 10 − 1	Series-saying
C. 4 − 2, 5 − 2, 6 − 2, 7 − 2	Series-saying
D. 8 − 2, 9 − 2, 10 − 2, 11 − 2	Series-saying
E. 1 − 0, 2 − 0, 3 − 0, 4 − 0, 5 − 0, 6 − 7 − 0, 8 − 0, 9 − 0	Three numbers—subtraction (1, 0, 1) (2, 0, 2) (3, 0, 3) (4, 0, 4)
F. 1 − 1, 2 − 2, 3 − 3, 4 − 4, 5 − 5, 6 − 6, 7 − 7, 8 − 8, 9 − 9	Three numbers—subtraction (1, 1, 0) (2, 2, 0) (3, 3, 0) (4, 4, 0)
G. 6 − 3, 8 − 4, 10 − 5, 12 − 6	Three numbers—subtraction (6, 3, 3) (8, 4, 4) (10, 5, 5) (12, 6, 6)
H. 5 − 3, 6 − 3, 7 − 3, 8 − 3	Series-saying
I. 9 − 3, 10 − 3, 11 − 3, 12 − 3	Series-saying
J. 3 − 2, 4 − 3, 5 − 4, 6 − 5	Three numbers—subtraction (3, 2, 1,) (4, 3, 1) (5, 4, 1) (6, 5, 1)
K. 7 − 6, 8 − 7, 9 − 8, 10 − 9	Three numbers—subtraction (7, 6, 1) (8, 7, 1) (9, 8, 1) (10, 9, 1)
L. 5 − 3, 6 − 4, 7 − 5	Three numbers—subtraction (5, 3, 2) (6, 4, 2) (7, 5, 2)
M. 8 − 6, 9 − 7, 10 − 8, 11 − 9	Three numbers—subtraction (8, 6, 2) (9, 7, 2) (10, 8, 2) (11, 9, 2)
N. 6 − 3, 7 − 4, 8 − 5, 9 − 6	Three numbers—subtraction (6, 3, 3) (7, 4, 3) (8, 5, 3) (9, 6, 3)
O. 10 − 7, 11 − 8, 12 − 9	Three numbers—subtraction (10, 7, 3) (11, 8, 3) (12, 9, 3)
P. 14 − 7, 16 − 8, 18 − 9	Three numbers—subtraction (14, 7, 7) (16, 8, 8) (18, 9, 9)
Q. 8 − 4, 9 − 4, 10 − 4, 11 − 4	Series-saying
R. 12 − 6, 13 − 6, 14 − 6, 15 − 6	Series-saying
S. 9 − 5, 10 − 6, 11 − 7	Three numbers—subtraction (9, 5, 4) (10, 6, 4) (11, 7, 4)
T. 13 − 7, 14 − 8, 15 − 9	Three numbers—subtraction (13, 7, 6) (14, 8, 6) (15, 9, 6)
U. 10 − 4, 11 − 4, 12 − 4, 13 − 4	Series-saying
V. 14 − 7, 15 − 7, 16 − 7	Series-saying
W. 17 − 8, 17 − 9, 12 − 8	Three numbers—subtraction (17, 9, 8) (12, 8, 4)
X. 11 − 5, 12 − 5, 13 − 5, 14 − 5	Series-saying
Y. 15 − 8, 16 − 9, 13 − 9	Three numbers—subtraction (15, 8, 7) (16, 9, 7) (13, 9, 4)
Z. 11 − 6, 12 − 7, 13 − 8, 14 − 9	Three numbers—subtraction (11, 6, 5) (12, 7, 5) (13, 8, 5) (14, 9, 5)

FIGURE 6.4   Sequence of Multiplication Facts

Series-Saying Format is Format 6.2.
Three-Number Format is Format 6.3.

Sets of New Facts	*Relationship Format*
A. Any problem with a one	Series-saying
B. $5 \times 2, 5 \times 3, 5 \times 4, 5 \times 5$	Series-saying
C. $2 \times 2, 3 \times 2, 4 \times 2, 5 \times 2$	Series-saying
D. $2 \times 5, 3 \times 5, 4 \times 5, 5 \times 5$	Three numbers—multiplication
E. $2 \times 2, 2 \times 3, 2 \times 4, 2 \times 5$	Three numbers—multiplication
F. Any problem with a zero	
G. $5 \times 6, 5 \times 7, 5 \times 8, 5 \times 9$	Series-saying
H. $2 \times 6, 2 \times 7, 2 \times 8, 2 \times 9$	Series-saying
I. $6 \times 5, 7 \times 5, 8 \times 5, 9 \times 5$	Three numbers—multiplication
J. $6 \times 2, 7 \times 2, 8 \times 2, 9 \times 2$	Three numbers—multiplication
K. $2 \times 0, 3 \times 0, 4 \times 0, 5 \times 0$	Series-saying
L. $0 \times 6, 0 \times 7, 0 \times 8, 0 \times 9$	Three numbers—multiplication
M. $9 \times 2, 9 \times 3, 9 \times 4, 9 \times 5$	Series-saying
N. $4 \times 2, 4 \times 3, 4 \times 4, 4 \times 5$	Series-saying
O. $2 \times 9, 3 \times 9, 4 \times 9, 5 \times 9$	Three numbers—multiplication
P. $2 \times 4, 3 \times 4, 4 \times 4, 5 \times 4$	Three numbers—multiplication
Q. $9 \times 6, 9 \times 7, 9 \times 8, 9 \times 9$	Series-saying
R. $4 \times 6, 4 \times 7, 4 \times 8, 4 \times 9$	Series-saying
S. $6 \times 9, 7 \times 9, 8 \times 9, 9 \times 9$	Three numbers—multiplication
T. $6 \times 4, 7 \times 4, 8 \times 4, 9 \times 4$	Three numbers—multiplication
U. $3 \times 6, 3 \times 7, 3 \times 8, 3 \times 9$	Series-saying
V. $6 \times 6, 6 \times 7, 6 \times 8, 6 \times 9$	Series-saying
W. $6 \times 3, 7 \times 3, 8 \times 3, 9 \times 3$	Three numbers—multiplication
X. $7 \times 6, 8 \times 6, 9 \times 6, 3 \times 3$	Three numbers—multiplication
Y. $7 \times 7, 8 \times 7, 9 \times 7$	Series-saying
Z. $7 \times 8, 8 \times 8, 9 \times 8$	Three numbers—multiplication

FIGURE 6.5   Sequence of Division Facts

Three-Number Format is Format 6.3.

Sets of New Facts	*Relationship Format*
A. any number divided by 1	Three numbers—division (8, 1, 8) (4, 1, 4) (7, 1, 7)
B. any number divided by itself	Three numbers—division (3, 1, 3) (9, 1, 9) (8, 1, 8) (2, 1, 2)
C. $10 \div 5, 15 \div 5, 20 \div 5, 25 \div 5$	Three numbers—division (2, 5, 10) (3, 5, 15) (4, 5, 20) (5, 5, 25)
D. $4 \div 2, 6 \div 2, 8 \div 2, 10 \div 2$	Three numbers—division
E. $10 \div 2, 15 \div 3, 20 \div 4, 25 \div 5$	Three numbers—division
F. $0 \div 1, 0 \div 2, 0 \div 3, 0 \div 4, 0 \div 5, 0 \div 6, 0 \div 7,$	Three numbers—division
$\quad 0 \div 8, 0 \div 9, 9 \div 3$	Three numbers—division
G. $4 \div 2, 6 \div 3, 8 \div 4, 10 \div 5$	Three numbers—division
H. $30 \div 5, 35 \div 5, 40 \div 5, 45 \div 5$	Three numbers—division
I. $12 \div 2, 14 \div 2, 16 \div 2, 18 \div 2$	Three numbers—division
J. $30 \div 6, 35 \div 7, 40 \div 8, 45 \div 9$	Three numbers—division
K. $12 \div 6, 14 \div 7, 16 \div 8, 18 \div 9$	Three numbers—division
L. $18 \div 9, 27 \div 9, 36 \div 9, 45 \div 9$	Three numbers—division
M. $8 \div 4, 12 \div 4, 16 \div 4, 20 \div 4$	Three numbers—division
N. $18 \div 2, 27 \div 3, 36 \div 4, 45 \div 5$	Three numbers—division
O. $8 \div 2, 12 \div 3, 16 \div 4, 20 \div 5$	Three numbers—division
P. $54 \div 9, 63 \div 9, 72 \div 9, 81 \div 9$	Three numbers—division
Q. $24 \div 4, 28 \div 4, 32 \div 4, 36 \div 4$	Three numbers—division
R. $54 \div 6, 63 \div 7, 72 \div 8, 81 \div 9$	Three numbers—division
S. $24 \div 6, 28 \div 7, 32 \div 8, 36 \div 9$	Three numbers—division
T. $18 \div 3, 21 \div 3, 24 \div 3, 27 \div 3$	Three numbers—division
U. $36 \div 6, 42 \div 6, 48 \div 6, 54 \div 6$	Three numbers—division
V. $18 \div 6, 21 \div 7, 24 \div 8, 27 \div 9$	Three numbers—division
W. $42 \div 7, 48 \div 8, 54 \div 9$	Three numbers—division
X. $49 \div 7, 56 \div 7, 63 \div 7$	Three numbers—division
Y. $56 \div 8, 64 \div 8, 72 \div 8$	Three numbers—division

Exercises for Memorizing

Practice to aid memorization of basic facts can be provided in a number of ways: paired drill in which students practice with each other, teacher drill in which the teacher presents facts to a group, worksheet exercises, flash card exercises in which students are given a specific set of facts to study independently, and fact games. Memorization exercises should be cumulative. That is, newly introduced facts receive intensive practice, while previously introduced facts receive less intensive, but still systematically planned, practice.

Setting Up a Program to Promote Mastery

A program to facilitate basic fact memorization should have the following components:

1. a specific performance criterion for introducing new facts
2. intensive practice on newly introduced facts
3. systematic practice on previously introduced facts
4. adequate allotted time
5. a record-keeping system
6. a motivation system

PERFORMANCE CRITERION We consider mastery of a basic fact as the ability of students to respond immediately to the fact question. For example, after the teacher asks students the answer to 8 + 7, the students immediately answer "15." Students should practice a new set of facts until they are able to answer each member of the new set and members of previously introduced sets immediately.

An acceptable criterion of performance for an oral exercise, assuming students say an entire statement, would be a rate of a fact each two seconds. The criterion for written exercises depends on the students' motor coordination. That is, rate criteria for written work should be based on the speed with which students are able to write numerals. Obviously, a student who writes numerals slowly will not be able to complete a worksheet as quickly as a student whose motor skills are more developed and is able to write numbers more quickly. Our basic recommendation is that the criterion be set at a rate that is about 2/3 of the rate at which the student is able to write digits. A student's writing ability can be easily determined by giving a one-minute timed test. The student would be instructed to write the numbers 1 through 9 as many times as he could. It would be appropriate to provide several practice trials before the timing. The student's writing rate is determined by counting up the number of digits written during this one-minute period. By multiplying that number by 2/3, the teacher can estimate how many digits a student should be able to write as answers during a one-minute fact timing. For example, a student who writes 60 digits in one minute should write 40 digits in one minute in a fact timing (60 × 2/3 = 40).

INTENSIVE PRACTICE AND SYSTEMATIC REVIEW In addition to providing intensive practice on new facts, the teacher must provide practice on previously taught facts. Unless earlier introduced facts are systematically reviewed, students are likely to forget them. We recommend that daily practice of new facts be followed immediately by review of previously introduced facts. (See sections on materials later in this chapter.)

ADEQUATE ALLOTTED TIME The amount of time allocated to fact practice must be sufficient. We recommend that teachers allocate 10–15 minutes per day for basic fact learning activities. This time allotment is much more than what is provided in most classroom schedules. Teachers should keep in mind that work on basic math facts is time well spent. Children who know facts will be able to compute efficiently and are more likely to encounter success in later problem-solving activities.

RECORD-KEEPING SYSTEM A record-keeping system is needed to monitor student progress so that the teacher knows when a student needs additional encouragement and when a student is ready to progress to the next set of facts. This system should involve a minimum of paperwork, so that little time is taken from actual fact practice.

MOTIVATION A motivational system should be integrated within the record-keeping procedure. The motivation system must be carefully designed so that students see a clear relationship between working hard and receiving recognition for their work.

Manageability is an important aspect of any instructional program and is especially important in a fact program. Procedures must be simple. Materials must be easy to prepare, pass out, collect, and score. Teachers cannot follow procedures that consume inordinate amounts of time.

TWO FACT MASTERY PROGRAMS

Two examples of fact mastery programs are presented below. The first program is designed for teachers working with homogeneous groups of students who are all functioning near the same instructional level. The second program is designed for teachers working with heterogeneous groups, groups composed of students functioning at different levels or for one-to-one tutoring in which an adult or a peer tutors a student.

Homogeneous Group Program

The homogeneous group system is designed for teachers working with a group of students functioning at approximately the same level. The basic system consists of teacher-directed instruction, with students completing daily exercises on a fact worksheet. In these exercises the teacher first presents a drill in which the students orally practice newly introduced facts. The oral drill is followed by a written exercise on which the students are timed.

MATERIALS   The system requires specially prepared sequences of worksheets for each type of fact: addition, subtraction, division, and multiplication. A worksheet would be prepared for each set listed in Figures 6.2–6.5. Each worksheet would be divided into two parts. The top half of the worksheets should provide practice on new facts, including facts from the currently introduced set and from the two preceding sets. More specifically, each of the facts from the new set would appear four times. Each of the facts from the set introduced just earlier would appear three times, and each of the facts from the set that preceded that one would appear twice. If this pattern were applied to sets, each containing four facts, the top part of the worksheet would have 36 facts: 16 new facts (4 × 4), 12 facts from the previously learned set (4 × 3), and 8 facts from the set before that (4 × 2).

The bottom half of the worksheet should include 30 problems. Each of the facts from the currently introduced set would appear twice. The remaining facts would be taken from previously introduced sets. All previously introduced facts would appear just one time. *Note:* At the beginning of a fact program, students will not know many facts; thus, facts from previous sets may appear several times on the bottom half of the worksheet. Only when 30 facts have been introduced can each fact appear just once. On the other hand, after more than 30 facts have been introduced, review should be planned so that each fact appears at least once every second or third worksheet.

Figure 6.6 is a sample worksheet for introducing facts according to the guidelines for worksheet construction. The new set consists of 5 + 6, 5 + 7, 5 + 8, and 5 + 9. Each of these facts appears four times in the top half. The previously introduced set includes 7 + 8, 7 + 9, and 4 + 9. Each of these facts appears three times. Finally, the next earlier introduced set included 6 + 5, 7 + 5, 8 + 5, and 9 + 5. Each of these facts appears twice. The top half of the worksheet has 33 facts. The bottom half of the worksheet includes the four facts from the new set, each written twice, along with previously introduced facts, each appearing just once.

PRETESTING   Before beginning instruction, teachers should determine which type of fact to start with (addition, subtraction, multiplication, division) and where students should be placed in that fact program.

Groups with students who know few facts would start at Set A. Students who know more facts would begin at later points. To determine the set at which students might begin, the teacher administers a written pretest that includes the 100 basic facts with the easier facts listed at the top. The teacher allows students two minutes to work as many problems as they can. A teacher with 10 or more students in a group will have to compromise when selecting a starting point. As a general rule we recommend a point slightly lower than the average starting point for the students in the group.

GROUP ORAL PRACTICE   The teacher begins the lesson with a group drill in which the students orally practice the facts on the top half of the worksheet. The students say each problem in unison as the teacher signals. The teacher begins the lesson by instructing students on the procedure: "When I signal, you'll read the first problem and say the answer. Then you'll touch the next problem and figure out the answer. When I signal again, you'll read that problem and say the answer."

The teacher then instructs the students to touch the first problem. After allowing two or three seconds for students to figure out the answer, the teacher says, "Get ready" and signals by clapping her hands. After the students respond, the teacher instructs them to touch the next problem, pauses to let them figure out the answer, then says, "Get ready" and signals. The teacher should keep her talk to a minimum. "Next problem" (pause). "Get ready" (signal). "Next problem" (pause). "Get ready" (signal).

The teacher repeats this signaling procedure with each fact across the first line of the worksheet. The teacher repeats the line until students are able to answer each fact correctly with no more than a two second thinking pause. This may take several repetitions of the entire line. The same procedure is repeated with each subsequent line on the top half of the worksheet.

FIGURE 6.6   Sample Worksheet

```
  5      8      5      6      7      5      4      5      7      5      7
 +6     +5     +8     +5     +9     +7     +9     +6     +8     +9     +9

  5      7      5      7      5      5      4      5      4      7      5
 +8     +5     +7     +8     +6     +8     +9     +9     +9     +9     +7

  8      5      5      6      5      7      5      9      7      5      9
 +5     +6     +9     +5     +7     +5     +8     +5     +8     +9     +5
```

```
  5      6      7      4      5      9      7      5      4      5
 +8     +4     +5     +7     +6     +8     +9     +9     +8     +7

  8      7      8      5      8      9      7      5      8      4
 +9     +8     +5     +6     +7     +5     +7     +8     +4     +9

  9      6      5      7      6      4      5      9      6      6
 +7     +7     +9     +4     +9     +6     +7     +4     +5     +8
```

TIMED TEST   The timed test is done on the bottom half of the worksheet. The teacher sets a specified time. A minute and 15 seconds would be a realistic goal for intermediate grade students. The teacher allows the students a minute or two to study the bottom half of the worksheet, then tells them to get ready for the test. The teacher tells the students how much time they have and to start. At the end of the specified time, the teacher says, "Stop," has the students trade papers, and reads the answers. Students are to mark all mistakes, write the total number correct at the top of the page, and then return the worksheet to its owner.

MASTERY CRITERIA   After the lesson, the teacher inspects the students' papers and records the number of facts each student answered correctly on the written timed drill. In the next lesson the teacher either repeats the same worksheet or presents the worksheet for the next set of facts. The teacher presents the next worksheet if 3/4 or more of the students answered 28 of the 30 facts correctly. The teacher repeats the same worksheet if less than 3/4 of the students answered 28 facts correctly. Keep in mind that students will likely need anywhere from three days to two weeks to master a set. During this time the teacher should keep presenting the relationship exercises for the new fact set and encourage the students.

SUMMARY   The advantage of this system is that it allows the teacher to coordinate the presentation of relationship activities and memorization exercises. Also, the system makes monitoring the performance of the students relatively easy. The disadvantage of this group system is that it does not allow individual students to progress at optimal rates. However, if only one or two students are performing at a much lower rate than other students in the group, the teacher could provide extra practice for those students.

Heterogeneous Group Program

The heterogeneous group program is designed for teachers working with a group of students who demonstrate significant differences in their knowledge of facts. This system also can be adapted for use in tutoring programs (peer tutoring, cross-age tutoring, or tutoring by adult volunteers).

MATERIALS   Prior to the beginning of the school year, teachers should make booklets for each type of fact: addition, subtraction, division, and multiplication. The booklets would consist of the worksheets for each fact set. The same worksheets used in the homogeneous system would be used in the heterogeneous system. Two types of booklets should be prepared, one with answers and one without (i.e. the test booklet). The answer book could be used in subsequent years, while the test booklets would need to be replaced annually.

PRETESTING   Students may start with different types of facts (addition, subtraction, multiplication, division) and at various sets within a type of fact. Pretesting to determine a starting set can be done in a group setting or individually. In a group setting, the teacher would administer a written pretest that includes the 100 basic facts with the easier facts listed at the top.

As mentioned previously, the teacher allows students two minutes to work as many problems as they can. Students who answer 30 or more facts in two minutes might start at set G. Students who answer 45 or more might start at set M. Students who answer 60 or more might start at set R. Students who are able to answer 85 or more facts in the two-minute pretest probably do not need to be placed in a fact program for that type of fact.

Individual testing will allow for a more accurate starting point for most students. To test individuals, the teacher would use the sequences in Figures 6.2–6.5. The teacher begins by testing the facts in set A, then set B. and so on. The teacher continues testing until reaching a set in which the student makes two or more errors. (Any fact problem that a student cannot answer within several seconds should be counted as wrong.) This set would be the student's starting point.

DAILY ROUTINE   In this program, students work in pairs. As a general rule, teachers should pair students who are working near the same level. Each student has one booklet with answers and one booklet without answers. The student with the answer sheet acts as a tutor, while the other student acts as the pupil.

The teacher has each student practice the top half of the worksheet twice. Each practice session is timed. The teacher says, "Get ready, go," and starts a stopwatch; the student practices by saying complete statements (e.g., 4 + 2 = 6), rather than just answers. Saying the entire fact statement makes it easier for the tutor to follow along. If the student makes an error, the tutor corrects by saying the correct statement and having the student repeat the statement. The teacher allows students a minute and a half when practicing the top part and a minute when practicing the bottom half. After the allotted time, the teacher has the second student begin practicing. This procedure is repeated twice for the facts on the top half and twice for the facts on the bottom half of the worksheet.

After allowing each student to practice the top and bottom sections of their individual fact sheets twice, the teacher tells the students to get ready for a test. Students work in their individual test booklets. The teacher stops students at the end of a minute. The students are to stop answering immediately. The students trade test booklets and answer booklets to correct each other's work. They count the number of facts answered correctly and record that number across from the letter for the respective set of facts on the student's record form (see Figure 6.7 and the discussion under Student Record Form).

The next day, the same procedure is followed. However, if a student answered all but two of the facts correctly on the previous day's testing, the student moves on to the next worksheet in the sequence. The teacher begins the lesson by having students inspect their record forms to determine the series students are to practice.

Cooperative student behavior is essential to make this system work. The teacher should provide strong positive consequences for cooperative behavior among students. Rules for the activity might include (1) talking softly, (2) following teacher instructions, and (3) honestly recording performance. Students may be tempted to record inaccurate scores on the test. To guard against cheating, the teacher must monitor student performance carefully during practice. If a student performs quite poorly during practice, yet turns in an excellent testing record, testing may be inaccurate. These students should be tested by the teacher to ensure accuracy of the recorded performance.

STUDENT RECORD FORM   A record form that can be used during this exercise appears in Figure 6.7. In the first column, the worksheet letters are listed. Across from each letter are seven columns. These columns are used to record the number of facts answered correctly on a test. The first day the student does a particular worksheet, the number of facts answered correctly is written in the first column across from that worksheet letter. The second day, the number is written in the second column across from the worksheet letter, and so on. On the right side of the chart is a progress rocket. Each time the student meets the criterion for a worksheet (28–30 correct problems), the student shades in the space for that worksheet on the rocket. On the next lesson, the student works on the next worksheet in the sequence.

MODIFICATIONS   The heterogeneous group program requires extensive preparation by the teacher at the beginning of the school year, because several booklets of worksheets must be made. Also, instruction will be necessary to teach students the procedure. The advantage of this system, though, is that once worksheets are prepared and students know what to do, the system provides the individualization needed to allow each student to progress at her optimal rate.

This system also is easily adapted for use in tutoring programs. Whether same-age students work together in pairs (peer-tutoring), older students work with younger students (cross-age tutoring), or adults work with individual students (volunteer or parent tutoring), the same materials and basic set of proce-

FIGURE 6.7   Student Record Form

page	TRY 1	TRY 2	TRY 3	TRY 4	TRY 5	TRY 6	TRY 7		page
Z									Z
Y									Y
X									X
W									W
V									V
U									U
T									T
S									S
R									R
Q									Q
P									P
O									O
N									N
M									M
L									L
K									K
J									J
I									I
H									H
G									G
F									F
E									E
D									D
C									C
B									B
A									A

dures can be used. That is, students would practice orally with feedback from their tutors, then take a timed test and record their performance.

If students require additional practice for mastery, the teacher or tutor can make flash cards for particularly difficult facts and use the flash cards prior to the oral worksheet practice. The flash cards can be sent home for additional practice (see next section on Parental Involvement) or turned into a game that might be played at recess. Flash cards are an excellent way to provide cumulative review, as well. Tutors might begin each session with a flash card review of the 15 previously introduced facts before introducing a new set.

Motivation is an important factor in all fact mastery programs. If students practice at home or at other times during the school day, their learning rate will likely increase. Teachers can encourage students to study by establishing incentive programs based on their performance. The incentives need not be material rewards, but might include time earned on a computer, extra minutes at recess, or other activities that are highly desirable.

Parental Involvement

Parents would like to help their children at home, but they are often afraid they will not know what to do, how to do it, or whether they will interfere with what the teacher is doing at school. Math fact practice is a good way to involve parents. Teachers should try to secure a commitment from parents to work with their children on facts at home for about ten minutes, three or four days a week. Teachers could easily ensure that this practice is coordinated with classroom activities. If possible, parents should be invited to a training session where the teacher would explain the fact system she is using and review suggestions for working with children at home.

The teacher should prepare a tutoring guide for the parents, specifying exactly how to implement a home practice program. During the training session, the teacher would demonstrate recommended procedures and talk about motivation. Teachers need to remember to encourage parents to interact with their children in positive ways so that home practice becomes an opportunity for students to experience success. A communication system should be set up to inform parents about which facts they should include in the exercises. A weekly letter including the facts to work on might be sent home along with progress reports.

Additional Practice Activities

Supplemental exercises should be available for practicing facts throughout the school day. One exercise that is motivating for most students is the math fact race. The teacher puts a scorecard on the board with one row for teacher points and one for student points:

☺ T	
☺ S	

The teacher then presents a fact or shows a flash card, pauses a second or two, and calls out a student's name. The teacher then hesitates a second more and says the answer. If the student responds correctly before the teacher says the answer, the students get the point. Note that pausing *before* calling on a student (but after stating the fact) will increase the probability that all students will attend to the question.

The race game can also be modified so that one group of students competes with another group. The teacher divides the class in half, placing an equal number of higher and lower performers in each group. The teacher conducts the game by saying a fact, pausing a second or two, and then calling on a student. The student earns a point for her team if she responds correctly.

Note that the games should be played in a way to avoid embarrassing low-performing students. Rules encouraging appropriate behavior should be discussed before playing the game and enforced during the game. Rules such as "No arguing" or "No complaining" are helpful in playing the game.

During free times, students can play board games in which the students pick a card from a deck of fact flash cards. If they say the fact correctly, they get to hit the spinner and move their marker on the board the number of spaces indicated by the spinner.

REMEDIAL STUDENTS

Many remedial students will rely on their fingers to figure out facts. Teachers should not initially discourage students from using their fingers, since memorizing basic facts may require months and months of practice. Teachers may tell students that eventually they will not have to use their fingers to figure out facts, but for the time being, using fingers is fine, except during fact memorization exercises. Teachers can expect some lower-performing students to be inaccurate even when using their fingers. These students may be divided into two groups: those who have an effective finger strategy to figure out facts but are careless, and those students who do not have any effective finger strategy.

The errors made by a student will indicate whether or not he has an effective finger strategy. Students whose answers are correct about 80–90% of the time, and when wrong are usually just one number off (e.g., $15 - 9 = 5$, $8 + 6 = 15$, $9 + 7 = 15$), probably have an effective strategy but are careless in applying it, counting too quickly or not coordinating counting and moving their fingers. The remediation procedure for these students is simply to provide daily exercises in conjunction with a strong incentive program. Students would be given worksheets containing 30–50 basic addition and subtraction facts. The incentives should be contingent on the number of problems worked correctly. Daily exercises would be continued until students performed with over 95% accuracy consistently for about a week.

Students who miss more than 20% of basic facts and/or make what seem to be random errors, having answers several numbers away from the correct answer (e.g., $15 - 8 = 4$, $8 + 6 = 19$, $9 - 3 = 8$), are likely not to have an effective strategy to figure out facts. The teacher should watch these students as they work problems in order to determine the students' specific deficits. The teacher would then provide remediation or, if the students are quite confused, teach them an alternative strategy. Below are finger strategies, one for addition and two for subtraction, that could be taught to students who by third grade have not developed an effective strategy for figuring out addition or subtraction facts.

For addition, the strategy would involve the following:

1. Noting which of the addends is smaller and putting up that number of fingers (e.g., in $8 + 5$ the student puts up five fingers, in $3 + 6$ the student puts up three fingers).
2. Counting from the other addend, saying one number for each finger (e.g., in $8 + 3$, student puts up three fingers and counts "eeighht, 9, 10, 11").

The teacher would demonstrate the strategy with several problems, then provide guided practice by asking, "Which number is smaller? . . . Hold up your fingers . . . Count and figure the answer." Daily supervised practice would be provided until the student performed at a 95% accuracy level for about two weeks on a group of about 30–40 random addition facts.

The strategy for subtraction facts would not be introduced until students were proficient in figuring out addition facts. One of two possible finger strategies might be taught for figuring out basic subtraction facts: a counting-backward strategy or an algebra-based counting forward strategy.

In the counting-backward strategy, the student puts up the number of fingers representing the number being subtracted. For example, in $12 - 7$ the student puts up seven fingers, says the larger number, then counts backward for each raised finger ("twelve, 11, 10, 9, 8, 7, 6, 5"). Note that the student does not count a raised finger when saying the larger number.

In the algebra counting strategy, the student counts from the smaller number to the larger number (e.g., to work $11 - 6$, the student counts from 6 to 11, putting up a finger each time she counts).

If the student does not have too much difficulty with counting backward, we recommend that the counting-backward strategy be taught, since the steps are basically the same as the addition strategy, except for the direction students count. Another advantage of the backward strategy is that students are less likely to become confused when renaming is introduced. Regardless of which strategy is taught, the teacher would provide daily practice on a group of 30–40 random subtraction facts.

COMMERCIAL PROGRAMS

Basic Facts

INSTRUCTIONAL STRATEGIES   In most programs, addition and subtraction facts are taught by emphasizing fact families. In several programs, alternative strategies that organize facts differently also are taught. This emphasis on teaching related facts is in keeping with current research on basic fact acquisition.

One caution about initial teaching procedures for addition and subtraction facts, however, involves the use of pictures. While pictures aid students in using a counting strategy to solve computation problems, pictures are a deterrent to memorization; if pictures are available, some students invariably will resort to counting the pictures instead of trying to remember the answer. For example, in one program a third of the exercises given to students for basic facts practice contain illustrations. For those problems, students need only count the pictures and write the answer, rather than recall the answers from memory. The amount of actual fact practice provided is thereby reduced. Teachers need to remember that if the objective of an exercise is to promote acquisition of facts, then no pictures or other prompts should be available to students during the activity.

PRACTICE AND REVIEW   The most important aspect of any fact program is the provision of adequate practice to develop mastery. A critical part of adequate practice is the cumulative review of previously introduced facts mixed with the presentation of new facts. This type of practice and review is not present in most basal programs. For example, in the third grade level of one program, all basic addition facts are introduced in only three lessons (six student practice pages). Those same facts (sums to 18) are not reviewed until six lessons later, when the relationship between addition and subtraction is taught. The program does not provide another opportunity for students to practice addition facts in that level.

Practice provided for learning basic multiplication facts is often less than adequate, as well. Basal programs typically teach basic multiplication facts within a single unit. Multiplication facts are introduced most often in sets of common factors, e.g., 3×0, 3×1, 3×2, 3×3, etc. (see Figure 6.8). Note that all of the three facts are introduced at once.

One type of fact practice noticeably absent from the programs we examined was fluency practice (i.e., timed fact drills). Whereas programs traditionally address issues of accuracy (number right, number wrong), they have not included exercises whereby students must meet a specified rate criterion as well. For students to be able to recall facts quickly in more complex computation problems, research tells us the students must know their math facts at an acceptable level of "automaticity." Therefore, teachers using these programs must be prepared to supplement by providing more practice, as well as by establishing rate criteria that students must achieve.

FIGURE 6.8 Excerpt from a Basal Math Program

STUDENT OBJECTIVE
To know the multiplication facts for 3.

TEACHING SUGGESTIONS

Act Out Multiplication Word Problems with Models (Materials: counters) Ask the students to use their counters to act out the stories you tell.

"There are 3 wheels on each tricycle. The Baxters have 2 tricycles. How many tricycle wheels do they have?" (6)

"There are 3 tennis balls in each can. Chris has 4 cans. How many tennis balls does Chris have?" (12)

There are 3 ice-cream cones. Each cone has 3 scoops on it. How many scoops are there altogether?" (9)

"There are 3 puppets in each package. Nancy bought 5 packages. How many puppets did she buy?" (15)

Encourage the students to make up stories.

Skip-Count by Threes Have students skip-count by threes through 30 (3, 6, 9, 12, 15, 18, 21, 24, 27, 30). As an extension, skip-count backward by threes from 30. (30, 27, 24, 21, 18, 15, 12, 9, 6, 3)

Review Orally the Multiplication Facts with 3 as a Factor Have students repeat aloud the multiplication facts with 3 as a factor through 3×9 and 9×3.[3]

Source: *Holt Mathematics,* Grade 4 Teacher's Edition (Copyright 1985 Holt Publishing Co., Inc.).

APPLICATION ITEMS: FACTS

1. Your principal asks you to describe the procedure you are using to facilitate learning basic facts. Assume that you are using the heterogeneous fact program system in your text. Write a description of the system.

2. The parents of the children in your class want to know why you spend so much time on memorization activities. What would your reply be?

3. Assume you are constructing worksheets for subtraction facts. More specifically, you are now preparing a worksheet for Set U. (a) List the facts that would appear on the upper half of the worksheet. Next to each fact write how often it would appear on the top half. (b) Describe the guidelines you would use in preparing the bottom half of the student worksheet.

4. You are presenting the relationship format to prepare students for the facts in Set M of the multiplication sequence. Write what you do.

5. You are going to train a volunteer to work with a new student who is not fluent with multiplication facts. Write out directions for a volunteer who will work with this student.

6. Assume the students have learned the basic multiplication facts in sets A through M in the fact sequence of this text. Which computation problems would be appropriate to assign to students, and which would not be appropriate?

34	82	34
×5	×6	×9

65	87	48
×7	×8	×2

FORMAT 6.1   Format for Plus 1 Facts

PART A: NEXT NUMBER

TEACHER	**STUDENTS**

1. When I put my hand down, you say the next number.

2. *(Hold up hand)* One, two, three, four, fiiive.

   (Drop hand.)   6

   To correct: My turn. One, two, three, four, fiiive
(drop hand) six.

   New problem. Tell me the next number: three, four, five, six,
seevven? *(Drop hand. Repeat step 2 with 3, 4, 5 and 7,
8, 9.)*   8

3. When I put my hand down, you say the next number. Siiiix.
(Drop hand.)

   To correct: My turn; sssiiix *(drop hand)* seven.   7

   *Repeat step 3 with 8, 4, 9, 2, 5. Give individual turns to
several students.)*

PART B: PLUS 1 RULE WITH STRETCH PROMPT

1. Everyone listen to the rule. When you plus one, you say the
next number. My turn. Fooouur plus one equals five. Eeiight
plus one equals nine.

2. Get ready to tell me the answers to some plus one
problems. Remember to say the next number. Five plus
one, fiiive plus one equals . . . *(Signal.)*   6

   Yes, 5 + 1 = 6.

   To correct: Listen: 5. *What number comes
next? So 5 plus 1 equals 6.*

3. Three plus one. Thhreee plus one equals? (Signal.)
Yes, 3 + 1 = 4   4

   *(Present step 3 with examples like the following until
students answer all +1 problems in a row correctly:
9 + 1, 7 + 1, 2 + 1, 8 + 1, 4 + 1.)*

PART C: PLUS 1 RULE WITHOUT PROMPT

1. Remember, when you plus 1 you say the next number.

2. Eight plus one equals . . . (Pause, then signal.) "Say the   9
whole statement.   8 + 1 = 9

3. *(Repeat step 2 with the following examples: 4 + 1, 7 + 1,
5+ 1, 9 + 1.)*

FORMAT 6.2   Format for Series Saying

PART A: READING STATEMENTS

TEACHER	**STUDENTS**

(Write the following problems on the board.)

5 + 2 = 7
6 + 2 = 8
7 + 2 = 9
8 + 2 = 10

1. Everybody, I'll touch them. You read. Get ready. *(Point to numerals and symbols in each statement. Repeat step 1 until students can read statements at a rate of a statement each three seconds.)*	5 + 2 = 7 6 + 2 = 8 7 + 2 = 9 8 + 2 = 10

PART B: READING STATEMENTS WITH ANSWERS ERASED

1. Now I'm going to erase the answers. *(Erase answers.)* Now read the statement and tell me the answer. *To correct: Respond with students until they appear able to respond without assistance.*	5 + 2 = 7 6 + 2 = 8 7 + 2 = 9 8 + 2 = 10

PART C: SAYING STATEMENTS

1. Now I'll make it even harder and erase everything. *(Erase everything)* Get ready to say the statements starting with 5 + 2. *(Either clap or snap fingers to set pace for students to respond.)* *(Repeat Part C until all students respond correctly and then present individual turns.)*	5 + 2 = 7 6 + 2 = 8 7 + 2 = 9 8 + 2 = 10

PART D: RANDOM FACT DRILL

(Write facts in random order on board.)

7	5	6	8
+2	+2	+2	+2

1. When I signal, say the whole statement with the answer.	
2. *(Point to left of 7 + 2, pause 2 seconds, then touch board.)*	7 + 2 = 9
3. *(Repeat step 2 with remaining facts.)*	
4. *(Repeat steps 2 and 3 with only a one-second pause.)*	
5. *(Repeat step 4 until students can respond to all facts with the one-second pause.)*	

PART A: STRUCTURED BOARD PRESENTATION

TEACHER	**STUDENT**

1. *(Write the following boxes and numbers on the board.)*

☐ 8
　 2

_____ + _____ = _____
_____ + _____ = _____

I want to make addition statements using the numbers 8 and 2. What is the big number that goes with 8 and 2? *(Pause.)*	10
I'll write the big number in the big box. *(Write 10 in the big box.)* What is 8 plus 2? *(Write 8 + 2 = 10.)*	10
2. We can make another addition statement. If 8 + 2 = 10, then 2 + 8 = 10. (Write 2 + 8 = 10.) Say the statement that begins with 8. Say the statement that begins with 2.	8 + 2 = 10 2 + 8 = 10
3. *(Erase statements.)* Let's say both statements we can make with the numbers 8, 2, and 10. Say the statement that begins with 8. Say the statement that begins with 2.	8 + 2 = 10 2 + 8 = 10

4. *(Write the following boxes and numbers on the board.)*

☐ 5
　 2

What's the big number that goes with 5 and 2? *To correct:* What does 5 + 2 equal?	
Say an addition statement using those numbers. Start with 5.*(Pause.)*	5 + 2 = 7
Say the other addition statement that starts with 2. *(Pause.)*	2 + 5 = 7

(Repeat step 4 with 6 and 2; 9 and 2.)

PART B: DISCRIMINATION PRACTICE

1. Now let's see if you can tell me the answers to some problems. What is 2 + 6? *(Pause.)*	8

(Repeat step 1 with 2 + 8, 2 + 5, 2 + 7. Repeat Part B until students are able to respond to any fact with only a one-second pause.)

PART C: SUPERVISED WORKSHEET

☐ 2　　☐ 6　　☐ 2　　☐ 8
　 7　　　 8　　　 5　　　 2

__ + __ = __ | __ + __ = __ | __ + __ = __ | __ + __ = __
__ + __ = __ | __ + __ = __ | __ + __ = __ | __ + __ = __

1. Fill in the big number and write the two addition statements that can be made from those numbers.

FORMAT 6.4 Format for Three Number Fact Family: Subtraction/Division Facts

PART A: STRUCTURED BOARD PRESENTATION

TEACHER	STUDENTS
1. *(Write the following lines and symbols on the board.)*	

_____ − _____ = _____
_____ − _____ = _____

TEACHER	STUDENTS
What big number goes with 5 and 3? *(Pause.)*	8
To correct: 5 + 3 = what number?	
(Write 8 in box.)	
2. We can use the numbers 5, 3, and 8 to figure out subtraction statements. When you subtract, you always start with the big number. What is the big number? I'll write 8 at the start of these subtraction problems.	8
3. Eight minus three. What will I end up with? Say the first statement. *(Write 8 − 3 = 5.)*	5
Eight minus five.	8 − 3 = 5
What will I end up with?	3
Say the second statement. *(Write 8 − 5 = 3.)*	8 − 5 = 3
4. Say both subtraction statements.	8 − 5 = 3
	8 − 3 = 5

(Repeat steps 1–4 with 3 and 4; 6 and 3.)

PART B: STRUCTURED WORKSHEET

1. *(Give students worksheets with problems similar to these.)*

a. ▨ 7 ▨3 ▨4	b. ▨ 8 ▨5 ▨3	c. ▨ 9 ▨3 ▨6
__ + __ = __	__ + __ = __	__ + __ = __
__ + __ = __	__ + __ = __	__ + __ = __
__ − __ = __	__ − __ = __	__ − __ = __
__ − __ = __	__ − __ = __	__ − __ = __

TEACHER	STUDENTS
1. Touch box a. You have to use the three numbers to make up statements. First, say the addition statements.	
2. Say an addition statement that starts with 3. *(Pause.)*	3 + 4 = 7
Say the other addition statement.	4 + 3 = 7
Write the addition statements.	
3. Now we'll write the subtraction statements. Which number will go first in both subtraction statements?	7
Say the subtraction fact that begins 7 − 3	7 − 3 = 4
Say the subtraction fact that begins 7 − 4.	7 − 4 = 3
Write the subtraction statements.	

(Repeat steps 1–3 with remaining examples.)

CHAPTER 7

Addition

TERMS AND CONCEPTS

Addition   Addition is (a) the process of combining smaller sets to form a larger set and then determining the total number of the larger set, or (b) the union of two disjoint sets. Disjoint sets have no members in common.

Addend   The numbers of the smaller sets in an addition statement (e.g., in 4 + 3 = 7, the addends are 4 and 3).

Missing Addend   A problem type in which students solve for an addend (e.g., 6 + □ = 9).

Sum   The number of the new set formed by combining the smaller sets (e.g., in 4 + 3 = 7, the sum is 7).

Commutative Law of Addition   The sum is the same, regardless of the order in which the numbers are added (e.g., 4 + 3 = 7 and 3 + 4 = 7).

Associative Law of Addition   Any method of grouping may be used to obtain the sum of several addends:

(1 + 2) + 3 = 6 or 1 + (2 + 3) = 6

Identity Element for Addition   When any whole number and zero are added, the result is the whole number.

Renaming   Converting a sum of 10 or more to the number of tens groups and the number of units; e.g., 17 is renamed as 10 and 7. In 19 + 28, the sum in the ones column (17) is renamed as 10 and 7 so that the 10 can be written in the tens column. This process had previously been called carrying. When used in addition, renaming is quite similar to expanded notation. In subtraction, a tens number is usually renamed as one ten and the number of remaining tens; e.g., 70 is renamed 10 and 60. In a problem such as 74 − 16, the 70 is renamed so that a ten and the 4 can be combined, allowing a student to subtract a 6 from 14. Six tens remain in the tens column.

Regrouping   The same process as renaming, except it is carried out with objects or counters rather than numerals; just as 8 + 4 can be renamed 10 + 2, so ||||||||||| can be regrouped as ||||||||| ||

SKILL HIERARCHY

Our discussion of addition is divided into two parts. The first part discusses strategies designed to establish a conceptual understanding of the process of addition. These strategies, usually taught with concrete objects or representations, are usually introduced in kindergarten or first grade. The second part addresses teaching students to work problems that require them to rely on mental computation rather than on representations of concrete objects. The second stage begins during the latter part of first grade

Instructional Sequence and Assessment Chart

Grade Level	Problem Type	Performance Indicator		
1a	Begin fact memorization	See Chapter 6		
1b	Adding a two-digit and a one- or two-digit number; no renaming	35 +21	64 +23	35 + 2
2a	Adding three single-digit numbers	1 3 +2	4 4 +3	1 3 +5
2b	Adding two three-digit numbers; no renaming	325 +132	463 +124	386 +100
2c	Adding a three-digit and a one- or two-digit number; no renaming	326 + 21	423 + 5	570 + 21
2d	Adding one-, two-, and three-digit numbers; no renaming	4 21 + 2	14 71 + 10	21 14 + 33
2e	Adding two two-digit numbers; renaming from ones to tens	37 +46	48 +14	57 +27
2f	Adding a three-digit and a one-, two-, or three-digit number; renaming from ones to tens	247 +315	258 + 13	276 + 8
3a	Complex facts; adding a single-digit number to a teen number—sum below 20.	Test students individually; teacher asks: 13 + 3 =	14 + 4 =	12 + 2 =
3b	Adding two two- or three-digit numbers; renaming from tens to hundreds	374 +261	83 +43	187 + 81
3c	Adding two three-digit numbers; renaming from ones to tens and tens to hundreds	376 +185	248 +164	437 +275
3d	Adding three two-digit numbers; renaming—ones column totals less than 20.	98 14 +12	39 16 +23	74 24 +12
3e	Adding three or four numbers; renaming from ones to tens and from tens to hundreds—sums of columns below 20.	385 6 24 +120	157 23 245 + 3	8 156 280 + 42
4a	Complex facts; adding a single number to a teen number—sum 20 or over	Test students individually; teacher asks: 16 + 6 =	18 + 8 =	17 + 6 =
4b	Adding three two-digit numbers—ones column ntotals 20 or more	28 17 +28	29 16 +35	38 18 +15
4c	Adding three, four, or five multi-digit numbers; renaming in all or some columns totals 20 or more	892 1486 38 286 + 35	8 4086 85 193 + 242	3856 2488 1932 +1583

and continues into the intermediate grades. For purposes of remediation, teachers should not revert to the conceptual introduction but should consider teaching basic facts and the operations specified in the Instructional Sequence and Assessment Chart.

During the beginning stage, students are taught to solve simple addition problems with concrete or semi-concrete objects representing each addend. For example, when solving the problem 4 + 2, the students are taught to draw four lines under the numeral 4 and two lines under the numeral 2. The students then figure the sum by counting all of the lines. Note that counting, numeral, and equality preskills must be mastered in order to work these problems. Missing addend problems in which an addend must be computed (e.g., 4 + □ = 7) are also presented during this stage. An understanding of equality is also essential to solving missing addend problems.

In the second stage, when multi-digit numbers are added, students work problems without making concrete representations for each addend. A new pre-skill necessary for solving column addition problems is knowledge of basic addition facts. (The 100 possible combinations of single-digit addends are referred to as basic addition facts.) The ability to accurately and quickly respond to a fact problem is a component skill of all multi-digit problems. Too little attention is usually given to the process by which students learn to memorize basic addition facts. In order to aid the teacher in teaching this critical preskill, we have devoted an entire chapter to the process of teaching addition, subtraction, multiplication, and division facts (see Chapter 6).

The first type of column problem introduced involves adding multi-digit numbers in which the sum in each column is less than 10; thus, renaming is not required (36 + 13). The next major type of problem involves adding two or more multi-digit numbers in which the sum of one or more columns is greater than 10 and requires renaming (36 + 15). The initial problem in this group would involve adding two double-digit numerals such as 45 + 37. Problems with hundreds and thousands numbers are introduced after students have been taught to read and write those numerals.

The third major type of problem involves addition of three or more multi-digit numbers. The difficulty of these problems increases as the sum of each column becomes greater. For example, adding 23 + 14 + 32 is not difficult, since a sum never reaches 10. On the other hand, in a problem such as 39 + 16 + 27, the sum for the first two numbers is more than 10 (9 + 6 = 15). The student must not only rename

but also be able to figure out facts in which a single-digit number is added to a two-digit number. The sum of the first two digits in the ones column, 9 and 6, is 15. The students must then add 7 to 15 to figure the sum of the ones column. We refer to problems in which a student must mentally add a single-digit number to a two-digit number as *complex addition facts*. A great deal of practice is necessary for students to master complex addition facts.

The Instructional Sequence and Assessment Chart includes our recommended instruction and assessment sequence.

INTRODUCING THE CONCEPT

The major objective of beginning addition instruction is to develop a conceptual understanding of addition as a union of disjoint sets. Most educators agree that, at this stage, demonstrations should involve concrete objects. Math educators recommend a variety of methods for introducing addition. Using the term *sets* and giving demonstrations of joining two sets are suggested in some commercial programs:

Demonstrations through number lines also are suggested:

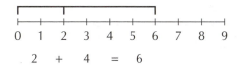

The direct instruction strategies recommended in this text use lines as semi-concrete objects to represent the members of sets. While nothing is wrong with using concrete manipulatives, having students draw lines has several advantages. Drawing lines graphically demonstrates equality (the same number of lines are on both sides of the equal sign); teachers can more readily monitor student performance with groups of students; and the lines provide a written record of student performance, which makes diagnosis of skill deficits easier.

A unique feature of the direct instruction strategies for introducing the addition process is the integration of the equality principle into the strategy. It is important that initial strategies demonstrate the application of the equality principle, since a grasp of equality is necessary for success in more complicated exercises, e.g., $7 + n = 12$.

Equality can be taught by presenting a functional definition and a series of positive and negative examples. The definition is functional in that it describes a condition that must be met for the equality principle to apply. *We must end with the same number on this side and the other side of the equal sign.* Format 7.1 includes a format for introducing equality. This format should be presented during the beginning stage before addition is introduced. The format includes three parts. In Part A, the teacher introduces the equal sign and equality rule. In Part B, the teacher demonstrates instances when the equality rule applies and does not apply. Diagrams like the one below in which lines are written inside two adjoining circles are written on the board.

The teacher leads the students in determining whether or not an equal sign would be drawn between the circles. Part C is a less structured worksheet exercise similar to Part B. Note that in Parts B and C students are asked to say the rule. Saying the rule may be quite difficult for lower-performing students. To ease this difficulty, the teacher might first model, lead, and test, saying just the first half of the rule: *We must end with the same number.* Lower performers may need five to ten corrected repetitions. After several days, the teacher would provide practice in saying the last half of the rule and then the entire rule.

Making lines for each addend and then counting the lines is referred to as *addition the slow way.* Students draw the appropriate number of lines under each numeral:

$$4 + 2 = \square$$
$$\text{IIII} \quad \text{II}$$

Students count the lines, then draw the same number of lines on the other side of the equal sign and write the answer in the box:

$$4 + 2 = \boxed{6}$$
$$\text{IIII} \quad \text{II} \quad \text{IIIIII}$$

By counting the lines one by one and drawing the same number on the other side, the concept of

equality is reinforced. Note that in this strategy *plus* is used as a verb; students are taught "The plus sign says to count all the lines." Later the term *addition* is introduced.

Problems with missing addends are introduced after students have demonstrated mastery of beginning addition exercises. In solving problems with missing addends:

$$4 + \square = 7$$
$$\text{IIII} \quad \text{IIIIIII}$$

The teacher points out that the sides are not equal. The students must add lines to make the sides equal and then write the numeral representing the number of lines added.

After the students can solve addition and missing addend problems, using a line-drawing strategy, a new strategy, called *addition the fast way,* is introduced. In addition the fast way, students make lines only under the numeral that is added, count the lines, beginning with the first numeral (fooouurr, five, six), and then write the answer in the box. Addition the fast way represents a transition from the semi-concrete stage in which objects are drawn to represent each member of the set to the stage in which no concrete representations are used. A similar fast-way strategy can be taught for missing addend problems.

Addition the Slow Way

Addition the slow way is an important strategy, since it is the first problem-solving strategy taught. The following preskills are those that students should have mastered before addition the slow way is introduced:

1. identifying and writing the numerals 0–10 and the symbols +, −, =, and $\square$
2. equality rule
3. reading an equation
4. drawing the appropriate number of lines to represent a numeral
5. counting the lines in two groups
6. writing the numeral that represents a set of objects

The format for teaching students to work addition problems the slow way appears in Format 7.2. In Part A, the teacher works the problem on the board. The teacher draws circles around the sides of the equal sign:

$$\boxed{5 + 2} = \bigcirc$$

to emphasize the concept of *side.* The steps in the strategy are summarized in the Summary Box 7.1.

Summary Box 7.1: Beginning Addition Strategy

---

1. Students read equation, 5 + 2 = how many?

2. Students recite equality rule: "You must end up with the same number on this side AND the other side."

3. Students draw lines under the first addend; then under the second addend.

4. Students count all lines on that side of the equal sign.

5. Students apply the equality rule and makes lines under the box on the other side of the equal sign.

6. Students write a numeral to represent the number of lines.

When presenting Part A, the teacher should repeat a problem until students can correctly respond to all of the questions. If a student hesitates or responds incorrectly, the teacher should repeat the question, model the correct answer, then repeat the question again, and ask the students to respond. Following the correction, all the steps from the beginning would be repeated one more time. This last presentation serves as a demonstration of how all the steps fit together.

Part B is a structured worksheet exercise and Part C is a less-structured worksheet exercise. Example selection for all worksheet exercises should include only numerals that students can identify and write. Sums should not exceed 10. On the worksheets, spaces should be left under numerals for students to draw lines. Once they develop 80–90% accuracy in working the problems, students no longer need supervised practice. Eight to ten problems should appear daily on student worksheets for several more weeks. Note that on worksheets, spaces are drawn below each numeral to prompt drawing the lines.

Missing Addend Strategy

The strategy discussed in this section teaches students to find the missing addend in a problem like this, 5 + □ = 8. The strategy is based on the equality rule *(You must end with the same number on both sides of the equal).* Students are presented this form of problem to enhance their understanding of the equality principle and to demonstrate that the equality principle may be used to solve a variety of problem types.

To solve this simple form of missing addend problems, the students first find the side of the equal sign that tells how many they end with. The teacher then points out that the sides are not equal until the students end with the same number on both sides. The teacher then directs the students to draw lines on the side with the box so that the sides will be equal and to fill in the missing numeral.

Format 7.3 includes the format for presenting the missing addend strategy. Part A teaches students the component skill of determining the side to start working on. The exercise points out that since a box doesn't tell how many lines to draw, it can't be the side to start on. Parts B and C are structured board and worksheet exercises, respectively. Note that in step 5 of Part B and step 7 of Part C the teacher reminds the students that the lines under a box tell what numeral goes in the box. This prompt prevents errors like 5 + 7 = 7 in which students write how many lines are on the whole side in the box.

Part D is a less-structured worksheet exercise. Worksheets for this part include an equal mixture of missing addend and regular addition problems. In Part D, the teacher leads the students through steps designed to teach the students when to apply the missing addend strategy. The teacher then instructs the students to make both sides equal and finally to fill in the missing numeral. Lower-performing students may need a great deal of practice on this part and on the supervised practice part before they can discriminate when and how to apply the regular addition and missing addend strategies. Examples should be limited to problems in which the sum is 10 or less. This limitation is suggested to prevent the tasks from becoming too cumbersome.

When the missing addend is zero, as in 8 + □ = 8, the teacher can use this wording to replace steps 6, 7, and 8 in Part C:

6. This is a special kind of problem. The sides are already equal. Eight on both sides. So you shouldn't make any more lines. You plus zero lines. Write a zero in the box.
7. Eight plus how many equals 8?
8. Say the whole statement.

Teachers should present two similar problems on the last day that Part C is presented, for example, $8 + \square = 8$ and $2 + \square = 2$. Teachers should continue to present problems in which the missing addend is zero in Part D and Part E.

Addition the Fast Way

Addition the fast way (see Format 7.4) is taught as a transitional step between the strategy in which students draw lines for each member of the sets represented by each addend and later exercises in which students memorize addition facts. When time for math instruction is limited, teachers can skip addition the fast way and move directly into fact teaching (see Chapter 6). The addition the fast way strategy differs from addition the slow way in that the student draws lines only to represent the addend following the plus:

$$7 + 4 = \square$$
$$||||$$

When solving the problem, the student starts counting at the number represented by the numeral in the first addend position and then counts the lines (e.g., in the problem above, students count "7777, 8, 9, 10, 11"). Then the student writes the numeral representing the sum in the box on the other side of the equal sign. The student does not draw lines under the box. The only new preskill for this strategy is rote counting beginning at a number other than 1.

Addition the fast way would be introduced when students are able to work a mixture of addition and missing addend problems with 80–90% accuracy. Teachers can expect some students to have difficulty coordinating counting from a number other than 1 and touching lines. For students who consistently have difficulty with this step, the teacher should present an exercise focusing solely on this component skill. The teacher might write a series of problems in which the lines are drawn:

$$
\begin{array}{cc}
5 + 3 & 7 + 2 \\
||| & || \\
3 + 4 & 9 + 5 \\
|||| & |||||
\end{array}
$$

The teacher would model and test counting until the students could do four problems in a row correctly. For example, the teacher teaches $5 + 3$ saying "Fffiiiveee," then touches each line and counts "6, 7, 8." The teacher would then test by presenting another example, $7 + 2$, touching 7 and saying "get it going," to indicate that students begin with 7 and then count each line.

Example selection criteria for addition the fast way problems are somewhat different from those for

addition the slow way. Larger numerals can be written in the first addend position since the student no longer has to draw lines to represent that amount. The second addend, however, should remain a smaller number (e.g., 1–8). Teachers must design the problems so that the sum is represented by a numeral the students have been taught to write.

After students work addition problems the fast way accurately (in Part D), subtraction instruction can begin (see Chapter 8). After students work addition problems fluently (in Part E), memorization of addition facts should begin (see Chapter 6).

Diagnosis and Remediation

This section presents basic procedures for diagnosing and remedying errors in beginning addition. The teacher first decides whether the problem is one of "can't do" or "won't do." In this section, we consider only the "can't do" problems. The basic steps below apply to diagnosing and remedying errors on any type of problem.

1. The teacher analyzes worksheet errors and hypothesizes about the cause of each error.
2. The teacher interviews the student to determine the cause of the error, if it is not obvious.
3. The teacher provides reteaching through board and/or worksheet presentations.
4. The teacher tests the student on a set of problems similar to the ones on which the original errors were made.

Once students begin working problems independently using a specific strategy, the errors they make on their worksheets fall into two main categories: (Fact errors are not possible at this stage because facts are not used, nor have they been taught.)

1. Component skill errors—those errors that indicate a deficit on one or more of the component skills that make up the strategy.
2. Strategy errors—errors indicating problems with the application of the strategy (Strategy errors often are the result of a student's forgetting certain steps in the procedure.)

Our discussion of diagnosis and remediation of each problem-solving strategy will address both types of errors. The similarities in the suggested remediation for each type of error should be noted.

COMPONENT SKILL ERRORS Component skill errors may be made on symbol identification and writing, counting and/or drawing lines, and application of the equality rule. When errors are due to component skill deficits, error patterns are more readily apparent. Therefore, a teacher will often be able to determine the cause of these errors by a careful analysis of worksheets. For example, on an addition the fast way worksheet, a student made the following errors:

a. $(6 + 2) = \boxed{7}$
   $||$

b. $(2 + 3) = \boxed{4}$
   $|||$

c. $(7 + 4) = \boxed{10}$
   $||||$

By analyzing the errors made by the student, the teacher can determine whether the student was having trouble coordinating counting from a number or incorrectly said the number representing the first group while touching the first line in the second group. For example, in problem A above, the student may have touched the first line under 2 while saying "sssiix" and then would have said "7" when touching the second line.

To remedy a component skill error, the teacher would present practice exercises on the component skill in isolation for several lessons before returning to the more advanced problems. For example, to remedy the errors made by the student above, the teacher would present an exercise on coordinating counting and touching lines. The teacher would focus on that one skill until the student reached a criterion of about 90% correct responses on the examples. Then the teacher would give the student addition problems to work independently.

Another possible component error involves symbol identification. If a student missed a problem because of numeral misidentification (e.g., identifying 6 as 9), the teacher would focus on the numeral 6 in numeral identification exercises for several lessons. During this time, the student would not be asked to solve problems including the numeral 6.

STRATEGY ERRORS A strategy error indicates a fundamental lack of understanding of how to sequence the steps in the problem-solving strategy. A strategy error would occur when, after drawing lines under each numeral, the student writes the next number in the counting sequence (10) in the box instead of the total number of lines counted (9). This

behavior clearly indicates that the student is not employing the strategy.

$$3 + 6 = 10$$
$$|||\ \ ||||||$$

To remedy a strategy error, the teacher reintroduces the format to the student, beginning with the structured board presentation, then progresses to the structured and less-structured worksheet presentations. A common strategy error students make when solving problems with missing addends involves adding the addend and the sum: $6 + \boxed{15} = 9$. Such errors indicate students are not applying the equality principle. For these types of errors, the teacher would begin with the structured board presentation, Part B of Format 7.3, then progress to Parts C and D.

DIRECT INSTRUCTION PROCEDURES FOR MULTI-DIGIT ADDITION PROBLEMS

Column addition problems may be divided into three groups. Simplest are those that do not require renaming:

$$\begin{array}{r} 24 \\ +15 \\ \hline \end{array}$$

Next are problems with two multi-digit addends, where renaming is necessary:

$$\begin{array}{r} 424 \\ + 317 \\ \hline \end{array}$$

Most difficult are problems with more than two multi-digit addends with renaming:

$$\begin{array}{r} 671 \\ 424 \\ +317 \\ \hline \end{array}$$

Students work column addition problems by using their knowledge of facts. Therefore, problems should be constructed from facts the students have been taught.

Problems Not Requiring Renaming

Column addition problems without renaming are usually introduced in first grade after students have learned to read and write numerals through 99 and are able to figure out mentally about 25 basic addition facts. Remember that basic addition facts include all possible pairings in which the addends are single-digit numbers. Students need many months of practice before they have memorized all basic facts.

However, the introduction of multi-digit addition problems need not be delayed until students have memorized all basic addition facts. Initial examples, however, should be designed to include the easier addition facts. Exercises to help memorize basic addition facts are discussed in detail in Chapter 6.

The procedure for teaching students to work these problems is relatively simple. The teacher has the students read the problem, then points out the place-value columns, telling students to first add the ones and then to add the tens. Teaching students to always begin working in the ones column helps prevent errors on more difficult renaming problems. Although students can compute the correct answer if they begin in the tens column on problems that don't require renaming, they will eventually have difficulty when they start working problems that do require renaming.

Therefore, students should be taught to always begin solving the problem in the ones column.

$$
\begin{array}{llll}
24 & 24 \text{ BUT} & 24 & 24 \\
+12 \quad \text{then} & \underline{12} \quad \text{NOT} & +17 \quad \text{then} & +17 \\
\overline{3} & \overline{36} & \overline{3} & \overline{311}
\end{array}
$$

After learning where to solve the problem, students add the ones and then the tens, writing the sum for each column. The teacher asks about the number of tens rather than the quantity represented by the tens number; that is, for

$$
\begin{array}{r}
34 \\
+21 \\
\end{array}
$$

the students indicate they are adding three tens and two tens, not 30 and 20, to remind students they are working in the tens columns. Because the teaching procedure is quite simple, we do not include a format in the book for this problem type. A teacher would, however, first use a structured board presentation, then structured and less-structured worksheet exercises. The transition from structured board to independent worksheet can be made in about four lessons.

Problems Requiring Renaming

Problems requiring renaming are usually introduced during second grade. Preskills include working addition problems without renaming, reading and writing numerals, figuring out basic addition facts, and expanded notation with teen and tens numbers.

PRESKILL   A unique preskill for renaming involves adding three single-digit numbers. For example, when adding tens in

$$
\begin{array}{r}
1 \\
37 \\
+29 \\
\hline
6 \\
\end{array}
$$

the student must add 1 + 3 to get the sum of 4, then add the sum to 2. Adding three numbers is significantly more difficult for low performers than adding two numbers. When adding three numbers, the student must add the first two numbers, remember the answer, and then add the third number to that sum.

Adding three single-digit numbers should be taught several weeks prior to the introduction of renaming problems. The format for teaching students a strategy to solve these problems appears in Format 7.5. The format contains only three parts: a structured board presentation, a structured worksheet presentation, and supervised practice. Since relatively few steps are involved, a less-structured worksheet format is not needed.

The most common error made on this format occurs in step 6 of Part A and step 4 of Part B when students are asked to identify the next two numbers to be added. Students often respond with the second and third numbers instead of the sum of the first two numbers and the third number. For example, in the following problem

$$
\begin{array}{r}
2 \\
3 \\
+4 \\
\end{array}
$$

the students answer 3 + 4 rather than 5 + 4. In Part A, the teacher tries to prompt the correct response by referring to that question as the "hard part." If students do make the error, the teacher must model and test the answer and then repeat the entire problem from the beginning. ("Now we're adding 5 + 4. What are we adding now? What is 5 + 4? . . . Let's do the whole problem again from the beginning.")

There are two example selection guidelines for this format. In about half of the examples, the top numeral should be 1, since in most renaming a 1 will be carried to the tens column. Initially, the sum of the three single digits should be 10 or less, so that students will be able to concentrate on adding the three numbers rather than figuring out more difficult basic facts.

INTRODUCING THE PROBLEMS   The first type of renaming problem should involve adding a two-digit numeral to another one- or two-digit numeral. Renaming is explained to students by pointing out that a tens number may not appear in the ones column and, therefore, must be carried to the tens column. For example, leading the students through the problem

$$37$$
$$+25$$

$$283$$
$$+\ 185$$

the teacher asks the students what 7 + 5 equals. After the students say 12, the teacher says, "We have a problem. Twelve equals one ten and two ones. We can't have a ten in the ones column. So, we put the one ten at the top of the tens column (teacher writes 1 over 3) and the two ones below the line" (teacher writes 2 under 5). Format 7.6 can be used for introducing renaming.

While Part A focuses student attention on the fact that they cannot have a ten in the ones column, Part B sets up the chain of steps the students will follow when working problems on their own. The vocabulary used in this format was selected to foster the students' understanding of the operation. For example, under step 5 in Part A, it is important to remind the students that they are adding tens ("How many tens do we end up with?") so that they remember the values of the numbers and do not just think of the numbers as individual numerals. Note that in Part B, step 3, the teacher prompts the students less on determining what 13 equals. Instead of just telling the students that 13 = 10 + 3, the teacher encourages the students to figure out the answer by themselves.

A common error made on renaming problems involves carrying the wrong number. For example, in working the problem 37 + 27, the student carries the 4 and writes 1 under the ones column. If the students write the numerals in the wrong places, the teacher should not merely model where to write the numbers but should ask students the critical questions (Part B, step 3) so that they can see why the numerals need to be in the appropriate places. After the students correctly answer the questions, the teacher can demonstrate how to put a ten on top of the tens column.

If a teacher notices that a student hesitates in answering on a particular step, the teacher should say the answer, repeat the question, and have the student respond again. After using this correction procedure, the teacher should then present the entire problem to give students the opportunity to successfully work through all of the steps in the strategy.

As students learn to read and write larger numbers, renaming problems with these numbers are introduced. First, problems in which students carry a hundred to the hundreds column are introduced. The format for presenting problems in which the students must rename a sum from the tens column would be very similar to the format for renaming a sum from the ones column (Format 7.6). For example, the students are working this problem:

After asking the students what eight tens + eight tens equal, the teacher would say, "We have a problem. Sixteen tens equal one hundred plus six tens. We can't have a hundred in the tens column, so we put it at the top of the hundreds column (teacher writes 1 over 2) and put the six tens here" (teacher writes 6 under answer line in tens column).

Problems in which students rename twice, from the ones column and then from the tens column, are introduced next. These problems and future problem types will require just a 2-3 day pattern of introduction, since once students understand the process of renaming, they usually have little difficulty generalizing. Lower-performing students, however, may need more supervised practice with worksheets containing a variety of problem types.

When introducing the strategy using the structured board and worksheet parts of a format, the teacher should use only examples of the type being introduced. When presenting the less-structured and supervised parts of the format, the teacher should give the students a cumulative review worksheet. Worksheets are designed to provide cumulative review so that previously taught types of problems receive systematic practice. One-third to one-half of the problems on the worksheet should be of the most recently introduced type. The others should be addition problems of previously introduced types and subtraction problems. The problems should be written in random order. Several examples of the new problem type can appear at the beginning of the worksheet. Otherwise, no more than two or three problems of the same type should appear consecutively.

Cumulative review is especially important when introducing renaming. A student cannot be said to have mastered renaming until he can discriminate when renaming is appropriate. Addition problems that do not require renaming must be included so that students do not get into the habit of always putting a 1 at the top of the tens column. Likewise, subtraction problems must be included so that the students receive continued practice discriminating addition from subtraction.

An example of a worksheet for a lesson that takes place several days after introducing double renaming (i.e., from ones to tens and from tens to hundreds) appears in Figure 7.1. Note that over one-third of the problems contain double renaming. Of the other addition problems, several involve just renaming from the tens to the hundreds columns, and several involve no renaming at all. About one-third of the problems are subtraction problems.

Summary Box 7.2: Addition with Renaming

---

1. Students read the problem.

2. Students begin adding in the ones column.

3. If the sum of the ones column is 10 or more, students determine they must rename.

4. Students use expanded notation to determine the number of tens and ones in the sum of the ones column.

5. Students rename by putting the tens in the tens column and the ones under the line in the ones column.

6. Students add the first two tens in the tens column, then add the next ten to that sum.

7. Students write the sum of tens under the line in the tens column.

FIGURE 7.1   Sample Worksheet for Adding with Renaming

```
 356     486     395     495     386
+277    +281    -243    +235    -241

 489      37     523     924     924
+232     +28    +206    -201     +31

 372     938     356     284     565
+472    -214    +217    +382    +265

  87      87     299     468      98
 +47     -47     +91    -354     +97
```

Three or More Addends

The last major problem type includes those problems with three or more multi-digit addends. Some of these problems are particularly difficult because the student is required to mentally add a number represented by a single-digit numeral to a number represented by a two-digit numeral. For example, note the problems below:

```
  36                    47
  16 ]12 + 4            24 ]11 + 3
 +24                   +13
```

```
      5839
      2467 ]16 + 9
      3589
     +2849 ]25 + 9
```

Note that in each problem the sum of the first two addends in the ones column is a teen number (12, 11, and 16). The next step in each problem involves adding a single-digit number to a teen number (i.e., 12 + 4, 11 + 3, 16 + 9). As mentioned earlier, we call facts in which a single-digit number is added to a two-digit number *complex addition facts.* Learning

complex addition facts is a critical preskill that takes many months of practice to master. Teachers should begin practice exercises on this preskill after students know about 50 basic addition facts. Students progressing at an average rate in a developmental program would be introduced to these problems sometime in early- to mid-second grade.

The first type of complex fact introduced would be that in which a single-digit number is added to a teen number, and the total does not exceed 19 (e.g., 14 + 3, 15 + 2, 15 + 3, 15 + 4). Format 7.7 shows how to present this skill. The students learn to transform a complex fact into two simple facts; e.g., students transform 16 + 3 into 10 + 6 + 3, add 6 + 3, then add 10 + 9. Note that daily practice on this skill would continue for about 30 days to develop fluency.

After students can solve this first type of complex addition fact mentally, they can begin column addition problems involving three or more numbers that require renaming. These problems can be introduced with a relatively simple format. The teacher has the students add all the numbers in the ones column. After the sum of the ones column is computed, the students carry the ten and write the remaining ones under the line. An analogous procedure would be followed with the tens, hundreds, and thousands columns. Note that examples should be carefully selected so that students do not encounter complex addition facts that have not been previously taught.

The second type of complex addition fact includes facts in which a single-digit number is added to a teen number and the sum totals 20 or more (e.g., 16 + 6 = 22, 18 + 7 = 25, 14 + 7 = 21, 15 + 8 = 23). This type of fact would be introduced in late third or early fourth grade. There are 44 more difficult complex addition facts (see Table 7.1). These

Table 7.1   Complex Addition Facts

	Sums greater than 20					Sums less than 20							
1.	11 + 9					11 + 1	11 + 2	11 + 3	11 + 4	11 + 5	11 + 6	11 + 7	11 + 8
2.	12 + 8	12 + 9					12 + 1	12 + 2	12 + 3	12 + 4	12 + 5	12 + 6	12 + 7
3.	13 + 7	13 + 8	13 + 9					13 + 1	13 + 2	13 + 3	13 + 4	13 + 5	13 + 6
4.	14 + 6	14 + 7	14 + 8	14 + 9					14 + 1	14 + 2	14 + 3	14 + 4	14 + 5
5.	15 + 5	15 + 6	15 + 7	15 + 8	15 + 9					15 + 1	15 + 2	15 + 3	15 + 4
6.	16 + 4	16 + 5	16 + 6	16 + 7	16 + 8	16 + 9					16 + 1	16 + 2	16 + 3
7.	17 + 3	17 + 4	17 + 5	17 + 6	17 + 7	17 + 8	17 + 9					17 + 1	17 + 2
8.	18 + 2	18 + 3	18 + 4	18 + 5	18 + 6	18 + 7	18 + 8	18 + 9					18 + 1
9.	19 + 1	19 + 2	19 + 3	19 + 4	19 + 5	19 + 6	19 + 7	19 + 8	19 + 9				

complex facts can be introduced in sets of two or three facts.

Format 7.8 shows how to teach this more difficult type of complex addition fact. Students transform a fact with a sum over 20 in the following way: 17 + 9 becomes 10 + 7 + 9, and then students add 7 + 9. Then they add the sum of 16 to 10. In Part A students learn to add the 10 to teens numbers (e.g., 14 + 10, 18 + 10). This skill is used in Part B (e.g., the last step in adding 19 + 3 is adding 10 and 12; the last step for 13 + 8 is adding 10 and 11). Part C provides supervised practice on the new complex facts and those introduced in the previous set.

Part D, an independent worksheet, should include a variety of problems, including problems that yield a sum of 20 or more and some that yield sums less than 20. This mix is needed to prevent students from possibly overgeneralizing and always adding 10 to a complex addition fact (e.g., 14 + 4 = 28). Worksheet exercises to develop fluency in this skill would be similar to those discussed in Chapter 6. A set of two or three complex facts would be introduced each several days. The new facts would appear several times on the independent worksheet along with previously introduced facts. Problems should be written horizontally. Instructions on the worksheet should tell students to work the problems mentally. The number of practice problems should increase as more complex facts are introduced.

SELF-CHECKING After students become proficient in working renaming problems with three addends, they should be taught to check their answers. A checking procedure for addition is adding from the bottom digit in each column, assuming the students start with the top digit in each column when they originally work the problem. The teacher introduces checking on a worksheet exercise. Students complete the first problem

and the teacher says, "Here's how to check your work to make sure you have the right answer. Start with the bottom number and add up the column. What are the first two numbers? . . . What's the answer? . . . What's the answer for the next two numbers? . . . Is that what you wrote in the answer for ones and at the top of the tens column? . . . Let's start from the bottom again . . . What are the first two numbers you add in the tens column? . . . What's the answer for the next two numbers? . . . Is that what you wrote for the answer?"

Determining whether students check their work is difficult because checking doesn't require any additional writing. An exercise to encourage checking involves giving students already worked problems about half of which have incorrect answers. The teacher would instruct the students to check the answers and correct mistakes.

Diagnosis and Remediation

As mentioned previously, once the teacher has determined that the errors on student worksheets are not caused by a lack of motivation, the teacher must identify specific skill deficits and provide remediation accordingly. Students make three major types of errors: facts, component, and strategy. In the area of addition, the most common errors involve facts, the component skills of renaming (either carrying the wrong number or failure to carry), and inattention to the sign in the problem.

FACT ERRORS Fact errors cause most column addition errors. Such errors are sometimes easy to identify, as in the problems below:

a. *11*
   357
+ 248
—————
 606

b. *1*
   228
+ 744
—————
 971

c. *1*
   648
+ 281
—————
 919

Note that in each example, the student missed the problem because of a fact error (e.g., in problem a the student wrote 16 for 7 + 8). In some cases, however, teachers will not be able to easily determine if a fact error caused the incorrect answer. For example, in the following problems, the errors could have been caused by failing to add the carried number or by a fact deficit. In problem d the student might have incorrectly added 1 + 5 + 4 in the tens column or simply failed to add the carried ten.

$$
\begin{array}{ll}
\text{d.}\quad \overset{\textit{1}}{}357 & \text{e.}\quad \overset{\textit{1}}{}228 \\
\underline{+\ 248} & \underline{+\ 743} \\
\textbf{595} & \textbf{961}
\end{array}
$$

In order to determine the specific cause of the errors, the teacher should look for error patterns. For example, the teacher should check the problems with errors to see if the same facts were consistently missed. Also, the teacher should utilize the information she has about the student's performance on recent fact worksheets. To confirm the diagnosis, the teacher should observe the student reworking some of the missed problems.

The remediation procedure depends on the nature of the fact errors. If a student consistently misses the same facts, the teacher merely provides extra practice on those facts. On the other hand, some students will be erratic in their performance, answering a fact correctly one time and missing it the next. For such students, the teacher should increase the incentives for accurate work.

A final note on facts concerns teachers who work with older remedial students who rely on their fingers to figure out basic facts. Unfortunately, since lower-grade classrooms often do not provide adequate practice on fact mastery, many students may be using their fingers to figure out basic facts. Teachers should be careful not to forbid the students to use their fingers if that is their only strategy for deriving an answer. Rather, the teacher should ensure that students are using a finger strategy that is relatively efficient and that students use the strategy accurately. Mistakes in finger operations may occur because a student makes errors in counting or does not coordinate putting up his fingers and counting (i.e., the student does not put up a finger for each number counted).

If the cause of the fact errors is determined to be an inappropriate finger strategy, the teacher would devote several minutes each day reviewing that strategy. Keep in mind that correcting a finger strategy deficit is done only with students who have not mastered their basic facts and have no other strategy

to use. In addition to correcting the finger strategy, teachers should spend more instructional time reviewing the exercises recommended in Chapter 6 to facilitate basic fact mastery. The ultimate goal of fact remediation is to teach students to master their facts and to stop relying on finger counting altogether.

COMPONENT ERRORS The first component skill deficit involves renaming. Note the errors in the problems below:

$$
\begin{array}{ll}
& \overset{\textbf{5}}{}39 \\
\overset{\textbf{6}}{}48 & 27 \\
\underline{+\ 28} & \underline{+19} \\
\textit{121} & \textit{112}
\end{array}
$$

The student carried the ones instead of the tens. Errors in which students carry the wrong number are quite serious because they indicate a fundamental misunderstanding of basic place value concepts. A possible remediation exercise for the component skill would involve a set of problems containing boxes where the sum of the ones column and the carried number are to be recorded. For each problem, the teacher would tell the student the sum of the numbers in the ones column, then ask how many tens and ones make up that sum. The students answer, then fill in the numbers. The remediation set would contain approximately 10 examples that look similar to the following.

$$
\begin{array}{cccc}
\square & \square & \square & \square \\
68 & 45 & 24 & 86 \\
\underline{+19} & \underline{+29} & \underline{+18} & \underline{+67} \\
\square & \square & \square & \square
\end{array}
$$

The first three to four examples in the remediation set should all be problems in which renaming is required. However, the examples in the remediation set should also contain some discrimination examples in which renaming is not required, so that students do not get into the habit of always writing a 1 above the tens column. If students demonstrate place value deficits during the remediation, the teacher may need to reteach expanded notation. After students are able to do four to six modified problems in a row filling in the correct numbers, the teacher leads the students through a set of four to six addition problems using Part C of Format 7.6, then has them do four to six problems with no teacher direction. This remediation procedure is repeated until students' performance on renaming problems is 90% or better.

A component skill deficit similar to renaming the wrong number involves not renaming the ten at all.

Problems in which students fail to rename the ten look like the following:

```
  48        32
 +36       +19
 ───       ───
  74        41
```

Since the student wrote the ones number in the appropriate place, it is likely that the student just forgot to carry the ten to the tens column. The remediation procedure for this error pattern is the same as for the previously discussed error in which the student carried the ones instead of the tens. Again, remember it is necessary to individually test students to determine if the error resulted from a renaming error or from a fact error.

Failure to attend to the sign is a common cause of errors in column addition problems. This deficit is characterized by worksheet errors in which the wrong operation is performed:

```
  342       304
 +131      −201
 ────      ────
  211       505
```

If such errors occur on more than 10% of the problems, a special worksheet should be given including an equal mix of addition and subtraction problems in random order:

```
 37    28    47    38    47    86    48
−15   +13   +24   −16   +25   −23   +20
```

The teacher would present the less structured worksheet exercises, instructing students to circle and say the sign before working each problem.

STRATEGY ERRORS   Strategy errors are caused by incorrectly carrying out several steps in the strategy. An example of one type of strategy error appears below:

```
  35        68
 +27       +18
 ───       ───
 512       716
```

This is quite a serious error, indicating the student does not understand the concept of renaming. The remediation procedure for all strategy deficits involves reteaching the format for that particular type of problem. The teacher presents several problems using a structured board presentation, then leads the students through several worksheet problems using the structured, then less-structured parts of the format.

A summary of the deficits common to column addition and the diagnosis and remediation procedures appropriate for each appear in Figure 7.2.

FIGURE 7.2   Diagnosis and Remediation of Addition Errors

Sample Patterns	Diagnosis	Remediation Procedures	Remediation Examples
Fact Errors			

a. 46   253 *1*
    +17   +174
    ──   ───
    64   *447*
	Basic fact errors. Student doesn't know the fact 6 + 7.	Emphasize 6 + 7 in fact memorization exercises. See Chapter 6.	

Component Skill Errors			

b. *3*   *2*
    46   53
   +17   +29
   ──   ──
   81   *91*
	Renaming errors. Student carries the ones to the tens column, writes the tens in the ones column.	Steps from structured worksheet exercise that focus on renaming. (Format 7.6, Part B, steps 1–3)	10 problems in this form:
			  □ □
			  69 46
			 +36 +29
			  □ □

c. 46   25
    +17   +17
    ──   ──
    53   *32*
	Renaming errors. Student forgets to carry.	Same as above.	Same as above.

d. 49   253
    +17   −174
    ──   ───
    32   *427*
	Sign discrimination error. Student subtracts instead of adding, vice versa.	Less-structured worksheet exercise. Have students circle the sign before working each problem. (Format 7.6, Part C, steps 1, 4)	Mix of addition and subtraction problems.

Strategy Errors			

e. 46   253
    +17   +174
    ──   ───
   513 *3127*
	Student does not carry; Writes the entire number in the sum.	Test and/or teach appropriate preskills. Present format beginning with structured board exercise. (Format 7.6, Part A)	

Unless otherwise noted, following each remediation procedure the teacher needs to give students worksheets similar to the ones on which the original errors were made in order to test whether the remediation was effective.

COMMERCIAL PROGRAMS

Addition: Regrouping

INSTRUCTIONAL STRATEGIES In most programs, students are taught a strategy for regrouping in addition by using bundles of sticks or other manipulatives. The steps in the strategy (with minor variations) in four basals we reviewed are

Step 1 - Add the ones
Step 2 - "Trade" if equal to 10 or more
Step 3 - Add the tens

See Figure 7.3 for an example of a page from a basal presentation book. The strategies for addition with regrouping appear to be straightforward. Our analysis reveals, however, that the programs may not be sufficiently addressing necessary prerequisite skills or providing enough systematic guided practice to ensure student success.

PREREQUISITE SKILLS Often basals attempt to teach the prerequisite place-value skills by having students trace numbers already placed in the proper columns. Then students are expected to progress from tracing numbers to independently solving problems. The problem with tracing should be obvious. If the numbers are placed for the students, students do not have to think about where to place them. As a result, some students will have difficulty on similar problems when the prompts are removed.

The remedy to this potential problem is to include intermediate steps in the strategy that require students to identify where they are going to write their answers *before* they write them. Then teachers can correct any errors that occur and prevent error patterns from forming.

Another major problem results from the lack of coordination between basic fact teaching and the facts students encounter in regrouping problems. Students often do not receive adequate practice to memorize basic facts before they encounter these facts in workbook exercises. Thus, students will often use their fingers to figure out the facts, which can slow down or interfere with learning the computation process.

FIGURE 7.3   A page from a basal program that includes picture representation.

STUDENT OBJECTIVE
To add 2-digit numbers, with regrouping from ones to tens.

TEACHING SUGGESTIONS

Demonstrate 2-digit addition with a model.
(Materials: ones and tens, a Tens and Ones mat for each child) Write an addition problem on the chalkboard. Ask the children to use their ones and tens to show the two sets on their mats.

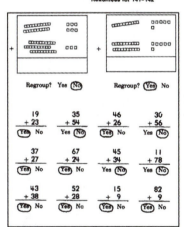

Ask them to join the two sets together and if they have more than 10 ones, to trade 10 ones for 1 ten. "Did you make a trade?" Write the little *1* over the *3*. "How many ones were you left with? (2) How many tens do you have now?" (6) Write it.

```
  1
  37
+ 25
  62
```

Provide the children with other addition problems to work through with their ones and tens.

READINESS

For students who need help with addition.

Readiness for 141–142

Copymaster S93 or Duplicating Master S93

Ask the children to decide whether or not each problem will require trading (regrouping). Ask them to mark *Yes* or *No*.

USING THE PAGES

Discuss the example at the top of page 141. Provide the children with ones and tens. Practice skip-counting by 10. Assign pages 141 and 142.

··· MENTAL-MATH NOTE ·············

The Shortcut character introduces mental math as well as paper-and-pencil shortcuts. After the children have completed page 142, provide them with oral practice using the shortcut to add 9 to different numbers.

·······························

CLASSWORK/HOMEWORK

Textbook Assignments	Basic	Enriched
all exercises	✓	✓
Extra Practice set 22 page 319	✓	
Optional Materials		
Readiness Worksheet	✓	✓
Basic Worksheet	✓	
Enrichment Worksheet		✓
Excursion Worksheet		✓
Creative Problem Solving section 6	✓	✓

141  ▦ **Concrete Materials**   ◪ **Mental Arithmetic**   ⁕ **Cooperative Learning Groups**   ◤ **Problem Formulation**

APPLICATION ITEMS: ADDITION

1. Describe the problem type that each example below represents. List the problems in the order they are introduced. Write the grade level when each type is typically introduced.

   a. 462
      +371

   d. 84
      +13

   b. 35
      16
      +24

   e. 348
      +135

   c. 46
      87
      +19

   f. 368
      +259

2. Below is an excerpt from the independent worksheet to be given to students who have just demonstrated accuracy in solving problem type 2e, adding two two-digit numbers, renaming from ones to tens columns. The teacher has made some errors in constructing the worksheet.

   a. Indicate the inappropriate examples.
   b. Identify any omitted problem types that should be included on the worksheet.

   Worksheet

   a. 462
      +183

   b. 75
      +16

   c. 141
      +324

   d. 38
      +26

   e. 582
      + 15

   f. 1
      3
      +6

   g. 46
      +15

   h. 617
      +124

   i. 58
      +25

3. At the beginning of the unit, the teacher tested Leslie. Her performance on the performance indicators for problem types 2e–3c appear below.

   Specify the problem type with which instruction should begin for Leslie. Explain your answer.

   Performance Indicators

   2e.
   ¹37   ¹48   ¹57
   + 46 + 14 + 27
   ‾83‾ ‾61‾ ‾84‾

   3a. 13 + 3 = *16*
       14 + 4 = *18*
       12 + 2 = *14*

   3c.
   ¹276   ¹248   ¹437
   +185   +365   +285
   ‾461‾ ‾512‾ ‾622‾

   Student: Leslie

   2f.
   ¹247   ¹258   ¹276
   +315   + 13   + 8
   562 *272* *284*

   3b. 374   248   437
       +261   +364   +285
       535 *511* *652*

4. Below are 11 problems that appeared on the worksheets to be done independently by the students in Mrs. Ash's math group. Next to each student's name are the problems missed by the student. For each student, specify the probable cause or causes of the student's errors.

   Describe the remediation procedure. Be specific. For each remediation, indicate the format and the part of that format you would begin remediation with. If no format appears in the book for that problem type, indicate the page in the text that discusses that problem type.

37	364	57	36	48	72	58	57	48	34	514
+26	+212	−23	+22	+28	+26	−32	+34	−24	+26	+ 23

   Errors: Bill
   ³37   ⁶48
   + 26   + 28
   ‾91‾   ‾121‾

   Ann
   37   48   34
   + 26   + 28   + 26
   ‾513‾ ‾616‾ ‾510‾

   Julie
   37   ¹48
   + 26   − 28
   ‾11‾   ‾72‾

5. The following is an excerpt from the Missing Addend Format (Format 7.3). Student responses are included. Specify teacher wording for the correction required.

Missing Addend Format

PART B: STRUCTURED BOARD PRESENTATION

TEACHER   **STUDENTS**

(Write the following $4 + \boxed{} = 6$
problem on the board.) | | | | | | | | | |

4. We want to end with the same number on both sides.
    (Point to $4 + \boxed{}$.) "How many on this side now?"   4
    "Think. How many do we have to end with on this side?"   4

---

6. Specify a diagnosis and remediation for each of the students listed below.

    a. For each student, describe the probable cause or mistaken strategy responsible for the errors.

    b. For each remediation, indicate the format and the part of that format you would begin remediation with. If no format appears in the book for that problem type, indicate the page in the text that discusses that problem type.

Student A

$3 + \boxed{7} = 7$ $5 + \boxed{8} = 8$
    | | | | | | |

$4 + \boxed{9} = 9$ $2 + \boxed{6} = 6$
    | | | | | | | | |

Student B

$6 + 3 = \boxed{8}$ $7 + 2 = \boxed{8}$
    | | | | |

$2 + 4 = \boxed{5}$ $3 + 5 = \boxed{7}$
    | | | | | | | | |

7. Write the wording the teacher uses in the structured worksheet part in presenting the following problem:

    162
    +283

8. Below are worksheets made by several teachers for the less structured part of the format for teaching students to work problems with renaming from the ones to tens columns. Two teachers constructed unacceptable lists. Identify these teachers and tell why each is unacceptable. For the unacceptable lists, specify what could be done to make the list acceptable.

    a.   37   37   237   481   374   48   786
        +25   −25   + 86   +110   −213   +24   +346

    b.   48   78   37   58   73   57
        +26   +25   + 8   +24   +28   +18

    c.   47   47   385   68   28   74   92   75   342
        +25   −25   +214   +48   +36   +23   −31   +38   + 26

FORMAT 7.1   **Format for Equality Introduction**

PART A: STRUCTURED BOARD PRESENTATION

TEACHER	STUDENTS

(Write the following problem on the board.)

$$ \left(| | | | | \right) = \left(| | | | | \right) $$

1. *(Point to equal sign.)* This is an equal sign. What is this?	Equal
2. Here's a rule: We must end with the same number on this side *(point to left side of equal)* and on the other side of the equal.	
3. *(Point to left side.)* Let's see if we end with the same number on this side and on the other side.	
4. *(Point to left side.)* Count the lines on this side as I touch them." *(Point to each line as students count.)*	1, 2, 3, 4, 5
5. How many did we end with on this side?	5
6. So we must end with 5 on the other side. *(Point to right side.)*	
7. Let's count the lines. *(Point as students count.)* Did we end with 5?	1, 2, 3, 4, 5 Yes

So the sides are equal. We ended with the same number on this side and the other side.

PART B: LESS STRUCTURED BOARD PRESENTATION

(Write the following problem on the board.)

1. Listen to the equal rule: We must end with the same number on this side and on the other side of the equal. Say the equal rule. *(Repeat rule with students until they can say it without assistance.)*

2. Let's see if the sides are equal.

3. *(Point to left side.)* How many do we end with on this side? *(Pause, signal.)*   4

4. *(Point to right side.)* How many do we end with on this side? *(Pause, signal.)*   2

5. Do we end with the same number on this side? *(Point to right side.)* And the other side? *(Point to left side.)*   No

6. Are the sides equal?   No

7. The sides are not equal, so I don't write an equal sign.

   (Repeat 1–7 with several examples, half equal and half unequal. Give individual turns to several students.)

FORMAT 7.1   **(continued)**

TEACHER	**STUDENTS**

PART C: LESS STRUCTURED WORKSHEET

(Give students worksheet with these problems.)

a.    d.

b.    e.

c.

f.

1. Touch problem a.
2. Say the equal rule.

We must end with the same number on this side and the other side of the equal.

3. Count and see if the sides are equal. *(Pause.)* Are the sides equal?

No

> *To correct: (Point to left side).* Count these lines. Tell me how many you end with. *(Point to right side.)* Count these lines. Tell me how many you end with. Did you end with the same number on this side and the other side?

4. Do you write in an equal?

No

5. *(If answer to 3 is yes)* Write the equal.

(Repeat steps 1–5 with remaining problems.)

FORMAT 7.2   **Format for Teaching Addition the Slow Way**

PART A: STRUCTURED BOARD PRESENTATION

TEACHER	**STUDENTS**

1. *(Write the following problem on the board.)*

     5 + 3 = ☐
     ____ ____ ____

Read the problem.

5 + 3 = how many?

(Point to the equal sign.) What is this?

Equal

2. Listen to the equal rule: We must end with the same number on this side of the equal *(Circle 5 + 3.)* and on the other side. *(Circle box.)*

3. *(Point to 5.)* How many in the first group? I'll draw five lines under the 5. Count as I draw the lines. *(Draw five lines.)*

5
1, 2, 3, 4

4. *(Point to +3.)* This says "Plus three." Plus tells us to draw more lines, so I draw three more lines under the 3. Count as I draw the lines. *(Draw three lines.)*

1, 2, 3

(continued on next page)

FORMAT 7.2   (continued)

TEACHER	STUDENTS
5. We've drawn all the lines on this side. Let's count and see what we end with. Count as I touch the lines. *(Touch lines.)*	1, 2, 3, 4, 5 , 6, 7, 8
What number did we end with?	8
We must end with the same number on this side and the other side.	
6. (Point to 5 + 3.) We must end with 8 on this side. So what number must we end with on the other side?	8
I'll draw the lines. You count and tell me when to stop. *(Draw lines under box.)*	1, 2, 3, 4, 5, 6, 7, 8, stop

$5 + 3 = \square$

|||| ||| |||||||

To correct: If children don't say stop after 8, keep drawing lines, then say, We made a mistake. You have to tell me to stop. *(Repeat from step 5.)*

7. The lines under a box tell what numeral goes in the box. How many lines are under the box?	8
So what number goes in the box?	8
(Write 8 in the box.) What does 5 + 3 equal?	8
8. Say the whole statement.	5 + 3 = 8
9. *(Repeat steps 1–8 until students can answer with no errors. Repeat steps 1–9 with several problems.)*	

PART B: STRUCTURED WORKSHEET PRESENTATION

(Here is a sample worksheet item.)

    a.   5 + 3 = $\square$

    ____   ____   ____

1. Touch problem a.	
2. Read the problem as I clap. Get ready. *(Clap at one-second intervals.)*	5 + 3 = how many?
3. How many in the first group?	5
Make the lines.	Students draw 5 lines.
4. The next part of the problem says plus 3. What do you do when you plus 3?	Make three more lines.
5. Make the lines under the 3.	Students draw 3 lines.
6. Let's count all the lines on that side. Put your finger over the first line. *(Check.)* Touch and count the lines as I clap. *(Clap one clap per second.)*	1, 2, 3, 4, 5, 6, 7, 8
7. How many lines did we end with?	8
8. So how many must we end with on the other side of the equal?	8
9. Make the lines and write the numeral.	
10. What does 5 + 3 equal?	8
11. Say the statement. *(Repeat steps 1–11 with remaining problems.)*	5 + 3 = 8

FORMAT 7.2   **(continued)**

TEACHER	STUDENTS

PART C: LESS STRUCTURED WORKSHEET

(Give students worksheets with problems.)

1. Touch problem a.

2. Read the problem. → 6 + 3 = how many?

3. First you make six lines, then you plus. How do you plus 3? → Make 3 more lines.

4. Make the sides equal and fill in the missing numeral. *(Check.)*

5. What does 6 + 3 equal? → 9

6. Say the statement. *(Repeat steps 1–5 with remaining problems.)* → 6 + 3 = 9

FORMAT 7.3   **Format for Solving Missing Addends**

PART A: PRESKILL: SIDE TO START ON

TEACHER	STUDENTS

(Write the following problems on the board.)

$4 + \square = 6$
$1 + \square = 3$
$3 + 2 = \square$
$8 + \square = 9$
$5 + 3 = \square$

1. Listen: I'm going to tell you something about the side you start with. You start with the side that tells how many lines to draw. Listen again: You start with the side that tells how many lines to draw.

2. My turn. *(Point to 4 + $\square$ in the first problem.)* Can I start on this side? No. How do I know? Because the box does not tell me how many lines to draw. *(Point to 6.)* Can I start on this side? Yes. How do you know? Because a 6 tells how many lines to draw.

3. Now it is your turn. *(Point to 4 + $\square$ in the first problem.)*
   Can I start on this side? → No
   How do you know? → Because a box does not tell how many lines to draw

4. *(Point to 6.)* Can I start on this side? *(Repeat steps 1–4 with remaining problems.)* → Yes

PART B: STRUCTURED BOARD PRESENTATION

(Write the following problem on the board.)

$4 + \square = 6$

____ ____ ____

1. Read this problem. → 4 + how many = 6

(continued on next page)

FORMAT 7.3   (continued)

TEACHER	STUDENTS
2. This is a new kind of problem. It doesn't tell us how many to plus. We have to figure out how many to plus. What must we figure out?	How many to plus
3. We use the equal rule to help us. The equal rule says we must end with the same number on this side. *(Point to 4 + ☐)* and on the other side of the equal. *(Point to 6.)* First we figure the side we start counting on. *(Point to 4 + ☐)* Do I start counting on this side? Why not?	No. The box does not tell how many lines to make
(Point to 6.) Do I start counting on this side? Yes. The 6 tells me to make six lines. *(Draw six lines under the 6.)*	Yes
4. We want to end with the same number on both sides. *(Point to 4 + ☐)* How many on this side now? I'll draw four lines. *(Draw four lines under 4.)* Think. How many do we need to end with on this side?	4 6
To correct: We want to end with the same number we end with on the other side. What number do we end with on the other side?	
We have 4. We want to end with 6. Count as I make the lines. Tell me when to stop. *(Point to 4.)* How many in this group? Get it going. *(Draw lines under box as students count.)*	4 444, 5, 6, stop
To correct: If students do not say stop after saying 6, tell them, We ended with 6 on the other side. We must end with 6 on this side. *(Then repeat from step 4.)*	
5. What number did we end with? We made the sides equal. Are we going to write 6 in the box?	6 No
To correct: If children say yes, We must count the lines under the box to see what number goes in the box.	
The number of lines under the box tells us what numeral to write in the box. What numeral? *(Write 2 in box.)*	2
6. 4 + how many equals 6? Say the whole statement. *(Repeat steps 1–6 with remaining problems.)*	4 + 2 = 6

PART C: STRUCTURED WORKSHEET PRESENTATION

(Below is a sample worksheet Item.)

   a.   5 + ☐ = 8
      ___ ___ ___

1. Touch problem a. Read the problem.	5 + how many = 8
2. Touch the side you start counting on.	Students touch side with 8.
3. Make the lines under the 8.	Students make 8 lines.
4. Touch the side that says "5 plus how many."	Students touch that side.

FORMAT 7.3   (continued)

TEACHER	STUDENTS
5. How many do we have on that side now? Make five lines under the five.	5 Students make 5 lines.
6. Think: How many do we have to end with on that side?	8
To correct: We want to make the sides equal. We ended with 8 on the other side so we must end with 8 on this side.	
7. Touch the 5. You have five lines so far. Make more lines under the box so that we end with 8 on that side.	Students draw more lines.
How many did you end with on that side?	8
Are you going to write 8 in the box? No, the lines under the box tell us what numeral to write in the box.	No
8. Count the lines you made under the box and write the numeral. 5 plus how many equals 8?	Students write 3.
Say the whole statement.	3 5 + 3 = 8

PART D: LESS-STRUCTURED WORKSHEET

(Give students a worksheet with an equal mix of addition and missing addend problems.)

a. 5 + 3 = ☐   d. 3 + 4 = ☐
b. 4 + ☐ = 6   e. 6 + ☐ = 7
c. 3 + ☐ = 8   f. 5 + 3 = ☐

1. Touch problem a. Read the problem.	5 + 3 equals how many?
2. Touch the side you start counting on.	
3. Make the lines on that side and get ready to tell me how many you end with. *(Pause.)* What do you want to end with?	8
4. Touch the other side. *(Pause.)* What do you want to end with?	8
5. Make lines to make the sides equal.	Students make lines.
6. Count the lines under the empty box and write the numeral.	Students write 8 in the box.

FORMAT 7.4   **Format for Teaching Addition the Fast Way**

PART A: STRUCTURED BOARD PRESENTATION

TEACHER	STUDENTS
1. *(Write the following problem on the board.)*	
5 + 3 = ☐	5 + 3 equals how many?
───	
I'll touch and you read.	
2. We're going to work this problem a fast way. We draw lines under the number after the plus. *(Point to + 3.)* What does this say?	+3

(continued on next page)

FORMAT 7.4 (continued)

TEACHER	STUDENTS
So how many lins are we going to draw? I'll make the lines. *(Draw 3 lines under the 3.)*	3
3. Watch me count the fast way. *(Touch 5 and then each line.)* Fiiiivvve, six, seven, eight.	5
Now it's your turn to count the fast way. How many are in the first group? Get it going . . . Count. *(Touch 5 for two seconds and then touch each line.)*	5555, 6, 7, 8
4. How many did we end with on this side? So how many must we end with on the other side?	8
I'll write an 8 in the box. *(Write 8 in the box.)*	8
5. Read the whole statement. *(Repeat steps 1–5 with 7 + 4, 9 + 5.)*	$5 + 3 = 8$

PART B: STRUCTURED WORKSHEET

(Write the following problem on the board.)

$4 + 2 = \square$

――――

1. *(Point to 4 + 2 = □.)* Touch this problem on your worksheet. *(Pause.)* Read the problem out loud. Get ready. *(Clap for each symbol.)*	4 + 2 equals how many?
2. Let's work this problem the fast way. Touch the numeral after the plus. *(Pause.)* How many lines are you going to plus? Make the lines under the 2. *(Check.)*	2
3. Touch the 4 and get ready to count the fast way. Four. Get it going. *(Clap as students touch and count.)* Count.	ffoouurrr, 5, 6
To correct: *(Teacher models.)* My turn . . . *(If necessary, moves student's finger as he counts.)*	
4. How many did you end with on the side you started with? How many must you end with on the side with the box? Yes, 6 equals 6. What numeral will you write in the box? Do it.	6 6 6
5. Read the whole statement.	$4 + 2 = 6$

PART C: LESS-STRUCTURED WORKSHEET

1. *(Read problem and determine side.)* Everybody, read problem one on your worksheet. Get ready. *(Clap for each symbol.)*	4 + 3 equals how many?
2. *(Work problem.)* Now you're ready to plus lines and count the fast way. What are you going to do?	Plus the lines and count the fast way.
Do it. *(Check students as they work.)*	
3. Read the whole statement.	$4 + 3 = 7$

FORMAT 7.5   **Format for Adding Three Single-Digit Numbers**

PART A: STRUCTURED BOARD PRESENTATION

TEACHER	STUDENTS

1. *(Write the following problems on the board.)*

```
 1      1      3
 3      2      1
+2     +4     +6
```

You're going to learn how to work a special kind of problem today. Read this problem.	$1 + 3 + 2$
2. Watch me work it. First I add 1 plus 3. What do I add first? What is 1 plus 3? *(Pause.)*	$1 + 3$ 4
3. 1 plus 3 = 4. Now I add 4 plus 2. What do I add next? What is 4 + 2? *(Pause.)*	$4 + 2$ 6
4. So I write the 6 below the equal.	
5. Let's see if you remember. What are the first numbers I add?	$1 + 3$
6. What is 1 + 3? *(Pause.)* Here's the hard part. What are the next numbers I add?	4 $4 + 2$
To correct: (If student says 3 + 2, repeat steps 2–6.) What is 4 + 2? *(Pause. Write 6.)*	6
7. Read the problem now.	$1 + 3 + 2 = 6$

    (Repeat with two more examples. Give individual turns to several students on steps 1–7.)

PART B: STRUCTURED WORKSHEET PRESENTATION

(Students have worksheets with 10 problems of the type below.)

```
 2      1      5
 4      4      2
+3     +3     +2
```

1. Touch problem one. Read it.	$2 + 4 + 3$
2. Touch the first numbers you add. *(Monitor responses.)* What are they?	$2 + 4$
3. What is 2 + 4? *(Pause.)*	6
4. Now tell me the next numbers you add. *(Pause.)* Yes, 6 + 3.	$6 + 3$
5. What is 6 + 3? *(Pause, signal.)* Write 9 below the line.	9
6. Read the problem now. *(Repeat Part B with two more examples.)*	$2 + 4 + 3 = 9$

FORMAT 7.6 **Format for Adding Two Numerals with Renaming**

PART A: STRUCTURED BOARD PRESENTATION

TEACHER

STUDENTS

(Write the following problems on the board.)

36	48	26
+27	+26	+16

1. Read this problem as I point.   36 + 27 = how many?
2. What column do we start working in?   the ones column
3. What are the first two numbers we're going to add?   6 + 7

   To correct: Point to 6 and 7. Repeat step 3.

4. We have a problem. Thirteen equals one ten and three ones. We can't have a ten in the ones column, so we put the one ten at the top of the tens column. Where do we put the ten?   on top of the tens column

   (Write 1 over 3.) We write three ones under the ones column. Where do we put the three ones? *(Write 3 under 7.)*   under the ones column

5. What are the first two numbers to add in the tens column?   1 + 3

   What does 1 + 3 equal? *(Pause.)*   4

   Now what two numbers will we add?   4 + 2

   What is 4 + 2?   6

   How many tens do we end up with?   Six tens

   We end up with six tens, so I'll write 6 under the tens column. *(Write 6 in the tens column.)*

6. We are finished. *(Point to 63.)* What does 36 + 27 equal?   63

   Read the problem and say the answer.   36 + 27 = 63

   (Repeat steps 1–5 with remaining problems.)

PART B: STRUCTURED WORKSHEET PRESENTATION

(Students have worksheets with the following problems.)

45	57	36	47
+38	+37	+16	+26

1. Touch the first problem on your worksheet. Read the problem.   45 + 38 = how many?
2. What column do you start working?   the ones

   What are the first two numbers you're going to add?   5 + 8

   What is 5 + 8? *(Pause.)*   13

3. There's a problem. What does 13 equal?   one ten and three ones

   Can we have a ten in the ones column?   no

   So where do you put the ten?   on top of the tens column

   Write a 1 on top of the tens column. *(Monitor student responses.)* Thirteen equals one ten and three ones.

   How many ones are left?   3

FORMAT 7.6   (continued)

TEACHER	STUDENTS

    Write them under the ones column.

    (Check.)

4. Look at the tens column. What are the first two numbers to
   add in the tens column?   1 + 4

   What is 1 + 4? *(Pause.)*   5

   Now what numbers will you add?   5 + 3

   What is 5 + 3?   8

   How many tens do you end up with?   Eight tens

   Write the tens under the tens column.

   (Monitor student responses.)

5. You're finished. What does 45 + 38 equal?   83

   Read the problem and say the answer.   45 + 38 = 83

   (Repeat steps 1–5 with remaining examples.)

PART C: LESS-STRUCTURED WORKSHEET

*(Give students a worksheet containing some problems that
involve renaming and some that do not.)*

```
 47    53    42    78
+25   +24   -31   +18

 78    56    75    26
+21   +36   -23   +43
```

1. Everyone, read problem one on your worksheet. What type   47 + 25
   of problem is this, addition or subtraction?   Addition

2. What are the first two numbers you add?   7 + 5

   What is 7 + 5? *(Pause.)*   12

3. Do you have to move a ten over to the tens column?   yes

4. Now work the problem on your own. *(Pause.)*

5. What does 47 + 25 equal?   72
   (Repeat steps 1–5 with remaining problems.)

FORMAT 7.7   **Format for Complex Addition Facts with a Total Less than 20**

PART A: STRUCTURED PRESENTATION

TEACHER	STUDENTS

1. I want to add 15 + 3 in my head.

2. Fifteen equals 10 + 5, so when we add 15 + 3 we add 10
   and *(pause)* 5 + 3. When we add 15 + 3 we add 10 and
   what numbers?   5 + 3

(continued on next page)

FORMAT 7.7 (continued)

TEACHER	STUDENTS
3. What is 5 + 3? *(Pause.)*	8
What is 10 + 8?	18
So what is 15 + 3?	18
4. Say the whole statement.	15 + 3 = 18
(Repeat steps 1–4 with 14 + 2, 11 + 4, 14 + 3, 15 + 3, 12 + 2. Give individual turns on steps 1–3.)	

PART B: LESS STRUCTURED PRESENTATION

TEACHER	STUDENTS
1. Listen: 14 + 3. What does 14 equal?	10 + 4
2. So when we add 14 + 3, we add 10 plus what numbers?	4 + 3
3. What is 4 + 3? *(Pause.)*	7
4. Say the whole statement.	14 + 3 = 17
5. What is 14 + 3?	17
(Repeat with 14 + 5, 12 + 3, 16 + 3, 13 + 4, 15 + 3. Give individual turns to several students.)	

PART C: SUPERVISED PRACTICE

TEACHER	STUDENTS
1. What does 11 + 4 equal? *(Pause.)*	15
To correct: (Use step 1 from Part B.) Say the whole statement.	11 + 4 = 15
(Repeat step with 17 + 2, 14 + 5, 12 + 6, 16 + 3, 11 + 6, 13 + 5. Give individual turns to several students.)	

FORMAT 7.8 Format for Complex Addition Facts with a Total More Than 20

PART A: PRESKILL: PLUS 10 FACTS

TEACHER	STUDENTS
1. Fourteen + 10 is 24. What is 14 + 10?	24
Say the statement. *(Repeat with 17 + 10, 12 + 10.)*	14 + 10 = 24
2. What is 13 + 10?	23
To correct: (Tell answer. Repeat question.) Say the statement. *(Repeat step 2 with 10 + 10, 18 + 10, 11 + 10, 13 + 10, 15 + 10. Repeat question until all are consecutively answered correctly.)*	13 + 10 = 23
3. *(Give individual turns to several students.)*	

FORMAT 7.8   (continued)

TEACHER	STUDENTS
PART B: STRUCTURED BOARD PRESENTATION	
1. When we add 15 + 7, we add 10 and what numbers?	5 + 7
2. What is 5 + 7? *(Pause.)*	12
What is 12 + 10?	22
So what is 15 + 7?	22
Say the whole statement.	15 + 7 = 22
(Repeat steps 1 and 2 with 17 + 7, 16 + 5.)	
PART C: SUPERVISED PRACTICE	
1. What does 15 + 7 equal? *(Pause.)*	22
To correct: When we add 15 and 7, we add 10 and what? What is 5 + 7? What is 10 + 12? So what is 15 + 7?	
2. *(Repeat step 1 with 17 + 7, 16 + 5, 18 + 8, 15 + 5, 17 + 8.)*	
PART D: INDEPENDENT WORKSHEET	

(Give students worksheets with a mix of complex facts that total 20 or more and complex facts that total less than 20.) Work these problems in your head. Write the answers.

CHAPTER 8

Subtraction

TERMS AND CONCEPTS

Subtraction   The removal of a subset from a set. Subtraction is the inverse of addition.

Subtrahend   Quantity to be taken away.

Minuend   Original quantity from which an amount will be subtracted.

Difference   The quantity remaining after the subtrahend is taken away from the minuend.

Renaming   Rewriting a numeral as a greater unit and a lesser unit; e.g., in 75 − 19, 75 is renamed as 60 + 15.

Borrowing   A term formerly used to describe subtraction with regrouping or renaming.

Regrouping   Rearranging a quantity of *objects* (not numerals) as a greater and lesser than unit; for example, |||||||||||||||||||||||||||| can be regrouped as ||||||| | | | | | | | | | | | | | |.

SKILL HIERARCHY

Subtraction instruction, like addition instruction, may be divided into two stages (see the Instructional Sequence and Assessment Chart). During the first stage, introducing the concept, the teacher presents strategies for solving simple subtraction problems with a single-digit minuend, such as 9 − 6 = ☐; the strategy at this stage involves semi-concrete objects that represent each member in the subtraction problem. The counting, numeral, and equality preskills on the subtraction skill hierarchy are the same as for addition. After subtraction has been taught, problems with a missing subtrahend can be presented. In these problems, all numerals should be below 10 to simplify computation (e.g., 7 − ☐ = 3 and 5 − ☐ = 3). Again, the strategy would involve using semi-concrete objects to represent the numerals in a problem. Note that for the purposes of remediation, when working with older students, teachers should not revert to the conceptual introduction but should teach basic facts and the multi-digit operations specified in the Instructional Sequence and Assessment Chart.

In the multi-digit operations stage, which usually begins late in first grade, students compute basic facts mentally (without semi-concrete prompts). Basic subtraction facts are the 100 possible combinations in which a one-digit subtrahend is subtracted from a one- or two-digit minuend and the difference is a one-digit number. Procedures for teaching students to answer and eventually memorize basic subtraction facts are discussed in Chapter 6.

Three basic types of column subtraction problems are included in the multi-digit operations stage. The

Instructional Sequence and Assessment Chart

Grade Level	Problem Type	Performance Indicator			
1a	Conceptual introduction				
1b	Subtracting a one- or two-digit number from a two-digit number; no renaming	57 −20	45 − 3	28 − 4	
2a	Subtracting a one- or two-digit number from a two-digit number; renaming required	54 −18	46 − 9	70 −38	
2b	Subtracting a one-, two-, or three-digit number from a three-digit number; renaming tens to ones	382 − 37	393 −174	242 − 6	
3a	Subtracting a two- or three-digit number from a three-digit number; renaming from hundreds to tens	423 −171	418 − 83		
3b	Subtracting a two- or three-digit number from a three-digit number; renaming from tens to ones and hundreds to tens	352 −187	724 −578	534 − 87	
3c	Tens minus 1 facts	70 − 1 = □ 40 − 1 = □ 80 − 1 = □			
3d	Subtracting a two- or three-digit number from a three-digit number, zero in tens column; renaming from tens to ones and hundreds to tens	503 − 87	504 − 21	700 − 86	905 −164
3e	Subtracting a three- or four-digit number from a four-digit number; renaming from thousands to hundreds	4689 −1832	5284 −4631	3481 −1681	
3f	Subtracting a one-, two-, three-, or four-digit number from a four-digit number; renaming required in several columns	5342 − 68	6143 − 217	5231 −1658	
4a	Subtracting a two-, three-, or four-digit number from a four-digit number; a zero in either the tens or hundreds column	4023 − 184	5304 −1211	5304 − 418	
4b	Hundreds minus 1 facts	700 − 1 = □ 400 − 1 = □ 800 − 1 = □			
4c	Subtracting a one-, two-, three-, or four-digit number from a four-digit number; a zero in the tens and hundreds column	4000 −1357	2001 −1453	8000 −4264	
4d	Same as 4c, except 1,000 as top number	1000 − 283	1000 − 82	1000 − 80	
4e	Same as 4c, except 1,100 as top number	1100 − 241	1100 − 532	1100 − 830	

Instructional Sequence and Assessment Chart (continued)

Grade Level	Problem Type	Performance Indicator		
4f	Subtracting involving five- and six-digit numbers; renaming	342,523 − 18,534	480,235 − 1,827	38,402 −15,381
5a	Thousands minus 1 facts	5000 − 1 = ☐ 3000 − 1 = ☐ 1000 − 1 = ☐		
5b	Subtracting from a number with four zeroes	80000 − 826	50000 − 8260	10000 − 284

---

easiest is the problem in which the subtrahend is smaller than the minuend in each column; renaming is not required:

$$
\begin{array}{r}
49 \\
-24 \\
\hline
\end{array}
$$

In the second type of problem, one or more columns have a subtrahend which is larger than the minuend:

$$
\begin{array}{r}
374 \\
- 28 \\
\hline
\end{array}
\qquad
\begin{array}{r}
5437 \\
-2859 \\
\hline
\end{array}
$$

Such problems require renaming or "borrowing":

$$
\begin{array}{rcl}
34 & \text{becomes} & \overset{2\;\;1}{\cancel{3}4} \\
-15 & & -15 \\
\end{array}
$$

Students need not have memorized all basic subtraction facts before problems with renaming are introduced. They should, however, know enough facts to allow teachers to include a variety of renaming problems.

The third type includes more complex column subtraction problems that require renaming. Included are problems with zeroes in the minuend:

$$
\begin{array}{rcl}
306 & \text{becomes} & \overset{291}{3\cancel{0}6} \\
-216 & & -219 \\
\end{array}
$$

$$
\begin{array}{rcl}
\text{and}\ \ 4000 & \text{becomes} & \overset{3991}{4\cancel{0}\cancel{0}0} \\
-258 & & -258 \\
\end{array}
$$

and problems with renaming in consecutive columns:

$$
\begin{array}{r}
421 \\
-247 \\
\hline
\end{array}
\ \text{or}\
\begin{array}{r}
6342 \\
-4971 \\
\hline
\end{array}
$$

A more complete listing of problems types and a suggested sequence of introduction appears in the Instructional Sequence and Assessment Chart.

INTRODUCING THE CONCEPT

Subtraction is usually introduced in first grade through demonstrations with semi-concrete objects. A number of alternative demonstrations are suggested in elementary mathematics textbooks. Among these are diagrams using pictures of objects; e.g., 5 − 3 is represented as

Another approach is the use of number lines; e.g., 8 − 3 is represented as

This text recommends a strategy that uses lines as semi-concrete objects. The strategy teaches minusing as crossing out; e.g., 7 − 4 is represented as

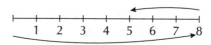

We recommend delaying the introduction of subtraction until students have demonstrated mastery of the regular addition strategy. However, subtraction may be introduced prior to or after addition problems with missing addends.

Beginning Subtraction Strategy

In the crossing-out strategy recommended here, the student first draws the number of lines for the minuend, then subtracts by crossing out the number of lines indicated by the subtrahend:

$$6 - 4 = \boxed{}$$
$$| \; | \; \cancel{| | | |}$$

Next, the student counts the remaining lines and draws an equal number of lines on the other side of the equal:

$$6 - 4 = \boxed{}$$
$$| \; | \; \cancel{| | | |} \quad | \; |$$

Finally, the student writes the numeral representing that set of lines:

$$6 - 4 = \boxed{2}$$
$$| \; | \; \cancel{| | | |} \quad | \; |$$

Format 8.1 shows the format for introducing subtraction. Note that *minus* is used as a verb: "How many lines are you going to minus?" Since students have already learned to identify the minus sign, they learn that the minus sign tells them to cross out lines. Later, the term *subtraction* is introduced, and students learn that a minus tells them to subtract.

In parts A and B of the format, the teacher presents structured board and worksheet exercises focusing solely on the preskill task of crossing out lines and counting the remaining lines. Since line drawing is a fine motor skill, many students in beginning arithmetic instruction may require extensive practice before they become proficient in crossing out the appropriate number of lines. Part C is a structured worksheet exercise in which the teacher leads students as they work entire problems, drawing lines for the first group, crossing out lines for the amount to be "minused," counting how many lines they end with, and then applying the equality rule. The minuend in subtraction problems should be 10 or less so that drawing lines does not become too cumbersome. Part D, the less-structured worksheet exercise, is the critical part of the format. The worksheet includes a mix of addition and subtraction problems. Instructionally naive students often have difficulty

discriminating which of the two similar problem-solving strategies to use. The format must provide a great deal of systematic practice in helping students make this discrimination. The less-structured and supervised practice worksheets would also contain an equal mix of addition and subtraction problems. Supervised practice is continued until students can work problems with 80–90% accuracy.

Missing Subtrahend Problems

Missing subtrahend problems (e.g., $7 - \square = 3$, $8 - \square = 1$) can be introduced when the students are able to do a worksheet including a mix of addition, regular subtraction, and addition problems with missing addends with 80–90% accuracy. Since the strategy for working this type of problem is relatively difficult to teach (students must circle some lines and cross out the remaining lines), we recommend not presenting the strategy during the beginning stage unless specified by the school district's curriculum guidelines. The missing addend problems provide an ample demonstration of the equality principle.

The strategy for missing subtrahend problems includes the steps shown in Summary Box 8.1.

A specific format is not included for missing subtrahend problems, since many programs do not teach the skill. The format would be similar to that for the missing addend operation. The teacher would have the students (1) draw lines under the numeral, (2) circle the number of lines representing the difference, (3) cross out the remaining lines, and (4) count up crossed-out lines and write the appropriate numeral in the empty box.

The teacher would introduce the entire strategy in structured board and worksheet exercises, stressing the equality principle. Finally, the teacher would present a less-structured worksheet exercise that includes a mix of subtraction, missing subtrahend, addition, and missing addend problems.

Diagnosis and Remediation

Diagnosis and remediation procedures for beginning subtraction problems are very similar to those discussed for beginning addition problems. The basic steps below apply to diagnosing and remedying errors:

1. The teacher analyzes worksheet errors and hypothesizes the cause of the errors.
2. The teacher interviews the students to determine the cause of the errors, if the cause is not obvious.

Summary Box 8.1: Subtraction: Missing Subtrahend Strategy

1. Students read problem.

2. Students draw lines under minuend.

3. Students determine the number they must end with on both sides.

4. Students circle three of the seven lines since they must end with three to make sides equal.

5. Students cross out uncircled lines.

6. Students count crossed-out lines and write numeral in the box.

Seven minus how many equals three?

$7 - \square = 3$
|||||||

$7 - \square = 3$
⑴⑴⑴||||

$7 - \square = 3$
⑴⑴⑴╫╫╫

$7 - \boxed{4} = 3$
⑴⑴⑴╫╫╫

---

3. The teacher provides reteaching through board and/or worksheet presentations.
4. The teacher tests the student on a set of problems similar to the ones on which the original errors were made.

Once students begin working problems independently on their worksheets, their errors usually fall into two main categories:

1. Component skill errors that indicate a deficit on one or more of the component skills that make up the strategy.
2. Strategy errors in which steps are omitted, applied in the wrong order, or replaced by incorrect steps. Strategy errors are remedied by reintroducing the structured board or worksheet format. Until the remedy is complete, problems of that type should not appear on the independent worksheets.

COMPONENT SKILL ERRORS Component skill errors are often difficult to diagnose. Note that in this problem the student's error may have resulted from misidentifying 3 as 4 or simply not crossing out the correct number of lines: $9 - 3 = \boxed{5}$

The teacher can determine the specific cause of errors by looking for patterns. If a student works all of the problems correctly except those that include the numeral 3, the cause of errors would be the misidentification of the numeral 3. In addition to looking for patterns, the teacher can observe students working problems, asking the students to read each problem, and describe what they are doing as they work it.

Once the teacher determines the specific component skill deficit, he works on that specific skill for several lessons. If the skill is one that would cause

students to miss many problems (e.g., a skill such as crossing out lines), the teacher would not present any subtraction problems until the students could perform the component skill independently. If the component skill is one which causes students to miss just some problems (e.g., numeral misidentification), the teacher excludes subtraction problems with that feature from independent worksheet assignments until the students demonstrate mastery of that component skill.

A common component skill error, which occurs soon after subtraction appears on worksheets, is confusing signs and adding rather than subtracting. Teachers can expect most students to make this error occasionally. However, a remediation procedure is necessary when the error occurs frequently (in more than 10% of problems). The remediation procedure involves reintroducing the less-structured worksheet format that provides guided practice on discriminating addition and subtraction problems.

Fact Memorization

Students need an understanding of the subtraction operation, which the crossing-out strategy provides. However, students also must learn to memorize the subtraction facts to reduce difficulties in learning multi-digit operations. Fact memorization instruction should begin as soon as students reach the 80–90% accuracy criterion during supervised practice.

MULTI-DIGIT SUBTRACTION PROBLEMS

This section deals with subtraction problems with multi-digit numbers. A critical component skill of multi-digit problems is renaming (borrowing). Two basic renaming strategies are suggested in mathematics texts. The first, the additive balancing or equal addends method, involves adding a tens unit to both the subtrahend and the minuend. In solving a problem with two digit numbers, the tens unit is added to the ones column of the top numeral, while the tens unit is added to the tens column of the bottom numeral:

$$
\begin{array}{r} 73 \\ -\,48 \\ \hline 25 \end{array}
\quad \text{becomes} \quad
\begin{array}{r} \overset{1}{7}3 \\ -\,5\,48 \\ \hline 25 \end{array}
$$

This involves application of the compensation principle for subtraction: The difference between two numbers is unaltered by the addition of the same amount to both terms. In turn, the compensation principle includes the equality principle. Since few students know the compensation principle, and many don't know the equality principle, the equal addends strategy tends not to be understood by most students.

The second method, sometimes called the decomposition or borrowing method, involves renaming the minuend so that a unit from a higher-order column is written in a lower-order column:

$$
\begin{array}{r} 73 \\ -\,48 \\ \hline 25 \end{array}
\quad \text{becomes} \quad
\begin{array}{r} \overset{6}{\cancel{7}}\overset{1}{3} \\ -\,48 \\ \hline 25 \end{array}
$$

Note that the minuend 73 has been rewritten as 60 and 13.

Teaching Procedure

The direct instruction procedures are based on the renaming (borrowing) method, since this method is used by most teachers in North America. The procedures emphasize knowing when to rename and the mechanics of renaming. The conceptual understanding of renaming is also emphasized, but in separate exercises from those for teaching the mechanics of working problems. This separation is done to simplify the formats for teaching the mechanics.

Three main groups of problems are discussed in this chapter: (1) problems that do not require renaming, (2) problems that require renaming and in which the student may "borrow" from the next column, and (3) problems requiring renaming in two consecutive columns, including problems with a zero in the column that must be renamed.

Column Subtraction—No Renaming

Since column subtraction problems that do not require renaming are taught in basically the same way as addition problems that do not require renaming, we have not included a format. Also, as was the case for addition, we recommend not introducing column problems until students have memorized approximately 12 facts. In working subtraction problems, students subtract in the ones column and then in the tens column. Also, as in addition, students read the number of tens in the tens column, rather than the quantity represented by the numerals: They would say, "Three tens minus two tens," rather than "30 minus 20."

Subtraction with Renaming

Simple renaming problems include types 2a, 2b, 3a, and 3b from the Instructional Sequence and Assessment Chart. Problem type 2a is the first subtraction problem type that involves renaming. It is usually introduced during mid-second grade. The three preskills for solving this problem type are (1) the place-value-related skills inherent in reading and writing numerals over 10, (2) knowledge of at least six facts that can be used for borrowing (i.e., facts in which the first number is ten or more), and (3) a conceptual understanding of renaming. Format 8.2 includes a format to teach the concept of regrouping (with objects), which builds the foundation for renaming (with numerals).

Format 8.2 presents a diagram showing several packages, each of which contains 10 objects and several single objects. The teacher tells a story that involves giving away some of those objects: "Bill has 34 nails. He wants to give 8 nails to his sister." The teacher points out that to give 8 nails to his sister, Bill will have to open a package of 10. The teacher erases one pack of 10 nails and draws 10 single nails. The teacher then erases 8 nails and counts the remaining packages and single nails. This format, with similar examples, would be presented for several days prior to introducing the renaming format.

The procedures for introducing the computation for renaming appears in Format 8.3. The format contains five parts. In Part A, students discriminate when renaming is necessary. This discrimination is critical in preventing mistakes in which students subtract the smaller from the larger number regardless of which number is on top (e.g., in 74 – 38 students take 4 from 8). The teacher presents this rule: "When we take away more than we start with, we must rename." This rule is not intended to be absolutely mathematically correct, but is meant to serve as a functional rule to teach the concept. After presenting this rule, the teacher leads students in applying the rule. The teacher points to the top number in the ones column and asks the students how many they are starting with, then points to the numeral below it and asks whether they must rename if they take away that number. Example selection is critical in this format. The teacher must include an unpredictable mix of problems, some requiring renaming and some not.

Part A should be presented for several lessons. The teacher should then test each student individually on a set of about seven problems, asking of each, "Do we have to rename in this problem?" Student performance determines what the teacher does next. If students miss no more than one of the seven problems, the teacher can present Part B, in which the strategy for working problems is presented. If students miss more than one question, Part A would be presented for several more lessons.

Part B introduces the renaming component skill. The teacher explains to the students that they rename by borrowing a ten and putting it with the ones number. In 75 − 38, they borrow a ten from the seven tens and put it with the five ones. After modeling several problems, the teacher tests students, making sure they can follow the steps for renaming.

Parts C and D are structured board and worksheet exercises in which the entire strategy is presented. Part E is a less-structured worksheet exercise that includes an equal mix of problems that do and do not require renaming. Supervised practice exercises should be included in lessons until students can perform with 80–90% accuracy. After several days of supervised practice with only subtraction problems, the teacher should include some addition problems for discrimination practice.

Problems requiring renaming become more difficult as the number of digits in the minuend and subtrahend increase. The structured format for presenting each new problem type is quite similar to the structured format just discussed. For example, when problems involving renaming hundreds are introduced, the teacher would first ask the students to identify what they are starting with and taking away in the tens column and then ask if it is necessary to rename to work the problem. The teacher then leads students through solving the problem. In multi-digit problems that require renaming in several columns, the teacher leads the students through working each column always asking, "What does the column tell us to do? . . . Must we rename?"

The examples for the less-structured, supervised practice, and independent worksheets should in-clude a mix of the currently introduced and previously introduced problem types. When the first problems requiring borrowing from tens are introduced, about ¾ of the problems should involve subtraction and ¼, addition. Of the subtraction problems, only about ½ should require renaming. When problems involving borrowing from the hundreds are introduced, ½ of the subtraction problems should require borrowing from the hundreds; ¼, from the tens; and ¼ should not require borrowing.

Some addition problems should also be included. Figure 8.1 is an example of a worksheet that could be presented after problems requiring borrowing from the hundreds are taught. Note the mixture of problem types: c, e, h, and j require borrowing from hundreds; b and i, from tens; a and g do not require renaming; and d and f are addition.

SELF-CHECKING   After students become proficient in working renaming problems, they should be taught to check their answers. A checking procedure for subtraction is adding the subtrahend and the difference. The teacher introduces checking on a worksheet exercise. After the students complete the first problem, the teacher says,

> Here's how to check your answer to a subtraction problem. Add the bottom two numbers. What's the answer? . . . Is that the same as the top number in the problem? So your answer is correct.

To demonstrate why the checking procedure works, teachers should use simple problems like 12 − 8 = 4. The teacher uses the same questions: "Add the bottom two numbers . . . What's the answer? . . . Is that the same as the top number? . . ." With familiar facts, students more readily see that the procedure "makes sense." The same type of exercise suggested for encouraging students to use the addition self-check can be used to encourage students to check their subtraction work. Teachers would give students a worksheet with some problems worked correctly and some incorrectly. Students would be asked to find the problems worked incorrectly by using the self-check strategy.

FIGURE 8.1   Sample Worksheet with Renaming Problems

a. 392	b. 346	c. 423	d. 728	e. 547
− 81	−118	−180	+324	− 83

f. 547	g. 285	h. 248	i. 347	j. 236
+38	−84	−58	−109	−46

Complex Renaming Problems

This group includes problems in which several consecutive columns must be renamed. First we discuss problems that do not include zeroes in the minuend. Working such problems does not involve new skills, just applying the renaming skill in consecutive columns. Errors often occur because students become confused over the crossed-out digits. When the problem 327 − 149 is worked, the number in the tens column is 11, neither digit of which comes from the original problem:

$$\begin{array}{r} 2\!\!\!/1_1 \\ \cancel{3}\cancel{2}7 \\ -149 \\ \hline 178 \end{array}$$

An important aspect of the teaching procedure is closely monitoring students as they write on their worksheets. Students who are not careful will make errors because of extensive crossing out and rewriting. Therefore, teachers should stress precisely where numerals are to be written.

Students encounter more difficulty with problems that require renaming zero. Types 3d, 4a, 4c, 4d, 4e, and 5b from the Instructional Sequence and Assessment Chart are examples of problems in which a number with a zero is renamed. The basic strategy students are taught is to rename several digits at once. For example, in the problem

$$\begin{array}{r} 304 \\ -\ 87 \end{array}$$

students treat the three hundreds as thirty tens. By doing this, they rename by borrowing one ten from the thirty tens), the 30 is crossed out and replaced with 29:

$$\begin{array}{r} 29_1 \\ \cancel{3}\cancel{0}4 \\ -\ 87 \end{array}$$

Students would follow a similar procedure when working problems containing zeroes in both the tens and hundreds columns:

$$\begin{array}{r} \cancel{3}\cancel{0}\cancel{0}2 \\ -\ 89 \end{array}$$

The students would treat the 3000 as 300 tens, crossing out the 300, writing 299 in its place and putting a ten in the ones column. This procedure was suggested by Cacha (1975) as a means of simplifying renaming that involved zeroes.

A preskill for solving problem types that involve renaming numbers with zeroes is learning the tens-numbers-minus-1 facts, e.g., 60 − 1, 90 − 1, 40 − 1.

These facts would be presented about a week prior to introducing problems such as

$$\begin{array}{r} 407 \\ -129 \end{array}$$

The format for teaching tens-numbers-minus-1 facts consists of two steps. First, the teacher says a tens number (a two-digit number ending in zero) and asks the students to indicate what number precedes it. "What number comes before 80?" Second, the teacher introduces the rule that when you minus 1, you say the number that comes just before. Then the teacher has the students apply the rule to a series of examples. The entire procedure appears in Format 8.4.

Once students have mastered the tens-minus-1 preskill, they can be presented with the format for renaming numbers with a zero, which appears in Format 8.5. The format has three parts. Part A includes a board demonstration by the teacher of how to work the problem. Part B includes steps in which the teacher guides students through solving problems on their worksheets. Part C is a less-structured worksheet guide. During the structured board and worksheet exercises, each problem should require renaming. In Part C, the less-structured worksheet exercise, students would be presented with a mix of problems—half would require renaming and half would not. For example, a typical worksheet might look like Figure 8.2. In about half of the problems, the numbers in the ones column require borrowing; while in the other half of the problems, borrowing in the ones column is not required. The mix is very important to prevent students from developing the misrule of always borrowing when they see a zero in the tens column. The importance of mixing problems on the less-structured, supervised practice and independent worksheets cannot be overemphasized. If the examples used are not carefully designed to provide discrimination practice, the students might develop a serious misrule of always crossing out the hundreds number and zero, as in the problem below:

$$\begin{array}{cc} 2_9 & 3_9 \\ \cancel{3}\cancel{0}2 & \cancel{4}\cancel{0}2 \\ -\ 41 & -\ 52 \\ \hline 251 & 340 \end{array}$$

Problem types become more complex as the number of digits increases, particularly the number of zeroes involved in renaming. In problem type 4c of the Instructional Sequence and Assessment Chart, numbers with two zeroes are renamed, as in

$$\begin{array}{r} 3004 \\ -\ 86 \end{array}$$

FIGURE 8.2   Worksheet Problems for Renaming with Zeroes

1. 402	2. 503	3. 305	4. 302	5. 504
– 69	–161	– 65	– 86	–128
6. 703	7. 500	8. 300	9. 700	10. 206
– 42	– 36	– 40	– 4	– 36
11. 508	12. 500	13. 300	14. 501	15. 302
– 32	– 26	– 20	– 61	– 48

The preskill for this type of problem is hundreds-minus-1 facts (e.g., 800 – 1, 300 – 1). The teaching procedure for hundreds-minus-1 facts would be basically the same as for tens-minus-1 facts. The teacher presents the structured board and worksheet formats using basically the same wording as in Format 8.5. The only difference is that the teacher points out that in a problem such as

$$3004$$
$$-\ 128$$

students borrow from 300 tens. "What are you going to borrow one ten from? What is 300 minus 1 ? . . . So cross out 300 and write 299." Again, the less-structured worksheet exercise would be the critical part of the format. The worksheet should include a mix of problems like that in Figure 8.3.

In some problems, students must rename in the ones column. In some problems, students rename in the tens column. In still others, students must rename in the hundreds column. Teachers can expect students to need a great deal of supervised practice on this before they reach an acceptable accuracy criterion.

Two additional problem types that may cause students difficulty require borrowing from the numbers 10, 100, 1000, or 1100 (problem types 4d and 4e). Problems in which the student must borrow from 10, 100, or 1000 may cause difficulty because the students do not replace each digit with another digit as in

$$799_1$$
$$\cancel{8}\cancel{0}\cancel{0}4$$

FIGURE 8.3   Sample Worksheet: Renaming with Two or More Zeroes

a. 3004	b. 3004	c. 3001	d. 7005	e. 7005
– 289	– 302	–1394	–2101	–2104
f. 7005	g. 6000	h. 6000	i. 4000	
–1149	– 80	– 8	– 50	

Instead, they only replace two of the three digits, as in

$$99$$
$$1\cancel{0}\cancel{0}$$

$$99_1 \qquad 799_1$$
$$\cancel{1}\cancel{0}\cancel{0}4 \text{ with } \cancel{8}\cancel{0}\cancel{0}4$$

Without instruction, students may write the nines in the wrong columns:

$$99$$
$$\cancel{1}\cancel{0}\cancel{0}0$$
$$-\ 193$$
$$\overline{9807}$$

The teaching procedure for these problems need not be elaborate. The teacher merely models working several problems and then supervises students as they work the problems.

Diagnosis and Remediation

FACT ERRORS   Basic fact errors will usually be obvious. For example, in problems a and b below, the student has made obvious errors involving the facts 13 – 6 and 12 – 8, respectively.

a.	$\overset{3}{\cancel{4}}\overset{_1}{3}5$	b.	$\overset{4}{\cancel{5}}\overset{_1}{2}8$
	–162		–186
	$\overline{283}$		$\overline{352}$

The remediation procedure for fact errors depends on their frequency. An occasional error is addressed by stressing the missed fact in practice exercises. A pattern in which students make several errors on different facts requires a more complete remediation procedure. First, the teacher determines the strategy used by the students to derive the basic facts. This can be done by observing students as they work problems. Teachers may find lower-performing students relying on their fingers. The remediation procedure for such students is discussed in Chapter 6. Other students may not rely on using their fingers but, nonetheless, may be inaccurate, answering a basic fact correctly in one problem, but incorrectly in the next problem. The remediation procedure for such students involves first working on developing accuracy in computing basic facts. The emphasis on facts should result in improved performance on column subtraction problems. If, however, the student continues making random fact errors in column subtraction problems, the teacher may tentatively consider the problem to be one of motivation and consider implementing strategies to increase student motivation.

STRATEGY ERRORS Errors caused by failure to rename are illustrated below. In problem a, the error is in the ones column. In problem b the error is in the hundreds column.

$$\begin{array}{cc} \text{a.} & 342 \\ & -128 \\ \hline & \mathit{226} \end{array} \qquad \begin{array}{cc} \text{b.} & 2584 \\ & -1827 \\ \hline & \mathit{1307} \end{array}$$

Again, the frequency of the error must be considered before remediation is planned. An occasional error, occurring no more than in 1 out of 10 problems, needs no extensive remediation. The teacher merely has students rework the problem. More frequent errors of this type require more in-depth remediation, beginning with Part A of Format 8.3. Part A focuses on when renaming is required. The teacher writes several problems similar to the ones missed by the student. The teacher points to each column in a problem, asking if renaming is required to work that column. This exercise is continued until students can respond correctly to four or five problems consecutively. Next the teacher leads the students through a structured worksheet exercise with several problems (Part D in Format 8.3), then through less-structured worksheet problems (Part E). Finally, the teacher has students work a group of problems as she closely monitors. This set of problems should include a mix of problem types so that the teacher can be sure students are discriminating when renaming is required. The exercise is continued daily until students perform accurately on independent assignments for several days in a row.

COMPONENT SKILL ERRORS These errors in the mechanics of borrowing are illustrated below:

$$\begin{array}{cc} \text{a.} & \overset{1}{3}\overset{}{5} \\ & -16 \\ \hline & \mathit{29} \end{array} \qquad \begin{array}{cc} \text{b.} & \overset{6}{5}\overset{1}{4} \\ & -28 \\ \hline & \mathit{46} \end{array} \qquad \begin{array}{cc} \text{c.} & \overset{20}{3}\overset{1}{\cancel{0}}2 \\ & -54 \\ \hline & \mathit{8} \end{array}$$

In problem a, the student forgot to subtract a ten from the three tens after borrowing. This error is not uncommon when borrowing is first introduced. For remediation, students are given practice rewriting two-digit numerals. Teachers might use the following wording:

> You're going to practice renaming. Touch the first numeral (check). What do you do first to rename this number? Do it. Write a 1 to show one ten. Remember to cross out and write a new tens number.

The error in problem b indicates the student is adding rather than subtracting the ten when renaming. The remediation procedure begins with the teacher drawing attention to the fact that when you borrow a ten you must *take away* a ten. The teacher then follows the same procedure as described for problem a.

The error in problem c indicates either that the student is having difficulty with tens-numbers-minus-1 facts or is confused regarding the strategy to use. The teacher would watch the student work several problems. If the problem relates to tens-minus-1 facts, the teacher would reteach tens-minus-1 facts (e.g., 60 − 1, 30 − 1, 80 − 1, etc.) from Format 8.4. When students demonstrate mastery of tens-minus-1 facts, they would be presented with the less-structured part of the format for that type of problem. If the error reflects a strategy error, the teacher repeats the entire format.

A special group of problems that may cause students difficulty are problems with a zero in the ones column of the minuend or subtrahend:

$$\begin{array}{cc} 70 \\ -34 \end{array} \qquad \begin{array}{cc} 74 \\ -30 \end{array}$$

Students often become confused working problems with zero, answering 70 − 34 as 44 or 74 − 30 as 40. If teachers note errors with this problem type, a special exercise comprised of problems like the ones below should be given. Teachers would first review minus-zero facts, pointing out that when you minus zero you end with the same number you start with, then lead students through working the problems. The exercise is continued until students can work the problems with 90% accuracy for several days in a row.

$$\begin{array}{cccc} 60 & 64 & 40 & 43 \\ -34 & -30 & -20 & -20 \end{array}$$

$$\begin{array}{ccc} 40 & 78 & 70 \\ -23 & -30 & -38 \end{array}$$

A summary of the diagnosis and remediation procedures for subtraction appears in Figure 8.4.

COMMERCIAL PROGRAMS

Subtraction: Renaming

INSTRUCTIONAL STRATEGIES As in addition with renaming, most basal programs advocate the use of manipulatives when introducing renaming in subtraction. Interestingly, many programs we examined also include picture representations of the manipulatives on the introductory pages (e.g., pic-

FIGURE **8.4**   Diagnosis and Remediation of Subtraction Errors

Sample Patterns		Sample Diagnosis	Remediation Procedures	Remediation Examples
a. 3̸1̸ 4̸37 −180 ‾‾‾‾ 2̸47	63 −28 ‾‾‾ 3̸4	Fact error: 13 − 8	Emphasis on 13 − 8 in fact drill.	
b. 1̸ 34 −18 ‾‾‾ 26	1̸ 352 − 71 ‾‾‾‾ 3̸81	Component skill: Student did not rename column borrowed from.	You're going to practice rewriting. Touch the first numeral (check). What do you do first to rewrite this number? . . . Do it. Write a 1 to show one ten. Remember to cross out and write a new number for the first digit.	For examples, present a worksheet with these numerals: a. 27 b. 38 c. 71 d. 42
c. 34 −18 ‾‾‾ 24	72 −36 ‾‾‾ 4̸4	Strategy: Renaming not done.	Present renaming format starting with Part A, in Format 8.3.	Examples specified for Format 8.3.
d. 2̸9̸1̸ 3̸0̸4̸ − 21 ‾‾‾‾ 2̸713	5̸1̸ 6̸4 −24 ‾‾‾ 3̸10	Strategy: Renaming was done unnecessarily.	Same as c	Same as c
e. 7̸1̸ 6̸3 −48 ‾‾‾ 35	3̸1̸ 6̸1 − 2 ‾‾‾ 3̸9	Fact error: Minus 1.	a. Present minus-1 facts b. Present less-structured worksheet for the particular problem type.	Mix: some problems require renaming, and some do not. Renaming problems sample all types introduced to date.
f. 35 −14 ‾‾‾ 49		Component skill: Sign discrimination; student added instead of subtracting.	a. Present less-structured part of Format. Have student circle sign, then work the problem.	Equal mix of addition and subtraction.
g. 2̸11̸ 3̸04 − 26 ‾‾‾‾ 2̸88		Component skill: Problems with zero in tens column; inappropriate renaming.	a. Present tens-minus-1 preskill (if necessary). b. Present the format for renaming numbers with zeroes (Format 8.5)	6–8 problems Examples specified for Format 8.5
h. 2̸9̸1̸ 3̸0̸2̸ − 41 ‾‾‾‾ 2̸511	3̸9̸1̸ 4̸0̸2̸ − 52 ‾‾‾‾ 3̸410	Strategy: Renaming unnecessarily.	Format 8.5, Part C	Example specified for Format 8.5

tures of sticks, etc.; see Figures 8.5 and 8.6). However, little direction is given to the students on how to work the problems without the manipulatives.

PREREQUISITE SKILLS Most programs identify key prerequisite skills and preteach these skills before the instructional strategy is introduced. However, often the prerequisites are introduced with only a few examples the same day or a day before the strategy instruction. Teachers should allow time for

students to master the prerequisites prior to introducing the strategy. Also, they should determine whether *all* necessary prerequisites have been addressed. (See this chapter for a thorough discussion of the preskills to teach before introducing a renaming strategy.)

PRACTICE AND REVIEW Most programs provide an average of 15 to 20 pages of initial practice on two-digit subtraction problems with renaming.

FIGURE 8.5 A page from a basal program that includes picture representation.

STUDENT OBJECTIVE
To subtract 2-digit numbers, with regrouping from tens to ones.

TEACHING SUGGESTIONS

Practice subtraction with models. (Materials: tens and ones, Tens and Ones mat) Write

$$\begin{array}{r} 34 \\ -18 \\ \hline \end{array}$$

on the chalkboard. "What should you put on your mats?" (3 tens and 4 ones) "Can you take 8 ones away from your 4 ones? (No) What can you do?" (Trade 1 of the tens for 10 more ones.)

Ask the children to trade one of their tens for 10 more ones. Show them how to record what they have done.

"We took one of the tens to the bank, leaving us with 2 tens." "We traded the ten for 10 more ones. That gives us 14 ones."

"Now do you have enough ones to take 8 away?" (Yes) Have the children take 8 ones off the mat. "How many ones are left? (6 ones) How many tens should we take away?" (1 ten) Have the children take 1 ten off the mat. "How many tens are left?" (1 ten) On the chalkboard, show the children how to record what they have done.

READINESS

For students who need help with subtraction.

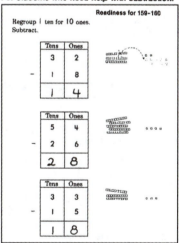

Copymaster S96 or Duplicating Master S96

Ask the children to draw the trade, crossing out 1 ten and drawing in 10 ones, and then cross out the amount to be subtracted and write the amount that is left.

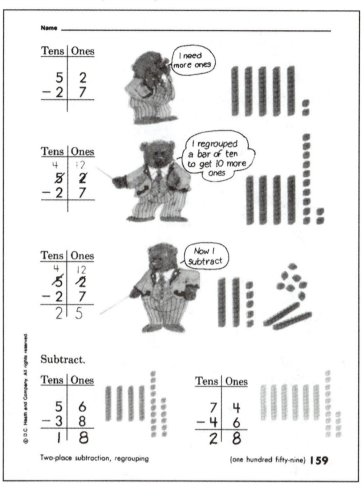

Two-place subtraction, regrouping

(one hundred fifty-nine) **159**

USING THE PAGES

Provide the children with tens and ones. Discuss the bear's and the turtle's demonstrations of regrouping on pages 159 and 160. Have the children make check marks by the problems that will require regrouping. A few problems will not require regrouping. Assign the pages.

•• **ERROR-ANALYSIS NOTE** ••••••••••••

Rather than regrouping the tens, some children may subtract the smaller ones digit from the larger ones digit—for example,

$$\begin{array}{r} 61 \\ -28 \\ \hline 47 \end{array} \quad \text{instead of} \quad \begin{array}{r} 5\,11 \\ \cancel{6}\,\cancel{1} \\ -28 \\ \hline 33 \end{array}$$

Have these children use ones and tens materials. See the Teaching Suggestions.

CLASSWORK/HOMEWORK

Textbook Assignments	Basic	Enriched
all exercises	✔	✔
Keeping Skills Sharp	✔	✔
Optional Materials		
Readiness Worksheet	✔	✔
Basic Worksheet	✔	
Enrichment Worksheet		✔
Creative Problem Solving section 7	✔	✔

▨ **Concrete materials**   ❖ **Cooperative Learning Groups**

Source: From *Heath Mathematics* Teacher's Edition, Level 2 by Rucker et al. Copyright © 1987 by D.C. Heath & Company. Reprinted by permission of Houghton Mifflin Company. All rights reserved.

While this is an adequate amount of practice initially, little further review of subtraction typically occurs until the next level of the series. This lack of review can be attributed to the spiral curriculum design employed by the majority of math programs. To maintain student success over time, adequate review on a continual basis must be provided.

FIGURE 8.6 A page from a basal program that includes picture representation.

STUDENT OBJECTIVES

To subtract any two whole numbers with one regrouping.
To solve word problems using subtraction with regrouping.

TEACHING SUGGESTIONS

Subtract with regrouping. (Materials: ones, tens, hundreds, a place-value mat for each student)
Write this subtraction problem on the chalkboard:

$$\begin{array}{r} 54 \\ -28 \\ \hline \end{array}$$

"How many blocks will you put on your mat? (54) How many are you going to take away? (28) Can you take 8 ones from the 4 ones? (No) What can you do?" (Trade 1 ten for 10 ones.)

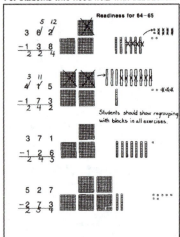

Ask the students to subtract the ones and then the tens. Demonstrate this on the chalkboard.

READINESS

For students who need help with subtraction.

Readiness for 64–65

Students should show regrouping with blocks in all exercises.

Copymaster S84 or Duplicating Master S84

Draw 3 hundreds, 6 tens, and 2 ones on the chalkboard. We want to take away 138 blocks. There are not enough ones. Cross off 1 ten and draw 10 ones. How many ones do you have now? (12) How many tens do you have now?" (5) Demonstrate how to record this in the example at the left. "Cross off 8 ones. How many ones do you have now? Write **4** in the ones place. Cross off 3 tens. How many tens do you have now? Write **2** in the tens place. Cross off 1 hundred. How many hundreds do you have now? Write **2** in the hundreds place."

 **Concrete Materials**  **Mental Arithmetic**

In this example, 1 ten is regrouped for 10 ones.

EXAMPLE 1.

$$\begin{array}{r} 54 \\ -29 \\ \hline \end{array}$$

Step 1. Not enough ones. Regroup 1 ten for 10 ones.

$$\begin{array}{r} {}^{4\ 14}\!5\!4 \\ -29 \\ \hline \end{array}$$

Step 2. Subtract ones. Subtract tens.

$$\begin{array}{r} {}^{4\ 14}\!5\!4 \\ -29 \\ \hline 25 \end{array}$$

In this example, 1 hundred is regrouped for 10 tens.

EXAMPLE 2.

Step 1. Subtract ones.

$$\begin{array}{r} 426 \\ -152 \\ \hline 4 \end{array}$$

Step 2. Not enough tens. Regroup 1 hundred for 10 tens.

$$\begin{array}{r} {}^{3\ 12}\!4\!2\!6 \\ -152 \\ \hline 4 \end{array}$$

Step 3. Subtract tens.

$$\begin{array}{r} {}^{3\ 12}\!4\!2\!6 \\ -152 \\ \hline 74 \end{array}$$

Step 4. Subtract hundreds.

$$\begin{array}{r} {}^{3\ 12}\!4\!2\!6 \\ -152 \\ \hline 274 \end{array}$$

64

USING THE PAGES

Discuss the examples on page 64. Provide place-value materials for the students who need them. Assign page 65.

.... **ERROR-ANALYSIS NOTE** ....

Some students may regroup when it is not necessary—for example,

$$\begin{array}{r} {}^{7\ 17}\!8\!7 \\ -26 \\ \hline \end{array} \text{ instead of } \begin{array}{r} 87 \\ -26 \\ \hline 61 \end{array}$$

Have these students look at exercises 1–15 and find the two exercises that do not require regrouping. (Exercises 7 and 15)

CLASSWORK/HOMEWORK

Textbook Assignments	Basic	Average	Enriched
Exercises 1–32	✔		
Exercises 1–34		✔	
Exercises 6–36			✔
Extra Practice set 15 page 366	✔		
Optional Materials			
Readiness Worksheet	✔	✔	
Basic Worksheet	✔		
Enrichment Worksheet		✔	✔
Excursion Worksheet			✔
Creative Problem Solving section 3	✔	✔	✔

APPLICATION ITEMS: SUBTRACTION

1. Below are Mary's and Alex's performances on a set of performance indicators. Specify the problem type with which instruction should begin for each student.

Mary

3a.
```
   3      3      1
  4̶23    4̶18    2̶2̶8
 -171   - 83   -137
 ‾252‾  ‾335‾  ‾91‾
```

3b.
```
   4₁     1₁     2₁
  35̶2    72̶4    53̶4
 -187   -578   - 87
 ‾245‾  ‾266‾  ‾567‾
```

3c. 70 – 1 = **69**
    40 – 1 = **39**
    80 – 1 = **79**

3d.
```
   4      4 ₁
  5̶03    5̶04    700
 - 87   - 26   - 86
 ‾486‾  ‾428‾  ‾786‾
```

3e.
```
              4₁
  4689    5̶284    3481
 -1832   -4631   -1681
 ‾3257‾  ‾653‾   ‾2201‾
```

Alex

3a.
```
   3₁     3₁     1
  4̶23    4̶18    2̶28
 -171   - 83   -137
 ‾252‾  ‾335‾  ‾91‾
```

3b.
```
   4₁     1₁     2₁
  35̶2    72̶4    53̶4
 -187   -578   - 87
 ‾245‾  ‾266‾  ‾567‾
```

3c. 70 – 1 = **69**
    40 – 1 = **39**
    80 – 1 = **79**

3d.
```
  49,    49     69
  5̶0̶3    5̶04    7̶0̶0
 - 87   - 26   - 86
 ‾415‾  ‾478‾  ‾614‾
```

3e.
```
   1
  4689    5284    3481
 -1832   -4631   -1681
 ‾3857‾  ‾1453‾  ‾2200‾
```

2. Below is an excerpt of the independent worksheet to be given to students who have just demonstrated accuracy in solving problem type 3a. The teacher made some errors in constructing the worksheet.

   a. Indicate the inappropriate examples and specify the problem type.

   b. Identify any omitted problem types that should be included on the worksheet.

a.	524	b.	504	c.	324	d.	533
	−186		−328		−192		−261

e.	824	f.	602	g.	523	h.	65
	−161		−159		−186		−32

3. Describe the problem type that each example below represents. List the problems in the order they are introduced. Write the grade level when each problem type is typically introduced.

63	353	48	523	346	503
−18	−182	−23	−486	−128	− 87

(continued)

4. Below are 12 problems which appeared on the worksheet to be done independently by the students in Mr. Dean's math group. Next to each student's name are the problems missed by the student.

For each student:

a. Specify the probable cause or causes of the student's error.

b. Describe the remediation procedure. Be specific (i.e. format part)

```
   4023        4702        8346         342        7304         430
  -1857       -2563       -1895        +185       -1286         -82

   2036        3248        3852         402        3826        8306
  - 518       -1026       +1624        - 81       -  63       -1243
```

James
```
        39          29
       4̶0̶2        8̶3̶0̶6
      - 81      - 1243
       311        7053
```

Debbie
```
      391,        69,
     4̶0̶2̶3       4̶7̶0̶2
    - 1857      - 2563
      2165        1138
```

Dylan
```
       79
      4̶7̶0̶2
    - 2563
      2̶2̶39
```

Jack
```
      342        3852
    + 185      + 1624
      157        2̶2̶2̶8
```

5. Specify the wording the teacher would use in the structured worksheet presentation for the problem

$$\begin{array}{r} 314 \\ -182 \\ \hline \end{array}$$

6. In presenting Format 8.3, Part A, a board format for introducing renaming problems, the teacher asks for this problem, "Must we rename?" The student says "No." Specify the wording the teacher uses in making the correction.

$$\begin{array}{r} 57 \\ -28 \\ \hline \end{array}$$

7. Below are partial worksheets made by several teachers for the less structured part of the format for teaching students to work problems that require borrowing from the hundreds column. Two teachers constructed unacceptable lists. Identify these teachers and tell why each list is unacceptable. For each unacceptable list, specify what could be done to make the list acceptable.

a.	342	623	483	362	534	235	427	329	427
	−181	−182	−193	−181	−184	+132	−193	−152	−121
b.	383	432	342	282	346	425	524	473	392
	−195	−150	−186	−195	−138	+132	−187	−197	−161
c.	428	328	526	48	362	364	325	436	329
	−368	−209	−385	−29	−182	−148	+132	−214	+142

FORMAT 8.1   **Format for Subtraction with Lines**

PART A: STRUCTURED BOARD PRESENTATION—PRESKILL OF MINUSING LINES

TEACHER	**STUDENTS**

(Write the following problem and lines on the board.)

6 – 2
| | | | | |

1. Everyone, read this problem.	6 – 2
This is a minus problem. What kind of problem is this?	A minus problem
2. *(Point to minus 2.)* What does this say? Minus 2 tells us to cross out two lines.	Minus 2
What does minus 2 tell us to do? Watch me cross out two lines. *(Draw two minuses through two lines and count each time.)* Minus 1, Minus 2.	Cross out two lines.
3. Let's see how many lines we have left. I'll touch and you count.	1, 2, 3, 4
How many did we end up with? *(Repeat steps 1–3 with 7 – 4, 5 – 3.)*	4

PART B: STRUCTURED WORKSHEET—PRESKILL OF MINUSING LINES

(Students have worksheets with four to six problems like the one below.)

6 – 2
| | | | | |

(Note that the lines under the first numeral in each problem are already drawn.)

1. Touch problem a on your worksheet. *(Check.)* Read the problem.	6 – 2
What kind of problem is this?	A minus problem
2. Touch the first group. How many lines are in the first group?	6
How many lines are you going to minus?	2
Minus the lines. *(Check that students minus two lines.)*	
To correct: When you minus 2, you cross out two lines.	
3. Now count and see how many lines you have left. *(Pause.)* How many did you end with?	4
(Repeat steps 1–3 with remaining examples.)	

PART C: STRUCTURED WORKSHEET—ENTIRE STRATEGY

5 – 3 = ☐

1. Touch this problem on your worksheet. *(Point to first problem.)* Read the problem.	5 – 3 = how many?
2. What kind of problem is this?	A minus problem
Touch the first group. How many lines are you going to draw?	5
Draw five lines under the 5.	

(continued on next page)

FORMAT 8.1   (continued)

TEACHER	STUDENTS
3. How many lines are you going to minus? Minus the lines. *(Monitor worksheet responses.)*	3
4. Now count and see how many lines you end with. *(Pause.)* How many?	2
5. So how many must you end with on the other side of the equal?	2
Draw two lines and write the numeral in the box.	
6. Now read the whole statement.	5 − 3 = 2
Five minus three equals how many?	2
Say the statement again.	5 − 3 = 2

(Repeat steps 1–5 with remaining examples.)

PART D: LESS-STRUCTURED WORKSHEET

(Give the students a worksheet with an equal mix of addition and subtraction problems.)

a. 4 + 3 = ☐   f. 7 − 0 = ☐
b. 8 − 2 = ☐   g. 8 − 2 = ☐
c. 7 − 5 = ☐   h. 2 + 4 = ☐
d. 5 − 4 = ☐   i. 5 + 3 = ☐
e. 7 + 0 = ☐

1. This worksheet is tricky. In some problems you plus and in some problems you minus. When you plus you make more lines. What do you do when you plus?	Make more lines.
When you minus you cross out lines. What do you do when you minus?	Cross out lines.
2. Touch problem a. Read it.	4 + 3 = how many?
Is that a plus or minus problem?	Plus problem
What do you do when you plus?	Make more lines.
3. Make the lines under the first group. Then plus/minus.	
4. Now make the sides equal and fill in the empty box.	

(Repeat steps 2–4 with the remaining problems.)

FORMAT 8.2   **Format for Teaching Regrouping**

TEACHER   **STUDENTS**

(Draw the following boxes on the board.)

| 10 | 10 | 10 |

1. A boy has nails. He has three packages with 10 nails in each package and 4 nails not in a package. Let's figure out how many nails he has in all. *(Point as you count.)* 10, 20, 30, 31, 32, 33, 34.

2. The boy wants to give 8 nails to his sister. We have a problem. He can't give 8 nails to his sister the way the nails are now. He has 4 nails and packages of 10 nails. He has to regroup the nails. When we regroup we put a group of 10 with the 4 nails. What do we do when we regroup in this problem?   Put a group of 10 with 4.

3. We open a pack of 10 nails *(Erase a group of 10 nails)* and put the 10 nails over here.

    (Draw the following on the board.)

    | 10 | | 10 | | | | | |
                         | | | | |

4. We still have 34 nails. They're just in different groups. We have two groups of 10 and a group of 14.
    Now let's give 8 away. *(Erase 8.)* Let's see how many we have left. *(Point to 6)* How many here? And two 10s equal   6
    how many?   20

    What is 20 and 6? Right, 26. The boy starts with 34. He   26
    gives away 8 and ends with 26.

5. *(Present one or two more problems.)*

FORMAT 8.3   **Format for Subtraction with Renaming**

Part A: When to Rename

TEACHER   **STUDENTS**

(Write the following problem on the board.)

$$\begin{array}{r} 75 \\ -49 \\ \hline \end{array}$$

(continued on next page)

FORMAT 8.3   (continued)

TEACHER	STUDENTS
1. Here's a rule about renaming with subtraction problems: When we take away more than we start with, we must rename. My turn. When must we rename? When we take away more than we start with. Your turn. When do we rename?	When we take away more than we start with.

(Repeat statement with students until they can say it by themselves.)

2. *(Point to the 5.)* What number are we starting with in the ones column?   5

We're starting with 5 and taking away 9. Must we rename? *(Pause and signal.)*   Yes

Right, we have to rename because we're taking away more than we start with; 9 is more than 5.

3. *(Write the following problem on the board.)*

```
  75
 −43
```

What number are we starting with in the ones column?   5

What are we taking away?   3

Must we rename if we take away 3? *(Pause, signal.)*   No

We don't rename. We're not taking away more than we start with.

4. *(Write the next problem on the board.)*

```
  38
 −27
```

What are we starting out with now in the ones column?   8

What are we taking away?   7

Must we rename? *(Pause, signal.)*   No

Why?   We're not taking away more than we start with.

5. *(Repeat step 4 with these problems.)*

```
  38      42      42      42
 −29     −37     −30     −33
```

(Give individual turns to several children.)

PART B: STEPS IN RENAMING

(Write these problems on the board.)

```
  53      75      92
 −26     −28     −15
```

FORMAT 8.3   (continued)

TEACHER	STUDENTS
1. *(Point to first problem.)* Read this problem.	53 – 26
The ones column tells us to start with 3 and take away 6. What does the ones column tell us to do?	Start with 3 and take away 6.
Do we have to rename? *(Pause, signal.)* Right. We start with 3 and take away more than 3.	Yes
2. Here's how we rename: First we borrow a ten from the five tens. What do we do first?	Borrow a ten from the five tens.
Next we put that ten with the three ones. What do we do next?	Put that ten with the three ones.
(Repeat steps 1 and 2 with the second and third problems.)	
3. Let's go back to the first problem. Read it.	53 – 26
What does the ones column tell us to do?	Start with 3 and take away 6.
Do we rename?	Yes
4. Tell me how we rename. What do we do first?	Borrow a ten from the five tens.
What do we do next?	Put that ten with the three ones.
(Repeat steps 3 and 4 with the remaining problems.)	

PART C: STRUCTURED BOARD PRESENTATION

(Write this problem on the board.)

```
  53
 −26
```

1. Read the problem.	53 – 26
What does the ones column tell us to do?	Start with 3 and take away 6.
Do we rename? *(Pause, signal.)*	Yes
To correct: What are we starting with in the ones column? Are we taking away more than 3? So, do we rename?	
2. What do we do first to rename?	Borrow a ten from the five tens.
(Point to 5.) If we borrow one ten from the five tens, how many tens will be left?	Four tens.
So I cross out the 5 and write 4 to show that four tens are left. *(Cross out 5 and write 4.)*	
3. We borrowed a ten. What do we do next? Right, put the ten with the three ones. *(Write 1 in front of 3.)*	Put the ten with the three ones.
Now we have 13 in the ones column.	
Figure out what 13 minus 6 is. *(Pause.)* What's 13 – 6? *(Pause, signal.)*	7
We write 7 in the ones column. *(Write 7 under the line.)*	

(continued on next page)

FORMAT 8.3   (continued)

TEACHER	STUDENTS
4. The tens column says four tens minus two tens. How many is four tens minus two tens? *(Pause, signal.)*	Two tens
We write 2 in the tens column. *(Write 2 under the line.)*	
5. What is 53 take away 26?	27
(Repeat steps 1–5 with remaining problems.)	

PART D: STRUCTURED WORKSHEET

(Give students worksheets with these problems.)

```
 92      86      64
-35     -17     -49
```

1. Read problem one on your worksheet.	92 – 35
2. What does the ones column tell you to do?	Start with 2 and take away 5.
Do you rename? *(Pause, signal.)*	Yes
3. What do you do first to rename?	Borrow a ten from the nine tens.
If you borrow a ten from the nine tens, how many will be left?	8
So cross out the 9 and write 8 above it. *(Check papers.)*	*(Students cross out the 9 and write 8.)*
4. What do you do now?	Put the ten with the two ones.
Do that. Put the ten with the two ones. *(Check papers.)* How many do you have in the ones column?	12
5. What is 12 minus 5? *(Pause, signal.)*	7
Write 7 under the line in the ones column.	
6. Look at the tens column. What does the tens column tell us to do?	Start with 8 and take away 3.
What is eight tens minus three tens?	Five tens.
Write 5 under the line in the tens column.	57
7. How many is 92 take away 35?	

(Repeat steps 1–7 with remaining problems.)

PART E: LESS-STRUCTURED WORKSHEET

(Give students a worksheet with a mixture of subtraction problems that do and do not require renaming.)

```
a.  84    b.  95    c.  46    d.  56    e.  78
   -23       -38        -8       -32       -38

f.  42    g.  34    h.  58
   -26       -26       -52
```

1. Touch problem a.
2. Read the problem.

FORMAT 8.3   (continued)

TEACHER	STUDENTS
3. Look at the ones column and get ready to tell me if you need to rename. *(Pause.)* Must you rename?	No
(If the answer is yes, present step 4. If the answer is no, go to step 5.)	
4. Where do you get the ten from?	
How many tens will you have left?	
5. Work the problem.	
(Repeat steps 1–5 with remaining problems.)	

FORMAT 8.4   **Format for Tens-Numbers-Minus-1 Preskill**

TEACHER	STUDENTS
1. I'll say numbers, and you say the number that comes just before. Listen: 60. What comes just before? *(Pause two seconds. Signal.)*	59
To correct: *(Tell answer, then repeat the problem.)*	
2. *(Repeat step 1 with 30, 80, 40, 70.)*	
3. Listen: When you minus 1 you say the number that comes just before. I'll say a problem, and you tell me the answer. Listen: 60 minus 1 is . . . *(Pause, signal.)*	59
To correct: *(Ask)* What number comes just before 60?	
(Repeat step 3 with 30 – 1, 80 – 1, 40 – 1, 70 – 1.)	

FORMAT 8.5   **Format for Renaming Numbers with Zeroes**

PART A: STRUCTURED BOARD PRESENTATION

TEACHER	STUDENTS
(Write this problem on the board.)	
$\begin{array}{r} 304 \\ -186 \\ \hline \end{array}$	
1. Read the problem.	304 – 186
2. What do we do in the ones column?	Start with 4 and take away 6.
Do we have to rename? *(Pause, signal.)*	yes

(continued on next page)

FORMAT 8.5 (continued)

TEACHER	STUDENTS
3. We have a problem. We can't borrow from zero tens. So we have to borrow from the thirty tens. We're going to borrow one ten from thirty tens. *(Circle 30 with finger.)*	
What are we going to borrow one ten from?	Thirty tens
What is 30 tens minus 1 ten?	29 tens
So I cross out 30 and write 29 above it.	
4. Now I'll put the one ten with the four ones. What is one ten and four ones?	14
What is 14 minus 6? *(Pause, signal.)*	8
So I write 8 in the ones column.	
5. Now look at the tens column. How many tens are we starting with now?	9
What is 9 – 8?	1
So I write 1 under the tens column.	
6. How many hundreds are we starting with now?	2
What is 2 – 1?	1
So I write 1 in the hundreds column.	
7. What is the answer to this problem?	118

(Repeat steps 1–7 with these examples: 504 – 327, 602 – 148.)

PART B: STRUCTURED WORKSHEET

```
  406      905      403
 −287     −626     −248
```

1. Touch the first problem. Read it.	406 – 287
2. What does the ones column tell us to do?	Start with 6 and take away 7.
Do you have to rename? *(Pause.)*	Yes
3. Can you borrow one ten ten from zero tens?	No
Where are you going to get the one ten?	From forty tens
What is forty tens minus one ten?	Thirty-nine tens
Cross out the 40 and write 39 above it. *(Monitor responses.)* Now put the one ten with the six ones. *(Monitor responses.)*	
4. Now work the problem in the ones column.	
What is one ten and six ones?	16
What is 16 minus 7?	9
5. How many tens are you starting with now?	9
What is 9 – 8?	1
Write it.	
(Monitor responses.)	

FORMAT 8.5   (continued)

TEACHER	STUDENTS
6. How many hundreds are you starting with now?	3
What is 3 – 2?	1
Read the whole problem and say the answer.	406 – 287 = 119
(Repeat steps 1–6 with remaining examples.)	

PART C: LESS-STRUCTURED WORKSHEET

a.	804 −619	b.	905 −164	c.	609 −426
d.	605 −197	e.	302 − 42	f.	508 −349

1. Touch problem a.

2. Read the problem.   804 – 619

3. Look at the ones column and get ready to tell me if you need to rename. *(Pause.)* Do you need to rename?   Yes

   (If the answer is yes.) Where do you get the ten from?   From eighty tens

4. Work the problem.

   (Repeat steps 1–4 with remaining problems.)

CHAPTER 9

Multiplication

TERMS AND CONCEPTS

Multiplication   The process of combining a specific number of sets, each including an equal number of elements, into a single larger set.

Multiplicand   The number of units in each equal set.

Multiplier   The number of sets in the multiplication process.

Factors   The multiplicand and the multiplier in a multiplication problem.

Product   The answer in a multiplication problem. The number designating elements in the combined set of a multiplication problem; i.e., the sum of all the equal sets.

Commutative Property   The commutative property for multiplication states that changing the order of two numbers in a multiplication equation does not change the answer. If a and b are whole numbers, then $a \times b = b \times a$; e.g., $3 \times 4 = 4 \times 3$. The commutative property is very helpful in teaching multiplication facts. Once students learn that $3 \times 4 = 12$, they do not need to learn $4 \times 3 = 12$ as a new fact; rather, they can relate 4×3 to the known fact (3×4) and learn the new fact more quickly.

Associative Property   The associative property for multiplication states that if $a, b,$ and c are whole numbers, then $(a \times b) \times c = a \times (b \times c)$; e.g., $(3 \times 2) \times 4 = 3 \times (2 \times 4)$.

Identity Element   The identity element for multiplication is 1. Any number times 1 equals that number; e.g., $4 \times 1 = 4$, $6 \times 1 = 6$. (The identity element for addition is zero: $4 + 0 = 4$, $6 + 0 = 6$. However, in multiplication a factor of zero results in a product of zero: $4 \times 0 = 0$, $6 \times 0 = 0$.)

The identity element for multiplication is often applied in operations with fractional numbers. For example, before students add $\frac{1}{4}$ and $\frac{1}{2}$, they must change $\frac{1}{2}$ to an equivalent fraction by multiplying by a fraction equal to 1: $\frac{1}{2} \times \frac{2}{2} = \frac{2}{4}$. Students substitute $\frac{2}{4}$ for $\frac{1}{2}$ and complete the equation. Students must realize that multiplying by $\frac{2}{2}$ is acceptable only because the fraction equals the identity element for multiplication, which means the value of $\frac{1}{2}$ has not been changed.

Distributive Property   The distributive property of multiplication over addition says that if $a, b,$ and c are whole numbers, then

$$a \times (b + c) = (a \times b) + (a \times c)$$

This property is essential to understanding multiplication of multi-digit numbers such as 4×27. Expanded notation allows 27 to be rewritten as $20 + 7$. The problem 4×27 then

Instructional Sequence and Assessment Chart

Grade Level	Problem Type	Performance Indicator		
1a	Count by 10s to 100 Count by 2s to 20 Count by 5s to 60			
2a	Count by 9s to 90			
2b	One digit times one digit	$2 \times 7 =$ $9 \times 3 =$ $5 \times 6 =$		
2c	Missing factor multiplication; both factors are one-digit numbers	$2 \times \square = 8$ $5 \times \square = 10$ $9 \times \square = 36$		
2d	Count by 4s to 40 Count by 25s to 100 Count by 7s to 70 Count by 3s to 30			
3a	Count by 8s to 80 Count by 6s to 60			
3b	One-digit factor times two-digit factor; no carrying	43 × 2	31 × 5	32 × 4
3c	One-digit factor times two-digit factor; carrying	35 × 5	43 × 9	17 × 2
3d	One-digit factor times two- or three-digit factor; problem written horizontally	$5 \times 35 =$ $9 \times 34 =$ $7 \times 56 =$		
4a	One-digit factor times three-digit factor	758 × 2	364 × 5	534 × 9
4b	One-digit factor times three-digit factor; zero in tens column	405 × 3	302 × 5	105 × 9
4c	One-digit factor times three-digit factor; horizontal alignment	$352 \times 9 =$ $7 \times 342 =$ $235 \times 5 =$		
4d	Two-digit factor times two-digit factor	37 × 25	26 × 52	34 × 25
4e	Two-digit factor times three-digit factor	324 × 29	343 × 95	423 × 29
5a	Three-digit factor times three-digit factor	284 × 346	242 × 195	624 × 283
5b	Three-digit factor times three-digit factor; zero in tens column of multiplier	382 × 506	320 × 402	523 × 703

becomes $4 \times (20 + 7)$, which equals $(4 \times 20) + (4 \times 7)$. It is also important for later work with fractions, equations, and algebra.

SKILL HIERARCHY

Our discussion of multiplication is divided into two stages. The first stage involves presenting strategies designed to establish a conceptual understanding of the process of multiplication. These strategies are usually taught to students in second grade. The second stage deals with teaching students to work multi-digit problems in which students rely on mental computation rather than on representations of concrete objects. This stage typically begins during third grade and continues into the upper grades.

During the beginning stage, a procedure for solving simple multiplication problems with concrete or semi-concrete objects to represent the members in each group is presented. For example, when determining the total in an array such as the one below,

```
O  O  O  O
O  O  O  O
O  O  O  O
```

students are shown that they can count by 3, four times, and end with 12. When solving the problem, 3×4, the students are taught to hold up four fingers for the second factor and then skip count by 3s for each of the four extended fingers: 3, 6, 9, 12. (The teaching procedures for skip counting are discussed in Chapter 4.) Students should have mastered at least three skip counting series before multiplication is introduced.

Missing factor problems, in which one factor and the product are given and a missing factor must be computed (e.g., $4 \times \square = 12$), are also presented during this stage. In the missing factor strategy, students do not know the number of fingers to extend, since the second factor is represented by a box or unknown. For these problems, students hold up a fist and extend a finger every time they skip count, stopping at the product. In $3 \times \square = 15$ students extend a fist, count 3 (extending one finger), count 6 (extending a second finger), count 9 (extending a third finger), count 12 (extending a fourth finger), and count 15 (extending a fifth finger). They do not count beyond 15 because they must end with 15 on both sides of the equal sign. Since they extended five fingers, the unknown factor is 5: $3 \times \boxed{5} = 15$. The teacher then summarizes by asking how many 3s are in 15. Teachers working with intermediate grade remedial students who have some knowledge of

multiplication might consider beginning instruction immediately with basic fact exercises and not presenting finger strategies. Teaching finger strategies for multiplication to older remedial students could result in an overreliance on using fingers rather than memorizing facts.

In the second stage, when multi-digit numbers are multiplied, students work problems without holding up fingers for the second factor and without using skip counting. Since students do not skip count, a new preskill is implied, i.e., knowledge of basic multiplication facts. The 100 possible combinations of single-digit factors are referred to as basic multiplication facts. Exercises to facilitate memorization of basic facts can begin a month or so after students have learned to use the count-by strategy to work multiplication problems. (See Chapter 6 for a discussion of teaching basic facts.) Besides basic multiplication facts, renaming and advanced addition facts (adding a single digit to a multi-digit addend) are also preskills. Knowledge of advanced facts such as $72 + 4$ is required in many problems with multi-digit factors. For example, in working 95×8, students first multiply 5 times 8 and then must add the 4 from the 40 to 72, the product of 9×8:

$$
\begin{array}{r}
4 \\
95 \\
\times\ 8 \\
\hline
760
\end{array}
$$

The need for teaching advanced facts can be avoided by presenting a low-stress multiplication algorithm. In the low-stress multiplication algorithm, students write out the complete answer every time they multiply. This strategy requires no carrying:

$$
\begin{array}{r}
32 \\
\times\ 24 \\
\hline
8 \\
120 \\
40 \\
600 \\
\hline
768
\end{array}
$$

Then they add the products, a process that seldom involves advanced facts. The major disadvantage of the low-stress algorithm, which is discussed at the end of this chapter, is its limited acceptance in U.S. schools.

Another preskill for multi-digit operations is expanded notation. When students multiply 34×7, they should understand that they are multiplying 4×7 and 30×7, which assumes the expanded notation skill of translating 34 into 30 and 4 (see Figure 9.1).

FIGURE 9.1   Using Expanded Notation to Explain Multi-Digit Multiplication

$$\begin{array}{ccc} 27 & 20 & 7 \\ \times 4 & \times 4 & \times 4 \\ \hline & 80 & 28 \end{array} = 108$$

$$20 \times 4 \quad + \quad 7 \times 4$$
$$80 \quad + \quad 28 \quad = 108$$

There are two basic types of multi-digit problems. The first type involves a single-digit factor and a multi-digit factor. This type includes problems that do not require renaming and problems that do require renaming. In the easier group, the first product is less than 10 and renaming is not required; for example, 32 × 3 does not require renaming in the first product (2 × 3 = 6). Problems in the harder group, such as 32 × 7, require renaming; in 2 × 7 = 14 the 10 from 14 is carried. The second major type of problem involves multiplying two multi-digit numbers (e.g., 32 × 13, 189 × 43, or 342 × 179). A more detailed specification of the various multiplication problem types appears in the Instructional Sequence and Assessment Chart.

INTRODUCING THE CONCEPT

The meaning of multiplication can be conveyed in various ways. Underhill (1981) lists five: sets, arrays, linear models, cross products, and addition. Jerman and Beardslee (1978) suggest that the most common ways of introducing the concept are equivalent sets and cross products. Multiplication as cross products is illustrated for 2 × 3 in Figure 9.2. Note that the display symbolized by 2 × 3 contains six pairs of objects as the product and the display symbolized by 3 × 5 contains 15 pairs of objects as the product. The product, formed by all possible pairings of two sets, is also called the Cartesian product. Multiplication as equivalent sets is illustrated for 2 × 3 as

BEGINNING MULTIPLICATION

Single-Digit Multiplication

Multiplication with single-digit factors can be introduced when students have mastered three count-by

FIGURE 9.2   Multiplication as Cross Products

		3		
	a	b	c
2	•	•a	•b	•c
	△	△a	△b	△c

and for 3 × 5 as

			5			
		a	b	c	d	e
	□	□a	□b	□c	□d	□e
3	○	○a	○b	○c	○d	○e
	△	△a	△b	△c	△d	△e

series (e.g., 2s, 5s, 9s) and are able to read and write all numerals between 1 and 99. Single-digit multiplication is typically introduced in mid-second grade. The format for teaching it is divided into five parts (see Format 9.1). Since an equivalent-sets representation is easier for students to understand than a Cartesian product, we introduce the multiplication concept in Part A with illustrations of equivalent sets. The students are shown a group of equivalent sets and told they can figure the total a "fast way" when each set has the same number. After verifying that each set has the same number, the teacher demonstrates how to write the problem as a multiplication problem. Next, the teacher demonstrates how to use skip counting to determine the total. In the final step of Part A, students count the members of the sets one at a time to verify that the answer derived through multiplication is correct. Part A should be included only the first two or three days the format is presented.

In Part B, students learn to translate a multiplication statement into terms that indicate how the problem is to be solved. For example, in initial problems, the multiplication sign (×) is read as "count by." Students are taught to read the multiplication statement $5 \times 2 =$ as "count by 5, two times." By reading the statement this way, students know exactly what to do to derive an answer. "Count by 5, two times" tells them to extend 2 fingers for the number of times they skip count and then to skip count by 5s. After several weeks, students learn to read problems in the conventional manner (e.g., 4×3, is read as "4 times 3").

When reading multiplication problems in Part B, students begin with the multiplication sign, saying "count by" and then say the first number; 5×3 is read "count by 5, three times." Since translating multiplication problems differs from reading addition or subtraction problems, in which students read in a strict left to right order, multiplication problems require a slightly different signal. The teacher should point under both the numeral and the times sign when having students translate problems. With low-performing students, the teacher may even need to point under the sign first, then point to the first number to emphasize that the multiplication sign is read before the numeral.

In Part C, the teacher guides students in solving several multiplication examples in a structured board presentation. First, students read and translate a problem. They hold up the appropriate number of fingers. Then the teacher models skip counting while touching each extended finger. Next the students skip count each time they touch an extended finger. Finally, the students work three new problems without any teacher modeling.

Part D is the structured worksheet presentation. The teacher has the students extend the appropriate number of fingers, identify the skip counting number, and then work the problem. Part E is the less-structured worksheet part of the format, where students work a set of problems on their own with the teacher carefully monitoring their performance. After students demonstrate accuracy during group instruction, they are given five to ten problems daily in independent worksheet exercises.

When having the students count and touch their fingers in step 2, Part C, the teacher must be sure that students coordinate saying the numbers with touching their extended fingers. Low-performing students may say the first number in the skip counting series before touching the first extended finger; in 2×5, for example, students may say "two" and then, when they touch their finger, count 4, continuing to count 6, 8, 10, 12. The correction for this error is to model, then lead by actually guiding the student's hand to coordinate touching and counting, and then test by watching while the student touches and counts alone. The teacher should then present a series of examples for the students to practice only the touching and counting and not the entire sequence of steps in Part C. Instead of presenting all of the steps, the teacher would tell the student the problem and how many fingers to hold up and then have the student touch and count. For example, the teacher would present a series of examples using this wording: "You're going to count by 5, three times. Hold up three fingers. Good. Now count by 5. Remember to touch each finger as you count by 5." With this correction, the teacher is providing intensive practice on an important component skill prior to reintroducing the strategy.

There are two example selection guidelines for this format. First, example selection should be coordinated with count-by instruction. The first digit in the multiplication problem should be taken from a skip counting series the students have previously mastered. For example, a problem such as 6×7 would not be included until students have mastered counting by 6s. As a general rule, problems with a specific number as the first digit should be included in multiplication tasks after students have reviewed that count-by series for about two weeks. Second, there should be a mix of problems. As a general rule, no more than two or three problems in a row should have the same numeral as the multiplicand or multiplier. Below is an example of an acceptable set of examples:

5×2	2×2
2×4	5×4
9×3	9×1
9×5	5×3

The mix of problems helps to ensure that students develop the habit of carefully attending to both factors.

Missing Factor Multiplication

Missing factor multiplication, or algebra multiplication, is not only a useful skill in its own right, but is also a critical preskill for the simple division strategies, which are discussed in the next chapter. In order to solve a missing factor multiplication problem, students must determine the number of times they count by a certain number. For example, in the problem $5 \times \square = 15$, students figure out how many times they have to count by 5 to get to 15. Students extend a finger every time they skip count; they extend one finger when they say 5, a second when they say 10, and a third when they say 15. The three extended fingers represent the answer.

Missing factor multiplication problems can be introduced after students have demonstrated mastery in solving regular multiplication problems. A time frame of at least three to four weeks between the introduction of regular multiplication and problems with missing factors is recommended to enable students to develop this mastery.

The format appears in Format 9.2. In Part A, students learn to translate the problem type; $5 \times \square = 20$ is translated as "Count by 5 how many times to end with 20?" Next the strategy is modeled. The teacher holds up a closed fist to indicate that the number of times to count is unknown and then extends a finger every time she skip counts. Then the teacher tests the students by guiding them through several examples. In Part B, the structured worksheet, students apply the strategy as the teacher guides them to hold up a fist, to identify the skip counting number and the product, and to extend a finger each time they count. Part C is the less-structured worksheet. In that part, students are taught to discriminate between regular problems and algebra problems (e.g., $2 \times 8 = \square$, $2 \times \square = 8$).

Example selection guidelines are basically the same as for regular multiplication. The first factor in the problem should represent a count-by series the students have mastered. Different numbers should appear as the first factor. Independent practice worksheets should include an equal mix of regular multiplication and multiplication problems with missing factors.

Diagnosis and Remediation

Four errors—two component skill and two strategy—account for the majority of errors in beginning multiplication. The first type of error results from skip counting incorrectly. Students may either forget a number or switch from one series to another while counting. Although this count-by component skill error is usually obvious on worksheets, it can only be diagnosed accurately by asking students to work problems aloud. A worksheet illustrating this count-by component skill error appears below:

$$5 \times 4 = 20 \qquad 9 \times 3 = 27$$
$$10 \times 3 = 30 \qquad 10 \times 6 = 60$$
$$2 \times 7 = 14 \qquad 9 \times 5 = 47$$
$$9 \times 6 = 50 \qquad 5 \times 2 = 10$$

Note that of the eight problems on the worksheet, only two were missed. Both these missed problems had 9 as one factor and a number of 5 or more as the other factor. The errors indicate that the student may have had difficulty remembering the higher numbers in the count-by-9 series. To remedy the count-by skill deficit, the teacher provides practice on counting by 9s for several lessons. The student shouldn't be required to solve any multiplication problems involving counting by 9 until he has demonstrated that he can accurately count by 9s.

The second error pattern is one in which answers are consistently off by one count-by number. For example, in regular multiplication problems a student might answer a set of problems like this: $9 \times 6 = 63$, $7 \times 6 = 49$, $5 \times 6 = 35$. Quite often the cause of this error is that the student says the number for the first group and then begins counting as opposed to touching and counting simultaneously. For example, a student working 4×3 may say the number 4 before touching his fingers and then say 8, 12, and 16 as he touches the three raised fingers.

To remedy this type of error, the teacher would present Part C, the structured board part of the multiplication format, correcting by modeling and leading. The exercise would be continued until the students are able to respond correctly to four consecutive problems. Several days of practice on this exercise should be provided before students are given problems to work independently again.

The third type of error occurs when students confuse the multiplication and addition operations. The remediation procedure involves presenting the less-structured format for regular multiplication, which includes a mix of multiplication and addition problems. For remediation purposes, the teacher could instruct students to circle the sign in the problems before working them.

The fourth type of error common to single-digit multiplication occurs when students confuse regular and missing factor multiplication, writing $5 \times \boxed{50} = 10$ or $2 \times \boxed{8} = 4$. The remediation procedure

FIGURE 9.3 Diagnosis and Remediation of Single-Digit Multiplication Errors

Error Patterns	Diagnosis	Remediation Procedures	Remediation Examples
a. $9 \times 6 = 51$ $8 \times 4 = 32$ $6 \times 5 = 30$ $9 \times 3 = 26$	Component skill: Student doesn't know count-by-9 series.	Part B—Count-by Preskill Format 4.5.	Practice on counting by 9s.
b. $9 \times 6 = 63$ $8 \times 4 = 40$ $6 \times 5 = 36$	Component skill: Student not coordinating touching and counting.	Part C—Format 9.1 for single-digit multiplication.	Regular multiplication problems.
c. $9 \times 6 = 15$ $8 + 4 = 12$ $6 \times 5 = 11$	Strategy: Student is confusing addition with multiplication; not attending to the sign in the problems.	Less-structured worksheet of regular multiplication format, Format 9.1. Instructions to circle the sign before working the problem.	Mix of addition and multiplication problems.
d. $2 \times \boxed{16} = 8$ $6 \times 5 = \boxed{30}$ $9 \times 6 = \boxed{54}$ $4 \times \boxed{32} = 8$	Strategy: Student is confusing regular multiplication and missing factor multiplication.	Less-structured worksheet of format for problems with missing factors, Format 9.2.	Mix of regular multiplication problems and problems with missing factor.

involves reviewing the less-structured part of the missing-factor multiplication format, which contains a mixture of regular and algebra multiplication problems. The teacher should present the less-structured worksheet presentation with about 10 problems, observing and correcting errors. This remediation is continued daily until students correctly answer 9 of 10 problems without teacher assistance for several days in a row. The diagnosis and remediation information is summarized in Figure 9.3.

MULTI-DIGIT MULTIPLICATION

There are two algorithms presented in most commercial programs to solve problems with a multi-digit factor. One algorithm is commonly referred to as the long form or low-stress algorithm. The other algorithm is referred to as the short form. Both forms are illustrated in Figure 9.4.

Both algorithms are based on the distributive property of multiplication, which states that the product of a multiplier and a multiplicand will be the same as the sum of a series of products from multiplying individual number pairs. For example, $3 \times 24 = (3 \times 20) + (3 \times 4)$.

The advantages of the long-form algorithm are that it does not alternate between multiplication and addition and seldom requires renaming. Moreover, it clearly shows the distributive property of multiplication. Its disadvantage, however, is that in problems involving multi-digit factors, many numerals must be written as partial products:

$$
\begin{array}{r}
245 \\
\times\,37 \\
\hline
35 \\
280 \\
1400 \\
150 \\
1200 \\
6000 \\
\hline
9065
\end{array}
$$

The advantage of the short-form algorithm lies in its relative efficiency in solving problems with multi-digit factors and its widespread usage. Its disadvantage lies with the difficulty a student may have in understanding the process when he alternates between addition and multiplication and with the inclusion of complex addition facts.

In this section we discuss in detail the procedures for teaching the short-form algorithm, primarily because it is the one used in most classrooms. The

FIGURE 9.4 Two Algorithms for Multi-Digit Multiplication

Long Form	Short Form
$\begin{array}{r} 232 \\ \times\,7 \\ \hline 14 \\ 210 \\ 1400 \\ \hline 1624 \end{array}$	$\begin{array}{r} 21 \\ 232 \\ \times\,7 \\ \hline 1624 \end{array}$

section on the short-form algorithm is divided into two parts. The first addresses problems in which one of the factors is a single digit number and the other factor a multi-digit number. The second part deals with problems in which each factor is a multi-digit number.

Single-Digit Factor and Multi-Digit Factor

Multiplication problems in which a single-digit factor and multi-digit factor are multiplied usually are introduced during mid-third grade. This group of problems includes problems 3b through 4c on the Instructional Sequence and Assessment Chart.

PRESKILLS Three preskills necessary to work these problems are (1) multiplication facts, (2) place value skills, including expanded notation and placing a comma in the proper position when writing an answer in the thousands, and (3) complex addition facts in which a single digit number is added to a two-digit number.

Basic multiplication facts include all of the possible combinations of single-digit factors. Memorizing basic facts is a very demanding and lengthy process. It is not realistic to imagine that most students will have memorized all basic multiplication facts by mid-third grade. Therefore, initially, problems should be limited so that they include only basic facts the teacher is sure students have memorized. As students learn more basic facts, these should be integrated into multiplication problems.

When introducing multiplication facts to students, teachers may find multiplication maps useful (see Table 9.1). Each map is designed to facilitate learning multiplication facts for a particular series. Students who are able to visualize the maps in their minds initially learn and remember facts more easily.

Each map has a unique pattern. For 9s, the second digit decreases by 1, while the first digit increases by 1. For 5s, the last digit of the numbers in the first column is 5; the last digit of the numbers in the second column is zero. For 4s, the second digits repeat after 20 (4, 8, 2, 6, 0). The pattern for 3s shows that all values below the top row have a second digit 1 less than the digit above it. For 7s, the second digit of each number is 1 more than the digit above it. It is helpful to let students discover the patterns after introducing a particular map. If *they* find it, they will remember it longer.

Teachers need to provide lots of practice with the number map in addition to practicing the count-bys orally. Practice activities may require students to write in missing digits, write missing numbers, or complete blank maps.

The place value skill of expanded notation is needed if the student is to understand the renaming procedure in the short-form algorithm. Procedures for teaching place value concepts appear in Chapter 5.

The second place value skill, placing a comma, seems trivial but needs to be taught. After completing problems with larger numbers, students are expected to place a comma in the answer. The procedure is simple. The teacher presents the following rule: The comma is written between the hundreds and the thousands. Then the teacher models and tests application of the rule. The teacher writes a series of three-, four-, and five-digit numbers on the board, then demonstrates how to find where to place the comma. Starting at the ones column, the teacher points to each numeral, saying "ones, tens, hundreds, thousands," and then places the comma between the hundreds and the thousands columns. After modeling several examples, the teacher tests the students.

Complex addition facts involve adding a single digit number to a two digit number mentally (e.g., $35 + 7$, $27 + 3$, $42 + 5$). Complex addition facts were discussed earlier in the addition chapter as a preskill for adding a series of multi-digit numbers. This type of addition fact is found in the short-form multiplication algorithm, when the student adds the carried units to the product of a column. For example, in the problem 35×9, the student first multiplies 9×5 and gets 45. A 4 is carried to the tens column and a 5 written under the ones column:

$$
\begin{array}{r}
4 \\
35 \\
\times 9 \\
\hline
5
\end{array}
$$

The student then multiplies 9×3 for a product of 27. Next, the student must mentally add the advanced addition fact, $4 + 27$:

$$
\begin{array}{r}
4 \\
35 \\
\times 9 \\
\hline
315
\end{array}
$$

There are easier and more difficult types of complex addition facts. In the easier type, the sum has the same number of tens as the original two-digit addend: $\underline{6}4 + 3 = \underline{6}7$, $\underline{4}3 + 5 = \underline{4}8$, $\underline{7}5 + 4 = \underline{7}9$. In the more difficult type, the sum has a tens number one higher than the original two-digit addend: $\underline{3}6 + 7 = \underline{4}3$, $\underline{5}8 + 8 = \underline{6}6$, $\underline{4}8 + 4 = \underline{5}2$, $\underline{4}9 + 9 = \underline{5}8$.

Instruction on complex addition facts would begin in early second grade. First, students are taught to add a single-digit number to a teen num-

Table 9.1   Multiplication Maps for 9s, 5s, 3s, 7s, and 4s

9s

9	9	9	9	9
18		__8	1__	
27	27	__7	2__	
36		__6	3__	
45	45	__5	4__	
54		__4	5__	
63	63	__3	6__	
72		__2	7__	
81	81	__1	8__	
90		__0	9__	90

5s

5 10	5	__ 1__	5 __0	5
15 20	15	1__ 2__	__5 __0	
25 30	25	2__ 3__	__5 __0	30
35 40	35	3__ 4__	__5 __0	
45 50	45	4__ 5__	__5 __0	45

3s

3 6 9	__ __ __	3 6 9	3
12 15 18	1__ 1__ 1__	__2 __5 __8	
21 24 27	2__ 2__ 2__	__1 __4 __7	24
30	3__	__0	

7s

7 14 21	__ __ __	7 14 21	7
28 35 42	2__ 3__ 4__	__8 __5 __2	
49 56 63	4__ 5__ 6__	__9 __6 __3	56
70	7__	__0	

4s

4 8 12 16 20	__ __ 1__ 1__ 2__	4 8 __2 __6 __0
24 28 32 36 40	2__ 2__ 3__ 3__ 4__	__4 __8 __2 __6 __0

ber: 14 + 3, 16 + 2, then 17 + 6, 15 + 8, etc. After several months of practice with teen numbers, students are introduced to advanced facts with tens numbers, first with easier facts (e.g., 24 + 3, 38 + 2), then with more difficult facts (e.g., 49 + 6, 45 + 8). Practice would be continued for many months to develop fluency. Procedures for teaching both the easier and more difficult types of complex addition facts appear in Chapter 7.

STRATEGY Column multiplication is introduced with simple problems involving no renaming. The product of the numbers in the ones column should be less than 10:

$$\begin{array}{cccc} 34 & 43 & 31 & 32 \\ \times 2 & \times 2 & \times 5 & \times 4 \end{array}$$

When presenting this type of problem, the teacher points out that the student first multiplies the ones and then the tens. A format is not included, since it would be quite similar to the one that involves renaming (see Format 9.3).

Problems with carrying are introduced several days after noncarrying problems have been presented. In Part A of the format (Format 9.3), the structured board presentation, the students break the problem into two parts. The two parts for 5 × 47 are 5 × 7 and 5 × 4 tens. After multiplying in the ones column, the teacher models how to carry, multiply the second part of the problem, add the carried number, and write the answer. Parts B and C provide structured and less-structured worksheet practice.

Note in the format the balance between explaining to students the rationale for the procedure and providing clear guidance in the mechanics of working the problem. Also note the use of a place value grid. The purpose of the grid is to initially prompt the students to place numerals from the product in the proper column. Proper placement of numerals in the product, though not a critical component of these problem types, is critical in problems with two multi-digit factors. The place value grid would appear on students' worksheets for about a week and then be dropped. The day the grid is dropped, the teacher would lead the students through several problems, pointing out the need to write numerals in the proper position. The teacher would also examine students' worksheets carefully for column alignment errors.

Multi-digit problems written horizontally are introduced after students can correctly work vertically aligned problems. The teacher presents a strategy in which the students rewrite the problem vertically, writing the one-digit factor under the multi-digit factor. In later grades, the teacher presents a strategy in which students multiply horizontally, writing the product and carrying:

$$\overset{12}{5 \times 324} = \mathbf{1620}$$

This strategy would be taught prior to introducing fraction multiplication and division problems with multi-digit divisors, both of which involve horizontal multiplication:

$$\frac{5}{4} \times 324 \qquad 324\overline{)1620}^{\,5}$$

Problems with a one-digit factor and a three-digit factor (e.g., 243 × 5 and 342 × 9) are introduced in late third grade. The format for presenting problems of this type is essentially the same as the format for introducing problems with a two-digit factor. The same basic explanation for carrying from the ones to the tens column would be used in presenting carrying from the tens to the hundreds column. In 543 × 5 students multiply the four tens and add the carried ten. Then the teacher explains that they can't have 21 tens in the tens column, so they write a 2 over the hundreds column to show 20 tens and 1 ten is written under the tens column. Note that, at this point, the teacher need not require the students to say that 20 tens equal 200 but simply to write the 2 in the hundreds column.

A special problem type includes a zero in the tens column of the three-digit factor (e.g., 403 × 5 and 306 × 2). Students may have trouble adding the carried ten to zero. This type of problem is introduced a week after problems with three-digit factors are introduced. Several problems of this subgroup should be presented daily for about two weeks. The first several days the teacher models a few problems, then closely supervises students as they work the problems.

EXAMPLE SELECTION   Two rules govern example selection. First, the basic facts included in problems should be those that the student has already mastered. Second, less-structured, supervised practice, and independent worksheets should include a mixture of problems. About 45% of the worksheet should contain problems of the most currently introduced type, and about 45% should be previously introduced multiplication problems. About 10% of the worksheet should contain addition problems to keep students in the habit of examining the sign in a problem carefully before working it.

SELF-CHECKING   In mid-fourth grade, or whenever students become proficient in multiplying by a one-digit factor and dividing by a one-digit divisor, students should be taught to check their answers. A checking procedure for multiplication is to divide the answer by the one-digit factor. If the quotient equals the other factor, the answer is correct. The teacher introduces checking on a worksheet exercise. After her students complete the first multiplication problem (e.g., 7 × 35), the teacher says, "Here's how to check your work to make sure you have the right answer. We multiplied by 7, so we divide 7 into the answer. If you end with 35, your answer is correct. What's the answer to the multiplication problem? Divide 7 into 245. . . . Write the problem and work it. . . . Is the answer the same as the top number in the multiplication problem? . . . So the answer for the multiplication problem must be correct."

Determining whether students check their work in multiplication is easier than in addition because checking requires writing a division problem. An exercise to encourage checking is to give students already worked problems, half of which have incorrect answers. The teacher would instruct the students to check the answers, and find the mistakes.

Two Multi-Digit Factors

Problems with two multi-digit factors are usually introduced during mid-fourth grade and include four problem types (types 4d, 4e, 5a, and 5b from the Instructional Sequence and Assessment Chart). The simplest problems involve two two-digit factors. Next in difficulty are problems with a two-digit factor and a three-digit factor. This type is introduced during late fourth grade. The last type, which is presented during fifth grade, includes two three-digit factors.

The preskills for introducing problems with two multi-digit factors include the preskills for problems with a one-digit and multi-digit factor (i.e., basic multiplication facts, place value skills, complex addition facts) and a new preskill, column addition with renaming, which is required when the student must add the partial products.

Format 9.4 shows how to present problem type 4d, in which both factors are two-digit numbers. We recommend using a place value grid the first several weeks this problem type appears. Examples of problems worked in a grid appear in Figure 9.5. The grids should already be predrawn on students' worksheets. Although drawing the grids provides extra work for the teacher, it saves instructional time that would be used to teach students how to draw them properly. The important part of the task for the student is filling in the numbers in the appropriate columns.

In Part A, the teacher simply presents the numbers in the order in which they are multiplied. For example, in the problem:

$$\begin{array}{r} 52 \\ \times\ 37 \end{array}$$

"We multiply 7 × 2, then 7 × 5, then 3 × 2, then 3 × 5." This part focuses simply on mechanics. Part B is a structured board presentation in which the teacher models the steps in solving a problem. Note in steps 3 and 5 that the teacher summarizes what has been done to that point: "First we multiplied 52 × 7, now we'll multiply 52 by 3 tens." Step 3 also points out that when multiplying by the tens number, a zero must first be placed in the ones column. This step is critical.

$$\begin{array}{r} 25 \\ \times\ 37 \\ \hline \mathit{175} \\ \underline{\hspace{1em}0\hspace{0.3em}} \end{array}$$

FIGURE 9.5 Using a Place-Value Grid in Multi-Digit Multiplication

Part C is a structured worksheet presentation. Step 4 of Part C, during which the teacher leads students in multiplying by the tens number, is the step in which students are most likely to have difficulty. Note the wording is very specific regarding where numerals are placed. Part D is a less-structured worksheet presentation. It includes problems with a two-digit factor and problems with a one-digit factor as the bottom factor, as well as some addition problems with a one-digit factor.

Diagnosis and Remediation

The specific cause of errors will sometimes be obvious, as in problem a, and sometimes not obvious, as in problem b. In problem a, we can readily assume the student made a fact error, multiplying 7 × 6 and writing 58.

$$\text{a.}\quad \begin{array}{r} 5 \\ 36 \\ \times\ 7 \\ \hline \mathit{268} \end{array} \qquad \text{b.}\quad \begin{array}{r} 4 \\ 36 \\ \times\ 7 \\ \hline \mathit{242} \end{array}$$

In problem b, we cannot be sure of the error. The student may have multiplied wrong or added wrong. If the cause of the error is not clear, the teacher should have the students rework the problem in front of her so that she can ascertain the specific cause.

FACT ERRORS The remediation procedure for basic fact errors depends on the number of fact errors made by the student. If a student makes a few fact errors, the teacher simply records the facts the student missed and incorporates them into practice exercises for the next several lessons. If a student makes fact errors on more than 10% of the problems, the teacher should test the student individually to determine what action to take. The teacher would test the student verbally on the facts missed (e.g., What is 8 × 7? 9 × 4? 8 × 6?). If the student responds correctly to the missed facts, the teacher should tentatively consider the cause of errors to be the student's hurrying through the problems and not exercising enough care. The remediation procedure would involve increasing motivation to perform accurately. If the student's performance indicates he does not know many basic facts, the teacher should devote more time to basic facts and, if possible, limit problems to include only basic facts the student knows or give students alternative strategies for figuring out facts (e.g., a fact table).

COMPONENT SKILL ERRORS Many of the component skill errors in column multiplication have to do with addition. Renaming errors may involve either (1) carrying the wrong number or carrying a number to the wrong column:

$$\begin{array}{cc} \overset{2}{58} & \overset{1}{312} \\ \underline{\times 9} & \underline{\times 7} \\ 477 & 2274 \end{array}$$

or (2) forgetting to add the carried number:

$$\begin{array}{cc} \overset{7}{58} & \overset{1}{82} \\ \underline{\times 9} & \underline{\times 7} \\ 452 & 564 \end{array}$$

If students make frequent errors (more than 10%) in which they carry the ones number to the tens column, the error might be caused by the students not understanding the place value concept. The teacher would test the students on the tasks in the writing tens number format (see Format 5.8) and if necessary, teach these place value skills in the context of writing numbers. When the students consistently respond correctly to place value tasks, such as how many tens in 57, the teacher would present the multiplication format, beginning with the structured worksheet exercise.

If students miss many problems because they fail to add the carried number, the teacher would present the structured worksheet part of the format again and then progress to the less-structured worksheet exercise, emphasizing the need to carry the added tens.

Addition mistakes account for a sizable proportion of student errors. Below are several examples of addition errors:

$$\begin{array}{cc} \overset{5}{88} & \overset{3}{34} \\ \text{a.}\ \underline{\times 7} & \text{b.}\ \underline{\times 9} \\ 626 & 296 \end{array}$$

$$\begin{array}{c} \overset{5}{28} \\ \text{c.}\ \underline{\times 7} \\ 186 \end{array}$$

Although, as mentioned earlier, we cannot be absolutely sure that the students' errors resulted from addition mistakes, the probability is high that they did. For example, in problem a, the student added 5 to 56 and ended incorrectly with a sum of 62. If students make frequent addition errors, the teacher would place extra emphasis on teaching complex addition facts, i.e., facts in which the first addend is

a two-digit number and the second addend a one-digit number. Teachers working with older students who have little knowledge of basic addition facts should permit students to use their fingers in computing complex addition facts; however, they should insist on accuracy. Practice should be provided on worksheets that include just complex addition facts. Worksheets of this type would be provided daily until students performed at 95% accuracy for several days.

Students often have difficulty with problems that have a zero in the tens column:

$$\begin{array}{c} 306 \\ \underline{\times 7} \end{array}$$

Students may multiply the carried number:

$$\begin{array}{c} \overset{24}{306} \\ \underline{\times 7} \\ 2382 \end{array}$$

or treat the zero as if it were a 1:

$$\begin{array}{c} \overset{14}{306} \\ \underline{\times 7} \\ 2212 \end{array}$$

The remediation procedure for errors of this type begins with testing and, if necessary, teaching times-zero facts: "When you multiply by zero you end up with zero. What is 5×0? 8×0? 3×0?" The teacher would then give students a worksheet containing 10–20 problems. Half of the problems would contain a zero in the tens column, a fourth of the problems would include a 1 in the tens column, and another fourth of the problems would have another numeral in the tens column. The teacher would lead the students through several problems using a structured worksheet presentation, then present a less-structured worksheet exercise with several examples, and finally have the students work the problems without assistance.

Errors unique to problems with two multi-digit factors include not writing a zero in the ones column when multiplying by tens:

$$\begin{array}{c} 46 \\ \underline{\times 24} \\ 184 \\ \underline{92} \end{array}$$

and inappropriately recording the partial products so that numbers are added in the wrong columns:

$$
\begin{array}{r}
425 \\
\times\ 37 \\
\hline
2975 \\
12750 \\
\hline
42455
\end{array}
$$

Both errors can be identified by closely examining worksheet errors.

To remedy the first error, caused by forgetting the zero, the teacher would lead students through about three multiplication problems using Part D of Format 9.4, the less-structured worksheet of the format for a two-digit factor times a two-digit factor. In Part D, the teacher prompts students to write a zero when multiplying by tens but does not guide them on every step. The students would complete the rest of the worksheet independently. The worksheet should contain 4–5 multi-digit problems with a one-digit factor mixed and about 10–15 multiplication problems with two-digit factors. Using some problems with single-digit factors provides better practice than having students work only problems that require inserting a zero. Students must remember and apply the rule about zeroes correctly, rather than writing a zero by every problem. The practice exercise is done daily until students respond correctly to 9 of 10 multiplication problems for several consecutive lessons.

To remedy errors caused by students' inadvertently writing numbers in the wrong columns, the teacher should point out the errors to the students and remind them to carefully align the columns. Often, just providing feedback on why the students missed the problems is enough to encourage students to be more careful. However, if students continue to make column alignment errors, the teacher should reintroduce the use of the place value grid. The teacher should lead students through working the first couple of problems using Part C in Format 9.4, the structured worksheet, and have the students complete the remaining problems independently. The teacher should probably continue having students use the grid for several days, then have students work problems without the grid.

Students may also answer problems incorrectly because of an error in adding the partial products. In problem a below, the student failed to carry. In problem b, the student made a basic fact error:

$$
\begin{array}{cc}
\text{a.} & \text{b.} \\
\begin{array}{r}
688 \\
\times\ 94 \\
\hline
2752 \\
61920 \\
\hline
63672
\end{array}
&
\begin{array}{r}
688 \\
\times\ 94 \\
\hline
2752 \\
61920 \\
\hline
64572
\end{array}
\end{array}
$$

Carrying errors often result from sloppiness. Teachers should insist that students write neatly. The remediation for carrying errors might involve giving the students a worksheet with about 10 problems. In each problem, the multiplication would be done already. The students' tasks would be to add the partial products. After the students can perform accurately on this worksheet, the teacher would supervise students as they worked entire problems on their own.

STRATEGY ERRORS Strategy errors indicate that the student simply has not learned the steps in the algorithm. Below are examples of student performance that indicate a strategy deficit:

$$
\begin{array}{cc}
\begin{array}{r}
428 \\
\times\ 3 \\
\hline
12624
\end{array}
&
\begin{array}{r}
32 \\
\times\ 57 \\
\hline
160224
\end{array}
\end{array}
$$

The remediation for such errors involves presenting the entire format for the particular problem type, beginning with the structured board presentation. The diagnosis and remediation information is summarized in Figure 9.6.

COMMERCIAL PROGRAMS

Multiplication: Multiplying by Two or More Digits

INSTRUCTIONAL STRATEGIES Often when teaching multi-digit multiplication, examples are given with arrows to display the order in which digits are to be multiplied. However, the actual strategy is not clearly defined in the teacher directions, and often the teacher is told to simply work through repeated examples to model the strategy (see Figure 9.7).

Some basals use various multiplication algorithms to teach multiplication "shortcuts." Because the teacher directions often are vague, it is easy to see why the authors warn teachers that most students will have difficulty at first with this type of multiplication algorithm. (See Figure 9.8 for such an algorithm.)

Practice and Review

Many commercial programs do not include a sufficient number of examples in their initial presentations to enable students to develop mastery of complex multiplication. Also, they often fail to provide an adequate variety of problem types to allow students to practice when to apply various steps in the strategies.

FIGURE 9.6   Diagnosis and Remediation of Multi-Digit Multiplication Errors

Error Patterns	Diagnosis	Remediation Procedures
Two-Digit Factor + One-Digit Factor		
a. $\begin{array}{r} 34 \\ 156 \\ \times\ 7 \\ \hline 1090 \end{array}$	Fact error: Student makes an error in problems containing the factor 6 × 7.	Drill on fact 6 × 7.
b. $\begin{array}{r} 8 \\ 46 \\ \times\ 3 \\ \hline 201 \end{array}$ $\begin{array}{r} 32 \\ 156 \\ \times\ 7 \\ \hline 1074 \end{array}$	Component skill: Student carries the ones and writes the tens in the ones column.	Present place-value exercise for writing tens numbers (Format 5.8). Then begin with structured worksheet exercise for multiplication (Format 9.3).
c. $\begin{array}{r} 46 \\ \times\ 3 \\ \hline 128 \end{array}$ $\begin{array}{r} 156 \\ \times\ 7 \\ \hline 752 \end{array}$	Component skill: Student does not carry the tens.	Begin with structured worksheet exercise (Format 9.3).
d. $\begin{array}{r} 1 \\ 46 \\ \times\ 3 \\ \hline 148 \end{array}$ $\begin{array}{r} 34 \\ 156 \\ \times\ 7 \\ \hline 982 \end{array}$	Component skill: Student does not add the carried number correctly.	Teach complex addition facts. Present worksheets containing complex addition facts.
Problems Containing Zero		
a. $\begin{array}{r} 1 \\ 406 \\ \times\ 3 \\ \hline 1238 \end{array}$ $\begin{array}{r} 24 \\ 106 \\ \times\ 7 \\ \hline 982 \end{array}$	Component skill: Student multiplies the carried number.	Test and teach times-zero facts. Begin with structured worksheet exercise (Format 9.3).
b. $\begin{array}{r} 1 \\ 406 \\ \times\ 3 \\ \hline 1248 \end{array}$ $\begin{array}{r} 4 \\ 106 \\ \times\ 7 \\ \hline 712 \end{array}$	Fact error: Student multiplies the zero as if it were a 1.	Test and teach times zero facts.
c. $\begin{array}{r} 406 \\ \times\ 3 \\ \hline 1208 \end{array}$ $\begin{array}{r} 106 \\ \times\ 7 \\ \hline 702 \end{array}$	Component skill: Student does not carry tens.	Modify Format 9.3 to include single-digit times three-digit factor with zero in the tens column.
Two-Digit Factor x Two-Digit Factor		
a. $\begin{array}{r} 1 \\ 46 \\ \times 23 \\ \hline 138 \\ 92\ \\ \hline 230 \end{array}$ $\begin{array}{r} 4 \\ 56 \\ \times 17 \\ \hline 392 \\ 56\ \\ \hline 448 \end{array}$	Component skill: Student does not write zero in ones column when multiplying by tens.	Begin with less structured exercise (Format 9.4). Include mix of problems with two-digit factor and one-digit factor on bottom of problem.
b. $\begin{array}{r} 1 \\ 46 \\ \times 23 \\ \hline 138 \\ 920 \\ \hline 9338 \end{array}$ $\begin{array}{r} 4 \\ 56 \\ \times 17 \\ \hline 392 \\ 560 \\ \hline 5992 \end{array}$	Component skill: Addition error; student doesn't align numbers in columns appropriately.	Make worksheets including place-value grid. Begin with structured exercise (Format 9.4).
c. $\begin{array}{r} 96 \\ \times 78 \\ \hline 768 \\ 6720 \\ \hline 6488 \end{array}$	Component skill: Addition error; student doesn't carry when adding partial products.	Give worksheet focusing on adding partial products, then supervised practice on multiplication problems.

FIGURE 9.7 (*Source:* From *Addison-Wesley Mathematics* Grade 5, 2nd edition by Eicholz et al. Copyright © 1987 by Addison-Wesley Publishing Company. Reprinted by permission.)

Exercises 13–30 This skill was originally taught on pages 116–117. Direct students' attention to second box and review the idea that when multiplying by a 1-digit number we first multiply the ones, then the tens, then the hundreds. Work through the example, making sure students understand how to make appropriate trades, where to write the digits in the answer, and how to write the necessary zeros in the partial products.

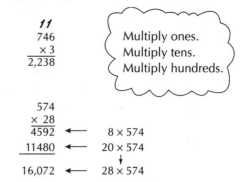

```
 11
746
× 3
2,238
```

Multiply ones.
Multiply tens.
Multiply hundreds.

```
  574
×  28
 4592   ←  8 × 574
11480   ←  20 × 574
              ↓
16,072  ←  28 × 574
```

FIGURE 9.8 (*Source:* From *Heath Mathematics* Teacher's Edition, Level 4 by Rucker et al., Copyright © 1987 by D.C. Heath & Company. Reprinted by permission of Houghton Mifflin Company. All rights reserved.)

STUDENT OBJECTIVE
To multiply multiples of 10 by 2-digit and 3-digit numbers.

TEACHING SUGGESTIONS

Multiply by multiples of 10. (Materials: ones, tens, hundreds) Write these examples on the chalkboard or overhead projector:

```
 12    12    12    12    12
×20   ×30   ×40   ×50   ×60
```

Ask the students to lay out a 12 by 20 rectangular array.

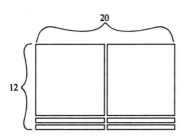

Most students will have difficulty at first with this type of multiplication algorithm, but they will be aware of how easy it is if they follow the steps:

1. Multiply 2 by 12:   24
2. Then multiply 24 by 10:   240

Explain to the students that there is a shortcut for finding such products as 20 × 12.

1. Describe the problem type each example below represents. List the problems in the order they are introduced. Write the grade level when each type is typically introduced.

   a. 758   b. $9 \times 4 = \square$ c. 3×26 d. 34
   $\underline{\times\ 2}$ $\underline{\times\ 2}$

   e. 37   f. 258   g.   37   h. $5 \times \square = 20$
   $\underline{\times\ 2}$ $\underline{\times\ 37}$ $\underline{\times\ 24}$

2. At the beginning of a unit, the teacher tested Jack. His performance on the performance indicators for problem types 3b–4b appears below. Specify the problem type with which instruction should begin. Explain your answer.

Jack

3b.   43   31   32   3c. $\overset{1}{3}\overset{2}{5}$ 43 17   3d. $5 \times 35 = \mathbf{175}$
     $\underline{\times\ 2}$ $\underline{\times\ 5}$ $\underline{\times\ 4}$ $\underline{\times\ 5}$ $\underline{\times\ 9}$ $\underline{\times\ 2}$ $9 \times 34 = \mathit{296}$
     86 *155* *128*   *165* *377* *34* $7 \times 56 = \mathit{392}$

4a.   758   364   534   4b.   403   302   105
     $\underline{\times\ 2}$ $\underline{\times\ 5}$ $\underline{\times\ 9}$ $\underline{\times\ 5}$ $\underline{\times\ 5}$ $\underline{\times\ 9}$
    1516 *1820* *4806*   *2105* *1600* *1305*

3. Below are 10 problems that appeared on the worksheet to be done independently by the students in Mrs. Ash's math group. Next to each student's name are the problems missed by the student. For each student, specify the probable cause or causes of the student's error. Describe the remediation procedure.

   24   342   61   23   203   60   21   28   432   48
  $\underline{\times 37}$ $\underline{\times\ 7}$ $\underline{\times 84}$ $\underline{\times 53}$ $\underline{\times\ 5}$ $\underline{\times\ 9}$ $\underline{\times 43}$ $\underline{\times 73}$ $\underline{\times\ 6}$ $\underline{\times 37}$

Jill   *Alice*   *Sam*
  203   48   28   203   60
$\underline{\times\ \ 5}$ $\underline{\times 37}$ $\underline{\times 73}$ $\underline{\times\ \ 5}$ $\underline{\times\ 9}$
1105   *338* *84*   *1065* *549*
               1440 *1980*
              1778 *2064*

Jean   *Sarah*
  24   23   28
$\underline{\times 37}$ $\underline{\times 53}$ $\underline{\times 75}$
168   *69* *140*
 72   *1150* *1960*
240   *1119* *2000*

4. A student makes the following errors on the less-structured worksheet presentation:

$$\overset{7}{4}3$$
$$\underline{\times\ 9}$$
$$2$$

Assume this type of error occurs frequently. What would the teacher do?

5. Write the wording the teacher would use in the structured worksheet part of a format in presenting the problem.

$$304$$
$$\underline{\times\ 7}$$

6. A student's worksheet assignment contains the following worked problems:

$$3 \times \boxed{\mathit{27}} = 9 \qquad\qquad 2 \times \boxed{\mathit{12}} = 6$$

What error is the student making? Describe the remediation procedure.

FORMAT 9.1 **Format for Single Digit Multiplication**

PART A: PICTORIAL DEMONSTRATION

TEACHER	**STUDENTS**

(Write the following boxes on the board.)

  5   5   5

1. We're going to learn a fast way to work problems that talk about the same number time and time again. *(Point to each column and ask)* How many in this group?   5

   Are we talking about the same number time and time again?   Yes

2. When we talk about the same number time and time again, we make a times problem. What number are we talking about time and time again?   5

   So we write 5. *(Write 5.)* How many 5s do we have?

   To correct: Count the groups of five. *(Point to each group as students count.)*   3

   So I write times 3. *(Write × 3.)*

3. The problem says what? 5×3

   We figure out 5 times 3 a fast way. We count by 5s three times: *(Point to each group of 5 as you count.)* 5, 10, 15. There are 15 in all.

4. Let's count by 1s and make sure 15 is right. *(Point to each member as students count.)* Are there 15?   Yes
   So we can count the fast way when we talk about the same number time and time again. *(Repeat steps 1–4 with the following boxes.)*

PART B: ANALYZING PROBLEMS

(Write these partial problems on the board.)
  5 ×
10 ×
  2 ×
  9 ×

Reading Partial Problems

1. *(Point to ×.)* This sign tells you to count by. What does it tell you to do?   Count by

2. *(Point to 5 ×.)* So this tells you to count by 5. What does this tell you to do?   Count by 5.

3. *(Point to 10 ×.)* What does this tell you to do?   Count by 10.

4. *(Point to 2 ×.)* What does this tell you to do?   Count by 2.

FORMAT 9.1   **(continued)**

TEACHER	STUDENTS

5. *(Point to 9×.)* What does this tell you to do? *(Repeat step 5 with all examples.)*   — Count by 9.

Reading Entire Problems

6. *(Point to 5×.)* What does this tell you to do?   — Count by 5.

   (Write 3 after 5×: 5 × 3.) Now this problem tells you to count by 5 three times. What does this problem tell you to do? *(Pause, signal.)*   — Count by 5, three times.

7. *(Point to 10×.)* What does this problem tell you to do?   — Count by 10.

   (Write 4 after 10.) What does this problem tell you to do now? *(Pause, signal.)*   — Count by 10, four times.

8. *(Point to 2×.)* What does this problem tell you to do?   — Count by 2.

   (Write 5 after 2×.) What does this problem tell you to do now? *(Pause, signal.)*   — Count by 2, five times.

9. *(Point to 9×.)* What does this problem tell you to do?   — Count by 9.

   (Write 4 after 9×: 9 × 4.) What does the problem tell you to do now?   — Count by 9, four times.

10. Let's start over. *(Point to 5 × 3.)* What does this problem tell you to do?   — Count by 5, three times.

   (Repeat step 10 with each problem. Give individual turns to several students.)

PART C: STRUCTURED BOARD PRESENTATION

(Write this problem on the board.)

$2 \times 5 = \square$

1. What does this problem tell us to do? *(Point to problem as students read.)*   — Count by 2, five times.

   How many times are we going to count?   — 5

   So I'll put up five fingers. Watch me count by 2, five times: *(Count and touch fingers.)* 2, 4, 6, 8, 10.

2. Now it's your turn to count by 2, five times. How many times are you going to count?   — 5

   Hold up your fingers. *(Monitor students' responses.)* You're counting by 2, five times. What number are you going to count by?   — 2

   Touch a finger every time you count. Counting by 2. Get ready, count. *(Clap at intervals of two seconds.)*   — Students touch an extended finger every time they count: 2, 4, 6, 8, 10.

   What number did you end with?   — 10
   So I'll write a 10 in the box. *(Write 10.)*

3. *(Write the problem below on the board.)* $2 \times 3 = \square$

   What does this problem tell us to do? *(Pause, signal.)*   — Count by 2, three times.

   How many times are you going to count?   — 3

(continued on next page)

FORMAT 9.1 (continued)

TEACHER	STUDENTS
Hold up your fingers. *(Monitor students' responses.)* What number are you going to count by?	2
Get ready to count. *(Clap at intervals of two seconds.)*	Students touch an extended finger every time they count 2, 4, 6.
How many did you end with?	6
So I'll write 6 in the box. *(Write 6.)* When we count by 2, three times what do we end with?	6

4. *(Repeat step 3 with $5 \times 4 = \square$, $10 \times 3 = \square$, $2 \times 4 = \square$, $9 \times 3 = \square$.)*

(Give individual turns to several students.)

PART D: STRUCTURED WORKSHEET

a. $5 \times 3 = \square$
b. $10 \times 4 = \square$
c. $2 \times 6 = \square$

1. Touch problem a. What does the problem tell you to do?	Count by 5, three times.
How many times are you going to count?	3
Hold up your fingers. *(Monitor responses.)*	Students hold up three fingers.
What number are you counting by?	5
2. Get ready. Count. *(Clap at intervals of one second.)*	Students count 5, 10, 15, touching each extended finger.
When you count by 5, three times what do you end with?	15
Write 15 in the box.	

(Repeat steps 1 and 2 with remaining problems.)

PART E: LESS STRUCTURED WORKSHEET

(Students have worksheets with variety of multiplication and addition problems.)
a. $5 \times 4 = \square$
b. $5 + 4 = \square$
c. $10 \times 3 = \square$
d. $10 \times 5 = \square$
e. $10 + 5 = \square$

1. Touch problem a. Put your finger under the sign. What does the problem tell you to do, plus or count by?	Count by
Say the problem.	Count by 5, four times.
Work it and write how many you end with in the box.	

(Repeat step 1 with remaining problems.)

FORMAT 9.2   **Format For Missing Factor Multiplication**

TEACHER	STUDENTS

PART A: STRUCTURED BOARD PRESENTATION

(Write the problem below on the board.)

$5 \times \square = 20$

Model and Test Translation

1. Here's a new kind of problem. Here's what it tells us to do. *(Point to each symbol as you read.)* Count by 5, how many times, to end with 20?

2. *(Point to $\square$.)* Does this problem tell how many times we count by 5?   No

   Right, we have to figure out how many times we count by 5.

3. Your turn to read the problem. I'll touch and you read. *(Touch ×, then 5, $\square$ = and 20. Repeat step 3 until students respond acceptably.)*   Count by 5 how many times to end with 20.

Model Strategy

4. Let's work this problem. What are we going to count by?   5

   Do we know how many times we count?   No

   I hold up a fist to show that I don't know how many times to count. How many are we going to end with?   20

5. My turn. I'm going to count by 5 and end with 20. *(Begin with a closed fist, then hold up a finger each time you count.)* Five, ten, fifteen, twenty. I put up a finger each time I counted. Here's how many times I counted. How many?   4

   So how many 5s in 20?   4

   I write a 4 in the space. *(Write 4 in box.)*

Test Strategy

6. Now it's your turn. Erase 4 in the space. Say what the problem tells us to do. *(Point to $5 \times \square = 20$.)*   Count by 5 how many times to end with 20.

   You have to figure out how many times we count. What do you have to figure out?   How many times we count.

   What are you counting by?   5

   Do you know how many times to count?   No

   So hold up a fist. What number are you going to end with?   20

7. Each time I clap you count and put up a finger. *(Students are to hold up a finger each time you clap. Clap at two-second intervals.)*   Students count 5, 10, 15, 20, putting up a finger each time they count.

   Now count your fingers and see how many times you counted. *(Pause.)* How many 5s in 20?   4

   Yes, so what do we write in the space? Right. *(Write 4.)*   4

   (Repeat steps 5 and 6 with $2 \times \square = 14$, $10 \times \square = 30$, $9 \times \square = 36$, $2 \times \square = 6$.)

(continued on next page)

FORMAT 9.2   (continued)

TEACHER	STUDENTS

PART B: STRUCTURED WORKSHEET

a. $5 \times \square = 20$
b. $2 \times \square = 10$
c. $10 \times \square = 40$
d. $9 \times \square = 18$
e. $5 \times \square = 30$

1. Touch problem a. What does the problem tell you to do?

Count by 5 how many times to end with 20.

2. What do you have to figure out?

How many times we count.

Put up your fist. What are you counting by?

5s

What are you going to end with?

20

3. Count and put up a finger each time you count. Get ready. Count. (Clap at two-second intervals.)

(Students count 5, 10, 15, 20, putting up a finger each time they count.)

How many times did you count?
Write 4 in the box.
(Repeat steps 1–3 with remaining problems.)

4

PART C: LESS STRUCTURED WORKSHEET

(Students have worksheets with an equal mix of regular and missing factor problems.)

a. $5 \times \square = 10$
b. $9 \times 3 = \square$
c. $2 \times \square = 8$
d. $2 \times 6 = \square$

1. Touch problem a.
2. What does the problem tell you to do?

Count by 5 how many times to end with 10?

3. What are you counting by?

5

4. Does the problem tell you how many times to count?

No

5. Show me what you hold up.

Students hold up fist.

6. Work the problem and write the answer in the box.
   (Repeat steps 1–6 with remaining problems.)

FORMAT 9.3   **Format for One-Digit Factor Times Two-Digit Factor—Renaming**

PART A: STRUCTURED BOARD PRESENTATION

TEACHER	STUDENTS
(Write the problem below on the board.)	

$$\begin{array}{r} 47 \\ \times\ 5 \\ \hline \end{array}$$

TEACHER	STUDENTS
1. Read the problem.	5 times 47
2. First we multiply 5 × 7.	
3. What do we do first? Next we multiply 5 × 4 tens.	Multiply 5 times 7
4. What do we do next? *(Repeat steps 1–4 until students respond acceptably.)*	Multiply 5 times 4 tens.
5. What is 5 × 7? We can't write 35 in the ones column. We must carry the tens. How many tens are in 35?	35 3

I put 3 above the tens column and put a plus sign in front of it to remind us to plus those tens.

$$\begin{array}{r} 47 \\ \times\ 5 \\ \hline 5 \end{array}$$

TEACHER	STUDENTS
6. Thirty-five has three tens and how many ones? I write the 5 under the ones column. Now we multiply 5 × 4 tens. How many tens is 5 × 4 tens? *(Pause, signal.)*	5 20
7. Now we add the three tens we carried. What is 20 + 3? *(Pause, signal.)*	23

Yes, 23 tens. I write 2 hundreds and 3 tens in the answer.

$$\begin{array}{r} 47 \\ \times\ 5 \\ \hline 235 \end{array}$$

TEACHER	STUDENTS
8. What does 5 × 47 equal?	235

(Repeat steps 1–8 with the problems below.)

$$\begin{array}{ccc} 36 & 42 & 34 \\ \times\ 2 & \times\ 9 & \times\ 5 \end{array}$$

PART B: STRUCTURED WORKSHEET

(Students have worksheet with these problems.)

a. $\begin{array}{r} 25 \\ \times\ 9 \\ \hline \end{array}$ b. $\begin{array}{r} 14 \\ \times\ 7 \\ \hline \end{array}$ c. $\begin{array}{r} 48 \\ \times\ 2 \\ \hline \end{array}$ d. $\begin{array}{r} 76 \\ \times\ 5 \\ \hline \end{array}$ e. $\begin{array}{r} 37 \\ \times\ 2 \\ \hline \end{array}$

(continued on next page)

FORMAT 9.3 (continued)

TEACHER	STUDENTS
1. Read problem a.	9 times 25
What numbers do we multiply first?	9×5
What is 9×5? *(Pause, signal.)*	45
How many tens in 45?	4
Write plus 4 over the tens column. How many ones in 45?	5
Write the 5 under the ones column.	
2. What numbers do we times next?	9×2
What is 9×2? *(Pause, signal.)*	18
What do we do now?	Add 4.
What is $18 + 4$? *(Pause, signal.)*	22
Write 22 next to the 5 under the line. What is 9×25? Read the whole problem.	225 $9 \times 25 = 225$
(Repeat steps 1 and 2 with remaining examples.)	

PART C: LESS STRUCTURED WORKSHEET PRESENTATION

(Students have worksheets with these problems.)

a. $\begin{array}{r} 35 \\ \times\ 5 \\ \hline \end{array}$ b. $\begin{array}{r} 79 \\ \times\ 2 \\ \hline \end{array}$ c. $\begin{array}{r} 35 \\ +\ 5 \\ \hline \end{array}$

d. $\begin{array}{r} 64 \\ \times\ 9 \\ \hline \end{array}$ e. $\begin{array}{r} 83 \\ \times\ 5 \\ \hline \end{array}$ f. $\begin{array}{r} 83 \\ +\ 5 \\ \hline \end{array}$

1. Read problem a.	5 times 35
What type of problem is this?[1]	Times
What will you do first?	Multiply 5×5.
What is 5×5? *(Pause, signal.)*	25
Carry the tens in 25 and write the ones.	
2. What numbers do we times next?	5×3
Then what do you do?	Add the 2.
Work the rest of the problem. *(Pause.)*	
3. What is 5×35?	175
(Repeat steps 1–3 with remaining problems.)	

[1]If the problem is addition, tell students to work the problem.

FORMAT 9.4   **Format for Two-Digit Factor Times Two-Digit Factor**

TEACHER	STUDENTS

PART A: ORDER OF MULTIPLYING

(Write these problems on the board.)

```
  5 8
× 4 3
```

```
  2 7
× 9 5
```

```
  4 2
× 5 7
```

1. *(Point to 58 × 43.)* Read the problem.   **43 times 58**

   Here's how we work multiplication problems with two numbers on the bottom. First we multiply all the numbers on the top by this number. *(Point to 3.)* Then we multiply all the numbers on the top by this number. *(Point to 4.)*

2. My turn. *(Point to numbers as you say them.)* First we multiply: 3 × 8, then 3 × 5, then 4 × 8, then 4 × 5.

3. *(Point to 3.)* What numbers do we multiply first?   **3 × 8**

   (Point to 3.) What numbers do we multiply next?   **3 × 5**

   (Point to 4.) What numbers do we multiply next?   **4 × 8**

   (Point to 4.) What numbers do we multiply next?   **4 × 5**

   (Repeat steps 2 and 3 with remaining problems. Give individual turns.)

PART B: STRUCTURED BOARD PRESENTATION

(Point to the problem below.)

```
  5 8
× 4 3
```

1. Read the problem.   **43 times 58**

2. What numbers do we multiply first?   **3 × 8**

   What is 3 × 8? *(Pause, signal.)*   **24**

   (Point above tens column.) What number do I write here?   **2**

   (Point under ones column.) What number do I put here?   **4**

   What numbers do we multiply next?   **3 × 5**

   What is 3 × 5? *(Pause, signal.)*   **15**

   What else do we do?   **Add 2**

   What is 15 + 2?   **17**

(continued on next page)

FORMAT 9.4   *(continued)*

TEACHER	STUDENTS

There are no more numbers on top to multiply so I write the 17 under the line next to the 4.

3. We multiplied 3 × 58. What is 3 × 58?   174
   I cross out the 2 we carried and the 3 to show we're finished with those numbers.

```
    2
   5 8
 × 4 3
 1 7 4
```

Now we multiply 4 tens × 58. Tens numbers have a zero so we put a zero in the ones column to show we're multiplying tens. How do we show we're multiplying by tens?   Put a zero in the ones column.
(Write 0 under 4.)

Now we multiply 4 × 8, then 4 × 5. What is 4 × 8? *(Pause, signal.)*   32

(Point above tens column.) What number do I write here?   3

(Point next to zero.) What number do I write here?   2
(Write numbers.)

```
     3
    5 8
  × 4 3
  1 7 4
2 3 2 0
```

4. Now what number do we multiply?   4 × 5

   What is 4 × 5? *(Pause, signal.)*   20

   What do we do now?   Add 3.

   What is 20 + 3? *(Pause, signal.)*   23

   Where do I write the 23?   Next to the 2

5. First we multiplied 3 × 58 and ended with 174. Then we multiplied 40 × 58 and ended with 2320. Now let's add those numbers and figure out what 43 × 58 equals. What is 4 + 0?   4

   What is 7 + 2?   9

   What is 1 + 3?   4

   What is nothing and 2?   2

6. We're finished adding. I'll put in the comma. Where does it go?   Between the 2 and 4

   What does 43 × 58 equal?   2,494

   (Repeat steps 1–6 with remaining problems on board.)

(continued on next page)

FORMAT 9.4   (continued)

PART C: STRUCTURED WORKSHEET

TEACHER	STUDENTS

(Students have worksheets with problems such as these.)

a.
$$\begin{array}{r} 2\,8 \\ \times\,3\,6 \\ \hline \end{array}$$
b.
$$\begin{array}{r} 6\,4 \\ \times\,2\,8 \\ \hline \end{array}$$
c.
$$\begin{array}{r} 8\,7 \\ \times\,4\,5 \\ \hline \end{array}$$

1. Touch problem a on your worksheet. Read the problem.	36×28
What numbers are you going to multiply first?	6×8
What is 6×8 *(Pause, signal.)*	48
Write it; don't forget to carry the tens. *(Monitor responses.)*	
2. What do you multiply next?	6×2
What is 6×2? *(Pause, signal.)*	12
What do you do now?	Add 4.
What is $12 + 4$? *(Pause, signal.)*	16
Write 16 next to the 8. *(Monitor responses.)*	
3. Are you done multiplying by 6? Cross out the 6 to show you're finished and cross out the carried number. *(Monitor responses.)*	yes
4. We multiplied 6×28. Now we multiply 30×28. What do you write to show that you are multiplying by tens?	Write a zero.
Write it. *(Monitor responses.)* What numbers do you multiply now?	3×8
What is 3×8? *(Pause, signal.)*	24
Write the 4 next to the zero. Write the 2 over the 2. *(Monitor responses.)*	
5. Now what are you going to multiply?	3×2
What is 3×2? *(Pause, signal.)*	6
What do you do now?	Add 2.
What is $6 + 2$? *(Pause, signal.)*	8
Write it. *(Monitor responses.)*	
6. We multiplied 6×28 and 30×28. Add the sums to see what 36×28 equals, then put in the comma. *(Pause.)* What is 36×28? *(Repeat with several examples.)*	1008

(continued on next page)

FORMAT 9.4 (continued)

PART D: LESS STRUCTURED PRACTICE

TEACHER   **STUDENTS**

(Give students worksheets with a mix of multiplication problems with two-digit and one-digit factors and some addition problems.)

1. Touch problem _____. Read the problem. What kind of problem is this?

2. What numbers do you multiply first?
   What numbers do you multiply next?
   What numbers do you multiply next?
   What numbers do you multiply next?

3. What are you going to do just before you start to multiply by 5 tens?
   Right, don't forget to write the zero. Work the problem.

Division

TERMS AND CONCEPTS

Division   The inverse of multiplication. When a student divides, he is finding a missing factor; 16 ÷ 8 can be expressed as $8 \times \square = 16$.

Measurement Division   Performed when a set of elements is to be separated into equivalent subsets. The answer is the number of subsets; e.g., John has six hats and separates them into groups of two hats. How many groups will he have?

Partitive Division   Performed when a set of elements is to be separated into a given number of subsets. The answer is the size of each subset; e.g., John has six hats and separates them into three groups. How many hats will be in each group?

Dividend   The number being divided. It corresponds to the product in a multiplication problem:

$$6 \text{ in } 2\overline{)6}$$

Divisor   The factor that is given in a division problem. It is written in front of the division sign:

$$2 \text{ in } 2\overline{)6}$$

Quotient   The factor solved for in a division problem. It is written above the division sign:

$$3 \text{ in } 2\overline{)6}^{\,3}$$

Commutativity   The commutative property does not hold:

$$a \div b \neq b \div a$$
$$6 \div 2 \neq 2 \div 6$$
$$3 \neq \frac{1}{3}$$

Associativity   The associative property does not hold:

$$(a \div b) \div c \neq a \div (b \div c)$$
$$(8 \div 4) \div 2 \neq 8 \div (4 \div 2)$$
$$2 \div 2 \neq 8 \div 2$$
$$1 \neq 4$$

Distributivity   The distributive property over addition and subtraction holds:

$$(a + b) \div c = (a \div c) + (b \div c)$$
$$(8 + 4) \div 2 = (8 \div 2) + (4 \div 2)$$
$$12 \div 2 = 4 + 2$$
$$6 = 6$$

The distributive property is used extensively in the division algorithm:

Instructional Sequence and Assessment Chart

Grade Level	Problem Type	Performance Indicator
3a	One-digit divisor and one-digit quotient; no remainder.	$3\overline{)15}$ $2\overline{)12}$ $5\overline{)20}$
3b	One-digit divisor and quotient with remainder.	$5\overline{)38}$ R $2\overline{)9}$ R $5\overline{)22}$ R
3c	Division equation with ÷ sign; no remainder; single-digit divisor and quotient.	$8 \div 2 = \square$ $20 \div 5 = \square$ $36 \div 9 = \square$
4a	One-digit divisor; two- or three-digit dividend; two-digit quotient; no remainder.	$5\overline{)85}$ $2\overline{)172}$ $2\overline{)54}$
4b	One-digit divisor; two- or three-digit dividend; two-digit quotient; remainder.	$5\overline{)87}$ $2\overline{)173}$ $2\overline{)55}$
4c	One-digit divisor; two- or three-digit dividend; quotient has two digits, one of which is zero; remainder	$5\overline{)53}$ $9\overline{)274}$ $9\overline{)360}$
4d	One-digit divisor; two- or three-digit dividend; two-digit quotient; express remainder as fraction.	Write the remainders as fractions. $5\overline{)127}$ $2\overline{)91}$ $9\overline{)364}$
4e	One-digit divisor; three- or four-digit dividend; three-digit quotient.	$5\overline{)635}$ $2\overline{)1343}$ $2\overline{)738}$
4f	Same as 4e; zero in quotient.	$5\overline{)2042}$ $2\overline{)1214}$ $5\overline{)520}$
4g	Four-digit quotient; one-digit divisor, four- or five-digit dividend.	$5\overline{)8753}$ $2\overline{)11325}$ $9\overline{)36286}$
4h	Rounding to the nearest 10.	76 rounds off to _____ 10s 405 rounds off to _____ 10s 297 rounds off to _____ 10s
4i	Two-digit divisor; one- or two-digit quotient; all estimation yields correct quotient.	$23\overline{)94}$ $56\overline{)857}$ $47\overline{)1325}$
4j	Same as above except estimation procedures yield quotient which is too large or small.	$24\overline{)82}$ $67\overline{)273}$ $35\overline{)714}$

$$4\overline{)48} = 4\overline{)40} + 4\overline{)8}$$

$$\begin{array}{c} 1 \\ 4\overline{)48} \end{array} = \begin{array}{c} 10 \\ 4\overline{)40} \\ 40 \end{array} + 4\overline{)8}$$
$$\underline{\quad 4 \quad}$$
$$8$$

$$\begin{array}{c} 12 \\ 4\overline{)48} \end{array} = \begin{array}{c} 10 \\ 4\overline{)40} \end{array} + \begin{array}{c} 2 \\ 4\overline{)8} \end{array} = 12$$
$$\begin{array}{ccc} 4 & 40 & 8 \\ \overline{8} & & \underline{-8} \end{array}$$

Note: The distributive property does not hold when the division operation precedes addition:

$$c \div (a + b) \neq c \div a + c \div b$$
$$8 \div (4 + 2) \neq 8 \div 4 + 8 \div 2$$
$$\frac{8}{6} \neq 2 + 4$$

SKILL HIERARCHY

As with all major operations, division is introduced in two stages: the conceptual stage and the multi-digit operation stage. During the conceptual stage, exercises providing concrete demonstrations of the division concept are presented. With concrete objects or pictures, the teacher illustrates how groups of objects can be divided into equal-sized small groups, first illustrating problems that have no remainder and later with problems that have a remainder.

During the operation stage, students are taught algorithms to solve division problems that have multi-digit quotients. A significant period of time is needed between the introduction of the conceptual stage and presentation of division algorithms. During that time, the teacher should present exercises to facilitate memorization of basic division facts. Once students know their division facts, division problems with one-digit divisors (and multi-digit quotients) can be introduced. Division problems with two-digit divisors are substantially more difficult and therefore are introduced later. A list of the specific problem types and when they are normally introduced appears in the Instructional Sequence and Assessment Chart.

INTRODUCING THE CONCEPT

There are at least four basic ways to provide concrete demonstrations of division:

1. *Removing equivalent disjoint subsets:* A picture of 6 fish is shown. The teacher says, "Let's put these fish in little bowls. We'll put 2 in each bowl. Let's see how many bowls we'll need. We put 2 in the first bowl. That leaves 4, then we put 2 in the second bowl. Then we put 2 in the third bowl. We need three bowls if we put 2 fish in each bowl."

2. *Arrays:* A group of objects aligned in equal piles is an array:

The teacher says, "Let's see how many sets of 6 there are in 30." The teacher counts each set of 6 as he circles them and then summarizes, "There are 5 sets of 6 in thirty."

3. *Linear models,* usually characterized by use of a number line: in multiplication, students start at 0 and jump to the right; e.g., 3 × 4 may be demonstrated as making 4 jumps of 3. Division problems are illustrated by saying, "If we start at 12, how many jumps of 4 do we make to get back to 0?"

4. *Repeated subtraction:* This way of introducing division is similar to the removal of equivalent disjoint subsets. The teacher says, "We want to find out how many groups of 4 are in 12. Here's one way to find out. We keep subtracting 4s until

we run out. We subtract 4 from 12. That equals 8. Then we subtract 4 from 8. That equals 4, and 4 from 4 equals zero." The teacher then has students count the number of times they subtracted to derive the answer.

Direct instruction procedures introduce the division concept through disjoint sets. Removing equivalent disjoint sets was selected since it can easily illustrate the relationship between multiplication and division, as well as the concept of remainder. Initial direct instruction exercises teach students to remove equivalent sets by circling groups of lines.

Students must have mastered two preskills prior to the introduction of division. The first preskill is knowledge of basic multiplication facts. Students need not have memorized all multiplication facts before division is introduced, but they should at least have memorized multiplication facts with 2 and 5 as factors. A second preskill is column subtraction with renaming, which often is required when students subtract to find a remainder.

Division is usually presented during the midpart of the third grade. Exercises to teach division facts are introduced about a week or two after the concept of division is introduced. Teachers present facts in related series (e.g., the facts with 5 as a divisor). Ample practice to enable students to develop fluency with a set of facts must be provided before a new set is introduced. Cumulative review of all previously introduced facts must also be provided. Practice exercises to teach basic division facts usually are provided daily for many months.

The concept of remainder is introduced after students have learned about 20 division facts. More specifically, we recommend that students know the division facts with divisors of 2 and 5 before the remainder concept is introduced. Similar to the introduction of division without remainders, the first exercises in which students are introduced to remainders require the students to circle groups of lines. After several days, exercises to teach students to compute quotients mentally in problems with remainders would be presented. Practice on division facts with remainders would continue for several months.

Problems Without Remainders

The procedure for introducing division appears in Format 10.1. The format contains four parts. Part A begins with the teacher modeling and testing the translation of a division problem. For example, the problem 5)20 is read as "5 goes into 20 how many times" rather than "20 divided by 5." The purpose of this translation is to draw attention to the divisor, since it specifies the size of the equivalent groups—the critical feature in using lines to solve division problems. Also, the translation facilitates the use of multiplication facts. Note that the students are taught to translate problems so that they are read as a form of missing-factor multiplication.

Part B is a structured board exercise in which the teacher demonstrates with lines the process of taking a big group and making smaller, equal-sized groups. When working the problem, the teacher points out the function of the numbers in a problem. In $5\overline{)20}$, the 20 tells how many lines in all, the 5 tells how many in each group, and the 4 tells how many groups. One minor, but important, aspect of Part B deals with where the quotient is written. If the dividend is a two-digit number, the quotient is written over the last digit. For example, in the problem $5\overline{)20}$ the quotient 4 is written over the zero. The purpose of having students write the quotient in the correct place is to prepare them for using the traditional algorithm to solve problems with multi-digit quotients. Improper placement of digits in the quotient leads to various types of errors:

$$\begin{array}{r} 13 \\ 5\overline{)607} \\ \underline{5} \\ 17 \\ \underline{15} \\ 2 \end{array} \quad \text{or} \quad \begin{array}{r} 2.5 \\ 5\overline{)1.26} \\ \underline{10} \\ 26 \\ \underline{25} \\ 25 \end{array}$$

Parts C and D are structured and less-structured worksheet exercises. In both exercises, students are given problems for which lines are already drawn. Note that a variety of divisors can be included in these exercises, since knowledge of facts is not required. Students just make groups the size of which are defined by the divisor. Note also that students are only assigned two or three problems a day for practice. This exercise is designed to provide a conceptual basis for understanding division. Therefore, teachers need only develop accuracy in such exercises; fluency is not as important at this point.

Division Facts

A week or so after students have been introduced to division through the line-circling exercises described in Format 10.1, exercises to facilitate mastery of basic facts can begin. Exercises that demonstrate the relationship between multiplication and division facts would be presented first, e.g., exercises in which students must generate both multiplication and division facts from fact number families.

$$3 \times 4 = 12 \qquad\qquad 4 \times 3 = 12$$

$$\begin{array}{r} 4 \\ 3\overline{)12} \end{array} \qquad\qquad \begin{array}{r} 3 \\ 4\overline{)12} \end{array}$$

After relationship exercises are presented for several days for a set of facts, those facts would be incorporated into memorization exercises. We recommend that students continue saying the facts in the statement form "5 goes into 20 four times" rather than "20 divided by 5 equals 4," because the former uses the language form presented when division problems with multi-digit quotients are introduced. Procedures to teach basic facts are discussed in more depth in Chapter 6.

Problems with Remainders

The concept of remainders is an important skill in and of itself and is also a preskill for the short-form division algorithm involving multi-digit quotients. Problems with remainders can be introduced when the students have learned division facts with divisors of 2 and 5, which is usually two to four weeks after division is introduced.

Format 10.2 shows how to introduce the remainder concept. In Part A, the teacher writes a problem on the board and has the students read it. After students read the problem, the teacher draws lines. For $5\overline{)13}$, the teacher draws 13 lines. The teacher then asks the students for the number in each smaller group and begins drawing circles around groups of 5 lines. After drawing two groups, the teacher points out that he cannot draw a circle around the last lines because there are not 5 lines. The teacher tells the students that only two groups of 5 can be made and that the other lines are called the remainder. The teacher then states the answer to the problem: 5 goes into 13 two times, with a remainder of 3.

In Part B and Part C, the students are given a worksheet with several division problems involving remainders. Next to each problem is a diagram illustrating the problem. For example, next to the problem

$$5\overline{)17}$$

17 lines would be drawn with circles around groups of 5 lines:

$$5\overline{)17} \quad (|||||) \ (|||||) \ (|||||) \ ||$$

The diagram is drawn so that the teacher may concentrate on the mechanics of where to write the number of groups, how to figure out how many parts are used (multiply 5 × 3), where to write the number of parts used (under the 17), and how to compute the remainder (subtract 17 minus 15). Note that practice on this exercise would be continued just for a week or two, since the exercise is designed primarily to teach a conceptual understanding.

Remainder Facts

As mentioned earlier, students should have been taught at least 20 division facts before the remainder concept is introduced. About a week after the remainder concept is introduced, exercises to teach students to mentally compute division facts that include remainders should begin with problems like those below:

$$5\overline{)27} \qquad 6\overline{)34}$$

This skill is a critical preskill for division problems with multi-digit quotients, since most of these problems involve remainders. For example, in

$$3\overline{)147}$$

students must first determine that 3 goes into 14 four times with a remainder. After multiplying 3 × 4, they then subtract to compute the exact remainder. Format 10.3 shows how to teach students to mentally compute division facts with remainders.

Part A uses a diagram like the one below to introduce remainder facts. The teacher would write numbers in a single row, circling numbers that are all multiples of a particular divisor. In the example below, numbers with a divisor of 5 are circled.

⓪ 2 3 4 ⑤ 6 7 8 9
⑩ 11 12 13 14 ⑮ 16 17 18
19 ⑳ 21 22 23 24 ㉕

If the teacher is introducing the second part of a series, the teacher writes the higher numbers in the series. For example, if the second half of the five series is being introduced, the teacher writes in a single row:

㉕ 26 27 28 29 ㉚ 31 32 33
34 ㉟ 36 37 38 39 ㊵ 41 42
43 44 ㊺ 46 47 48 49 ㊿

After writing the series on the board, the teacher points out that the circled numerals are the numbers that 5 goes into without a remainder. The teacher then models answering the question of how many times 5 goes into various numbers, for example, "5 goes into 23 four times with a remainder; 5 goes into

10 two times with no remainder; 5 goes into 9 one time with a remainder." (Note that at this point the quantity of the remainder is not stated.) The teacher then tests the students on a set of examples.

In Part B, the teacher tests the students on various numbers, letting the students refer to the diagram. Part C is a supervised worksheet exercise designed to provide practice that will facilitate fluency in determining division facts. In Part C, the students are given a set of about 30 worksheet problems. The students write the quotient, then multiply and subtract to figure out the remainder. The teacher leads the students through several problems and then has them complete the work independently.

Parts A and B need to be presented only when the first several sets of facts are introduced. Once students have learned to compute division facts mentally with 2s and 5s and 9s, problems with other divisors can be introduced without using the diagram as a prompt.

The sequence in which new division facts with remainders are introduced would parallel the sequence in which basic division facts without remainders are introduced (see Chapter 6 on Basic Facts for the suggested sequence for introducing division facts). About two weeks after a set of division facts with a particular divisor has been taught, division facts with remainders for the same divisors and quotients would be presented. For example, after students master the division facts for 5s:

$$\text{e.g., } 5\overline{)30} \qquad 5\overline{)35} \qquad 5\overline{)40} \qquad 5\overline{)45}$$

problems with the same divisor and quotient but with remainders are introduced:

$$\text{e.g., } 5\overline{)32} \qquad 5\overline{)41} \qquad 5\overline{)43}$$
$$5\overline{)48} \qquad 5\overline{)36} \qquad 5\overline{)38}$$

The daily worksheet exercise would include about 30 problems. In half of the problems, the divisor would be derived from the set currently being introduced; in the other half of the problems, the divisor would be a number introduced in earlier sets. Although most problems would involve remainders, about a fifth without remainders would be included to prevent students from developing the potential misrule that all problems must have remainders.

Finally, several problems in which the quotient is zero should be included:

$$5\overline{)3} \qquad 9\overline{)6} \qquad 2\overline{)1}$$

Teaching students to mentally compute the answer to such problems prepares them for long division problems in which zero is in the quotient, such as

FIGURE 10.1   Sample Worksheet Exercise

7)18	9)46	7)26	7)31	2)7	5)32	7)35	9)27
7)4	7)17	9)58	9)65	7)27	5)3	7)41	9)53
5)30	7)11	7)25	7)32	9)31	5)18	7)3	7)25
9)49	9)26	5)48	2)17	7)36	7)28	7)19	7)36

$$\frac{104 \; R4}{5)524}$$

Figure 10.1 is a sample worksheet exercise based on the assumption that students have previously mastered problems with divisors of 2, 5, and 9 and are being introduced to the first half of the 7s series.

Worksheet exercises like Figure 10.1 would be presented daily for several months. Students who develop fluency in computing division facts with remainders are less likely to have difficulty when more complex division problems are introduced.

Diagnosis and Remediation

Determining the cause of errors while introducing the division concept is fairly easy. The more common causes, other than not knowing basic facts, are component skill errors:

1. writing quotients that are either too small or too large
2. subtracting incorrectly
3. confusing the placement of the quotient and remainder

FACT ERRORS   Basic fact errors are illustrated below:

a. $\dfrac{5}{7)33}$ b. $\dfrac{4}{9)42}$ c. $\dfrac{4}{7)32}$
$\underline{30}$ $\underline{38}$ $\underline{26}$

As usual, the remediation procedure for basic fact errors depends on the number of fact errors the student makes. If a student makes just an occasional fact error, the teacher simply records the facts the student misses and incorporates those facts into practice exercises for the next several lessons. If a student makes fact errors on more than 10% of the problems, he should be tested individually to determine what action to take next. If the teacher finds that the student responds correctly on the individual test to all the missed facts, the teacher should tenta-

tively conclude that the errors resulted from hurrying through the problems. The remediation procedure would be to increase the student's motivation to perform accurately. If the student's test performance indicates he does not know many previously introduced basic facts, he should be tested on all previously taught multiplication and division facts and provided systematic, intensive instruction on those facts. Also, for several weeks the teacher should carefully control the assignments given to the student so that only facts the student knows appear on worksheet problems.

COMPONENT SKILL ERRORS   One component skill error involves writing a quotient that is either too large or small. Examples of this error are illustrated below. Problems a and b are examples of computing too small a quotient; problems c and d are examples of computing too large a quotient.

a. $\dfrac{4}{5)28}$ b. $\dfrac{4}{7)35}$
$\underline{20}$ $\underline{28}$

c. $\dfrac{6}{6)32}$ d. $\dfrac{5}{4)19}$
$\underline{36}$ $\underline{20}$

If either type of error occurs in more than 10% of the problems students work independently, the teacher should present an exercise that teaches students to compare the remainder and divisor to determine the accuracy of their answer.

The content of the remedial exercise would depend on the type of error made. If the student wrote quotients that were too small:

$$\frac{6}{5)37}$$
$$\underline{30}$$
$$7$$

the teacher would present an exercise like the one in Format 10.4. That format contains an exercise in which students are given a worksheet comprised of division problems with the quotients written. In half of the problems the quotient is correct, and in the other half the quotient is too small:

$$
\begin{array}{r}
3 \\
9\overline{)38} \\
\underline{27} \\
11
\end{array}
$$

In Part A, the teacher tells students that they must compare the remainder and the divisor to see if they worked the problem correctly. Note that the term *divisor* is not used by the teacher. If students divide by 9, they are taught that the remainder must be smaller than 9; if they divide by 5, the remainder must be smaller than 5; if they divide by 3, the remainder must be smaller than 3, and so on. In Part B, the teacher leads students through determining if the quotient is correct by figuring the remainder and comparing it to the divisor. In problems in which the remainder is not smaller than the divisor, the teacher points out that another group can be made and instructs the student to cross out the answer and in its place write the next higher number. For example, in the problem

$$
\begin{array}{r}
2 \\
5\overline{)16} \\
\underline{10} \\
6
\end{array}
$$

the teacher has the students cross out 2 and write 3 as the answer. The student then erases 10, multiplies 3 × 5, and subtracts 15 from 16. The teacher would guide students through four problems and then have them work 8–10 problems on their own. The format is presented daily until students are able to successfully solve the problems for several consecutive days.

For errors such as

$$
\begin{array}{r}
7 \\
5\overline{)32}
\end{array}
$$

in which the answer is too large, the teacher should use the process illustrated in Format 10.5. In Part A, the teacher guides the students through a set of problems on the board, pointing out that if they can't subtract, the answer is too big, and the number in the answer must be made smaller. In Part B, the teacher has students work a set of remediation examples in which half of the problems have a quotient that is too large and half of the problems have a quotient that is correct. As with the previous format, this remediation format should be presented for several lessons.

Column subtraction errors are easy to spot and usually result from a failure to rename. Problems a and b below illustrate subtraction errors.

$$
\begin{array}{cc}
\begin{array}{r}
5 \\
\text{a. } 7\overline{)41} \\
\underline{35} \\
14
\end{array}
&
\begin{array}{r}
7 \\
\text{b. } 9\overline{)71} \\
\underline{63} \\
12
\end{array}
\end{array}
$$

The remediation procedure includes giving students a worksheet with about 10 problems in which borrowing is necessary. The teacher guides students through the first several problems and then has students work the remaining problems on their own. For example, in the problem

$$
\begin{array}{r}
5 \\
7\overline{)41} \\
\underline{35}
\end{array}
$$

the teacher would have the students identify the problem in the ones column, ask if they can subtract 5 from 1, then prompt students to regroup.

The final type of error involves confusing placement of the quotient and remainder. The remediation procedure would be to present Part C of Format 10.3 with several problems and then supervise the students as they work several more problems.

A summary of the diagnosis and remediation procedures for beginning division appears in Figure 10.2.

MULTI-DIGIT PROBLEMS

The second stage of instruction in division focuses on multi-digit problems, which become quite complex. Multi-digit quotients are grouped in this text according to the number of digits in the divisor. Problems with one-digit divisors are discussed first, followed by a discussion of problems with two-digit divisors.

Two algorithms are taught in most commercial programs. One is commonly referred to as the long form; the other, the short form. The long-form and short-form division algorithms are illustrated below:

$$
\begin{array}{ll}
\textit{LONG FORM} & \textit{SHORT FORM} \\
& \begin{array}{r} 54 \end{array} \\
\begin{array}{r}
7\overline{)382} \\
\underline{350} \quad 50 \\
32 \\
\underline{28} \quad 4 \\
4 \quad \rule{2cm}{0.4pt} \\
54
\end{array}
&
\begin{array}{r}
7\overline{)382} \\
\underline{35} \\
32 \\
\underline{28} \\
4
\end{array}
\end{array}
$$

The advantage of the long-form algorithm is that it presents a clear interpretation of what is involved in division. The disadvantage is that most intermediate-grade teachers expect students to use the short-form algorithm. The advantage of the short-form

FIGURE 10.2   Diagnosis and Remediation of Beginning Division Errors

Error Patterns	Diagnosis	Remediation Procedures	Remediation Examples
Component Skill Errors			
$\dfrac{4}{7\overline{)35}}$ $\underline{32}$	Fact error: 35 ÷ 7	High percentage of fact errors—provide systematic fact instruction. Low percentage of fact errors—increase motivation, include missed facts in fact drills.	See Chapter 6
$\dfrac{3}{6\overline{)24}}$ $\underline{18}$	Component skill: Student computes a quotient that is too small.	Format 10.4, "Remediation for Division with Remainders—Quotient Too Small."	Partially worked problems, containing quotients. Half of the quotients should be too small, half of them should be accurate: $\dfrac{3}{9\overline{)42}}$ $\dfrac{6}{9\overline{)56}}$
$\dfrac{4}{7\overline{)26}}$ $\underline{28}$	Component skill: Student computes a quotient that is too large.	Format 10.5, "Remediation for Division with Remainders—Quotient Too Large."	Partially worked problems combining quotients—half of the quotients should be too large, half of them should be accurate.
$\dfrac{7}{8\overline{)62}}$ $\underline{56}$ $\overline{14}$	Component skill: Student incorrectly subtracts.	Lead student through subtraction.	Partially worked problems containing accurate quotients in which students must subtract.
$\dfrac{1 \ R4}{7\overline{)29}}$ $\underline{28}$ $\overline{1}$	Component skill: Student misplaces remainder and quotient.	Part C of Format 10.3.	

algorithm is the relatively easy set of preskills that must be mastered prior to introducing division problems. The disadvantage of the short-form algorithm is that students may not understand why it works.

In this section, we discuss in detail the procedures for teaching the short-form algorithm. We discuss this algorithm because it is the algorithm most programs eventually encourage students to use. Remember, as mentioned earlier, we believe that lower-performing students will be more successful if just one algorithm is presented. The basic steps of the short-form algorithm are presented in Format 10.6.

One-Digit Divisors

Problems with one-digit divisors and multi-digit quotients are usually introduced in late third or early fourth grade. Students should know at least 30 to 40 basic division facts and the corresponding remainder facts prior to the introduction of this type of problem.

Two factors affect the difficulty level of single-digit divisor problems: the number of digits in the quotient and the presence of a zero in the quotient. The more digits in the quotient, the more difficult a problem will be. For example, the first problem below is more difficult than the second problem

$$5\overline{)835} \qquad 5\overline{)125}$$

because the former will have a three-digit quotient while the latter will have a two-digit quotient. Each additional numeral in the quotient requires an extra set of computations. Similarly, a problem such as the first one below is more difficult than the second

$$5\overline{)52} \qquad 5\overline{)85}$$

because in the former problem the quotient contains a zero. Without careful instruction, students are likely to leave out the zero.

$$\dfrac{1}{5\overline{)52}}$$
$$\underline{5}$$

This section discusses procedures for teaching students to work all of these problem types.

PROBLEMS WITH A TWO-DIGIT QUOTIENT Format 10.7 shows the process to use for introducing division problems with two-digit quotients. The format includes five parts. In Part A, the students are taught how to determine the part of the problem to work first. This important preskill is necessary since division problems are worked a part at a time. For example, when working the problem

$$5\overline{)375}$$

the student first works the problem

$$5\overline{)37}$$

then, after multiplying and subtracting:

$$
\begin{array}{r}
7 \\
5\overline{)375} \\
\underline{35} \\
25
\end{array}
$$

the student divides 5 into 25. The strategy to determine which part to work first involves comparing the divisor with the first digit of the dividend. If the first digit of the dividend is at least as big as the divisor, only the first digit of the dividend is underlined. For example, in this problem the 9 is underlined:

$$7\overline{)\underline{9}45}$$

because the part of the problem to work first is 7 goes into 9. If the first digit of the dividend is not at least as big as the divisor, students are taught to underline the first two digits of the dividend. For example, in this problem 23 is underlined:

$$7\overline{)\underline{23}6}$$

because the part of the problem to be worked first is 7 goes into 23. Note that in presenting this important preskill, the teacher does not use the words *divisor* or *dividend,* but rather refers to "the number dividing by" and "dividing into".

Examples must be carefully selected for Part A. In half of the problems, the first digit of the dividend should be smaller than the divisor. In the other half of the problems, the first digit of the dividend should be the same or larger than the divisor. A variety of divisors can be included since students are not actually working the problems at this point. Below is a sample set of problems appropriate to use when teaching this preskill.

a. $7\overline{)\underline{243}}$ b. $5\overline{)\underline{85}}$ c. $4\overline{)\underline{235}}$

d. $7\overline{)\underline{461}}$ e. $9\overline{)\underline{362}}$ f. $8\overline{)\underline{89}}$

Part B of this format is a worksheet exercise in which the students practice underlining the part of the problem they work first. The teacher guides the students through several problems, then has the students work the rest on their own. The teacher repeats this

part daily until students can perform accurately without teacher assistance. Part C is a structured board exercise in which the teacher demonstrates the entire short-form algorithm. Format 10.6 shows the basic steps in that algorithm illustrated with the problem

$$7\overline{)238}$$

Parts D and E in Format 10.7 are structured and less-structured worksheet exercises. Note that the teacher specifies where digits in the quotient are to be written. The first digit in the quotient is to be written over the last underlined digit:

$$
\begin{array}{cc}
3 & 1 \\
7\overline{)\underline{23}8} \quad & 8\overline{)\underline{82}}
\end{array}
$$

Each succeeding numeral is to be written over the succeeding digit in the dividend:

$$
\begin{array}{r}
613 \\
7\overline{)\underline{42}91}
\end{array}
$$

As mentioned earlier, placing the digits of the quotient in the proper position helps students in solving problems with zeroes in the quotient as well as with problems containing decimals.

The example selection guidelines for all worksheet exercises remain the same as for Parts A and B, except that since students work the problems, the divisors should be limited to familiar facts. Half of the problems should have two-digit dividends, and half should have three-digit dividends. All problems should have two-digit quotients. Below is a sample set of problems that might appear in an exercise. This worksheet assumes students have learned division facts with 2, 9, 5, and 7 as divisors.

a. $5\overline{)87}$ b. $9\overline{)324}$ c. $5\overline{)135}$

d. $7\overline{)86}$ e. $2\overline{)134}$ f. $7\overline{)94}$

g. $2\overline{)156}$ h. $7\overline{)79}$ i. $2\overline{)29}$

ZERO IN THE QUOTIENT Problems with zero as the last digit of a two-digit quotient

$$7\overline{)143} \qquad 2\overline{)81} \qquad 5\overline{)153}$$

require special attention. These problems would be introduced several weeks after division problems with two-digit quotients have been presented.

The critical part of the format occurs after students subtract and bring down the last digit. For example, in

$$
\begin{array}{r}
3 \\
7\overline{)214} \\
\underline{21} \\
4
\end{array}
$$

Summary Box 10.1   Division: The Short-Form Algorithm

---

1. Students read the problem.

2. Students underline the part of the problem that they work first.

3. Students compute the underlined part and write the answer above the last underlined digit.

4. Students multiply, subtract, and bring down the next number.

5. Students read the "new" problem and compute a quotient.

6. Students write the answer above the digit they just brought down.

7. Students multiply and subtract to determine the remainder.

8. Students say the problem and answer.

---

the teacher asks, "7 goes into 4 how many times?" Since the answer is zero, the teacher writes a zero above the 4. The teacher may have to model the answer for the first several problems. The format would be presented for several days. Thereafter, three or four problems with a quotient ending in zero should be included in daily worksheet exercises.

QUOTIENTS OF THREE OR MORE DIGITS Problems with quotients of three or more digits are introduced only when students have mastered problems with two-digit quotients. No preskills or board exercises need be presented. The teacher merely presents the less-structured part of Format 10.7 for several days. The teacher emphasizes the need to keep bringing down digits until an answer has been written above the last digit of the dividend.

Problems with a zero as one of the three digits in the quotient are introduced only after students can solve problems without zeroes in the quotient. Problems with a zero as the last digit could be introduced a week or so after problems with three-digit quotients have been introduced. These problems should cause students relatively little difficulty, since two-digit quotients with a zero would have been taught earlier. On the other hand, problems with a zero as the second digit of a three-digit quotient:

$$\begin{array}{r} 103 \\ 5\overline{)515} \end{array} \qquad \begin{array}{r} 407 \\ 2\overline{)814} \end{array}$$

will be difficult for many students. A structured worksheet exercise (Part D of Format 10.7) should be presented. After bringing down the first number,

$$\begin{array}{r} 1 \\ 5\overline{)517} \\ 5 \end{array}$$

the teacher can say, "The next part says 5 goes into 1; 5 goes into 1 zero times, so I write 0 in the answer. What is zero times 5? So I write zero under the 1. Now we subtract and bring down the next number."

The teacher presents the structured worksheet exercise for several days with three or four problems. Next, a supervised worksheet exercise containing about 10 problems, three or four of which have zero as the middle digit, would be presented. Supervised practice is continued until students develop accuracy.

Problems with quotients of four or more digits are usually presented in late fourth grade or early fifth. For students who have mastered all types of problems with three-digit quotients, these longer problems should cause little difficulty.

SELF-CHECKING After students become proficient in working division problems with remainders, they should be taught to check their answers. A checking procedure for division is to multiply the divisor and quotient and add the remainder, if there is one. The teacher can introduce self-checking on a worksheet exercise in which the problems are already worked and about half of them have incorrect answers. The teacher would instruct the students to check their answers using the self-checking strategy and to correct mistakes.

Two-Digit Divisors

Solving problems with two-digit divisors requires the integration of numerous component skills into a fairly lengthy strategy. The steps in the short-form algorithm are outlined in Format 10.8.

The complexity of problems with two-digit divisors is affected mainly by whether or not the estimating, or rounding off, procedure produces a correct quotient. In some cases, the estimate may yield a quotient that is too large. For example, in the problem

$$53\overline{)203}$$

students round off 53 to 5 tens and 203 to 20 tens, and then determine how many 5s in 20. The estimated quotient, 4, when multiplied by 53 equals 212, which is too large to be subtracted from 203. Since the estimate yielded too large a quotient, the actual quotient must be 3, not 4.

In contrast, other estimates may yield a quotient that is too small. For example, in the problem

$$56\overline{)284}$$

when 56 is rounded off to 6 tens and 284 is rounded off to 28 tens, the estimate is a quotient of 4. However, 56 × 4 is 224, which when subtracted from 284 leaves a difference of 60, from which another group of 56 could be made. Since the estimated quotient yields too small a quotient, the actual quotient must be one larger than 4.

Problems in which the estimated quotient is too large or too small are more difficult and should not be introduced until students can work problems in which the estimated quotients prove to be correct.

PRESKILLS   Students should have mastered all of the component skills needed to solve division problems with one-digit divisors before problems with two-digit divisors are introduced. Additional preskills are rounding off numbers to the nearest tens unit, which is discussed next, and multiplying multi-digit numbers, which was discussed in the previous chapter.

Rounding off numbers to the nearest tens unit is a critical skill for problems with two-digit divisors. The first part of the strategy teaches students to estimate how many groups the size of the divisor can be made from the dividend. For the problem,

$$54\overline{)186}$$

the teacher asks, "How many times does 54 go into 186?" The estimate is derived by rounding off and expressing both the divisor and dividend as tens units: 54 is rounded to 5 tens and 186 is rounded to 19 tens. The students then figure out how many fives in 19.

Format 10.9 shows how to teach students to round off numbers to the nearest tens unit. In Part A, the teacher models and tests converting a tens number that ends in 0 to a unit of tens: 340 equals 34 tens, 720 equals 72 tens, 40 equals 4 tens. The teacher repeats a set of six to eight examples until the students can respond correctly to all of the examples. In Part B, the teacher models and tests rounding numbers that end in any digit to the near-

est tens unit. The teacher writes a numeral on the board and asks the students if the number is closer to the tens number preceding it or following it. For example, after writing 238 on the board, the teacher asks the students if 238 is closer to 230 or 240. After the students respond, "240" the teacher asks, "So how many tens is 238 closest to, 23 tens or 24 tens?"

Part C is a worksheet exercise in which the student must write the tens unit closest to the number (e.g., 342 = ☐ tens). Students may require several weeks of practice to develop mastery in this skill. However, division problems with two-digit divisors should not be introduced until mastery of this preskill is demonstrated.

There are several example selection guidelines for this format: (1) half of the numbers to be transformed should have a numeral less than 5 in the ones column, while the other half of the numbers should have 5 or a numeral greater than 5; (2) about two-thirds of the examples should be three-digit numbers and one-third, two-digit numbers, so that practice is provided on the two types of numbers students will have to round off, and (3) numbers that may cause particular difficulty for students should not be included in initial exercises.

Two types of numbers may cause difficulty: (1) numbers in which the last two digits are 95 or greater (e.g., 397, 295, 498), which require rounding off to the next hundreds grouping (397 rounds off to 40 tens, and 295 rounds off to 30 tens), and (2) numbers that have a zero in the tens column (e.g., 408, 207, 305). Special emphasis should be given to these two types of examples about a week after the format is initially presented.

PROBLEMS WITH CORRECT ESTIMATED QUOTIENTS   Initially, division problems with two-digit divisors should be limited to problems in which the estimated quotients prove to be correct. Also, the initial problems should involve a one-digit quotient. Problems containing a two-digit quotient can usually be introduced several days after problems with a one-digit quotient are presented.

The process for teaching correct estimated quotients with two-digit divisors appears in Format 10.10. It includes four parts. Parts A and B teach component skills unique to the short form algorithm: horizontal multiplication and estimating a quotient by rounding off the divisor and dividend.

Part A teaches students to multiply the estimated quotient and divisor, which are written horizontally, and to place the product below the dividend. In the problem

$$57\overline{)391}$$

the estimated quotient 6 and the divisor 57 are multiplied. The student first multiplies 6×7, which is 42. The 2 is placed under the 1 in the dividend, and the 4 is carried over the 5 in the divisor:

$$\overset{4\quad6}{57\overline{)391}}$$
$$\underline{2}$$

The student then multiplies 6×5 and adds the carried 4. The total 34 is written under the 39 in the dividend:

$$\overset{4\quad6}{57\overline{)391}}$$
$$\underline{\mathbf{342}}$$

Part B presents the rounding off strategy to determine the estimated quotient. The teacher writes a problem on the board and next to the problem writes a box with a division sign:

$$37\overline{)1582}\qquad \boxed{\;)\overline{}\;}$$

The rounded off problem is written in the box. The teacher has students read the problem and determine the part to work first (e.g., 37 goes into 158) and then underline those numbers in the dividend. The students then round off 37 to 4 tens and 158 to 16 tens and write the rounded off problem in the box:

$$\boxed{4\overline{)16}}$$

After rounding off, the students figure out the answer to the rounded-off problem and write the answer above the last underlined digit in the original problem:

$$\overset{4}{37\overline{)\underline{158}2}}\qquad \boxed{4\overline{)16}}$$

Parts A and B can be introduced at the same time. Also note that both parts contain two sections. In the first section of each part, the teacher presents several problems on the board. In the second section, the teacher leads the students through several worksheet problems and then has them work several problems on their own. Each day, the students should work more problems on their own. If the students can work at least four of the five problems correctly, they are presented the next day with Part C, in which the entire strategy is introduced. If students miss two or more problems, they continue working on Parts A and/or B. Students must be able to perform the multiplication and estimation skills accurately before the entire strategy is presented.

Part C is a structured worksheet exercise in which students are guided through all the steps in the strategy. For about the first two weeks, the boxes to do the rounding off should be written on students' worksheets. A sample problem on a worksheet would look like this:

$$37\overline{)1582}$$

The upper box is for writing the rounded-off problem for the first part of the problem; the lower box is for writing the rounded-off problem for the second part of the problem.

Two example selection guidelines are important to this format. First and foremost, all of the problems must yield estimated quotients that are correct. Second, in half of the problems, the first two digits in the dividend must be less than the divisor:

$$37\overline{)2431}\qquad\qquad 52\overline{)4681}$$

while in the other problems, the first two digits must be greater than the divisor:

$$37\overline{)441}\qquad\qquad 52\overline{)838}$$

Several problems with a one-digit quotient should be included in supervised and independent worksheets. The mixture of problems ensures that students will use the steps of determining which part to work first.

PROBLEMS WITH INCORRECT ESTIMATED QUOTIENTS   In a minor, but still significant, proportion of problems with two-digit divisors, one or more estimated quotients will prove to be incorrect. For example, in the problem

$$39\overline{)155}$$

the estimated quotient would prove too large, since 4×39 equals 156. Problems in which the estimated quotient is incorrect should be introduced about a week after students have developed accuracy in working problems in which the estimates are correct. The first problems presented should result in a one-digit quotient. The steps for presenting these problems appear in Format 10.11.

The format includes two parts. Part A focuses only on the component skill of determining if the estimated quotient is correct and what to do if it is not correct. Separate sequences of steps are indicated for problems in which the estimated quotient is too large and for problems in which the estimated quotient is too small. The rules in the format are designed to minimize student confusion (i.e., If you can't subtract, make the answer smaller; if the remainder is too big, make the answer bigger).

In Part A, the students are given a worksheet on which the estimated quotient is written in each problem. The worksheet includes a variety of problems. One-third of the problems have a quotient that is a multiple too large:

$$\frac{5}{34)\overline{146}}$$

One-third of the problems have a quotient that is a multiple too small:

$$\frac{4}{36)\overline{193}}$$

The final third of the problems contain the estimated quotients that are correct:

$$\frac{5}{28)\overline{153}}$$

Students first multiply the quotient and divisor. If the product of these two numbers is greater than the dividend, the teacher points out that the answer must be less. In the problem

$$\frac{5}{34)\overline{146}}$$
$$\underline{170}$$

the teacher says, "We can't subtract. We must make the answer smaller. Cross out the 5 and write 4." In problems in which the estimated quotient is too small, the teacher has the students compare their remainder to the divisor. If the remainder is as big or bigger than the divisor, the quotient is to be made larger. For example, in the problem

$$\frac{4}{36)\overline{193}}$$
$$\underline{144}$$
$$49$$

the teacher points out that another group of 36 can be made from 49, so the answer is made bigger. The 4 in the answer is erased and replaced with a 5.

A special type of problem yields an estimated quotient of 10 or above. For these problems, the teacher introduces a rule that no matter how high the answer to the rounded-off problem, the highest number used in an answer is 9. Then, even though rounding off

$$24)\overline{228} \quad \text{as} \quad 2)\overline{23}$$

yields 11 as an estimated quotient, the student would still use 9 as the quotient. Several problems of this type should be included in the exercises.

Practice on problems yielding an incorrect quotient would be continued daily for several weeks. During this time, problems would be limited to those that have one-digit quotients. Problems with multi-digit quotients would not be introduced until students are successful at working problems with single-digit quotients. The teacher should prepare worksheets containing a variety of problems. In some problems, the estimate for the first digit of the quotient should prove too large or too small, while the estimate for the second digit proves correct. For example, in the problem

$$64)\overline{1803}$$

only the estimate for the first numeral in the quotient is incorrect (3 is too large). In other problems, the estimate for the first digit of the quotient would be correct while the estimate for the second part would be incorrect. For example, in the problem

$$64)\overline{3317}$$

the estimate for 64 into 331 is correct, while the second part of the problem, 64 into 117, yields an estimated quotient that is too large. Finally, in some problems the estimate for both numerals of the quotient would be incorrect. Figure 10.3 includes sets of problems that can be used in these exercises.

Problems in which the estimated quotient is too small are particularly difficult for students. In order to prepare students for this format, the teacher should present an exercise for several days prior to introducing Format 10.11, focusing on when a remainder is too big. In this exercise the teacher

---

Summary Box 10.2   Division: Double-Digit Division

1. Student reads the problem.

2. Student underlines the part to be worked first.

3. Student writes the rounded-off problem.

4. Student computes the division problem using the estimate from the rounded-off problem.

5. Student multiplies and determines if he can subtract.

6. Student adjusts the quotient if the estimate is not correct (using the rules: If you can't subtract, make the answer smaller; if the remainder is too big, make the answer bigger).

7. Student computes the division problem and reads the problem with the answer.

FIGURE 10.3 Examples of Two-Digit Divisor Problems with Single-Digit Quotients

Estimate Yields Quotient That Is Correct

34)102	82)591	37)1723	72)3924	73)2308	53)230	27)94	52)2731
53)1752	29)2150	48)268	51)78	68)1528	27)941	51)2398	39)94
90)673	80)7485	19)813	86)5000	40)289	48)269	12)384	41)987
25)896	67)242	82)370	89)6703	58)1256	16)415	32)197	11)48
45)968	93)5780	42)534	75)183	28)154	36)2000	84)991	60)2486

Estimate Yields Quotient Too Large

73)289	84)246	91)632	64)3321	53)1524	16)60	23)170	13)68
93)2724	24)900	44)216	72)354	82)2401	52)1020	31)1500	31)180
54)102	71)3520	41)2450	72)2815				

Estimate Yields Quotient Too Small

26)185	35)175	38)193	35)1651	25)1852	46)283	86)260	75)300
37)2483	47)1898	57)342	29)114	48)3425	46)1823	85)6913	45)238
58)232	36)1892	16)861	17)698				

Problems in Which Estimated Quotient Is Greater Than 9

23)214	21)200	34)312	73)725	74)725	43)412	24)238	14)120
13)104	32)304						

writes about six problems with two-digit divisors on the board and models how to determine if the remainder is too big.

Diagnosis and Remediation

Division problems may be worked incorrectly for numerous reasons. Common errors made by students are summarized in the diagnosis and remediation chart in Figure 10.4. The remediation procedures usually involve presenting a structured worksheet exercise focusing on the particular component skill error made by the students. Remember, when students miss more than 10–20% of the problems due to a specific type of error, a remediation procedure is needed. When examining student worksheets, the teacher should not only look for the reason why students missed a problem but also should examine problems solved correctly, noting if the students rounded off correctly. Students who round off incorrectly may solve problems correctly but may have done much unnecessary computing. Students who make rounding-off errors in 10–15% or more of the problems should receive intensive

remediation in rounding off. The teacher would review the rounding-off formats for several days before reintroducing the less-structured presentation.

COMMERCIAL PROGRAMS

Division: Renaming with Single- and Double-Digit Divisors

INSTRUCTIONAL STRATEGIES The initial strategy presented for division with remainders does not vary significantly in the major programs. The strategy usually includes these steps:

Step 1—Divide tens
Step 2—Regroup
Step 3—Divide ones

As with strategies presented for other basic operations, the strategy appears straightforward. However, upon closer inspection we find that critical steps in the strategy are omitted, thereby making use of the strategy more difficult, especially for

FIGURE 10.4 Diagnosis and Remediation of Multi-Digit Division Errors

Error Patterns	Diagnosis	Remediation Procedures
One-Digit Divisor Problems		
a. 64 7)483 45 33 28 5	Fact error: Student makes a fact error (6 × 7 = 45).	Depends on frequency of fact error. High % fact errors—provide systematic fact instruction. Low % fact errors—increase motivation, include missed facts in fact drills.
b. 56 7)413 35 43 42 1	Component skill: Student makes a subtraction error (41 − 35 = 4).	Less-structured worksheet part of Format 10.7. Remind students to borrow.
c. 81 6)493 48 13 6 7	Component skill: Student computes an incorrect quotient. Too small.	Remediation formats (Formats 10.4 and 10.5) for incorrect quotients. Problems should have divisor that was in problem missed.
d. 49 6)288 24 48 54	Component skill: Student computes an incorrect quotient. Too large.	
e. 335 7)23458 21 24 21 38 35 3	Component skill: Student computes an incomplete quotient: does not bring down a digit.	Less-structured worksheet exercise (Format 10.7).
f. 514 4)20568 20 5 4 16 16 0	Component skill: Student computes an incomplete quotient: does not write a quotient for the last digit.	Less-structured worksheet exercise focusing on need to keep working problems until each digit after underlined part has a digit over it.
g. 12 7)714 7 14 14 7 5)352 35 2	Component skill: Student computes an incomplete quotient in problems with zero in the quotient.	Structured worksheet focusing on problems of this type.

continued on next page

low-performing students. In some programs students are encouraged to "think through" these critical steps. Also, the use of pictures tends to direct student attention away from necessary steps in the computation process, such as how to align numbers in the problem or when and where to subtract (see Figure 10.5). In fact, it is unclear from the teacher's manual whether students are supposed to operate on the pictures or on the numerals first. Naive students would require more explicit instruc-

FIGURE 10.4 continued

Error Patterns	Diagnosis	Remediation Procedures
Two-Digit Divisor Problems		
h. $\begin{array}{r} 4 \\ 39\overline{)155} \\ 156 \\ \hline 1 \end{array}$ $\begin{array}{r} 2 \\ 25\overline{)78} \\ 50 \\ \hline 28 \end{array}$	Component skill: Student computes quotient that is too large or too small.	Present format for problems in which estimated quotient is incorrect (Format 10.11).
i. $\begin{array}{r} 7 \\ 27\overline{)2248} \\ 189 \end{array}$	Component skill: Student computes an incomplete quotient because of misplacement of products.	Present structured worksheet exercise (Format 10.10). Focus on where to place digits when multiplying.

FIGURE 10.5 Excerpt from a Basal Mathematics Textbook. (*Source:* From *Heath Mathematics* Teacher's Edition, Level 5 by Rucker, et al. Copyright © 1987 by D.C. Heath & Company. Reprinted by permission of Houghton-Mifflin Company. All rights reserved.)

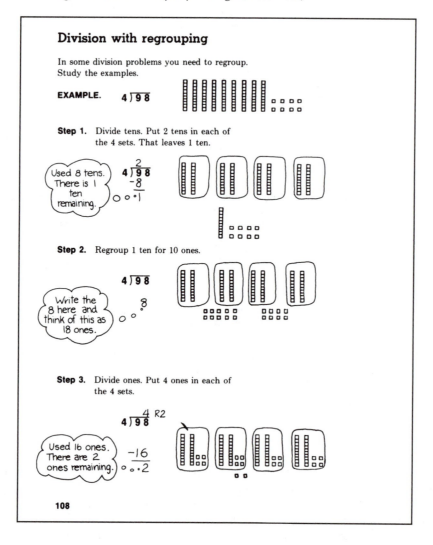

tion on all steps of this computation process to master this skill.

The strategies for division with two-digit divisors that appear in the leading basals are again quite similar. Even in initial lessons, students are assumed to have mastered sophisticated prerequisites such as determining where to begin working the problem or estimation. Figure 10.6 is an example of an initial lesson on two-digit divisors taken from a program. The problem the teacher writes on the board is $20\overline{)1897}$. The strategy is outlined in four basic steps: regroup thousands, regroup hundreds, regroup tens, and regroup tens again. The process of estimating the answer is already completed for the student. Whether students can estimate on their own is a question. Also, since many errors in division are caused by writing quotients in the wrong columns, the omission in many programs of provisions for teaching students how to align columns in division is noteworthy. In the example provided, the answer is not written for the students, so there is not even a model of where to write the answers.

FIGURE 10.6   Excerpt from the Teacher's Edition of a Basal Mathematics Textbook. (*Source:* From *Heath Mathematics* Teacher's Edition, Level 6 by Rucker et al. Copyright © 1987 by D.C. Heath & Company. Reprinted by permission of Houghton Mifflin Company. All rights reserved.)

Using the Pages

Work the example on page 84 on the chalkboard. Go over each step in detail. "There are not enough thousands to put any thousands into each of 20 groups. We regroup the thousand into 10 hundreds. Look at the 18 hundreds. There are not enough hundreds to put any hundreds into each of 20 groups. Regroup the 18 hundreds into 180 tens. Look at the 189 tens. Using the multiplication facts at the top of the page, notice that there are enough tens to put 9 tens into each of 20 groups. That uses 180 tens and leaves 9 tens. Regroup the 9 tens into 90 ones, so we have 97 ones. Again, using the multiplication facts at the top of the page, we can see that there are enough ones to put 4 ones into each 20 groups (but not enough to put 5 ones in each group.) This uses 80 ones and leaves 17 ones."

Assign exercises from pages 84 and 85. Discuss the procedure with individual students as they work. Check to be sure that students are placing digits in the quotient properly.

APPLICATION ITEMS: DIVISION

1. Describe the problem type that each example below represents. List the problems in the order they are introduced. Write the grade level when each type is typically introduced.

$5\overline{)128}$ $5\overline{)23}$ $2\overline{)136}$ $5\overline{)20}$ $5\overline{)153}$

$27\overline{)122}$ $5\overline{)736}$ $27\overline{)136}$ $5\overline{)526}$

2. Below is an excerpt from the independent worksheet to be given to students who have just demonstrated accuracy in solving problems with a one-digit divisor and a three-digit quotient (type 4e). The teacher has made some errors in constructing the worksheet.

   a. Indicate any inappropriate examples.
   b. Identify any omitted problem types that should be included on the worksheet. (Assume that students know all basic division facts.)

   $7\overline{)932}$ $5\overline{)1432}$ $3\overline{)1214}$ $5\overline{)3752}$

   $2\overline{)714}$ $9\overline{)1436}$ $5\overline{)823}$ $6\overline{)1443}$

3. Below are eight problems that appeared on a worksheet to be done independently by the students in Ms. Adams' math group. Below each student's name are the problems missed by the student. For each student, specify the probable cause or causes of the student's errors. Describe the remediation procedure.

(continued on next page)

APPLICATION ITEMS: DIVISION (CONTINUED)

$6\overline{)8324}$ $4\overline{)12385}$ $7\overline{)493}$ $8\overline{)7200}$ $5\overline{)5214}$ $7\overline{)9222}$ $5\overline{)8253}$ $9\overline{)72990}$

Barbara

```
       8332R2              925
  9) 72990            8) 7200
     70                  70
     29                  20
     27                  16
      29                 40
      27
       20
       18
        2
```

Randy

```
       396R1             142R4
  4) 12385            5) 5214
     12                  5
     38                  21
     36                  20
      25                 14
      24                 10
       1                  4
```

Fred

```
       131R5
  7) 9222
     7
     22
     21
      12
       7
       5
```

4. Below is an error made by Charles on a worksheet assignment. Describe what the teacher says in making the correction.

```
       4R40
  36) 184
     144
      40
```

5. Write the structured worksheet part of a format to present this problem:

$7\overline{)213}$

6. Specify the wording the teacher uses to correct the following errors:

a. $27\overline{)482}$ $\boxed{3\overline{)48}}$

b. $27\overline{)482}$ $\boxed{2\overline{)4}}$

7. Below is an excerpt from the independent worksheet to be given to students who have just demonstrated accuracy in solving problems with two-digit divisors and one- or two-digit quotients, in which estimating produces proper quotient. Indicate the inappropriate examples.

$23\overline{)989}$ $34\overline{)148}$ $76\overline{)793}$

$58\overline{)2938}$ $31\overline{)283}$ $49\overline{)1638}$

FORMAT 10.1   **Format for Introducing Division**

| TEACHER | STUDENTS |

PART A: TRANSLATING DIVISION PROBLEMS

(Write these problems on the board.)

$$\begin{array}{cccc} 3 & 9 & 5 & 4 \\ 5\overline{)15} & 2\overline{)18} & 6\overline{)30} & 3\overline{)12} \end{array}$$

$$\begin{array}{ccc} 5 & 4 & 7 \\ 4\overline{)20} & 7\overline{)28} & 3\overline{)21} \end{array}$$

1. This is a division problem. What kind of problem?

   A division problem

   It says *(Point to 5.)* 5 goes into *(point to 15.)* 15 *(Point to 3.)* three times. What does the problem say? *(Point to 5, then 15, then 3 as students answer. Repeat step 1 with the problems below.)*

   5 goes into 15 three times.

   $$\begin{array}{cc} 9 & 5 \\ 2\overline{)18} & 6\overline{)30} \end{array}$$

2. *(Point to* $3\overline{)12}$*)* What does this problem say? *(Point to 3, then 12, then 4 as students answer. Repeat step 2 with the problems below.)*

   3 goes into 12 four times.

   $$\begin{array}{ccc} 5 & 4 & 7 \\ 4\overline{)20} & 7\overline{)28} & 3\overline{)21} \end{array}$$

   (Give individual turns to several students.)

PART B: STRUCTURED BOARD PRESENTATION

(Write on board: $5\overline{)15}$*)*

1. What kind of problem is this?

   A division problem

   This problem says 5 goes into 15. What does this problem say? *(Point to 5, then 15.)*

   5 goes into 15.

   We have to find out how many times 5 goes into 15. When we divide we start with a big group and make equal-sized smaller groups. *(Write 15 lines on board.)*

   | | | | | | | | | | | | | | |

2. This is a group of 15 lines. I want to divide this group of 15 lines into smaller groups. Each smaller group will have 5 lines in it. How many lines in each smaller group?

   5

3. I'll touch the lines. You count. *(Touch five lines.)* This is a group of 5, so I'll put a circle around it. *(Circle five lines.)* *(Repeat step 3 with remaining groups of five lines.)*

   1, 2, 3, 4, 5

4. We divided 15 into groups of 5. Let's count the groups. *(Touch each group.)*

   1, 2, 3

5. How many times does 5 go into 15? I write the 3 above the last digit in 15. *(Write* $5\overline{)15}$ with 3 above*)*

   3

   Say what the problem tells us.

   5 goes into 15 three times.

   (Repeat steps 1–5 with $2\overline{)8}$*)*

(continued on next page)

FORMAT 10.1   (continued)

PART C: STRUCTURED WORKSHEET

TEACHER	**STUDENTS**

a. 5)‾20‾   b. 2)‾8‾   c. 2)‾12‾

| | | | | | | | | | | | | | | | | | | | | | | | | | | | | | | | | | | | | | | | |

1. Touch problem a. That problem says 5 goes into 20. What does the problem say?

5 goes into 20.

2. We have to find out how many groups of 5 we can make from 20. There are 20 lines under the problem. Make groups of 5 lines each *(Check students' papers.)*

3. How many groups did you make?

4

Write 4 above the last digit in 20. *(Monitor.)*

Students write 4.

4. Now the problem says 5 goes into 20 four times. What does the problem say now?

5 goes into 20 four times.

(Repeat steps 1–4 with remaining problems.)

PART D: LESS STRUCTURED WORKSHEET

1. Touch problem a.

Students touch 2)‾10‾.

| | | | | | | | | |

2. What does the problem say?

2 goes into 10.

3. How many in each group?

2

4. Make the groups and write how many groups over the last digit in 10.

Students make circles around each two lines. Students write 5.

5. Read the problem and answer.

2 goes into 10 five times.

FORMAT 10.2   **Format for Introducing Division with Remainders**

TEACHER	**STUDENTS**

PART A: INTRODUCING REMAINDERS

(Write this problem on board.)

5)‾13‾

1. *(Point to 5)‾13‾.)* What does the problem say?

5 goes into 13.

2. First let's solve the problem by making lines. The problem asks how many groups of 5 in 13, so I'll draw 13 lines. *(Make 13 lines on the board.)* The problem asks how many groups of 5 in 13. So I'll put a circle around each group of 5. *(Count out each group of 5 aloud; after circling each group, say,)* Here's a group of 5. *(After counting the last 3 lines, say,)* We only have 3 left so we can't make a group of 5.

   | | |

(continued on next page)

FORMAT 10.2   (continued)

TEACHER	STUDENTS
3. Now let's see how many groups of 5 there are; count the groups as I touch them. *(Touch groups as students count.)*	1, 2
4. How many groups of 5 in 13?	2
Yes, there are two groups. *(Write $5\overline{)13}$ with 2 above.)*	
5. Are there lines left over?	Yes
We call those lines the remainder. How many lines are left over?	3
6. We say that 5 goes into 13 two times with a remainder of 3. How many times does 5 go into 13?	Two times with a remainder of 3.

(Repeat steps 1–6 with the problems below.)

$2\overline{)9}$ $9\overline{)21}$

PART B: STRUCTURED WORKSHEET

a. $5\overline{)23}$ (|||||) (|||||) (|||||) (|||||) |||

b. $2\overline{)7}$ (||) (||) (||) |

c. $9\overline{)25}$ (|||||||||) (|||||||||) |||||||

d. $5\overline{)14}$ (|||||) (|||||) ||||

1. Read problem a.	5 goes into 23.
2. The problem asks how many groups of 5 we can make from 23. Next to the problem are 23 lines. A circle has been drawn around each group of 5 lines. How many groups of 5 are there?	4
Write 4 on the line above the 3.	
3. We want to figure out how many lines we used up, so we multiply 4 times 5. How do we figure how many lines we used up?	Multiply 4×5.
4. What is 4×5? *(Pause, signal.)*	20
5. Write 20 under the 23. We started with 23 and used up 20 so write a minus sign in front of the 20. Read the subtraction problem we just wrote.	$23 - 20$
Subtract and write the remainder. What is 23 minus 20?	3
6. We're all finished; 5 goes into 23 four times with a remainder of 3. How many times does 5 go into 23?	four times with a remainder of 3

(Repeat steps 1–6 with problems b and c.)

(continued on next page)

FORMAT 10.2 **(continued)**

TEACHER	STUDENTS

PART C: LESS-STRUCTURED WORKSHEET

TEACHER	STUDENTS
1. Read problem _____ .	_____ goes into _____ .
How many times does _____ go into _____ ?	
(Pause, signal.)	_____ times
Write _____ above the _____ in _____.	
How do we figure how many lines we used?	Multiply _____ times _____ .
2. What is _____ times _____ ?	_____
3. Write _____ under the _____. Put in the minus	
sign.	
4. Subtract. *(Remind students to borrow when applicable.)*	
What is the remainder?	_____
5. How many times does _____ go into _____ ?	_____ times with a remainder
	of _____

FORMAT 10.3 **Format for Introducing Remainder Facts**

TEACHER	STUDENTS

PART A: STRUCTURED BOARD PRESENTATION

(Write these numbers on the board in a single row.)

⓪ 1 2 3 4 ⑤ 6 7 8 ˙9

⑩ 11 12 13 14 ⑮ 16 17 18

19 ⑳ 21 22 23 24 ㉕

TEACHER	STUDENTS
1. Listen: 5 goes into the circled numbers without a remainder. Say the numbers that 5 goes into without a remainder.	0, 5, 10, 15, 20, 25
2. Five goes into the other number with a remainder. *(Point to 1, 2, 3, 4.)* These are numbers 5 goes into zero times with a remainder.	
3. My turn: How many times does 5 go into 2? Five goes into 2 zero times with a remainder.	
How many times does 5 go into 2?	zero times with a remainder
How many times does 5 go into 4?	zero times with a remainder
4. *(Point to 5.)* Five goes into 5, one time. *(Point to 6, 7, 8, 9.)* These are numbers 5 goes into one time with a remainder.	
How many times does 5 go into 8?	one time with a remainder
How many times does 5 go into 6?	one time with a remainder
5. *(Repeat step 4 using 5 goes into 15 and then 5 goes into 19 and 5 goes into 17.)*	
6. *(Repeat step 4 using 5 goes into 20, 5 goes into 24, 5 goes into 21.)*	

(continued on next page)

FORMAT 10.3 (continued)

TEACHER	STUDENTS

PART B: LESS-STRUCTURED BOARD PRESENTATION

(Write these numbers on the board in a single row.)

⓪ 1   2   3   4   ⑤   6   7   8   9
⑩ 11 12 13 14 ⑮ 16 17 18
19 ⑳ 21 22 23 24 ㉕

1. Say the numbers 5 goes into without a remainder.

                                         5, 10, 15, 20, 25

2. *(Point to 13.)* Think, 5 goes into 13 how many times? *(Pause, signal.)*

                                         Two times with a remainder

    To correct: (Point to 10.) Five goes into 10 two times. *(Point to 11, 12, 13, 14.)* These are the numbers 5 goes into two times with a remainder. Five goes into 13, two times with a remainder. *(Repeat step 2.)*

3. *(Repeat step 2 with 20, 24, 0, 3, 9, 16.)*

PART C: STRUCTURED WORKSHEET

a. $5\overline{)22}$ b. $5\overline{)16}$ c. $5\overline{)10}$ d. $5\overline{)7}$

1. Read problem _____

                                      _____ goes into _____.

2. How many times does _____ go into _____ ? *(Pause, signal.)*

    To correct: (If student says number too low:

$$\overset{3}{5\overline{)22}}$$

    say,) We can make another group of five—5 times 4 is 20. *(If student says number too high:*

$$\overset{5}{5\overline{)22}}$$

    say,) 5 × 5 is 25. That's too big.

3. Write _____ above the _____ in _____ .

                                        Student writes quotient over last number in dividend.

    What do you multiply?

                                          _____ times _____

    Multiply and subtract. *(Pause.)* What is the remainder? How many times does _____ go into _____ ?

                                          _____ times with a remainder of _____

    (Repeat steps 1–3 with several more problems and then have students work the rest on their own.)

FORMAT 10.4 **Remediation for Division with Remainders—Quotient Too Small**

PART A: RECOGNIZING QUOTIENTS THAT ARE TOO SMALL

TEACHER	**STUDENTS**
(Write this problem on the board.)	
5)‾28‾	
1. This problem says 5 goes into 28. We're figuring 5 into a number, so the remainder must be smaller than 5.	
2. What does the problem say?	5 goes into 28.
3. So what do you know about the remainder?	It must be smaller than 5.
4. *(Repeat steps 1–3 with* 7)‾23‾ 2)‾13‾ 6)‾14‾ 5)‾27‾ 3)‾24‾.)	

PART B: WRITING THE CORRECT ANSWER

a. $\dfrac{4}{5)\overline{28}}$ b. $\dfrac{4}{7)\overline{31}}$ c. $\dfrac{2}{9)\overline{24}}$

d. $\dfrac{3}{9)\overline{43}}$ e. $\dfrac{8}{5)\overline{42}}$ f. $\dfrac{5}{2)\overline{13}}$

g. $\dfrac{6}{2)\overline{15}}$ h. $\dfrac{5}{5)\overline{28}}$

1. Problem a says 5 goes into 28 four times. We figure the remainder by multiplying 5×4 and then subtracting. Do that on your paper.	
2. What's the remainder?	8
3. Here's a rule: *If the remainder is too big, we make the answer bigger.* What do we do if the remainder is too big?	Make the answer bigger.
4. Is the remainder too big?	Yes
So what must we do?	Make the answer bigger.
The remainder is more than 5. So 5 can go into 28 another time. Cross out the 4 and write 5. *(Check.)* Now erase 20; multiply and subtract to figure the new remainder. What's the new remainder?	3
(Note: If the answer to step 4 is no, tell students,) so the answer is correct. Let's go to the next problem.	
5. Is the remainder too big?	No
So the answer is correct. Read the problem.	5 goes into 28, 5 times with a remainder of 3.
6. *(Repeat steps 1–5 with several problems, and then have students work remaining problems on their own.)*	

FORMAT 10.5   **Remediation for Division with Remainders—Quotient Too Large**

PART A: RECOGNIZING QUOTIENTS THAT ARE TOO LARGE

TEACHER	STUDENTS
(Write the problem below on the board.)	

$$\begin{array}{r} 6 \\ 5\overline{)28} \\ \underline{30} \end{array}$$

TEACHER	STUDENTS
1. What does this problem say?	5 goes into 28 six times.
2. The problem is worked for you, but there is something wrong. Can you subtract 30 from 28?	No
3. Here's a rule: If you can't subtract, make the answer smaller. What do you do if you can't subtract?	Make the answer smaller.
4. We make the answer one smaller. What is one smaller than 6?	5
(Erase 6 and write 5.) What is 5 times 5?	25
5. *(Erase 30 and write 25.)* Can you subtract 25 from 28?	Yes
What is 28 − 25?	3
Read the problem.	5 goes into 28 five times with a remainder of 3.
6. *(Repeat steps 1–5 with several examples.)*	

PART B: WRITING THE CORRECT ANSWER

$$\text{a.} \quad \begin{array}{r} 6 \\ 5\overline{)28} \end{array} \qquad \text{b.} \quad \begin{array}{r} 4 \\ 7\overline{)31} \end{array} \qquad \text{c.} \quad \begin{array}{r} 2 \\ 9\overline{)24} \end{array}$$

$$\text{d.} \quad \begin{array}{r} 5 \\ 9\overline{)43} \end{array} \qquad \text{e.} \quad \begin{array}{r} 8 \\ 5\overline{)42} \end{array} \qquad \text{f.} \quad \begin{array}{r} 7 \\ 2\overline{)13} \end{array}$$

TEACHER	STUDENTS
1. Look at the problems on your worksheet. Some of the answers are too big. You'll have to fix them.	
2. Look at problem a. What is 6 × 5?	30
3. Can you subtract 30 from 28?	No
What must you do?	Make the answer one smaller
(Note: Do step 4 only if answer to step 3 is no.)	
4. Cross out the 6. What do you write? Work the problem.	
(Repeat steps 2–4 with five or six problems, and then have students complete the worksheet on their own.)	

FORMAT 10.6   Basic Steps in the Short-Form Algorithm

TEACHER	STUDENTS
1. Read the problem.	7 goes into 238.
2. Underline the part you work first.	Students underline 7)$\overline{238}$.
3. Say the underlined part.	7 goes into 23.
4. Write the answer above the last underlined digit.	$\begin{array}{r} 3 \\ 7\overline{)238} \end{array}$
5. Multiply 3 × 7, subtract, and then bring down the next number.	$\begin{array}{r} 3 \\ 7\overline{)238} \\ 21 \\ \hline 28 \end{array}$
6. Read the new problem.	7 goes into 28.
7. Write the answer number above the digit you just brought down.	$\begin{array}{r} 34 \\ 7\overline{)238} \\ 21 \\ \hline 28 \end{array}$
8. Multiply and subtract to determine the remainder.	$\begin{array}{r} 34 \\ 7\overline{)238} \\ 21 \\ \hline 28 \\ 28 \\ \hline 0 \end{array}$
9. Say the answer.	7 goes into 238, 34 times.

FORMAT 10.7   Format for Division with Two-Digit Quotients

PART A: DETERMINING WHERE TO BEGIN

TEACHER	STUDENTS
1. When a division problem has lots of digits, we work the problem a part at a time. We always begin a problem by underlining the first part we work. Sometimes we underline just the first digit. Sometimes we underline the first two digits.	
2. *(Write the following problem on the board.)* 6)$\overline{242}$ Read the problem.	6 goes into 242.
We're dividing by 6. If the first digit in the number we're dividing is at least as big as 6, we underline the first digit in 242. If 6 can't go into the first digit, we underline the first two digits. Look at the number we're dividing into. The first digit we're dividing into is 2. Is 2 at least as big as 6?	No
So we underline the first two digits. *(Underline 24.)* 6)$\overline{242}$	
The underlined problem says 6 goes into 24. What does the underlined problem say?	6 goes into 24.

(continued on next page)

FORMAT 10.7   (continued)

TEACHER	**STUDENTS**

(Repeat step 2 with these problems.)

a. 5)87   b. 9)328   c. 4)38
d. 6)62   e. 3)245   f. 7)832

PART B: WORKSHEET ON DETERMINING WHERE TO BEGIN

a. 7)248   b. 3)527   c. 7)486   d. 5)532
e. 5)234   f. 6)184   g. 6)932
h. 4)128   i. 4)436   j. 8)264

1. Touch problem a. Read the problem.   **7 goes into 248.**

   You're going to underline the part of the problem you work first. What are you dividing by?   **7**

   Is the first digit you're dividing into at least as big as 7?   **No**

   So what do you underline?   **24**

   Underline 24. Say the underlined problem.   **7 goes into 24.**

   (Repeat step 1 with five problems. Then have students underline the part they work first in renaming problems.)

PART C: STRUCTURED BOARD PRESENTATION

(Write the following problem on the board:)
5)213

1. Read this problem.   **5 goes into 213.**

   Tell me the part to underline. *(Pause. Underline 21.)* 5)21̲3   **21**

   To correct: Look at the first digit. Is 2 at least as big as 5?   **No**

   So what do you underline?   **21**

   What does the underlined problem say?   **5 goes into 21.**

2. How many times does 5 go into 21? *(Pause.)*   **4**

3. I'll write the 4 over the last digit underlined.
   (Write the following:)

   $$\frac{4}{5)213}$$

4. Now multiply 4 × 5. What is 4 times 5? *(Pause. Write 20.)*   **20**
   Now I subtract 20 from 21. What is 1 – 0?   **1**
   (Write 1.)

5. *(Point to 3.)* What's the next digit after the underlined part?   **3**

   I bring it down and write it after the 1.
   (Write the steps in the problem so far.)

   $$\frac{4}{5)213}$$
   $$\frac{20}{13}$$

   What number is under the line now?   **13**

(continued on next page)

FORMAT 10.7 (continued)

TEACHER	STUDENTS

6. The next part of the problem says 5 goes into 13. What does the problem say now? — 5 goes into 13.

How many times does 5 go into 13? *(Pause.)* — 2

I write the 2 above the digit I brought down. *(Write this step in the problem.)*

```
   42
5)213
   20
   13
```

7. Now I multiply and subtract. What is 2 × 5? *(Pause.)* — 10

I write 10 under the 13. *(Write 10.)* What is 13 minus 10? *(Pause.)* — 3

8. The problem is finished. Every digit after the underlined part has a digit over it. 5 goes into 213, 42 times with a remainder of 3. How many times does 5 go into 213? *(Repeat steps 1–8 with 7)94   2)135   3)65)* — 42 times with a remainder of 3.

PART D: STRUCTURED WORKSHEET

(Write the following problem on the board.)
3)137

1. Touch the problem. Read the problem. — 3 goes into 137.

What numbers do you underline? *(Pause.)* — 13

2. Underline 13. What does the underlined problem say? — 3 goes into 13.

3. How many times does 3 go into 13? — 4
Write 4 above the last digit you underlined.

4. What numbers do you multiply? — 4 × 3

What is 4 × 3? — 12

5. Write 12 under 13, then subtract. What is 13 – 12? — 1

6. What is the next digit in the number you're dividing into? *(Pause.)* — 7

Bring down the 7 and write it next to the 1.
```
    7
3)137
   12
   17
```

7. What number is under the line? — 17

What does this part of the problem say? — 3 goes into 17.

How many times does 3 go into 17? *(Pause.)* — 5

8. Write the 5 above the digit you brought down. *(Monitor student responses.)*

9. What numbers do you multiply? — 5 × 3

What is 5 × 3? — 15

Write 15 under 17 and subtract. What is 17 – 15? — 2

Is there another number to bring down? — No

(continued on next page)

FORMAT 10.7   (continued)

TEACHER	STUDENTS
10. Every digit after the underlined part has a digit over it. So you finished the problem. What's the remainder?	2
How many times does 3 go into 137?	45 with a remainder of 2.
(Repeat steps 1–10 with remaining problems.)	

PART E: LESS-STRUCTURED WORKSHEET

(Write the following problem on the board.)
4)69

TEACHER	STUDENTS
1. Touch the problem. Read the problem.	4 goes into 69.
Underline the part you work first.	4)6̲9
Say the underlined problem.	4 goes into 6.
How many times does 4 go into 6?	1
2. Write the 1, multiply, subtract, and then bring down the next digit. *(Pause.)* What number is under the line now?	29
3. Say the new problem.	4 goes into 29.
How many times does 4 go into 29?	7
Write 7 in the answer. Then multiply and subtract. *(Pause.)* Is there another number to bring down?	No
Is the problem finished?	Yes
4. How many times does 4 go into 69?	17 with a remainder of 1.
(Repeat steps 1–4 with remaining problems.)	

FORMAT 10.8   Short-Form Algorithm—Two-Digit Divisors

TEACHER	STUDENTS
1. Read problem a.	37 goes into 1586.
2. Underline the part to work first.	37)1̲5̲8̲6
3. Read the first part.	37 goes into 158.
4. Estimate the quotient as tens units.	37 is converted to 4 tens. 158 is converted to 16 tens. 4 goes into 16 four times.
5. Place estimated quotient above last underlined digit, then multiply and subtract.	$$\begin{array}{r} 4 \\ 37\overline{)1586} \\ 148 \\ \hline 10 \end{array}$$
6. Compare the difference and divisor to see if quotient is correct. Bring down the next number in dividend.	$$\begin{array}{r} 4 \\ 37\overline{)1586} \\ 148 \\ \hline 106 \end{array}$$
7. Read the new problem.	37 goes into 106.

(continued on next page)

FORMAT 10.8   (continued)

TEACHER	STUDENTS
8. Estimate the quotient for the next problem.	37 is converted to 4 tens. 106 is converted to 11 tens. 4 goes into 11 two times.
9. Place estimated quotient above the last digit brought down, then multiply and subtract.	
10. Compare difference and divisor to see if quotient is correct.	

$$\begin{array}{r} 42 \\ 37\overline{)1586} \\ \underline{148} \\ 106 \\ \underline{74} \\ 32 \end{array}$$

FORMAT 10.9   Format for Rounding to Nearest Tens Unit

PART A: EXPRESSING NUMBERS AS TENS UNITS

TEACHER	STUDENTS
(Write on board: 190)	
1. What number?	190
Another way of saying 190 is 19 tens. What's another way of saying 190?	19 tens
2. *(Repeat step 1 with 80, 230.)*	
3. What's another way of saying 140?	14 tens
4. *(Repeat step 3 with 280, 30, 580, 420, 60, 500, 280, 40, 700.)*	

PART B: STRUCTURED BOARD PRESENTATION

(Write on board: 186.)	
1. What number?	186
2. Is 186 closer to 180 or 190?	190
To correct: If we have at least 5 in the ones column. We round off to the next higher tens unit. How many ones in 186? So we round off to 190.	
So is 186 closer to 18 tens or 19 tens? *(Pause.)*	19 tens
To correct: 186 is closer to 190. How many tens in 190?	

3. *(Repeat step 2 with these examples.)*

142	14 tens or 15 tens
83	8 tens or 9 tens
47	4 tens or 5 tens
286	28 tens or 29 tens
432	43 tens or 44 tens
27	2 tens or 3 tens
529	52 tens or 53 tens

(continued on next page)

FORMAT 10.9   (continued)

PART C: STRUCTURED WORKSHEET

TEACHER	STUDENTS

Worksheet

Round off these numbers to the nearest ten. Write how many tens in the rounded off number:

142 __ tens	87 __ tens	537 __ tens	497 __ tens
287 __ tens	426 __ tens	248 __ tens	321 __ tens
825 __ tens	53 __ tens	632 __ tens	503 __ tens
546 __ tens	182 __ tens	428 __ tens	278 __ tens
932 __ tens	203 __ tens	561 __ tens	426 __ tens

1. *(Call on a student to read the directions.)* Read the first number.   142

2. Think: 142 is closest to how many tens?   14 tens

   To correct: is 142 closer to 140 or 150? So is 142 closer to 14 or 15 tens? *(Write the answer.)*

3. Write 14 in the blank. *(Repeat steps 2–3 with several more examples.)*

FORMAT 10.10   Format for Correct Estimated Quotients with Two-Digit Divisors

PART A: PRESKILL—MULTIPLYING QUOTIENT TIMES DIVISOR

I. Board Presentation

TEACHER	STUDENTS

(Write the problem below on the board.)

$$54\overline{)231}\quad\overset{4}{}$$

1. This problem says 54 goes into 231, four times. What does the problem say?   54 goes into 231 four times.

2. We have to figure out the remainder. We multiply 4 times 54. What do we multiply? 4×54

3. When I multiply 4×54, first I multiply 4×4, then I multiply 4×5. What is 4×4?   16

   I write the 6 under the last underlined digit and carry the 1.

   (Write the problem below on the board.)

   $$\overset{1}{54}\overline{)231}\atop 6\quad\overset{4}{}$$

4. Now I multiply 4×5 and add the 1 I carried. What is 4×5?   20

   And one more is?   21

   I write the 21 in front of the 6.

(continued on next page)

FORMAT 10.10   (continued)

TEACHER	STUDENTS

(Write this step of the problem on the board.)

```
      4
54)231
   216
```

5. What is 4 × 54? — 216

6. We subtract 216 from 231 to figure out the remainder. Can we start with 1 and subtract 6? — No

We must borrow. *(Write this step:)*

```
  2 1
2 3̸ 1.
```

What is 11 minus 6? — 5

What is 2 minus 1? — 1

7. 54 goes into 231 four times with a remainder of 15. Say that. — 54 goes into 231 four times with a remainder of 15.

(Repeat steps 1–7 with the problems below.)

```
      3           4
48)156      94)413
```

II. Worksheet

```
a.      3     b.      6     c.      5
  27)103       46)278       14)80
```

1. Read problem a. — 27 goes into 103 three times.

2. You need to multiply 3 × 27. When you multiply 3 × 27, what do you multiply first? — 3 × 7

3. What is 3 × 7? — 21

Write the 1 and carry the two tens.

To correct: Write the 1 under the 3. *(Pause.)* Carry the two tens above the 2 in 27.

4. Now what do you multiply? — 3 × 2

What is 3 × 2? — 6

Add the 2 you carried. What's the answer? — 8
Write the 8.

5. Figure out the remainder. Be careful to borrow in the tens column.

6. What is the remainder? — 22
Yes, 27 goes into 103 three times with a remainder of 22. Say that. — 27 goes into 103 three times with a remainder of 22.

(Repeat steps 1–6 with several problems; then have students work the rest independently.)

(continued on next page)

FORMAT 10.10   (continued)

TEACHER	STUDENTS

PART B: PRESKILL—ESTIMATING

I. Board Presentation
(Write the problem and the box below on the board.)

37)932   [ ) ___]

1. What does the problem say?	37 goes into 932.
2. We have to underline the part we work first. Does 37 go into 9?	No
Does 37 goes into 93?	Yes
So I underline the first two digits.	
3. I'll read the part we work first; 37 goes into 93. Say the part we work first.	37 goes into 93.
4. To find out how many times 37 goes into 93, we must round off. The box next to the problem is for rounding off.	
5. First I round off 37; 37 is rounded off to how many tens? *(Pause and then write the four.)*	4

[4) ___]

Ninety-three is rounded off to how many tens? *(Pause and then write the 9.)*	9

[4)9 ___]

Read the rounded-off problem	4 goes into 9.
6. Four goes into nine how many times?	2
So in the problem we started with, I write 2 over the last underlined digit. *(Write the 2.)*	2

$$\frac{2}{37)\underline{932}}$$

(Repeat steps 1–6 with 24)136   52)386   34)942.)

II. Worksheet

a. 79)246   [ ) ___]   b. 49)538   [ ) ___]

c. 27)943   [ ) ___]   d. 36)193   [ ) ___]

1. What does problem a say?	79 goes into 2463.
2. What digits do you underline? *(Pause.)*	246
Underline the part you work first. Say the underlined problem.	79 goes into 246.
3. Let's write the rounded-off problem for 79 into 122 in the box. How many tens does 79 round off to? *(Pause.)*	8

(continued on next page)

FORMAT 10.10   (continued)

TEACHER	STUDENTS
Write 8 in the box. How many tens does 246 round off to? *(Pause.)*	25
Write 25 in the box. Read the rounded-off problem.	8 goes into 25.
Three goes into twenty-five how many times?	3

4. Write the answer in the problem you started with. Write it above the last underlined digit.

   (Repeat steps 1–4 with three more problems; then have students work the next problems on their own.)

PART C: STRUCTURED WORKSHEET

(Write the sample problem on the board.)

38)1432

1. Read the problem.	38 goes into 1432.
Underline the part you work first.	
What did you underline?	143
Read the underlined problem.	38 goes into 143.
2. Write the rounded-off problem in the box. How many tens does 38 round off to? *(Pause.)*	4
Write 4. How many tens does 143 round off to? *(Pause.)*	14
Write 14. Read the rounded-off problem.	4 goes into 14.
3. Four goes into fourteen how many times? Write 3 above the last digit you underlined.	3
4. Now we multiply 3 times 38. What is 3×8? *(Pause.)* Write 4 below the last underlined digit and carry the 2. *(Pause.)* Now multiply 3×3 and add 2. *(Pause.)*	24
What's the answer? *(Pause.)*	11
Write 11 next to the 4.	
5. Now subtract 114 from 143. *(Pause.)* What is 143 minus 114?	29
6. Let's see if there's a second part to work. Is there a digit after the underlined part to bring down?	yes
(If the answer to step 6 is no, skip steps 7–10; go directly to step 11.)	
7. Bring down that digit, what number is under the line now?	292
Say the new problem.	38 goes into 292.
8. Let's write the rounded-off problem in the second box. How many tens does 38 round off to?	4
Write 4. How many tens does 292 round off to?	29

(continued on next page)

FORMAT 10.10   (continued)

TEACHER	STUDENTS
Write 29. Read the rounded-off problem.	4 goes into 29.
9. How many times does 4 go into 29? Write 7 in the problem you started with. Write it above the 2 you brought down.	7
10. Now we multiply 7 × 38. What do you multiply? Multiply and write the answer below 292.	7 times 38
(Pause.) What is 7 × 38?	266
Subtract 292 – 266 to find the remainder. (Pause.) What's 292 – 266?	26
Are there any more digits to bring down?	No
11. So you're done with the problem. How many times does 38 go into 1432?	37 times with a remainder of 26.
(Repeat steps 1–11 with remaining problems.)	

PART D: LESS-STRUCTURED WORKSHEET

(Write the sample problem on the board.)

18)604

TEACHER	STUDENTS
1. Read the problem.	18 goes into 604.
Underline the part you work first. What did you underline?	60
Read the underlined problem.	18 goes into 60.
2. Write the rounded-off problem in the upper box. (Pause.) Say the rounded-off problem.	2 goes into 6.
3. Write the answer, then multiply. (Pause.) Say the subtraction problem.	60 – 54
Subtract 60 – 54. (Pause.) What is 60 – 54?	6
4. What do you do next? Do it.	Bring down the 4.
5. Say the new problem.	18 goes into 64.
6. Write the rounded-off problem in the second box. (Pause.) Say the rounded-off problem.	2 goes into 6.
7. Write the answer, then multiply and subtract. (Pause.) What is the remainder?	10
8. Are you finished? How many times does 18 go into 604?	33 times with a remainder of 10.

FORMAT 10.11   **Format for Incorrect Estimated Quotients**

PART A: STRUCTURED WORKSHEET

TEACHER			STUDENTS

a. $\dfrac{4}{37\overline{)142}}$ b. $\dfrac{5}{48\overline{)299}}$ c. $\dfrac{5}{48\overline{)299}}$

d. $\dfrac{4}{79\overline{)315}}$ e. $\dfrac{3}{46\overline{)192}}$ f. $\dfrac{3}{52\overline{)148}}$

g. $\dfrac{4}{82\overline{)318}}$ h. $\dfrac{5}{34\overline{)178}}$ i. $\dfrac{2}{26\overline{)81}}$

1. The answers to some of these problems are wrong. To find the wrong answers, you figure out the remainder. If you can't subtract, you must make the answer *smaller*. If you find a remainder, but it is too big, you must make the answer *bigger*.	
2. Touch problem a. What does the problem say?	37 goes into 142 four times.
3. What are you going to multiply? Do the multiplication. Write the minus sign and stop.	4 times 37.
4. Say the subtraction problem.	142 – 148
5. Can you subtract 142 minus 148? We can't subtract, so we must make the answer smaller.	No
6. So you have to cross out the 4 and write a 3 above it. Do it, then erase the 148.	
7. Now multiply 3 × 37.	
8. Read the subtraction problem now.	142 – 111
9. Subtract and figure out the remainder. That's all we do for now.	31

(Steps 4a–8a are for problems in which the estimated quotient is too small.)

(The problem is)

$\dfrac{5}{48\overline{)299}}$

4a. Say the subtraction problem.	299 – 240
Can you subtract 240 from 299? Subtract. *(Pause.)*	Yes
5a. What is the remainder?	59
Is the remainder too big?	Yes
To correct: (Ask.) What are we dividing by? Is the remainder at least as big as 48?	
You can make another group. So we make the answer bigger. Cross out the 5 and write 6. Erase 240.	
6a. Now multiply 6 × 48.	
7a. Read the subtraction problem now. Subtract.	299 – 288

(continued on next page)

FORMAT 10.11   (continued)

TEACHER	STUDENTS
8a. What's the answer?	11
Can we make another group of 48?	No
So we're all finished.	

(Repeat steps 1–9 or 4a–8a with three of the remaining problems. Have students work the remaining problems on their own.)

PART B: LESS-STRUCTURED WORKSHEET

a. 42)197   b. 36)203

c. 58)232

1. Touch problem a. Read the problem.   42 goes into 197.

2. Underline the part you work first.

3. Write the rounded-off problem. Say the rounded-off problem.   4 goes into 20.

4. What is the answer?   5
    Multiply 5 × 42. *(Pause.)* Can you subtract?   No

    (Note: Present step 5 or 6.)

5. *(If the answer to step 4 is no, say,)* So what must you do? Fix your answer then multiply and subtract.

6. *(If the answer to step 4 is yes, say,)* Subtract _____ from _____ . What is the remainder? Is the remainder too big? *(Continue if answer is yes.)* So what must we do? Erase _____ and write _____ then multiply and subtract. *(Pause.)* What is the remainder? Is that remainder too big? So we're finished. Say the whole answer.

    (Repeat steps 1–6 with remaining problems.)

CHAPTER 11

Problem Solving

This chapter discusses procedures for teaching students to apply the four basic operations (addition, subtraction, multiplication, and division) to word problems, stories that present situations requiring a mathematical solution. Because mathematical terms and properties were introduced in the chapters for each operation, no new terms or properties are presented here. Nor does this chapter include all of the important problem-solving strategies. Procedures for teaching problem-solving strategies for problems that include fractions, percent, decimals, time, money, and measurement are all addressed in later chapters on those topics.

There are two basic groupings of math story problems: addition/subtraction and multiplication/division. Addition and subtraction word problems are introduced together to provide discrimination practice. For the same reason, multiplication and division word problems are taught together. Multiplication and division story problems are introduced as soon as students have mastered previously introduced types of story problems and have been taught to solve multiplication and division computation problems. Story or word problems are usually introduced soon after a new operation has been mastered.

Addition and subtraction problems are usually introduced in late first grade. Analysis of addition and subtraction problems in commercial mathematics programs revealed three main problem types:

temporal sequence problems, classification problems, and comparison problems. Simple versions of these three types of one-step problems are usually introduced by the end of second grade. Both initial and more sophisticated strategies for solving these problem types are introduced in this chapter.

Multiplication and division problems are usually introduced during third grade. In most initial problems, the multiplication or division operation is signaled by the presence of the word *each* or *every*. Later, the words *a* and *per* serve as signals for multiplication or division. Multiplication and division problems that do not contain key words are obviously more difficult. See the Instructional Sequence and Assessment Chart for a recommended sequence of introduction.

Besides the two basic groupings of story problems, there are also problems with large numbers, multi-step problems, and problems with distractors. Problems with larger numbers are usually more difficult because the computation is more difficult and the operation required is often less obvious. Multi-step problems usually appear in third grade and require students to perform two or more steps, usually involving two or more different operations, to solve the problem. The simplest type of multi-step problem involves adding three numbers. Multi-step problems become more difficult as the number and type of computations to be performed increase. The third type of these more difficult story problems con-

Instructional Sequence and Assessment Chart

Grade Level	Problem Type	Performance Indicator
1–2a	Addition/subtraction simple action problems with key words.	Bill had 7 apples. He got 3 more from the store. How many apples does he have in all?
		Lisa had some apples. She bought 3 more. She ended up with 12 apples. How many apples did she start with?
2a	Addition/subtraction temporal sequence problems	Carlos had 7 apples. He gave 3 to his sister. How many does he have left?
2b	Addition/subtraction comparison problems.	Bill is 7 years old. Alice is 5 years old. How much older is Bill?
		Hole A is 5 feet deep. Hole B is 7 feet deeper than Hole A. How deep is Hole B?
		Hole A is 5 feet deep. Hole B is 7 feet deep. How much deeper is Hole B?
2c	Addition/subtraction classification problems.	Eight men are in the store. Three women are in the store. How many people are in the store?
		Ramona had 4 hats; 3 of the hats are blue. How many hats are not blue?
		Jill sold 5 hats in the morning. She sold 2 hats in the afternoon. How many hats did she sell?
2d	Multi-step problems: add three numbers.	Bill ran 5 miles on Monday, 3 miles on Tuesday, and 4 miles on Wednesday. How many miles did he run altogether?
3a	Multiplication/division problems with the word *each* or *every*.	Bill has 4 boxes. In each box there are 6 pencils. How many pencils does Bill have?
		Tammy jogs 5 miles every day. How far will she jog in 3 days?
		There are 20 students. The teacher wants to divide them into 4 equal groups. How many students will be in each group?
3b	Multiplication/division problems with the word *per* or a phrase using *a*.	The ABC Company makes pens. They put 5 pens in a box. How many pens are in 3 boxes?
		Rosa runs 2 miles per day. How many days will it take her to run 8 miles?
3c	Addition/subtraction problems with larger numbers.	Bill ran 214 miles in January and 158 miles in February. How many more miles did he run in January?
		There are 153 students in the school. If there are 61 girls in the school, how many boys are there?

Instructional Sequence and Assessment Chart (continued)

3d	Multiplication/division problems with larger numbers.	There are 35 students in every class. There are 5 classes in the school. How many students are in the school?
		Jean worked 2 days. If she makes $16 a day, how much did she make?
		Jill has 215 pencils. She wants to make bundles with 5 pencils in each bundle. How many bundles can she make?
3e	Division problems with remainders.	There are 22 students. The teacher wants to divide them into 4 equal groups. How many students will be in each group?
		A mother wants to divide a pie equally among her children. The pie has 19 pieces. There are 9 children. How many pieces should she give to each child?
3f	Addition/subtraction problems with distractors.	There are 20 blue pencils, 5 red pencils, and 16 yellow pens in a bag. How many pencils are in the bag?
		Bill weighed 120 pounds. He ran 5 miles. Now he weighs 117 pounds. How much did he lose?
		Bill had 12 hats; 5 hats were old. He gave away 3 old hats. How many hats does he have left?
4a	Division and multiplication problems with larger numbers (two-digit divisor or multi-digit factors).	Sarah wants to save $385. If she puts $35 in the bank each month, how many months will it take her to save the $385?
		A factory produces 325 cars a day. How many cars will it produce in 25 days?
		A pound of apples costs 60¢. How much will 20 pounds of apples cost?
4b	Multi-step problems: three numbers; the sum of two numbers is subtracted from the third number.	Julie sold 12 pencils in the morning. Ann sold 15 in the afternoon. How many more must they sell before they've sold 50 altogether?
		Timmy weighed 84 pounds. He lost 4 pounds in May and 7 pounds in June. How much did he weigh at the end of June?
		Jean sold 10 pens in the morning. She began with 18. If she sells 2 more, how many will she have left?
4c	Three numbers: two quantities are multiplied; the product is added or subtracted from a third number.	Tom has 3 pens in each pocket. He has 5 pockets. Ann has 16 pens. Who has more pens? How many more?
		Ann has $7. If she works 4 hours and earns $3 each hour, how many dollars will she have at the end of the day?

Instructional Sequence and Assessment Chart (continued)

4d	Three numbers: two quantities are added. The sum is divided or multiplied.	There are 10 boys and 20 girls in the class. Each row can sit 5 students. How many rows will there be? Jill earns $2 every morning and $4 every afternoon. How much will she earn in 6 days?
5a	Four numbers: two sets of quantities are multiplied; the product of each is added.	Pam ran 5 miles a day for 3 days, and 6 miles a day for 2 days. How many miles did she run altogether? Tammy bought 3 cakes and 2 drinks. A cake cost 10¢. A drink cost 15¢. How much did Tammy spend?
5b	Five numbers: two sets of quantities are multiplied; the product of each is added; the sum is subtracted or added to a given quantity.	Bill needs $30. He worked 5 hours on Monday for $2 an hour. He worked 2 hours on Tuesday for $3 an hour. How much more money does he need? Bill weighed 135 pounds in May. He gained 3 pounds each month for the next 2 months. Then he gained 5 pounds each month for the next 3 months. How much does he weigh now?

tains irrelevant quantities or information that distracts students from successfully solving the problem. More information about these three problem types will be discussed later in the chapter.

Teachers also should be aware that story problems become more difficult as the problems include unfamiliar vocabulary and use more complex syntax. The two problems that follow illustrate the importance of vocabulary and syntax:

a. Miles wrote 6 sentences. The teacher crossed out 2 of them. How many are left?

b. When the teacher read Andrew's paper, she deleted 15 sentences and 3 commas. He had initially written 52 sentences. How many sentences did he have at the end?

Both of these word problems are temporal sequence problems, i.e., problems that state the original amount and the amount of decrease. Problem b is more difficult for several reasons. First, problem b contains more difficult vocabulary. Students may not be familiar with the words *deleted* and *initially*. If a student does not understand *deleted,* she has no basis for solving the problem. Second, the amount that Miles began with is stated first in problem (a), but in problem (b) it is stated *after* the amount of the decrease. When the smaller number appears first, students are more likely to add. The third difficulty is the presence of the quantity 3, a distractor that must be ignored. Finally, the numerals in problem (b) are larger and the operation requires renaming. Teachers must be sure that students receive ample practice with problems containing these complexities to ensure student mastery.

Some mathematics approaches introduce problem-solving activities to students before the students have been taught efficient strategies for how to approach them. Commercial programs often suggest that students work word problems by using counters to represent values or acting out the story. These approaches frequently confuse students in that the students fail to see the relationship between their actions to solve the problem and how to generate the appropriate algorithm. Another obstacle is the amount of time required to present some of the activity-based strategies. Some of these suggested activities may not be the most productive use of instructional time. In this chapter, we present generalizable problem-solving strategies that are useful and efficient. We endorse the use of more activity-based strategies as an *introduction* to the concepts in word problems and also as opportunities for students to apply the strategies once they have mastered them.

ADDITION AND SUBTRACTION PROBLEMS

The procedures for teaching addition and subtraction problems are divided into two parts. The first part introduces the concept of story problems to first grade students or remedial second graders through the use of illustrations. The second part teaches a more sophisticated generalizable problem-solving strategy that enables students to solve temporal sequence, classification, and comparison problems. The generalizable strategy is more sophisticated because it must accommodate the difficulties caused by variations in word usage. The same verb *(lost)* appears in examples (a) and (b), but the usage is such that addition is called for in (a) and subtraction in (b).

a. Nicole gave away 7 stickers. Maria gave away 3 more stickers than Nicole. How many stickers did Maria give away?

b. Nicole had 15 stickers. Then she gave away 7 stickers. How many stickers does she have now?

Other usage problems occur when the verb gives no information about whether to add or subtract: "Corey had four pets; three were dogs. How many were not dogs?" The difficulties in usage can only be resolved through the careful teaching of a strategy. Illustrating story problems, a strategy found in many programs, is not as useful a strategy due to its limited generalizability. Drawing pictures is rarely a viable option when students encounter word problems in "real-life" settings. Also, as problems become more complex and use larger numbers, drawing pictures would not be a practical or efficient strategy. Pictures can assist in introducing word problems, but illustrations must later be replaced by a strategy that teaches students the relationships between the words in a problem and the mathematics algorithm they must use to solve the problem.

Introducing the Concept

Word problems can be introduced when students can work a page of addition and subtraction problems, using a line strategy, with 80–90% accuracy. It is not necessary that students know how to solve missing-addend problems or have memorized any basic facts in order to be introduced to word problems.

About three weeks prior to the introduction of word problems, the teacher should present a preskill format designed to teach students how to translate four key phrases—*get more, get rid of, end with,* and

how many—to symbols. The phrase *get more* translates to a plus sign, *get rid of* to a minus sign, *end with* to an equal sign, and *how many* to an empty box. The teacher should say each new phrase and tell students its translation. For example, the teacher might say, "Listen: When you *get more,* you write a plus sign. What do you write for *get more?*" Each second or third day, the teacher would introduce a new phrase and would review the phrases introduced earlier.

After the students know these four terms, the teacher presents another preskill exercise in which the teacher says a common verb and asks if the verb translates to a plus or a minus sign. Several common verbs—*buys, loses, sells, eats, finds, gives away, breaks,* and *makes*—should be presented. The teacher equates each verb with getting more or getting rid of before asking the students to translate the verb to a sign. For example, the teacher asks, "When you buy something, do you get more or get rid of something? So when you buy something do you plus or minus?"

The format for introducing word problems (see Format 11.1) is presented when the students have mastered the preskills outlined above. The format includes 2 parts. In Part A, a structured board presentation, the teacher begins story problem instruction by demonstrating on the chalkboard how a written or verbal story problem can be solved with semi-concrete objects (pictures). In solving problems such as "There were six children. Two children went home. How many were left?" pictures or actions are easily used to illustrate the problem.

After demonstrating how a verbal or written word problem can be illustrated, the teacher demonstrates how a verbal or written story problem may be expressed numerically, translating it phrase by phrase into an equation.

There were six children.	6
Two children went home.	−2
How many were left?	

In Part B, the structured worksheet exercise, the teacher gives students a worksheet with a set of problems. If students can decode the words in the story, they read the problems. If the students do not have adequate decoding skills, the teacher should read the problems to them. The teacher has the students read each entire problem and then reread it phrase by phrase. After reading each phrase, students are directed to draw the appropriate picture. Then, students read the problem again phrase by phrase and write the appropriate symbols. After completing the equation, students are encouraged to figure out the answer by counting the pictures.

Example selection for word problems is very important. The verbs in stories should be fairly common terms such as *buy, give away, make, break, find, lose*. Also, problems should contain words that the students are able to decode, and the problems initially should be relatively short. A random mix of addition and subtraction problems should be used so that students must discriminate between the two types of problems.

For the first several weeks, the last sentence in word problems should say "ends with how many?" These words can be literally translated to the symbols = □. After several weeks, final sentences such as "How many does she have now?" and "How many does she have in all?" can be presented. The teacher explains that these sentences mean the same as "ends with how many" and thus can be translated into the symbols = □.

A Number-Family Problem-Solving Strategy

Most word problems cannot be translated phrase by phrase into an equation. Therefore, we recommend teaching a strategy that encourages students to integrate their knowledge of the fact number-family concepts with basic language skills involving temporal sequencing, comparisons, and classification. The number-family strategy is based on the concept that three numbers can be used to form four math statements. For example, the numbers 2, 5, and 7 yield $2 + 5 = 7$, $5 + 2 = 7$, $7 - 5 = 2$, and $7 - 2 = 5$. In a typical problem, two of the numbers in the family are provided. Students place these numbers where they belong in the family and then determine whether the missing number is obtained by adding or subtracting.

The strategy is applied to word problems in that if the total number of a fact family is given, the problem requires subtraction. For example, "Kyle had two snakes. Now he has seven snakes. How many more snakes did he get?" The last sentence asks about how many more, not about the total. So one of the numbers in the problem, 2 or 7, must be the big number, the total. The phrase "Now he has 7" indicates that 7 is the total number. Students then subtract 2 from the total number; $7 - 2 = 5$. Kyle got 5 more snakes.

If the total number of the fact family is not given, the problem requires addition. For example, "There are five dogs. There are two cats. How many pets?" The total number, the number that tells how many pets, is not given—dogs are pets and cats are pets, so *pets* has to refer to the total number. Therefore, the math sentence would be $5 + 2 = 7$ pets.

A standard diagram is used in teaching the number family strategy. In learning the number family

strategy to solve basic facts, students are taught that the big number goes at the end of the arrow. If the big number is not known, a box goes at the end of the number family arrow. These conventions might appear to be difficult in the beginning, but the strategies are useful in allowing students to see the relationships between the concepts in the word problem and the values that are given. (See Format 11.2.) Very careful guided practice is required to teach students the linguistic elements in a story problem that tell whether or not the total number is given.

PRESKILL FOR THE NUMBER FAMILY STRATEGY An essential preskill for the number family word problem strategy is figuring out the missing number when two of the three numbers in a fact family have been given. Students are taught that if the total number is given, they subtract to find the missing number. For example, if 9 and 4 are given and 9 is the total, or big number, they subtract 4 from 9 to find 5, the missing number. On the other hand, if the total number is not given, they add the two given numbers. For example, if 9 and 4 are given and students are told that neither is the total number, they add $9 + 4$ to find 13, the missing number. Students should be able to compute these facts mentally rather than using lines. Consequently, problems should be limited to basic facts that students already know.

This preskill, which is presented in Format 11.2, should be taught approximately two or three weeks before temporal sequence problems are first introduced, normally sometime during the second grade. Note that this format is similar to those used in Chapter 6 to teach basic facts. In that chapter, the phrases "big numbers" and "small numbers" were used. Those phrases can be replaced by the phrases "total number" and "parts of the total" when preparing students to solve story problems. These phrases are substituted to prevent students from cuing on every larger number as the "big" number.

When presenting the preskill diagrams, the teacher shows an arrow with two boxes over the arrow and a larger box at the end of the arrow. Below are examples of the diagrams. In problem (a) the total number is given, while in problem (b) the total number is not given. The line below the diagram is for writing the equation to find the missing number.

a. 6 □ → 8   b. 6 2 → □
_____   _____

Format 11.2 has four parts. Part A introduces the rule about what to do when the total number is given: "When the total number is given, you subtract." After telling students the rule, the teacher demonstrates its application, writing on the board a diagram in which the total number is given:

$$2 \quad \square \longrightarrow \boxed{8}$$

$$8-2=6$$

The teacher points out that, because the total number is given, the students must subtract to figure out the missing number ($8 - 2 = 6$). And when they subtract, they must start with the total number.

Part B introduces the rule about what to do when the total number is not given: "When the total number is not given, you add." After telling students the rule, the teacher demonstrates its application, writing on the board a diagram in which the total number is not given:

$$3 \quad 7 \longrightarrow \square$$

$$3+7=10$$

The teacher points out that because the total number is not given, the two given numbers must be added to figure out the missing number ($3 + 7 = 10$). Note that if students do not understand the terms *add* and *subtract,* the teacher can use *plus* and *minus* instead.

Part C is a structured worksheet with diagrams, half of which give the total number and half of which do not.

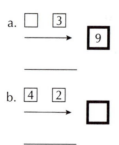

The student's task is to write the appropriate equation on the line under each arrow and to figure out the missing number. In problem (a), the total number is given; therefore, the student would write the subtraction problem $9 - 3$ on the line to figure

out the missing number. In problem (b), the total number is not given; so the students would write the addition problem $4 + 2$ on the line to derive the answer.

Part D is a less-structured worksheet exercise in which the teacher asks students whether they add or subtract and then has them work the problem. In parts C and D, the problems should not be written in a predictable order. Addition and subtraction problems should appear randomly.

TEMPORAL SEQUENCE PROBLEMS In these types of problems, a person or thing starts out with a specified quantity, and then an action occurs, e.g., *finds, loses, buys, sells,* that results in the person or thing ending up with more or less. There are four basic types of temporal sequence problems. (See Table 11.1) Two are types in which a verb indicates that the person ended up with more, e.g., *gets, buys, makes.* Two are types in which a verb indicates that the person ends up with less, e.g., *loses, eats, sells.*

The problems in Table 11.1 illustrate why students cannot rely solely on the verb to determine what operation is called for. Even though the presence of verbs such as *buys, gets,* and *finds* usually indicates addition, there are a significant number of problems with those verbs that require subtraction. Likewise, students will encounter story problems with verbs that usually indicate subtraction but that are solved by adding. For example: "Michael lost 17 pounds. Now he weighs 132 pounds. How much did he weigh before?"

The strategy presented in the format for temporal sequence problems (Format 11.3) teaches the students to look at the overall structure of a word prob-

Table 11.1 Four Types of Action Problems

- Verb indicates ending up with more.
   Addition
   James had 12 apples. He bought 17 more apples. How many apples did he end up with?
   Subtraction
   James had 12 apples. He bought more apples. Now he has 17 apples. How many apples did he buy?

- Verb indicates ending up with less.
   Addition
   James had lots of apples. He sold 17 of the apples. He ended up with 12 apples. How many apples did he start with?
   Subtraction
   James had 17 apples. He sold 12 apples. How many apples did he end up with?

---

lem. The format utilizes the number-family concept. A story problem gives two quantities of the three quantities that make up a number family. If the quantity that represents the total is given in the problem, the students subtract to determine the missing quantity. If the quantity that represents the total is not given in the problem, the students add to determine the missing quantity.

The procedure for writing these problems is very specific. The first-named item in the problem is the first value students write in the number-family diagram. The next item named is the next value written in the diagram in the family. Before students work with actual word problems, they should be provided with sufficient practice opportunities to ensure that they understand how to use the diagrams correctly. The teacher would introduce the diagram using minimal statements containing values. For example: "You have 81. You lose some. You end up with 69." The teacher provides two values and an unknown and has students place the values along an arrow according to the rules about getting more or getting less. The rules simply stated are: When you get more, you place the values forward on the arrow. When you get less, you place the values backward on the arrow. This preskill enables students to practice using the diagram before they are required to solve a problem. (See Part A in Format 11.3.)

When students have mastered placing the values correctly along the arrow, they practice with problems that give information, so that students determine whether to go forward along the arrow or backward along the arrow. (See Part B in Format 11.3.) To determine where the values go, students must determine whether the problem ends up with more or less. The items always go along the arrow, with the first value at one end of the arrow or at the other end. Which end to start writing the values on depends on whether students will end up with more than the first value or less than the first value. Students apply the rules: If you get more, you put the values forward along the arrow; if you get less, you put the values backward along the arrow. The example selection for the problems must be such that they indicate which value to write first, next, and last. Then determination of writing the values forward or backward depends on whether you are getting more or less.

Below is a series of steps a student would take to solve problems. The arrow is used as a prompt for students. The first problem is a subtraction problem that contains a verb that usually indicates addition. The second problem is an addition problem that contains a verb that usually indicates subtraction.

Subtraction Problem
Samantha had 36 books. Then she bought some more books. She ended up with 57 books. How many books did Samantha buy?

1. The problem talks about spending money, but the question is about how many books, rather than how much money. So the total will be how many books Nicole ends up with. She is getting more books, so the values go forward along the arrow. She starts out with 36 books, the first value. The word *some* in the problem indicates the missing value and is represented by a box. 57 is the last value stated in the problem and is therefore written at the end of the arrow when going forward along the arrow.

2. Now that the values are placed correctly around the arrow, students can readily see that the total, or big number, is given, but one of the small numbers is missing in the number family. The number-family rule states that if the total number is given, you subtract to figure out the answer.

$$57 - 36 = 21 \text{ books}$$

Addition Problem
Matt had some money. Then he lost 14 dollars. Now he has 2 dollars. How many dollars did he have before he lost those dollars?

1. The problem talks about losing money. That means Matt ended up with less. So the values go backwards along the arrow. The first value is "some" or box, for how many. The second value is $14 and the last value is $2. Starting at the end of the arrow and going backwards, the problem is written:

2. Now that the problem is written along the arrow, students determine that the total, or big number is missing. When the total number in a number family is missing you add the two small numbers to find the answer.

The format for teaching students to work temporal sequence problems appears in Part C in Format

11.3. Part C, which is introduced when students have mastered the exercises in Part B, is a structured worksheet exercise. The teacher leads students through working a set of problems. First, he has the students read a problem and decide if the problem talks about getting more or getting less. As mentioned previously, students are taught that if you get more, you place the values forward along the arrow. If you get less, you place the values backward along the arrow. After the values are in place along the arrow, students apply their knowledge of the number family rule: If the total, or big number, is missing, you add. If a small number is missing, you subtract.

Part D is a less-structured worksheet exercise in which the teacher asks the students to determine which direction to place the values along the arrow. After the values have been placed, students answer questions about whether they add or subtract, according to whether the big number or the small number in the number family is missing.

Example Selection When selecting examples for this format, the teacher constructs sets of four problems. An exercise might include two sets of four problems for a total of eight problems. Each set should contain two addition and two subtraction problems. One addition problem should have a verb that indicates ending up with more. One addition problem should have a verb that indicates ending up with less. Likewise, one subtraction problem should have a verb that indicates ending up with more, and one subtraction problem should have a verb that indicates ending up with less. The problems should be written in random order. Problems introduced initially should contain common verbs. Sentences should be relatively simple. All problems should result in equations that the students are able to work. For example, if students have not learned to regroup, subtraction problems should be limited to problems that do not require regrouping.

COMPARISON PROBLEMS   A comparison problem addresses two quantities and the difference between them. There are two basic types of comparison problems. In one type, a quantity is stated describing an attribute of one object, e.g., weight, length, height, or age. Also stated is the difference between that object and another object: "Brendan is 7 years old. Colleen is 3 years older. How old is Colleen?" The student is asked to find the quantity of the other object. In the second type of problem, the quantities of two objects are stated and the student is asked to find the difference between them: "Brendan is 7 years old. Colleen is 10 years old. How much

older is Colleen?" Both types of comparison problems are introduced concurrently.

A two-step strategy for solving comparison problems involves (1) determining which object represents the bigger quantity and (2) determining whether the bigger quantity is given or not given. For example: "Andrew got 10 problems correct. Josh got 2 fewer problems correct than Andrew. How many problems did Josh get correct?" In this problem, the number of problems Josh answered correctly is fewer, so the number of problems Andrew answered correctly represents the bigger number. Because the number of problems Andrew answered correctly is given, the problem requires subtraction.

Format 11.4 shows how to present comparison problems. The format includes three parts. Part A is a preskill format designed to teach students to determine the big number. Note that this part assumes that students understand comparative words such as *deeper, shallower, thicker, thinner, bigger, smaller, heavier, lighter.* Students who have difficulty with Part A may not understand the meaning of the comparatives. Teachers should test students' understanding with diagrams or illustrations. For example, the teacher could present illustrations of two holes and ask, "Show me the hole that is deeper."

Another useful strategy for helping students determine which object is greater is to practice with sentences that compare two things without numerical values. For example:

a. The lake is closer than the city.
b. Brad worked longer than Ryan did.
c. The bird stored fewer nuts than the raccoon stored.

Students would write partial number families for these sentences by placing the first letter of the object having the greater value at the end of the number value arrow. For example, in (a), the lake is closer than the city, so the city must be the big number. Students would write the number family:

After students have mastered placing two values correctly in the number family, they are taught to write a number family with values included, but still not using complete comparison story problems. For example, (a) would now read "The lake is 23 miles closer than the city." Initially, students are taught to cover up the 23 and read the sentence first without the number: The lake is closer than the city. This helps them make the decision about which object is farther away, the lake or the city. After placing the lake and the city correctly on the number line, they place the number 23 at the beginning of the number family so it looks like this:

23   L
————————→ C

Comparison word problems are constructed with two names of items and the difference number. (In the previous example, *lake* and *city* are the two names, and 23 is the difference number.) Whether the sentence tells about something greater or something smaller, the difference number is always a small number and it is always the first small number in the family.

If students have trouble constructing these word-problem number families correctly, teachers should not try to give them a linguistic clue to look for, but instead help them understand the information given in the problem. An example of this type of correction would involve the following types of questions: "If Chandra got money back after buying a video game at the store, which is more, the amount that she started with, or the price of the video game?" If students still do not understand the relationship, the teacher might ask, "If something costs more than you have, do you get change? If you get change, you must have *more* money than the object costs." Once students have figured out which is the big number and which is the small number, the difference number is easy to identify. The difference number is the amount more or the amount less.

Part B is a structured worksheet with complete story problems. Using the same example, the problem would be completed to read: "The lake is 23 miles closer than the city. The city is 59 miles away. How far away is the lake?" Using the number family format above, students practice filling in the values that are given in the problem:

23   L   59
————————→ C

Since one of the small numbers is missing in the number family, the number sentence would be written:

59 − 23 = ☐

The critical step in Part B occurs when the teacher asks if the problem gives a number for the total. Students may not read the problem carefully and may give a wrong answer. For example, if a problem states that Rachel is 12 years older than Sally, who is 7 years old, the total will tell how old Rachel is. When examining the problem, the students may misread the words *Rachel is 12 years older* as *Rachel is 12 years old,* and write 12 as the total number.

If this type of error occurs frequently, the teacher should do a verbal practice exercise that just focuses on this step. For each problem, the teacher would tell the students what the total number tells about and ask if the problem gives a number for the total; e.g., "The total number will tell how old Rachel is. Does a number in the problem tell how old Rachel is?" The teacher does the verbal exercise with a set of six to eight problems.

Part C is a less-structured worksheet exercise in which the teacher leads students in applying the strategy.

Example Selection Each example set should include the following types of examples to provide discrimination practice.

1. Two addition problems in which one quantity is stated. The difference indicates the other quantity is greater:

    Bill dug a hole 6 feet deep. Tim dug a hole 2 feet deeper than Bill's hole. How deep is the hole Tim dug?

    Bill dug a hole 6 feet deep. Bill's hole is 2 feet shallower than the hole Tom dug. How deep is the hole Tom dug?

2. One subtraction problem in which one quantity is stated. The difference indicates the other quantity is smaller:

    Bill dug a hole 6 feet deep. Jim dug a hole 2 feet shallower than Bill's hole. How deep is the hole Jim dug?

3. One subtraction problem in which both quantities are stated. Students must determine the difference.

    Bill dug a hole 6 feet deep. Jim dug a hole 2 feet deep. How much deeper is Bill's hole?

Two addition problems are included in each set so that there will be an equal mix of addition and subtraction problems.

CLASSIFICATION PROBLEMS   Format 11.5 gives the steps for teaching students to work classification problems using the number-family strategy. Part A is designed to provide practice in the language preskill of identifying class names for groups of objects. The teacher says a superordinate class and two related subclasses and asks the students to tell which is the biggest class. This exercise assumes that students already understand the idea of classification. Teachers working with very low-performing students may find that more extensive teaching in this language skill is necessary.

In Part B, a structured worksheet exercise, the teacher introduces classification story problems. Students are given a worksheet with six to eight problems. Part B begins with the teacher reminding the students that when the total number in a fact family is given, they must subtract to find the answer; when the total number is not given, they must add. The teacher then states a problem and identifies the three groups mentioned in the problem: "There are five children. Two of the children are girls. How many are boys? This problem mentions children, girls, and boys." After telling students the three groups, the teacher asks which word tells about all the things in this problem. Students are shown how to write the word *children* under the number-family line to show the big category or class that the story problem is talking about. They use *G* for girls and *B* for boys. The word *all* is placed at the end of the number family in writing all classification problems.

$$\underset{\text{Children}}{\overset{G \qquad\qquad B}{\underline{\hspace{3cm}} \rightarrow \text{All}}}$$

After students write the number family correctly, they are shown how to go back to the problem and determine which values are known. In this problem, we know the number of girls and the number of children. Students cross out *G* and *All* and place the values above as shown:

$$\underset{\text{Children}}{\overset{\overset{2}{\cancel{G}} \qquad\qquad B \quad \overset{5}{\cancel{All}}}{\underline{\hspace{3cm}} \rightarrow}}$$

Students would apply the number-family rule, and since a small number is missing, they would subtract to find out the number of boys:

$$5 - 2 = \square$$

Part C is a less-structured worksheet exercise. After reading a problem, the students write the name of the big class under the number-family line and the word *all* at the end of the line. They use the first letter of each word describing the subordinate classes within the big class and write each letter above the number-family arrow. Then they go back and cross out the letters that stand for the values that are given or the word *all*.

Example Selection There are several example selection guidelines. First, there should be an equal mix of addition and subtraction problems. Second, problems should initially be written in a relatively short form with few extraneous words. Third, relatively common classes should be used. A sample set of four problems appears below:

a. There were 75 cars in all. 15 were green cars. The rest were red cars. How many red cars were there?
b. Lauren had red marbles and blue marbles. She had 23 red marbles and 16 blue marbles. How many marbles did she have in all?
c. Tasha had golf balls and tennis balls. She had 43 balls in all. 14 were golf balls. How many were tennis balls?
d. Jason had Christmas boxes and birthday boxes. He had 81 boxes in all. 43 were birthday boxes. How many were Christmas boxes?

During the first week that classification problems are introduced, the key words in the problem can be underlined to prompt the students. For example, in problem (a) above, the words *cars, red,* and *green* could be underlined.

While students are learning to solve classification problems, they should continue to solve temporal sequence and comparison problems. After they have demonstrated mastery of classification problems, the teacher should give students worksheets that include a mix of classification, comparison, and temporal sequence problems. Worksheets should still include six to eight problems daily, with one-third representing each type of problem. When students first encounter a mix of problems, they must again receive teacher direction to be sure that they can discriminate the different kinds of problems that they are solving. Even though students have been successful at solving temporal sequence, comparison, and classification problems independently, teachers should not assume students will be equally successful when two or three types are mixed on the same worksheet.

Reading Tables An important skill related to working classification problems involves the application of classification logic in solving problems using tables. Table problems are an efficient way of presenting a lot of data and of reinforcing logic skills and number facts. Students are introduced to the idea that values in rows and columns are added to obtain totals. (See Parts A and B in Format 11.6.) To find the total for a row or column, students use a running total. This process is a great deal like adding three columns with three or more numbers. In a beginning table exercise, students learn that columns go vertically and rows horizontally. After students have sufficient practice adding both columns and rows of numbers in tables, headings are presented. These headings tell about the numbers in the columns and rows. For example:

Hours Worked

	Mon.	Tues.	Weds.	Total
Josh	5	4	10	19
Jane	4	7	1	12
John	2	5	3	10
Total	11	16	14	

Students practice touching both headings and moving their fingers together until they touch in a particular cell. For example, students place one finger on *Tuesday* and move downwards, and another finger on *John*, and move across until they meet at 5. After working with several examples, students should be ready to answer questions about a number in a particular cell, e.g., how many hours did Mary work on Wednesday? Who worked the most hours on Monday? Who worked the most hours in all?

After students have become familiar with reading tables and adding data in rows and columns, the teacher can demonstrate how to apply the number-family strategy to solving problems in tables. Students first are introduced to the concept that tables with rows and columns work like number families. Instead of just a line for the cells, the tables in the early problems should have arrows for the rows and columns. The arrows remind the students that each row and column works like a number family. The first two numbers in the row or column are small numbers. The total is the big number. (See Part C in Format 11.6.)

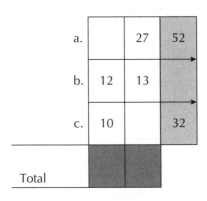

Here is the number family for row a:

A small number is missing in that row. Students would then apply the number-family rule: If the small number is missing, you subtract. If the big number is missing, you add. Since a small number is missing in this example, you would subtract to find the missing number in the row. 52 − 27 = 25. Looking at row b, you write the number family:

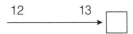

Since the big number is missing, you add to find the missing number in the family and write it in the table: 12 + 13 = 25.

Teachers may want to separate the introduction of the number family in rows and the number family in columns, first working only with rows, then only with columns, and finally solving for unknown cells in both.

The final step involves teaching students how to use information from the word problem by placing the values correctly in tables and answering questions about the data. (See Part D in Format 11.6.) Using tables to solve classification problems involves identifying the related objects or actions, one of which is a superordinate class to the other objects or actions; e.g., boys and girls are children; red apples and green apples are apples; running and walking are ways people move; buying hats in the morning and buying hats in the afternoon are part of buying hats all day. Classification problems appear in two forms. In the addition form, two subordinate actions or objects are given, and the student has to figure out the total or superordinate quantity: "There are six girls and four boys in our class. How many students are there?"

In the subtraction form, the total or superordinate group is given, along with the amount of one subordinate group. Students must subtract to figure the number for the other subordinate group: "There are ten children in our class. Six are girls. How many are boys?"

Part D in Format 11.6 illustrates how teachers can teach students to record information, use the number-family strategy to complete the table, and then answer questions using the information from the table. Note that teaching all parts of the Format 11.6 would take a considerable amount of time. However, it should be clear that teaching students to use tables is an efficient and logical approach to solving several types of problems.

MULTIPLICATION AND DIVISION PROBLEMS

Multiplication and division operations are used to solve word problems that deal with equal-sized groups. These problems are stated in three basic forms. If a problem gives the number of groups and the number in each group, the problem is a multiplication problem: "Carlos has three piles of toys. There are two toys in each pile. How many toys does Carlos have in all?" The equation representing that problems is $3 \times 2 = \square$. If the problem gives the total and asks either how many groups or how many in each group, the problem is solved with division: a) "Carlos has six toys. He puts two toys in each pile. How many piles does he end up with?" $6 \div 2 = 3$; b) "Carlos has six toys. He wants to put the toys in three piles. How many toys will he put in each pile?" $6 \div 3 = 2$. Once the students determine that the problem is addressing equal-sized objects or groups, they will know that it is either a multiplication or a division problem. Then the students can apply the same number-family strategy to determine whether the big number is given and, therefore, whether they must multiply or divide to solve the problem.

Multiplication and division problems almost always contain a word or phrase that tells the students that the problem is talking about equal-sized groups. Most of the problems contain the word *each* or *every*. Other indications are the use of the word *per* or phrases like *in a box* or *in a dozen:* "John walked four miles per day. How many miles did John walk in three days?" or "There were three balls in a box. There were six boxes. How many balls in all?"

Multiplication and division word problems should not be introduced until students have achieved mastery of addition and subtraction problems, and have a working knowledge of basic multiplication and division facts.

Word problems requiring multiplication and division may be first introduced using coins. Initially, students do not solve the problems, but learn to set up the number families correctly. The strategy is to start with knowledge students already have about the value of coins and proceed to statements in the same form that do not involve coins. If someone has 4 dimes, they have 10×4, or 40 cents. Illustrations for problems show either the number of coins for the example or the number of cents for the example.

Students complete the number family by following the convention of writing the value of each coin as the first small number of the number family. The number of coins then is the second small number in the family. The total amount (cents) is the big number. (See Format 11.7.) For example:

$$\overset{10}{\underset{\longrightarrow}{}} \overset{D}{\underset{C}{}}$$

The next step in the strategy would be to introduce problems where no coins are shown. For example:

a. You have nickels. You have 45 cents in all. How many nickels do you have?

$$\overset{N}{\underset{\longrightarrow}{}} \underset{C}{}$$

To work problem a, students write the value of each nickel as the first small number and 45 as the big number for total cents, or cents in all. The answer is then obtained by recalling the missing small number of the number family (5, 45, and ?), or by seeing how many times you count by 5 until you get to 45.

$$\overset{5 \quad N}{\underset{\longrightarrow}{}} \overset{\mathbf{45}}{\underset{C}{}}$$

b. You have quarters. You have 5 quarters. How many cents do you have in all?

$$\overset{\mathbf{25}}{\underset{\longrightarrow}{}} \overset{5}{\underset{C}{}}$$

For problem b, the value of each quarter is written as the first small number, and 5 is written for the second small number. The number of cents is the large number in the number family and can be obtained by counting by 25, five times.

The coin strategy can be applied to a range of other types of examples. After students have mastered writing coin problems in number families, they are taught how to analyze the language in a multiplication/division problem. They are taught that statements about what *each* member is worth tell about small numbers. Also, they are taught that the word following *each* refers to a small number. For example: "Each brick weighs 3 pounds." Brick is a small number. The weight of each brick is the other small number. The total number of pounds would be the big number.

$$\overset{3}{\underset{\longrightarrow}{}} \overset{B}{\underset{P}{}}$$

In the beginning, students are not asked to figure out the answer to these types of problems, but rather to practice putting them in number families. Then, after students are able to master number-family writing, complete problems are presented. Students are taught that one sentence in each problem tells how to make the number family. That sentence is the one that tells about each thing. (See Format 11.8.)

Sometimes students have difficulty determining the big number. For the sentence, "Each sack has 10 cookies," the big number is cookies and sack is a small number. But if students think about the big number as the size of things, they may reverse the components. Since sacks are generally bigger than cookies, the students may think that sack is the big number. Teachers need to remind students that they are counting objects, not measuring size. If students use the information about *each* in this sentence, they can identify one of the objects as the big number. "Each sack has 10 cookies." The word following *each* is *sack*. Sack is the small number. The only other name in the sentence is *cookies,* so *cookies* must be the big number.

MULTI-STEP WORD PROBLEMS

Frequently students work problems that require both addition and subtraction. These multi-step problems are usually difficult for students, but are easily processed using number families. For example:

Shane spends $12 on stamps. Then he spends $32 on a video game. If he ends up with $6, how much did he start out with?

Because this problem contains the word *spends,* students tend to use subtraction to solve the problem, regardless of the fact that there are several steps required by the problem. Using the number-family analysis guards against this kind of mistake.

An adaptation of the number-family strategy can easily be used to solve this money problem. (See Format 11.9.) In this adaptation, usually used with money problems, the values in the number family are labeled *in, out,* and *end up. In* is always the big number, *out* and *end up* are the small numbers. These words refer to the direction of the flow of money. This adaptation facilitates the use of the strategy with multi-step problems such as the one above.

end up	out	in
	$12	
$6	$32	
	$44	$50

Applying the number-family strategy, students realize that this problem requires adding both *out* numbers and then adding the *end up* number to arrive at the *in,* or big number, the answer to the problem.

Initially, students practice multi-step problems with only one value for both *in* and *out.* Although these are not multi-step problems, they establish important conventions: (1) If a sentence tells the amount that somebody has, that is an *in* number. The sentence *Caley had $15* gives a number for *in.* If a sentence tells about a gain, it tells about a value for *in. McKenzie collected 34 stamps* tells the gain in stamps. 34 is the number for *in.* (2) Values for *out* tell about losses or reductions. *Howard gave away 3 apples* tells about *out. 1500 gallons leaked out of the tanker* tells about *out.* (3) The value for *end up* is the amount that is left, or the difference between the amount *in* and the amount *out.* In most problems, the amount for *end up* is the amount the person has after the final loss or gain the problem describes. Simple problems that refer to only three values permit students time to practice these conventions before proceeding to multi-step problems. For example:

a. Maria starts a savings account with $567. Later she takes some money out of her account, which leaves a balance of $329. How much money went out?

b. A florist starts out with no carnations. She buys 59 carnations and later sells 47 of them. How many carnations did she end up with?

c. Daniel had an empty fruit crate. He put some oranges in the crate. Then he gave away 23 of those oranges. The crate still has 19 oranges in it. How many oranges did he put in the crate?

After students have mastered the number-family conventions, more difficult problems are introduced. These have more than one value for *in* or more than one value for *out.* These values are shown stacked under the appropriate heading in the number family, as with the first example.

end up	out	in
	$12	
$6	$32	
	$44	$50

After students have mastered multi-step problems with many values for either the *in* or *out* headings, they are introduced to problems with multiple values for both headings. For example:

At the beginning of the work day the elevator in the Federal Building is empty. Then 5 people get on the elevator. It stops at the fifth floor and 2 more people get on. On the next floor, 4 people get off. On the seventh floor 7 people get on, and 8 people get off. How many people are still on the elevator?

end up	out	in
	4	5
	8	2
		7

12   7
→ 14

The number-family strategy also can be applied to word problems that discuss an individual's goals. The names for the values in the number family become *goals, now,* and *difference.* This type of problem is more difficult because it is not only a multi-step problem, but *goal* may be a big number or a small number. There are two parts to the rule used to determine when *goal* is a big number or small number:

a. If the *goal* is to have a smaller amount than the current amount, the goal is a small number.

Dif   G   N
→

b. If the *goal* is an amount that is more than the current amount, the goal is a big number.

Dif   N   G
→

The *goal* is what the person originally sets out to do. The *difference* is what remains to be done in order to reach the *goal.* The values for *now* include any current amount and any past amount. There may be more than one value for *goal* and *now,* but there is always only one *difference* number. For example:

Nancy's goal is to buy new tires for her bike, a bicycle helmet, and knee pads. The tires both cost $29, the helmet $38, and the knee pads $17. Nancy mowed the lawn and earned $15. Then she washed the windows and earned $20. How much more money does she need to reach her goal?

First, students determine whether the goal is the big number or the small number. Since her goal is a larger amount than she now has, *goal* is a big number. Next, they make the family with the names appropriately placed. Then they put in the values for the problem.

Dif	N	G
	$15	$29
	20	38
	$35	17
		$84

→

Students work the vertical problems first, or those for *now* and *goal.* Nancy's goal is to earn $84, enough money to buy the items that she wants. She has earned $35 so far. The last step is to work the horizontal problem for the main arrow. Since the first small number (difference) is missing, students subtract to find the answer. *Goal* ($84) minus *now* ($35) equals $49, so she is $49 away from reaching her goal, or the difference between *now* and *goal.*

DISTRACTORS

A distractor is information given in a word problem that is not necessary to find the solution of the problem. It is called a distractor because students are accustomed to using all of the information that a problem provides, and it distracts them from the correct calculations. For example:

Stefanie had 4 stuffed dogs, 2 stuffed rabbits, 2 stuffed pigs, and 5 stuffed cats in her collection. 4 of the stuffed animals are very old. How many stuffed animals does Stefanie have in her collection?

Since the problem asks how many stuffed animals Stefanie has in her collection, the irrelevant information is about the old animals and must be ignored in order to solve the problem correctly.

Students are most often introduced to problems with distractors in early intermediate grades. Several practice problems should be given in which students state what they have been asked to solve and cross out the information that they don't need to know to solve the problem. Problems with distractors should be distributed throughout the math curriculum and practiced frequently until students can easily discern relevant information in solving a problem.

DIAGNOSIS AND REMEDIATION

Teachers should be checking students' math work daily. In doing so, every effort should be made to determine the possible cause for errors. Determining the reason for the errors should then guide the teacher's instruction in the remediation procedure. There are at least five possible causes for errors in solving story problems: (1) fact errors, (2) computation errors, (3) decoding errors, (4) vocabulary errors, and (5) translation errors.

FACT ERRORS   If the student chooses the correct operation and writes the problem correctly, but fails to arrive at the correct answer, that is a fact error. An example of a fact error is:

There were 9 boys and 14 girls in the gifted class. How many students were there?

$$9 + 14 = 22$$

The equation is written using the correct numbers and the correct operation, but the student failed to add correctly. The remediation process would not require repetition of word problem strategies, but some extra practice on memorization of basic facts.

COMPUTATION ERRORS A computation error is one that a student makes in one or more parts of computing an answer. For example, failure to rename correctly or to remove the decimal point from the divisor before dividing would be computational errors. Errors of this sort do not require reteaching of the word-problem strategies, but remediation in the type of computation that is giving the student difficulty. If the student is repeatedly making errors in removing the decimal point from the divisor before dividing, reteaching this strategy is essential.

DECODING ERRORS Reading a word or words in a problem incorrectly is a decoding error. For example, if a student reads *bought* instead of *broke* in the following problem, he would use the wrong operation: "Taryn had 8 crayons. She bought 6. How many does she have now?" The decoding error would cause the student to subtract 6 from 8, for a solution of 2 crayons, rather than add 6 + 8. Finding out if the error is a decoding one is easy to determine. Teachers should simply have the student read the problem aloud.

Teachers can help students who have difficulty decoding words in story problems by presenting difficult words in board exercises before students encounter them in word problems. Teachers of students who are unable to decode written story problems easily should not require students to read the problems, but should read the problems to the student.

VOCABULARY ERRORS Vocabulary errors are caused by students not knowing the meaning of key words in the story problems. For example, in the following problem, students must know that *receives* means "to get more."

Curt has 18 pairs of socks. He receives 4 more pairs for his birthday. How many socks does he have now?

Teachers can easily determine if the error is vocabulary related by simply asking the student what the word *receive* means. If necessary, the meaning of crucial vocabulary words should be taught prior to teaching the word problems.

TRANSLATION ERRORS If a student fails to translate a problem into the correct equation and uses the wrong operation, he has made a translation error. For example:

Andrew now has 7 video games. He started out with 2 video games that he received for his birthday. How many more video games has he gotten since then?

$$7 + 2 = 9$$

In this problem, the student added instead of subtracting. It is not uncommon for students to divide or add instead of multiplying, or subtract instead of dividing. The teacher begins remediation after determining if the same type of problem is consistently missed. If that specific error is an area of weakness for the student, she should be given a special worksheet exercise using the less-structured format of the lesson for that particular problem type. The worksheet should include at least 10 problems, half of which are of the difficult type, the other half a similar type. Students should not be allowed to work on this type of problem independently until they are able to perform with a 90% accuracy rate for several days in a row.

CALCULATORS When and how to use calculators in the teaching of mathematics can be a controversial topic. If students are having difficulties with computation, we endorse the use of calculators to prevent teachers from having to delay instruction in problem-solving. Using the calculators permits students to concentrate on reading problems and writing them correctly. When less time is spent doing the actual calculations, more time can be spent on mastering the word-problem strategies. Student motivation for solving problems seems to increase with the use of calculators. Teachers must note, however, that some students may require explicit instruction on the use of calculators before they are able to use them correctly.

COMMERCIAL PROGRAMS

The major concerns about the manner in which story problems are presented in basal programs are inadequate provisions for practice and review and inadequate strategy teaching.

Practice

Three critical aspects of providing adequate practice are providing enough examples of a problem type to develop and maintain mastery, providing distributed practice across the textbook, and providing adequate discrimination practice. Although recently published editions show improvement, most basal programs still provide limited discrimination practice. For example, after students have been introduced to multiplication and division problems, textbooks rarely contain pages containing a mix of addition, subtraction, multiplication, and division story problems. Teachers must be prepared to construct worksheets to provide discrimination practice.

The number of story problems appearing in basal series has increased in most recent editions of basal programs. However, the relatively long periods with no review are still a concern. These long gaps result from the unit approach in programming. When units dealing with measurement, geometry, place value, or fractions are presented, story problems are often not mentioned. Many students will require daily practice, which would have to be provided from another program, from supplemental workbook or ditto exercises, or from supplemental worksheets prepared by the teacher.

Strategy

Most commercial programs simply do not provide step-by-step teaching procedures for story problems. The teacher's guide may instruct teachers to explain why the problems call for a certain operation, but it does not provide the teacher with specific wording and strategies or specific correction procedures.

APPLICATION ITEMS: STORY PROBLEMS

1. Tell what story problem type each of the following problems represents. Use the types described in the Instructional Sequence and Assessment Chart.

   a. Jim has 15 green apples and 17 red apples. He wants to split them equally among his four friends. How many apples should he give to each friend?

   b. Ann has been running for 2 months. She runs 5 miles each day. How many miles will she run in 10 days?

   c. There are 20 balls in the toy closet. Eight of the balls are baseballs. How many of the balls are not baseballs?

   d. Jill has 2 pens in each pocket. She has 8 pens. How many pockets does she have?

   e. Amy had 8 dollars. She spent 3 dollars. How many dollars does she have left?

   f. A girl is 15 years old. Her brother is 2 years younger. How old is her brother?

2. Story problems can be made easier or more difficult by changing one or more aspects. Name several ways in which problems can be made more difficult. For each problem in the item above, change or add to the problem to increase its level of difficulty in some way.

3. Tell the possible cause of the following errors. When there is doubt as to the cause of the error, tell what the teacher does to find out the specific cause. Specify the remediation procedure called for if errors of this type occur frequently.

   a. Jill's team scored 54 points. The other team scored 19 points fewer. How many did the other team score? $\boxed{36}$ points

   b. The ABC Company produced 1,534 pool tables last year. This year production decreased by 112 pool tables. How many pool tables did the ABC Company produce this year? $\boxed{1,646}$ pool tables

   c. Tim baked 6 cakes every week. He baked for 18 weeks. How many cakes did he bake? $\boxed{3}$ cakes

   d. Tara took 20 shots in the basketball game. She made 15 shots. How many shots did she miss? $\boxed{35}$ shots

   e. There are 10 boys and 20 girls in the class. Each row can seat 5 students. How many rows will there be? $\boxed{35}$ rows

   f. There are 28 students. The teacher wants to divide them into 4 equal groups. How many students will be in each group? $\boxed{6}$ students

   g. A factory produces 325 cars a day. How many cars will it produce in 25 days? $\boxed{8,105}$ cars

4. Write a structured worksheet format using tables to guide students through solving this problem:

28 vehicles went past our house. 12 of the vehicles were cars. How many vehicles were not cars?

5. Write a structured worksheet format to guide students through solving this problem: Ann runs 5 miles every day. So far she has run 20 miles. How many days has she run?

FORMAT 11.1   **Format for Introducing Problem-Solving Concepts**

PART A: PRESKILL: PICTURE DEMONSTRATION

Addition Problem

TEACHER	**STUDENTS**

1. Listen: Ann has seven apples. She gets three more apples. She ends with how many apples?

2. Let's draw a picture of that problem. Ann has seven apples. *(Draw the illustration below on the board.)*

She gets three more apples, so I draw three more. *(Draw three more apples.)*

3. Let's write the equation. Here's the first sentence again. Ann has seven apples. How many apples does Ann have?   7

I write seven under the seven apples. *(Write 7.)*

Here's the next sentence. She gets three more apples. How many more apples did she get?   3

Yes, Ann gets three more. What do I write for gets three more? *(Write + 3.)*   plus 3

The problem says she ends up with how many apples? So I write equals and a box, like this: *(Write = □: 7 + 3 = □.)*

4. Read the equation.   7 + 3 equals how many?

Let's count and see how many we end up with. *(Touch pictures of apples as students count.)*   1, 2, 3, 4, 5, 6, 7, 8, 9, 10

So Ann ends with 10 apples. *(Write 10 in the box.)*

Subtraction Problem

1. Listen: Ann has seven apples. She gives away three apples. She ends with how many apples?

2. Let's draw a picture of that problem. Ann has seven apples, so I draw seven apples. *(Draw apples.)*

She gives away three apples, so I'll cross out three apples. *(Cross out three.)*

(continued on next page)

FORMAT 11.1 (continued)

TEACHER	STUDENTS

Ø Ø Ø ⌀ ⌀ ⌀ ⌀

3. Let's write the equation. Here's the first sentence again. Ann has seven apples. How many apples did Ann have? — **7**

I'll write a 7. *(Write 7.)*

Here's the next sentence. She gives away three apples. How many apples did she give away? — **3**

What do I write for gives away three apples? — **minus 3**

Yes, she gives away three, so we write minus three. *(Write – 3.)*

The problem says she ends with how many apples? So I write equals and a box.

Write = □ *(7 – 3 =* □ *)*

4. Read the equation. — **7 – 3 equals how many?**
   Let's count the apples that are left and see how many she ends with. *(Touch the remaining apples.)* — **1, 2, 3, 4**

So, Ann ends with four apples. *(Write 4 in the box.)*

(Repeat addition or subtraction steps 1–4 with several more problems.)

PART B: STRUCTURED WORKSHEET

(Give students a worksheet that contains a mix of addition and subtraction problems and includes a box and the word for the unit answer, like this:)

---

a. Jim has six marbles. He finds two more marbles.
   He ends with how many marbles?
   □ marbles
b. Jim has six marbles. He gives away two marbles.
   He ends with how many marbles?
   □ marbles

---

1. Touch problem A. Listen: Jim has six marbles. He finds two more marbles. He ends with how many marbles?

○ ○ ○ ○ ○ ○   ○ ○

2. Let's draw a picture of that problem. Jim has six marbles. Draw the marbles. *(Wait while the students draw on their papers, then draw the marbles on the board.)* — Students write:

○ ○ ○ ○ ○ ○   ○ ○ ○ ○ ○ ○

FORMAT 11.1   (continued)

TEACHER	STUDENTS

He finds two more marbles. Draw those. *(Wait, then draw the marbles on the board.)*

Students write:

◯ ◯ ◯ ◯ ◯ ◯   ◯ ◯   ◯ ◯ ◯ ◯ ◯ ◯   ◯ ◯

3. Let's write the equation.

Read the first sentence again.   Jim has 6 marbles.

How many marbles did Jim have?   6

Write 6 under the 6 marbles.
(Wait, then write 6 on board.)   Student write 6.

Read the next sentence.   He finds 2 more marbles.

How many more marbles did he get?   2

Yes, Jim finds two more. What do you write for finds two more?   Plus 2

Yes, write + 2. *(Write + 2 on board.)*   Student writes + 2.

The problem says he ends with how many marbles? So, what do you write?   Equals box

Write equals how many. *(Write = ☐ on board: 6 + 2 = ☐).*   Students write = ☐.

4. Read the equation.   6 + 2 equals how many?

Let's count and see how many we end with. *(Touch pictures of marbles as students count.)*   1, 2, 3, 4, 5, 6, 7, 8

Write 8 in the box after the equal sign.   Students write 8.

Now, write 8 in the answer box next to the word marbles. Jim ends with 8 marbles.   Students write 8 in box next to the word marbles.

Subtraction Problem

1. Touch the next problem. Listen: Jim has six marbles. He gives away two marbles. He ends with how many marbles?

2. Let's draw a picture of that problem. Jim has six marbles. Draw the marbles. *(Wait while students draw on their papers, then draw the marbles on board.)*

Students write:

◯ ◯ ◯ ◯ ◯ ◯   ◯ ◯ ◯ ◯ ◯ ◯

He gives away two marbles. Cross them out. *(Wait, then cross out two.)*

Students cross out marbles:

⊘ ⊘ ◯ ◯ ◯ ◯   ⊘ ⊘ ◯ ◯ ◯ ◯

(continued on next page)

FORMAT 11.1   (continued)

TEACHER	STUDENTS
3. Let's write the equation. Jim has 6 marbles. How many marbles did Jim have?	6
Write a 6. *(Write 6 on board.)*	Students write 6.
How many did he give away?	2
What do you write for gives away two marbles?	minus 2
Yes, he gives away two, so write minus two. *(Write – 2 on board.)*	Students write – 2.
The problem says he ends with how many marbles, so what do you write?	equals box
Write it. *(Write = ☐ on board: 6 – 2 = ☐).*	Students write = ☐.
4. Read the equation.	6 – 2 equals how many?
Let's count the marbles that are left and see how many he ends with. *(Touch the remaining marbles.)*	1, 2, 3, 4
Write 4 in the box after the equal sign. *(Write 4 in the box.)*	Students write 4.
Now write 4 in the answer box next to the word *marbles*. Jim ends with 4 marbles.	Students write 4 in answer box.
(Repeat addition or subtraction steps 1–4 with several more problems.)	

FORMAT 11.2   Fact Family Preskill Format—Finding the Missing Family Member

Part A: Subtracting Rule

TEACHER	STUDENTS
1. *(Write this diagram on the board.)*	

2. Three numbers go together to make a fact family. *(Point to 8.)*

The total number is always at the end of the arrow.

(Point to 2.) This number is part of the total.

(Point to 6.) Here's the other part of the total.

2̲ 6̲
⟶ ☐

(Erase the 8.) Sometimes, we don't know the total and we have to figure it out.

FORMAT 11.2   (continued)

TEACHER	STUDENTS

2 ☐
⟶ 8

(Write the 8 back in; erase the 6.) Sometimes, we don't know part of the total and we have to figure it out.

3. *(Write the following diagram on the board.)*

3 ☐
⟶ 10
___

Is the total number given in this problem?   yes

Here's the rule: When the total number is given, we subtract. The total number is 10. So I start with 10 and subtract 3. *(Write 10 – 3 on the bottom line.)* What is 10 – 3?   7

So, I write equals 7. *(Write = 7 on the line.)*

Now I write 7 in the empty box. *(Write 7 in box.)*

The numbers 3 and 7 are the parts of the total. The number 10 is the total number.

4. *(Write the following diagram on the board.)*

☐ 5
⟶ 12
___

Is the total number given?   yes

What do we do when the total number is given?   subtract

Remember, when you subtract, you start with the total number. What problem do I write on the line?   12 – 5

(Write 12 – 5 on the line.) What is 12 – 5?   7

(Write = 7 on the line.) What number goes in the empty box? *(Write 7 in the box.)*   7

(Repeat step 3 with these problems.)

2 ☐   ☐ 4
⟶ 10   ⟶ 7
___   ___

PART B: ADDITION RULE

1. *(Write the following problem on the board.)*

3 5
⟶ ☐
___

(continued on next page)

FORMAT 11.2   (continued)

TEACHER	STUDENTS

2. In this problem, the total number is not given. When the total number is not given, we add.

     Is the total number given in this problem?   no

     Watch. The parts are 3 and 5, so I add 3 and 5. *(Write 3 + 5 on the line.)* What is 3 + 5?   8

     So, I write equals 8. *(Write = 8 on the line.)*
Now, I write 8 in the empty box. The numbers 3 and 5 are the parts of the total. The number 8 is the total.

3. *(Write the following problem on the board.)*

     Is the total number given?   no

     What do we do when the total number is not given?   add

     What problem do I write on the line? *(Write 7 + 2 on the line.)*   7 + 2

     What is 7 + 2? *(Write = 9 on the line.)*   9

     What number goes in the empty box? *(Write 9 in the box.)*   9

     (Repeat step 3 with the problems below.)

PART C: STRUCTURED WORKSHEET

1. You have to figure out the missing number in all these problems. It might be the total number or it might be part of the total.

     If the total number is given, what must you do?   subtract

     If the total number is not given, what must you do?   add

FORMAT 11.2   (continued)

TEACHER	STUDENTS
(Repeat step 1 until students answer correctly.)	
2. Touch the first problem.	
Touch the box for the total.	Students touch the box after the arrow.
Is the total given?	no
So what must you do?	add
What problem do you write on the line?	3 + 2
Write it.	Students write 3 + 2.
What is 3 + 2?	5
Write an equals sign and the answer.	Students write = 5
Fill in the empty box.	Students write 5 in box.
(Repeat step 2 with remaining problems.)	

PART D: LESS STRUCTURED WORKSHEET

(Give students a worksheet like that in Part C.)

1. Touch the first problem.

2. Is the total number given or not given?

3. Do you add or subtract?

4. Write the equation on the line and write the answer.

   (Repeat steps 1–5 with all problems.)

FORMAT 11.3   Temporal Sequence Word Problems

PART A: PRESKILL—DETERMINING DIRECTION FOR USING DIAGRAMS

TEACHER	STUDENTS

1. *(Write the following statements on the board.)*
  a. You have 81. You lose some. You end up with 59.
  b. You have 81. You find some. You end up with 129.	

2. Listen while I read problem a. You have 81. You lose some. You end up with 59.	
What is the first value in this problem?	81
What is the second value?	box
What is the third value?	59
3. Now you have to figure out whether you put the values in forward along the arrow or backward. Here are the rules: If you *get more*, you put them in forward along the arrow. If you *get less*, you put them in backward along the arrow.	

(continued on next page)

FORMAT 11.3 (continued)

TEACHER	STUDENTS
4. Listen while I read the first part of problem a again. You have 81. You lose some. Are you getting more or less?	less
5. So do you go forward or backward along the arrow?	backward
6. That is correct. You go backward along the arrow starting with the first value. Tell me what to write first.	81
Tell me what to write next.	box
Tell me what to write last.	59

(Write the following diagram on the board.)

59

————————————→ 81

7. *(Repeat for problem b.)*

8. Remember, you write the values for the parts in the same order as they are in the problem. All you have to do is figure out whether you go backward or forward on the number-family arrow.

   To correct: If the students have trouble figuring out whether they are getting more in a problem or getting less, read the first parts of the problem carefully: You have some. You lose 56. Are you getting more or getting less if you lose some? So do the values go forward or backward along the arrow?

PART B: PRESKILL—DETERMINING IF THE PROBLEM TELLS ABOUT GETTING MORE

1. *(Give students a worksheet with a standard mix of addition and subtraction problems. Under each problem is a number-family diagram.)*	
James had 14 apples. He bought some more apples. Now he has 25 apples.	
2. Remember the rules about writing problem sentences. If the problem tells about getting more, you write the values forward on the arrow. If the problem tells about getting less, write the values backward on the arrow.	
3. Touch problem 1. I'll read it. James has 14 apples. He bought some more apples. Now he has 25 apples.	
That problem has the word *bought*. When you buy, you get more. Remember, in problems that tell about getting more, you write the numbers forward on the arrow. Write the values in the correct place.	*Students write values.*
4. Touch problem 2. I'll read it. Jill had 19 apples. She lost some apples. Now she has 15 apples. Does that problem tell about getting more? Which way will you write the values?	No Backward

FORMAT 11.3   **(continued)**

TEACHER	**STUDENTS**

5. Read problem 3 to yourselves. If the problem tells about getting more, write the values forward on the arrow. If the problem tells about getting less, write the values backward on the arrow.

Students write values above arrow.

(Repeat step 4 with the remaining problems.)

PART C: STRUCTURED WORKSHEET

1. *(Give students a worksheet like that used in Parts A and B with 6-8 problems.)*

2. We're going to work these problems. First we'll see if the total tells about getting more or getting less. Then we'll put the values in the diagram and work the problem.

3. Read problem 1 to yourself and figure out if it tells about getting more or getting less. Does the problem tell about getting more or getting less?

4. Remember the rules: If the problem tells about getting more, you write the values forward on the arrow. If the problem tells about getting less, you write the values backward on the arrow. Does the problem tell about getting more or getting less? So which way will you write the values?

5. Complete the diagram. Now write the equation and figure out the answer. What is the answer?

Students write the equation and the answer.

(Repeat steps 1–4 with the remaining problems.)

PART D: LESS-STRUCTURED WORKSHEET

1. *(Give students a worksheet with temporal sequence problems.)*

2. Read the problem to yourself and figure out whether you write the values forward or backward.

3. Write the values on the diagram.

Students write values on diagram.

4. Write the equation and figure out the answer.

Students write the equation and the answer.

5. Read the last sentence in the problem and write the whole answer—the number and the word.

Students write answer.

(Repeat steps 1–4 with the remaining problems.)

FORMAT 11.4 Format for Comparison Problems

Part A: Preskill—Determining the Total Number

TEACHER	STUDENTS

1. Comparison problems tell you about two persons or things. Here are some words you'll see in comparison problems: *bigger, older, smaller, taller, wider.* If the problem tells about two people and has a word that ends in *er,* you know it's a comparison problem.

2. Let's practice figuring out which person or thing in a comparison problem tells about the big number.

3. Listen: A dog weighs 7 pounds. A cat weighs 3 pounds more than the dog. Who does that problem tell about?   A dog and a cat.

4. Listen to the problem again. *(Repeat problem.)* Who is heavier?   The cat.

5. So the big number tells how many pounds the cat weighs.

   (Repeat steps 3–5 with the problems below.)

   Jill is 10 years old. Brian is 8 years younger. Who is older?

   Hole A is 6 feet deep. Hole B is 4 feet deep. Which hole is deeper?

   Jack ran 8 miles. Ann ran 2 miles more. Who ran farther?

   Jane weighs 60 pounds. Ann is 5 pounds lighter. Who is heavier?

   A yellow pencil is 5 inches long. A blue pencil is 3 inches longer. Which pencil is longer?

Part B: Structured Worksheet

1. *(Give students worksheets with problems written in the form below.)*

---

a. Tom's stick is 2 feet long.
   Bill's stick is 5 feet longer.
   How long is Bill's stick?

   □ □
   ⟶ □
   _____

   Answer: _____

---

b. Jack is 10 years old.
   Bill is 2 years younger.
   How old is Bill?

   □ □
   ⟶ □
   _____

   Answer: _____

FORMAT 11.4   (continued)

TEACHER	STUDENTS

2. Read the first problem.

3. Who does the problem tell about?

    Which is longer, Bill's stick or Tom's stick?

    Write *Bill* on the line under the total box.

4. Read the problem again. *(Pause.)*

    Does a number in the problem tell how long Bill's stick is?

5. The problem does not give a number for the total. The numbers in the problem tell about parts of the total. Write those numbers in the boxes on the arrows.

6. Write the equation and figure out the answer.

    (Repeat steps 1–5 with the remaining problems.)

STUDENTS column:

Tom and Bill

Bill's stick

Students write *Bill.*

no

Students write numbers in the boxes.

PART C: LESS-STRUCTURED WORKSHEET

1. *(Give students worksheets written in this form.)*

Alex is 14 years old. Doug is 3 years younger.
How old is Doug?

□ □

⟶ ☐   Answer: _____

_____

2. Read the problem.

3. Write the word that tells about the big number under the total box.

4. See if the big number is given in the problem. Then write the numbers in the boxes.

5. Write the equation and figure out the answer.

6. Write the whole answer on the number line.

(Repeat steps 1–5 with the remaining problems.)

FORMAT 11.5   **Format for Classification Story Problems**

PART A: LANGUAGE TRAINING

TEACHER   **STUDENTS**

1. I'll say some class names. You tell me the biggest class.
   Listen: cats, animals, dogs. What is the biggest class?   animals

   (Repeat step 1 with: hammer, saw, tool; vehicle, car, truck;
   men, women, people; girls, boys, children.)

PART B: STRUCTURED WORKSHEET

1. *(Give students a worksheet with 6–8 problems written like*
   those below.)

---

a. There are 8 *children*. Three are *boys*. How many are *girls*?

b. Jill has 5 *hammers* and 4 *saws*. How many *tools* does she have?

---

2. Let's review some rules you already know. If the total
   number is given, what do you do?   subtract

   If the total number is not given, what do you do?   add

3. In some problems we don't see words like *find, lose, buy,*
   or give away. So we have to use a different way to do these
   problems.

4. Touch the first problem. I'll read it. There are 8 children:
   3 are boys. How many are girls? The problem talks about
   children, boys, or girls. Which is the big class, children,
   boys, or girls?   children

   If children is the big class, then the number of children is
   the total number. So write *children* on the line under the
   total box.   Students write *children*.

5. Listen. *(Repeat the problem.)* Children is the total number.
   Does the problem tell how many children?   yes

   So the total number is given. What is the total number?   8

   Write 8 in the box for the total number.   Students write 8.

> Note: If the first answer is "no," tell the students,
> "The total is not given, so we don't write anything
> in the box for the total."

FORMAT 11.5   (continued)

TEACHER	STUDENTS
6. Now we write the values for boys and girls in the boxes over the arrow. How many boys?	3
Write 3 in the first box.	Students write 3.
We don't know how many girls, so we don't write anything in the other box.	
7. Is the total number given?	yes
So what do you do to work out the problem?	subtract
I start with 8 children and subtract 3 boys to find out how many girls.	
Write the equation and figure out the answer.	Students write $8 - 3 = 5$.
If there are 8 children and 3 are boys, how many are girls?	5
(Repeat steps 3–5 with remaining problems.)	

PART C: LESS STRUCTURED WORKSHEET

1. *(Give students worksheet with problems in this form.)*

Jerry has 7 pets. 4 are *dogs*.
How many are *cats*?

Answer: _____

2. Touch problem one.

3. Read the problem. Then write the name for the big class under the total box.	Students write name for big class.
4. Write the numbers in the number family boxes.	Students write numbers.
5. Write the equation and figure out the answer.	Students write equations.
6. Write the whole answer on the number line.	Students write answer.
(Repeat steps 1–5 with remaining problems.)	

FORMAT 11.6 Using Tables to Solve Problems

PART A: INTRODUCING ROWS AND COLUMNS IN A TABLE

TEACHER	STUDENT

1. *(Write the table below on the board.)*

6	6	1	
2	3	2	
1	1	2	

2. This is a table problem. To work this kind of problem, you have to add the numbers in each column and the numbers in each row. Remember that columns go up and down. Rows go side to side. Point to show me which way columns go. *(Check to make sure that students go up and down.)* Point and show me which way rows go. *(Check to make sure that students point side to side. Repeat to correct.)*

3. *(Touch the first column.)* I'll read the numbers in the first column: 6, 2, 1.

4. *(Touch the second column.)* Read the numbers.   6, 3, 1

5. *(Touch the third column.)* Read the numbers.   1, 2, 2

6. *(Touch the top row.)* I'll read the numbers in the top row. 6, 6, 1.

7. *(Touch the middle row.)* Your turn. Read the numbers in the middle row.   2, 3, 2

8. *(Touch the bottom row.)* Read the numbers in the bottom row.   1, 1, 2

PART B: FINDING TOTALS IN TABLES

1. Go back to the first column. The numbers are 6, 2, 1. Here's how you work the problem. You add 6 and 2. What's the answer?   8

2. Then you add 8 and 1. What's the answer?   9

3. 9 is the *total* for the first column. *(Write 9 at the bottom of the first column.)*

4. Your turn. Add the numbers in the next column and raise your hand when you know the answer. *(Wait for students to solve the problem.)* The numbers in this column are 6, 3, and 1. What is the answer, everyone?   10

5. *(Repeat procedure with last column.)*

FORMAT 11.6   (continued)

TEACHER	STUDENTS

6. The numbers for the top row are 6, 6, and 1.
   What is 6 plus 6?   12

   What's 12 plus 1? *(Write 13 at the end of the row.)*   13

7. Your turn. Add the numbers in the middle row and raise
   your hand when you have the answer. *(Wait for students to
   solve the problem.)* The numbers in this row are 2, 3, and 2.
   What is the answer, everyone?   7

8. *(Repeat procedure with last row.)*

PART C: USING THE NUMBER-FAMILY STRATEGY TO SOLVE FOR MISSING DATA

1. *(Write the following table on the board.)*

2. This is a table with arrows for the rows and columns. The
   arrows show you something interesting about the table.
   Each row and column works just like a number family. The
   first two numbers in the row are the small numbers. The
   total is the big number.

3. *(Touch row a.)* A number is missing in that row. Is the
   missing number a big number or a small number?   a small number

   (Write the following diagram on the board.)

   $$\xrightarrow{\hspace{2cm} 38 \hspace{2cm}} 45$$

4. So do you add or subtract to find the missing number?   subtract

5. Say the subtraction problem.   45 minus 38.

6. *(Touch row b. Write the diagram below on the board.)*

   $$\xrightarrow{\hspace{1cm} 15 \hspace{1cm} 11 \hspace{1cm}}$$

   Here is the number family for that row. Is the missing
   number a small number or the big number?   the big number

7. So do you add or subtract to find the missing number?   add

8. Say the addition problem.   15 plus 11

9. *(Touch the bottom row, c.)* Is the missing number a small
   number or the big number?   a small number   *(continued on next page)*

FORMAT 11.6 (continued)

TEACHER	STUDENTS
10. So do you add or subtract?	subtract
11. Say the subtraction problem.	31 minus 12
12. Your turn. Write the problem and the answer for each row. Write the column problem for rows a, b, and c. *(Wait for students to finish the problems.)*	
13. Everyone, read the problems and the answers. Get ready: row a, row b, row c.	45 minus 38 equals 7. 15 plus 11 equals 26. 31 minus 12 equals 19.
14. What is the missing number in row a? *(Write 7 in row a.)* What is the missing number in row b? *(Write 26 in row b.)* What is the missing number in row c? *(Write 19 in row c.)*	7 26 19
15. Figure out the totals for each column. *(Wait for students to finish the column problems.)*	
16. Read the totals for the columns: first column, second column,	34 68

PART D: USING TABLES TO SOLVE WORD PROBLEMS

1. *(Students have worksheets with several problems that are similar to the one below.)*
   Facts: There are 23 red cars on Al's lot. The total number of red and green cars on Jim's lot is 43. The total number of green cars on both lots is 30.

	Red cars	Green cars	Total for both colors
Jim's lot			
Al's lot			
Total for both lots			

Questions

    a. Are there fewer green cars or red cars on both lots?
    b. How many green and red cars are on Al's lot?
    c. There are 31 cars of some color on Jim's lot. What color?
    d. Are there more green cars on Jim's lot or Al's lot?

TEACHER	STUDENTS
2. We're going to use a table to answer the questions listed above. First we need to fill in any missing information from the facts that are given. Read the first fact. Write the value from that fact in the correct place in the table. *(Repeat step 1 with the remaining facts.)*	There are 23 red cars on Al's lot.
3. Now you have enough information to complete the table using the number-family strategy. If one of the small numbers is missing, what do you do?	subtract

FORMAT 11.6   (continued)

TEACHER	STUDENTS
If one of the totals is missing, what do you do?	add

4. Now that table is complete, read question one and raise your hand when you know the answer. *(Call on an individual student to answer question 1.)* Everyone, write the correct answer next to the question.

Students write answer.

5. *(Repeat step 3 for each question.)*

To correct: If students make a mistake locating the correct information, have them put their fingers on the cell that has the information to answer the question. Monitor where students are placing their fingers to determine if they are able to read the table. If they have problems locating the correct cells, then reteach Part C of this format, adding a question about the information represented in each row and column.

FORMAT 11.7   Introduction to Multiplication and Division Word Problems

TEACHER   **STUDENT**

1. *(Write the following diagrams on the board.)*

$$\begin{array}{c} \underline{\quad\quad}\ D \\ \longrightarrow\ C \end{array}$$

⊗⊗⊗
⊗⊗⊗

2. What coins are shown in this problem?   dimes

3. How many cents is each dime worth?   10

4. So 10 is the first small number. *(Write 10.)*

$$\begin{array}{cc} 10 & D \\ \multicolumn{2}{c}{\longrightarrow\ C} \end{array}$$

5. How many dimes are there?   6

6. So I cross out D and write 6. *(Cross out D and write 6.)*

$$\begin{array}{cc} & 6 \\ 10 & \cancel{D} \\ \multicolumn{2}{c}{\longrightarrow\ C} \end{array}$$

7. To figure out how many cents, you multiply 10 times 6. How many cents? *(Cross out C and write 60.)*   60

$$\begin{array}{cc} & 6 \\ 10 & \cancel{D} \\ & \quad 60 \\ \longrightarrow & \cancel{C} \end{array}$$

(continued on next page)

FORMAT 11.7 **(continued)**

TEACHER	STUDENTS

8. *(Repeat steps 1–6 with similar problems using nickels, dimes, and quarters. Later problems do not need to show the coins, but describe them as in the following problems.)*
   a. You have nickels. You have 35 cents in all. How many nickels do you have?
   b. You have dimes. You have 9 dimes. How many cents do you have in all?
   c. You have nickels. You have 8 nickels. How many cents do you have in all?
   d. You have quarters. You have 5 quarters. How many cents do you have in all?
   e. You have dimes. You have 40 cents in all. How many dimes do you have?

FORMAT 11.8 **Setting up Multiplication and Division Word Problems**

TEACHER	STUDENT

1. *(Write the following problems on the board.)*
   a. Each box holds 7 cans. You have 35 cans. How many boxes do you have?

   b. Each room had 10 lights. There were 8 rooms. How many lights were there in all the rooms?

   c. Each dog had 9 bugs. There were 7 dogs. How many bugs were there on all the dogs?

   d. Each cat had 9 fleas. There were 36 fleas in all. How many cats were there?

   e. Each boy ate 2 hot dogs. There were 5 boys. How many hot dogs were eaten by all the boys?

2. These are word problems. To work them, you have to make multiplication number families. One sentence in each problem tells how to make the family. That sentence tells about each thing.

3. Listen while I read problem a. Each box holds 7 cans. You have 35 cans. How many boxes do you have? The first sentence gives you information for making the number family. Each box holds 7 cans. There are more cans than boxes. So cans is the big number.

4. What do we write to stand for box?   B
   (Write the following diagram on the board.)

   B
   ———————————▶

FORMAT 11.8   (continued)

TEACHER	STUDENT

What do we write to show cans?

C

(Write the following diagram on the board.)

      B
————————→ C

If can is the big number and box is a small number, what is
the other small number?

7

(Write the following diagram on the board.)

  7   B
————————→ C

5. Here is the number family. The next sentence tells you that
   you have 35 cans, so we put that in the number family.
   (Write the following diagram on the board.)

  7   B
          35
————————→ ~~C~~

6. Our number family shows a big number and a small number.
   You find the missing small number by finding out how many
   7s are in 35.

7. How many boxes do you have?

5

   (Write the final diagram on the board.)

      5
  7   ~~B~~
          35
————————→ ~~C~~

8. *(Repeat steps 1–5 using problems b, c, d, and e.)*

FORMAT 11.9   **Introducing Multi-Step Word Problems**

TEACHER	STUDENT

PART A

1. *(Write the following problems on the board.)*

   a. A wallet is empty. $432 goes into that wallet. Then some
      money goes out of that wallet. The wallet ends up with
      $85. How much went out?

   b. A florist starts without any roses. She picks up 87 roses.
      She sells 54 roses. How many roses does she end up with?

(continued on next page)

FORMAT 11.9   (continued)

TEACHER	**STUDENT**

   c. Chandra had an empty basket. She put some eggs in
      the basket. Then she gave away 37 of those eggs. The
      basket still had 14 eggs in it. How many eggs did Chandra
      put in the basket?

   end up   *out*   *in*

   ———————————————————→

2. Listen while I read problem a. A wallet is empty. $432 goes
   into that wallet. Then some money goes out of that wallet.
   The wallet ends up with $85. How much went out?

3. In this problem, some money goes into the wallet, and some
   money goes out of the wallet. How much money does the
   wallet end up with? $85

   So I will write $85 under "end up" in the number family.
   (Write $85 on the board.)

   end up   *out*   *in*

   $85

   ———————————————————→

4. Do we know how much money went out of the wallet?   no

   So we do not know the other small number.

5. Do we know how much money went into the wallet?   yes

6. How much money went into the wallet? So we can write that
   for the big number. *(Write $432 under "in" on the
   board.)* $432

   end up   *out*   *in*

   $85

   ———————————————————→ $432

7. Now that we know two numbers for the number family, we
   can figure out the third number. What is missing, a big number or a small number?   a small number

8. How do we find a missing small number?   subtract

9. Say the subtraction problem. $432–$85

10. *(Repeat for problems b and c.)*

PART B

1. *(Write the following problems on the board.)*
   a. Josh had $17 in the bank. Later he put $12 in the bank.
      The next day he went to the bank and took out $11.50. How
      much money did Josh end up with in the bank?

FORMAT 11.9   (continued)

TEACHER	STUDENT

b. A water tank had some water in it. 250 gallons were taken from the tank. Then another 720 gallons were taken from the tank. The tank still had 1150 gallons in it. How many gallons were in the tank in the beginning?

c. A farmer had 534 bales of hay. She fed 247 bales to her cattle. She sold 85 bales to a neighbor. She threw 4 bales away, because they were moldy. How many bales did she end up with?

2. Listen while I read problem a: Josh had $17 in the bank. Later he put $12 in the bank. The next day he went to the bank and took out $11.50. How much money did Josh end up with in the bank? The first part of the problem tells about the two values that went in the bank. Here is the number family:

   end up   *out*   *in*

   ———————————————▶

3. What is the first value that went in the bank? $17
   (Write $17 in the number family.)

   end up   *out*   *in*
                              $17

   ———————————————▶

4. What is the second value that went in the bank? $12
   (Write $12 on the board.)

   end up   *out*   *in*
                              $17
                              12

   ———————————————▶

5. Do we know how much Josh took out of the bank?   yes

   How much? $11.50

   So we write $11.50 in the number family.
   (Write $11.50 on the board.)

   end up   *out*   *in*
                              $17
              $11.50   12

   ———————————————▶

(continued on next page)

FORMAT 11.9   (continued)

TEACHER	STUDENT

6. Now we need to add the amounts that went into the bank.
   Say the problem.

   $17 plus $12

   What is the total?
   (Write $29 on the board.)

   $29

```
    end up          out      in
                            $17
                  $11.50     12
    ──────────────────────→ $29
```

7. Now that we have two numbers in the number family, we
   can figure out the other number.

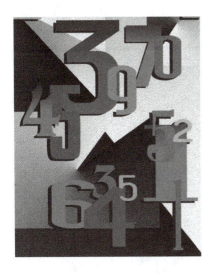

CHAPTER 12

Fractions

TERMS AND CONCEPTS

Fractions   A fraction is a numeral of the form y/x where x ≠ 0. Fractions involve division into equal-sized segments and a statement regarding the number of segments present, used, or acted upon. For example, "John ate ¼ of a pie" implies that a pie was divided into four equal parts and that John ate one of those parts.

Numerator   The top number in a fraction.

Denominator   The bottom number in a fraction.

Proper Fraction   A fraction whose numerator is less than its denominator.

Improper Fraction   A fraction whose numerator is equal to or greater than the denominator.

Mixed Number   An improper fraction expressed as a whole number and a fraction.

Greatest Common Factor   Largest factor of both the numerator and the denominator; e.g., the greatest common factor for ⁴⁄₈ is 4.

Lowest Common Denominator   The least common multiple of the denominators; e.g., the lowest common denominator for ⅓ + ½ + ¼ is 12.

Rational Numbers   Rational numbers can be expressed as the quotient of two integers. (Rational numbers can be negative, −¾ or −⁷⁄₂, as well as positive, ¾ or ⁷⁄₂. The chapters in this text discuss only positive rational numbers.) Fractions,

decimals, ratios, proportion, and percent could all be considered different forms of rational numbers. Rational numbers are usually represented in one of the following ways:

1. Portioning off units from a total number of units

   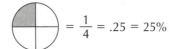
   $$= \frac{3}{10} = .3 = 30\%$$

2. Portioning off subsets of a group of subsets

   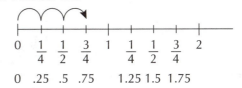
   $$= \frac{2}{3} = .67 = 66\tfrac{2}{3}\%$$

3. Dividing a whole figure into equal parts

   $$= \frac{1}{4} = .25 = 25\%$$

4. Number line

0	¼	½	¾	1	1¼	1½	1¾	2

   0   .25   .5   .75   1.25 1.5 1.75

SKILL HIERARCHY

We have included a Skill Hierarchy Chart in this chapter because fractions comprise one of the most complex sets of skills covered in elementary mathematics.

Skill Hierarchy Chart

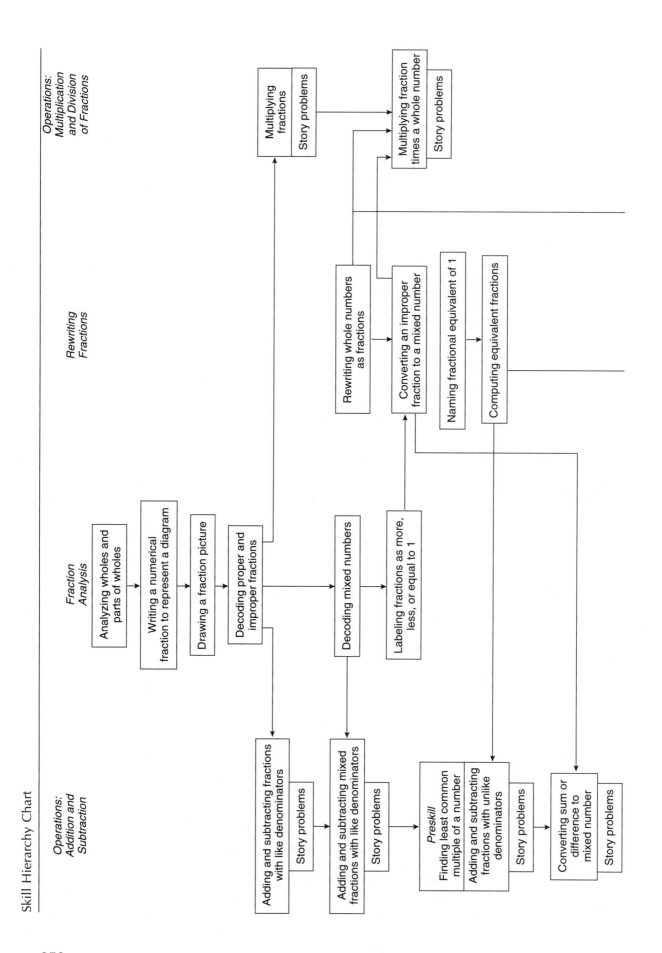

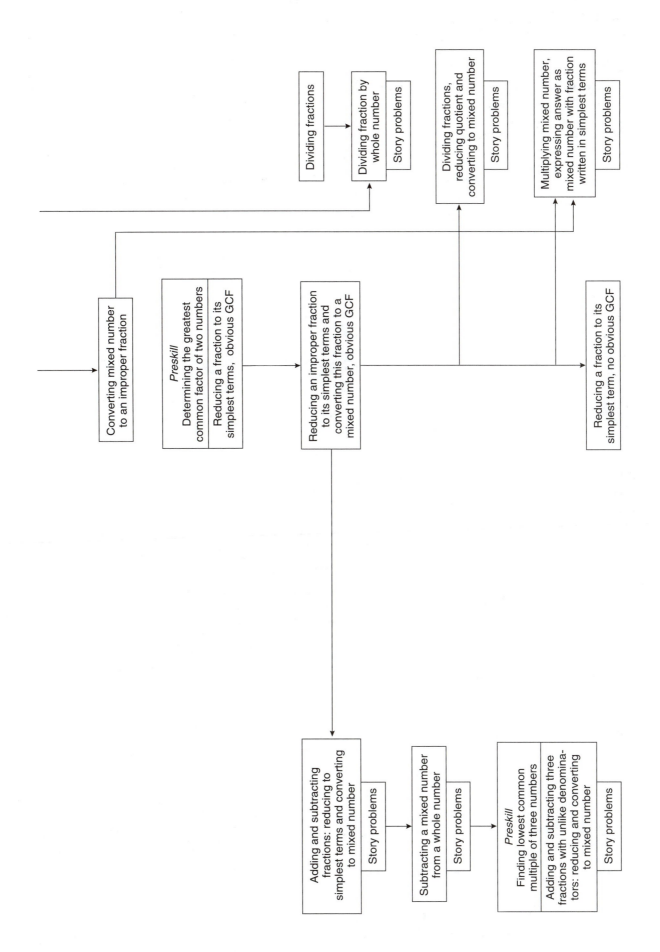

Dividing fractions

Dividing fraction by whole number

Story problems

Dividing fractions, reducing quotient and converting to mixed number

Story problems

Multiplying mixed number, expressing answer as mixed number with fraction written in simplest terms

Story problems

Converting mixed number to an improper fraction

Preskill
Determining the greatest common factor of two numbers

Reducing a fraction to its simplest terms, obvious GCF

Reducing an improper fraction to its simplest terms and converting this fraction to a mixed number, obvious GCF

Reducing a fraction to its simplest term, no obvious GCF

Adding and subtracting fractions: reducing to simplest terms and converting to mixed number

Story problems

Subtracting a mixed number from a whole number

Story problems

Preskill
Finding lowest common multiple of three numbers

Adding and subtracting three fractions with unlike denominators: reducing and converting to mixed number

Story problems

Instructional Sequence and Assessment Chart

Grade Level | *Problem Type* | *Performance Indicator*

1-2a   Identifying fractions that correspond to diagrams

a. Circle the picture that shows ²/₄.

b. Circle the picture that shows ⁴/₄.

c. Put X on the line below the picture that shows ⁴/₃.

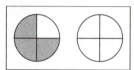   

_____   _____

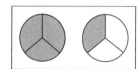

_____

d. Put X on the line below the picture that shows ³/₂.

_____ _____ _____

1-2b   Drawing diagrams to correspond to fractions

$\frac{3}{4}$ =

$\frac{2}{3}$ =

$\frac{3}{2}$ =

Instructional Sequence and Assessment Chart (continued)

Grade Level	Problem Type	Performance Indicator
1-2c	Reading and writing fractions expressed as fractions	Write these fractions: a. two-thirds $= \dfrac{\square}{\square}$ b. five-halves $= \dfrac{\square}{\square}$ c. four-fifths $= \dfrac{\square}{\square}$ (Test students individually. "What does this say: $\dfrac{2}{3}$ $\dfrac{4}{5}$ $\dfrac{5}{2}$?")
2d	Determining whether a fraction is more than, equal to, or less than 1	Write *more than, less than,* or *equal to* in each blank. $\dfrac{4}{3}$ is _____ 1 $\dfrac{7}{7}$ is _____ 1 $\dfrac{5}{6}$ is _____ 1
2e	Adding and subtracting fractions with like denominators	$\dfrac{3}{5} - \dfrac{2}{5} =$ _____ $\dfrac{4}{7} - \dfrac{2}{7} =$ _____ $\dfrac{3}{5} + \dfrac{1}{5} =$ _____
2f	Multiplying fractions	$\dfrac{3}{5} \times \dfrac{2}{3} =$ _____ $\dfrac{2}{5} \times \dfrac{3}{5} =$ _____ $\dfrac{2}{2} \times \dfrac{3}{5} =$ _____
3a	Reading and writing mixed numbers	Write two and one-third _____ Write four and two-fifths _____ Write six and one-half _____ (Test students individually. "Read these numbers: $2\dfrac{1}{4}$ $3\dfrac{2}{5}$ $7\dfrac{3}{9}$.")
3b	Adding and subtracting mixed numbers: fractions with like denominators	$5\dfrac{4}{7} - \dfrac{2}{7} =$ _____ $3\dfrac{2}{5} - 1\dfrac{2}{5} =$ _____

continued

Instructional Sequence and Assessment Chart (continued)

Grade Level	Problem Type	Performance Indicator
3c	Story problems: Adding and subtracting mixed numbers and fractions with the same denominator	Bill ran $2\frac{2}{4}$ miles on Monday and $3\frac{1}{4}$ miles on Tuesday. How many miles did he run altogether? _____ miles Jack had $4\frac{2}{8}$ pounds of nails. Bill had $2\frac{3}{8}$ pounds of nails. How much more did Jack have? _____ pounds of nails Bob worked $2\frac{1}{2}$ hours on Monday and 3 hours on Tuesday. How many hours did he work altogether? _____ hours
4a	Rewriting fractions as mixed numbers	$\frac{12}{5} = $ _____ $\frac{8}{3} = $ _____ $\frac{21}{9} = $ _____
4b	Rewriting whole numbers as fractions	$9 = \dfrac{\square}{\square}$ $6 = \dfrac{\square}{\square}$ $8 = \dfrac{\square}{\square}$
4c	Multiplying fractions by a whole number; converting answers to whole numbers	$\frac{2}{3} \times 6$ $\frac{1}{3} \times 12$ $\frac{3}{5} \times 20$
4d	Multiplying fractions by whole numbers and converting answers to mixed numbers	$\frac{2}{5} \times 14$ $\frac{3}{7} \times 8$ $\frac{2}{9} \times 15$
4e	Story problems: multiplying fractions by whole numbers	There are 15 children in class. Two-thirds are boys. How many boys in the class? Jack has to study for 30 hours. He has done half of the studying. How many hours did he study? Ann's coach told her to run $\frac{3}{4}$ of a mile a day. How many miles will she run in 5 days?
4f	Writing a fraction as an equivalent to one whole group	$1 = \dfrac{\square}{4}$ $1 = \dfrac{\square}{7}$
4g	Rewriting fractions as equivalent fractions with larger denominators	$\frac{2}{5} = \dfrac{\square}{10}$ $\frac{3}{4} = \dfrac{\square}{12}$ $\frac{2}{3} = \dfrac{\square}{9}$

Instructional Sequence and Assessment Chart (continued)

Grade Level	Problem Type	Performance Indicator
4h	Finding the lowest common multiple of two small numbers	Find the lowest common multiple of 6 and 4 _____ Find the lowest common multiple of 5 and 10 _____ Find the lowest common multiple of 5 and 2 _____
4i	Adding and subtracting fractions with unlike denominators	$\frac{3}{4} - \frac{2}{3} = \frac{\square}{\square}$ $\frac{2}{5} + \frac{3}{10} = \frac{\square}{\square}$ $\frac{1}{2} - \frac{1}{3} = \frac{\square}{\square}$ $\frac{2}{6} + \frac{1}{2} = \frac{\square}{\square}$
4j	Comparing value of fractions	Which is greater: $\frac{2}{3}$ or $\frac{4}{5}$? $\frac{4}{5}$ or $\frac{2}{3}$? $\frac{2}{7}$ or $\frac{1}{2}$?
4k	Story problems: adding and subtracting fractions with unlike denominators	Bill painted $\frac{1}{2}$ of the wall. Jane painted $\frac{1}{4}$ of the wall. How much of the wall have they painted altogether? Tom ate $\frac{1}{3}$ of the pie, and Jack ate $\frac{1}{2}$ of the pie. How much of the pie did they eat?
4l	Determining all factors of a given number	Write all the numbers that are factors of 12. Write all the numbers that are factors of 8.
4m	Determining the greatest common factor	What is the greatest common factor of 8 and 12? What is the greatest common factor of 4 and 8? What is the greatest common factor of 12 and 15?
4n	Reducing a fraction to its simplest terms	Reduce these fractions to their simplest terms: $\frac{12}{18} = \frac{\square}{\square}$ $\frac{16}{20} = \frac{\square}{\square}$ $\frac{6}{18} = \frac{\square}{\square}$
4o	Adding fractions, reducing and converting to mixed numbers	Add these fractions; reduce the answers to simplest terms. Write answers as mixed numbers. $\frac{4}{6} + \frac{2}{5} =$ _____ $\frac{2}{4} + \frac{2}{3} =$ _____ $\frac{6}{10} + \frac{4}{5} =$ _____

continued

Instructional Sequence and Assessment Chart (continued)

Grade Level	Problem Type	Performance Indicator
4p	Converting mixed numbers to improper fractions	$2\frac{1}{4} = \frac{\square}{4}$ $3\frac{1}{2} = \frac{\square}{2}$ $1\frac{3}{5} = \frac{\square}{5}$
5a	Subtracting mixed numbers from whole numbers	$8 - 1\frac{2}{3} = $ _____ $9 - 2\frac{3}{5} = $ _____ $7 - 4\frac{1}{2} = $ _____
5b	Finding the lowest common multiple of three numbers	Find the lowest common multiple of 3, 6, and 4. Find the lowest common multiple of 2, 4, and 5. Find the lowest common multiple of 2, 5, and 10.
5c	Adding and subtracting three fractions with different denominators	Add these fractions and write the answers with fractions written in simplest terms: $\frac{3}{5} + \frac{1}{2} + \frac{3}{6} = $ _____ $\frac{2}{3} + \frac{2}{4} + \frac{1}{6} = $ _____ $\frac{3}{4} + \frac{1}{2} + \frac{2}{5} = $ _____
5d	Multiplying mixed numbers	$7\frac{3}{4} \times 3\frac{1}{2} = $ _____ $2\frac{3}{5} \times 4 = $ _____ $5 \times 2\frac{1}{2} = $ _____
5e	Dividing fractions	$\frac{3}{4} \div \frac{2}{5} = $ _____ $\frac{5}{6} \div \frac{2}{3} = $ _____ $\frac{7}{9} \div \frac{1}{3} = $ _____
5f	Dividing fractions by whole numbers	$\frac{2}{3} \div 4 = $ _____ $\frac{3}{5} \div 2 = $ _____ $\frac{2}{4} \div 7 = $ _____

Instructional Sequence and Assessment Chart (continued)

Grade Level	Problem Type	Performance Indicator
5g	Dividing mixed numbers by whole numbers	$3\frac{1}{2} \div 3 = $ _____ $2\frac{1}{5} \div 2 = $ _____ $7\frac{1}{2} \div 4 = $ _____
5h	Story problems: division involving fractions	Two girls picked $5\frac{1}{2}$ pounds of cherries. They want to split up the cherries equally. How much will each one get? Bill has 35 inches of ribbon. He wants to make shorter ribbons. If each ribbon is $\frac{1}{2}$" long, how many ribbons can he make?

This complexity is understandable, since the entire range of operations discussed in other sections of the book is applicable to fractional numbers. Unfortunately, fractions do not represent a simple extension of familiar skills. While early instruction on whole numbers covers counting by groups of 1 or more than one, that instruction does not help students generalize to groups of less than one. For example, in addition and subtraction of whole numbers, members of a second group relate to the members of the first group based on one-to-one correspondences. For example, in the problem $4 + 3$, students increase the first set in units of 1 (5,6,7), producing the answer 7. To solve $4 - 3$, students decrease the first set in units of 1, producing the answer 1. In multiplication and division of whole numbers, a second group is related to the first group based on a one-to-many correspondence. For example, in solving for 8×2, students count units of 8 for each member of the second group (8, 16), producing the answer 16. In $16 \div 2$, students determine the answer by counting 1 for each unit of 2 in 16 (1,2,3,4,5,6,7,8), producing the answer 8.

In operations containing fractions, the correspondences involve fractional numbers. For example, to solve $\frac{2}{3} \times 4$ students count units of $\frac{2}{3}$ for each member of the second group. While students can quickly learn to count 2, 4, 6, 8 for 2×4, counting $\frac{2}{3}$, $\frac{4}{3}$, $\frac{6}{3}$, $\frac{8}{3}$, for $\frac{2}{3} \times 4$ is not easy. The problem $\frac{2}{3} \times \frac{4}{7}$ is even less comprehensible because students have no experiential basis for counting $\frac{4}{7}$ths times. Therefore, the learning of fractional correspondences with both whole numbers and other fractions requires instruction in new strategies.

Another major difficulty with fractions is the incompatibility of different units. Addition and subtraction can be carried out only with equivalent units. Whole numbers represent a simple type of equivalent unit, so they can be added and subtracted in any combination. In contrast, fractional numbers do not represent one type of unit: All thirds represent equivalent units and all fourths represent equivalent units, but thirds are not the same as fourths. Consequently, thirds and fourths cannot be added or subtracted as such. Prior to adding or subtracting fractions, the fractional units must be transformed into a common unit:

$$\frac{1}{4} + \frac{2}{3} = \frac{3}{12} + \frac{8}{12} = \frac{11}{12}$$

The necessity to transform or rewrite fractional numbers is a major source of difficulty in teaching fractions. (This is one reason for the appeal of decimals; they have the uniform base of multiples of 10.)

Instruction in fractions can be organized around the three main groupings of fraction topics outlined in the Skill Hierarchy: fraction analysis, rewriting fractions, and operations (addition, subtraction, multiplication, and division of fractions).

Since application of fraction skills depends on an understanding of fractional numbers, initial instruction on the concepts and conventions characterizing fractions is critical. Therefore, early instruction must address fraction analysis skills such as constructing diagrams to represent fractions, writing the fraction represented by diagrams, decoding fractions, and determining if a fraction is proper or improper.

The second area, rewriting fractions, includes the following skills:

1. Rewriting an improper fraction as a mixed number: $^{13}/_2 = 6^1/_2$
2. Rewriting a proper fraction using the smallest possible denominator (reducing fractions): $^6/_8 = ^3/_4$
3. Rewriting a fraction as an equivalent fraction: $^2/_5 = ^4/_\square$
4. Rewriting a mixed number as an improper fraction: $2^1/_2 = ^5/_2$

The third area, operations, includes addition, subtraction, multiplication, and division of fractions. These operations often require several rewriting fraction skills. For example, to work the problem $^3/_4 + ^5/_6$, the student must rewrite $^3/_4$ and $^5/_6$ as equivalent fractions with the same denominator: $^3/_4 = ^9/_{12}$ and $^5/_6 = ^{10}/_{12}$. The equivalent fractions $^{10}/_{12}$ and $^9/_{12}$ are then added to produce a sum of $^{19}/_{12}$, which must be converted to the mixed number $1^7/_{12}$. When working the problem $^4/_5 \times 1^3/_4$, the student must first convert the mixed number $1^3/_4$ to the improper fraction $^7/_4$. The student then multiplies $^4/_5 \times ^7/_4$, ending with a product of $^{28}/_{20}$, which can be converted to the mixed number $1^8/_{20}$. The fraction part of this mixed number can be reduced so that the final answer reads $1^2/_5$.

The Skill Hierarchy Chart is designed to help the reader see the interrelationships among various fraction skills. Note on the chart the numerous fractions skills that are component skills for other skills. A sequence for teaching fractions must be arranged so that all component skills for an advanced problem type have been presented before that problem type is introduced. Note also how the focus of instruction circulates. For example, simple addition and subtraction problems involving fractions with like denominators are introduced at a relatively early stage in the sequence of instruction. Problems involving adding and subtracting fractions with unlike denominators are not introduced until significantly later in the sequence, since several rewriting skills must be taught first. The Instructional Sequence and Assessment Chart suggests one possible order for introducing the important types of fraction-related problems. Teachers working with intermediate students will find it productive to test for and teach, when necessary, the skills appearing at the beginning of the sequence chart, since these skills lay the foundation for a conceptual understanding of fractions.

FRACTION ANALYSIS

Fraction analysis instruction usually begins in mid-second grade. The skills included in this area are listed below in their order of introduction:

1. Learning part/whole discrimination: Students learn to discriminate between whole units, the number of parts each unit is divided into, and the number of parts used.
2. Writing a numerical representation for a diagram of whole units divided into equal-sized parts and vice-versa:

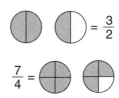

3. Reading fractions: $^3/_4$ is read as "three-fourths."
4. Determining whether a fraction equals, exceeds, or is less than one whole.
5. Reading mixed fractional numbers: $3^1/_2$ is "three and one-half."

The strategies in the fraction analysis section have been designed to introduce proper and improper fractions concurrently. This feature prevents students from learning the misrule that all fractions are proper fractions. Without adequate instruction, low-performing students often learn this misrule, as evidenced by the fact that they can usually decode and draw a picture of $^3/_4$ but are not able to generalize the skills to the example $^4/_3$. By introducing proper and improper fractions at the same time, teachers show students that the analysis applies to all fractions.

A second important feature of the analysis section is that students are taught initially to interpret what the denominator and numerator tell (e.g., in $^3/_4$ the 4 tells four parts in each whole unit, and 3 tells three parts are used), rather than to read the fraction in the traditional way (e.g., $^3/_4$ read as three-fourths). The interpretive reading of fractions enables students to represent a diagram as a numerical fraction and facilitates conceptual development.

A third important feature of fraction analysis is initial limitation of fractions to figures that have been divided into parts:

$$\frac{5}{4} = \bigoplus\bigoplus \qquad \frac{2}{3} = \bigcirc$$

To simplify initial learning, we recommend delaying the introduction of subsets until several months after fractions are introduced.

Part-Whole Discrimination

Format 12.1 shows how to introduce fractions to students. The goal of the format is to teach basic fraction (part-whole) concepts through the use of number lines, rather than separate groups. The reason for working with number lines from the onset is to ensure that students relate fractions to whole numbers. The specific objective is to teach students to discriminate between the number of parts in each whole unit and the number of whole units.

In the format, the teacher draws a number line on the board and divides each unit into an equal number of parts. The teacher tells the students that each unit is called a whole and then leads the students through determining how many parts are in each whole. Students complete the bottom number for units on the number line. They learn that the bottom number is the number of parts in each unit. (See Format 12.1.)

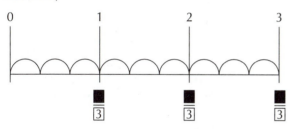

Each example set should include number lines divided into different numbers of parts. Each example should also include a number line of a different length. For example, the first number line might end with 5, with each section divided into two parts. The next number line might end with 3, and each unit might be divided into four parts. This format would be presented for several days.

Next, the students learn to write complete fractions for whole numbers on number lines. The bottom number is the number of parts in each unit. That number is the same for all whole units on a number line. The top number is the number of parts from the beginning of the number line.

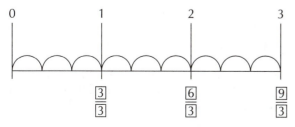

For the third step, students write three fractions for each number line, two "whole number" fractions and a fraction for a shaded part. To figure out the fractions, students first count the number of parts in each unit and write the bottom number for all the fractions. They then count the units from the beginning of each number line and write the top number for the fraction at one unit, the top number at two units, and the top number for the shaded part.

After students have worked with horizontal number lines for several days, teachers can introduce number lines that are vertically oriented. The procedure is the same. The number of parts in each unit is the bottom number of each fraction. The top number is the number of parts from the beginning of the number line.

After working with number lines until students can perform flawlessly, students work with groups that are "separated." Groups that are "separated" are figures, like circles or squares, that are divided into equal parts.

Format 12.2 includes a format for introducing groups that are "separated." The goal of the format is to teach basic fraction (part-whole) concepts through the use of diagrams. The specific objectives are to teach students to discriminate between the number of parts in each whole unit and the number of whole units.

In the format, the teacher writes a row of circles on the board and divides each into an equal number of parts. The teacher tells the students that each circle is called a whole and then leads the students through determining how many parts in each whole, or unit.

Each example set should include a different number of circles (wholes). Also the number of parts each whole is divided into should vary from set to set. For example, the first set might include three circles, each of which is divided into two parts. The next set might include five circles, each divided into four parts; the next two circles, each divided into three parts; etc. This format would be presented for several days.

Some students may not see the relationship between pictures of "separated" fraction groups and fractions on a number line. For that reason, it is very important to use the same language when teaching or correcting mistakes. Be sure to stress the word *each* if students have problems with the number-line examples. Remind them to count the parts in *each* unit.

Writing Numerical Fractions to Represent Diagrams

Exercises in which the students write a numerical fraction to represent a diagram (e.g., for students write $5/4$) would be presented after the students have had ample practice, usually several days, to master the part-whole concepts presented in Format 12.2. The format for writing numerical fractions appears in Format 12.3. In Part A, the structured board presentation, students learn that the bottom number of a fraction tells how many parts in each whole, while the top number of a fraction represents how many parts are used (i.e., shaded). Parts B and C are structured and less-structured worksheet exercises in which the students are to fill in the numerals to represent a diagram. Daily practice would be provided for several weeks followed by intermittent review.

Two guidelines are important for appropriate example selection for this skill. First, the number of parts in each whole unit, the number of whole units, and the number of parts used should vary from example to example. Second, the examples should include a mixture of proper and improper fractions. The examples should include some fractions that equal less than a whole unit:

$$\bigcirc = \frac{2}{3} \qquad \bigcirc = \frac{1}{4}$$

some examples that equal more than one unit:

$$\bigcirc\bigcirc\bigcirc\bigcirc = \frac{7}{2} \qquad \bigcirc\bigcirc = \frac{5}{4}$$

and just a few that equal one unit:

$$\bigcirc = \frac{4}{4} \qquad \bigcirc = \frac{2}{2}$$

During the first days, all examples would include circles divided into parts. After several weeks, other shapes (e.g., squares, rectangles, triangles) can be included in exercises.

Special attention should be given to examples containing a series of units that are not divided:

$$\bigcirc\bigcirc\bigcirc = \frac{3}{1}$$

These diagrams will need additional explanation. The teacher should point out that if a whole is not divided into parts, students should write a 1 on the bottom. The 1 tells that there is only one part in the whole unit. Examples which yield 1 as a denominator should not be introduced when fractions are initially presented, but can be introduced about a week after initial instruction. Thereafter, about 1 in every 10 diagrams should be an example with 1 as a denominator. These examples are important, since they present a conceptual basis for exercises in which students convert a whole number to a fraction (e.g., $8 = 8/1$).

Drawing Diagrams to Represent Fractions

Prior to constructing actual diagrams, students should practice completing fractions and shading in the correct fractional parts on the number line. Monitor the work carefully. Make sure that students are relating the information shown by the number lines to the fractions.

Translating numerical fractions into diagrams is a useful exercise for reinforcing a conceptual understanding of the part-whole fraction relationship. Constructing diagrams can be introduced when students are able to accurately fill in the numerals to represent a diagram. For most students, this should be a week or two after fraction analysis is introduced. The procedure is relatively simple, so we haven't included a format. The teacher should begin instruction by modeling how to divide circles into equal-sized parts, stressing the need to divide the circles so that each part is the same size. Examples can be limited to fractions with 2, 3, or 4 as denominators. This will allow for adequate discrimination without spending an inordinate amount of time teaching younger students to divide circles into more than four parts. After several days of practice dividing wholes into parts, the teacher would present a worksheet exercise, prompting the students as they draw diagrams. The teacher has the student say what each number tells, beginning with the bottom number. For $3/4$, the teacher would say, "Touch the bottom number. What does it tell you? . . . Draw four parts in each whole. . . . Touch the top number. . . . What does it tell you? . . . Shade in three parts." Figure 12.1 includes a sample worksheet. Note that each example has four circles. The purpose of keeping the number of circles constant is to prevent students from thinking that the number of whole units has something to do with the numerator and/or denominator.

FIGURE 12.1   Sample Worksheet for Drawing Diagrams from Numerical Fractions

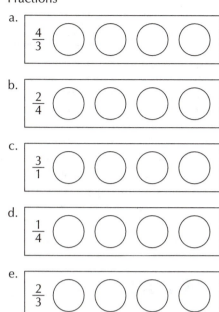

Decoding Fractions

When fractions are initially introduced, students are taught to say what each numeral in the fraction tells. The fraction ¾ is read as "four parts in each whole; three parts are used up." This translation is recommended since it specifies what to do (make four parts in each whole and then shade three parts), thus facilitating conceptual understanding.

Several weeks after fractions are introduced, reading fractions in the traditional way can be taught; e.g., ¾ is read as "three-fourths". Format 12.4 shows how to teach students to read fractions the traditional way. The teacher writes several fractions on the board and models how to read the fractions, testing after each example. Then the teacher tests students on reading the fractions without first providing the model. The correction is a model and test. After the initial correction, the teacher would use the alternating-test pattern to provide practice on the missed example.

This decoding-fractions format should be presented daily for about two or three weeks, then once each second or third day for about three or four weeks until students can accurately read fractions. Thereafter, students receive practice in reading fractions at the same time new fraction skills are introduced. For example, in adding fractions, students

receive practice decoding fractions in the step when they are asked to read the problem aloud.

Two example selection guidelines should be followed in teaching students to decode fractions. First, the introduction of fractions with the numbers 2, 3, or 5 as denominators should be delayed several lessons, because these denominators are not pronounced by adding the suffix "ths" to the number as is the case for sixths, ninths, and fourths. When a 2 appears as the denominator, students say "halves," not "twoths"; when a 3 appears, students say "thirds" not "threeths"; when a 5 appears, students say "fifths," not "fiveths." These denominators need to be introduced one at a time, using a model-and-test procedure. Fractions with 2 as a denominator might be introduced first. When introducing 2 as a denominator, about half of the examples in the teaching set should contain 2 in the denominator, while the other half should represent a variety of previously introduced denominators:

$$\frac{1}{2} \quad \frac{1}{4} \quad \frac{3}{2} \quad \frac{3}{8} \quad \frac{5}{2} \quad \frac{5}{7} \quad \frac{1}{6} \quad \frac{4}{2}$$

When students have mastered denominators of 2, they would be introduced in the same way to fractions with 5, then 3, as denominators. A second example selection guideline addresses the numerators. In about a fourth of the examples, the number 1 should be written as the numerator. These examples are included so that the students can see the difference between how a fraction is said when the numerator is 1 and when the numerator is more than 1; one-eighth versus four-eighths.

Determining if a Fraction Is More, Less, or Equal to One

Determining whether a fraction equals, exceeds, or is less than one whole is an important skill and also serves as a prerequisite for later exercises in which students are expected to convert an improper fraction like ¹⁶⁄₇ to a mixed number: 2²⁄₇. This skill can be introduced when students can accurately decode fractions the traditional way. The teaching process appears in Format 12.5. Part A is a pictorial demonstration in which the teacher draws diagrams representing fractions of various values (more than 1, less than 1, equal to 1) and asks the students if the picture shows one whole, more than one whole, or less than one whole.

In Part B, the teacher presents rules to be used in determining whether a numerical fraction equals, exceeds, or is less than one whole unit. First, students are taught the rule that when the top and bottom number of a fraction are the same, the fraction equals one whole. After this rule is presented, the teacher tests the students' application of the rule, using a series of numerical fractions, about half of which equal one whole:

$$\frac{5}{5} \quad \frac{6}{4} \quad \frac{4}{4} \quad \frac{9}{2} \quad \frac{9}{9} \quad \frac{5}{3} \quad \frac{7}{7} \quad \frac{2}{7} \quad \frac{8}{8}$$

Next, the teacher instructs students that when the top number of a fraction is greater than the bottom number, the fraction equals more than one whole; and when the top number is less than the bottom number, the fraction equals less than one whole. Finally, the students are shown fractions and asked to tell whether the fraction is equal to, more than, or less than 1. A structured worksheet exercise follows in which students must circle either *more, equal,* or *less* when given numerical fractions:

$$\frac{3}{4} \quad \text{more equal less}$$

$$\frac{8}{8} \quad \text{more equal less}$$

Note that in this format, the words *numerator* and *denominator* are not used. The purpose of excluding the terms is to avoid possible confusion for students who may be unclear about which number is the numerator and which is the denominator. Similarly, the term *improper fraction* is not included in the format. This term is best introduced in later grades.

Examples for Parts B, C, and independent practice should include a variety of problems. In about a third of the examples, the numerator and denominator of the fraction should be the same:

$$\frac{4}{4} \quad \frac{8}{8} \quad \frac{3}{3}$$

In another third, the numerator should be greater than the denominator:

$$\frac{7}{5} \quad \frac{3}{2} \quad \frac{4}{2}$$

In another third, the numerator should be less than the denominator:

$$\frac{2}{3} \quad \frac{4}{7} \quad \frac{3}{4}$$

Reading and Writing Mixed Numbers

The above diagram may be expressed as the improper fraction $\frac{9}{4}$ or as the mixed fractional number $2\frac{1}{4}$. Reading and writing mixed numbers can be introduced relatively early in the fraction sequence, as soon as students can correctly determine when a fraction equals, exceeds, or is less than one whole. However, the teacher must keep in mind that exercises designed to teach students to convert mixed numbers to improper fractions and vice versa would not be introduced until much later in the fraction sequence, since these conversions require students to know basic multiplication facts. Format 12.6 is designed to teach students to read and write mixed numbers. The format begins with a pictorial demonstration exercise in which students are taught to express the diagram of an improper fraction as a mixed number by counting the number of whole units shaded and writing that number, then determining the numerator and denominator of the remaining units. Below is a sample exercise:

Part B is designed to teach students to read mixed numbers. The teacher uses a model/test procedure, having students first say the whole number, then the fraction, then the mixed number. Note that the teacher emphasizes the word *and* when reading mixed numbers. The purpose of emphasizing *and* is to prevent errors in which the student either combines the whole number and the numerator, reading $4\frac{2}{3}$ as "forty-two thirds" or leaves out the numerator, reading $5\frac{1}{3}$ as "five thirds."

Part C is an exercise in which students are taught to write mixed numbers. The teacher gives students lined paper and pencil and points out that when students write mixed numbers, they are to make the whole number big and the numbers in the fraction small: "The big number should be written so that it touches the top and bottom of the line. Then write the fraction line in the middle of the space." The exercise begins with the teacher dictating a mixed number and having students first say and write the whole number, then say and write the fraction part of the mixed number.

REWRITING FRACTIONS

The procedures in this section all involve the process of changing a fraction from one form to another without changing its value, i.e., maintaining equivalency. Three main types of conversion skills are discussed:

1. Determining the missing number in a pair of equivalent fractions. Given a problem such as

$$\frac{3}{5} = \frac{\square}{10}$$

the student will determine the missing number. This problem type is a critical component skill for problems involving adding and subtracting fractions with unlike denominators.

2. Reducing fractions to their lowest terms. A fraction is said to be at its lowest term (or simplest form) when both the numerator and denominator have no common factor except 1:

$$\frac{20}{24} \text{ can be reduced to } \frac{5}{6}$$

3. Converting mixed numbers to improper fractions:

$$3\frac{1}{2} = \frac{7}{2}$$

and improper fractions to mixed numbers:

$$\frac{17}{5} = 3\frac{2}{5}$$

A general preskill for all rewriting skills is knowledge of basic multiplication and division facts. To perform all three types of conversion problems, students must be able to either multiply or divide. Thus, rewriting fraction skills usually are not introduced until early fourth grade.

The strategies presented here are designed so that students not only learn the necessary computation required to change fractions into parallel forms but also so that they understand the underlying concepts of equivalency that govern each strategy. Without understanding equivalency, students will be able to apply very few of the skills they learn. For example, if students do not understand that when the numerator and denominator are the same, the fraction is equal to 1, they will not understand why $\frac{3}{4}$ can be multiplied by $\frac{5}{5}$ to create the equivalent fraction $\frac{15}{20}$. Although the equivalency concept is relatively sophisticated, the language of the strategies is relatively simple because they are designed for elementary students.

Completing Equivalent Fractions

Instruction in equivalent fractions begins with problems in which the student must determine the missing numerator in an equivalent fraction:

$$\frac{3}{4} = \frac{\square}{12} \qquad \frac{1}{2} = \frac{\square}{10}$$

The basic strategy is to multiply the first fraction by a fractional equivalent to one whole. In working the first problem above, the student determines that to end up with an equivalent fraction that has 12 as a denominator the fraction $\frac{3}{4}$ must be multiplied by $\frac{3}{3}$:

$$\frac{3}{4} \times \frac{(3)}{(3)} = \frac{9}{12}$$

Equivalency is maintained since, by definition, the identity element for multiplication is 1. When multiplying $\frac{3}{4}$ by $\frac{3}{3}$, we are multiplying $\frac{3}{4}$ by a fraction that equals 1; therefore we are not changing the value of $\frac{3}{4}$.

PRESKILLS Several skills should be mastered prior to introducing equivalency problems: (1) knowledge of the terms *numerator* and *denominator,* (2) the ability to multiply fractions, and (3) the ability to construct a fraction that equals one whole.

The terms *numerator* and *denominator* are usually introduced in second or third grade. The teaching procedure is simple. The teacher tells students the numerator is the top number in a fraction and the denominator is the bottom number in the fraction. The teacher then provides practice by writing several fractions on the board and having students identify the numerator and denominator of each fraction. Daily practice is necessary so students won't forget or confuse the terms.

Multiplication of two fractions is also usually taught in third grade. Procedures for teaching this skill are presented later in this chapter.

Constructing fractions equal to one whole is introduced about two weeks prior to introducing equivalent fraction problems. Format 12.7 includes the preskill format for constructing fractions equal to 1. Part A is a board exercise in which the rule for constructing fractions equal to 1 is introduced: "When the top number is the same as the bottom number, the fraction equals 1." After introducing the rule, the teacher presents examples of its application, writing problems such as

$$1 = \frac{\square}{4}$$

in which the student must fill in the missing numerator of a fraction equal to one whole. The board exercise is followed by worksheet exercises of a similar nature.

FORMAT The format for computing equivalent fractions is shown in Format 12.8. Part A includes a pictorial demonstration introducing the concept of equivalent fractions. The teacher first defines the term *equivalent fractions,* explaining that fractions are equal when they show that equal portions of the wholes are used. The teacher then draws two circles on clear plastic, each divided into a different number of parts, but each with equal portions shaded:

The teacher points out that these fractions are equivalent since the same portion of each whole is shaded. The same demonstration is presented with a diagram in which nonequal proportions of the wholes are shaded:

The teacher points out that the fractions are not equivalent since the shaded portions of the wholes do not take up the same space.

Part B introduces a very critical rule: When you multiply by a fraction that equals 1, the answer equals the number you start with. The teacher tells students this rule, then presents a set of problems demonstrating the rule's application. In some of the problems, the original fraction is multiplied by a fraction that equals 1, and in some the original fraction is multiplied by a fraction not equal to 1. The students are to tell whether or not the answer will equal the original fraction.

Part C is a structured board exercise in which the teacher presents the strategy for working equivalency problems such as

$$\frac{3}{4} = \frac{\square}{20}$$

The teacher explains that the equal sign tells that the fractions are equal. The student's job is to find the missing numerator in the second fraction.

The teacher writes parentheses after the first fraction

$$\frac{3}{4}\left(\ \ \right) = \frac{\square}{20}$$

explaining that the students must multiply the first fraction by a fraction that equals 1, which will be written inside the parentheses. The parentheses indicate multiplication. The teacher demonstrates how to figure out the denominator to be written inside the parentheses by using a missing-factor multiplication strategy. In the problem above, the teacher asks, "4 times what number equals 20?"

The answer, 5, is written as the denominator inside the parentheses:

$$\frac{3}{4}\left(\frac{}{5}\right) = \frac{\square}{20}$$

The teacher then points out that since the fraction inside the parentheses must equal one whole, the numerator must be the same as the denominator. The missing number in the equivalent fraction can be determined by multiplying the numerator in the first fraction and the numerator in the second fraction:

$$\frac{3}{4}\left(\frac{5}{5}\right) = \frac{15}{20}$$

EXAMPLE SELECTION There are three example selection guidelines for this format. The denominator of the first fraction must be a number that can be multiplied by a whole number to end with the denominator of the second fraction. Therefore, problems such as

$$\frac{2}{3} = \frac{\square}{5} \qquad \frac{4}{5} = \frac{\square}{8} \qquad \frac{2}{3} = \frac{\square}{7}$$

would not be appropriate to include, while problems such as

$$\frac{2}{3} = \frac{\square}{6} \qquad \frac{4}{5} = \frac{\square}{10} \qquad \frac{2}{3} = \frac{\square}{9}$$

would be appropriate. Second, the numbers to appear in parentheses should vary from problem to problem. For example, in one problem the numerator and denominator in the second fraction could be four times bigger than the original:

$$\frac{3}{5} = \frac{\square}{20}$$

in the next problem, two times bigger:

$$\frac{5}{6} = \frac{\square}{12}$$

in the next, five times bigger:

$$\frac{2}{3} = \frac{\square}{15}$$

and so on. The third guideline is that all problems should require multiplication; i.e., the numbers in the fraction to be completed should be greater than the numbers in the first fraction.

Reducing Fractions

We recommend that reducing fractions be taught in two stages. During the first stage, which would be presented during late fourth grade, the teacher introduces a greatest common factor strategy. In this strategy, students are taught to reduce a fraction to its simplest terms by pulling out the greatest common factor of the numerator and denominator. For example, the fraction $9/15$ is reduced by pulling out a 3, which is the greatest common factor of 9 and 15. When the factor 3 is pulled out, $9/15$ becomes $3/5$.

The greatest common factor strategy is a viable strategy only for problems in which it is relatively easy to find the greatest common factor (e.g., $18/27$, $30/35$, $8/16$). Nearly all reducing problems students encounter in fourth and early fifth grade can be reduced to simplest terms using the GCF (greatest common factor) strategy. During the second stage, students are taught to reduce fractions in which the greatest common factor is difficult to determine.

PRESKILLS Teaching students to find the greatest common factor of two numbers is the critical preskill for reducing fractions. The greatest common factor of two numbers is the largest number that can be multiplied by whole numbers to end with the two target numbers. For example, the greatest common factor of 12 and 18 is 6. Six can be multiplied by whole numbers to end with 12 and 18.

The first step in teaching students to find the greatest common factor of two numbers is to teach them to determine all possible factors for a given number. For example, the numbers 1, 2, 3, 4, 6, and 12 are all factors of 12, since they can all be multiplied by another whole number to end with 12. Table 12.1 includes a list of the factors for the numbers 1 through 50. Once the students are able to easily determine all factors for a number, finding the greatest common factor is relatively easy.

Format 12.9 includes the format for teaching students to determine factors. In Part A, the teacher introduces the term *factor,* defining factors as any numbers that are multiplied together. In Part B, the teacher presents a strategy for figuring out all factors for a target number. The teacher writes the target number on the board and beside it writes spaces for each factor. For example, if the target is 15, the teacher writes 15 on the board and puts 4 blanks beside it, since four numbers (1,3,5,15) are factors of 15. The teacher then tells the students that they are going to find all of the numbers that are factors of 15 by asking if they can multiply a number by another number and end up with 15. The teacher always begins with the target number: "Is 15 a factor of 15?" The teacher then points out that they can find another factor by determining what number times that factor equals the target number. For example,

Table 12.1   Factors for 1 to 50

Number Factors* (other than the number itself and 1)[†]

4—2, 2	28—14, 2; 7, 4
6—3, 2	30—15, 2; 10, 3; 6, 5
8—4, 2	32—16, 2; 8, 4
9—3, 3	33—11, 3
10—5, 2	34—17, 2
12—6, 2; 3, 4	35—7, 5
14—7, 2	36—18, 2; 9, 4; 6, 6
15—5, 3	38—19, 2
16—4, 4; 8, 2	39—13, 3
18—6, 3; 9, 2	40—20, 2; 10, 4; 8, 5
20—10, 2; 5, 4	42—21, 2; 14, 3; 7, 6
21—3, 7	44—22, 2; 11, 4
22—11, 2	45—15, 3; 9, 5
24—12, 2; 8, 3; 6, 4	46—23, 3
25—5, 5	48—24, 2; 12, 4; 8, 6
26—13, 2	49—7, 7
27—9, 3	50—25, 2; 10, 5

* Factors are listed in pairs.
[†] Numbers not in list have only the number itself and 1 as factors.

after determining that 15 is a factor of 15, the teacher asks, "What number times 15 equals 15?" The answer, 1, is the factor of 15 that goes with 15. The teacher writes 15 in the first space and 1 in the last space.

The teacher then asks about other numbers, beginning with 10 and proceeding backward (10, 9, 8, 7 . . .): "Can we multiply 10 and end with 15? No, so 10 is not a factor of 15," and so on. The teacher instructs the students to say "stop" when she says a number that is a factor of the target number. When the students identify another factor of the target number, the teacher once again leads them in finding the other factor it goes with to produce the target number. If 15 is the target number, the students say "stop" after the teacher says 5. The teacher asks what number times 5 equals 15. The students answer 3. The teacher points out that 5 and 3 are both factors of 15. When target numbers over 20 are introduced, the teacher models the answer for the larger numbers. That is, the teacher tells the student any two-digit number that is a factor of the target number. For example, when introducing 28, the teacher says that 14 and 2 can be multiplied to equal 28.

Part C is a worksheet exercise. Target numbers are written on the worksheet, followed by spaces for each of the factors of that number. For the target number 7, only two spaces would be written, since 1 and 7 are the only factors for 7. For the number 12, six spaces would be written, since the numbers 12, 1, 6,

2, 4, and 3 are factors for 12. Students are to fill in the factors, beginning with the biggest factor.

The objective of this format is to develop student fluency in naming all possible factors of numbers. A systematic plan for introducing new target numbers and reviewing target numbers should be followed. One or two new target numbers can be introduced daily. (Table 12.2 contains a suggested sequence for introducing target numbers.) Part A of the format is used only with the first pair of target numbers. New numbers would be introduced using the board presentation in Part B. The worksheet exercise described in Part C could be done independently after the first several lessons. A target number should appear on practice worksheet exercises daily for several weeks after it is introduced. This practice is very important to developing fluency.

FORMAT FOR GREATEST COMMON FACTORS The format for teaching greatest common factors (Format 12.10) would be introduced when the students are able to determine the factors of any target number below 20. The format is relatively simple. The teacher defines the phrase *greatest common factor* as the largest number that is a factor of both target numbers. The teacher then leads the students through finding the greatest common factor. First, the teacher asks students what the largest factor of the smaller target number is and if that factor is also a factor of the other target number. For example,

assuming that 8 and 20 are the target numbers, the teacher asks what the largest factor of 8 is. The students reply, "8 is the largest factor of 8." The teacher then asks, "Is 8 a factor of 20?" Since the answer is no, the teacher asks the students to tell him the next largest factor of 8: "What is the next biggest factor of 8?" After the students answer 4, the teacher asks, "Is 4 a factor of 20? . . . So, 4 is the greatest common factor of 8 and 20."

After about five days of presenting the format, the teacher gives students worksheet exercises to work independently. The worksheet includes 8-12 problems daily in which students find the greatest common factor of two target numbers. A common error in independent exercises involves writing a common factor that is not the greatest common factor of the two target numbers; for example, writing 3 as the greatest common factor of 12 and 18. The correction is to point out to students that they can find a larger common factor.

Example selection guidelines are quite important. In about half of the problems, the greatest common factor should be the smaller of the two target numbers (e.g., 6, 18; 4, 8; 2, 10; 5, 20). If examples such as these are not included, students might develop the misrule that the smaller number is never the greatest common factor. This would result in errors in which the student might identify a 4 rather than an 8 as the GCF of 8 and 24. Examples should be limited to numbers for which students have been taught to find factors. Initially, both target numbers should be under 20. As students learn to determine factors for larger numbers, the larger numbers can be included. Several examples should be included in which 1 is the greatest common factor, as in 4 and 7 or 6 and 11. These prepare students for fractions that cannot be reduced (e.g., $\frac{4}{7}$, $\frac{6}{11}$).

FORMAT FOR REDUCING FRACTIONS The format for reducing fractions (see Format 12.11) would be introduced when students are able to determine the greatest common factor of any two target numbers below 20. The format includes three parts. Part A is a board exercise in which the teacher presents the strategy for reducing fractions. The teacher writes a fraction on the board with an equal sign next to it. Next to the equal sign are parentheses and a fraction bar for the reduced fraction:

$$\frac{12}{16} = \left(\quad\right)\underline{\quad\quad}$$

The fraction in which the numerator and denominator are the greatest common factor of the two tar-

Table 12.2 Sequence for Introducing Target Numbers and Their Factors

Day	Factors of These Numbers Are Introduced	Day	Factors of These Numbers Are Introduced
1	12, 7	16	27, 29
2	10, 3	17	28
3	16, 5	18	30, 31
4	8, 13	19	32, 33
5	4, 6, 9	20	34, 37
6	2, 17	21	35, 39
7	12, 19	22	36, 41
8	14, 23	23	38, 43
9	15	24	40, 47
10	18	25	42
11	20	26	44
12	21	27	45
13	22	28	46
14	24	29	48
15	25, 26	30	49
		31	50

get numbers will be written inside the parentheses. For example, the greatest common factor of 12 and 16 is 4. Thus, the fraction in the parentheses will be $\frac{4}{4}$, which equals 1. The teacher then asks, "12 equals 4 times what number?" The answer is 3, which is the numerator of the reduced fraction. The teacher then asks, "16 equals 4 times what number?" The answer is 4, which is the denominator of the reduced fraction. Since multiplying by 1 does not change the value of the fraction, $\frac{4}{4}$ can be crossed out. Crossing out the fraction equal to 1 leaves the reduced fraction:

$$\frac{12}{16} = \left(\frac{\cancel{4}}{\cancel{4}}\right)\frac{3}{4}$$

Part B is a structured worksheet exercise in which the teacher first asks for the greatest common factor of the numerator and denominator of a fraction; in $^{10}\!/_{15}$ the GCF is 5. The teacher then instructs the students to write the corresponding fraction equal to 1 in the parentheses. For example, the fraction written in parentheses for $^{10}\!/_{15}$ is $^5\!/_5$. The teacher then has the students determine the missing factors in the final fraction, which is the reduced fraction:

$$\frac{10}{15} = \left(\frac{5}{5}\right)\frac{2}{3}$$

There are three example selection guidelines for exercises on reducing fractions. First, the numbers should be ones for which students have been taught to find factors. At first, both the numerator and denominator should be below 25. As students learn to find factors for larger numbers, fractions with these larger numbers can be included.

Second, a third of the fractions should have the greatest common factor as the numerator. For example, in the fractions $^4\!/_{12}$, $^8\!/_{16}$, and $^5\!/_{20}$, the numerator is the greatest common factor. Third, about a third of the fractions should already be expressed in their simplest terms (e.g., $^4\!/_7$, $^3\!/_5$, $^6\!/_{11}$). Including several fractions already expressed in their simplest terms provides the students with the knowledge that not all fractions can be reduced. A sample set of items appears below:

a. $\dfrac{12}{15}$ b. $\dfrac{4}{8}$ c. $\dfrac{5}{7}$ d. $\dfrac{8}{12}$ e. $\dfrac{3}{5}$

f. $\dfrac{5}{15}$ g. $\dfrac{4}{12}$ h. $\dfrac{6}{9}$ i. $\dfrac{9}{11}$

Items b, f, and g are fractions in which the smaller number is a factor of the larger number. Items c, e, and i are fractions which are already expressed in their simplest terms and, therefore, cannot be reduced any further.

REDUCING FRACTIONS WITH LARGER NUMBERS   After several weeks of practice reducing fractions using the greatest common factor, students can be introduced to the concept of pulling out successive common factors. When the greatest common factor is difficult to find, students can reduce the fraction to its simplest terms by repeatedly pulling out factors. Note the examples below:

a. $\dfrac{45}{75} = \left(\dfrac{5}{5}\right)\dfrac{9}{15} = \left(\dfrac{3}{3}\right)\dfrac{3}{5} = \dfrac{3}{5}$

b. $\dfrac{24}{72} = \left(\dfrac{2}{2}\right)\dfrac{12}{36} = \left(\dfrac{6}{6}\right)\dfrac{2}{6} = \left(\dfrac{2}{2}\right)\dfrac{1}{3} = \dfrac{1}{3}$

This strategy is useful for problems with larger numbers. The teacher would guide students through sets of problems, pointing out clues students can use (e.g., If both the numerator and the denominator are even numbers, the fraction can still be reduced. If the numerator and denominator both end in either 5 or zero, the fraction can still be reduced). The teacher would present an exercise in which students check answers to determine if they're reduced to simplest terms. The teacher would give students a worksheet with problems similar to those below, some of which have not been reduced to their simplest terms. The students would be asked to find those fractions that can be further reduced and to reduce those fractions.

a. $\dfrac{64}{72} = \left(\dfrac{\cancel{4}}{\cancel{4}}\right)\dfrac{16}{18} =$ d. $\dfrac{65}{85} = \left(\dfrac{\cancel{5}}{\cancel{5}}\right)\dfrac{13}{15} =$

b. $\dfrac{45}{75} = \left(\dfrac{\cancel{5}}{\cancel{5}}\right)\dfrac{9}{15} =$ e. $\dfrac{48}{64} = \left(\dfrac{\cancel{2}}{\cancel{2}}\right)\dfrac{24}{32} =$

c. $\dfrac{21}{30} = \left(\dfrac{\cancel{3}}{\cancel{3}}\right)\dfrac{7}{10} =$ f. $\dfrac{56}{84} = \left(\dfrac{\cancel{2}}{\cancel{2}}\right)\dfrac{28}{42} =$

Converting Mixed Numbers and Improper Fractions

An improper fraction, one whose numerator is greater than its denominator, is a fraction that equals more than one whole. An improper fraction may be converted to a mixed number by dividing its numerator by its denominator. For example, to convert the fraction $^{13}\!/_5$ to a mixed number, we divide 13 by 5, which equals 2 with a remainder of 3. The remainder is written as the fraction $^3\!/_5$; the improper fraction $^{13}\!/_5$ is converted to the mixed number $2^3\!/_5$.

Converting a mixed number to an improper fraction requires the reverse operation, multiplication rather than division. Students first change the whole number into a fraction by multiplying the whole number by the number of parts in each whole, indicated by the denominator:

$$\text{for } 6 = \frac{}{4}, \text{ students write } \frac{24}{4}$$

To determine the equivalent improper fraction for a mixed number, after students multiply the whole number they add the numerator of the fraction:

$$3\frac{1}{2} = \frac{6+1}{2} = \frac{7}{2}$$

On the Instructional Sequence and Assessment Chart, we recommend that converting improper fractions to mixed numbers be introduced in early fourth grade. Students apply this skill when they rewrite their answers after adding or multiplying fractions. Converting a mixed number to an improper fraction should not be introduced until several months later. The time between the introduction of these two conversion skills is recommended to decrease the probability of students' confusing the two operations. Converting mixed numbers to and from improper fractions requires that students have a good understanding of the difference between a whole unit and parts of a unit. Therefore, students should have mastered all the fraction analysis skills presented earlier.

CONVERTING IMPROPER FRACTIONS TO MIXED NUMBERS The format for converting improper fractions to mixed numbers appears in Format 12.12. Part A is a pictorial demonstration in which the teacher shows how to construct a diagram to figure out how many whole units an improper fraction equals.

Part B is a structured board presentation in which the teacher presents the strategy of dividing the numerator by the denominator. Note the special emphasis given to explaining how to write the remainder as a fraction. The teacher explains that the denominator of the fraction in the mixed number must be the same denominator as in the original fraction.

Part C is a structured worksheet exercise. The division symbol, along with boxes for the whole number and the fraction remainder, are written as prompts on the students' worksheets:

$$\frac{11}{4} = \boxed{}\,\frac{\boxed{}}{\boxed{}}\,\overline{)}$$

The teacher begins the exercise by instructing the students to look at the fraction and determine

whether it is less than one whole, one whole, or more than one whole. If the fraction is less than 1, students are instructed to leave the fraction as it is. If the fraction equals 1, they write = 1. If the fraction equals more than 1, they are instructed to divide and write the answer as a mixed number.

Part D is a less-structured worksheet exercise in which students convert improper fractions to mixed numbers with minimal teacher prompting. Teachers should insist that students write the whole number part of the answer and the fraction part of the answer neatly. Teachers should watch for students writing answers in which the numerator of the fraction could easily be mistaken for a whole number:

$$5\overline{)17}^{\,32/5}$$

Examples should be selected to provide appropriate discrimination practice. First, there should be a mixture of problems. About half of the fractions should translate to a mixed number; about a fourth should translate simply to a whole number (e.g., $6/3$, $16/4$, $10/5$); finally, about a fourth should be proper fractions. Including proper fractions ensures that students do not develop the misrule of inappropriately converting all fractions to mixed numbers (e.g., $3/4 = 1\frac{1}{4}$).

After students have had several weeks of practice converting improper fractions to mixed numbers and reducing fractions to their lowest terms, they can be given exercises in which they must first convert the fractions to mixed numbers then reduce the fractions. No special format is required for such exercises. The teacher gives students a worksheet with directions similar to these: "Change any fraction that equals one or more wholes to a mixed number. Then reduce the fractions." A set of examples would include a mix of proper and improper fractions, some of which can be reduced and some of which are written in their simplest form. A sample set might include these fractions:

$$\frac{16}{12} \quad \frac{6}{8} \quad \frac{9}{7} \quad \frac{14}{6} \quad \frac{5}{7}$$

$$\frac{8}{24} \quad \frac{20}{8} \quad \frac{9}{12} \quad \frac{24}{10}$$

Exercises of this type would be continued for several months to develop fluency.

CONVERTING MIXED NUMBERS TO IMPROPER FRACTIONS The format for converting mixed numbers to improper fractions appears in Format 12.13. The format includes three parts. Part A teaches the component skill of translating any whole number into an improper fraction by multiplying the number of whole units by the number of parts in each whole:

In $6 = \dfrac{}{4}$, students multiply 6×4

Since this component skill is very important, both a board and a worksheet exercise are presented.

Part B, a structured board presentation, teaches the strategy to convert a mixed number into an improper fraction. First, the students determine the fraction equivalent to the whole number; then they add the fraction portion of the mixed number. For example, with $6\frac{3}{4}$, students multiply 6×4 and then add 3 to determine the answer:

$$6\frac{3}{4} = \frac{24 + 3}{4} = \frac{27}{4}$$

In order to ensure that students understand the purpose of the computations, the teacher might have students "check" several problems by drawing the diagram to illustrate the improper fraction or mixed number.

OPERATIONS—ADDING AND SUBTRACTING FRACTIONS

There are three basic problem types in addition and subtraction of fractions. The first type includes addition/subtraction problems that have like denominators:

$$\frac{3}{8} + \frac{1}{8} + \frac{2}{8} = \frac{\square}{\square} \qquad \frac{7}{9} - \frac{3}{9} = \frac{\square}{\square}$$

Problems of this type can be introduced during the primary grades, since relatively few preskills are required to work the problems. The students learn that to work such problems they work only across the numerators; the denominator remains constant:

$$\frac{2}{5} + \frac{1}{5} = \frac{3}{5} \qquad \frac{7}{9} - \frac{3}{9} = \frac{4}{9}$$

The second type includes problems with unlike denominators. Problems in this group are limited, however, to those in which the lowest common denominator is relatively easy to figure out. Problems of this type are usually introduced during fourth grade. The strategy for solving these problems involves first figuring out the lowest common denominator, rewriting each fraction as an equivalent fraction with that denominator, and then working the problem:

$$\frac{5}{6} \quad \text{becomes} \quad \frac{5}{6}\left(\frac{2}{2}\right) = \frac{10}{12} \quad \text{which} \quad \frac{10}{12}$$
$$-\frac{3}{4} \qquad\qquad -\frac{3}{4}\left(\frac{3}{3}\right) = \frac{9}{12} \quad \text{becomes} \quad -\frac{9}{12}$$
$$\qquad\qquad\qquad\qquad\qquad\qquad\qquad\qquad\qquad \frac{1}{12}$$

The third type includes problems in which the lowest common denominator is difficult to determine. These problems usually have a lowest common denominator that is a relatively large number. For example, in the problem, $\frac{5}{13} + \frac{3}{18}$, the lowest common denominator is 234. To solve this problem, students must be taught a strategy that involves factoring. Since the discussion of the procedures to teach this strategy would take many pages and since this type of problem is often not introduced until junior high, we have not included it.

Fractions with Like Denominators

Adding and subtracting fractions with like denominators is a relatively simple operation that can be introduced after fraction analysis skills have been taught, sometime in second or third grade. A format for teaching students to add and subtract fractions with like denominators appears in Format 12.14. Part A is a pictorial demonstration in which the teacher demonstrates adding fractions. In Part B, the teacher presents the rule that students can only add and subtract fractions in which each whole has the same number of parts.

Parts C and D are structured and less-structured worksheet exercises in which the students are presented with a set of addition and subtraction problems. Half of the problems should have like denominators:

$$\frac{3}{4} - \frac{1}{4} \qquad \frac{4}{7} + \frac{2}{7}$$

and half different denominators:

$$\frac{3}{4} - \frac{1}{3} \qquad \frac{5}{7} + \frac{2}{3}$$

Students are instructed to cross out the problems with unlike denominators and work the problems with like denominators. The problems with unlike denominators are included to prevent errors caused by students' ignoring the denominators.

During the first week or two of instruction, adding and subtracting fraction problems should be written horizontally. When students are able to work problems written horizontally, vertically aligned problems should be introduced:

$$\frac{3}{4} \qquad \frac{4}{8} \qquad \frac{5}{7}$$
$$-\frac{1}{4} \qquad +\frac{3}{8} \qquad +\frac{2}{3}$$

The teacher introduces vertically aligned problems with a board and structured worksheet exercise. Teachers should not assume that because students can work horizontally aligned problems, they will all be able to work vertically aligned problems.

Problems with Mixed Numbers

Adding and subtracting mixed numbers in which the fractions have like denominators:

$$3\frac{2}{5} - 1\frac{1}{5}$$

can be introduced when students can read and write mixed numbers and can add and subtract fractions with like denominators. The teaching procedure is relatively simple: The students first work the fraction part of the problem, then the whole number part of the problem. Both horizontally and vertically aligned problems should be presented.

Fractions with Unlike Denominators

Adding and subtracting fractions with unlike denominators is usually introduced during fourth grade. A strategy for solving problems with unlike denominators is outlined in Summary Box 12.1. Note the integration of several component skills.

PRESKILLS There are two preskills that should be mastered before the format for adding and subtracting fractions with unlike denominators is introduced: (1) finding the least common multiple of two numbers and (2) rewriting a fraction as an equivalent fraction with a given denominator (see Format 12.8).

The least common multiple of two numbers is the smallest number that has both numbers as factors. For example, the least common multiple (LCM) of the numbers 6 and 8 is 24 since 24 is the smallest number that has both 6 and 8 as factors. Likewise, the LCM of 6 and 9 is 18 since 18 is the smallest number that has 6 and 9 as factors.

Format 12.15 shows how to teach students to figure out the least common multiple of two numbers. This format assumes that students are able to say the skip-counting series for 2s through 9s. About two months prior to introducing the least common multiple, the teacher should begin reviewing the skip-counting series. (See Chapter 4 for teaching skip counting.) Students who know their basic multiplication facts should have little trouble learning the series.

The strategy students are taught requires them to say the skip-counting series for each target number and to select the smallest number appearing in both series. This strategy is viable for examples in which

---

Summary Box 12.1: Steps for Problems with Unlike Denominators

1. $\frac{3}{4} + \frac{1}{6}$

   Students read problem and say, "The problem can't be worked as it is because the denominators are not the same."

2. $\frac{3}{4} + \frac{1}{6}$

   Students determine that the least common multiple of 4 and 6 is 12. Thus 12 is the least common denominator. Both fractions must be rewritten with denominators of 12.

3. $\frac{3}{4}\left(\frac{3}{3}\right) + \frac{1}{6}\left(\frac{2}{2}\right)$

   Students determine the fraction by which each original fraction must be multiplied to equal 12.

4. $\frac{3}{4}\left(\frac{3}{3}\right) + \frac{1}{6}\left(\frac{2}{2}\right)$ $\frac{9}{12} \quad \frac{2}{12}$

   Students rewrite each fraction so that it has a denominator of 12.

5. $\frac{3}{4}\left(\frac{3}{3}\right) + \frac{1}{6}\left(\frac{2}{2}\right) = \frac{11}{12}$ $\frac{9}{12} \quad \frac{2}{12}$

   Students work the problem with equivalent fractions.

the target numbers are small. A more sophisticated strategy would need to be taught to figure the least common multiple of larger numbers for which the students could not say the skip-counting series. This more sophisticated strategy, which involves factoring, is not discussed in this text.

The format includes two parts. In Part A, the teacher writes count-by series for two numbers on the board so that students can visually find the least common multiple. The teacher also introduces the term *multiple*. Part B is a worksheet presentation in which the teacher leads students in finding the least common multiple for several pairs of numbers and then monitors as students complete the worksheet on their own. Daily practice on worksheet exercises involving finding the least common multiple of two numbers would be continued for several weeks.

There are two example selection guidelines for the least common multiple format. First, in about half of the problems the larger number should be a multiple of a the smaller number. For the numbers 3 and 12, 12 is a multiple of 3. The least common multiple of 12 and 3 is 12. Likewise, the least common multiple of the numbers 2 and 8 is 8.

The second guideline pertains to the other half of the problems in which the larger number is not a multiple of the lower number. In these problems both target numbers should be below 10.

FORMAT The format for adding and subtracting fractions with unlike denominators appears in Format 12.16. The format has three parts. Part A is a structured board presentation. This part begins with the teacher writing a problem on the board and asking the students if the fractions can be added (or subtracted) as they are. After the students determine the fractions cannot be added (or subtracted) because the denominators are not the same, the teacher tells the students that they can work the problem by rewriting the fractions so that both have the same denominator. The teacher then demonstrates the problem-solving strategy outlined earlier: writing the least common multiple of both denominators; multiplying each fraction by the fraction of 1, which enables it to be rewritten with the lowest common denominator; and then adding (or subtracting) the rewritten fraction.

In Parts B and C, the structured and less-structured worksheet exercises, the teacher leads students through working problems. Note that Format 12.16 includes problems in which both fractions are rewritten. In many problems, only one fraction will need to be rewritten (e.g., in ¾ + ⅛, only ¾ needs to be rewritten as ⁶⁄₈). When initially presenting this type of problem, the teacher has the students write the fraction ($\frac{1}{1}$) next to the fraction that does not need to be rewritten:

$$\frac{3}{4}\left(\frac{2}{2}\right) + \frac{5}{8}\left(\frac{1}{1}\right)$$

After several weeks, the teacher can explain that if the denominator of the rewritten fraction is to be the same, nothing need be done to that fraction.

There are two example selection guidelines. The first addresses the manner in which problems are written. During the first two weeks, all problems should be written horizontally. When students can work horizontal problems, they can be introduced to vertically aligned problems.

The second guideline pertains to the variety of problems. Half of the problems should have denominators in which the larger denominator is a multiple of the smaller denominator. For example, in the problem

$$\frac{3}{5} + \frac{2}{10}$$

the larger denominator, 10, is a multiple of the smaller denominator, 5. In the other half of the problems, the denominators should both be one-digit numbers:

$$\frac{3}{5} + \frac{2}{3} \qquad \frac{3}{4} + \frac{2}{5} \qquad \frac{5}{6} - \frac{1}{4}$$

Several problems involving adding and subtracting fractions with like denominators should also be included. A sample set of problems appears below. Note that problems c and f have like denominators. Problems b, e, and g have a lower denominator which is a multiple of the larger denominator. In problems a, d, and h, both fractions must be rewritten.

a. $\frac{3}{4} + \frac{2}{5}$ b. $\frac{7}{9} - \frac{2}{3}$ c. $\frac{5}{6} - \frac{1}{6}$

d. $\frac{5}{6} - \frac{4}{9}$ e. $\frac{1}{5} + \frac{3}{10}$ f. $\frac{4}{9} + \frac{3}{9}$

g. $\frac{7}{10} - \frac{1}{2}$ h. $\frac{3}{4} - \frac{2}{3}$

Reducing and Rewriting Answers as Mixed Numbers

The skills of reducing fractions to their lowest common terms and converting an improper fraction to a mixed number can be integrated into problems after students have had several weeks of practice working problems with unlike denominators. Students should be given problems that require them to convert the answer to a mixed number (when necessary) and/or reduce. Teachers should lead students through determining the correct answers for several days. Daily practice with six to eight problems should continue for several weeks.

More Complex Problems with Mixed Numbers

A rather difficult problem type involving mixed numbers is illustrated below:

$$\begin{array}{r} 8 \\ -3\frac{2}{4} \\ \hline \end{array}$$

This is a subtraction problem involving renaming. The student must rewrite the 8 as 7 and $\frac{4}{4}$ to work the problem. Prior to introducing such a problem, the teacher would present an exercise like the one below in which the student must rewrite a whole number as a whole number and a fraction equivalent to 1 (e.g., $6 = 5 + \frac{4}{4}$).

$$6 = \boxed{5} + \frac{\square}{4} \qquad 9 = \boxed{8} + \frac{\square}{6}$$

$$6 = \boxed{5} + \frac{\square}{3}$$

In leading students through this preskill exercise, the teacher points out that they have to take one whole away from the original whole number and rewrite that one whole as a fraction. Once this preskill is taught, students should have little difficulty with problems that involve renaming.

Comparing Fractions

Students are often asked to compare the values of fractions. For example, which has the greater value, $\frac{1}{5}$ or $\frac{1}{3}$? Which has the lesser value, $\frac{2}{3}$ or $\frac{5}{9}$? During second and third grade, students usually are asked to compare fractions with numerators of 1 but with different denominators. The students can be prepared for early comparison questions by pictorial demonstrations illustrating that the more parts a unit is divided into, the smaller the size of each part. The rule is "The bigger the denominator, the smaller the value of each part." The demonstrations can then be followed by a rule application exercise in which the teacher presents pairs of fractions asking which fraction has a greater value.

In later grades, students are asked to compare fractions that have numerators other than 1 (e.g., $\frac{3}{4}$ and $\frac{5}{9}$). The strategy for comparing the two fractions involves rewriting fractions so that they have common denominators (e.g., $\frac{3}{4}$ would be rewritten as $\frac{27}{36}$ and $\frac{5}{9}$ as $\frac{20}{36}$).

Once fractions have been rewritten so they have common denominators, their values are readily apparent. Procedures for teaching students to rewrite fractions with common denominators would be the same as those discussed in the early steps of the format to add and subtract fractions with different denominators: determining the least common multiple of the denominators and multiplying each fraction by a fraction equal to 1.

Word Problems

The basic guideline for introducing fraction word problems is that a new type of problem should be integrated into word problem exercises as soon as the students can accurately compute problems of that type. Story problems involving adding and subtracting fractions with like denominators should be introduced after students work such problems independently. Story problems with unlike denominators should be introduced only after students have mastered the strategy for adding/subtracting that type of problem. All of the various types of addition and subtraction problems described in the problem-solving chapter (Chapter 11) would be included in the exercises. Figure 12.2 is a sample of problems that could be included on a worksheet given to students shortly after they learn how to add/subtract mixed numbers with fractions that have like denominators. Note the variety of story problem types (e.g., classification, action, and comparison).

FIGURE 12.2 Sample Story Problem Worksheet with Mixed Numbers and Like Denominators

1. Tina ran $3\frac{2}{5}$ miles in the morning and $2\frac{1}{5}$ miles in the afternoon. How many miles did she run altogether?
2. We had $\frac{3}{4}$ of an inch of rain on Monday and $\frac{1}{4}$ of an inch of rain on Tuesday. How much more rain did we have on Monday?
3. Ricardo's cat weighed $14\frac{2}{6}$ pounds. If the cat gains $3\frac{1}{6}$ pounds, how much will it weigh?
4. Joan bought $6\frac{2}{4}$ pounds of meat. After she cooked the meat it weighed $2\frac{1}{4}$ pounds. How much less does it weigh now?

OPERATIONS—MULTIPLYING FRACTIONS

There are three types of multiplication fraction problems. The first type, which involves multiplying two proper fractions, is usually introduced in third grade:

$$\frac{3}{4} \times \frac{2}{5} \qquad \frac{4}{9} \times \frac{1}{3}$$

The second type, which also is usually introduced during third or fourth grade, involves multiplying a fraction and a whole number:

$$\frac{3}{4} \times 8$$

This type of problem is important since it occurs often in story problems. The third type of problem, usually introduced in fifth grade, involves multiplying one or more mixed numbers:

$$5 \times 3\frac{2}{4} \qquad 4\frac{1}{2} \times 2\frac{3}{5} \qquad \frac{3}{4} \times 2\frac{1}{2}$$

Multiplying Proper Fractions

Multiplying proper fractions can be introduced several weeks after students have learned to add and subtract fractions with like denominators. The steps for multiplying fractions are presented in Format 12.17. Note that no pictorial demonstration is included since it would be too complex. The reason why multiplying proper fractions is taught at this point is that it is a prerequisite for equivalent fraction tasks and for the second type of multiplication problem, a fraction times a whole number.

The format includes two parts. In Part A, the structured board presentation, the teacher presents the rule about multiplying fractions, "Work top times the top and bottom times the bottom," and demonstrates how to apply the rule to several problems. Part B is a structured worksheet presentation. Note that the examples in this part include an equal mix of multiplication problems and problems that involve addition and subtraction of like denominators. This mix is essential to provide students with practice in remembering the difference between the multiplication strategy (multiply across the top and bottom) and the addition/subtraction strategy (work only across the top). Part B begins with a verbal exercise in which the teacher asks students how they work a particular type of problem (i.e., "What do you do when you multiply fractions? What do you do when you add or subtract fractions?").

Multiplying Fractions and Whole Numbers

Problems that involve multiplying a fraction and a whole number are important because they have many real-life applications. For example, consider the following problem: "A boat engine called for $\frac{2}{3}$ quarts of oil for every gallon of gasoline. John had 9 gallons of gas. How much oil did he need?"

Multiplying fractions and whole numbers in word problems can be introduced when students have mastered multiplying proper fractions and converting an improper fraction to a mixed number. The steps in the problem-solving strategy are outlined in the summary box below:

Summary Box 12.2:   Multiplying Fractions and Whole Numbers

1. Student reads the problem.	$\frac{3}{4} \times 8$
2. Student changes the whole number into a fraction.	$\frac{3}{4} \times \frac{8}{1}$
3. Student multiplies numerators and denominators.	$\frac{3}{4} \times \frac{8}{1} = \frac{24}{4}$
4. Student converts product into a whole number or mixed number.	$\frac{3}{4} \times \frac{8}{1} = \frac{24}{4} = 6$

Picture demonstrations of what takes place when multiplying a whole number by a fraction might precede the introduction of the format. In these demonstrations, the teacher explains that the bottom number tells how many groups to form and the top number tells how many groups are used. For example, for the problem $\frac{2}{3} \times 12$, the following diagram might be drawn:

$$||||\qquad ||||\qquad ||||$$

The teacher first draws 12 lines and says, "I've made three groups. Now I'm going to circle two of the groups." The teacher then circles two groups.

$$\big(||||\big)\quad\big(||||\big)\quad ||||$$

The teacher counts the lines within the circles: "We end up with 8. $\frac{2}{3} \times 12 = 8$."

The format for teaching students to work such problems appears in Format 12.18. Part A introduces an essential component skill, converting a whole number to a fraction. Any whole number may be converted to a fraction by putting it over a denominator of 1. Part B is a structured board presentation. Part C is a structured worksheet presentation. Note that the worksheet is set up with a prompt for the students. After a fraction bar for the answer is a division box:

$$\frac{3}{4} \times 8 = \underline{\qquad} = \overline{)\ \ } = \square$$

The division box serves as a prompt for the students to divide. The box serves as a prompt to write the whole number answer. This prompt should be used the first week this problem type is presented.

Examples should be carefully controlled. Some problems should have answers that are whole numbers:

$$\frac{3}{4} \times 8 = 6$$

and some should have answers that are mixed numbers:

$$\frac{2}{3} \times 7 = 4\frac{2}{3}$$

Initially, the whole number should be a relatively small number (e.g., below 20). As students learn to multiply and divide larger numbers, the examples should include hundreds and then thousands numbers:

$$\frac{3}{4} \times 2000$$

Multiplying Mixed Numbers

Multiplying a mixed number and a whole number is an important component skill for advanced map reading skills. For example, if 1 inch equals 50 miles, how many miles will $3\frac{1}{2}$ inches equal?

$$50 \times 3\frac{1}{2} = 175$$

Initially, we recommend a strategy in which the students convert a mixed number into an improper fraction before working the problem. See Summary Box 12.3. Problems in a and b in the Summary Box illustrate the steps in working these problems.

Summary Box 12.3:   Multiplying Mixed Numbers

Steps	*Problems*	
	a. $5\frac{1}{2} \times 3\frac{2}{4} =$	b. $5 \times 2\frac{3}{4} =$
1. Convert mixed number to improper fraction.	$\frac{11}{2} \times \frac{14}{4} =$	$\frac{5}{1} \times \frac{11}{4} =$
2. Multiply.	$\frac{11}{2} \times \frac{14}{4} = \frac{154}{8}$	$\frac{5}{1} \times \frac{11}{4} = \frac{55}{4}$
3. Convert answer to mixed number.	$\frac{154}{8} = \dfrac{19\frac{2}{8} = 19\frac{1}{4}}{8\overline{)154}}$	$\frac{55}{4} = \dfrac{13\frac{3}{4} = 13\frac{3}{4}}{4\overline{)55}}$

Later, a more sophisticated strategy involving the distributive property may be introduced for problems in which a whole number and mixed number are multiplied. The students first multiply the whole number factor by the whole number from the mixed number factor, then multiply the whole number factor by the fraction, and finally add the products. This process is shown below:

$$5 \times 3\frac{1}{2} = (5 \times 3) + \left(5 \times \frac{1}{2}\right)$$

$$= \quad 15 \quad + \quad 2\frac{1}{2}$$

$$= 17\frac{1}{2}$$

OPERATIONS—DIVIDING FRACTIONS

Dividing fractions is usually introduced in fifth grade. Fraction division problems may be divided into three types. First are those in which a proper fraction is divided by a proper fraction:

$$\frac{2}{3} \div \frac{3}{4} \qquad\qquad \frac{4}{5} \div \frac{2}{7}$$

This type of problem, while having little practical application, is introduced first since it prepares the students for the second type of problem in which a fraction is divided by a whole number:

$$\frac{3}{4} \div 2$$

Problems such as the one above have everyday application. For example, John has ³⁄₄ pound of candy. He wants to split the candy up equally among his two friends. How much candy should he give to each friend?

The third type of problem involves dividing a mixed number:

$$3\frac{1}{2} \div 4 \qquad\qquad 5\frac{1}{2} \div 2\frac{1}{3}$$

The strategy taught to solve division problems involves inverting the second fraction, changing the sign to a times sign, and then multiplying (e.g., ³⁄₄ ÷ ²⁄₃ is worked by inverting ²⁄₃ so that the problem reads ³⁄₄ × ³⁄₂ = ⁹⁄₈). Because a lengthy explanation is needed for the rationale for this procedure, we recommend presenting the strategy in the elementary grades without rationale. The teacher simply presents the rules: "We cannot divide by a fraction

number; we must change the problem to a multiplication problem. Here's how we do that: we invert the second fraction and change the sign." The teacher illustrates the meaning of invert as she demonstrates solving the problem.

Problems in which students divide by a whole number are solved by first converting the whole number to a fraction and then inverting that fraction:

$$\frac{3}{4} \div 2 = \frac{3}{4} \div \frac{2}{1} = \frac{3}{4} \times \frac{1}{2} = \frac{3}{8}$$

Problems that include a mixed number are solved by converting the mixed number to an improper fraction, inverting, and multiplying.

The relationship between fractions and multiplication-division number families is very important. Teachers should introduce the line in fractions as another way of saying "divided by." The fraction ½ can also be read "1 divided by 2." After students have practiced reading fractions both these ways, they learn that multiplication number families can be turned up on end.

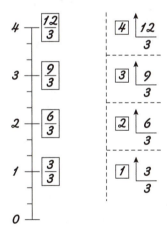

Students practice identifying the big number and the two small numbers. Later, students apply this knowledge to number lines.

Students complete the fractions for the number lines. The fraction for 1 on the number line is ³⁄₃. The fraction for two is ⁶⁄₃. Next to the numbers on the number line, students complete the number families that are turned on end. The number that goes in the box is the whole number on the number line. The numbers for the fractions are the vertically-oriented numbers in the family.

This relationship is very important. It shows how multiplication-division number families imply fractions, and vice versa. The relationship between multiplication-division number families is emphasized when students learn to read fractions as division problems. Students should be presented this concept as an introduction to dividing fractions, and as early as third grade. After mastering reading fractions as division problems, students learn to write regular division problems as fractions.

Story Problems—Multiplication and Division

Multiplication and division story problems can be introduced when students can solve the respective problem types. Multiplication story problems with fractions usually involve figuring out what a fractional part of a specified group equals. Here is a typical problem:

> There are 20 children in our class; $\frac{3}{4}$ of the children are girls. How many girls are in the class?

This type of problem is introduced shortly after students can solve problems in which a fraction and a whole number are multiplied (e.g., $\frac{3}{4} \times 12$). As an intermediate step to prepare students for the story problems, the teacher can present problems like these:

$$\frac{3}{4} \text{ of } 12 = \frac{\square}{\square} = \square \qquad \frac{2}{3} \text{ of } 9 = \frac{\square}{\square} = \square$$

Students would be taught that *of* in this problem can be translated to *times*. The problem $\frac{3}{4}$ of 12 would be converted to $\frac{3}{4} \times 12$ and then worked:

$$\frac{3}{4} \times \frac{12}{1} = \frac{36}{4} = 9$$

As students are able to solve operations with larger numbers, the examples in the story problems should include larger numbers. Instead of $\frac{2}{3}$ of 12, a problem might ask $\frac{2}{3}$ of 126.

The most common type of division story problem involves dividing a fraction by a whole number. Here is an example of this type of problem:

> John has $\frac{2}{3}$ of an apple left. He wants to share it equally with his 2 friends. How much of the apple should he give to each friend?

This type of problem can be introduced when students can work problems in which a fraction can be divided by a whole number.

DIAGNOSIS AND REMEDIATION

Students may miss fraction problems for one or a combination of the following reasons:

1. *A computational error* (e.g., dividing 18 by 3 and ending with 5, multiplying 7×8 and ending with 54). If a student misses a problem solely because of a computational error, the teacher need not spend time working on the fraction skill but should reteach the specific computational skill.
2. *A component skill error.* The student makes an error on a previously taught fraction skill, which causes the student to miss the current type of problem. For example, when working the problem $\frac{2}{3} \times 12$, the student converts 12 to the fraction $\frac{1}{12}$ instead of $\frac{12}{1}$, writing $\frac{2}{3} \times \frac{1}{12} = \frac{2}{36}$. The remediation procedure involves reteaching the earlier taught component skill. In the example given, the teacher would first reteach the student how to convert a whole number to a fraction. When the student's performance indicates mastery of the component skill, the teacher leads the student through solving the original type of problem, using the structured worksheet part of the appropriate format.
3. *A strategy error.* A strategy error occurs when the student does not correctly chain the steps together to solve a problem. For example, when attempting to convert $\frac{12}{4}$ to a whole number, the student subtracts 4 from 12, ending with 8. The remediation procedure involves reteaching the strategy beginning with the structured board part of the format.

The following sections give examples of common errors made on the various types of fraction problems along with suggestions for remediation.

Reading and Writing Fractions and Mixed Numbers

Students should read a problem as the first step in any part of the format. If the teacher notes the student reading a fraction or mixed number incorrectly, the teacher should reintroduce the reading format, stressing the particular type of fraction missed. For example, if a student reads $5\frac{1}{3}$ as $\frac{5}{3}$, the teacher would present the formats for reading mixed number.

Adding and Subtracting Fractions

When adding fractions with like denominators, students will usually make (1) strategy errors or (2) computational errors. Note the problems below:

a. $\dfrac{7}{9} - \dfrac{2}{9} = \dfrac{5}{0}$

b. $\dfrac{4}{8} + \dfrac{2}{8} = \dfrac{6}{16}$

c. $\dfrac{7}{9} - \dfrac{2}{9} = \dfrac{6}{9}$

d. $\dfrac{4}{8} - \dfrac{2}{8} = \dfrac{7}{8}$

Problems a and b illustrate strategy errors. The student does not know that the denominators are not added or subtracted. The remediation procedure involves reintroducing the format for adding and subtracting fractions, beginning with Part A. Problems c and d, on the other hand, indicate computational errors. The student knows the strategy but missed the problems because of basic fact errors. The remediation procedure depends on the number of problems missed. If a student misses less than 10% of the problems because of computational errors, the teacher merely works on the particular fact missed, writing the fact for the student and testing him periodically on it for several days. If the student misses more than 10% of the problems because of computational errors, the teacher must work on improving fact accuracy through instituting a stronger motivational system and/or providing more practice on basic facts. In neither case must the teacher reintroduce the adding and subtracting fraction format.

Problems involving adding or subtracting fractions with unlike denominators may be missed because of

fact, component skill, or strategy deficits. Note the problems in the Summary Box below. The cause of each error and the suggested remediation procedures are provided for many common mistakes.

COMMERCIAL PROGRAMS

Fractions: Adding and Subtracting Fractions with Unlike Denominators

INSTRUCTIONAL STRATEGIES The main concern regarding the way fractions are taught is the lack of specificity generally found in the instruction. Structured teaching presentations become particularly important when more complex strategies are introduced. For example, Figures 12.3 and 12.4 show the initial instruction for subtracting mixed numbers with regrouping in a fifth grade text. These are particularly difficult problems, requiring a thorough understanding of fraction analysis skills. Note the minimal guidance provided in the teacher's guide. The teacher demonstrates one example on the board, and there is a model of one problem in the student's text. There is no demonstration for subtracting a mixed number from a whole number, yet nine problems are of this type. Considering that not only must students rename but in many problems

---

Summary Box 12.4   Errors in Addition with Unlike Denominators

Error Patterns	Diagnosis	Remediation Procedures
1. $\dfrac{4}{5} + \dfrac{2}{3} = \dfrac{4}{5\left(\times 3\right)} + \dfrac{2}{3\left(\times 5\right)} = \dfrac{6}{15}$ *15* *15*	Component error: student failed to multiply numerator.	Present Format 12.16 beginning with Part A.
2. $\dfrac{4}{8} + \dfrac{2}{4} = \dfrac{4(\times 4)}{8(\times 4)} + \dfrac{2(\times 8)}{4(\times 8)} = \dfrac{32}{32}$ *16* *16* *32* *32*	Component skill error: student did not find least common multiple. Note that answer is correct.	Teacher points this out but emphasizes it's important to find the least common multiple. Extra practice on finding LCM.
3. $\dfrac{4}{5} + \dfrac{2}{3} = \dfrac{6}{8}$	Strategy error: student adds denominators.	Present entire format for fractions with unlike denominators (12.16) over, beginning with Part A.
4. $\dfrac{5}{6} + \dfrac{2}{4} = \dfrac{5(\times 2)}{6(\times 2)} + \dfrac{2(\times 3)}{4(\times 3)} = \dfrac{15}{12}$ *10* *5* *12* *12* *12* *12*	Computational errors: student multiplied 2×3 incorrectly.	Teacher works on 2×3 fact. No reteaching of fraction format necessary.

FIGURE 12.3 Excerpt from a Basal Mathematics Textbook Teacher's Edition (From *Heath Mathematics,* Grade 5 Teacher's Edition, by Walter E. Rucker, Clyde A. Dilley, and David A. Lowry, pp. 312–313. Copyright © 1987 by D.C. Heath & Company. Reprinted by permission.)

STUDENT OBJECTIVE
To subtract mixed numbers by finding a common denominator and regrouping.

TEACHING SUGGESTIONS

Learn about regrouping with subtraction of fractions. Write this problem on the chalkboard:

$$6\tfrac{1}{3}$$
$$-2\tfrac{2}{3}$$

We must regroup 1 one to $\tfrac{3}{3}$ before we can subtract. Work through the steps on the chalkboard:

$$6\tfrac{1}{3} = 5\tfrac{4}{3}$$
$$-2\tfrac{2}{3} = 2\tfrac{2}{3}$$
$$\overline{\phantom{-2\tfrac{2}{3}}\;3\tfrac{2}{3}}$$

Of course, this can be done in shorter steps, but at this time focus on the renaming procedure so that the fractions can be subtracted.

READINESS

For students who need help with mixed numbers.

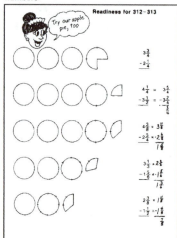

Copymaster S126 or Duplicating Master S126

Draw this example on the chalkboard:

$$4\tfrac{1}{2}$$
$$-2\tfrac{3}{4}$$

"We can't subtract $\tfrac{3}{4}$ from $\tfrac{1}{2}$, so we use a whole circle and the half circle to make $\tfrac{4}{4}$ and $\tfrac{2}{4}$ which totals $\tfrac{6}{4}$." Demonstrate. "Now we can subtract $\tfrac{3}{4}$." Demonstrate by crossing off three $\tfrac{1}{4}$ segments. "How many fourths do we have now? (3) Now subtract 2 whole circles."

Guide the students through the exercises. Have them rewrite each problem on the right side of the page after they draw the regrouping.

❖❖ **Cooperative Learning Groups**

More about subtracting mixed numbers

Sometimes you have to regroup before you subtract.

EXAMPLE. $8\tfrac{1}{4}$
$-3\tfrac{3}{8}$

Step 1.
Change to a common denominator.

$$8\tfrac{1}{4} = 8\tfrac{2}{8}$$
$$-3\tfrac{3}{8} = 3\tfrac{3}{8}$$

Step 2.
Since $\tfrac{2}{8}$ is less than $\tfrac{3}{8}$, regroup 1 as $\tfrac{8}{8}$.

$$8\tfrac{1}{4} = 8\tfrac{2}{8} = 7\tfrac{10}{8}$$
$$-3\tfrac{3}{8} = 3\tfrac{3}{8} = 3\tfrac{3}{8}$$

Step 3.
Subtract.

$$8\tfrac{1}{4} = 8\tfrac{2}{8} = 7\tfrac{10}{8}$$
$$-3\tfrac{3}{8} = 3\tfrac{3}{8} = 3\tfrac{3}{8}$$
$$\overline{4\tfrac{7}{8}}$$

$$8\tfrac{1}{4} = 8\!\!\!\!\diagdown^{7}\tfrac{\overset{10}{\cancel{2}}}{8}$$
$$-3\tfrac{3}{8} = 3\tfrac{3}{8}$$
$$\overline{4\tfrac{7}{8}}$$

Here is how I find the difference.

EXERCISES
Subtract. Write the difference in simplest form.

1. $5\tfrac{1}{4} = 5\tfrac{1}{4} = 4\tfrac{5}{4}$
    $-2\tfrac{1}{2} = 2\tfrac{2}{4} = 2\tfrac{2}{4}$
    $\overline{2\tfrac{3}{4}}$

2. $6\tfrac{1}{8} = 6\tfrac{1}{8} = 5\tfrac{9}{8}$
    $-3\tfrac{3}{4} = 3\tfrac{6}{8} = 3\tfrac{6}{8}$
    $\overline{2\tfrac{3}{8}}$

3. $7\tfrac{2}{3} = 7\tfrac{8}{12} = 6\tfrac{20}{12}$
    $-4\tfrac{3}{4} = 4\tfrac{9}{12} = 4\tfrac{9}{12}$
    $\overline{2\tfrac{11}{12}}$

4. $6 = 5\tfrac{4}{4}$
    $-2\tfrac{1}{4} = 2\tfrac{1}{4}$
    $\overline{3\tfrac{3}{4}}$

5. $9 = 8\tfrac{3}{3}$
    $-5\tfrac{2}{3} = 5\tfrac{2}{3}$
    $\overline{3\tfrac{1}{3}}$

6. $7 = 6\tfrac{8}{8}$
    $-3\tfrac{5}{8} = 3\tfrac{5}{8}$
    $\overline{3\tfrac{3}{8}}$

312

USING THE PAGES

Go through the exposition on page 312. Have the students work exercises 1–6 on scratch paper while you work them on the chalkboard. Keep a close check on the students' work and the way they record it. Assign exercises 7–28.

⋯⋯ **ERROR-ANALYSIS NOTE** ⋯⋯⋯⋯⋯⋯⋯

When a mixed number is subtracted from a whole number, some students may not regroup but just write the fraction as part of the answer—for example,

$$\frac{6}{-4\tfrac{2}{3}}\ \ \text{instead of}\ \ \frac{\overset{5}{\cancel{6}}\tfrac{3}{3}}{-4\tfrac{2}{3}}$$
$$\overline{2\tfrac{3}{3}}\qquad\qquad\overline{1\tfrac{1}{3}}$$

Point out to these students that since they are subtracting more than 4 from 6, their answer must be less than 2. They need to regroup.

○○○○○○ → ○○○○○⦿
Subtract $4\tfrac{2}{3}$ ⟶ ∅∅∅∅○⦿

CLASSWORK/HOMEWORK

Textbook Assignments	Basic	Average	Enriched
Exercises 1–26	✓		
Exercises 1–28		✓	
Exercises 7–28			✓
Keeping Skills Sharp	✓	✓	✓
Extra Practice set 53 page 377	✓		
Optional Materials			
Readiness Worksheet	✓	✓	
Basic Worksheet	✓		
Enrichment Worksheet		✓	✓
Excursion Worksheet		✓	✓
Creative Problem Solving section 11	✓	✓	✓

FIGURE 12.4 Excerpt from a Basal Mathematics Textbook Teacher's Edition (From *Heath Mathematics*, Grade 5 Teacher's Edition, by Walter E. Rucker, Clyde A. Dilley, and David A. Lowry, pp. 312–313. Copyright © 1987 by D.C. Heath & Company. Reprinted by permission.)

7. $9\frac{5}{9}$ $-4\frac{1}{9}$ $\overline{5\frac{4}{9}}$	8. $8\frac{4}{5}$ $-2\frac{3}{5}$ $\overline{6\frac{1}{5}}$	9. $5\frac{3}{4}$ $-1\frac{1}{2}$ $\overline{4\frac{1}{4}}$	10. $9\frac{5}{6}$ $-4\frac{2}{3}$ $\overline{5\frac{1}{6}}$	11. $7\frac{1}{2}$ $-2\frac{1}{3}$ $\overline{5\frac{1}{6}}$	12. $9\frac{3}{4}$ $-4\frac{2}{3}$ $\overline{5\frac{1}{12}}$
13. 8 $-3\frac{1}{2}$ $\overline{4\frac{1}{2}}$	14. 6 $-4\frac{3}{5}$ $\overline{1\frac{2}{5}}$	15. 12 $-3\frac{7}{10}$ $\overline{8\frac{3}{10}}$	16. 11 $-5\frac{3}{4}$ $\overline{5\frac{1}{4}}$	17. 15 $-6\frac{3}{8}$ $\overline{8\frac{5}{8}}$	18. 16 $-9\frac{4}{5}$ $\overline{6\frac{1}{5}}$
19. $9\frac{1}{4}$ $-3\frac{1}{2}$ $\overline{5\frac{3}{4}}$	20. $8\frac{1}{2}$ $-4\frac{3}{4}$ $\overline{3\frac{3}{4}}$	21. $7\frac{3}{8}$ $-2\frac{3}{4}$ $\overline{4\frac{5}{8}}$	22. $10\frac{2}{3}$ $-8\frac{5}{6}$ $\overline{1\frac{5}{6}}$	23. $11\frac{1}{8}$ $-6\frac{3}{4}$ $\overline{4\frac{3}{8}}$	24. $12\frac{2}{3}$ $-8\frac{5}{6}$ $\overline{3\frac{5}{6}}$

25. Diane is $8\frac{3}{4}$ inches taller than her little brother. If Diane is $58\frac{1}{2}$ inches tall, how tall is her brother? $49\frac{3}{4}$ inches

26. One week, David watched $6\frac{1}{4}$ hours of television. The next week he watched 8 hours of television. How much more did he watch the second week? $1\frac{3}{4}$ hours

27. In basketball, the rim of the basket is 10 feet above the floor. Stan can jump up and reach $7\frac{1}{4}$ feet above the floor. How much higher must he jump to touch the basket rim? $2\frac{3}{4}$ feet

28. A share of certain stock sold for $32\frac{5}{8}$ dollars. Two weeks later it sold for $34\frac{1}{8}$ dollars a share. How much did the value of the stock increase? $1\frac{1}{2}$ dollars

---

KEEPING SKILLS SHARP

Add or subtract.

1. 8.4 $+3.29$ $\overline{11.69}$	2. 7.34 -2.6 $\overline{4.74}$	3. 13 $+89.2$ $\overline{102.2}$	4. 87 -9.6 $\overline{77.4}$	5. 0.67 $+5.6$ $\overline{6.47}$	6. 9 -2.57 $\overline{6.43}$

7. $37 + 8.6$ 45.6 8. $37 - 8.6$ 28.4 9. $2.6 + 0.57$ 3.17 10. $2.6 - 0.57$ 2.03

313

PRACTICE

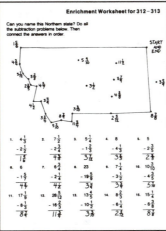

Basic Worksheet for 312–313

Available as Copymasters, Duplicating Masters, and Workbooks

ENRICHMENT

Enrichment Worksheet for 312–313

Can you name this Northern state? Do all the subtraction problems below. Then connect the answers in order.

LESSON FOLLOW-UP

REINFORCEMENT   ***ERROR ANALYSIS***

Diagnosis and remediation. Identify the students having difficulty and work with them individually. You may want to select exercises from this lesson for these students to work on the chalkboard while you watch. As necessary, go back to page 312 and emphasize the sequence of steps to follow.

ENRICHMENT

Build a number. (Materials: digit cards) Pair students and give them a deck of digit cards. As they draw in turn, they complete a mixed number. The student building the larger number wins one point. The first student to get 5 points wins the game.

CHALLENGE

An excursion on adding and subtracting decimals.

Excursion Worksheet for 310–313

1. One player is X and the other is O.
2. Taking turns, each player picks two decimal cards and adds or subtracts.
3. The player marks the answer on the game board.
4. The first player to get five marks in a line wins.

GAME BOARD

6.14	10.25	2.14	3.25	1.11
4.45	7.25	3.5	12.39	5.14
9.05	7.94	6.25	7.95	5.8
4.7	4.44	9.14	5.55	1.8
1.2	3.34	2.8	6.84	1.1

6.75 5.64 3.5 2.3 1.2 0.5

Copymaster S192 or Duplicating Master S192

After the students have played a few games, set up a tournament to determine the class champion.

they must also first rewrite the fractions with common denominators, it is highly likely that some students will have difficulty. Note that the only reference to a correction procedure suggests that the teacher work with those students having difficulty on an individual basis (see Figure 12.4).

REVIEW The second focus of concern with instruction in fractions has to do with the amount of review provided in the programs. In grades one through three, only one to three weeks are typically devoted to fraction skills. Minimal review is presented on fraction skills after the unit is presented. Because of this minimal review, it is highly likely that many students will not retain fraction-related skills taught in these earlier grades. In intermediate grades, the critical fraction analysis skills taught in early grades are briefly reviewed prior to teaching new skills. The amount of practice provided in the programs must be significantly supplemented if the students are to develop mastery. Teachers must not go on to a new skill until students have mastered preskills. When the more complex fraction skills are introduced in the intermediate grades, the programs tend to provide enough initial practice (with all of the supplemental worksheets available). However, the practice usually is concentrated in a short amount of time with little systematic review built into the program outside of the fractions units themselves, as in the earlier grades. Low-performing students require continual review if they are to maintain acquired skills.

APPLICATION ITEMS: FRACTIONS

1. Below are various fraction-related problems. Describe the type each problem represents. List the types in their order of introduction.

   a. $\dfrac{2}{3} - \dfrac{1}{3}$

   b. Circle the picture that shows $\dfrac{2}{4}$.

   c. Read this fraction: $\dfrac{3}{5}$

   d. $\dfrac{3}{4} + \dfrac{2}{5}$

   e. $5\dfrac{4}{7} - 3\dfrac{2}{7}$

   f. $\dfrac{12}{5} = \Box$

   g. $\dfrac{3}{5} = \dfrac{\Box}{10}$

   h. $5\dfrac{1}{2} \times 3$

   i. $3\dfrac{4}{5} = \dfrac{\Box}{5}$

2. Write a structured worksheet presentation for teaching students how to solve the following type of problem:

   Draw a picture for this fraction: $\dfrac{3}{4} = \bigcirc \bigcirc$

3. A teacher is presenting the first lesson in which she is teaching students to decode fractions in the traditional manner (e.g., $^2\!/_3$ is read as two-thirds). Below are four sets of examples. One set is appropriate. Tell which set is appropriate. Tell why the other three sets are not appropriate.

   a. $\dfrac{2}{3}$ $\dfrac{1}{2}$ $\dfrac{4}{5}$ $\dfrac{7}{3}$ $\dfrac{1}{4}$ $\dfrac{2}{9}$ $\dfrac{3}{2}$ $\dfrac{1}{5}$

   b. $\dfrac{1}{8}$ $\dfrac{1}{4}$ $\dfrac{1}{9}$ $\dfrac{1}{6}$ $\dfrac{1}{5}$ $\dfrac{1}{7}$

   c. $\dfrac{1}{8}$ $\dfrac{3}{4}$ $\dfrac{7}{6}$ $\dfrac{1}{6}$ $\dfrac{2}{8}$ $\dfrac{9}{4}$ $\dfrac{1}{4}$

   d. $\dfrac{3}{4}$ $\dfrac{7}{9}$ $\dfrac{8}{4}$ $\dfrac{2}{9}$ $\dfrac{4}{6}$ $\dfrac{8}{6}$ $\dfrac{5}{7}$

4. A student writes the mixed number five and one-third as $\frac{5}{3}$. Specify the wording the teacher uses in making the correction.

5. Specify the wording the teacher uses in making the correction for the following error:

$$\frac{3}{4} = \frac{\boxed{3}}{8}$$

6. Cross out the examples below that would not be included in an early equivalent fraction exercise.

a. $\frac{2}{3} = \frac{\square}{9}$ b. $\frac{5}{7} = \frac{\square}{28}$ c. $\frac{3}{4} = \frac{\square}{6}$

d. $\frac{4}{5} = \frac{\square}{20}$ e. $\frac{3}{5} = \frac{\square}{20}$ f. $\frac{4}{6} = \frac{\square}{10}$

7. Below are four sets of examples constructed by the teacher for an early reducing fraction exercise. One set is appropriate. Three are not appropriate. Identify the inappropriate sets. Tell why they're inappropriate.

a. $\frac{8}{12}$ $\frac{7}{9}$ $\frac{6}{18}$ $\frac{4}{6}$ $\frac{5}{20}$ $\frac{2}{3}$

b. $\frac{8}{12}$ $\frac{6}{18}$ $\frac{4}{6}$ $\frac{5}{20}$ $\frac{3}{12}$ $\frac{6}{8}$

c. $\frac{8}{12}$ $\frac{7}{9}$ $\frac{10}{15}$ $\frac{12}{20}$ $\frac{3}{5}$ $\frac{6}{8}$

d. $\frac{4}{7}$ $\frac{5}{20}$ $\frac{22}{36}$ $\frac{8}{16}$ $\frac{18}{34}$ $\frac{5}{9}$

8. Write the structured worksheet presentation used in leading students through reducing the fraction $\frac{12}{18}$ to its lowest terms.

9. Below are sets of examples prepared by various teachers for an exercise in which students convert improper fractions to mixed numbers. Tell which sets are inappropriate.

a. $\frac{9}{5}$ $\frac{11}{3}$ $\frac{9}{3}$ $\frac{12}{7}$ $\frac{14}{5}$ $\frac{12}{4}$

b. $\frac{9}{4}$ $\frac{3}{7}$ $\frac{8}{2}$ $\frac{7}{5}$ $\frac{8}{3}$ $\frac{5}{9}$ $\frac{9}{3}$ $\frac{7}{3}$

c. $\frac{9}{5}$ $\frac{3}{7}$ $\frac{5}{2}$ $\frac{4}{9}$ $\frac{7}{3}$ $\frac{9}{2}$

10. Below are sets of examples prepared by several teachers for an independent worksheet exercise focusing on adding and subtracting fractions with unlike denominators. Tell which sets are inappropriate. Explain why.

a. $\frac{6}{14} - \frac{3}{8}$ $\frac{5}{8} + \frac{1}{5}$ $\frac{4}{9} - \frac{5}{12}$ $\frac{3}{8} + \frac{2}{8}$

b. $\frac{3}{8} + \frac{1}{5}$ $\frac{5}{7} - \frac{1}{4}$ $\frac{3}{8} + \frac{2}{8}$ $\frac{3}{5} + \frac{2}{3}$ $\frac{2}{3} - \frac{1}{2}$ $\frac{4}{7} - \frac{2}{5}$

c. $\frac{3}{4} - \frac{2}{3}$ $\frac{4}{9} - \frac{2}{9}$ $\frac{2}{9} + \frac{2}{3}$ $\frac{5}{7} - \frac{1}{2}$ $\frac{3}{8} + \frac{1}{4}$ $\frac{3}{7} + \frac{2}{7}$

(continued)

11. Below are problems missed by students. These examples are typical of the errors made by students. Specify the diagnosis and remediation for each student.

    William

    $$\frac{7}{8} - \frac{1}{6} = \frac{6}{2}$$

    Ann

    $$\frac{5}{9} + \frac{2}{5} = \frac{5}{9}\left(\frac{5}{5}\right) + \frac{2}{5}\left(\frac{9}{9}\right) = \frac{5}{9}\left(\overset{25}{\frac{5}{5}}\right) + \frac{2}{5}\left(\overset{18}{\frac{9}{9}}\right) = \frac{42}{45}$$

    Samuel

    $$\frac{4}{5} + \frac{1}{2} = \frac{4}{5}\left(\frac{2}{2}\right) + \frac{1}{2}\left(\frac{5}{5}\right) = \frac{4}{5}\left(\overset{8}{\frac{2}{2}}\right) + \frac{1}{2}\left(\overset{5}{\frac{5}{5}}\right) = \frac{13}{10} = \frac{3}{10}$$

    Jean

    $$\frac{3}{5} + \frac{2}{3} = \frac{3}{5}\left(\frac{5}{3}\right) + \frac{2}{3}\left(\frac{3}{5}\right) = \frac{3}{5}\left(\overset{15}{\frac{5}{3}}\right) + \frac{2}{3}\left(\overset{6}{\frac{3}{5}}\right) = \frac{21}{15}$$

12. Write a structured worksheet exercise to lead students through solving this problem:

    $$8 - 3\frac{4}{5}$$

13. Specify the diagnosis and remediation procedures for each student.

    Jim $\frac{6}{7}$ of 28 = $\frac{162}{7}$ = $23\frac{1}{7}$

    Sarah $\frac{6}{7}$ of 28 = $\frac{6}{196}$ = $\frac{3}{98}$

    William $\frac{6}{7}$ of 28 = $\frac{168}{7}$

FORMAT 12.1   **Format for Introducing Fractions**

TEACHER   **STUDENTS**

(Write the following diagram on the board.)

1.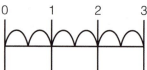

2. *(Touch line A.)* Pretend that I've drawn inches on the board.
   (Point to 1.) Here's one inch.
   (Point to 2.) Here's two inches.
   (Point to 3.) Here's three inches.

FORMAT 12.1   **(continued)**

| **TEACHER** | **STUDENT** |

3. Listen: Each inch is divided into parts. Each hump is a part.
   (Draw a line under the first inch.)

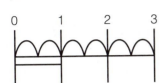

4. Look at the first inch. How many parts are in the first inch?   2
   (Signal.)
   (Underline the next inch.)

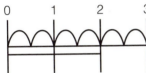

5. Look at the second inch. How many parts are in the second   2
   inch? *(Signal.)*
   (Underline the third inch.)

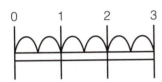

6. Look at the next inch. How many parts are in the next inch?   2
   (Signal.)

7. If I drew another inch, how many parts would be in that   2
   inch? *(Signal.)*
   To correct:

    a. *(Students do not understand the number of parts in
   each unit. They do not write the same bottom number
   or the correct bottom number for all the fractions.)*

    *(First, have them show you the first unit on the number
   line.)* Use your fingers. Show me where the first unit
   starts and where it stops. Now start at the beginning
   and count the parts in that unit. How many parts are
   in that unit? Now do the same thing for the next unit.
   Mark the beginning and the end of the unit. Now start
   at the beginning and count the number of parts in that
   unit. How many parts are in that unit? There were 3
   parts in the first unit and 3 parts in this unit. So how
   many parts are in EACH unit?   3

    *(Repeat the procedure until students who have
   problems are performing flawlessly. Note that some of
   them may have serious problems because they don't
   understand that the second unit starts where the first
   unit ends.)*

(continued on next page)

FORMAT 12.1 **(continued)**

TEACHER	STUDENT
b. *(Students don't write the correct top number.)*	
(If students seem to make chronic mistakes, touch different places on the number line and say,) Let's say you're going to write a fraction right here. Figure out the top number of that fraction. Count from the beginning and write the number.	

FORMAT 12.2 **Format for Part-Whole Discrimination**

PART A: STRUCTURED BOARD PRESENTATION

TEACHER	STUDENTS
1. *(Write the following circles on the board.)*	

TEACHER	STUDENTS
2. *(Point to the first circle.)* This is a whole unit. What is this? *(Point to the second circle.)* This is a whole unit. What is this? How many units?	a whole unit. a whole unit 2
3. Each whole unit has parts. The parts are all the same size. Let's see how many parts are in each whole unit.	
4. *(Point to first unit.)* Count the parts as I touch them. Touch each part in the first circle. How many parts in this whole unit?	1,2,3 3
5. *(Point to the second circle.)* Now let's count the parts in this whole unit. *(Touch each part as students count.)*	1,2,3
6. How many parts in each whole unit?	3 parts
7. Yes, three parts in each whole unit. Say that.	3 parts in each whole unit
8. Now think: How many whole units? Yes, there are two whole units with three parts in each unit. *(Repeat steps 1-7 with other examples.)*	2

FORMAT 12.3 **Format for Writing Numerical Fractions**

PART A: STRUCTURED BOARD PRESENTATION

TEACHER	**STUDENTS**

1. *(Write the following circles on the board.)*

2. We're going to learn to write fractions. Fractions tell us how many parts in each whole unit and how many parts are used.

3. The bottom number of a fraction tells how many parts in each whole. What does the bottom number tell? *(Signal.)*   How many parts in each whole.
   Look at this picture and think how many parts in each whole?   4

   To correct: Let's see how many parts are in each whole. *(Point to first circle.)* Count the parts as I touch them. *(Touch each part in the first circle. Repeat same procedures with next two circles.)* There are four parts in this whole, and four parts in this whole. There are four parts in each whole.

   So what is the bottom number of the fraction?   4
   I'll write 4 as the bottom number. That tells us four parts in each whole. What does the 4 tell us?   4 parts in each whole

4. The top number tells us how many parts are used. What does the top number tell us?   How many parts are used.

   We find how many parts are used by counting the shaded parts? *(Point to each shaded part.)* Count as I touch the parts. How many parts are shaded?   1,2,3,4,5 / 5

   So I write 5 as the top number of the fraction. *(Write 5 on top.)* That tells us five parts are used. What does the 5 tell us?   5 parts are used.

5. I'll say what the fraction tells us. *(Point to 4.)* Four parts in each whole. *(Point to 5.)* Five parts are used.

6. You say what the fraction tells us. *(Point to 4. Signal. Point to 5. Signal. Repeat step 5 until students respond without hesitation. Give individual turns to several students.)*   4 parts in each whole / 5 parts are used.

7. *(Repeat steps 1-4 with the problems below.)*

a. b.

c.

(continued on next page)

FORMAT 12.3 (continued)

PART B: STRUCTURED WORKSHEET

TEACHER	STUDENTS

1. *(Give students a worksheet with problems like those that follow.)*

a.   d.

b.   e.

c.   f.

2. Touch picture a. You're going to write the fraction for the picture.

3. First we write how many parts in each whole. Where do you write the number of parts in each whole?   in the bottom box
   Look and see how many parts in each whole. *(Pause.)*
   How many parts in each whole?   3
   Where do you write 3? Write the number.   in the bottom box

4. Now we write the number of parts used. Where do you write the number of parts used?   on the top
   Count the shaded parts. *(Pause.)* How many parts were used?   4
   (Signal.) Count the shaded parts. *(Pause.)* How many parts are used *(Signal.)* Write the 4.   3 parts in each whole

5. Touch the bottom number. *(Pause.)* What does that tell us?   4 parts are used.
   Touch the top number. What does that tell us? *(Repeat step 4 until students answer without hesitation. Give individual turns to several students on step 4. Repeat steps 1-4 with remaining diagrams.)*

PART C: LESS-STRUCTURED WORKSHEET

(Give students a worksheet similar to the one in Part B.)

1. Touch problem a.

2. Where do you write how many parts in each whole unit?   on the bottom

3. What do you write on the top? Write the numbers.   How many parts are used.

FORMAT 12.3 (continued)

TEACHER	STUDENTS
4. Touch the bottom number. What did you write? What does it tell us?	_____ parts in each whole.
5. Touch the top number. What did you write? What does the top number tell us?	_____ parts are used.
(Repeat steps 1–5 with remaining problems.)	

FORMAT 12.4 **Format for Reading Fractions**

PART A: STRUCTURED BOARD PRESENTATION

TEACHER

(Write the following fractions on the board.)

$$\frac{4}{9} \quad \frac{1}{9} \quad \frac{3}{4} \quad \frac{1}{4} \quad \frac{6}{7} \quad \frac{1}{7} \quad \frac{2}{4} \quad \frac{1}{4}$$

1. So far we've learned what fractions tell us to do. Today we're going to learn to read fractions a new way. My turn to read this fraction. *(Point to 4.)* Four *(Point to 9.)* Ninths.

2. Your turn. *(Point to 4, then 9.)*

3. *(Repeat steps 1 and 2 with half the examples on the board.)*

4. *(Repeat step 2 only with the remaining examples.)*

   To correct: Model correct answer; repeat.

STUDENTS

Four-ninths

FORMAT 12.5 **Format for Determining Whether a Fraction Equals, Exceeds, or Is Less Than One Whole**

PART A: PICTORIAL DEMONSTRATIONS

TEACHER

1. I'll draw a picture on the board. You tell me if we use up more than one whole, less than one whole, or just one whole. *(Draw the diagram below.)*

2. Did I shade more than one whole, less than one whole, or just one whole? *(Signal.)*

   Yes, less than one whole unit. Each circle has four parts, but I only shaded three parts.

STUDENTS

less than one whole unit

(continued on next page)

FORMAT 12.5 (continued)

TEACHER	STUDENTS

(Repeat step 2 with the examples below.)

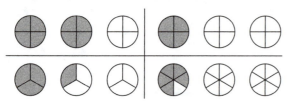

PART B: STRUCTURED BOARD PRESENTATION

1. We're going to learn some rules so we can tell if a fraction equals one whole or equals more or less than one whole without drawing a picture.

2. First rule: A fraction equals one whole when the top number and bottom number are the same. When does a fraction equal one whole?

   (Write on board:)

   $\dfrac{4}{4}$

   STUDENTS: when the top number and bottom number are the same

3. *(Point to the fraction.)* Does this fraction equal one whole?

   STUDENTS: yes

   How do you know?

   STUDENTS: the top number and bottom number are the same.

   (Repeat step 3 with the problems below.)

   $\dfrac{7}{4}$ $\dfrac{2}{3}$ $\dfrac{5}{5}$ $\dfrac{1}{4}$ $\dfrac{8}{8}$

4. Listen to these new rules: If the top number is *more* than the bottom number, the fraction equals *more* than one whole. When does a fraction equal more than one whole?

   STUDENTS: when the top number is more than the bottom number

   If the top number is *less* than the bottom number, the fraction equals *less* than one whole. When does a fraction equal less than one whole?

   STUDENTS: when the top number is less than the bottom number

5. *(Write on board:)*

   $\dfrac{3}{5}$

   Is the top number the same as the bottom number?

   STUDENTS: no

   So does the fraction equal one whole?
   Is the top number more or less than the bottom number?

   STUDENTS: no
   less

   So does the fraction equal more or less than one whole?
   How do you know?

   STUDENTS: less than one whole
   The top number is less than the bottom number.

   Yes, 5 parts in each whole and only 3 parts are used.

   (Repeat step 5 with the problems below.)
   $\dfrac{3}{4}$ $\dfrac{3}{3}$ $\dfrac{3}{2}$ $\dfrac{4}{5}$ $\dfrac{4}{4}$ $\dfrac{4}{2}$

FORMAT 12.5   (continued)

PART C: STRUCTURED WORKSHEET

TEACHER	STUDENTS

1. *(Give students worksheets with problems like these.)*

a. $\frac{5}{4}$ more equal less   b. $\frac{7}{7}$ more equal less   c. $\frac{3}{7}$ more equal less

2. In these problems you have to tell if a fraction is more than one whole, equals one whole, or is less than one whole.

3. Read the fraction in problem a.   Five-fourths

4. Does the fraction equal one whole?   no

5. Is the top number more or less than the bottom number?   more

   So does the fraction equal more or less than one whole?   more than one whole

   Put a circle around the word *more*.

   (Repeat steps 1-4 with remaining problems.)

FORMAT 12.6   **Format for Reading and Writing Mixed Numbers**

PART A: PICTORIAL DEMONSTRATIONS

TEACHER	STUDENTS

1. *(Write the following diagrams on the board.)*

2. You're going to learn how to write the fraction in this picture a new way.

3. First, let's write the fraction the old way. How many parts in each whole? *(Pause.)*   4

   Where do I write it? Do it.   on the bottom

4. How many parts are used? *(Pause.)*   14

   Where do I write it? Do it.   on the top

5. Now we're going to write the fraction as a mixed number. A mixed number has a whole number, and a fraction. What does a mixed number have?   a whole number and a fraction

6. First we count the number of wholes used up. Count as I point. How many wholes are used up?   3

   So I write 3 in the box. *(Write 3 in the box.)*

7. Now we write the fraction to tell about the whole not used up. *(Point to the last circle.)*

(continued on next page)

FORMAT 12.6   (continued)

TEACHER	STUDENTS

What do I write as the bottom number in the fraction?
(Write 4.)

To correct: There are four parts in each whole.

4

What do I write as the top number in the fraction?
(Write 2.)

2

To correct: There are two parts shaded. The fraction that tells about the whole not used up says two-fourths.

8. The mixed number says three and two-fourths. What does the mixed number say?
There are three whole units used up and 2/4 of another whole unit used up.

3 and $\frac{2}{4}$

(Repeat steps 2-7 with these examples.)

a.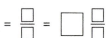

b.

c.

PART B: STRUCTURED BOARD PRESENTATION

1. *(Write the following on the board.)*

   $2\frac{1}{3}$

2. A mixed number is a whole number and a fraction. What is a mixed number?

   a whole number and a fraction

3. *(Point to:)*

   $2\frac{1}{3}$

   What's the whole number?

   2

   What's the fraction?

   $\frac{1}{3}$

4. Read the mixed number.

   two and one third

   (Repeat steps 2 and 3 with these problems.)

   $5\frac{2}{7}$ $7\frac{1}{2}$ $3\frac{4}{5}$ $6\frac{1}{2}$

FORMAT 12.6 (continued)

TEACHER	STUDENTS

PART C: STRUCTURED WORKSHEET

(Give students lined paper.)

1. Listen: two *and* three-fourths. Say that.
   What is the whole number?

   I write 2 so that it takes up the whole space:

   $\overline{2}$

2. Listen: two and three-fourths. What's the fraction?

   I write the fraction line in the middle of the space next to the 2. Then I write the fraction numbers small. *(Write the number.)*

   $2\frac{3}{4}$

3. What is the mixed number?

   (Repeat steps 1-3 with the problems below.)

   $7\frac{1}{2}$ $4\frac{2}{5}$

4. Now it's your turn. You're going to write the mixed number five and two-thirds. What mixed number are you going to write?

5. Listen: $5\frac{2}{3}$. What is the whole number? Write it. Make it big so that it touches both lines. *(Monitor responses.)*

6. Listen: $5\frac{2}{3}$. What is the fraction? Put the fraction line right in the middle of the space next to the 5. Then write $\frac{2}{3}$.

   Write the numbers small.

   (Repeat step 2 with these numbers.)

   $7\frac{2}{4}$ $9\frac{1}{3}$ $7\frac{1}{2}$ $5\frac{3}{8}$

7. Listen: $3\frac{4}{6}$. Say it.

   Write it. *(Monitor responses. Repeat step 7 with these numbers.)*

   $7\frac{2}{4}$ $9\frac{1}{3}$ $7\frac{1}{2}$ $5\frac{3}{8}$

STUDENTS responses:

1. two and three-fourths
   2

2. three-fourths

3. two and three-fourths

4. five and two-thirds

5. 5

6. $\frac{2}{3}$

7. three and four-sixths

FORMAT 12.7   **Preskill: Constructing Fractions Equal to 1**

PART A: STRUCTURED BOARD PRESENTATION

TEACHER	**STUDENTS**
1. Here's a rule: When the top number is the same as the bottom, the fraction equals one whole. When does a fraction equal one whole?	when the top number is the same as the bottom number
2. *(Write the following on the board.)*	

$$\frac{\square}{5}$$

What number is on the bottom of this fraction?	5
What fraction with a 5 as a denominator equals one whole?	$\frac{5}{5}$

To correct: A fraction equals 1 when the top number is the same as the bottom number. What's the bottom number? What must the top number be? *(Repeat step 2.)*

Yes, five-fifths equals one whole.

(Repeat step 2 with these problems.)

$$\frac{\square}{8} \qquad \frac{\square}{3} \qquad \frac{\square}{6} \qquad \frac{\square}{9}$$

PART B: STRUCTURED WORKSHEET

1. *(Give students worksheets with examples like these.)*

   a. $1 = \dfrac{\square}{4}$ b. $1 = \dfrac{\square}{7}$

   c. $1 = \dfrac{\square}{4}$ d. $1 = \dfrac{\square}{7}$

2. When does a fraction equal one whole?	when the top number is the same as the bottom number
3. Touch problem a. It says 1 equals how many fourths? Read the problem.	1 equals how many fourths?
4. Tell me the fraction with 4 as a denominator that equals one whole. Yes, four-fourths equals one whole.	$\frac{4}{4}$
5. Fill in the missing number.	Students write 4 in box.

   (Repeat steps 1-4 with remaining problems.)

FORMAT 12.8 Format for Computing Equivalent Fractions

PART A: PICTORIAL DEMONSTRATIONS

TEACHER	STUDENTS
1. Fractions are equivalent when they show the same amounts. *(Draw these figures on clear plastic sheets. The circles should have the same radius. Use a different color for each figure.)*	

TEACHER	STUDENTS
2. This is a picture of 4/8. *(Point to first figure.)* This is a picture of ½. *(Point to second figure.)*	
3. Would a person who had 4/8 of a pie have the same portion as a person who had ½ a pie?	yes
To correct: (Place one figure on top of the other. Outline the shaded part.) See, the shaded portion is the same size in both pies.	
4. So are 4/8 and ½ equivalent fractions?	yes
5. Yes, 4/8 and ½ both use up the same amount of a whole. *(Repeat steps 1-3 with these pairs.)*	

a.
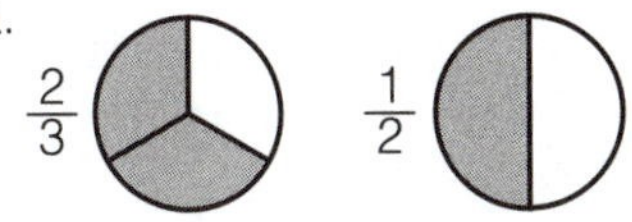

b.
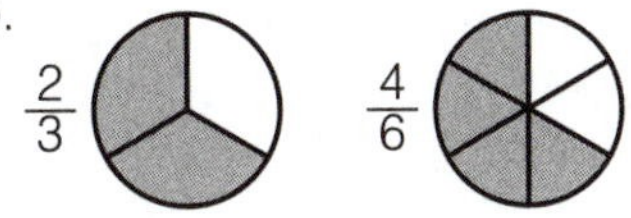

c.
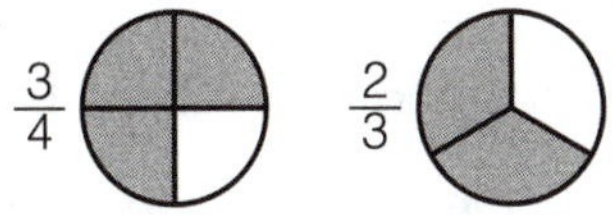

PART B: MULTIPLYING OR DIVIDING BY 1

TEACHER	STUDENTS
1. When you multiply by 1, the answer equals the number you start with.	
2. *(Write the following problem on the board.)* $\frac{3}{8} \times 1$	
What number do we start with?	$\frac{3}{8}$
Will our answer equal 3/8?	yes
How do you know?	We are multiplying by 1.
(Repeat step 2 with these problems.) $\frac{1}{2} \times 1$ $\frac{1}{4} \times 5$	

(continued on next page)

FORMAT 12.8   (continued)

TEACHER	STUDENTS

3. Here's a rule about fractions: When you multiply by a fraction that equals 1, your answer equals the number you start with. Listen, again. *(Repeat rule.)*

4. *(Write the following problem on the board.)*

$$\frac{4}{8} \times \frac{2}{2}$$

What fraction do we start with?

What are we multiplying ⅘ by?

$\frac{4}{8}$

$\frac{2}{2}$

5. Does ⅔ equal 1?   yes

So will our answer equal ⅘?   yes

How do you know?   We are multiplying by a fraction that equals 1.

(Repeat steps 4 and 5 with the problems below.)

$$\frac{4}{8} \times \frac{4}{4} \qquad \frac{5}{6} \times \frac{3}{6}$$

$$\frac{5}{6} \times \frac{2}{3} \qquad \frac{3}{9} \times \frac{8}{8}$$

$$\frac{7}{2} \times \frac{9}{9} \qquad \frac{2}{4} \times \frac{4}{4}$$

PART C: STRUCTURED BOARD PROBLEMS

1. *(Write the following problem on the board.)*

$$\frac{2}{3}\left(\ \ \right) = \frac{\square}{12}$$

2. We don't change the value of a fraction when we multiply it by a fraction that equals 1.

3. These parentheses mean times. We're going to multiply ⅔ by a fraction that equals 1. We have to figure out the fraction that equals 1.

4. We are going to end with a fraction that has the same value as ⅔. *(Point to 12.)*

What's the bottom number of the fraction we end with?   12

Three times what number equals 12?   4

So we multiply by a fraction that has a denominator of 4.

5. *(Write 4 inside parentheses.)*

$$\frac{2}{3}\left(\frac{}{4}\right) = \frac{\square}{12}$$

FORMAT 12.8   (continued)

TEACHER	STUDENTS

6. The fraction inside the parentheses must equal 1. If the bottom number is 4 what must the top number be?

    (Write a four in the numerator inside parentheses.)

$$\frac{2}{3}\left(\frac{4}{4}\right) = \frac{\square}{12}$$

    Yes, we multiply ⅔ by ⁴⁄₄. What do we multiply ⅔ by?

Students: 4

Students: $\frac{4}{4}$

7. We figured out the fraction of 1 we're multiplying by. Let's multiply and figure out how many twelfths, ⅔ equals . Two times four equals how many? *(Pause.)*

Students: 8

    (Write the problem on the board.)

$$\frac{2}{3}\left(\frac{4}{4}\right) = \frac{8}{12}$$

8. We multiplied ⅔ by a fraction that equals 1 and ended with ⁸⁄₁₂; ⅔ has to equal ⁸⁄₁₂.

    (Repeat steps 3-7 with these problems.)

$$\frac{3}{5} = \frac{\square}{10} \qquad \frac{2}{3} = \frac{\square}{15} \qquad \frac{2}{7} = \frac{\square}{21}$$

PART D: STRUCTURED WORKSHEET

1. *(Give students a worksheet with problems similar to these.)*

    a. $\frac{3}{4}\left(\frac{}{}\right) = \frac{\square}{8}$ b. $\frac{5}{9}\left(\frac{}{}\right) = \frac{\square}{27}$ c. $\frac{1}{4}\left(\frac{}{}\right) = \frac{\square}{20}$

    d. $\frac{2}{5}\left(\frac{}{}\right) = \frac{\square}{20}$ e. $\frac{3}{5}\left(\frac{}{}\right) = \frac{\square}{35}$ f. $\frac{2}{3}\left(\frac{}{}\right) = \frac{\square}{12}$

2. Touch problem a.

3. It says ¾ equals how many eighths? What does the problem say?

Students: ¾ equals how many eighths?

4. We have to multiply ¾ by a fraction that equals 1. What is the bottom number of the fraction we start with?

Students: 4

    What is the bottom number of the fraction we end with?

Students: 8

    Four times what number equals 8?

Students: 2

    Write 2 as the bottom number in the parentheses.

5. We're multiplying ¾ by a fraction that equals 1. What fraction with a denominator of 2 equals one whole?

Students: two halves

    Write 2 as a numerator in the parentheses.

(continued on next page)

FORMAT 12.8   (continued)

TEACHER	STUDENTS

6. We figured out the fraction of 1. Now what do we multiply to figure out the missing numerator?

3×2

What is 3×2? *(Pause, signal.)*

Write 6 in the box.

6

7. What fraction equals ¾?

$\dfrac{6}{8}$

8. How do you know that ¾ equals ⁶⁄₈?

We multiplied by a fraction that equals 1

(Repeat steps 1-7 with remaining problems.)

PART E: LESS-STRUCTURED WORKSHEET

1. *(Give students a worksheet with problems like the one below. Note that parentheses aren't written in.)*

   a. $\dfrac{5}{6} = \dfrac{\square}{12}$ b. $\dfrac{3}{4} = \dfrac{\square}{20}$ c. $\dfrac{1}{3} = \dfrac{\square}{12}$

   d. $\dfrac{1}{5} = \dfrac{\square}{20}$ e. $\dfrac{2}{5} = \dfrac{\square}{15}$ f. $\dfrac{3}{7} = \dfrac{\square}{14}$

2. Touch problem a. Read the problem.

$\dfrac{5}{6} = \dfrac{\square}{12}$

3. We must multiply ⁵⁄₆ by a fraction that equals 1. To keep the fractions equal, put parentheses next to ⁵⁄₆.

4. Look at the numbers and get ready to tell me what we must multiply ⁵⁄₆ by. *(Pause.)*

two halves

   To correct: What is the bottom number of the fraction we start with? What is the bottom number of the fraction we end with? Six times what number equals 12? That's the denominator. The fraction we're multiplying equals 1. What fraction goes in the parentheses?

   Write two halves in the parentheses.

5. Multiply and write in the missing numerator.

6. What fraction does ⁵⁄₆ equal?

$\dfrac{10}{12}$

(Repeat steps 1-5 with remaining problems.)

FORMAT 12.9   **Preskill: Format for Determining Factors**

PART A: INTRODUCING THE CONCEPT

TEACHER	**STUDENTS**

1. *(Write the problems below on the board.)*
   $5 \times 3 = 15$
   $9 \times 2 = 18$
   $7 \times 6 = 42$

2. Factors are numbers that are multiplied together.

3. Read the first problem. $5 \times 3 = 15$

   What numbers are being multiplied?   5 and 3

   So 5 and 3 are factors of 15. What are two factors of 15?   5 and 3

4. Look at the board and tell me two factors of 18.   9 and 2

5. Look at the board and tell me two factors of 42.   7 and 6

PART B: STRUCTURED BOARD PRESENTATION

1. *(Write the following diagram on the board.)*
   12 (_____ _____ _____ _____ _____ _____)

2. We want to list all of the factors for 12 beginning with the
   biggest factor. Listen: A number multiplied by 1 always
   equals itself. So is 12 a factor of 12?   yes

   Yes, 12 is a factor of 12. What number times 12 equals 12?   1

   Twelve and 1 are factors of 12; 12 is the biggest factor of
   12; 1 is the smallest factor of 12. *(Write 12 and 1:*
   $\underline{\quad 12 \quad}$ _____ _____ _____ $\underline{\quad 1 \quad}$ *)*

3. Let's find the next largest number we can multiply and end
   with 12. I'll say some numbers. You say stop when I come
   to a number that is a factor of 12. Listen: 10 *(pause),*
   9 *(pause),* 8 *(pause),* 7 *(pause),* 6 *(pause),* . . . Yes, 6 is   stop
   the next biggest factor of 12.

   To correct: If students say stop at 10, 9, 8, 7. say, We
   can't multiply that number and end with 12. *If students
   don't say stop at 6, say,* We can multiply 6 and end with 12.
   So 6 is a factor of 12.

   6 times what number equals 12?   2
   So 2 is the other factor that goes with 12. *(Write 6 and 2:*
   $\underline{\quad 12 \quad} \underline{\quad 6 \quad}$ _____ _____ $\underline{\quad 2 \quad} \underline{\quad 1 \quad}$ *)*

3. Let's find the next largest factor of 12. I'll say some
   numbers. You say stop when I come to a factor of 12.

   Listen: 5 *(pause),* 4 *(pause)* . . .   stop
   Yes 4 is a factor of 12. Four times what other number
   equals 12?   3
   So 3 is the other factor that goes with 4.

   (Write 4 and 3: 12 6 4 3 2 1)

(continued on next page)

FORMAT 12.9   (continued)

TEACHER	STUDENTS
Tell me all the factors of 12.	12, 6, 4, 3, 2, 1
(Repeat Part B with other new example(s) for that day.)	

PART C: STRUCTURED WORKSHEET

1. *(Give students a worksheet with the following directions and problems.)*
   List all the factors for each number.
   List the biggest factors first.
   a. 10 ____ ____ ____ ____
   b. 12 ____ ____ ____ ____
   c. 7 ____ ____

2. Touch a. There are four spaces next to the 10. That means there are four numbers that are factors for 10.

3. What is the biggest factor of 10?	10
What is the other factor that goes with 10 to equal 10?	1
Write 10 in the first space. Write 1 in the last space.	
4. What is the next biggest factor of 10? *(Pause.)*	5
What is the other factor that goes with 5 to equal 10? *(Pause.)*	2
Write 5 and 2 in the next two spaces.	
5. Say all the factors of 10.	10, 5, 2, 1

(Repeat steps 1-4 with new target numbers. Have students do the rest of problems on their own.)

FORMAT 12.10   Format for Determining the Greatest Common Factor (GCF)

PART A: STRUCTURED WORKSHEET

TEACHER	STUDENTS
1. *(Present students with a worksheet similar to the one below.)*	
a. What is the greatest common factor of 12 and 16? _____	
b. What is the greatest common factor of 10 and 5? _____	
c. What is the greatest common factor of 4 and 7? _____	
d. What is the greatest common factor of 10 and 15? _____	
e. What is the greatest common factor of 18 and 9? _____	
f. What is the greatest common factor of 12 and 9? _____	
2. Find problem a on your worksheet. Read the directions.	What is the greatest common factor of 12 and 16?
Let's find the greatest common factor of 12 and 16. The greatest common factor is the largest number that is a factor of 12 and 16. What is the largest number that is a factor of 12?	12

FORMAT 12.10   (continued)

TEACHER	STUDENTS
Is 12 a factor of 16?	no
Twelve cannot be the greatest common factor of 12 and 16. Why?	because 12 is not a factor of 16
3. What is the next largest factor of 12? *(Pause.)*	*6*
Is 6 a factor of 16? *(Pause.)*	no
So 6 is not a factor of 12 and 16. Why?	because 6 is not a factor of 16
4. What is the next largest factor of 12? *(Pause.)*	*4*
Is 4 also a factor of 16? *(Pause.)*	yes
So what number is the greatest common factor of 12 and 16?	4
5. Write 4.	

(Repeat steps 1–4 with remaining examples.)

FORMAT 12.11   Format for Reducing Fractions

PART A: STRUCTURED BOARD PRESENTATION

TEACHER	STUDENTS
1. *(Write the following problem on the board.)* $$\frac{8}{12} = \left(\ \ \right)\underline{\quad}$$	
2. We're going to reduce this fraction. We reduce by pulling out the greatest common factor of the numerator and denominator. How do we reduce a fraction?	pull out the greatest common factor of the numerator and denominator.
3. We want to reduce $\frac{8}{12}$. What is the greatest common factor of 8 and 12? *(Pause.)*	4
To correct: Tell correct answer. Explain why student's answer is incorrect.	
4. So we pull out the fraction $\frac{4}{4}$. What fraction do we pull out of $\frac{8}{12}$?	$\frac{4}{4}$
(Write the new fraction on the board.) $$\frac{8}{12} = \left(\frac{4}{4}\right)\underline{\quad}$$	
5. Let's figure out the top number of the reduced fraction. *(Point to symbols as you read.)* Eight equals four times what number? *(Pause.)*	2
(Write the 2.) $$\frac{8}{12} = \left(\frac{4}{4}\right)\frac{2}{\quad}$$	

(continued on next page)

FORMAT 12.11   (continued)

TEACHER	STUDENTS

6. Let's figure out the bottom number of the reduced fraction. *(Point to symbols as you read.)* Twelve equals four times what number? *(Pause, signal.)*
   (Write the 3.)

   $$\frac{8}{12} = \left(\frac{4}{4}\right)\frac{2}{3}$$

   3

7. The fraction in parentheses equals 1. We don't change the value of a fraction when we multiply by 1. So we can cross out ¼. *(Cross out.)* When we pull out the fraction of 1, the reduced fraction is ⅔. What is the reduced fraction?

   $$\frac{2}{3}$$

8. Read the statement.

   (Repeat steps 1–7 with these problems.)

   $$\frac{8}{12} = \frac{2}{3}$$

   $$\frac{15}{20} = (\ ) \underline{\quad} \qquad \frac{9}{36} = (\ ) \underline{\quad} \qquad \frac{16}{24} = (\ ) \underline{\quad}$$

PART B: STRUCTURED WORKSHEET

1. *(Give students a worksheet with problems like those below.)*

   a. $\dfrac{10}{15} = (\ ) \underline{\quad}$ b. $\dfrac{12}{16} = (\ ) \underline{\quad}$

   c. $\dfrac{8}{24} = (\ ) \underline{\quad}$

2. We're going to reduce these fractions. How do you reduce fractions?

   pull out the greatest common factor of the numerator and denominator.

3. Touch problem a. Read the fraction.

   ten-fifteenths

4. What is the greatest common factor of 10 and 15? *(Pause.)*

   5

5. So what fraction do you write in the parentheses?

   Write it.

   $$\frac{5}{5}$$

6. The numbers across the top of the fraction say 10 equals 5 times what number? What do the numbers across the top say?

   10 equals 5 times what number

7. What do the numbers across the bottom say?

   15 equals 5 times what number

8. Fill in the numerator and denominator in the reduced fraction. *(Pause.)*

   Students write 2 and 3.

   Cross out the fraction of 1 in the parentheses.

   Students cross out $\dfrac{5}{5}$

9. What is the reduced fraction?

   $$\frac{2}{3}$$

10. Read the statement.

    (Repeat steps 1–9 with remaining problems.)

    $$\frac{10}{15} = \frac{2}{3}$$

FORMAT 12.11   (continued)

TEACHER	STUDENTS

PART C: LESS-STRUCTURED WORKSHEET

1. *(Present a worksheet like the following. Note that parentheses are not written.)* Reduce these fractions:

a. $\dfrac{15}{20}$ b. $\dfrac{8}{12}$ c. $\dfrac{6}{18}$

d. $\dfrac{4}{7}$ e. $\dfrac{8}{16}$ f. $\dfrac{5}{8}$

2. How do you reduce a fraction?

Pull out the greatest common factor of the numerator and denominator.

3. Read fraction a.

Fifteen-twentieths

4. Make an equal sign. Then write parentheses on the other side of the equal.

Students write $\dfrac{15}{20} = \left(\quad \right)$

5. What fraction are you going to write in the parentheses? *(Pause.)*

$\dfrac{5}{5}$

   To correct: What is the greatest common factor of _____ and _____ ? *(Repeat step 4.)*

6. Write five-fifths in the parentheses. Then figure out the reduced fraction. *(Pause.)*

7. Cross out the fraction of 1.

8. What is the reduced fraction?

$\dfrac{3}{4}$

   To correct: Read the top numbers of the fractions. What's the answer? Read the bottom numbers of the fractions. What's the answer?

9. Read the statement.

$\dfrac{15}{20} = \dfrac{3}{4}$

   (Repeat steps 1–8 with remaining problems.)

FORMAT 12.12   **Format for Converting Improper Fractions to Mixed Numbers**

PART A: PICTORIAL DEMONSTRATION

TEACHER	STUDENTS

1. *(Write the following diagram on the board.)*

$\dfrac{13}{5}$ ◯ ◯ ◯

2. *(Point to $^{13}\!/_{5}$.)* Read this fraction.

thirteen-fifths

3. Does $^{13}\!/_{5}$ equal more than one whole unit?

yes

4. Let's make a picture and see how many whole units $^{13}\!/_{5}$ makes.

(continued on next page)

FORMAT 12.12 (continued)

TEACHER	STUDENTS

5. How many parts in each whole? *(Draw the following circles on the board.)* — 5

6. How many parts do we use up? *(Shade in 13 parts.)* — 13

7. Let's see how many whole units are used. *(Point to first circle.)* Is this whole unit all used up? — yes

(Point to second circle.) Is this whole unit all used up? — yes

(Point to third circle.) Is this whole unit all used up? — no

How many whole units are used up? — 2

Two whole units are used up. Let's look at the last unit and count. How many parts are used up? — 3

And how many parts in each whole? — 5

So, we can say ⅗ of a unit. We have 2 whole units and ⅗ of another unit. *(Write 2 ⅗.)*

PART B: STRUCTURED BOARD PRESENTATION

1. We're going to learn a fast way to figure out how many whole units a fraction makes. We divide by the number of parts in each whole unit. What do we do to figure out how many whole units? — Divide by the number of parts in each whole unit.

(Write the following on the board.)

$$\frac{13}{5}$$

Read this fraction. — thirteen-fifteenths

Is this fraction equal to, more than, or less than one unit? — more than one unit

2. I want to figure out how many whole units this fraction makes. How many parts in each whole? — 5
So I divide by 5.

(Write the problem.)

$$5\overline{)13} \quad \square\frac{\square}{\square}$$

3. Let's divide. *(Point to box.)* How many 5s in 13? — 2
(Write 2.) We have two whole units. *(Point under 13.)* What number do I write here? — 10

FORMAT 12.12   (continued)

TEACHER	STUDENTS

(Write –10 under 13.)

4. We use up 10 parts in two wholes. Now let's subtract and see how many parts we have left. What is 13 – 10?   3

5. Since we started with a fraction, we write the remainder as a fraction. Remember, there are five parts in each whole. *(Point to 5 in 5)‾13‾.)*

So we write 5 on the bottom of the fraction. *(Write 5.)* How many parts are remaining?   3

So I write 3 on the top of the fraction.

(Write the 3.)

6. Tell me the mixed number for the fraction ¹³⁄₅ . $2\dfrac{3}{5}$

Yes, 2⅗ is the same as ¹³⁄₅.

7. *(Write = 2⅗ next to ¹³⁄₅.)*

Read the statement. $\dfrac{13}{5} = 2\dfrac{3}{5}$

(Repeat steps 1–7 with ¹²⁄₇ and ⁹⁄₄.)

PART C: STRUCTURED WORKSHEET

1. *(Give students a worksheet with problems like the following ones.)*

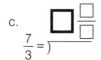

2. Touch problem a. Read the fraction.   eleven-fourths

Is ¹¹⁄₄ less than 1, equal to 1, or more than 1?   more than 1

So you have to change ¹¹⁄₄ to a mixed number. How many parts in each whole? So you divide 4 into 11.   4

(continued on next page)

FORMAT 12.12 (continued)

TEACHER	STUDENTS
3. Write the division problem.	Students write 4)$\overline{11}$
How many 4s in 11?	2
We can make two whole units. Write the 2 in the big box. Multiply and subtract to find how many parts are left. How many parts are left?	3
4. Now let's figure out the fraction remainder. The bottom number of the fraction tells how many parts in each whole. How many parts in each whole?	4
So write 4 on the bottom of the fraction.	Students write 4 in the bottom box of the fraction
What do you write for the top number? Write it.	3
5. What mixed number does $^{11}\!/_4$ equal?	$2\dfrac{3}{4}$
Say the whole statement.	$\dfrac{11}{4} = 2\dfrac{3}{4}$

(Repeat steps 1–4 with remaining problems.)

PART D: LESS-STRUCTURED WORKSHEET

1. *(Present a worksheet like the following.)* Rewrite the fractions that equal more than 1 as mixed numbers.	

a. $\dfrac{12}{5}$ b. $\dfrac{3}{4}$

c. $\dfrac{15}{4}$ d. $\dfrac{5}{5}$

2. Some of these fractions equal more than one whole unit. If a fraction equals more than one whole unit, change it to a mixed number. What are you going to do if a fraction equals more than one unit?	Change it to a mixed number.
If the fraction does not equal more than one group, don't do anything.	
3. Touch problem a. Read the fraction.	twelve-fifths
Does the fraction equal more or less than one unit?	more than one unit
The fraction equals more than one unit, so what must you do?	Change it to a mixed number
What do you divide by?	5
Say the division problem. Write the problem and work it. *(Pause.)* Remember to write the whole number as a big number and the numerator and denominator small.	5 goes into 12
4. Twelve-fifths equals what mixed number?	$2\dfrac{2}{5}$

(Repeat steps 1–3 with remaining problems.)

FORMAT 12.13   **Format for Converting Mixed Numbers to Improper Fractions**

PART A: CONVERTING WHOLE NUMBERS

TEACHER	**STUDENTS**

Board Presentation

1. *(Write the following problem on the board.)*

$$6 = \frac{\square}{4}$$

2. This problem says six wholes equal how many fourths? What does the problem say?

    STUDENTS: 6 wholes equal how many fourths?

3. We want to figure out how many parts are used when we have six wholes. How many parts in each whole?

    STUDENTS: 4

4. We're talking about the same number again and again, so we multiply 6 × 4. What numbers do we multiply?

    STUDENTS: 6 × 4

5. What is 6 × 4? *(Pause, signal.) (Write 24 in box.)*

    STUDENTS: 24

6. Yes, six whole units equal 24 fourths. If we use six whole units and there are 4 parts in each unit, we use 24 parts.

(Repeat steps 1–4 with the problems below.)

$$5 = \frac{\square}{3} \qquad 2 = \frac{\square}{6} \qquad 4 = \frac{\square}{5} \qquad 6 = \frac{\square}{3}$$

Worksheet

1. *(Give students worksheets with problems such as the ones below.)*

    a. $5 = \dfrac{\square}{3}$ b. $2 = \dfrac{\square}{4}$

    c. $7 = \dfrac{\square}{2}$ d. $5 = \dfrac{\square}{9}$

2. Touch problem a.

3. Read the problem.

    STUDENTS: 5 equals how many thirds?

4. How many parts in each whole unit?
   How many whole units?

    STUDENTS: 3
    STUDENTS: 5

5. What do we do to figure out how many parts are used up?

    STUDENTS: multiply

   Yes, we multiply 5 × 3. Multiply and write your answer in the box.

6. Five equals how many thirds?
   Say the whole statement.

    STUDENTS: 15 thirds
    STUDENTS: 5 = 15 thirds

   (Repeat steps 1–5 with half the problems, and then tell students to do the rest by themselves.)

PART B: STRUCTURED BOARD PRESENTATION

1. *(Write the following problem on the board.)*

$$6\frac{1}{4} = \frac{}{4}$$

2. This problem says 6¼ equals how many fourths. What does this problem say?

    STUDENTS: $6\frac{1}{4}$ equals how many fourths?

(continued on next page)

FORMAT 12.13   (continued)

TEACHER	STUDENTS
3. First we figure out how many fourths in six whole units. Then we add on ¼. *(Write + between 6 and ¼.)* What do we do first?	Figure out how many fourths in six whole units.
4. There are six wholes with four parts in each whole. What do I do to figure how many parts are used?	Multiply 6 × 4.
5. What is six times four? *(Pause.)*	24

(Write the 24.)

$$6\frac{1}{4} = \frac{24}{4}$$

6. How many parts are used in the last whole?	1
7. I add one part. *(Write +1 in the numerator.)*	

$$6\frac{1}{4} = \frac{24 + 1}{4} =$$

8. What is 24 + 1?	25

(Write the following on the board.)

$$\frac{25}{4}$$

9. So 6¼ equals ²⁵⁄₄. Say that.

$6\frac{1}{4}$ equals $\frac{25}{4}$

(Repeat steps 1–8 with these fractions.)

$$3\frac{2}{5} \qquad 7\frac{3}{4} \qquad 2\frac{3}{7} \qquad 5\frac{1}{4}$$

PART C: STRUCTURED WORKSHEET

1. *(Present a worksheet like the one below.)*
   Convert these mixed numbers to improper fractions.

   a. $3\frac{1}{2}$ = _____ = _____

   b. $7\frac{3}{5}$ = _____ = _____

   c. $4\frac{2}{5}$ = _____ = _____

   d. $2\frac{3}{4}$ = _____ = _____

2. Read the mixed number in problem a.	$3\frac{1}{2}$
3. How many parts in each whole unit?	2
Write 2 as the denominator in the new fraction.	Students write 2.

FORMAT 12.13   (continued)

TEACHER	STUDENTS
4. First we see how many halves in three whole units. Then we add ½. How do we figure out how many halves in three wholes? *(Pause.)*	Multiply 3×2.
How many halves in three wholes? *(Pause.)*	6
Write 6.	Students write 6.
5. How many parts in the last whole?	1
Write +1.	Students write $\dfrac{6+1}{2}$
6. What is $^6\!/_2$ plus ½?	$\dfrac{7}{2}$
Write equals $^7\!/_2$.	Students write $= \dfrac{7}{2}$.
7. What fraction does 3½ equal?	$\dfrac{7}{2}$
(Repeat steps 1–6 with remaining problems.)	

FORMAT 12.14   **Format for Adding and Subtracting Fractions with Like Denominators**

PART A: PICTORIAL DEMONSTRATION

TEACHER	STUDENTS
1. *(Draw the following circles and lines on the board.)*	

$$\underline{\quad} \;+\; \underline{\quad} \;=\; \underline{\quad}$$

TEACHER	STUDENTS
2. Let's write a problem that will tell us how many parts are used in these wholes.	
3. How many parts in each whole?	4
(Write the denominators.)	

$$\frac{\quad}{4} + \frac{\quad}{4} = \frac{\quad}{4}$$

We're talking about wholes with four parts in each whole.

4. *(Point to first circle.)* How many parts are used in this whole?   3

(continued on next page)

FORMAT 12.14   (continued)

TEACHER	STUDENTS

(Write the following on the board.)

$\dfrac{3}{4}$

(Point to second circle.) How many parts are used in this whole?   2

(Write the following on the board.)

$\dfrac{3}{4} + \dfrac{2}{4} =$

5. How many parts are used altogether?   5

(Write the following on the board.)

$\dfrac{5}{4}$

6. What does ¾ + ²⁄₄ equal? $\dfrac{5}{4}$

(Repeat steps 1–5 with the problem below.)

_____ + _____ = _____

PART B: STRUCTURED BOARD PRESENTATION

1. We can only add and subtract fractions with the same number of parts in each whole. Listen again. *(Repeat rule. Write this problem.)*

$\dfrac{3}{4} + \dfrac{2}{5} =$

2. Read this problem.

3. *(Point to ¾.)* How many parts in each whole?   4

   (Point to ²⁄₅.) How many parts in each whole?   5

4. Can we add these fractions?   no

5. Right. We can only add fractions that have the same bottom number.

(Repeat steps 2–5 with the problems below.)

$\dfrac{3}{5} + \dfrac{2}{5}$ $\dfrac{5}{7} - \dfrac{3}{9}$ $\dfrac{3}{9} + \dfrac{3}{5}$

$\dfrac{4}{7} + \dfrac{2}{7}$ $\dfrac{5}{7} - \dfrac{5}{9}$ $\dfrac{4}{9} - \dfrac{3}{9}$

(Give individual turns.)

FORMAT 12.14   (continued)

TEACHER	STUDENTS

Part C: Structured Worksheet

1. *(Write the following problems on the board.)*

   a. $\dfrac{3}{5} + \dfrac{1}{5} =$ _____

   b. $\dfrac{3}{5} + \dfrac{2}{7} =$ _____

   c. $\dfrac{4}{7} - \dfrac{2}{7} =$ _____

   d. $\dfrac{5}{9} - \dfrac{2}{3} =$ _____

   e. $\dfrac{7}{9} \times \dfrac{1}{9} =$ _____

   f. $\dfrac{3}{4} - \dfrac{1}{4} =$ _____

   g. $\dfrac{6}{9} - \dfrac{2}{8} =$ _____

   h. $\dfrac{6}{9} + \dfrac{2}{9} =$ _____

   i. $\dfrac{5}{7} + \dfrac{3}{5} =$ _____

2. Remember, you can only add and subtract fractions that tell about the same number of parts in each whole.

3. Touch problem a. Read the problem. → $\dfrac{3}{5} + \dfrac{1}{5}$

4. Can we add these fractions the way they are now? → yes

   (If the answer to step 3 is no, say to students,) You can't work the problem, so cross it out. *(If the answer to step 3 is yes, do steps 4–6.)*

5. We're talking about fractions with five parts in each whole so the answer will have five parts in each group. Write 5 as the bottom number in the answer.

6. Look at the top numbers. They tell the number of parts used. What is 3 + 1? → 4

   So what do you write for the top number in the answer? Write it. → 4

7. Read the whole problem. → $\dfrac{3}{5} + \dfrac{1}{5} = \dfrac{4}{5}$

   (Repeat steps 1–6 for the remaining problems.)

Part D: Less Structured Worksheet

1. *(Give students a worksheet with a mix of four addition and four subtraction problems. About half of the problems should have like denominators.)*

2. Read the first problem. If you can work it, write the answer. If you can't work the problem, cross it out. *(Monitor student performance.)*

FORMAT 12.15   Preskill: Format for Finding the Least Common Multiple

PART A: STRUCTURED BOARD PRESENTATION

TEACHER	STUDENTS
1. *(Write the following numbers on the board.)* 3 6 9 12 15 18 5 10 15 20 25	
2. *(Point to 3.)* These numbers are multiples of 3. Say them.	3, 6, 9, 12, 15, 18
(Point to 5.) These numbers are multiples of 5. Say them.	5, 10, 15, 20, 25
3. What is the smallest number that is a multiple of 3 and 5?	15
Yes, 15 is the least common multiple of 3 and 5. *(Repeat steps 1 and 2 with these examples: 2 and 8, 6 and 8, 3 and 9.)*	

PART B: WORKSHEET PRESENTATION

1. *(Write the number which is the least common multiple for each pair of numbers.)*
   a. The LCM of 6 and 9 is _____.
   b. The LCM of 8 and 6 is _____.
   c. The LCM of 5 and 2 is _____.
   d. The LCM of 5 and 4 is _____.
   e. The LCM of 6 and 12 is _____.
   f. The LCM of 4 and 3 is _____ .
   g. The LCM of 6 and 2 is _____ .
   h. The LCM of 4 and 12 is _____ .
   i. The LCM of 5 and 3 is _____ .
   j. The LCM of 3 and 9 is _____ .

2. The instructions tell us to find the least common multiple of the numbers. LCM means least common multiple. In problem a you must find the least common multiple of 6 and 9. The least common multiple is the lowest number that is in both count-by series.

3. Say the numbers that are multiples of 6. *(Stop students at 30.)*	6, 12, 18, 24, 30
4. Say the numbers that are multiples of 9. *(Stop students at 45.)*	9, 18, 27, 36, 45
5. What is the least common multiple of 9 and 6? *(Pause, signal.)*	18

Write it in the space.

(Repeat steps 1–4 with several more problems, and then have students work the rest of the problems on their own.)

FORMAT 12.16   **Format for Adding and Subtracting Fractions with Unlike Denominators**

PART A: STRUCTURED BOARD PRESENTATION

TEACHER	**STUDENTS**

1. *(Write the following problem on the board.)*

$$\frac{2}{3} + \frac{1}{4} = \underline{\hspace{3cm}}$$

2. Read this problem.

$\frac{2}{3} + \frac{1}{4}$

   Can we add these fractions the way they are written?

no

3. To work this problem, we must rewrite the fractions so they both have the same denominator. First, we figure out the least common multiple of the denominators. What is the denominator of the first fraction?

3

   What is the denominator of the second fraction?

4

4. What is the least common multiple of 4 and 3? *(Pause, signal.)*

12

   To correct: Say the numbers that are multiples of 3. Say the numbers that are multiples of 4. What is the least common multiple?

5. We must rewrite each fraction as equivalent fractions with denominators of 12. *(Write 12 under each denominator.)*

$$\frac{2}{3} + \frac{1}{4}$$
12 12

   I want to rewrite ⅔ as a fraction that has 12 as a denominator. Remember, I don't want to change the value of ⅔. What fraction do I multiply ⅔ by to end with a fraction that has a denominator of 12? *(Pause, signal.)*

$\frac{4}{4}$

   To correct: What is the denominator of ⅔? What must I multiply 3 by to end with 12? So I must multiply ⅔ times ⁴⁄₄. What do I multiply ⅔ by?

   (Write ¼ in parentheses.)

$$\frac{2}{3}\left(\frac{4}{4}\right) + \frac{1}{4}$$
   12   12

   What is 2 × 4? *(Pause, signal.)*

8

   (Write 8.) What is 3 × 4? *(Pause, signal.)*

12

   (Cross out ⅔. Write the 12.)

$$\overset{8}{\cancel{\frac{2}{3}}}\left(\cancel{\frac{4}{4}}\right) + \frac{1}{4}$$
   12   12

   We rewrote ⅔ as ⁸⁄₁₂. What did we rewrite ⅔ as?

$\frac{8}{12}$

(continued on next page)

FORMAT 12.16   (continued)

TEACHER	STUDENTS

6. Now let's rewrite ¼ as a fraction that has 12 as a denominator. Remember, I don't want to change the value of ¼. What fraction must I multiply ¼ by? *(Pause, signal.)* $\frac{3}{3}$

   To correct: What is the denominator of ¼? What do I multiply 4 by to end with 12? So I must multiply ¼ by ⅔. What do I multiply ¼ by?

   (Write ⅓.)

   $$\frac{2}{3}\left(\frac{4}{4}\right) + \frac{1}{4}\left(\frac{3}{3}\right)$$
   (with 8 written above, 12 12 written below)

   What is 1 × 3?   3

   (Write 3.) What is 4 × 3?   12

   (Cross out ¼. Write ³⁄₁₂.)

   $$\frac{2}{3}\left(\frac{4}{4}\right) + \frac{1}{4}\left(\frac{3}{3}\right)$$
   (with 8 and 3 written above, 12 12 written below)

   We rewrote ¼ as ³⁄₁₂. What did we rewrite ¼ as? $\frac{3}{12}$

7. Now the denominators are the same and we can add. The problem now says ⁸⁄₁₂ + ³⁄₁₂. What does the problem say? $\frac{8}{12} + \frac{3}{12}$

8. What is ⁸⁄₁₂ + ³⁄₁₂? $\frac{11}{12}$

   (Repeat steps 1–7 with the problems below.)

   $$\frac{4}{5} - \frac{7}{10} \qquad \frac{3}{6} - \frac{1}{4} \qquad \frac{1}{9} + \frac{2}{3}$$

PART B: STRUCTURED WORKSHEET

1. *(Give students worksheets with problems like the ones below.)*

   a. $\frac{5}{6} - \frac{2}{4} =$ d. $\frac{5}{10} - \frac{2}{5} =$

   b. $\frac{2}{9} + \frac{2}{3} =$ e. $\frac{7}{9} - \frac{2}{3} =$

   c. $\frac{2}{3} - \frac{3}{5} =$ f. $\frac{2}{5} - \frac{1}{3} =$

2. Read problem a. $\frac{5}{6} - \frac{2}{4}$

   Can we work the problem the way it is?   no

   (If the answer is yes, tell the students to work the problem. If the answer is no, continue the format.)

   Why not?   The denominators aren't the same.

3. What are the denominators?   6 and 4

FORMAT 12.16   (continued)

TEACHER	STUDENTS
What is the least common multiple of 6 and 4? *(Pause, signal.)*	12
Write 12 under each fraction.	
4. The first fraction says ⅚. Write parentheses next to it. What fraction do you multiply ⅚ by so that you'll end with a denominator of 12? *(Pause, signal.)*	$\frac{2}{2}$
Write two halves in the parentheses.	
To correct: The denominator is 6; 6 times what number equals 12? So we must multiply a fraction that has 2 as a denominator. We don't want to change the value of ⅚ so we multiply it by ²⁄₂.	
Let's multiply 5/6 by two halves and write the new fraction. What is 5 times 2?	10
Write 10 over the fraction. Five-sixths equals how many twelfths?	10 twelfths
(Cross out ⅚.)	
5. The second fraction says ²⁄₄. Write parentheses next to it. What fraction do you multiply ²⁄₄ by so that you'll end with a denominator of 12? *(Pause, signal.)*	$\frac{3}{3}$
To correct: (Same as step 3.)	
Multiply ²⁄₄ by ³⁄₃ and write the new fraction. *(Pause.)* Two-fourths equals how many twelfths?	$\frac{6}{12}$
(Check students' papers.) Cross out 2/4.	
6. Read the problem saying the rewritten fractions.	$\frac{10}{12} - \frac{6}{12}$
Can you work the problem now?	yes
How do you know?	The denominators are the same.
7. Work the problem and write the answer.	
8. What is the answer?	$\frac{4}{12}$

PART C: LESS-STRUCTURED WORKSHEET

1. *(Give students a worksheet like that for structured worksheet exercise.)*

2. Read problem a. Can we work the problem the way it is? *(If the answer is yes, tell students to work the problem. If the answer is no, continue the format.)*

   Why not?

3. What is the least common multiple of the denominators? *(Pause, signal.)* Write it under the fraction.

4. What fraction will you multiply the first fraction by so that it will have a denominator of _____ ? *(Pause, signal.)*

5. What fraction will you multiply the second fraction by so that it has a denominator of _____ ? *(Pause, signal.)*

6. Rewrite the fractions and work the problem. *(Pause.)*

7. What is your answer?

FORMAT 12.17 Format for Multiplying Two Proper Fractions

PART A: STRUCTURED BOARD PRESENTATION

TEACHER	**STUDENTS**
1. *(Write the following problem on the board.)* $$\frac{3}{4} \times \frac{2}{5} =$$	
2. Read this problem.	Three-fourths times two-fifths equals what number?
3. We work times problems with fractions by multiplying top times the top and bottom times the bottom. How do we work times problems with fractions?	top times the top; bottom times the bottom
4. First we multiply top times the top. What is 3×2? *(Pause, signal.)* *(Write the 6.)* $$\frac{3}{4} \times \frac{2}{5} = \frac{6}{}$$	6
5. Now we multiply bottom times the bottom. What is 4×5? *(Pause, signal.)* *(Write the 20.)* $$\frac{3}{4} \times \frac{2}{5} = \frac{6}{20}$$	20
6. What does $\frac{3}{4} \times \frac{2}{5}$ equal? *(Repeat steps 1–5 with several more problems.)*	$\frac{6}{20}$

PART B: STRUCTURED WORKSHEET

1. *(Give students worksheets with a mix of multiplication, addition, and subtraction problems.)* a. $\frac{3}{4} + \frac{2}{4} = \frac{\square}{\square}$ b. $\frac{3}{2} \times \frac{4}{2} = \frac{\square}{\square}$ c. $\frac{6}{3} - \frac{1}{3} = \frac{\square}{\square}$ d. $\frac{6}{3} \times \frac{1}{3} = \frac{\square}{\square}$	
2. When you times fractions, you work top times top and bottom times bottom. When you times fractions what do you do?	top times top and bottom times bottom
3. But when you plus or minus fractions, you work only across the top. When you add or subtract fractions, what do you do?	Work only across the top.
4. What do you do when you add or subtract fractions?	Work across the top.
What do you do when you times fractions?	top times top and bottom times bottom
(Repeat step 3 until firm.)	
5. Touch problem a. Read the problem.	$\frac{3}{4} + \frac{2}{4}$
What type of problem is this?	plus
What do you do when you plus fractions?	Work across the top.
Work the problem. *(Pause.)* What's the answer? *(Repeat step 4 with remaining problems.)*	

FORMAT 12.18   Format for Multiplying a Fraction and a Whole Number

PART A: CONVERTING A WHOLE NUMBER TO A FRACTION

TEACHER	STUDENTS

1. Listen to this rule: We can change a whole number into a fraction by giving it a denominator of 1. How do we change a whole number into a fraction? — Give it a denominator of 1.

2. *(Write on board: 3.)* What number is this? — 3
   How do I change it into a fraction? — Give it a denominator of 1.
   Watch me change 3 into a fraction.

   (Write 1 under 3.)

   $\frac{3}{1}$

   A 3 over 1 is the same as 3. I'll draw a picture to show you that $\frac{3}{1}$ equals 3.

   (Draw the following circles.)

   $\frac{3}{1} =$

   We have three wholes used up.

3. *(Write on board: 5.)* How do I change 5 into a fraction? — Give it a denominator of 1.

   Yes, 5 over 1 equals 5 wholes. *(Write the fraction.)*

   $\frac{5}{1}$

   (Repeat step 3 with 2, 9, 4, 8.)

PART B: STRUCTURED BOARD

1. *(Write the following problem on the board.)*

   $\frac{3}{4} \times 8 =$ _____ $= \overline{)} = \square$

2. Listen to this rule about multiplying fractions: A fraction can only be multiplied by another fraction. Listen again.

   (Repeat the rule.)

3. Read this problem. *(Point to $\frac{3}{4}$.)* — $\frac{3}{4} \times 8$

   Is this fraction multiplied by another fraction? — no

   So before we can work the problem we have to change 8 into a fraction. How do I change 8 into a fraction? — Give it a denominator of 1.

   (Write the problem.)

   $\frac{3}{4} \times \frac{8}{1} =$

4. Now we're ready to multiply across the top and bottom. What is 3×8? — 24

   (Write 24.)
   What is 4×1? — 4

   (Write $\frac{24}{4}$.)

(continued on next page)

FORMAT 12.18 (continued)

TEACHER	STUDENTS
5. Does $^{24}/_4$ equal more or less than one whole?	more
How do we figure out how many whole groups $^{24}/_4$ equals?	Divide 4 into 24.
Four goes into 24 how many times?	6
(Write 6 in box.)	
6. What does $^3/_4 \times 8$ equal?	6
(Repeat steps 2–5 with the problems below.)	

$$\frac{2}{3} \times 9 \qquad \frac{3}{5} \times 10 \qquad \frac{1}{4} \times 8$$

PART C: STRUCTURED WORKSHEET

1. (Give students worksheets with problems similar to the following problem:)

   a. $\frac{2}{3} \times 7 = $ _____ $= \overline{)} = \square$

2. Touch problem a. Read it.	Two-thirds times seven equals how many?
Is $^2/_3$ multiplied by another fraction?	No
So what do you have to do?	Change 7 into a fraction.
Do it. (Monitor responses.)	
3. Now multiply the fractions. (Monitor responses.) What fraction did you end up with?	$\dfrac{14}{3}$
4. Is $^{14}/_3$ more or less than one whole group?	more
How do you figure out how many whole groups?	Divide 3 into 14.
Divide—Don't forget to write the remainder as a fraction.	
5. What does $^2/_3 \times 7$ equal?	4 and $\dfrac{2}{3}$
(Repeat steps 1–4 with remaining problems.)	

FORMAT 12.19 Format for Writing Regular Division Problems from Fractions

TEACHER	STUDENTS
1. (Write the following on the board.)	

$$\frac{12}{3} \qquad \overline{)}$$

2. I'll show you how to write fractions as regular division problems. You just read the fraction as a division problem. Then you know what to write. I will read this fraction as a division problem. Remember that we read the big number first for a division problem. This fraction can be read as 12 divided by 3.

FORMAT 12.19   (continued)

TEACHER	STUDENTS

3. That's what I write: 12 divided by 3. 12 is the big number and 3 is the first small number. *(Write 3 and 12.)*

$\dfrac{12}{3}$ $3\overline{)12}$

(Write the next fraction.)

$\dfrac{40}{8}$

4. Here's another fraction. Read it as a division problem. Get ready. *(Signal.)*   40 divided by 8

5. I want to write it as a regular division problem. What do I write for the big number? *(Signal.)*   40

What do I write for the first small number? *(Signal.)*   8

(Write 8 and 40.)

$\dfrac{40}{8}$ $8\overline{)40}$

6. The answer to the division problem is the answer to the fraction problem. 40 divided by 8 equals what number?   5
(Write 5.)

$\dfrac{40}{8}$ $8\overline{)40}^{\,5}$

(Continue with other fraction examples until firm.)

CHAPTER 13

Decimals

TERMS AND CONCEPTS

Decimal Fractions   Fractions with a denominator of 10 or any multiple of 10: $\frac{1}{10}$, $\frac{1}{100}$, $\frac{1}{1000}$, etc.

Decimals   Decimals are similar to fractions in that they both deal with something that has been divided into equal parts. Decimals are restricted, however, to situations with 10 parts or any power of 10 (10, 100, 1000, etc.). In a decimal, the number of equal parts is not indicated by a denominator but rather through place value. The position of a number in relation to a decimal point expresses the number of equal parts. For example, one digit after the decimal point indicates 10 equal parts; two digits after the decimal point indicate 100 equal parts. The value of the digit represents the number of parts present, used, or acted upon. For example, .5 equals $\frac{5}{10}$ and .5 represents a division into 10 equal parts with 5 parts present.

Mixed Decimal   An expression consisting of a whole number and a decimal: e.g., 3.24, 18.05.

Percent   The symbol % is read "percent." It represents the ratio of two quantities with the denominator being hundredths. The fraction $\frac{2}{5}$ may be converted to an equivalent fraction, $\frac{40}{100}$, which in turn may be expressed as 40%. When presenting the various forms of rational numbers, teachers must consider their interrelatedness.

Problem-solving strategies designed for teaching fractions should be presented in a manner that will prepare students for decimals. Likewise, the strategies presented for decimals should prepare students for percent.

The Instructional Sequence and Assessment Chart illustrates the seven main areas covered in decimal instruction:

1. Reading and writing decimals and mixed decimal numbers
2. Converting decimals to equivalent decimals
3. Adding and subtracting decimals
4. Rounding off decimals
5. Multiplying decimals
6. Dividing decimals
7. Converting values between the decimal notation system and fraction notation system

The chart also illustrates the relationship of the various skill areas to one another with respect to the sequence of their introduction. Note that analyzing fractions is a preskill for decimals. Students must understand what the numerator and denominator in a fraction represent: the denominator signifying the parts in each whole; the numerator, the parts that are used. They must also understand the concept of whole units versus parts of a whole. An understanding of fraction analysis skills is critical, since deci-

Instructional Sequence and Assessment Chart

Grade Level	Problem Type	Performance Indicator
4a	Reading tenths and hundredths	Circle the correct decimal: five-tenths 5 .05 .5 four-hundredths 4 .04 .4 seventh-hundredths 70 .70 .07
4b	Writing tenths and hundredths	Write these fractions as decimal numbers: $\dfrac{5}{100} =$ $\dfrac{5}{10} =$ $\dfrac{19}{100} =$

4c	Reading mixed decimals; tenths and hundredths	Circle the correct mixed decimal:
		five and three-tenths
		   .53 5.03 5.3
		
		ten and four-hundredths
		   1.04 10.04 10.4
		
		eighteen and six-hundredths
		   18.6 1.86 18.06

4d	Writing mixed decimals: tenths and hundredths	Write the mixed decimal for each mixed number: $10\dfrac{14}{100}$ _____ $16\dfrac{3}{10}$ _____ $40\dfrac{18}{100}$ _____
4e	Column alignment: adding tenths, hundredths, and whole numbers	Write these problems in columns and work them: $8.23 + 12.1 + 6 =$ $7 + .3 + 45 =$ $.08 + 4 + .6 =$
4f	Subtracting tenths and hundredths from whole numbers	$5 - 3.2 =$ $8 - .34 =$ $7 - .3 =$
4g	Ordering mixed decimals	Rewrite these numbers in order, beginning with the smallest: 18.8 10.10 10.3 10.03 ____ ____ ____ ____
5a	Reading thousandths	Circle the correct decimal: five-thousands .05 .5 .005 .500 ninety-thousandths .90 .900 .090 .009

(continued on next page)

Instructional Sequence and Assessment Chart (continued)

Grade Level	Problem Type	Performance Indicator
5b	Writing thousandths	Write these fractions as decimals: $\dfrac{342}{1000} =$ $\dfrac{60}{1000} =$ $\dfrac{5}{1000} =$
5c	Multiplying decimals: one-digit or two-digit factor times three-digit factor	$\begin{array}{r} 7.14 \\ \times\,.5 \\ \hline \end{array}$ $\quad$ $\begin{array}{r} 214 \\ \times\,.7 \\ \hline \end{array}$
5d	Multiplying decimals: zero to be placed after decimal point	$\begin{array}{r} .1 \\ \times\,.7 \\ \hline \end{array}$ $\quad$ $\begin{array}{r} .02 \\ \times\,.8 \\ \hline \end{array}$
5e	Rounding off decimals	Round off these numbers to the nearest whole number: 8.342 _____ 7.812 _____ Round off these numbers to the nearest tenth: 8.34 _____ 9.782 _____ Round off these numbers to the nearest hundredth: 8.346 _____ 9.782 _____
5f	Dividing: whole number divisor, no remainder	$5\overline{)32.45}$ $\quad$ $7\overline{)215.6}$ $\quad$ $2\overline{).856}$
5g	Dividing by whole number: quotient begins with zero	$9\overline{).036}$ $\quad$ $9\overline{).36}$ $\quad$ $9\overline{).0036}$
5h	Rounding off where there is a 9 or 99 after the decimal	Round off these numbers to the nearest tenth: 9.961 _____ 19.942 _____ 29.981 _____ Round off these numbers to the nearest hundredth: 14.993 _____ 14.996 _____ 29.9982 _____
5i	Dividing: whole number divisor, zeroes must be added to dividend after decimal point	Divide and write answer as mixed decimal: $2\overline{)3}$ $\quad$ $5\overline{)3.1}$ $\quad$ $4\overline{)21}$
5j	Dividing: whole number divisor, rounding off	Divide: write answer to mixed decimal; round off to the nearest hundredth: $7\overline{)3.1}$ $\quad$ $9\overline{)7}$ $\quad$ $3\overline{)2}$

Grade Level	Problem Type	Performance Indicator
5k	Converting proper fraction to decimal; not rounding off required	Rewrite these fractions as decimal: $\dfrac{2}{5} =$　　　　$\dfrac{3}{4} =$ $\dfrac{3}{10} =$
5l	Converting proper fraction to decimal: rounding off required	Rewrite these fractions as decimals; round off to nearest hundredth: $\dfrac{3}{7} =$ $\dfrac{4}{6} =$ $\dfrac{2}{9} =$
5m	Multiplying mixed decimal by 10 or 100: no zeroes added	$10 \times 34.2 =$ $100 \times 34.52 =$ $10 \times 34.52 =$
5n	Multiplying mixed decimal by 10 or 100: zeroes added	$100 \times 34.2 =$ $100 \times 3.42 =$ $100 \times 342 =$ $10 \times 342 =$
5o	Dividing: divisor is decimal, no adding zeroes in dividend necessary	$.2\overline{)23.74}$　　$.2\overline{)14.26}$　　$.05\overline{).345}$
5p	Same as above: adding zero in dividend required	$.5\overline{)13}$　　$.50\overline{)275}$　　$.02\overline{)3.1}$　　$.05\overline{)2}$
5q	Converting decimal to fractions	Circle the correct answer: .75 equals　$\dfrac{1}{4}$　$\dfrac{5}{7}$　$\dfrac{2}{3}$　$\dfrac{3}{4}$ .8 equals　$\dfrac{4}{5}$　$\dfrac{8}{8}$　$\dfrac{1}{8}$　$\dfrac{2}{5}$ .67 equals　$\dfrac{1}{4}$　$\dfrac{2}{3}$　$\dfrac{6}{7}$　$\dfrac{1}{6}$
5r	Converting mixed numbers to mixed decimals	Rewrite these mixed fractions as mixed decimals: $2\dfrac{3}{5} =$ $7\dfrac{1}{4} =$

mals are explained as an alternative representation of fractions that have 10 or a multiple of 10 (100, 1000, etc.) as a denominator.

Also, note that reading and writing decimals are component skills for all the other decimal operations. Too frequently, an insufficient amount of instructional time is allotted to teaching students to accurately read and write decimals. Without adequate practice on these basic decimal reading and writing skills, students will encounter unnecessary difficulty when more advanced decimal skills are introduced.

READING AND WRITING DECIMALS AND MIXED DECIMALS

This section includes procedures for teaching students to read and write decimals and mixed decimals expressed as tenths, hundredths, and thousandths. Early direct instruction procedures for teaching students how to read and write decimals focus student attention on the number of digits after the decimal point (i.e., one digit after the decimal point indicates tenths; two digits after the decimal point indicate hundredths; three digits after the decimal point indicate thousandths).

Decimals and mixed decimals representing tenths and hundredths are usually introduced in fourth grade, while decimals and mixed decimals representing thousandths are introduced in fifth grade. The sequence for introducing these skills follows:

1. Reading decimals representing tenths or hundredths
2. Writing decimals representing tenths or hundredths
3. Reading and writing mixed decimals; decimals represent tenths or hundredths
4. Reading decimals representing thousandths
5. Writing decimals representing thousandths
6. Reading and writing mixed decimals; decimals represent thousandths

Note that students are taught to write decimal numbers immediately after they can read them.

Reading Decimals Representing Tenths and Hundredths

The format for reading decimals (Format 13.1) introduces students to decimals as an alternative system for writing fractions of tenths and hundredths. The teacher begins by writing two fractions on the board, one with 10 as a denominator and one with 100 as a denominator (e.g., $^4/_{10}$, $^{24}/_{100}$) and has students read

the fractions. Next, the teacher explains that there is another way to express fractions that have 10 or 100 as a denominator. In this alternative method, a decimal point is used in place of the denominator. The teacher explains that if one digit is written after the decimal point, the decimal tells how many tenths; but if two digits are written after the decimal point, the decimal tells how many hundredths. (If students are unfamiliar with the term *digit,* they should be told that a digit is any written numeral from 0 to 9.)

After telling students the rule regarding the number of digits after the decimal, the teacher has the students read a list of numbers comprised of an equal mixture of tenths and hundredths decimals. Several minimally different sets (e.g., .07, .70, .7 and .4, .04, .40) are included among the examples. Included in the minimally different sets would be three decimal numbers: a decimal representing tenths (e.g., .8) and two decimals representing hundredths. In one of these hundredth decimals, a zero would precede the numeral (.08) while in the other hundredth decimal, the zero would follow the numeral (.80). The purpose of these minimally different sets is to focus student attention on the number of digits following the decimal.

The correction for errors in reading decimals is to have students identify the number of places after the decimal and then model and test identifying the decimal. For example, if a student misreads .04 as four tenths, the teacher says, "How many digits after the decimal? So what does the 4 tell about?"

A critical teacher behavior for this format is monitoring student responses. To avoid student problems in confusing whole numbers and decimal numbers, teachers should be sure that students are adding the "ths" endings to tens, hundreds, and thousands. For example, teachers should be sure .40 is pronounced as "forty hundredths" not "forty hundreds." Individual turns should be given frequently during the first several lessons. Practice on reading decimal numbers would be presented daily for two or three weeks. After the first several lessons the teacher need not present all of the steps in Part A but would just write decimals on the board and have students read them (step 4).

Part B includes a worksheet exercise designed both to provide practice in reading decimals and to reinforce the relationship between decimal fractions and decimals. Students are given worksheets with two types of items. In the first type, a decimal number is written to the left of three fractions:

$$.8 = \quad \frac{8}{10} \quad \frac{8}{100} \quad \frac{1}{8}$$

The students read the decimal and then circle the fraction equivalent of the decimal number. In the second type of item, a fraction is written, and students must find the corresponding decimal among several similar-looking decimals:

$$\frac{4}{100} = \quad .4 \quad .40 \quad .04$$

About five of each type of item would appear daily on worksheets for several weeks.

Writing Decimals Representing Tenths and Hundredths

Writing decimals representing tenths and hundredths is introduced after students can read those decimals accurately. A format for teaching students to write these decimals appears in Format 13.2. The format includes three parts. Part A is a structured board format in which the teacher demonstrates how to write a decimal fraction as a decimal. The teacher writes a fraction on the board and has the students read it. The teacher then asks how many digits there must be after the decimal point and models writing the fraction as a decimal number. Special attention must be given to fractions with a hundred as the denominator and with a numerator of less than 10 (e.g., $7/100$, $4/100$, $1/100$). When presenting these examples, the teacher demonstrates that in order to make two digits after the decimal, a zero must be written immediately after the decimal point. For example, in writing $7/100$, the teacher would write .07.

Practice on writing decimal numbers should be provided daily for several weeks. This practice can be provided in the form of written worksheets containing fractions with 10 or 100 as the denominator. The students would be required to write the decimal equivalents.

The example selection guideline is basically the same as that for the reading decimals format. Several minimally different sets (e.g., $8/10$, $8/100$, $80/100$) would be included to provide students with the practice to determine when a zero is needed immediately after the decimal point. Several extra examples of hundredths fractions with a numerator below 10 also would be included to provide extra practice on this difficult type of decimal.

Reading and Writing Mixed Decimals: Tenths and Hundredths

When the students are able to read and write tenths and hundredths decimals without prompting from the teacher, mixed decimals, numbers formed by a whole number and a decimal (e.g., 9.3, 16.4, 27.02), can be introduced. Students are first taught to read mixed decimals, then write them. The format for these skills appears in Format 13.3. In Part A, the board presentation, the teacher introduces reading mixed decimals, explaining that the numerals before the decimal point represent whole numbers, while the numerals after the decimal point tell about the decimal number. The teacher then models and tests reading several numbers, having the students say the whole number, the decimal, and then the mixed decimal. Note that in reading mixed decimals, the teacher should heavily emphasize the word *and* (e.g., 15.03 should be read "fifteen *and* three hundredths"). This voice emphasis is designed to help students discriminate between the whole number and the decimal parts of the mixed decimal in preparation for writing mixed decimals. Reading mixed decimals is practiced daily for several weeks. No prompting is recommended after the first several days.

Part B, a structured worksheet exercise, includes two types of items. In the first type, a mixed fraction is written, and the student rewrites it as a mixed decimal:

$$12\frac{3}{100} \text{ is written as } 12.03$$

In the second type, the words representing a mixed decimal are written and the student must write the mixed decimal; e.g., twenty-eight and four hundredths is written as 28.04. This type of item is appropriate, of course, only for students able to decode well.

Reading and Writing Decimals Representing Thousandths

Decimals representing thousandths are introduced after students have mastered reading and writing decimals and mixed decimals representing tenths and hundredths. Thousandths decimals are taught with the same basic formats as used for reading and writing tenth and hundredth decimals (see Formats 13.1 and 13.2) with the added explanation that if there are three digits after the decimal point the decimal tells about thousandths.

During the first several lessons, examples should concentrate entirely on thousandth numbers. Minimally different groupings such as

.800	.080	.008
.004	.040	.400
.070	.007	.700

should be presented. In these sets, two of the three digits in each decimal are zeroes and one digit is a numeral other than zero. In each decimal, the nonzero digit is placed in another position:

$$.003 \quad .030 \quad .300$$

After several lessons comprised of just thousandth decimals, the teacher would present examples including tenths, hundredths, and thousandths. In these example sets, minimally different groupings should be included to focus student attention on the number of digits after the decimal point:

$$.4 \quad .04 \quad .004$$
$$.70 \quad .070 \quad .700$$

Writing decimals representing thousandths is particularly difficult because students must discriminate when to write two zeroes after the decimal point (e.g., .001, .009) from when to write one zero after the decimal point (e.g., .010, .090). Therefore, the teacher should be prepared to provide extensive practice on examples of this type.

EQUIVALENT DECIMALS

Equivalent decimals are decimals that have the same value. The mixed decimals 8.30 and 8.3 are equivalent since they both represent the same quantity. Converting a decimal, mixed decimal, or whole number to an equivalent mixed decimal is an important preskill for addition, subtraction, and division operations with decimal numbers. For example, when subtracting .39 from 5, students must convert 5 into 5.00. Students should be introduced to equivalent decimal conversions shortly after they can read and write decimals and mixed decimal numbers.

Format 13.4 shows how to teach students to convert decimals into equivalent decimals. Although the rewriting skill is simple, since the students simply add or take away zeroes, students should understand why adding or taking away zeroes is permissible. Part A illustrates the rationale behind adding zeroes by using equivalent fractions. The teacher demonstrates that changing a fraction like $\frac{3}{10}$ to $\frac{30}{100}$ involves multiplying by a fraction equal to 1 ($\frac{10}{10}$) and, therefore, does not change the value of the original fraction. Since $\frac{3}{10} = \frac{30}{100}$, then .3 = .30.

Part B is a structured board exercise demonstrating how to rewrite decimals. Part C is a worksheet exercise in which the students are given a chart containing columns for whole numbers, tenths, hundredths, and thousandths. The student's task is to write equivalent mixed decimals in other spaces

across the row. For example, 9.1 is written in the tenths column. The student would add a zero, writing 9.10 in the hundredths column; and add two zeroes, writing 9.100 in the thousandths column. For whole numbers, the teacher explains that a whole number is converted into a mixed decimal by writing a decimal point after the number and writing zero(es) after the decimal point.

ADDING AND SUBTRACTING DECIMALS AND MIXED DECIMALS

Addition and subtraction problems with decimals and/or mixed decimals can be divided into two groups for instructional purposes. The first group contains those problems in which each number in the problem has the same number of decimal places; e.g., in the problems below all numbers have decimals representing hundredths:

$$
\begin{array}{cc}
435.42 & 24.35 \\
+ 17.82 & - 1.48
\end{array}
$$

The second group is comprised of those problems in which the addends (in an addition problem) or the minuend and subtrahend (in a subtraction problem) have different numbers of digits after the decimal point:

$$
\begin{array}{ccc}
9.1 & 4 & 4.23 \\
- 3.87 & + 3.64 & - 3.645
\end{array}
$$

Decimals Having the Same Number of Places

Problems in which each number has the same number of digits after the decimal point can be introduced when students can read and write decimals and mixed decimals. Problems of this type are relatively easy. The only new step involves placing the decimal point in the answer. Because the teaching procedure is simple, no format has been included.

The first problems should be vertically aligned, so students can be taught to bring the decimal point straight down without first having to determine if the columns are properly aligned. For these problems, the teacher just instructs students to write the decimal in the answer below the other decimal points.

Problems written horizontally (e.g., 7.24 + 19.36) can be introduced shortly after the introduction of vertically aligned problems. For horizontal problems, we recommend teaching students to rewrite the problem so that the decimal points are in a column. When horizontal problems are introduced, teachers should monitor student worksheets daily to see that students align the numbers correctly.

Decimals with Different Number of Places

Problems in which each mixed decimal has a different number of digits after the decimal point are introduced after students are able to rewrite decimal numbers as equivalent decimal numbers by adding zeroes after the decimal. This typically would be only a week or two after the easier addition and subtraction problems are presented. The strategy for solving these more complex problems involves rewriting one or more of the mixed decimal numbers so that each mixed decimal in the problem has the same number of digits after the decimal point. Once the problem has been rewritten, students are instructed to bring the decimal point straight down, and then solve the problem. For example:

$$
\begin{array}{cc}
8.1 & \text{becomes} \quad 8.10 \\
-3.42 & \underline{-3.42}
\end{array}
$$

Horizontally written problems should be introduced once students can solve the vertical problems. The key to accurately solving horizontal problems is correctly aligning the numbers vertically. Without direct instruction, students are likely to misalign the numbers as illustrated below:

$$
3.72 + 18.4 \quad \text{becomes} \quad \begin{array}{r} 3.72 \\ +18.4 \\ \hline \end{array}
$$

The strategy for rewriting the decimal numbers so that each has the same number of digits after the decimal will prevent this alignment error from occurring. Format 13.5 shows how to present this type of problem.

Problems in which a decimal or mixed decimal is added to or subtracted from a whole number should receive special emphasis (e.g., 7 − 3.8, 8 − .43, 4.23 + 7 + 2.1, 9.2 − 3). Problems of this type would be introduced several days after problems with mixed decimals expressing various decimal fractions are introduced. The teacher reminds students that a whole number is converted to a mixed decimal by placing a decimal point after it and adding zeroes. The teacher models solving several problems. About half of the problems on students' worksheets should include problems with a whole number.

ROUNDING OFF DECIMALS

Rounding off is not only a useful skill in and of itself but is also a necessary component skill for decimal division and percent. An example of the use of rounding off in percentage problems occurs when converting $\frac{3}{7}$ to a percent: the 3 is divided by 7, which yields a decimal:

$$
7 \overline{)3.000} \quad {}^{.428}
$$

The decimal then is rounded off to hundredths to determine the approximate percent, 43%. Although rounding off decimals involves steps similar to those used in rounding off whole numbers, these two skills should not be introduced at the same time because of potential confusion. Rounding off whole numbers should have been presented many months before rounding off decimals is introduced.

Format 13.6 shows how to present rounding off decimal numbers to the nearest whole number, tenth, hundredth, or thousandth. The rounding off strategy taught in this format is comprised of three steps:

1. The students determine how many digits will appear after the decimal point when the number is rounded off; e.g., when rounding off to the nearest tenth, one digit will be left after the decimal.
2. The students count that number of digits and then draw a line. If 3.4825 is to be rounded to the nearest tenth, the students place a line after the digit in the tenth place, the 4: 3.4/825. The line serves as a prompt.
3. The students look at the numeral after the line. If it is a 5 or more they add another unit to the digit before the line. For example .54/7 rounded to the nearest hundredth is .55, since 7 appears after the line. If a number less than 5 appears after the line, no extra unit is added. For example, .54/2 is rounded to .54, since a number less than 5 follows the line.

There are three important example selection guidelines for this format:

1. Half of the decimals should require the addition of another unit; i.e., the numeral after the place to be rounded off should be 5 through 9. In the other half of the decimals, the numeral after the place to be rounded off should be less than 5.
2. The numbers should have two or three places after the place to be rounded off. These extra places reinforce the concept that only the digit immediately after the line determines if another unit is added.
3. Examples should include a mix of problems that require students to round off to the nearest tenth or to the nearest hundredth. The sample worksheet in Part B of the format shows an application of these guidelines.

A particularly difficult type of rounding-off problem arises when a unit is added to a 9, because the sum is 10. For example, rounding off .498 to the nearest hundredth requires students to add a whole unit to the nine-hundredths, which changes .498 to .50. Likewise, when rounding off 39.98 to the nearest tenth, the answer is 40.0. Problems of this type should be introduced after students have mastered easier rounding-off problems. When introducing the more difficult type, the teacher should model working several problems.

Most errors in rounding off occur because students do not attend to the relevant digit. A student is likely to round off .328 to .4 if she focuses on the 8 rather than the 2. The basic correction is to emphasize the steps in the strategy by asking the student:

1. How many digits will there be after the decimal when we round off to the nearest whole (or tenth or hundredth)?
2. Where do you draw the line?
3. What number comes just after the line?
4. So do you add another whole (or tenth or hundredth)?

MULTIPLYING DECIMALS

Although the concept of multiplying decimals is difficult to illustrate, teaching students to solve a multiplication problem with decimal numbers is relatively simple. A possible demonstration to illustrate the rationale of the multiplying decimal strategy can be done with decimal fractions like these:

$$\frac{32}{100} \times \frac{4}{10}$$

The answer, $^{128}/_{1000}$, would then be written as the decimal .128. The original problem would then be written in a decimal form: .32 × .4, and the teacher would point out the three decimal places in the two fractions and make three decimal places in the answer. "The total number of decimal places in the factors is the same as the number of decimal places as the answer: .32 has two places; .4 has one place. That's three decimal places. The answer has three decimal places, too."

Format 13.7 is a strategy for multiplying decimals or mixed decimal numbers. In the board presentation, the teacher introduces the strategy for figuring out where the decimal point goes in the answer. In the worksheet presentation, the teacher gives the student a worksheet with 10 to 15 multiplication problems that have answers and leads students in determining where to place the decimal point. Note that in the problems on the worksheet, the decimal point in the factors appears in several different positions.

The less-structured worksheet exercise includes a mix of multiplication and addition problems. The purpose of combining multiplication with addition is to ensure that students do not overgeneralize (to addition) the procedure of counting the places to determine where to put the decimal. A worksheet might include these examples:

9.4	9.4	3.2
× .5	+ .5	× .57

.32	40	18
+ .57	× 3	× .32

.18	31.4	3.14
+ .32	× .05	+ .05

Before the students work the problems, the teacher should remind them about placing the decimal point in different types of problems. "In addition problems, bring the decimal point straight down. In multiplication problems, count the digits after the decimal points in the numbers you multiply." The teacher should then carefully monitor the students as they work the first several problems.

A potentially confusing type of multiplication problem is one in which the students must place a zero in front of the digits in the answer. For example, when multiplying .4 × .2, the student must add a zero before the 8; .4 × .2 = .08. Likewise, in .5 × .01, the student must place two zeros after the decimal; .5 × .01 = .005. This type of problem would be introduced after the easier types of problems. The teacher models solving several problems of this type, and then includes about three such problems in daily worksheet assignments.

A common error found on independent seatwork occurs when students simply forget to put the decimal point in the answer. The correction is merely to inform the students that they forgot to put in the decimal point. However, if the error occurs frequently, the teacher should prepare worksheets with about 10 to 15 problems, two-thirds of which contain decimals. In presenting the worksheet, the teacher tells students that the worksheet was designed to try to fool them, that some of the problems require decimal points in the answer and some don't. The teacher then monitors closely as students complete the worksheet so that immediate corrections can be made.

DIVIDING DECIMALS

Dividing decimal numbers is the most difficult decimal operation. Division with decimal numbers can be introduced when students can read and write decimals and perform long division. When long division with whole numbers was taught, the teacher should have stressed placing the digits in the quotient over the proper places in the dividend. For example, when working the problem 186 ÷ 2, the quotient should be written as in example a, rather than in example b:

$$\begin{array}{cc} 93 & 93 \\ \text{a. } 2\overline{)186} & \text{b. } 2\overline{)186} \end{array}$$

If students have not learned to write numerals in the quotient in the proper position, errors of misplacing the decimal in the quotient are likely to occur.

$$\begin{array}{ccc} 9.3 & \text{rather than} & .93 \\ 2\overline{)1.86} & & 2\overline{)1.86} \end{array}$$

Procedures for teaching proper placement of the digits in the quotients of long division problems are discussed in Chapter 10.

Division problems with decimals can be categorized into four types of difficulty. The first three types have whole numbers as divisors.

1. Problems in which the quotient does not have a remainder and that require no conversion of the dividend:

$$\begin{array}{ccc} .69 & \text{or} & .03 \\ 5\overline{)3.45} & & 7\overline{).21} \end{array}$$

2. Problems in which the dividend must be converted to an equivalent decimal so that no remainder will be present:

$$\begin{array}{ccc} .7 & & .74 \\ 5\overline{)3.7} & \text{becomes} & 5\overline{)3.70} \\ \underline{3\ 5} & & \underline{3\ 5} \\ 2 & & 20 \\ & & \underline{20} \end{array}$$

3. Problems with a remainder that requires rounding off:

$$\begin{array}{c} .34\,|\,2 = .34 \\ 7\overline{)2.40\,|\,0} \\ \underline{2\ 1} \\ 30 \\ \underline{28} \\ 20 \\ \underline{14} \\ 6 \end{array}$$

4. Problems in which the divisor is a decimal or mixed decimal number and must be converted to a whole number

$$.4\,\overline{)61.32} \quad \text{becomes} \quad {}_{\curlywedge}4\,\overline{)61.\underset{\curlywedge}{3}2}$$

Decimal or Mixed Decimal Divided by a Whole Number

Division problems in which the dividend is a mixed decimal or decimal number and the divisor a whole number are usually introduced in late fourth or early-to-mid-fifth grade. An elaborate format is not required to introduce the problem type in which the divisor goes into the dividend without leaving any remainder:

$$\begin{array}{cc} 5\overline{)2.35} & 7\overline{)84.7} \end{array}$$

The teacher presents the rule that the decimal point must be written on the line directly above where it appears in the number being divided. For example, when dividing 69.26 by 6, the student writes the problem:

$$6\overline{)69.26}$$

then places the decimal point on the quotient line directly above the decimal in the dividend:

$$6\overline{)69.26}^{\,\cdot}$$

The teacher then leads students through working several sets of problems, emphasizing the need to place the digits in the quotient in their proper place.

There are two example selection guidelines for problems without remainders. First, the decimal point should appear in different positions in various problems:

$$\begin{array}{ccc} \text{a. } 5\overline{)3.725} & \text{b. } 2\overline{)184.6} & \text{c. } 9\overline{)1.836} \\ \text{d. } 7\overline{).364} & \text{e. } 5\overline{)23.5} & \text{f. } 5\overline{).215} \end{array}$$

Second, one or two problems in which a zero must be placed immediately after the decimal point should be included. In problems d and f above, the quotients are .052 and .043. The teacher may have to provide extra prompting on these problems by explaining that a digit must be written in every place after the decimal point. Therefore, in problem d, the teacher might say, "7 doesn't go into 3 so write a zero above the 3." Daily practice would include 6-10 problems.

The second type of decimal division problem requires the student to eliminate a remainder by rewriting the dividend as an equivalent decimal. For example, zeroes need to be added to the dividend in each of the following problems:

$$\begin{array}{cc} .62 & .75 \\ \text{a. } 5\overline{)3.1} = 5\overline{)3.10} & \text{c. } 4\overline{)3} = 4\overline{)3.00} \\[2mm] 1.725 & .4 \\ \text{b. } 2\overline{)3.45} = 2\overline{)3.450} & \text{d. } 5\overline{)2} = 5\overline{)2.0} \end{array}$$

This type of problem is introduced about 2 weeks after decimal division problems without remainders.

The preskill of converting a decimal to an equivalent decimal should be taught prior to the introduction of this problem type. These problems are not very difficult and, like the previous type, do not require a lengthy format. In introducing the problems, the teacher would explain that students should work them until there are no remainders. He then models working problems that require the addition of zeroes. For example, after bringing down the final digit, 9, of the dividend in this problem:

$$
\begin{array}{r}
5.6 \\
6\overline{)33.9} \\
\underline{30} \\
3\ 9 \\
\underline{3\ 6} \\
3
\end{array}
$$

the teacher would explain that he must keep dividing since he doesn't want a remainder, "I'll add a zero after the last digit in the decimal and divide again. Remember: adding zeroes after a decimal does not change the value of the number."

$$
\begin{array}{r}
5.65 \\
6\overline{)33.90} \\
\underline{30} \\
3\ 9 \\
\underline{3\ 6} \\
30 \\
\underline{30}
\end{array}
$$

Examples in these exercises should be designed so that the addition of one or two zeroes to the dividend eliminates a remainder. Several examples such as

$$
4\overline{)3} \quad \text{or} \quad 5\overline{)8}
$$

in which a whole number is the dividend should be included. These problems may require the teacher to remind students to write the decimal point first and then add zeroes after the whole number:

$$
4\overline{)3} \quad \text{becomes} \quad 4\overline{)3.0}
$$

The third type of decimal division problem requires rounding off. Students are usually instructed to work these problems to the nearest tenth, hundredth, or thousandth. Obviously, the preskill required is rounding off decimal numbers. The format for presenting this problem type appears in Format

13.8. In Part A, the teacher demonstrates how to work the problem. The student first reads the directions specifying to what decimal place (tenths, hundredths, thousandths) the answer is to be rounded. The teacher asks how many digits must be written after the decimal point in the answer, then instructs the students to work the problem until they have written that many digits. The teacher instructs the students to draw a line after that last digit in the answer and divide once more so they can decide how to round off the answer. The answer is then rounded off. If the numeral after the line is 5 or greater, another unit is added; if the numeral after the line is less than 5, no additional unit is added.

Special consideration should again be given to those problems in which a whole number is being divided by a larger whole number. These problems are very important, since they prepare students to compute percentages; e.g., "John made 4 out of 7 basketball shots. What is his percentage for making shots?" We recommend that students round off answers in this type of problem to the nearest hundredth, since percents are based on hundredths.

Dividing by a Decimal or Mixed Decimal

The fourth type of division problem has a decimal or mixed decimal divisor. Problems of this type are relatively difficult because students must multiply the divisor and dividend by 10 or a multiple of 10 to convert the divisor into a whole number. Both the dividend and divisor must be multiplied by the same number so that the numerical value represented by the problem is not altered. For example, to work the problem $8.7 \div .35$, students must multiply the dividend and divisor by 100, converting .35 to 35 and 8.7 to 870.

The preskill of moving the decimal to the right when multiplying by a multiple of 10 should be taught and practiced for several weeks before introducing division problems with decimal divisors. Format 13.9 teaches this preskill. Students are taught that when a decimal number is multiplied by 10, the decimal point moves one place to the right; when it is multiplied by 100, the decimal moves two places to the right; and when it is multiplied by 1000, the decimal point moves three places to the right.

Particularly difficult problems are those in which a zero must be added. For example, to multiply 8.7×100, the students must add a zero to the 8.7 so they can move the decimal point two places to the right: $8.7 \times 100 = 870$. The teacher will need to model several of these problems, explaining the need to add zeroes. "You have to move the decimal point two places to the right, but you've only got one decimal place to the right. Add a zero so you can move the decimal point two places."

The examples included in this preskill exercise should include a mix of problem types. The decimal point should not be placed in the same position from problem to problem. In half of the problems, 10 should be a factor, and in the other half, 100 should be a factor. Several problems should require that students add zeroes to a mixed decimal (e.g., 100 × 34.2, 100 × 14.2). Also, several problems should include a whole number that must be multiplied by a multiple of 10 (e.g., 10 × 34, 25 × 100). As the decimal point is moved over, zeroes are added. For example, with 15 × 100, the student writes 15 and then adds two zeroes: 1500. The teacher models working several of these problems, pointing out that a whole number can be converted to a mixed decimal by adding a decimal point after the last digit in the whole number (e.g., 15 is written as 15.).

Teachers can demonstrate that moving the decimal and adding a zero when multiplying by a multiple of 10 is valid by beginning with a problem like this:

$$\begin{array}{r} 3.4 \\ \times\ 10 \\ \hline 00 \\ 340 \\ \hline 34.0 \end{array}$$

The teacher would point out that when he multiplies by 10, the answer is 34, with the decimal point moved one place to the right and a zero added. Next the teacher would write this problem:

$$\begin{array}{r} 3.4 \\ \times\ 100 \\ \hline 00 \\ 000 \\ 3400 \\ \hline 340.0 \end{array}$$

and point out that when he multiplies by 100, the answer is 340, with the decimal point moved two places to the right.

Division problems with decimal or mixed decimal divisors are introduced when students have mastered multiplying by multiples of 10 and can work all types of problems in which the divisor is a whole number and the dividend a decimal or mixed decimal number. Format 13.10 shows how to teach students to work problems with a decimal or mixed decimal divisor.

In Part A, the teacher presents a rule: "We cannot divide by a decimal number" and demonstrates how the divisor and dividend must be revalued. Both the divisor and dividend are multiplied by whatever multiple of 10 is needed to change the divisor into a whole number. The teacher revalues the divisor first by moving the decimal point to the right. The dividend is revalued by moving the decimal point the same number of spaces to the right. Note in the format the demonstration of how to revalue a problem is kept relatively simple to avoid confusing students with lengthy explanations.

Two example selection guidelines are important in teaching division with decimal or mixed decimal divisor. First, the number of places in the divisor and dividend should vary from problem to problem. For example, a worksheet might include the following problems:

a. $.5\overline{)3.75}$ b. $.05\overline{)37.5}$ c. $2.5\overline{)75}$

d. $.2\overline{)0.1368}$ e. $.03\overline{)24}$ f. $.5\overline{)21.85}$

Changing the type of decimal divisor forces students to attend carefully to moving the decimal. A second guideline involves including some examples in which zeroes must be added to the dividend (e.g., problems b, c, and e above). After a week or so, some problems in which a decimal or mixed decimal is divided by a whole number should be included so that students will receive adequate practice applying the strategies to the various types of problems.

If the teacher wishes to demonstrate the validity of moving the decimal point, she begins with a division problem:

$$.5\overline{)2.4} = \frac{2.4}{.5}$$

"Let's work this division problem as a fraction. Dividing by a decimal is too hard, so I have to change .5 into a whole number. I do that by multiplying by 10. If I multiply the denominator by 10, what do I have to do to the numerator? . . . Right, ten-tenths equal 1, and when we multiply by 1 we don't change the value of the fraction."

The teacher writes this:

$$\frac{2.4}{.5} \times \frac{10}{10} = \frac{24}{5}$$

and says, "Now we can divide by a whole number." The teacher then writes this problem:

$$5\overline{)24}$$

CONVERTING FRACTIONS AND DECIMALS

Decimals and fractions are both numerical systems for representing part(s) of a whole. Converting a fraction to a decimal is an important skill in itself as well as a component skill of percent problems. Converting a decimal to a fraction is less important, since it has fewer practical applications.

Converting a Fraction to a Decimal

The strategy for converting a fraction to a decimal involves dividing the numerator by the denominator. For example, $\frac{3}{8}$ is converted to a decimal by dividing 8 into 3:

$$8\overline{)3.000}^{.375}$$

The preskills for this conversion strategy, which we discussed earlier in this chapter, are (1) decimal division problems in which a whole number is divided by a larger whole number (e.g., $3 \div 7$, $3 \div 5$) and (2) rounding off decimals.

Because students who have mastered these preskills should have no difficulty converting a fraction to a decimal, an elaborate format is not required. The teacher merely presents the rule: "To change a fraction into a decimal, divide the numerator by the denominator." The teacher then models application of the rule with several problems and supervises students as they complete a worksheet. Proper and improper fractions should be included in the exercise.

Initial examples used to illustrate this strategy should be limited to fractions that can be divided evenly to the nearest tenth, hundredth, or thousandth:

$$\frac{4}{8} = 8\overline{)4.0}^{.5}$$
$$\qquad\quad 4\ 0$$

Fractions that result in repeating decimals should not be introduced until several days later, since they require rounding off. When these problems are presented, instructions should specify to what place the decimal should be rounded off.

$$\frac{2}{3} \quad 3\overline{)2.0000}^{.6666}$$

Mixed numbers can be converted to a mixed decimal by first converting the mixed fraction to an improper fraction:

$$3\frac{2}{5} = \frac{17}{5} = 5\overline{)17.0}^{3.4}$$

$$5\frac{3}{4} = \frac{23}{4} = 4\overline{)23.00}^{5.75}$$

Conversion of a mixed number would be introduced about a week after the introduction of repeating decimal problems.

In a final type of problem, the denominator is a two-digit number (e.g., $\frac{8}{12}$, $\frac{15}{18}$). Students should be taught to first reduce the fraction to its lowest common terms before converting the fraction to a decimal:

$$\frac{8}{12} = \frac{3}{4} = 4\overline{)3.00}^{.75}$$

$$\frac{15}{18} = \frac{5}{6} = 6\overline{)5.000}^{.833}$$

Reducing is helpful, in that dividing by a one-digit divisor is easier than dividing by a two-digit divisor. If the fraction cannot be reduced, students must be able to work problems with a two-digit divisor. Daily practice including four to eight problems should be provided over a period of several weeks.

Converting a Decimal to a Fraction

Converting a decimal to a fraction can be presented when students have learned to read and write fractions and can reduce fractions to their lowest terms. The strategy for converting a decimal to a fraction involves the students' first rewriting the decimal as a decimal fraction, and then reducing this decimal fraction to its lowest terms. For example, the decimal .75 would first be converted to the fraction $\frac{75}{100}$, which in turn would be reduced to $\frac{3}{4}$.

Initially, students should be given a worksheet like the one below, and the teacher should lead students through completing several items.

Decimal	Decimal Fraction	Common Fraction
.8	$\frac{8}{10}$	$\frac{4}{5}$
.80		
.35		

After several lessons, the teacher could introduce a worksheet exercise like the one below. The teacher guides students in converting the decimal to a decimal fraction, and then reducing this fraction to its lowest terms.

Circle the fraction that is equivalent to the decimal number.

.60	$\frac{6}{9}$	$\frac{3}{6}$	$\frac{3}{5}$	$\frac{6}{6}$
.75	$\frac{2}{3}$	$\frac{3}{4}$	$\frac{5}{7}$	$\frac{7}{5}$
.8	$\frac{8}{5}$	$\frac{1}{8}$	$\frac{4}{5}$	$\frac{3}{5}$

DIAGNOSIS AND REMEDIATION

Students may miss decimal problems for one or a combination of the following reasons:

1. *A computational error.* For example, when working the problem 9.63 ÷ 9, the student writes 1.08 as the answer, The student's only mistake was dividing 9 into 63 incorrectly.

   If a student misses a problem solely because of a computational error, the teacher need not spend time working on the fraction skill but should reteach the specific computational skill.

2. *A component skill error.* The student makes an error on a previously taught decimal skill, which causes the student to miss the current type of problem. For example, when converting $^3/_7$ to a decimal, the student divides 3 by 7 correctly to 428, but then rounds off the answer to .42.

   The remediation involves reteaching the earlier taught component skill. In the example given, the teacher would first reteach students how to round off. When the students demonstrate mastery of the component skill, the teacher would lead the students through solving the original type of problem, using the structured worksheet part of the appropriate format.

3. *A strategy error.* A strategy error occurs when the student does not correctly follow the steps to solve a problem. For example, when attempting to convert $^3/_4$ to a decimal, the student divides 4 by 3. The remediation procedure involves reteaching the strategy, beginning with the structured board part of the format.

Summary Box 13.1, which describes diagnoses and remediation procedures for common errors made on the various types of decimal problems, appears below.

Summary Box 13.1:   Diagnosis and Remediation of Decimal Errors

Error Patterns	Diagnosis	Remediation Procedures
Adding or subtracting 3.5 + 2 = **3.7** 5 − .3 = **2**	Student does not convert whole number to mixed decimal.	Teach students to rewrite whole number as mixed decimal, see Format 13.4. Present structured worksheet on addition and subtraction problems, see Format 13.5.
Multiplying 3.45 × .5 **17.25**	Strategy error: placing decimal point in wrong position in answer.	Present Format 13.7. Be sure to include mix of addition and multiplication problems in less-structured worksheet exercise.
Dividing **46.1** 7)32.27	Component skill error: misalignment of digits in quotient	Present format for teaching long division from Chapter 10. Stress proper alignment of digits.
.63 .05)3.15	Strategy error: failure to rewrite divisor and dividend	Present Format 13.10.
Rounding off 3.729 **3.8** 8.473 **8.4**	Strategy error	Present Format 13.6.

APPLICATION ITEMS: DECIMALS

1. Describe the problem type that each example below represents. List the problems in the order they are introduced.

   a. $14.3 + 8.5$

   b. 7×34.8

   c. $9 - 3.28$

   d. Convert $^4\!/_7$ to a decimal.

   e. Convert $^2\!/_5$ to a decimal.

   f. Read this number 8.04.

   g. $.9\overline{)28}$

   h. $9\overline{)2.7}$

   i. $9\overline{)2.8}$

   j. Round off 3.4785 to the nearest hundredth.

2. Construct a structured board presentation to teach students to read decimals expressed as thousandths.

3. Below are the examples various teachers used in presenting reading decimals (tenths and hundredths). Tell which teacher used an appropriate set of examples. Tell why the other sets are inappropriate.

Teacher A	.04	.09	.08	.05	.01	.07
Teacher B	.7	.37	.48	.5	.28	
Teacher C	.7	.70	.07	.4	.40	.04

4. Specify the wording the teacher uses to present the following problem: $8 - .34 =$

5. Below is a set constructed by a teacher for a rounding-off exercise. It is inappropriate. Tell why.

   Round off 3.482 to the nearest tenth
   Round off 7.469 to the nearest hundredth
   Round off 4.892 to the nearest tenth
   Round off 6.942 to the nearest whole number

6. A student rounds off 3.738 to the nearest hundredth, writing 3.73. Specify the wording the teacher uses in making the correction.

7. Which problems below would not be included in the initial exercises teaching students to divide a whole number into a decimal or mixed decimal number? Tell why.

   a. $7\overline{)37.8}$ b. $4\overline{)23.5}$ c. $9\overline{)84.86}$

   d. $.7\overline{)34.3}$ e. $9\overline{)3.87}$ f. $2\overline{)1.46}$

8. Tell the probable cause of each student's error. Specify the remediation procedure for the type of error.

   Write this fraction as a decimal rounded off to the nearest hundredth: $^5\!/_7$.

   Jason

   $$\frac{5}{7} = 7\overline{)5.00}^{\,.614} = 7\overline{)5.00} = .61$$

   Jill

   $$\frac{5}{7} = 5\overline{)7.0}^{\,1.4}$$

   Samuel

   $$\frac{5}{7} = 7\overline{)5.0}^{\,.714} = .72$$
   $$\frac{4.9}{10}$$
   $$\frac{7}{30}$$

FORMAT 13.1   **Format for Reading Decimals**

PART A: STRUCTURED BOARD PRESENTATION

TEACHER	**STUDENTS**

1. *(Write the following fractions on the board.)*

    $\dfrac{3}{10}$ and $\dfrac{3}{100}$

2. Read these fractions.   three-tenths, three hundredths

3. We're going to learn another way to write tenths and hundredths. *(Write a decimal point on the board.)* This is a decimal point. What is this?   a decimal point

    One digit after the decimal point tells about tenths. What does one digit after the decimal tell about?   tenths

    Two digits after the decimal point tell about hundredths. What do two digits after the decimal point tell about?   hundredths

    Remember: If there is one digit after the decimal point, the number tells about tenths. If there are two digits after the decimal point, the number tells about hundredths.

4. *(Write .9 on board.)*
    Listen: There's one digit after the decimal point. The 9 tells about tenths. This says "nine tenths."

    (Write .09 on board.) Listen: There are two digits after the decimal point. The 9 tells about hundredths. This says "nine hundredths." Your turn.

5. *(Write .3 on the board.)*
    How many digits after the decimal point?   one

    What does the 3 tell about?   tenths

    Say the decimal number.   three-tenths

    To correct: How many digits after the decimal point? There is/are _____ digit(s) after the decimal so the _____ tells about _____. The decimal says _____

    (Repeat step 3 with .03, .30, .6, .60, .06, .58.)

6. *(Write on board: .7)*
    Say this decimal number.

    (Repeat step 4 with .70, .07, .9, .09, .90, .05, .4, .32.)

PART B: STRUCTURED WORKSHEET

1. *(Present a worksheet like the following.)*

    a. $.4 = \dfrac{4}{100} \quad \dfrac{4}{10} \quad \dfrac{40}{1000}$ d. $.61 = \dfrac{61}{100} \quad \dfrac{61}{10} \quad \dfrac{61}{1000}$

    b. $.40 = \dfrac{40}{100} \quad \dfrac{40}{10} \quad \dfrac{4}{10}$ e. $.06 = \dfrac{60}{100} \quad \dfrac{6}{100} \quad \dfrac{6}{10}$

    c. $.04 = \dfrac{40}{100} \quad \dfrac{40}{10} \quad \dfrac{4}{100}$ f. $.6 = \dfrac{6}{100} \quad \dfrac{6}{1000} \quad \dfrac{60}{100}$

(continued on next page)

FORMAT 13.1   (continued)

TEACHER	STUDENTS

g. $\dfrac{38}{100}$ = .3 .38 38.   j. $\dfrac{8}{100}$ = .80 .08 .080

h. $\dfrac{4}{100}$ = .40 .04 .4   k. $\dfrac{80}{100}$ = .80 .08 .8

i. $\dfrac{40}{100}$ = .40 .4 .04   l. $\dfrac{7}{10}$ = .70 .07 .7

TEACHER	STUDENTS
2. Read the decimal number next to a. We have to find the fraction that says .4.	4 tenths
3. Read the first fraction. *(Pause, signal.)*	4 hundredths
Read the next fraction. *(Pause, signal.)*	4 tenths
Read the next fraction. *(Pause, signal.)*	40 thousandths
4. The decimal says four-tenths. Draw a circle around the fraction that says four-tenths. *(Monitor student responses.)*	
5. Work problems b–f on your own. Remember to circle the fraction that says the same thing as the decimal.	
6. Read the fraction next to letter g. We have to find the decimal that says 38 hundredths.	38 hundredths
7. Read the first decimal.	3 tenths
Read the next decimal.	38 hundredths
8. It says the same thing as the fraction, so draw a circle around it. *(Monitor student responses.)*	
9. Work the rest of the problems on your own.	

FORMAT 13.2   **Format for Writing Decimal Numbers**

Part A: Structured Board Presentation

TEACHER	STUDENTS
1. *(Write on board:* $\dfrac{73}{100}$ *)*	
2. Read this fraction.	73 hundredths
3. I want to write 73 hundredths as a decimal.	
4. How many digits after the decimal point when a decimal tells about hundredths?	two
5. So I write a decimal point then 73. What do I write after the decimal point to write 73 hundredths?	73
6. *(Write .73.)* Read the decimal.	73 hundredths

(Repeat steps 1–5 with: $^{7}/_{10}$, $^{7}/_{100}$, $^{70}/_{100}$, $^{4}/_{100}$, $^{48}/_{100}$, $^{6}/_{10}$, $^{6}/_{100}$, $^{60}/_{100}$, $^{3}/_{100}$.)

(Note: When presenting fractions like $^{7}/_{100}$, the teacher says in step 4, "So I write a decimal point then zero seven.")

FORMAT 13.2   **(continued)**

PART B: LESS-STRUCTURED WORKSHEET

TEACHER   **STUDENTS**

1. *(Write these fractions as decimals.)*

   a. $\dfrac{4}{100}$ = _____   g. $\dfrac{32}{100}$ = _____

   b. $\dfrac{4}{10}$ = _____   h. $\dfrac{28}{100}$ = _____

   c. $\dfrac{40}{100}$ = _____   i. $\dfrac{9}{10}$ = _____

   d. $\dfrac{7}{100}$ = _____   j. $\dfrac{92}{100}$ = _____

   e. $\dfrac{7}{10}$ = _____   k. $\dfrac{9}{100}$ = _____

   f. $\dfrac{70}{100}$ = _____   l. $\dfrac{5}{10}$ = _____

2. Read the directions.   Write these fractions as decimals.

3. Read the fraction next to a.   4 hundredths

4. How many digits must there be after the decimal point for
   hundredths?   two

5. What do you write after the decimal point to say four
   hundredths?   zero four

6. Now write the decimal point and the numeral(s) to say
   seven hundredths.

   (Repeat steps 2–5 with remaining examples.)

FORMAT 13.3   **Format for Reading and Writing Mixed Decimals**

PART A: STRUCTURED BOARD PRESENTATION

TEACHER   **STUDENTS**

1. *(Write a decimal point on the board.)* The numerals on this
   side of the decimal point *(Motion to the left.)* tell about
   whole numbers. What do the numerals on this side of the
   decimal point *(Motion to the left.)* tell about? The numerals   whole numbers
   after the decimal point *(Motion to the right.)* tell about the
   decimal number.

2. *(Write on board: 2.4)* This is a mixed decimal. It has a whole
   number and a decimal number. It says two and four-tenths.
   What is this mixed decimal?   2 and 4 tenths

   What's the whole number in the mixed decimal?   2

   What's the decimal?   4 tenths

   Say the mixed decimal   2 and 4 tenths

   (Repeat step 2 with 9.03, 14.2, 16.23, 7.4, 9.03.)   *(continued on next page)*

FORMAT 13.3   (continued)

TEACHER	STUDENTS

3. *(Write on board: 8.4)* Say the mixed decimal.

   (Repeat step 3 with 8.04, 7.41, 19.2, 8.50, 19.02.)

PART B: STRUCTURED WORKSHEET

1. *(Write the mixed decimal.)*

   a. eight and four tenths = _____
   b. sixteen and two hundredths = _____
   c. five and sixteen hundredths = _____
   d. eleven and four tenths = _____
   e. eleven and four hundredths = _____
   f. eleven and forty hundredths = _____

   g. $17\frac{9}{10}$ =   _____

   h. $8\frac{45}{100}$ =   _____

   i. $16\frac{1}{100}$ =   _____

   j. $16\frac{5}{100}$ =   _____

   k. $16\frac{10}{100}$ =   _____

2. Read the words in a.   eight and four tenths

3. What's the whole number? Write it.   eight

4. What's the decimal number? Write it—Don't forget the   four-tenths
   decimal point. *(Monitor responses.)*

5. What mixed decimal did you write?   eight and four-tenths

   (Repeat steps 1–4 with problems b–f.)

6. Read the mixed number in problem g.   seventeen and nine-tenths

   (Repeat steps 2–5 with remaining problems.)

FORMAT 13.4   **Format for Converting Decimals into Equivalent Decimals**

PART A: DEMONSTRATION

TEACHER	STUDENTS

1. Listen to this rule: When we write zeroes after a decimal   When we write zeroes after a decimal
   number, we don't change the value of the number. Say that.   number, we don't change the value of
                                                                 the number.

2. *(Write on board: .3)*
   Read this decimal.   three-tenths

   I'll write a zero after the decimal. *(Add a zero: .30.)* Now
   read the decimal.   thirty-hundredths

   I changed 3 tenths to 30 hundredths by adding a zero after
   a decimal number.

FORMAT 13.4   (continued)

TEACHER	STUDENTS

3. I'm going to use fractions to show that 3 tenths equals 30 hundredths.

   (Write on board: $\frac{3}{10}$ *)*

   Read this.   three-tenths

   We start with 3 tenths and we end with 30 hundredths.

   (Write on board: $\frac{30}{100}$ *)*

   What do I multiply 10 by to make it 100?   10

   What do I multiply 3 by to make it 30?   10

   (Write on board: $\frac{3}{10}\left(\frac{10}{10}\right) = \frac{30}{100}$ *)*

   I multiplied 3 tenths by 10 tenths: 10 tenths equal 1. Remember, when we multiply by 1 we don't change the value of a number. So 3 tenths equals 30 hundredths. *(Write .3 = .30.)*

4. *(Repeat steps 2 and 3, changing .5 to .500.)*

5. Here's another rule about zeroes: If we cross out zeroes at the end of a decimal number, we don't change the value of the decimal. *(Write .50.)* Read this decimal number.   fifty hundredths

   I'll cross out the zero at the end of the decimal. *(Cross out zero: .50.)* Now what does this decimal say?   five tenths

6. Let's use fractions to show that 50 hundredths equal 5 tenths.
   (Write the problem on the board.)

   $$\frac{50}{100} = \frac{5}{10}$$

   Fifty equals 5 times what number?   10

   One hundred equals 10 times what number?   10

   (Write the rest of the problem.)

   $$\frac{50}{100} = \frac{5}{10}\left(\frac{10}{10}\right)$$

   To make 5 tenths into 50 hundredths we multiplied it by 10 tenths. Ten-tenths equals 1. When we multiply by 1 we don't change the value of a number, so .50 = .5.

   (Repeat steps 5 and 6 with $\frac{300}{1000} = \frac{3}{10}$.)

PART B: STRUCTURED BOARD PRESENTATION

1. *(Write on the board: 8.4.)*
   Read this number.   eight and four tenths

   I want to rewrite this mixed decimal so that the decimal tells about thousandths.

(continued on next page)

FORMAT 13.4   (continued)

TEACHER	STUDENTS
2. When we write a decimal that tells about thousandths, how many digits must there be after the decimal point?	3
3. I already have one digit after the decimal point, so how many zeroes must I add? *(Write 8.400.)*	2
4. Read the decimal number now.	eight and four-hundred thousandths
Did we change the value of 8.4?	no

No, 8.400 is the same as 8.4. When we add zeroes at the end of the decimal, we don't change its value.

(Repeat steps 1–4 changing 5.1 to 5.10; 9.300 to 9.3, 7 to 7.00, 9 to 9.0.)

PART C: LESS-STRUCTURED WORKSHEET

1. *(Give students a worksheet like this one.)*

Mixed Decimals

Tenths	Hundredths	Thousandths
3.7	_____	_____
_____	_____	_____
9.2	_____	_____
_____	_____	_____
_____	6.20	_____

2. *(Point across row a.)* You have to fill in the missing mixed decimal numbers. Every mixed decimal in a row must have the same value. Read the number closest to a.   three and seven tenths

3. Touch the space in the next column. The heading says hundredths. We must rewrite 3.7 so that the decimal expresses hundredths. How many digits must be after the decimal point for hundredths?   2

The mixed decimal 3.7 has one digit after the decimal. What must you do?   Add one zero

Write the mixed decimal in the hundredths column. What mixed number did you write in the hundredths column?   3.70

4. *(Repeat step 2 with the thousandths column.)*

(Repeat steps 2 and 3 with remaining examples.)

(Note: When converting whole numbers to mixed decimals, the teacher explains that a decimal point is written after the whole number. After the decimal point, zero(es) are added: one zero if the decimal expresses tenths, two zeroes if it expresses hundredths, and three zeroes if it expresses thousandths.)

FORMAT 13.5   **Format for Addition/Subtraction of Unlike Decimals**

PART A: STRUCTURED BOARD PRESENTATION

TEACHER	STUDENTS
1. When we add or subtract numbers containing decimals, we first rewrite them so they all have the same number of places after the decimal point.	
(Write on board: 13.7 – 2.14)	
2. Read this problem.	thirteen and seven tenths minus two and fourteen hundredths.
3. Which number has more places after the decimal point?	2.14
So we have to rewrite the problem so that each number is talking about hundredths.	
4. *(Point to 13.7.)* What can I do to 7 tenths to make it into a number with two places behind the decimal?	Add the zero after the 7.
Yes, I add a zero after the 7. *(Write 0 after 7: 13.70.)* Now we have 70 hundredths. Read the problem now.	13.70 – 2.14
5. To work the problem, I'll write the problem in a column, making sure the decimal points are lined up. *(Write and solve the problem.)*	

   13.70

– 2.14

   11.56

| 6. I'll write the decimal point in the answer. Remember, when we subtract numbers with decimals, we bring the decimal point straight down. *(Write the decimal point.)* | |

   13.70

– 2.14

   11.56

| Read the answer. | 11.56 |
| *(Repeat steps 1–6 with this problem: 18.9 – 3.425.)* | |

PART B: STRUCTURED WORKSHEET

1. *(Give students a worksheet like this one.)*
   a. 7.1 – 3.45   b. 16.345 + 8.3
   c. 51.43 + 6.85   d. 13.6 – 2.346
   e. 19.1 – 8.34   f. 96.4 + 86.4
   g. 4.5 + 6.35   h. 271. – 71.42

2. Read problem a on your worksheet.	7.1 – 3.45
3. Do the numbers have the same number of places after the decimal point?	no
4. Right. One number has tenths, and the other has hundredths. Which number has more places after the decimal?	3.45
So which number do you have to change?	7.1
What do you do to 7.1?	Add a zero after the 1.
Add the zero. *(Monitor responses.)* Now rewrite the problem in a column and work it. *(Pause.)* What is the answer? *(Pause, signal.)*	1.65
(Repeat steps 1–3 with several more problems.)	

FORMAT 13.6 **Format for Rounding Off Decimals**

PART A: STRUCTURED BOARD PRESENTATION

TEACHER	STUDENTS

1. *(Write on board: .376)*

2. I want to round off this decimal to the nearest hundredth. When we talk about hundredths, how many digits will we have after the decimal? — two

   I will count off two digits after the decimal point and then draw a line after that digit. *(Write .37/6.)*

3. When we round off a decimal, we must look at the number that comes after the line. If the number is 5 or more we must add another unit. What number comes after the line? — 6

   So must we add another hundredth? — yes

   If we had 37 hundredths and we add another hundredth, how many hundredths do we have? — 38

   So .376 rounded to the nearest hundredth is . . . — .38

   (Write .38.)

4. *(Repeat steps 1 and 2 with the following problems.)*
   .372 rounded to the nearest tenth
   .1482 rounded to the nearest hundredth
   .382 rounded to the nearest whole
   .924 rounded to the nearest hundredth

PART B: STRUCTURED WORKSHEET

1. *(Give students a worksheet like this one.)*
   a. Round .462 to the nearest tenth _____
   b. Round .428 to the nearest tenth _____
   c. Round .8562 to the nearest hundredth _____
   d. Round .8548 to the nearest hundredth _____
   e. Round .3467 to the nearest hundredth _____
   f. Round .3437 to the nearest hundredth _____
   g. Round .417 to the nearest tenth _____
   h. Round .482 to the nearest tenth _____
   i. Round .3819 to the nearest hundredth _____
   j. Round .3814 to the nearest hundredth _____

2. Touch problem a. What do we round off that decimal to? — to the nearest tenth

3. How many digits will be after the decimal point when you round off to the nearest tenth? — one

   Count one digit after the decimal point and draw a line.

4. Let's see if you add another tenth. What number comes just after the line? — 6

   So do you add another tenth? — yes

   You had four tenths. If you add a tenth, how many tenths do you have? — 5

   If you round off .462 to the nearest tenth, what do you have? — 5 tenths

   Write the answer on the line. — Students write .5.
   (Repeat steps 1–3 with remaining problems.)

FORMAT 13.6   (continued)

PART C: LESS STRUCTURED WORKSHEET

TEACHER	STUDENTS

(Give students a worksheet like the one given in Part B.)

1. Read item a.

2. Draw a line to show where you round off.

3. Round off and write your answer on the line.

4. Read your answer.

   (Repeat steps 1–4 with remaining problems.)

FORMAT 13.7   **Format for Multiplying Decimals**

PART A: STRUCTURED BOARD PRESENTATION

TEACHER	STUDENTS

1. *(Write the following problem on the board.)*

    $$\begin{array}{r} 34.2 \\ \times\ .59 \\ \hline 3078 \\ 1710\ \ \\ \hline 20178 \end{array}$$

2. We're multiplying mixed decimals so we have to put a decimal point in our answer. Here's a fast way to figure out where to write the decimal point in the answer. We count the places after the decimal points in both numbers we're multiplying.

3. I'll touch the numbers after the decimal points and count them: *(touch 2)* one *(touch 9)* two *(touch 5)* three. How many decimal places in both numbers?   **3**

4. So I write the decimal point in the answer so that there are three places after it. *(Point between 7 and 8.)* One place. *(Point between 1 and 7.)* Two places. *(Point between 0 and 1.)* Three places. I put the decimal point here. *(Point between 0 and 1.)*

5. How many places after the decimal point?   **3**

    Read the answer.   **20.178**

    (Repeat steps 1–4 with the problems below.)

    $$\begin{array}{r} 34.2 \\ \times\ \ 5 \\ \hline \end{array} \qquad \begin{array}{r} 34.2 \\ \times\ .7 \\ \hline \end{array} \qquad \begin{array}{r} 351 \\ \times\ .05 \\ \hline \end{array}$$

(continued on next page)

FORMAT 13.7   (continued)

PART B: STRUCTURED WORKSHEET

TEACHER   **STUDENTS**

1. *(Give students a worksheet like the following one.)*

a. 32.1	b. .321	c. 3.21	d. 321	e. 3.421
× .9	× .9	× 9	× .9	× .7
2889	2889	2889	2889	23947

f. 492	g. 4.92	h. .492	i. 49.2
× .53	× .53	× 5.3	× 53
1476	1476	1476	1476
24600	24600	24600	24600
26076	26076	26076	26076

j. 429	k. .32	l. 3.2	m. 3.2
× 53	× .05	× 5	× .05
1476	160	160	160
24600	000		000
26076	160		160

2. These problems are worked already. All you have to do is put in the decimal points.

3. Touch problem a.

4. How many places are after the decimal points in both numbers being multiplied? *(Pause, signal.)*   2

5. Where does the decimal point go in the answer?   Between the 7 and the 8

6. Write it.

7. Read the answer.   27.89

    (Repeat steps 2–6 with remaining problems.)

PART C: LESS-STRUCTURED WORKSHEET

1. *(Give students worksheet with a mix of multiplication and addition problems containing decimals and mixed decimals.)* Remember: When you multiply, you count the places after the decimal point. When you add, you bring the decimal point straight down.

2. Work problem a. *(Pause.)*

3. Where does the decimal point go?

    (Repeat steps 1–3 with remaining problems.)

FORMAT 13.8   **Format for Division with Decimals—Rounding Off**

PART A: STRUCTURED BOARD PRESENTATION

TEACHER	STUDENTS

1. *(Write the following instructions on the board.)*
   Work the problem, and express your answer to the nearest
   hundredth: 7)3.24

2. Read the problem.   7 goes into 3 and 24 hundredths

   The instructions tell us to work the problem to the nearest
   hundredth. How many digits after the decimal point when
   we have hundredths?   2

   So we work the problem until we have two digits after the
   decimal point.

   (Solve the problem.)

   ```
     .46
   7)3.24
    2 8
     44
     42
      2
   ```

3. We have hundredths in the answer, but we're not done
   because we have a remainder. We have to work the
   problem to thousandths and then round to hundredths.
   So I draw a line after the 6.

4. We have to divide one more time so we know how to round
   off. Here's what we do. We add a zero after the 4 in the
   number we're dividing. Remember, when you add a zero
   after the last digit in a decimal number, you don't change
   the value of the number.

   (Add a zero.)

   ```
     .46
   7)3.240
    2 8
     44
     42
      2
   ```

   Now we can divide again. We bring down the zero. *(Write 0
   next to 2.)* How many 7s in 20? *(Pause, signal.)*   2

   (Write 14 and 2.)

   ```
     .462
   7)3.240
    2 8
     44
     42
     20
     14
      6
   ```

4. Do I round off to 46 hundredths or 47 hundredths?   46 hundredths

   To correct: What number is after the rounding off line?
   That is less than 5, so we don't add another unit.

(continued on next page)

FORMAT 13.8 (continued)

TEACHER	STUDENTS

(Repeat steps 1–4 with the problems below.)

9)4̄ Round off to nearest tenth.
7)2̄6.3 Round off to nearest hundredth.
3)2̄ Round off to nearest hundredth.

PART B: STRUCTURED WORKSHEET

1. *(Give students a worksheet like the following one.)*
   a. Work these problems and round off to the nearest hundredth.
      1. 3)7̄.4 =   2. 6)5̄ =
   b. Work these problems and round off to the nearest tenth.
      3. 4)2̄.31 =   4. 7)3̄ =

2. Read the instructions for a.

       Work these problems and round off to the nearest hundredth.

   Read problem one.

       3 into 7.4

3. You have to round the problem to the nearest hundredth. How many digits will there be after the decimal point in your answer?

       2

   Work the problem. Stop after there are two digits after the decimal point. *(Monitor students' work.)*

   $$\begin{array}{r} 2.46 \\ 3\overline{)7.40} \\ \underline{6} \\ 1\,4 \\ \underline{1\,2} \\ 20 \\ \underline{18} \end{array}$$

4. You're not finished because you still have a remainder. Draw a line after the last digit in your answer. Now add a zero to 7.40 and divide again. *(Pause.)*

5. What numeral did you write after the line in the answer?

       6

   So do you add another hundredth?

       yes

   Write your rounded-off answer. What's your answer?

       2.47

PART C: LESS-STRUCTURED WORKSHEET

1. *(Give students a worksheet like the one given in Part B.)*

2. Read the instructions for a.

3. Read problem one.

4. Where are you going to draw the line for rounding off: after the first, second, or third digit behind the decimal point?

       second digit?

5. Work the problem and write your rounded-off answer.

FORMAT 13.9 Preskill: Multiplying Decimals by Multiples of 10

PART A: STRUCTURED BOARD PRESENTATION

TEACHER	STUDENTS
1. Here are some rules about multiplying decimals by 10 or 100: When you multiply by 10, you move the decimal one place to the right. What do you do to the decimal point when you multiply by 10?	Move it one place to the right.
When you multiply by 100, you move the decimal point two places to the right. What do you do with the decimal point when you multiply by 100?	Move it two places to the right.
2. *(Write on the board: 37.48 × 10)* Read the problem.	37.48 × 10
We're multiplying by 10. What do you do to the decimal point when you multiply by 10?	Move it one place to the right.
3. *(Write on the board: 37.48 × 10 = 3748)* The decimal point was between the 7 and the 4. If I move it one place to the right, where will the decimal be?	between the 4 and 8
(Write on board: 37.48 × 10 = 374.8) Read the answer.	374.8

4. *(Repeat steps 2 and 3 with the problems below.)*
   37 × 100
   8.532 × 10
   7.2 × 100
   25 × 100
   2.5 × 10

PART B: STRUCTURED WORKSHEET

1. *(Give the students a worksheet like the following one.)*

   a. 3.74 × 10 =   e. 16 × 100 =
   b. .894 × 100 =   f. 15 × 10 =
   c. 42.8 × 100 =   g. .0382 × 10 =
   d. 3.517 × 10 =   h. 49.2 × 100 =

2. When you multiply by 10, what must you do?	Move the decimal one place to the right.
When you multiply by 100, what must you do?	Move the decimal two places to the right.
3. Read problem a.	3.74 × 10
4. You're multiplying by 10, so what must you do to the decimal point?	Move it one place to the right.
5. Where will the decimal point be in the answer?	between the 7 and the 4
6. Write the answer.	Students write 37.4.
7. Read your answer.	37.4

   (Repeat steps 1–6 with remaining problems.)

FORMAT 13.10   Format for Dividing by Decimals

PART A: STRUCTURED BOARD PRESENTATION

TEACHER	STUDENTS

1. *(Write the following on the board.)*
   .5)51.75

2. Here's a rule about decimal division: We don't divide by a decimal number. *(Point to .5.)* We must change the divisor to a whole number.

3. *(Point to .5)51.75)* What is the divisor in this problem?   5
   Can we work the problem the way it is?   no
   What must we do?   Change the divisor to a whole number.

4. We make five-tenths a whole number by moving the decimal point. A number is a whole number when there are no digits after the decimal point. How many places must I move the decimal point over to the right to make .5 into a whole number? _____   one
   (Draw arrow: .5)51.75)
   I moved the decimal one place to the right. We have to move the decimal point the same number of places in the dividend. How many places to the right must we move the decimal point in the dividend?   one
   (Write on board: .5)51.7 5)
   Now we can work the problem. I write the decimal point on the answer line, and then divide.
   (Write on board: 5.)51 7.5)

5. I'll divide.
   ```
       10 3.5
   5.)51 7.5
      5
      01 7
       1 5
        2 5
        2 5
   ```

6. What's the answer?   103.5

   (Repeat steps 1–5 with the problems below.)
   .05)5.125   .7)28
   .0)21.9   .07)28

PART B: STRUCTURED WORKSHEET

1. *(Give students a worksheet like the following one.)*
   .05)3.25   .5)32   .04)92
   .3)9.6   .03)9.6

2. Read the first problem.   .05 into 3.25

3. What is the divisor?   .05

4. Cross out the decimal point and move it to the right to make a whole number.   Students write 05.)3.25

FORMAT 13.10 (continued)

TEACHER	STUDENTS
5. How many places did you move the decimal point to the right?	2
That's what you must do in the dividend. Cross out the decimal point and write it where it belongs. *(Monitor students' work.)*	Students write $.05.\overline{)3.25}$
6. Now write the decimal point where it will be in the answer.	Students write $.05.\overline{)3.25}$.
7. Work the problem.	
8. What's the answer?	65
(Repeat steps 1–7 with remaining problems.)	

CHAPTER 14

Percent and Ratio

TERMS AND CONCEPTS

Percent   A notation for hundredths.

Percentage   The number obtained by finding the percent of another number.

Ratio   The numerical expression of the relationship between two comparable quantities. Usually the ratio is the result of dividing the first quantity by the second.

The concepts of percentage and percent are applied frequently in real-life situations.

Percentage
Prices went up 15%.
The store is having a 20% reduction sale.
The loan charges are 8%.

Percent (Ratio)
Alice made 3 of 7 shots.
Mary worked 8 of 10 problems.
Carlos saw 2 of the 3 movies.

The introduction of percentage and ratio usually follows instruction on most of the basic fraction and decimal skills discussed in the earlier chapters.

Ratio problems require students to convert a numerical relationship (ratio) between two quantities into a percent. The fraction ¾ is converted to 75%. An example of a ratio application problem is "Ann made 3 of 7 shots. What percent of her shots did she make?"

Percentage problems require the student to figure out the quantity that represents a given percent of another quantity. For example, (a) What is 30% of 60? (b) You need to get 70% of the questions on the test correct to pass. If there are 20 problems on the test, how many must you get correct to pass?

Teachers should note that various decimal skills are preskills for percent and ratio problems. For example, to solve a percentage problem, the student must be able to multiply mixed decimals; to solve a ratio problem, the student must be able to convert a fraction to a decimal or mixed decimal and round off the decimal or mixed decimal number.

A specific sequence for introducing the major types of problems students encounter in the elementary grades appears in the Instructional Sequence and Assessment Chart. Note on the chart that we recommend introducing percentage-related skills before ratio-related skills.

PERCENTAGE PROBLEMS

Two types of percentage problems are common to elementary mathematics instruction. The easier type of problem states a percent and quantity and asks students to find the percentage:

Instructional Sequence and Assessment Chart

Grade Level	Problem Type	Performance Indicator
5a	Converting percentages to decimal figures	Write these percents as decimals: 45% = 15% = 6% = 1% =
5b	Determining a percent of a given number	What is 8% of 20? What is 25% of 12? What is 130% of 50?
5c	Simple percentage story problems	Jane took 20 basketball shots. She made 60% of her shots. How many shots did she make? Tara scored 5% of her team's points. Her team scored 60 points. How many points did Tara score? In May a store sold 300 shirts. In June the store sold 130% of what it sold in May. How many shirts did it sell in June?
5d	Converting a decimal to a percent	.32 = % .6 = % 3.4 = %
5e	Converting a fraction to a percent: percentage comes out even	Convert these fractions to percentages: $\frac{3}{5} =$ % $\frac{7}{10} =$ % $\frac{5}{4} =$ %
5f	Converting a fraction to a percent: rounding off required	$\frac{3}{7} =$ % $\frac{4}{9} =$ % $\frac{5}{3} =$ %
5g	Simple ratio story problems; total is given	Bill took 20 basketball shots. He made 12. What is his shooting percentage? Ann has 15 friends; 9 of her friends are from Texas. What percentage of her friends are from Texas?
6a	Complex percentage problems	Jill earned $80 in May. In June she earned 30% more than she did in May. How much did Jill earn in June? Tim borrowed $200. He must pay 9% interest. How much must he pay back altogether?

(continued on next page)

Instructional Sequence and Assessment Chart (continued)

Grade Level	Problem Type	Performance Indicator
6b	Complex ratio problems; total not given	I got A's on 5 tests and B's on 4 tests. What percent of the tests did I get A's on?
		There are 4 boys and 6 girls. What percent of the class is boys?
		Bill has 5 blue pens and 15 red pens. What percent of the pens are blue?

The teacher said that 70% was passing. There are 50 problems on the test. How many problems must I get to pass? (70% of 50 is .70 × 50 = 35)

The more difficult problem type requires the student to figure the percentage of an original quantity, then either add or subtract that amount from the original quantity:

Bill borrowed $80 from the bank. He must pay 8% interest on the loan. How much must he pay back to the bank? (.08 × 80 = 6.40, $80.00 + $6.40 = $86.40)

This problem type would not be introduced until students had a great deal of practice with the easier type.

Converting Percent to Decimal

Prior to introducing percentage problems, students should have mastered (1) multiplying decimal and mixed decimal numbers and (2) converting a percent figure to a decimal.

Format 14.1 introduces the percent concept and teaches students to convert a percent to a decimal. The format contains three parts. In Part A, the teacher simply presents the percent sign and teaches students to read percent numbers. In Part B, a structured board exercise, the teacher demonstrates how a percent number can be written as a decimal number by rewriting the numerals, deleting the percent sign, and placing a decimal point so that there are two decimal places. Part C is a structured worksheet exercise. Daily worksheet practice should continue for several weeks.

Example selection is quite important when teaching this format. One-third of the percent figures should be below 10%, one-third between 10 and 100%, and one-third over 100%. For example, a conversion exercise might include the following percents: 5%, 28%, 1%, 235%, 30%, 300%. Exposure to these problem types provides students with the practice needed to generalize the strategy to a wide range of examples. Percents below 10 are included to teach students that when converting a percent below 10 they must write a zero in front of the decimal number (e.g., 6% = .06, 1% = .01). Percents of 100 and above are included to show that a whole number can be produced (e.g., 354% = 3.54, 200% = 2).

Problems in which a percent that already includes a decimal, such as 87.5%, is converted to a decimal would not be included initially. Problems of this type require the students to add two more decimal places (e.g., 87.5% = .875). An adaptation of Format 14.1 would be used. The teacher would explain that two more decimal places must be added.

Simple Percentage Problems

Simple percentage problems are comprised of a quantity multiplied by a given percent; students must determine the percentage (e.g., 30% × 40 = 12). This problem type can be introduced after the students can translate percent to decimals and can accurately multiply decimal numbers.

Format 14.2 shows how to teach students to solve simple percentage problems. Part A is designed to teach students rules that will help them determine if their answers to subsequent problems are correct. The students are taught that if the problem asks for 100%, then the answer is the same as the number being multiplied (e.g., 100% × 20 = 20).

Likewise, if the percent is more than 100%, the answer is more than the number being multiplied; if less than 100%, the answer is less than the number being multiplied. Students then use the rules to predict the answers to some numerical problems. Although these rules appear to be extremely simple, by examining the errors of students who have not been explicitly taught this information, it is clear that many students never figure out these relationships on their own.

Part B is a structured board presentation in which the strategy for solving percentage problems is presented: Convert the percent to a decimal, then multiply that decimal and the amount given. Students apply the rules learned in Part A to check their answers.

Part C is a structured worksheet exercise in which the students solve problems. Note that when multiplying a two-digit and a three-digit number, the student should be instructed to write the two-digit number on the bottom. For example, in solving 125% × 60, the student writes:

$$\begin{array}{r} .125 \\ \times\ 60 \\ \hline \end{array}$$

Examples should include sets of three problems in which the same number is being multiplied. In one problem, the percent would be below 10%; in another problem, between 10 and 100%; and in another problem, more than 100%. For example, a sample set for an exercise might include these problems:

30% × 60	25% × 36
3% × 60	2% × 36
130% × 60	125% × 36

Including these three problem types in a set provides practice in the wide range of problems students will encounter.

Simple Percentage Story Problems

Simple percentage story problems state an amount and ask the student to determine a percentage. A distinguishing characteristic of these problems is the inclusion of the word *of.* Below are two typical simple percentage problems:

> There are 60 children in our school. 75% of the children are girls. How many girls are there in our school?

> Sarah made 60% of her shots. She took 20 shots. How many shots did she make?

Story problems of this type are introduced when students can solve problems such as 40% × 20 accurately. As preparation, teachers first give students

simple equations in which the word *of* is substituted for the times sign (e.g., 75% of 48). After several lessons, the teacher introduces story problems, modeling and testing how to solve them. After solving them, the teacher repeats the problem, asking whether students multiplied by more or less than 100%, and if the answer made sense. (e.g., "The problem said she got 60% of her shots in. She took 25 shots. We know the answer must be less than 25 because she made less than 100% of her shots.") A worksheet should include problems with a percent below 10, problems with a percent between 10 and 100, and problems with a percent above 100.

Complex Percentage Problems

Complex percentage problems usually give the percent that an original amount has either increased (or decreased) and asks the students to figure out the amount of the increase (or decrease) and the new total. These complex percentage problems should not be introduced until students have practiced simple percent problems for at least several weeks. This type of problem is illustrated below:

> The hat store sold 50 hats in May. In June the sales went up 20%. How many more hats did the store sell in June than May? How many hats did the store sell in June?

The teaching procedure involves the teacher modeling how to solve the problem: first computing the percentage increased or decreased by converting the percent to a decimal and then multiplying. This amount is then added to or subtracted from the original amount to determine the new total. For example, in the problem above, the student converts 20% to .20 and multiplies .20 × 50 to end with 10. The store sold 10 more hats in June than in May. This 10 is added to the 50 hats sold in May to determine that 60 hats were sold in June.

A special type of problem involves computing interest. (The term *interest* used here refers to simple interest. Compound interest would be presented in junior or senior high.) The teacher can explain the term *interest* to students by using an explanation similar to the one below. "When you borrow money from a bank, you must pay back the bank extra money. The extra money is interest. If the bank charges 10% interest, you must pay back the money you borrowed plus 10% of the amount you borrowed."

Figure 14.1 is a sample interest exercise. Students fill in missing amounts in a table that provides practice in determining interest for various loans. More

FIGURE 14.1   Sample Interest Exercise

Amount of Loan	Interest Rate for 1 Year	Amount of Interest for 1 Year	Amount to Be Paid Back at End of 1 Year
a. $500	5%	_____	_____
b. $500	8%	_____	_____
c. $1000	4%	_____	_____
d. $1000	7%	_____	_____

complex interest problems would be introduced in later grades.

RATIO PROBLEMS

In ratio problems, students must convert a fraction to a percent figure. Three basic types of ratio problems include:

1. Numerical problems for converting a fraction to percent.

$$\frac{2}{5} = 40\%$$

$$\frac{5}{4} = 125\%$$

2. Simple ratio story problems. In these problems, the total and one partial quantity are given. The student calculates the percent.

Sarah made 10 out of 20 shots. What percent of her shots did she make?

$$\frac{10}{20} = 50\%$$

3. Complex story problems. In these problems, the student is required to add the amounts given prior to determining a percent.

Ann got 10 shots in and missed 10 shots. What percent of her shots did she make?

$$10 + 10 = 20 \qquad \frac{10}{20} = 50\%$$

Converting a Fraction to a Percent

Converting a fraction to a percent can be introduced several weeks after students have mastered simple percentage problems. Format 14.3 teaches this conversion skill. The format assumes that students have previously mastered converting fractions to decimals by dividing the numerator by the denominator, which in turn requires students to divide and round off decimal numbers.

The format includes five parts. In Part A, the teacher presents a strategy for converting decimal numbers to percent numbers: "Write a percent sign and move the decimal point two places toward the percent sign." The wording for this procedure has been designed to aid students in determining the direction to move the decimal point. After presenting the rule, the teacher presents examples of its application in converting decimals to percents. Examples should include mixed decimals and decimal numbers with tenth, hundredth, and thousandth decimals.

Part B is a worksheet exercise in which students practice converting decimals to a percent. The teacher guides the students through several conversions, and then the students work the rest of the problems themselves. Several days of practice on this skill should be provided before introducing Part C. The examples selected for Parts A and B should include a mix of decimals, whole numbers, and mixed decimals. Decimals expressed as tenths, hundredths, and thousandths should be included, as well as one or two whole numbers and several mixed decimals. A sample set for a worksheet exercise might include these numbers: 3.2, .475, 6, .08, .4, .37, 2, 6.1, 35, .875, and .1. When converting a tenths decimal or whole number, the teacher tells the students the number of zeroes to add:

$$.1 = .10 = .10\% = 10\%$$

In Part C, a structured board exercise, the teacher presents the two-step strategy for converting fractions to a percent. "First convert the fraction to a decimal, and then convert that decimal to a percent." The teacher then demonstrates its application with several fractions.

Part D is a structured worksheet exercise in which students are given a worksheet with prompts to help make the conversion. A prompted problem looks like this:

$$\frac{3}{4} = .\underline{\hspace{2cm}} = \underline{\hspace{2cm}}\%$$

Part E is a less-structured worksheet exercise in which no prompts are written on the students' worksheets. There are two example selection guidelines for Parts C, D, and E:

1. Both proper and improper fractions should be included so that students can see that the strategy also applies to percents greater than 100 percent (e.g., $5/4 = 125\%$, $7/5 = 140\%$).
2. Problems should initially be limited to fractions that do not require rounding off to compute the percent. Problems requiring rounding off require an extra step and should not be introduced for several weeks. The fractions $3/4$, $1/2$, $7/5$, $7/10$, $6/8$, and $6/4$ are examples of fractions that do not require rounding off. The fractions $5/7$, $2/9$, $4/3$, $3/11$, and $6/5$ are examples of fractions that do require rounding off.

When problems requiring rounding off are introduced, the teacher tells the students to divide until the answer has three digits after the decimal and then instructs them to round off to the nearest hundredth. For example, when converting $5/7$ to a percent, the student divides to hundredths, then writes a line after the 1 (the hundredths number), divides once again, and then rounds off the answer to 71:

$$
\begin{array}{r}
.71|4 \\
7\overline{)5.00|0} \\
\underline{4\,9} \\
10 \\
\underline{7} \\
3\,0 \\
\underline{2\,8} \\
2
\end{array}
$$

For examples such as $2/3$ in which there is a repeating decimal, the teacher can demonstrate how to round off and express the answer as 66.7. This type of problem is potentially confusing and should not be introduced until students have mastered the rounding-off strategy.

After students have had several weeks of practice in converting fractions to decimals, the teacher can introduce the new steps of reducing the fraction before dividing, when possible. For example, $9/12$ can be reduced to $3/4$, so students would divide 3 by 4 instead of 9 by 12. Reducing fractions prior to dividing is especially helpful when dealing with two-digit denominators. If the denominator can be reduced to one digit, the division problem will be much easier.

A final consideration in teaching students to convert fractions to decimals involves providing students with adequate practice so that they can mem-

orize the percents that more common fractions represent. The percents for these fractions should be taught: $1/4$, $3/4$, $1/2$, $1/3$, $2/3$, $1/5$, $2/5$, $3/5$, $4/5$ as well as $1/10$, $2/10$, $9/10$. Students should receive adequate practice so that they can tell the percents these fractions represent instantaneously. To facilitate this memorization, the teacher provides flash card practice or another type of memorization exercise. However, this memorization practice would not begin until after several weeks of instruction on conversions to percents.

Simple Ratio Story Problems

In simple ratio story problems two related quantities are given, and students are asked to express the relationship between these two quantities as a percent figure. Most simple ratio problems deal with a subset of a total set. For example, shots made (subset) out of shots attempted (total set); girls (subset) out of children (total set); red apples (subset) out of apples (total set). Problems a and b are examples of this type of problem:

a. There were 20 problems on the test. Jack got 14 right. What percent of the problems did Jack get correct?

b. There are 12 children in our class; 8 are girls. What percent of our class are girls?

Simple percentage problems can be introduced when students have mastered converting fractions to a percent figure. The format for simple ratio problems contains three parts (see Format 14.4). In Part A, the board presentation, students are taught the component skill of converting the relationship expressed in the story to a fraction. The teacher presents the rule that the number that tells how many altogether is written as the denominator of the fraction; she then models and tests with several examples. For example, "Sheila took 12 shots; she made 10" translates to the fraction $10/12$.

Part B provides worksheet practice on converting ratio story problems to fractions. Part C is a less-structured worksheet in which the teacher guides students in rewriting a fraction as a percent figure. The teacher first asks students to write the fraction indicated by the problem and then to translate that fraction to a percent.

Practice problems should include as many real-life situations pertaining to the classroom as possible (e.g., What percent of the children are girls? What percent of the days has it rained?).

Complex Ratio Story Problems

In complex ratio story problems, the students must add the two quantities to derive a sum that will be the denominator of the fraction used to compute percent. For example, a problem may state there are four boys and six girls and ask for the percent of the children that are girls. For that problem, the quantities four and six must be added to determine the denominator, since the fraction is:

$$\frac{\text{girls}}{\text{boys and girls}}$$

Complex ratio story problems are not introduced until students have had several weeks of practice with simple ratio problems.

In Part A of Format 14.5, the teacher models how the total is derived for complex problems. "The problem asks what fraction of the children are girls, so the fraction will be girls over the children. How many children? So what do I write for the denominator?"

The examples used to teach complex ratio problems should include both simple and complex ratio problems, including sets of related problems such as a and b below:

a. There are 6 children in the club, and 4 are girls. What percent of the children are girls?

b. There are 4 boys and 6 girls in the club. What percent of the children in the club are girls?

Problem a is a simple ratio problem. Problem b is a complex ratio problem. Note that the total in both problems is the number of children. In problem a, the number of children is given. However, problem b does not tell the total, and the quantities 4 boys and 6 girls must be added. Presenting related simple and complex problems is necessary to provide students with practice in determining when the quantities should be added to figure the denominator of the fraction.

APPLICATION ITEMS: PERCENT AND RATIO

1. Below are errors made by students. Specify the probable cause of each error and describe a remediation procedure.

   a. What is 38% of 90?

   Jill

   $$\begin{array}{r} 90 \\ \times\,.38 \\ \hline 720 \\ 2700 \\ \hline 3420 \end{array} = 3420$$

   Tim

   $$\begin{array}{r} 90.00 \\ .38 \\ \hline 90.38 \end{array} = 90.38$$

   Sarah

   $$\begin{array}{r} 90 \\ .38 \\ \hline 720 \\ 270 \\ \hline 9.90 \end{array} = 9.9$$

   b. What is 5% of 60?

   Jack

   $$\begin{array}{r} 60 \\ \times\,.5 \\ \hline 30.0 \end{array} = 30$$

c. Bill took 15 shots; he made 12 of his shots. What percent of his shots did he make?

Tom

$$\frac{15}{12} = 12\overline{)15.0} \begin{array}{r} 1.25 \\ \underline{12} \\ 3\,0 \\ \underline{2\,4} \\ 60 \end{array} = 125\%$$

Zelda

$$\frac{12}{15} = 15\overline{)12.0} \begin{array}{r} .69 \\ \underline{9\,0} \\ 3\,00 \\ \underline{1\,35} \end{array} = 69\%$$

Elwin

$$\frac{12}{15} = 15\overline{)12.0} \begin{array}{r} .8 \\ \underline{12.0} \end{array} = 8\%$$

2. Specify the wording the teacher uses in correcting Tom's mistake.

3. Specify the wording the teacher uses in a structured worksheet presentation for converting $^3/_7$ to a percent.

4. Below are sets of examples teachers constructed for an exercise to teach students to convert percent figures to decimals. Tell which sets are inadequate and why.

Set A:	85%	94%	30%	62%	53%	6%
Set B:	40%	5%	135%	240%	7%	82%
Set C:	130%	20%	72%	145%	80%	360%

FORMAT 14.1   Format for Converting Percent to Decimal

PART A: READING AND WRITING THE PERCENT SIGN

TEACHER	STUDENTS
1. *(Write on board: %)* This is a percent sign. What is this?	a percent sign
2. *(Write on board: 42%)* This says 42%. What does this say?	42%
3. *(Repeat step 2 with 20%.)*	
4. *(Write on board: 30%)* What does this say?	30%
(Repeat step 4 with 8%, 142%, 96%, 300%.)	

PART B: STRUCTURED BOARD PRESENTATION

1. Percent means hundredths. What does percent mean?	hundredths
2. 87% means 87 hundredths. What does 87% mean?	87 hundredths
(Repeat step 2 with 50%, 214%.)	

(continued on next page)

FORMAT 14.1   (continued)

TEACHER	STUDENTS
3. What does 30% mean?	30 hundredths
(Repeat step 3 with 248%, 8%.)	
4. How many decimal places in a hundredths number?	two
5. Here's a rule for changing a percent number to a decimal number: Get rid of the percent sign and put in a decimal point so that there are two decimal places. How many decimal places must we have when we change a percent number to a decimal number?	two
6. *(Write on board: 236%)* Read this.	236%
I want to change this number to a decimal. What does 236% mean?	236 hundredths
How many decimal places in a hundredths number?	two
So I get rid of the percent sign and put in two decimal places. *(Write 2.36.)* Read this.	2 and 36 hundredths
Yes, 236% = 2.36.	
7. *(Write on board: 8%)* Read this.	8%
I want to change this number to a decimal. What does 8% mean?	8 hundredths
How many decimal places in a hundredths number?	two
So I get rid of the percent sign and put in two decimal places. *(Write .08.)* Read this	8 hundredths
Yes, 8% = .08.	
(Repeat steps 6 and 7 with 34%, 126%, 5%, 82%.)	

PART C: STRUCTURED WORKSHEET

1. *(Give students a worksheet with similar instructions and problems like those below.)*
   Change these percents to decimals:

   a. 35% = _____   e.   1% = _____
   b. 200% = _____   f. 192% = _____
   c.   6% = _____   g. 374% = _____
   d. 72% = _____   h.   2% = _____

2. Read the directions.	Change these percents to decimals.
3. Read the percent number in problem a.	35%
4. What does 35% mean?	35 hundredths
5. How many decimal places in a hundredths number?	two
6. Where will we write the decimal point?	in front of the 3
7. Write the decimal number.	Students write .35.
8. What decimal did you write?	35 hundredths
Yes, 35% equals 35 hundredths.	
(Repeat steps 1–7 with remaining problems.)	

FORMAT 14.2   **Format for Solving Simple Percentage Problems**

PART A: MORE/LESS THAN 100%

TEACHER	**STUDENTS**

1. *(Write on board: 100%)* I want to change 100% to a decimal, so I get rid of the percent sign and put in two decimal places.

(Write on board: 1.00) 100% equals what whole number?   **1**
Yes, 100% equals one whole. So when we multiply by 100%, we don't change the value of the number we're multiplying. The answer is the same as the number we're multiplying.

2. Here are some rules about other percents: If we multiply by more than 100%, our answer is bigger than the number we're multiplying. If we multiply by less than 100%, our answer is less than the number we're multiplying.

3. If you multiply by 100%, what do you know about the answer?   The answer is the same as the number we're multiplying.

4. If you multiply by less than 100%, what do you know about the answer?   The answer is less than the number we're multiplying.

Right, when the percent is less than 100, you multiply by a number less than 1. So the answer must be less than the number we're multiplying.

5. If you multiply by more than 100%, what do you know about the answer?   The answer is more than the number we're multiplying.

(Repeat steps 2–5 until students respond correctly.)

6. Here's a problem: 60% × 20. Say the problem.   60% × 20

What's the percent?   60

Is the answer more than 20, less than 20, or equal to 20? *(Pause, signal.)*   less than 20

To correct: Remember: If the percent is less than 100, the answer is less than the amount we're multiplying. Is the percent less than 100? So, tell me about the answer. *(Repeat step 6.)*   The answer is less than 20.

How do you know?   The percent is less than 100.

7. *(Repeat step 6 with 140% of 20, 100% of 20, 24% of 150, 100% of 150, and 60% of 150.)*

PART B: STRUCTURED BOARD PRESENTATION

1. *(Write on board: 75% × 20)* Read this problem.   75% times 20

What is the percent?   75

What is the amount?   20

Will the answer be more or less than 20?   less than 20

2. Here's how we find the exact answer. We change the percent to a decimal, then multiply. How do we find the exact answer?   Change the percent to a decimal and multiply.

(continued on next page)

FORMAT 14.2 (continued)

TEACHER	STUDENTS
3. First we write 75% as a decimal; 75% equals how many hundredths?	75
Yes, 75% can be written as 75 hundredths. *(Write .75.)*	

4. Now we multiply. *(Write the problem on the board.)*

$$\begin{array}{r} 20 \\ \times.75 \\ \hline 100 \\ \underline{1400} \\ 1500 \end{array}$$

We multiplied by a decimal number so I must put a decimal point in the answer. Where do I put the decimal point?	after the 5
So what whole number do we end with?	15
5. What is 75% times 20?	15
Write 75% × 20 = 15. Say the statement.	75% times 20 equals 15.
6. Let's see if that follows the rules. The amount we began with was 20. We were finding less than 100%. Our answer must be less than 20. Is 15 less than 20?	yes
So our answer makes sense.	

(Repeat steps 1–6 with these problems: 125% × 20, 5% × 20, 120% × 65, 12% × 65, 20% × 65.)

PART C: STRUCTURED WORKSHEET

a.   30% × 50 equals ☐
b. 130% × 50 equals ☐
c.   3% × 50 equals ☐
d. 25% × 72 equals ☐

FORMAT 14.3   **Format for Converting Decimals and Fractions to Percents**

PART A: CONVERTING DECIMALS TO PERCENT

TEACHER	STUDENTS
1. We change a decimal to a percent by adding a percent sign after the number and moving the decimal point two places toward the percent sign. Listen again.	
(Repeat rule.)	
(Write on board: .486)	
2. Read this decimal.	486 thousandths
I want to change this decimal to a percent number. First I write the percent sign after the number.	
(Write on board: .486%)	

FORMAT 14.3   **(continued)**

TEACHER	**STUDENTS**

3. Now I move the decimal point two places, toward the percent sign. What do I do?

(Erase decimal point. Move two places to right: 48.6%.)

Move the decimal point two places toward the percent sign.

4. What percent do we end with?

48.6%

(Repeat steps 1–4 with 1.4, 2, .73, .04.)

PART B: CONVERTING DECIMAL TO PERCENT WORKSHEET

1. *(Give students a worksheet with instructions and problems like the following one.)*
   Convert these decimals and mixed decimals to percent:

a. .38 = _____	e. 3 = _____	i. 7.3 = _____
b. 4.1 = _____	f. .542 = _____	j. .485 = _____
c. .7 = _____	g. .04 = _____	k. 8 = _____
d. .07 = _____	h. .4 = _____	l. .02 = _____

2. Read the instructions.

Convert these decimals and mixed decimals to percent.

3. Where do we write the percent sign?

after the number

4. What do we do to the decimal point?

Move it two places toward the percent sign.

5. Touch a. Read the number.

.38

6. Write the digits 3 and 8 in the space next to the decimal. Write in the percent sign.

7. What must you do to the decimal point?

Move it two places toward the percent sign.

Put in the decimal. What percent does 38 hundredths equal?

38%

(Repeat steps 4–6 with several more problems; then have students work the rest on their own.)

PART C: STRUCTURED BOARD PRESENTATION

1. *(Write the following fraction on the board):* ⁵⁄₄

   I want to write this fraction as a percent. Here's how we change a fraction to a percent. First we change the fraction to a decimal and then change that decimal to a percent. Listen again. *(Repeat procedure.)* Read this fraction.

   five-fourths

2. I want to change this fraction to a percent. First I change the fraction to a decimal. What do I do first? How do I change ⁵⁄₄ to a decimal?

   Change the fraction to a decimal. Divide 4 into 5.

   I'll work the problem. I divide until there is no remainder. *(Solve the problem.)*

(continued on next page)

FORMAT 14.3 (continued)

TEACHER	STUDENTS
$\frac{5}{4} = 4\overline{)5.00} = 1.25$ (quotient 1.25; 4; 1 00; 80; 20)	
What mixed decimal does 5⁄4 equal?	1 and 25 hundredths
3. First I changed the fraction to a decimal. Now I change the decimal to a percent. What do I do next?	Change the decimal to a percent.
I write the percent sign and move the decimal two places toward the percent sign. *(Write on board: 125%)*	
How many percent does 5⁄4 equal?	125 percent
(Repeat steps 1–3 with 3⁄5, 1⁄2, and 7⁄5.)	

PART D: STRUCTURED WORKSHEET

TEACHER	STUDENTS
1. *(Give students a worksheet with instructions and problems like the following.)* Change these fractions to percents: a. $\frac{3}{4} = \overline{)\quad}$ = . ______ = ______ % b. $\frac{2}{5} = \overline{)\quad}$ = . ______ = ______ % c. $\frac{8}{4} = \overline{)\quad}$ = . ______ = ______ %	
2. In these problems, you must figure out the percent a fraction equals. First you change the fraction to a decimal. What do you do first?	Change the fraction to a decimal.
How do you change 3⁄4 to a decimal?	Divide 4 into 3.
Divide 4 into 3. Don't forget to put the decimal point in the answer. *(Pause.)* What decimal does 3⁄4 equal?	75 hundredths
Write 75 hundredths in the space next to the division problem. Now you change the decimal to a percent.	
3. What do you do?	Change the decimal to a percent.
Do it and write your answer in the last space. *(Pause.)*	
4. What percent does 3⁄4 equal?	75%
(Repeat steps 1–3 with remaining problems.)	

PART E: LESS-STRUCTURED WORKSHEET

1. *(Give students a worksheet with instructions and problems like the following one.)*
   Change each fraction to a percent:

   a. $\frac{3}{4} =$ b. $\frac{5}{2} =$

   c. $\frac{3}{5} =$ d. $\frac{5}{4} =$

FORMAT 14.3   **(continued)**

TEACHER	STUDENTS
2. Read the directions.	Change each fraction to a percent.
3. Touch a.	
4. What is the first fraction?	$\dfrac{3}{4}$
What do you do first to ¾?	Make it a decimal.
Do it. Make ¾ into a decimal. *(Pause.)* What decimal does ¾ equal?	75 hundredths
5. Now write 75 hundredths as a percent. *(Pause.)* What percent does 75 hundredths equal?	75%
(Repeat steps 1–4 with remaining problems.)	

FORMAT 14.4   **Format for Simple Ratio Story Problems**

PART A: STRUCTURED BOARD PRESENTATION: TRANSLATING TO FRACTIONS

TEACHER	STUDENTS
1. Listen to this problem: Jill took 8 basketball shots; she made 4 of the shots. What fraction of the shots did she make? Listen again: Jill took 8 shots. She made 4 of the shots. What fraction of the shots did she make?	
2. The problem asks what fraction of her shots she made. The fraction will be how many she actually made, over how many she took altogether. The bottom number tells how many altogether. What does the bottom number tell?	how many altogether
How many shots did she take altogether?	8
So I write 8 on the bottom. *(Write the following on the board.)* $\dfrac{}{8}$	
3. The top number tells how many shots she made. How many shots did she make?	4
I write 4 on the top. *(Write the fraction on the board.)* $\dfrac{4}{8}$	
4. Ann took 8 shots. She made 4 shots. What fraction of her shots did she make?	$\dfrac{4}{8}$

(Repeat steps 1–4 with the examples below.)
  a. Jill has 8 pencils; 5 are blue. What fraction of her pencils are blue?
  b. The class has 8 students; 5 are girls. What fraction of the students are girls?
  c. There are 10 apples in a bag; 6 of the apples are red. What fraction of the apples are red?
  d. Bill saved $5 so far. He needs $8 altogether. What fraction of the money he needs does he have?

(continued on next page)

FORMAT 14.4 **(continued)**

PART B: WORKSHEET

TEACHER	**STUDENTS**

1. *(Give students a worksheet with instructions and problems like the ones below.)*
   Write the fractions for these problems:

   a. Jane made 12 out of the 16 shots she took during the game. $\frac{\square}{\square}$

   b. Alex has 15 friends; 10 of his friends live in California. $\frac{\square}{\square}$

   c. Sarah won 8 out of the 12 races she ran in last year. $\frac{\square}{\square}$

   d. Tim picked 30 flowers; 18 are roses. $\frac{\square}{\square}$

2. Read the directions.   Write the fractions for these problems.

3. Read problem a. What should the bottom number of the fraction tell?   how many altogether

   What number tells altogether?   16

   Say the fraction. $\frac{12}{16}$

   Write it.

   (Repeat step 2 with several problems and then have students do rest on their own.)

PART C: LESS-STRUCTURED WORKSHEET

(Give students a worksheet with problems like the ones below.)
a. Jean ran in 8 races. She won 2 of the races. What percent of the races did she win?
b. Ann's team won 6 out of 8 games. What percent of the games did Ann's team win?
c. Dina got 12 out of 15 problems correct on her test. What percent of the problems did she get correct?
d. Jill has 8 pencils; 4 of her pencils are red. What percent of her pencils are red?

1. Read problem a. The problem asks for a percent. To find the percent, first you write a fraction. *(Repeat the problem.)* What fraction do you write? *(Pause, signal.)* Write it. $\frac{2}{8}$

2. Now you change the fraction to a percent.

3. What percent of the races did she win?   25%

FORMAT 14.5   **Format for Complex Ratio Problems**

Part A: Determining the Fraction

TEACHER	**STUDENTS**

1. Listen to this problem: I'm going to tell you about the cars that a salesman sold in September. He sold 10 blue cars *(Write 10 blue cars on board.)* and 14 red cars *(Write 14 red cars on board.)* in September. What fraction of the cars he sold were red?

2. The problem asks for the fraction of the cars that were red, so the fraction will be the number of red cars sold, over the total number of cars sold. What should the bottom number tell?   the total number of cars sold

   How many cars were sold altogether? *(Pause.)*   24

   (Write the following on the board:)

   $$\frac{}{24}$$

   > *To correct:* Remember: The dealer sold 10 blue cars and 14 red cars. To find the total number of cars sold, what must you do? What is 10 and 14?   24

3. What does the top number tell?   the number of red cars sold
   How many red cars were sold?   14
   (Write the following on the board.)

   $$\frac{14}{24}$$

4. What fraction of the cars sold in September were red? $\frac{14}{24}$

   (Repeat steps 1–4 with several examples of both simple and complex ratio problems.)

Part B: Less-Structured Worksheet

(Adapt Part C from the simple ratio problem format in Format 14.4.)

CHAPTER 15

Telling Time

Telling time is not as easy for all students to learn as teachers sometimes assume. Its difficulty is due to the number of discriminations students must make when telling time. In the following list are discriminations that, if not properly taught, tend to cause errors, especially for low-performing students:

1. Direction the clock hands move
2. Discrimination of the minute hand from the hour hand
3. Discrimination of minutes (which are not represented by the numerals on the clock) from hours (which are represented by the numerals on the clock)
4. Vocabulary discrimination; for example, when to use *after* and when to use *before*.

Because of these potentially troublesome discriminations, we have divided instruction on telling time into three stages. First, students are taught a strategy for figuring out the time and expressing it as minutes after the hour. Second, when students have mastered minutes after the hour, alternate ways of expressing time as after the hour are taught, e.g., using a colon (8:40), quarter past, and half past. Third, students are taught a strategy for expressing time as minutes before the hour. See the Instructional Sequence and Assessment Chart for details and examples.

MINUTES AFTER THE HOUR

Preskills

The four major preskills for telling time are (1) knowledge of the direction in which the hands of the clock move, (2) discrimination of the hour hand from the minute hand, (3) counting by 5s, and (4) switching from counting by fives to counting by ones, which is needed to determine the number of minutes (e.g., 5, 10, 15, 16, 17, 18, 19).

The preskill of knowing which direction the hands on a clock move is critical if students are to figure out the correct hour. A convenient way to teach students about direction on a clock is to have them fill in the missing numerals on several clocks containing boxes instead of numerals:

By doing this exercise, students can develop the pattern of moving in a clockwise direction around the clock face. In the first exercises, some of the numerals should be included as prompts on the clock (e.g., 3, 6, 9, 12). After several lessons, how-

Instructional Sequence and Assessment Chart

Grade Level	Problem Type	Performance Indicator

2a   Expressing time as minutes after the hour—minute hand pointing to a number

a.

_____ minutes after _____

b.

_____ minutes after _____

c.

_____ minutes after _____

2b   Expressing time as minutes after the hour—minute hand not pointing to numbers

a.

_____ minutes after _____

b.

_____ minutes after _____

c.

_____ minutes after _____

2c   Time expressed with hour stated first

a. Put an X on the line under the clock that says 7:25.

_____   _____

_____   _____

(continued on next page)

Instructional Sequence and Assessment Chart (continued)

Grade Level	Problem Type	Performance Indicator

b. Put an X on the line under the clock that says 4:03

_____   _____

_____   _____

c. Put an X on the line under the clock that says 2:53

_____   _____

_____   _____

Grade Level	Problem Type	Performance Indicator	
3a	Expressing time as half past or quarter after or to the hour	○ quarter to 5 ○ half pat 5 ○ 5 o'clock ○ quarter after 5	○ half past 9 ○ quarter after 7 ○ quarter after 8 ○ quarter to 9

(continued on next page)

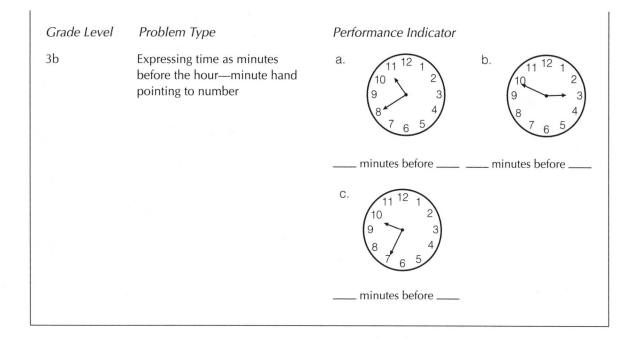

Grade Level	Problem Type	Performance Indicator

3b — Expressing time as minutes before the hour—minute hand pointing to number

a. ____ minutes before ____

b. ____ minutes before ____

c. ____ minutes before ____

ever, these prompts should be removed, and the students should fill in all the numbers themselves. Teachers need to monitor students carefully while they work to make sure they fill in numerals in the proper direction. Teachers also can use a clock with movable hands and ask students to move the clock hands in the appropriate direction to assess student understanding of the concept.

Counting by 5s is the initial way students are taught to determine the number of minutes. Students are taught to start at the top of the clock, say *zero*, and then count the numbers by 5s until reaching the minute hand. Later, the procedure is modified to teach students to determine the number of minutes when the minute hand is not pointing to a multiple of 5. In all procedures, however, the skill of counting by 5s, or knowledge of the relevant multiplication facts, is important. Procedures for teaching counting by 5s can be found in Chapter 4.

Discrimination of the hour hand from the minute hand is taught by describing each hand (the *short* hand is the hour hand, and the *long* hand is the minute hand) and then by providing discrimination practice in which students identify the hands. The teacher should present pictures of clocks and ask about each hand: "Which hand is this? How do you know it's the minute hand? Yes, the long hand is the minute hand." Commercial instructional clocks are well suited for this exercise, since teachers can manipulate the hands of the clock. The hands on the clock used for initial instruction should be easy to tell apart.

Units of 5 Minutes

The steps for teaching students to tell time by determining the number of minutes (in units of 5) after the hour is divided into five parts. (See Format 15.1.) Part A teaches students to read the hour. The teacher reminds students that the hour hand is the short hand and demonstrates how to figure out the hour by starting at the top of the clock and saying the numbers on the clock until reaching the hour hand.

Part B teaches students to determine the number of minutes after the hour. The teacher instructs students that the long hand is the minute hand and that the minute hand says to count by 5s. The teacher then models and tests figuring out the minutes. The students are taught to start at the 12, say *zero*, and then count by 5 for each number, stopping at the number to which the minute hand is pointing. All examples in this format would have the minute hand pointing directly to a number.

Part C includes a board demonstration of how the strategies for determining minutes and hours are combined into a complete strategy for figuring out the time. Parts D and E are structured and less-structured worksheet exercises in which the students are shown a clock and asked to write the time. Daily practice is continued for several weeks until students achieve fluency.

As a prompt to help students discriminate the hour and minute hands, we recommend that, for the first several days, teachers use illustrations like the one below, in which the minute hand is drawn longer than usual. Note that in the illustration, the minute hand extends outside the clock and is written as a thin line so that it does not block students' view of the numerals on the clock.

When constructing a set of examples, the teacher must be quite careful to include a wide range of problems. In half of the clocks, the hour hand should be pointing toward the right side of the clock; while on the other clocks, the hour hand should be pointing toward the left side of the clock. The same recommendation holds true for the minute hand. This helps prevent students from developing misrules that the strategies only apply to certain positions on the clock.

Also, examples should be arranged so that in half of the examples the minute hand is pointing to a number larger than the one to which the hour hand is pointing. If the minute hand were pointing to the smaller number in all the examples, students might inadvertently learn that the hand pointing to the smaller number is the minute hand.

For the first week or two, examples in which the minute hand is pointing to the 12 would be expressed as zero minutes after the hour. When students have demonstrated the ability to use the minutes-after strategy, the teacher can present the convention for saying *o'clock*. "When it's zero minutes after 4, we say it is 4 o'clock."

As students learn multiplication facts, they should be encouraged to use their knowledge of facts in determining the minutes, rather than always starting at the top and counting by 5s. The teacher would explain that in figuring out minutes, each number stands for a group of five. Therefore, when the minute hand points to 4, it is the same as four groups of five. Instead of counting, the minutes can be determined by solving 4×5.

Units of Single Minutes

After several weeks of practice expressing time with examples in which the minute hand points directly to a numeral, students can learn to express time when the minute hand is not pointing directly to a number. Note the example illustrated below:

No elaborate teaching format is required to introduce this skill. Students would be told that to count the spaces in between the numbers, they count by 1s. The teacher would then model the process of counting by 5s and switching to 1s: "5, 10, 15, 20, 21, 22, 23; the time is 23 minutes after 7."

ALTERNATE WAYS OF EXPRESSING TIME

Quarter After and Half Past

The terms *quarter after* and *half past* are introduced when students master expressing time as minutes after the hour: A *quarter after* means 15 minutes after; *half past* means 30 minutes after. Teachers

---

Summary Box 15.1: Stating Time as Minutes After the Hour

1. Students determine the hour by starting at the top of the clock and counting until they reach the hour hand. The time is stated as after _____.

2. Students determine the number of minutes after the hour by starting at the top of the clock, saying *zero*, and then counting by fives until they reach the minute hand.

3. Students practice determining the minutes after the hour.

working with lower-performing students would not introduce both terms at the same time. *Quarter after* might be introduced first. The instructional procedure consists of modeling and testing on several examples:

1. Another way of saying 15 minutes after 2 is a quarter after 2.
2. What's another way of saying 15 minutes after 2?
3. What's another way of saying 15 minutes after 8?

Next, an exercise in which the teacher states the time as a *quarter after* and the students restate it as minutes after would be presented: "If it's a *quarter after* 2, how many minutes after 2 is it?" The same procedure would be used to teach *half past* the hour. The final task would consist of a discrimination exercise including both *quarter after* and *half past* the hour time:

1. What's another way of saying 15 minutes after 6?
2. What's another way of saying 30 minutes after 6?
3. If it's half past 4, how many minutes after 4 is it?
4. If it's a quarter after 4, how many minutes after 4 is it?

Using a Colon

When students are able to express time as minutes after the hour, the colon system, in which the hour is written first, can be introduced: "3:14 is read as *three-fourteen,* which means 14 minutes after 3." The procedures for teaching students to identify time that is shown by a colon involve modeling and testing how to translate the time expressed as minutes after the hour to time expressed as the hour and then the minutes after: "Here's another way of saying 28 minutes after 5: *five-twenty-eight.* What's another way of saying 28 minutes after 5?"

The teacher models and tests several more examples, and then tests students on a series of four to six examples by saying the time as minutes after the hour and asking students to express it as hours then minutes after (e.g., "Tell me another way of saying 35 minutes after 4."). The teacher repeats the set of examples until students can respond correctly to all of them.

After several lessons, the teacher has students practice expressing time in a variety of ways:

"I'll say the time one way, and then say it another way. Listen: 8:24. I'll say the time the other way: 24 minutes after 8. Your turn: 8:24. Say the time the other way." Repeat with 4:15, 7:32, 9:28.

After learning to state the time as the hour then minutes after, students also can be taught how to read and write the time using a colon. A written task like the one below, in which students are required to express the time as both minutes after the hour and as the hour and then minutes, should be introduced next.

_____ minutes after _____

_____ : _____

Times of less than 10 minutes after the hour are particularly difficult, since a zero must be added when the time is expressed both verbally and in written form. For example, 8 minutes after 6 is written as 6:08 and stated as *"six oh eight."* This type of example should not be introduced until students have mastered easier ones. Several of these more difficult types should appear thereafter on worksheet exercises.

MINUTES BEFORE THE HOUR

Teachers should not introduce telling time as minutes before the hour until students can express time as minutes after the hour with accuracy and fluency. Students should demonstrate mastery by completing a worksheet of clocks with at least 90% accuracy at a rate of no more than 6 to 7 seconds per clock.

The procedure for teaching students to express time as minutes before the hour is somewhat similar to the one used in teaching students to express time as minutes after the hour. First, the teacher presents a strategy to figure out the hour, then a strategy to figure out the minutes, and then an exercise in which both strategies are applied to express the time (see Format 15.2).

The teacher first presents an exercise in which she places the hour hand between two numbers, then models and tests saying what hour it is after and what hour it is before. For example, if the hour hand were pointing between 5 and 6, the teacher would say the hour is after 5 and before 6. Next, the teacher shows students how to figure out the number of minutes before the hour. She points in a counterclockwise direction and tells the students that in figuring minutes before the hour they start at the 12 but count in this direction (pointing counterclockwise). The teacher models and tests several examples. The next exercise is a structured one in which

FIGURE 15.1 Student Errors in Telling Time

a.

b.

c.

d.

a. *30 minutes after 1*   b. *45 minutes after 8*   c. *15 minutes after 7*   d. *10 minutes after 4*

the teacher leads students through expressing the time as minutes before the hour.

During the first week that expressing time as minutes before the hour is presented, the minute hand should point directly to the numerals so that all minute times involve multiples of five. Examples in which the minute hand points to a line between the numerals are introduced later. Examples should be limited to times that are 30 minutes or less before the hour (i.e., the minute hand is pointing toward the center or the left part of the clock).

DIAGNOSIS AND REMEDIATION

Errors in telling time usually are caused by component skill errors. The remediation procedure is to reteach the component skill, then present several

structured worksheet examples, then several less-structured worksheet examples, and finally to provide supervised practice. Figure 15.1 shows some errors that might indicate a particular component skill error.

In examples a and b, the student's answer is 5 minutes more than the proper time. Probably the student is starting to count by 5s when touching 12 instead of saying *zero* when touching 12. The remediation would begin with the part of the format that teaches figuring out minutes after the hour.

The errors in examples c and d may be caused by the student's confusing the minute and hour hands. If this type of error occurs frequently, the teacher presents exercises focusing on discriminating the hour hand from the minute hand (see page 374). If the confusion is severe, the teacher might use examples in which the minute hand is elongated to serve as a prompt.

APPLICATION ITEMS: TELLING TIME

1. Below are sets of examples prepared by teachers to use in early exercises to teach telling time as minutes after the hour. Which sets are inappropriate and why?

   Set A: 15 minutes after 8   10 minutes after 7
   10 minutes after 9   5 minutes after 7

   Set B: 13 minutes after 2   25 minutes after 4
   37 minutes after 10   10 minutes after 9

   Set C: 20 minutes after 7   35 minutes after 4
   15 minutes after 2   30 minutes after 8

2. Tell the probable cause of each student's errors.

   a. *Tom*

30 minutes after 3   *50 minutes after 8*   *10 minutes after 11*

b. *Jessica*

50 minutes after *12*   *20* minutes after *9*   *35* minutes after *5*

c. *Peter*

30 minutes after *2*   *15* minutes after *8*   *50* minutes after *6*

3. Specify the wording the teacher uses in correcting the first error made by each student in problem 2. The wording will be different for each student.

FORMAT 15.1   Format for Expressing Time as Minutes After the Hour (Units of 5 Minutes)

PART A: DETERMINING THE HOUR

TEACHER   **STUDENTS**

1. *(Draw the following on the board.)*

2. One of the hands is missing on this clock. *(Point to the hour hand.)* This short hand is the hour hand. What is the short hand?   the hour hand

3. Let's figure out what hour the hand is after. We start at the top of the clock and say the numbers until we come to the hour hand. I'll touch; you say the numbers. Say stop when I come to the hour hand. *(Starting with 12, touch each numeral and then the hour hand as the children say the numbers.)*   12, 1, 2, 3, 4, 5, stop

4. What was the last numeral I touched?   5

(continued on next page)

FORMAT 15.1 **(continued)**

TEACHER	STUDENTS

5. The hour hand is after 5. So, the hour is after 5. Tell me about the hour.

  after 5

  (Repeat steps 1-4 with after 8.)

6. *(Point hour hand to after 5.)* Now let's figure out the hour a fast way, without counting. Look at the clock. What numeral is the hour hand after?

  5

  So tell me about the hour.

  after 5

  (Repeat step 5 with several more examples: after 9, after 2, after 6, after 3, after 10.)

PART B: MINUTES AFTER

1. *(Draw the following on the board.)*

2. This long hand is the minute hand. What is the long hand called?

  the minute hand

  The minute hand is very funny. It tells you to count by 5. What does the minute hand tell you to do?

  Count by 5.

3. Watch me figure out the minutes. *(Point to the minute hand.)* I touch the top of the clock and say zero. Then I count by 5 until I come to the minute hand. *(Touch the clock above 12.)* Zero. *(Starting with 1, touch each numeral as you count: 5, 10, 15, 20, 25.)*

4. Tell me about the minutes.

  25 minutes

5. Your turn. I'll touch the numerals; you count by 5. Remember to say zero when I touch the top of the clock. *(Touch the clock above 12 and then touch each numeral as the children count.)*

  0, 5, 10, 15, 20, 25

6. Tell me about the minutes.
  Yes, 25 minutes.

  25 minutes

  (Repeat steps 4–5 with five more examples: hand points to 3, hand points to 7, hand points to 2, hand points to 10, hand points to 4.)

(continued on next page)

FORMAT 15.1 **(continued)**

PART C: STRUCTURED BOARD PRESENTATION

TEACHER	**STUDENTS**

1. *(Draw the following on the board.)*

2. We're going to figure out what time this clock shows. First we'll figure out the minutes. Then we'll figure out the hour.

3. First the minutes. Which hand is the minute hand, the short hand or the long hand?   the long hand

4. What does the minute hand tell you to count by?   Count by 5.

   Where do you start counting?   at the top of the clock

   What do you say?   zero

   (Repeat step 3 until all questions are answered correctly.)

5. Counting by 5 to the minute hand. *(Touch the top of the clock and then the numerals as the children count.)*   0, 5, 10, 15

   How many minutes?   15
   I'll write the answer. *(Write 15 minutes under the clock.)*

6. We know it's 15 minutes, but we don't know about the hour. Look at the hour hand. Tell me about the hour.
   (Pause, signal.)   after 6

7. Yes, after 6. I'll write the answer. *(Write after 6.)* That's the time the clock shows, 15 minutes after 6. What time does the clock show? Say the time.   15 minutes after 6

   (Repeat steps 1–6 with 5 minutes after 7, 45 minutes after 4, 20 minutes after 2, 25 minutes after 10.)

PART D: STRUCTURED WORKSHEET

1. *(Give students a worksheet that includes about six to eight clocks like those below.)*

_____ minutes after _____   _____ minutes after _____

2. Everyone touch the first clock on your worksheet. First you'll figure out the minutes, then you'll figure out the hour.

(continued on next page)

FORMAT 15.1   (continued)

TEACHER	STUDENTS
3. Which is the minute hand?	the long hand
What does the minute hand tell you to count by?	Count by 5.
Where do you start counting?	at the top of the clock
What do you say at the top of the clock? Let's figure the minutes.	zero
4. Touch the 12. Count and touch as I clap. *(Clap once each second.)*	0, 5, 10, 15, 20, 25, 30, 35
How many minutes?	35 minutes
Write *35* in front of the word *minutes*.	
5. Touch the hour hand. Tell me about the hour. *(Pause, signal.)*	after 4
Yes, it says after 4. Write *4* in the next space.	
6. Now tell me what time that clock says.	35 minutes after 4
(Repeat steps 1–5 with each remaining clock.)	

PART E: LESS-STRUCTURED WORKSHEET

1. *(Give the students a worksheet like the one below.)*

_____ minutes after _____

2. Touch clock a. You're going to figure out the time and write it under the clock.

3. Figure out the minutes and write the minutes in the first blank. *(Monitor response.)* How many minutes?	20
4. Now figure the hour and write it in the last blank.	
5. Read what time the clock says.	20 minutes after 6

FORMAT 15.2   Format for Expressing Time as Minutes Before the Hour

PART A: DETERMINING THE HOUR

TEACHER	**STUDENTS**

1. *(Draw the following clock on the board.)*

2. In telling time, you've learned to say how many minutes after the hour. Another way of telling time is to say the number of minutes before the hour.

3. Look at this clock, what hour is it after?   4

4. The next bigger number tells you the hour it's before. Tell me the hour it's before.   5
   Yes, it's before 5. What is the hour?   before 5

5. *(Move the hour hand between 7 and 8.)* Tell me the hour by saying what hour it is before. *(Pause, signal.)*   before 8

   (Repeat step 4 moving the hand to five more positions: between 2 and 3, between 10 and 11, between 6 and 7, between 11 and 12, between 12 and 1.)

PART B: MINUTES BEFORE THE HOUR

1. *(Draw the clock below.)*

2. Now we'll figure out the minutes before the next hour. When we figure the minutes before the hour, we start at the 12 but we count this way *(Point ↲)* until we get to the minute hand. My turn: 0, 5, 10, 15, 20. It's 20 minutes before. How many minutes before?   20 minutes before

3. Show me which way you count to figure the minutes before the hour. Where do we start counting?   at the 12

   What do we say first?   zero

   (Move minute hand to 10.) Tell me how many minutes before. *(Pause, signal.)*   10 minutes before

   To correct: We're figuring out minutes before so we count this way (↲). I'll touch, you count.

   (Repeat step 2 with four more examples: hand pointing to 10, 8, 11, 7.)

(continued on next page)

FORMAT 15.2 **(continued)**

PART C: STRUCTURED BOARD PRESENTATION

TEACHER	**STUDENTS**
1. *(Draw the following clock on the board.)*	

_____ minutes before _____

2. Let's tell what time this clock says by telling how many minutes before the hour.

3. *(Point to the hour hand.)* Which hand is this?	the hour hand
What hour is it before? *(Pause. write 4.)*	4
4. *(Point to minute hand.)* Which hand is this?	the minute hand
How many minutes before 4 is it? *(Pause. Write 20.)*	20 minutes
To correct: Show me which way we count when we figure out minutes before. Count as I point.	
5. What time does the clock say?	20 minutes before 4
(Repeat steps 1–4 with additional times: 5 before 2, 25 before 8, 15 before 11, 10 before 12, 20 before 5.)	

PART D: STRUCTURED WORKSHEET

1. *(Give students worksheet with six to eight clocks. Under each clock is written:* _____ *minutes before* _____ *.)*

2. Let's find out what time these clocks say by finding out how many minutes before the hour.

3. Find the hour hand on clock a. What hour is it before? *(Pause, signal.)*	before 8
4. Now let's find out how many minutes before 8. Start at the top of the clock—remember which way to count. How many minutes before 8? *(Pause, signal.)*	20 minutes
5. What time does this clock say?	20 minutes before 8
Fill in the blanks.	
(Repeat with remaining examples.)	

CHAPTER 16

Money

The need for instruction in money-related skills is derived from their importance in daily activities. Included in this chapter are procedures for (1) determining the value of a group of coins, (2) counting change, (3) decimal notation for money, and (4) consumer skills. A more in-depth list of problem types appears in the Instructional Sequence and Assessment Chart.

DETERMINING THE VALUE OF A GROUP OF COINS

Preskills for determining the value of a group of coins include the ability to identify and tell the value of individual coins and knowledge of the 5, 10, and 25 count-by series.

Students are usually taught to identify coins in the first grade. This is a fairly simple preskill to teach, since many students will already be able to recognize several coins. A format similar to that used in symbol identification would be taught for coin identification. The teacher initially models and tests the name of the coin and then models and tests its value: "This is a nickel. What is this? . . . A nickel is worth 5¢. How much is a nickel worth? . . ." For this task, the teacher can use either real coins or pictures of coins.

The penny and nickel should be introduced first. After students can label and state their values, dimes can be introduced, followed by quarters. Note that the coins are introduced *cumulatively,* which implies that students must be able to discriminate the new coin from previously introduced coins before the teacher can present a new example.

The preskill for counting groups of similar coins is knowledge of the respective count-by series. Once students have learned the count-by series, they have little trouble applying the skill to coin counting. In teaching students to count groups of similar coins for the first time, the teacher indicates the value of the coin and then models counting. For example, "Here is a group of nickels. Each nickel is worth 5¢. To find out how many cents this group of nickels equals, I count by 5s. My turn." The teacher then counts by 5 as she touches each coin. After modeling, the teacher tests students on counting several sets of identical coins. Worksheet exercises like the one in Figure 16.1 should follow the oral presentation.

Problems in which students determine the value of a set of mixed coins are usually introduced in second grade and contain just two or three coins. In later grades, the number of coins to be counted increases. We recommend a two-step strategy: (1) grouping like coins together and (2) starting with the coin worth the most and counting all like coins, then switching to the next highest coin in the group and counting the value of that coin. For example, in counting two quarters, three dimes, and two nickels, students would begin counting the two quarters (25,

Instructional Sequence and Assessment Chart

Grade Level	Problem Type	Performance Indicator

1a   Value of single coins

= _____ ¢   = _____ ¢

= _____ ¢   = _____ ¢

1b   Determining value of groups of like coins

= _____ ¢

= _____ ¢

= _____ ¢

2a   Determining value of groups of different coins

= _____ ¢

= _____ ¢

= _____ ¢

(continued on next page)

Grade Level	Problem Type	Performance Indicator
2b	Adding dollars and cents	$1.32 $4.78 + $2.43 + $6.92
3a	Consumer skills: Verifying change from less that $1.00	You bought a soda that costs 20¢. You give the clerk a half dollar. The clerk gives you this change. Is it correct?

You bought a soda that costs 27¢. You give the clerk 35¢. The clerk gives you this change. Is it correct?

Grade Level	Problem Type	Performance Indicator
3b	Consumer skills: Specifying change	Write the coins you would need to make 27¢. Write the coins you would need to make 79¢. Write the coins you would need to make 43¢.
3c	Decimal notation: Reading and writing dollar and cents notations under 10 dollars	Write four dollars & six cents _____ Write nine dollars & thirty cents _____ Write one dollar & five cents _____

4a	Decimal notation: Subtracting dollars and cents from whole dollar figures	$15.00 − 1.35 =
		   9.00 − 8.20 =
		  10.00 − 6.16 =

4b	Consumer skills: Adding and subtracting whole dollars and dollar and cents amounts	Jack had $6. He spent $3.25. How much does he have left? If you had $4 and you got $2.15 more, how much would you have? Jan buys a shirt for $2.85. She gives the clerk a $5 bill. How much change does she get back?
4c	Consumer skills: Determining cost of purchase for two groups of items	You buy 3 pencils for 15¢ each and 5 pencils for 10¢ each. How much do you spend? You buy 4 pens for 30¢ each and 2 erasers for 12¢ each. How much do you spend? You buy 5 pens for 15¢ each and 3 erasers for 8¢ each. How much do you spend?

(continued on next page)

Instructional Sequence and Assessment Chart (continued)

Grade Level	Problem Type	Performance Indicator
4d	Consumer skills: How much can be bought with specified amount	Bill wants to buy pencils which cost 7¢ each. He has 2 dollar bills and a dime. How many pencils can he buy? Bill has 3 quarters. If spoons cost 5¢ each, how many spoons can he buy? Bill has 3 half dollars. If spoons cost 5¢ each, how many spoons can he buy?
4e	Consumer skills: Reading a price list	

Hamburger		Ice cream	
plain	35¢	cone	
cheese	50¢	small	40¢
bacon	70¢	large	60¢
fries add	20¢	sundae	
Soda		small	60¢
small	30¢	large	80¢
med.	40¢		
large	50¢		

Bill wants two hamburgers with cheese, one with fries, one without fries, a large soda, and two large ice cream cones. How much will all that cost?

Grade Level	Problem Type	Performance Indicator
5a	Consumer skills: Comparison shopping—unit cost	A 6 oz. package of rice made by ABC Company costs 96¢. A 5 oz. package made by the XYZ company costs 90¢. Which package of rice is the best buy? Tell why.

50), switch to the dimes (60, 70, 80) and switch once more to the nickels (85, 90).

A strategy beginning with higher-value coins is recommended over a strategy beginning with lower-value coins, since beginning with lower-value coins more often results in a difficult counting sequence. For example, to count a quarter, dime, nickel, and two pennies, the student would count 1, 2, 7, 17, 42; counting 25, 35, 40, 41, 42 is much easier.

A preskill for counting a group of unlike coins is knowledge of addition facts in which 10, 5, or 1 is added to a two-digit number ending in zero or 5 (e.g., 70 and 10 more is. . . .70 and 5 more is. . . .). This preskill can be taught using a model-test procedure in which the teacher models several problems and then tests students on a set of problems (e.g., 40 and 10 more, 40 and 5 more, 40 and 1 more, 45 and 5 more, 45 and 1 more, 80 and 5 more, 80 and 1 more, 20 and 10 more, 20 and 5 more).

Facts in which 10 is added to a two-digit number ending in 5 (35 + 10, 65 + 10) are particularly hard. They should not be introduced until the easier facts are mastered. Practice would be provided daily for several weeks, either orally or through worksheet exercises. If teachers use worksheets to provide this practice, they should write problems horizontally and indicate to students that they are to complete the problems mentally (not realign them vertically and compute).

To teach students to determine the value of a set of mixed coins, the teacher initially models by touching and counting the coins, and then tests, prompting students by telling the value of each coin. For example, if the teacher is having the students determine the value of a group of coins including

FIGURE 16.1   Coin Counting Worksheet

= _____ ¢

= _____ ¢

= _____ ¢

= _____ ¢

two quarters, three dimes, and a nickel, the teacher would start, pointing to the first quarter:

Teacher	Students
25 and *(pointing to next quarter)* 25 more is . . .	50
50 and *(pointing to the first dime)* 10 more is . . .	60
60 and *(pointing to next dime)* 10 more is . . .	70
70 and *(pointing to next dime)* 10 more is . . .	80
80 and *(pointing to nickel)* 5 more is . . .	85

COUNTING CHANGE

Three change-related skills are discussed in this section: (1) making equivalent change, which involves exchanging a group of smaller-valued coins for a larger-valued coin (e.g., two dimes and a nickel for a quarter), (2) giving change when the amount to be given is specified, and (3) verifying the change received from a purchase. These skills would most likely be taught in third grade. The primary preskill

for counting change is the ability to count groups of coins.

Making Equivalent Change

Giving equivalent change for a larger coin is not a complex skill to teach. However, two kinds of equivalent change exercises should be practiced. In the first type, the teacher has students first identify the value of a larger-value coin. Then the teacher has students determine the number of smaller-value coins equal to the original coin. In this exercise, students are always counting similar coins. In the second type of equivalent change problem, the students must count a set of different coins to determine whether or not a given amount of change is equivalent to the amount stated. Both types of exercises are illustrated in Format 16.1.

Initially, coin equivalency problems would include pennies, nickels, dimes, and quarters (e.g., a quarter equals two dimes and a nickel). Larger values, including dollar bills, would be introduced later.

Worksheet exercises like Figure 16.2 present a different application of the equivalency skill. In these exercises, students circle the appropriate more, less, or equal sign between two groups of

FIGURE 16.2 Worksheet on Equivalent Change

coins. To introduce this exercise, the teacher would lead the students in counting the coins in each group. After counting the coins, the students would be instructed to write the value of each group above the group. If the values are equal, the students would be instructed to circle the equal sign. If the values of the groups are not equal, the students would circle the appropriate *more than* or *less than* sign.

Verifying Change

The easiest way of verifying change received is to begin at the price of the item(s) and then count the coins received as change, beginning with the coin of least value. Students would then compare the number they derived to the amount given to pay for the purchase (see Format 16.2). For example, if a purchase of 36¢ is made and the student is given back four pennies and two nickels after paying the clerk a half dollar, the student would count 37, 38, 39, 40, 45, 50. The student then knows the change given is correct since she ends with 50¢, the value of the amount given to make the purchase.

Initial examples should be relatively easy, including small numbers of coins. Later examples can include a greater number of coins. An example appropriate for the introduction of the skill might consist of payment of 40¢ for an object costing 36¢. To verify the change in this example, students need count only pennies: 37, 38, 39, 40. A later example might involve payment of a dollar for an object costing 36¢, for which students would need to count pennies, dimes, and quarters: 37, 38, 39, 40, 50, 75, a dollar. (See Format 16.2.)

Problems involving more than one dollar would be introduced last. Note that the same strategy applies to counting change from dollars. The student counts the change to determine if the object's cost plus the change equals the payment price. For example, if an object costing 37¢ is paid for with a $10 bill, counting change would proceed as follows: 38, 39, 40, 50, 75, a dollar, 2, 3, 4, 5, 10 dollars. Again, practice would be provided on worksheet exercises

and through hands-on activities in which students exchange facsimiles of coins.

DECIMAL NOTATION IN MONEY

Money problems expressed in decimal notation typically are introduced in third grade. A typical problem may state that a 39¢ toy is paid for with a $5 bill and asks how much change should be given. The solution would be computed by subtracting 39¢ from $5 and would be expressed as $4.61. Specifying the exact coins would not be an appropriate response for this problem unless the problem asked students to specify the type of change that would be given. Since many application problems call for a specific amount rather than the coins used to make change, the decimal notation for money should be introduced in the primary grades, even if general decimal instruction has not begun.

Fortunately, decimal notation for money is relatively safe to introduce before more comprehensive decimal instruction is taught. The students can be told that the two numbers to the right of the decimal tell about cents, while the numbers to the left of the decimal tell about dollars. A format for teaching students to read and write dollar figures expressed with decimal notation appears in Format 16.3. Both parts of the format would be presented daily for two or three weeks. Six to eight examples should be included in each part.

Practice should include examples without dollars (e.g., $.45, $.30) and examples without cents (e.g., $5.00, $13.00). Students can be expected to have difficulty writing amounts between 1 and 9 cents because of the need to place a zero after the decimal: $7.03, $14.08. These examples, therefore, should not be introduced in the initial exercises. Concentrated practice on this type of example should be provided in later lessons. At that time, the teacher would explain that there must always be two digits after the decimal when writing money figures. The teacher would then model that when the number of cents is below ten, a zero and then the digit for the number of cents are written.

Story problems with money expressed in decimal notation should be introduced when students are able to read and write decimal notation for money. A common type of story problem that deserves special attention is illustrated below:

Jim bought a shirt for $3.62. He gave the clerk $10 bill. How much change will Jim receive?

Jill had $6. She was given $3.50 for working in the yard. How much money does she have now?

In these problems, a dollar amount is expressed without cents after the decimal point. When working the problem, students must write the dollar amount with a decimal point and two zeroes. The critical skill of aligning the numbers according to the decimal point was discussed in Chapter 13. The teacher would model working several problems of this type before assigning students to work them independently.

CONSUMER SKILLS

Three consumer skills are discussed in this section. The first, a skill taught in second or third grade, involves teaching students to pay for purchases with coins. The second, a skill taught in third or fourth grade, involves teaching students to read price lists and menus. The third, a skill taught in fourth or fifth grade, involves teaching unit pricing to make comparisons when shopping.

Making Purchases with Coins

When purchasing an item in a store, the student should use a strategy that allows her, as quickly as possible, to figure out the coins to give. We recommend that students begin counting with the largest-value coins. For example, if a student has an assortment of coins and wants to buy something costing 28¢, the fastest way to count the exact amount would be to use a quarter and three pennies. This skill can be taught by using real coins or facsimiles of coins. We recommend that the teacher introduce the rule, "When you count money to buy something, you start with the coins that are worth more." Next, the teacher would model several examples and then give students problems to solve. The steps for teaching this skill appear in Format 16.4.

A mistake often made by students is inappropriately allocating only pennies for the value of the ones (regardless of the other coins used). For example, when counting out 38¢, students might count

out 30¢ using a quarter and a nickel and then count out eight pennies, instead of using a quarter (25), a dime (35) and then 3 pennies. One way to prompt students to use larger coins when possible is to limit the number of pennies they are given (i.e., give students only four pennies). This procedure will force students to use nickels and dimes more wisely. As students become more adept at counting coins efficiently, the teacher can give them more pennies. Often, students will not have the appropriate coins to allow them to count an exact amount. For these situations, students must be taught to count an amount that exceeds the purchase price.

Format 16.5 teaches students to use the fewest coins to make a purchase. For example, with a purchase price of 69¢ and these coins—QQQDD—the coins that give a value closest to 69¢ are two quarters and two dimes; however, using up the larger coins is much easier, in this case three quarters.

Counting Change

Counting change is usually done by a clerk. Because most cash registers display the amount of change to give, students need to be able to reach the amount using the fewest number of coins. Format 16.6 outlines the procedure for teaching that skill. The format is written just for coins. However, the format easily can be altered to teach the skill with dollars. In the adaptation, the examples would include whole dollars and students wouldn't write letters for coins but rather the numbers that represent the bills (e.g., 20, 10, 5, and 1). Similar wording can be used: "Start with the bill worth the most and see how close you can get. Then try the next largest bill." After students have mastered change for coins and bills separately, mixed amounts can be presented. First tell the students to figure the bills. Check their answers. Then have them figure the coins and check their answers.

Reading Price Lists and Menus

Many price lists or menus utilize indentation systems to describe subcategories of a general group. Figure 16.3 includes a sample menu students might encounter in a fast food restaurant. Teachers should test students on reading various price lists and menus by asking students the prices of the items represented. Teachers can then give students story problems such as: "Jerry has 2 dollars. He wants to buy a small hamburger, large French fries, and a small ice cream. Does he have enough money? If so, how much change will he receive?"

FIGURE 16.3   Worksheet for Reading Menus

XYZ Fast Food Restaurant
MENU

Hamburgers		Ice Cream	
plain—small	$ .60	cones	
plain—large	$1.25	large	$.60
with cheese	add 10¢	small	$.50
French Fries		cups	
large	$ .60	large	$.50
small	$ .35	small	$.30

Unit Pricing

Unit pricing comparison shopping involves determining the relative cost of the same type of item when it appears in packages containing different quantities. For example, a 10 oz. bag of ABC soap costs 97¢ and an 8 oz. bag of XYZ soap costs 86¢. Which soap is a better buy? The teacher presents the rule: "To compare similar items in different size packages, we must divide to find the unit price." The teacher then models with several examples. For example, in comparing a 6 lb. package that costs 42¢ with a 5 lb. package that costs 40¢, the teacher points out that you must find the cost per pound (the unit price) and illustrates how this can be done by dividing the total cost by the number of pounds: 42 ÷ 6 = 7 and 40 ÷ 5 = 8. After computing the problems, it is easy to see that the 6 lb. package is a better buy, since it costs a penny less per pound.

APPLICATION ITEMS: MONEY

1. When counting a quarter, a dime, and two nickels, students count as specified below. Tell the probable cause of their errors. Specify what the teacher says to correct each student. (Assume students know the value of each coin.)

   Jill—25, 30, 35, 40
   Jim—5, 10, 20, 35

2. Tell the probable cause for each error below. Specify what the teacher says to correct each student.

   Jill had 5 dollars. She buys a pencil for 4 cents. How much money does she have left?

   Tom

   $$\begin{array}{r} 4 \\ \$5.00 \\ - .04 \\ \hline \$4.06 \end{array}$$

   Ann

   $$\begin{array}{r} 5 \\ - 4 \\ \hline 1 \end{array}$$

FORMAT 16.1   **Format for Making Equivalent Change**

PART A

TEACHER	STUDENTS
1. *(Show students real or pretend coins.)* I want to find out how many nickels equal one dime. How much is a dime worth?	10¢
So I count nickels until I get to 10. What do I count by when I count nickels?	5
Stop me when I get to 10. 5, 10 . . .	Students say "stop."
How many nickels did I count?	2

(continued on next page)

FORMAT 16.1   (continued)

TEACHER	STUDENTS
So how many nickels equal one dime?	2
(Repeat step 1 to help students figure out how many pennies are in a dime.)	
2. *(Review previously taught equivalencies.)*	
How many pennies in a nickel?	5
How many nickels in a dime?	2
How many pennies in a dime?	10

PART B

1. I gave a man a quarter and he gave me two dimes and a nickel. Let's figure out if these coins are worth the same as a quarter. How much is a quarter worth?	25¢
Let's count the coins and see if they're worth 25¢. I'll touch. You count.	10, 20, 25
Are those coins worth 25¢?	yes

FORMAT 16.2   Format for Verifying Change

PART A: STRUCTURED BOARD PRESENTATION

TEACHER	STUDENTS
1. *(Write the following on the board.)* 36¢ P P P P D Q Q	
2. *(Point to P.)* This stands for penny.	
(Point to D.) This stands for dime.	
(Point to Q.) This stands for quarter.	
(Point to each letter in random order and ask,) What does this stand for?	
3. *(Point to 36¢.)* John bought apples that cost 36¢. He gave the man a dollar. We're going to count the change John got and see if it's right. We'll count from 36 and see if we end with a dollar. *(Point to pennies.)* What do we count by for these?	1
(Point to dime.) What do we count by for this?	10
(Point to quarters.) What do we count by for these?	25
4. Let's count the change. Start with 36—count. *(Point to coins as students count.)*	37, 38, 39, 40, 50, 75, 100
Did we end with a dollar?	yes
(Repeat steps 2 and 3 with several more examples.)	

FORMAT 16.3 **Format for Decimal Notation for Money**

PART A: READING DECIMAL NOTATION

TEACHER	STUDENTS

1. *(Write the following on the board.)*
   $4.32

2. Here is the way to write dollars and cents. *(Point to the decimal point in $4.32.)* This dot is a decimal point. It divides dollars and cents. *(Point to 4.)* This tells us four dollars. *(Point to 32.)* These two numbers tell us about cents. I'll read the amount: Four dollars and thirty-two cents.

3. *(Write the following on the board.)*
   $3.62

   How many dollars?   3

   How many cents?   62

   Say the whole amount. $3.62

   (Repeat step 2 with $7.20, $.45,* $6.00, $.30*)

PART B: WRITING WITH DECIMAL NOTATION

1. *(Give each student a sheet of lined paper.)* You're going to write money amounts using a dollar sign and a decimal point.

2. Listen: Eight dollars and thirty-two cents. Say that. $8.32
   How many dollars?   8
   Write a dollar sign, then an 8.

3. Eight dollars and thirty-two cents. How many cents?   32
   Write a decimal point on the line. Then write 32.

4. What amount did you write? $8.32

   (Repeat steps 2–4 with these examples:
   $6.42, $.32, $4.10, $7.00, $.57, $9.00.)

*For examples with no dollars, the teacher should model the response on
 the first day the format appears.

FORMAT 16.4 **Format for Counting Coins to Reach an Exact Value**

PART A: STRUCTURED BOARD PRESENTATION

TEACHER	STUDENTS

1. Today you're going to count out money at your seats. I'll tell you how much something costs and you count out the

FORMAT 16.4 (continued)

TEACHER	STUDENTS
money to buy it. When you count out money to buy something, start with the coin that's worth more. If I want to buy something for 25¢, would I use 25 pennies or 1 quarter?	1 quarter
Why?	a quarter is worth more than a penny
Right, a quarter is worth more than a penny. If I want to buy something that costs 20¢, would I use nickels or dimes?	dimes
Why?	A dime is worth more than a nickel.

2. My turn. I want to buy a balloon that costs 31¢. I start with a quarter: 25, 30, 31. *(Write Q N P on board.)*

3. Your turn. *(Pass out coins, either real or facsimiles.)* A toy car costs 28¢. Start with the coin that's worth the most and count out 28¢.

    Students should put out a quarter and three pennies.

(Monitor student responses.)

(Repeat step 3 with several more examples.)

FORMAT 16.5   **Format for Counting Coins When You Don't Have the Exact Amount**

PART A

TEACHER	STUDENTS

1. I'm going to use the coins I have to buy something that costs 56¢.
   (Write 56¢. Below, write QQQDDD.)

   This is all the money I have to use. I start with the coin that has the greatest value. I get as close as I can. If I don't have the exact amount, I have to give more. I'll get the extra money back as change. Watch.
   (Circle a coin each time you count.)

   25, 50, 75.
   I paid more than 56¢, so I'll get some change back.

2. Your turn. Point to problem 1 on your worksheet.
   1. 36¢ QDDN

   Start with the coin worth the most. If you don't have exactly 36¢, count more than 36. Circle the coins you'll use. Raise your hand when you're done.

   (When most hands are raised) Tell me the coins you circled.   Q, D, N

3. *(Repeat step 2 with the problems below.)*
   2. 72¢ QDDDNNP
   3. 29¢ DDDNNPP

FORMAT 16.6   **Format for Counting Change**

PART A: STRUCTURED BOARD PRESENTATION

TEACHER	STUDENTS

(Write the following example on the board.)

73¢   Q
       D
       N
       P

1. When you make change, you have to figure out what coins to use. *(Point to each letter as you say)* I'm going to figure out how many quarters, dimes, nickels, and pennies I use to make 73¢. I start with the coin worth the most—a quarter. I count to get as close as I can to 73: 25, 50. I counted 2 times. So I write this to show 2 quarters. *(Write QQ.)*

   Now I count dimes. I've already got 50: 60, 70. I counted 2 times, so I write DD for 2 dimes. *(Write DD.)*

   Now I try to count nickels. I already have 70. I can't count any nickels. The first time I count by 5 I get 75 and that's too big. I don't write any N's. Now I count pennies. I still have 70: 71, 72, 73. I counted 3 times so I write PPP after the last d. *(Write PPP.)*

   I'm done. The answer is 2 quarters, 2 dimes, and 3 pennies—those coins make 73¢. Watch.
   (Point to each letter as you count: 25, 50, 60, 70, 71, 72, 73)

2. Your turn.
   (Write the following for problem 1: 48¢)

   Start with quarters. Get as close as you can to 48¢. Raise your hand when you know how many quarters. *(When most hands are raised)* How many quarters?   one
   (Write one Q after 48¢.)

   Now figure out how many dimes you need to get as close as you can to 48. Remember, you've already have 25¢ from the quarter. *(When most hands are raised)* How many dimes? *(Write DD after Q.)*   two

   Now figure out how many nickels you need to get as close as you can to 48¢. Remember, you already have 25, 35, 45¢. *(When most hands are raised)* How many nickels?   zero (or none)

   Zero nickels. If you count by 5 even one time, you get to 50¢, and that is bigger than 48¢. So you don't write anything for nickels. Figure out how many pennies you need to get to 48. Remember, you've already got 45¢. *(When most hands are raised)* How many pennies?   three
   (Write PPP after the last D.)

   Let's see if we have 48¢. Start with the Q and count the coins.

3. (Repeat step 2 with 55¢ and 82¢.)

CHAPTER 17

Measurement

CUSTOMARY AND METRIC UNITS

There are two basic measurement systems—the customary system, which is used in the United States and a few other countries, and the metric system, which is used in the majority of countries in the world.

The metric system has several advantages over the customary system. First, since the metric system uses the base 10 place value system, instruction in decimals directly relates to measurement skills. With customary units, different place value base systems are required for weight (16 ounces), length (12 inches, 3 feet), etc. Second, in the customary system there is no commonality among the units for various measurements, while there is commonality among the metric units. The prefixes in the metric system *(milli-, centi-, deci-, deka-, hecto-, kilo-)* are used in each area: length, weight, and capacity.

Table 17.1 includes the various customary and metric units for expressing length, weight, capacity, and temperature. Note the consistency of the metric system. The prefix in front of a unit tells the unit's relation to the base unit. At the same time, note how the various units in the customary system are different from one another.

Teachers need to check district and/or school policy regarding the extent and type of metric instruction expected in their classrooms. The question facing most teachers is not whether to teach about the

metric system but rather whether both systems should be taught simultaneously, and if not, which should be taught first. Unfortunately, there is no simple answer to this question. However, we have noticed that lower-performing students are likely to confuse facts from one system with the facts from another system when both systems are introduced concurrently. This information leads us to recommend that the two systems be taught independently of one another, preferably at different times during the year. Low-performing students should be familiar with common units from one system before the other system is introduced.

During the primary grades, measurement instruction is relatively simple. Common units and equivalences are introduced, and students use tools to measure objects to the nearest whole unit. During the intermediate grades, measurement instruction becomes more complex as less commonly used units are introduced and more sophisticated uses of measuring tools are presented. While in the early grades students measured to the nearest whole unit, in later grades they are taught to measure partial units (e.g., $3\frac{1}{8}$ inches). Also in the intermediate grades, conversion problems are introduced in which students must convert a quantity expressed as one unit to a larger or smaller unit (5 meters = 500 centimeters).

A sequence of major skills appears in the Instructional Sequence and Assessment Chart. Though not

Instructional Sequence and Assessment Chart

Grade Level	Problem Type	Performance Indicator
2a	Customary units: Length	_____ inches in a foot _____ feet in a yard About how long is a spoon? 6 inches 6 feet 6 yards About how tall is a person? 5 inches 5 feet 5 yards
2b	Customary units: Weight	_____ ounces in a pound _____ pounds in a ton About how much does a cat weigh? 8 ounces 8 pounds 8 tons About how much does a car weigh? 2 ounces 2 pounds 2 tons
2c	Customary units: Liquid capacity	_____ cups in a pint _____ pints in a quart _____ quarts in a gallon
3a	Metric units: Length	_____ centimeters in a meter About how long is a pen? 8 mm 8 cm 2 m 2 km About how long is a car? 2 mm 2 cm 2 m 2 km
3b	Metric units: Weight	_____ grams in a kilogram About how much does a pencil weigh? 75 mg 75 g 75 kg 75 cg About how much does a newborn baby weigh? 4 mg 4 g 4 kg 4 cg
3c	Metric units: Capacity	_____ milliliters in a liter How much water can we put in a baby bottle? 250 ml 250 dl 250 l 250 kl How much milk would a basketball hold? 3 ml 3 dl 3 l 3 kl
3d	Customary units: Length (tool—measure to nearest half-inch)	How long is the line? Circle the correct answer: 2 inches $2\frac{1}{2}$ inches 3 inches $3\frac{1}{2}$ inches
3e	Customary units: Length (tool)—using a ruler to the nearest fourth-inch	How long is the line? 3 inches $2\frac{3}{4}$ inches $3\frac{1}{4}$ inches $2\frac{1}{4}$ inches

(continued on next page)

Grade Level	Problem Type	Performance Indicator
4a	Customary units: Length conversions—inches, feet, yards	4 feet = _____ inches 2 yards = _____ feet 36 inches = _____ feet
4b	Customary units: Length (tool)—using a ruler to the nearest eighth-inch	 Make an X over 2¼ Make an R over 1½ Make a T over 2⅜ Make a B over 2¼

4c	Customary units: Operations—regrouping required	Circle the correct answer.
		  4 feet 5 inches
		+3 feet 8 inches
		8 feet 3 inches
		8 feet 1 inch
		7 feet 3 inches
		Circle the correct answer
		  3 weeks 4 days
		−1 week 6 days
		1 week 8 days
		2 weeks 8 days
		1 week 5 days

4d	Customary units: Area—volume	What is the area of a room 8 feet long and 10 feet wide? _____ What is the volume of a box 6 inches long, 8 inches wide and 4 inches high? _____
4e	Customary units: Story problems—renaming	Jill wants to make ribbons 6 inches long. How many feet of renaming material will she need to make 8 ribbons? Jill is 6 feet 2 inches. Her sister is 4 feet 10 inches. How much taller is Jill?

5a	Metric equivalencies—less common units	Circle the answer.
		A kilogram equals:
		1 gm 10 gm 100 gm 1,000 gm
		A hectogram equals:
		1 gm 10 gm 100 gm 1,000 gm
		A dekaliter equals:
		1 l 10 l 100 l 1,000 l
		A milliliter equals:
		  a tenth of a liter
		  a hundredth of a liter
		  a thousandth of a liter

(continued on next page)

Instructional Sequence and Assessment Chart (continued)

Grade Level	Problem Type	Performance Indicator
		A centigram equals:
		a tenth of a gram
		a hundredth of a gram
		a thousandth of a gram
		A decimeter equals:
		a tenth of a meter
		a hundredth of a meter
		a thousandth of a meter
5–6	Metric conversions	20 meters = _____ centimeters
		5000 centigrams = _____ grams
		500 kilometers = _____ meters
		3.6 meters = _____ centimeters
		46 grams = _____ kilogram
		2.7 liters = _____ deciliters

all possible items for customary and metric units are included, each type of item appears in at least one of the two systems of units.

INTRODUCING THE CONCEPT

Teachers working with beginning-level kindergarten or first grade students who have had no previous experience with measurement should demonstrate with concrete objects how to use consistent units as standards in measurement. Length can be introduced first. To illustrate measurement of length, before students are taught about abstract concepts of inches and feet, the teacher can present an exercise in which students measure the lengths of various strips of paper using paper clips as the measurement

Table 17.1   Metric and Customary Units for Measuring Length, Weight, and Capacity

Customary Units		
Length	Weight	Capacity
12 inches = 1 foot	16 ounces = 1 pound	2 cups = 1 pint
3 feet = 1 yard	2,000 pounds = 1 ton	2 pints = 1 quart
5,280 feet = 1 mile		4 quarts = 1 gallon

Metric Units			
Meaning of Prefix	Length	Weight	Capacity
thousandth	millimeter (mm)	milligram (mg)	milliliter (ml)
hundredth	centimeter (cm)	centigram (cg)	centiliter (cl)
tenth	decimeter (dm)	decigram (dg)	deciliter (dl)
whole	meter (m)	gram (g)	liter (l)
10 wholes	dekameter (dkm)	dekagram (dkg)	dekaliter (dkl)
100 wholes	hectometer (hm)	hectogram (hg)	hectoliter (hl)
1000 wholes	kilometer (km)	kilogram (kg)	kiloliter (kl)

standard. The teacher demonstrates how to measure the paper strip by laying the clips along the edge of the paper and determining that the paper is "X clips long." For example, in the illustration the slip of paper is three clips long:

Following the demonstration, students are given the opportunity to determine the lengths of several strips of paper using paper clips.

This exercise serves two purposes. First, it introduces students to the concept of measuring a specific attribute, e.g., length. Second, the exercise provides the opportunity to demonstrate how the units used for measurement are equivalent. The paper clips used in measuring length are always the same size.

Teachers can introduce weight measurement in the same way with a balance scale. First, the teacher demonstrates how the scale works. This is done by showing students that the weights on both sides of the scale are the same when the trays of the scale are the same height. Similarly, the teacher must show that when the weights are not the same, the side that is pushed down is heavier. Following the demonstration with a balance scale, the teacher introduces students to standard weights against which they will measure various objects. For example, blocks that weigh an ounce can be used as the measuring standard against which other objects can be measured.

For liquid capacity, the teacher can set out a number of empty cups, presents a water-filled container whose capacity is to be measured, and pour the contents into the cups, one at a time. The teacher then asks how many cups of water the container holds. Because of the potential mess involved in pouring liquids, this activity is best done as a teacher demonstration only.

PRIMARY GRADES

Common Units and Equivalencies

During the primary grades, students learn the more common units and their equivalencies. See Figure 17.1 for a table of commonly taught measurement facts. The basic procedure for introducing new units to students includes five steps. The teacher does the following:

1. Tells the function of the specific unit; e.g., "Inches tell how long something is. We use inches to measure objects that are not very big. Feet also tell how long something is. We use feet to measure objects that are pretty big."
2. Illustrates the unit; e.g., the teacher draws lines on the board and shows students the length of an inch or a foot. For demonstrating weight, the teacher might give students blocks weighing an ounce or a pound.
3. Demonstrates how to use measuring tools, measuring to the nearest whole unit.
4. Presents application exercises in which the students determine the tool that is appropriate to use when measuring an object; e.g., "What unit would we use to tell how long a piece of paper is? What unit would we use to tell how long the chalkboard is?"
5. Presents an equivalency fact; e.g., 12 inches equals one foot.

Application exercises (step 4) and equivalencies (step 5) should incorporate review of previously introduced units from all areas. For example, if students have learned inch, foot, ounce, pound, and pint, a representative set of questions would include: "What unit would we use to tell how tall a person is? What unit would we use to tell how much a person weighs? What unit would we use to tell how much a letter weighs? What unit would we use to tell how long a pencil is?"

Equivalency review might include these questions: "How many ounces in a pound? How many inches in a foot? How many pints in a quart?" Review can be provided daily in worksheet exercises. A sample worksheet appears in Figure 17.2.

In addition to worksheet exercises, the teacher should incorporate measuring tasks into daily activities. Scales, thermometers, rulers, and liquid containers should be readily accessible. Students should be encouraged to apply measuring skills with concrete objects.

The sequence and rate of instruction for measurement facts and skills must be carefully controlled. New information is introduced cumulatively. That is, a new piece of information is not introduced until mastery of prior skills and information is demonstrated. Also, review of prior information is incorporated into tasks that introduce new skills. The length units, inch and foot, are usually introduced first. Several weeks later, ounces and pounds might be introduced, and, several weeks after that, pints and quarts.

FIGURE 17.1 Measurement Facts

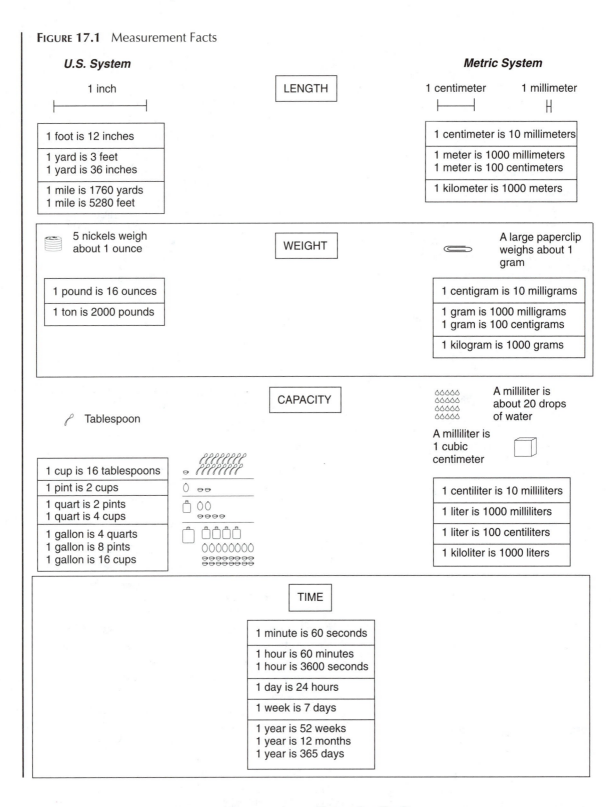

When the students demonstrate mastery of these smaller units, larger units (yard, ton, gallon) can then be introduced. A new set of units would be introduced only after students have mastered all the previous sets.

Measuring Tools

Calibrated measurement instruments include rulers, scales, thermometers, and speedometers. Every calibrated instrument is divided into segments representing specific quantities. The easiest type of instrument

FIGURE 17.2   Measurement Review Worksheet

Circle or fill in the answer.

				feet	pounds	inches	pints
1.	A pencil is about 6 _____ long.			feet	pounds	inches	pints
2.	A cat weighs about 8 _____.			feet	pounds	inches	pints
3.	A woman is about 5 _____ tall.			foot	pound	inch	pint
4.	He drinks a _____ of milk every day.			_____			
5.	How many inches in a foot?			_____			
6.	How many feet in a yard?			_____			
7.	How many ounces in a pound?			_____			
8.	How many pints in a quart?						
9.	About how many pounds does a dog weigh?			2	20	200	
10.	About how many feet high is a door?			8	80	800	

to read is one in which each line represents one unit. For example, on most thermometers each line represents 1 degree; likewise, on many bathroom scales each line designates 1 pound. Often instruments only label some of the lines that stand for quantities:

Those instruments require students to figure out what the unmarked lines represent before they are able to read them. Instruments like the ruler and scales found in grocery stores contain lines that represent fractions of a unit (e.g., ¼ inch, ⅛ pound).

In the early primary grades, students learn to measure length to the nearest inch (or centimeter) and weight to the nearest pound (or kilogram). In the late primary and intermediate grades, students learn to measure more precisely.

Measuring length with a ruler might be introduced first. The teacher explains that the numbers on the ruler indicate how many inches from the end of the ruler to the line corresponding to that numeral. The teacher then models using the ruler to measure several lines or objects, pointing out the need to properly align the front end of the ruler and the beginning of the line or object being measured. Finally, the teacher has the students use the ruler themselves. In order to make initial instruction more manageable, the teacher can give students worksheets with lines of various lengths (to the nearest inch).

For weight, the students put the object on the scale and read the number closest to the pointer. For capacity, the students fill the container with water, pour the water into a calibrated flask, and read the number closest to the water level. When teaching students to use measuring tools on which a line rep-

resents each unit but the relative value of each line is not shown:

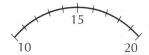

the teacher models how to count from the last given unit to the target unit. In the example below, the teacher models counting from 25, touching and counting each line—25, 26, 27, 28—to the quantity. A discussion on measuring to the nearest fraction of an inch appears later in this chapter.

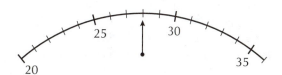

INTERMEDIATE GRADES

During the intermediate grades, the teacher follows these steps:

1. Presents and reviews all equivalencies
2. Teaches students more sophisticated uses of measuring tools (e.g., measuring to nearest ⅛ of an inch)
3. Teaches students to convert units to larger or smaller units
4. Presents measurement operations and story problems

To review previously introduced customary equivalencies, the teacher might prepare a handout, like the one previously presented in Figure 17.1, with the standard equivalencies written on it. Students who did not already know them would be asked to memorize these standard equivalencies. For students who have difficulty, the teacher can present verbal exercises to review the material.

Exercises in which students identify the most appropriate unit to measure various objects would follow the memorization exercise. A similar procedure should be used to review more common metric units as well.

Metric Equivalencies

In fifth or sixth grade, after decimals have been taught, exercises designed to teach students about the structure of the metric system should be presented. Format 17.1 shows the steps for teaching students the prefixes for the metric system. In Parts A and B, the teacher merely presents the meaning of the prefixes. The prefixes for units less than 1 (*milli-*, *centi-*, and *deci-*) are presented in Part A. Note that the teacher must emphasize the *th* ending of the words *thousandth, hundredth,* and *tenth,* so that students will note they are fractions and pronounce them correctly. In Part B the teacher presents the prefixes indicating units greater than 1 (*deka-, hecto-,* and *kilo-*). Depending on the level of students, a week or more of practice may be required to teach the meanings of these prefixes. The teacher would not go on to Part C, however, until the students demonstrate knowledge of all the metric prefixes.

Part C teaches students to use their knowledge of metric prefixes to tell the value of metric units. For example, the teacher models: Since *milli-* means a thousandth, *milligram* refers to a thousandth of a gram. Part D is a worksheet exercise in which students must find and circle the numerical representation of a specific metric unit. For example, a worksheet problem may ask for the amount that equals a centimeter, giving the following choices: 100 meters, .01 meter, .10 meter. Note that the ability to read decimal numbers is a prerequisite for this task. Daily worksheet exercises would continue for several weeks.

Abbreviations for metric units should also be introduced in a worksheet exercise. Teachers should not take for granted that students will be able to decode abbreviations. Several lessons should be devoted to teaching metric abbreviations.

Conversion Problems

This section addresses problems in which students must convert a quantity expressed as one unit into an equal quantity expressed in terms of a larger or smaller unit; for example, 3 feet can be converted to 36 inches, 2 meters to 200 centimeters.

The preskill for conversion problems is knowledge of equivalencies. Students cannot convert 5 kilograms to grams unless they know the number of grams in 1 kilogram. Conversion problems should not be taught until students know equivalencies.

There are three basic steps in any conversion problem: (1) determining whether the "new" unit is larger or smaller than the original unit, (2) determining what multiple the larger unit is in relation to the smaller unit, and (3) multiplying when converting to a smaller unit or dividing when converting to a larger unit. These steps are illustrated in Figure 17.3.

FIGURE 17.3   Steps in Basic Conversion Problems

	Problem a	Problem b	Problem c	Problem d
1. Determine whether the new quantity is a bigger (higher order) or smaller (lower order) unit.	48 inches = _____ feet. Change inches to feet. Feet is a bigger unit.	3 pounds = _____ ounces. Change pounds to ounces. Ounces is a smaller unit.	5 kilograms = _____ grams. Change kilograms to grams. Grams is a smaller unit.	300 centimeters = _____meters. Change centimeters to meters. Meters is a bigger unit.
2. Determine difference between units.	12 inches in a foot	16 ounces in a pound	1,000 kilograms in a gram	100 centimeters in a meter
3. Multiply if changing to a smaller unit. Divide if changing to a bigger unit.	Since change is to a bigger unit, division is called for. 48 inches ÷ 12 = 4 feet	Since change is to a smaller unit, multiplication is called for. 3 pounds × 16 = 48 ounces	Since change is to a smaller unit, multiplication is called for. 5 kilograms × 1000 = 5,000 grams	Since change is to a bigger unit, division is called for. 300 centimeters ÷ 100 = 3 meters

CONVERTING METRIC UNITS   Early intermediate grade teachers should limit examples to conversions with small quantities of common units (e.g., 5 meters = —————— centimeters). In the late intermediate grades, teachers can present the conversion strategy with larger numbers. Below is a description of the procedure for teaching conversion with metric units. Before the metric conversion strategy is introduced, students should know the equivalencies of the metric units, be able to read and write mixed decimals and decimal numbers, and be able to multiply and divide by multiples of 10 by moving the decimal point to the right or the left. When dividing, the decimal point is moved to the left. For example, when dividing by 10, the decimal point is moved one place to the left ($75 \div 10 = 7.5$); by 100, two places ($75 \div 100 = .75$); by 1000, three places to the left ($75 \div 1000 = .075$). When multiplying, the decimal point is moved to the right. Instructions for teaching multiplying decimals by multiples of ten appear in Format 13.9 in Chapter 13. A similar exercise would be used to teach students to divide by multiples of 10.

Before beginning conversion exercises, the teacher should give students worksheets like the one in Figure 17.4, designed to provide practice in dividing and multiplying by various multiples of 10. The discussion in Chapter 13 on multiplying decimals by multiples of 10 specifies example types to include in worksheet exercises. Students may require several weeks of practice to develop mastery. In some multiplication problems, students should have to add one or more zeroes (e.g., $100 \times 3.5 = 350.0$). In some division problems, students should have to add a zero in front of the original digits (e.g., $3.5 \div 100 = .035$). Such examples are difficult and require modeling.

A format for presenting the conversion strategy appears in Format 17.2. As mentioned earlier, this format assumes that students have been previously taught the metric equivalencies (e.g., when asked what a hectogram equals, they will say 100 grams). If students have not developed mastery in the preskills, they will find the conversion exercises quite difficult and frustrating. The format contains four parts: Parts A and B teach important component skills. Part A teaches students to determine whether they are changing the original unit to a bigger or smaller unit. Part B presents the rules: "When we change to a bigger unit, we divide; when we change to a smaller unit, we multiply." Part B concludes with an exercise in which the teacher writes sets of units on the board such as centigram → gram and leads the students in determining the appropriate operation.

For converting from grams to milligrams, the teacher might say "We're changing to milligram, which is a smaller unit than gram. So we multiply." For converting from meters to kilometer, similar teacher wording would be appropriate, "We're changing to kilometer, which is a bigger unit than meter. So we divide." Teachers raised in the United States may find that learning these rules themselves requires a good deal of practice, due to their own unfamiliarity with the metric system.

Part C is a structured board presentation in which the teacher presents all the steps in the conversion strategy. After the students determine whether to multiply or divide, the teacher leads them through deriving the number by which to multiply or divide. "There are 100 centigrams in a gram, so we divide by 100." Finally, the teacher demonstrates moving the decimal, as a quick way of multiplying or dividing by multiples of 10. For example, determining how many grams 2,135 centigrams equal requires division, since the new unit is bigger. Students divide by 100, since there are 100 centigrams in a gram. Therefore, the decimal point is moved two places to the left, and the answer is 21.35 grams. Part D is a structured worksheet exercise. Because this exercise incorporates several difficult component skills, a great amount of practice is necessary to develop mastery.

EXAMPLE SELECTION   Four example selection guidelines are important in teaching conversion problems:

1. In all problems, one of the units should be a base unit. The base units are grams, meters or liters.
2. In half of the problems, the students should convert a unit to a larger unit; while in the other half, the students should convert to a smaller unit.

FIGURE 17.4   Worksheet on Multiplying and Dividing by 10

a. $37 \times 100 =$ _____	b. $4 \div 1000 =$ _____	c. $53.2 \times 100 =$ _____	d. $7.04 \times 10 =$ _____
e. $4.8 \times 1000 =$ _____	f. $28.5 \div 10 =$ _____	g. $72 \times 1000 =$ _____	h. $.37 \times 100 =$ _____
i. $7 \div 100 =$ _____	j. $.37 \times 100 =$ _____	k. $5.43 \times 10 =$ _____	l. $.4 \times 1000 =$ _____
m. $37 \div 10 =$ _____	n. $4.2 \div 10 =$ _____	o. $72 \div 10 =$ _____	p. $38 \div 10 =$ _____
q. $52 \times 100 =$ _____	r. $4.8 \div 1000 =$ _____	s. $400 \div 1000 =$ _____	t. $52 \div 100 =$ _____

3. In half of the problems, the quantity of original units should be a whole number; while in the other half of the problems, the quantity should be a decimal or mixed number.
4. The amount the student multiplies or divides should vary from problem to problem: 10 in one problem, 1000 in the next, 100 in the next.

An example of an appropriate set of problems, following the guidelines, appears below. The answers are in parentheses.

142 centigrams = _____ grams (1.42)
9.8 grams = _____ milligrams (9800)
35 decigrams = _____ grams (3.5)
20 hectograms = _____ grams (2000)
4.35 grams = _____ milligrams (4350)

Note that the examples shown in Format 17.2 all refer to grams. The next day's unit might refer to liters or meters. In each lesson, a different type of unit is used.

CONVERTING CUSTOMARY UNITS Teaching students to convert quantities from one unit to another is more difficult in the customary system than in the metric system for three specific reasons: First, whereas in metric conversions the students always multiply or divide by a multiple of 10, in conversion problems with customary units, the number to multiply or divide by varies from problem to problem; converting inches to feet requires division by 12, and converting feet to yards requires division by 3.

A second reason for increased difficulty involves the procedures used when the converted unit is not a multiple of the original unit. In the customary system, the answer must be expressed in terms of a mixed number with two different units (e.g., 7 feet = 2 yards, 1 foot).

A final reason why customary conversions are more difficult is that conversions are sometimes made to a unit two or more steps removed. In the metric system the original unit is simply multiplied or divided by 10, 100, or 1000. In the customary system, several conversions may be required. For example, to convert gallons to cups, the student must first convert gallons to quarts, quarts to pints, then pints to cups.

The sequence for introducing conversion problems with customary units should be carefully controlled, with easier problems introduced first. The three basic types of conversion problems in the customary system are illustrated below:

1. Converting a quantity of a specified unit into a quantity of the next larger or smaller unit (Exam-

ples involve whole numbers only.):

28 days equal _____ weeks
6 feet equal _____ yards
24 inches equal _____ feet
4 weeks equal _____ days
2 yards equal _____ feet
2 feet equal _____ inches

2. Converting a unit into a mixed number (and vice versa) containing the next larger or smaller quantity:

27 inches equal _____ feet _____ inches
19 ounces equal _____ pound(s) _____ ounces
13 days equal _____ week(s) _____ days
2 feet 3 inches equal _____ inches
1 pound 3 ounces equal _____ ounces

3. Converting a unit into a unit twice removed:

2 yards equal _____ inches
2 quarts equal _____ cups
72 inches equal _____ yards
16 cups equal _____ quarts

The preskills for teaching conversion problems with customary units are knowledge of equivalents and knowledge of multiplication and division facts. Since measurement conversion tasks are usually introduced before students can divide by two-digit numbers, the teacher may choose to teach the students to count by 12s. Knowing this count-by series will help students in converting inches to feet and in determining dozens.

The format for introducing the first type of customary conversion problems (problems in which a unit is converted evenly into the next larger or smaller unit) would be basically the same as that for converting metric units (see Format 17.2). The teacher would have students (1) tell whether they are changing to a bigger or smaller unit, (2) tell whether they multiply or divide, and (3) tell by what number they multiply or divide. "We want to find how many ounces in 6 pounds. We're changing to a smaller unit, so we multiply. There are 16 ounces in a pound, so we multiply by 16."

The format for problems in which the conversion results in a remainder (e.g., 27 inches equal 2 feet 3 inches) is the same as for the previous type of problem except the teacher must explain what to do with the remainder. For example, in solving the problem 27 inches = _____ feet, after the students determine that 27 must be divided by 12, the teacher points out that since 12 goes into 27 with a remainder, the remainder tells the number of inches left. A structured worksheet presentation for converting from smaller to larger units when there is a remainder appears in Format 17.3.

The format for converting a mixed quantity to a lower unit appears in Format 17.4. When converting 2 feet 11 inches to inches, the teacher has the students cross out the 2 and write 24, the number of inches, above it. Then they add that quantity, 24 inches, to the 11 inches to end up with 35 inches.

Problems in which students must convert to a unit twice removed are quite difficult (e.g., 2 yards = _____ inches). The strategy we recommend involves having the students translate the quantity unit by unit. For example, in converting 2 yards to inches, the student would first convert 2 yards to 6 feet, then 6 feet to 72 inches.

Operations

This section deals with addition, subtraction, multiplication, and division operations with measurement units. As with most measurement-related skills, performing operations with customary units is more difficult than performing operations with metric units. The differences arise in problems that require renaming. Since the metric system uses a base 10 place value system, renaming presents no problems. Students merely apply the renaming skills they learned previously in decimal instruction. However, when working with customary units, there is no consistent base from which to work. The base for ounces is 16; for inches, 12; for feet, 3; etc. So students must be taught to use these bases rather than base 10.

Addition and subtraction problems with measurement units are usually introduced in fourth or fifth grade. The operations cause little difficulty in measurement problems that do not involve renaming:

$$
\begin{array}{lll}
\text{6 lb 4 oz} & \text{6 lb 4 oz} & \text{6 lb 4 oz} \\
\underline{\text{+1 lb 1 oz}} & \underline{\text{−1 lb 1 oz}} & \underline{\times\quad 2} \\
\text{7 lb 5 oz} & \text{5 lb 3 oz} & \text{12 lb 8 oz}
\end{array}
$$

$$
\begin{array}{ll}
\text{3 lb 2 oz} & \text{6.4 kg} \\
2)\overline{\text{6 lb 4 oz}} & \underline{\text{+1.1 kg}} \\
 & \text{7.5 kg}
\end{array}
\qquad
\begin{array}{l}
\text{6.4 kg} \\
\underline{\text{−1.1 kg}} \\
\text{5.3 kg}
\end{array}
$$

$$
\begin{array}{ll}
\text{6.4 kg} & \text{3.2 kg} \\
\underline{\times\quad 2} & 2)\overline{\text{6.4 kg}} \\
\text{12.8 kg} &
\end{array}
$$

Problems that do require renaming, on the other hand, are quite difficult:

$$
\begin{array}{ccc}
\overset{4}{\cancel{5}}\ \overset{18}{} & 1 & \overset{4}{\cancel{5}}\ \overset{14}{} \\
\cancel{5}\text{ lb }\cancel{2}\text{ oz} & \text{3 weeks 4 days} & \cancel{5}\text{ ft }\cancel{2}\text{ in} \\
\underline{-3\text{ lb }4\text{ oz}} & \underline{+1\text{ week }5\text{ days}} & \underline{-2\text{ ft }8\text{ in}} \\
1\text{ lb }14\text{ oz} & 5\text{ weeks }\cancel{0}\text{ days} & -2\text{ ft }6\text{ in} \\
 & 2 &
\end{array}
$$

A preskill for renaming problems is converting units, which was discussed previously. When working an addition problem, the teacher instructs students to always start working with the smaller unit. The difficult part of addition problems occurs after students have derived a sum that includes enough of the smaller unit to form a larger unit. In the problem

$$
\begin{array}{l}
\text{3 ft}\quad\text{8 in} \\
\underline{+\ \text{2 ft}\quad\text{6 in}} \\
\phantom{+\ \text{2 ft}\quad}\text{14 in}
\end{array}
$$

the students add 8 and 6 to end with 14 inches, which is more than 1 foot. The student must carry 1 to the feet column, cross out the 14, and write 2 to represent the remaining inches:

$$
\begin{array}{l}
\overset{1}{} \\
\text{3 ft}\quad\text{8 in} \\
\underline{+\ \text{2 ft}\quad\text{6 in}} \\
\phantom{+\ \text{2 ft}\quad}\cancel{14} \\
\phantom{+\ \text{2 ft}\quad}2
\end{array}
$$

The teacher leads students through sets of problems, renaming them when they must carry: "Remember, we're adding inches. How many inches in a foot? Yes, 12 inches in a foot. So if we have 12 or more inches in the inches column, we must carry a foot to the feet column."

Format 17.5 shows how to teach addition problems with renaming. The key in teaching the operations with customary units is teaching students *when* to rename and *what numbers* to use. Part A of the structured board presentation focuses on when renaming is appropriate. Part B provides practice in renaming with the appropriate numbers. Examples would include problems that require renaming and problems that do not require renaming. The examples in the format involve weight units; similar exercises would be done with length and capacity units.

After students can rename a variety of units when adding, they are given problems with subtraction. The difficult aspect of subtraction problems lies in renaming the minuend. For example, to work the problem

$$
\begin{array}{l}
\text{8 lb 4 oz} \\
\underline{-\ \text{3 lb 8 oz}}
\end{array}
$$

students must rename 8 pounds 4 ounces, borrowing a pound from 8 pounds, leaving 7 pounds, and increasing the ounces by 16 ounces (a pound) so there are 20 ounces:

$$
\begin{array}{r}
7 \quad 20 \\
\cancel{8}\ \text{lb}\ \cancel{4}\ \text{oz} \\
-\ 3\ \text{lb}\ \ 8\ \text{oz} \\
\end{array}
$$

We recommend that teachers introduce this skill by first presenting problems in which a mixed unit is subtracted from a whole unit. Following are examples of such problems:

$$
\begin{array}{ll}
3\ \text{ft} & 8\ \text{lb} \\
-1\ \text{ft}\ 4\ \text{in} & -2\ \text{lb}\ 5\ \text{oz} \\
\end{array}
$$

The teacher leads students through working these problems, pointing out the need to rename and how to rename: "We must borrow a foot from 3 feet. I'll cross out 3 feet and write 2. I borrowed a foot from 3 feet. How many inches in a foot? . . . So I write 12 in the inches column." After several days of practice, more difficult problems, in which two mixed numbers are involved, can be introduced. An example of a structured worksheet part of a format for subtraction problems with renaming appears in Format 17.6

Multiplication and division problems requiring renaming with measurement units are quite difficult. A strategy for working multiplication problems involves teaching the students to first multiply each unit. For example, in the problem

$$
\begin{array}{r}
5\ \text{ft}\ 7\ \text{in} \\
\times\ \ \ 4 \\
\end{array}
$$

the students first multiply 4 × 7 inches then 4 × 5 feet, writing the products for each:

$$
\begin{array}{r}
5\ \text{ft}\ 7\ \text{in} \\
\times\ \ \ \ \ 4 \\
\hline
20\ \text{ft}\ 28\ \text{in} \\
\end{array}
$$

After the products are written for each unit, the students rename, converting the smaller quantity and adding:

$$
\begin{array}{r}
5\ \text{ft}\ \ 7\ \text{in} \\
\times\ \ \ \ \ \ \ 4 \\
\hline
20\ \text{ft}\ \cancel{28}\ \text{in} \\
2\ \text{ft}\ \ 4\ \text{in} \\
\hline
22\ \text{ft}\ \ 4\ \text{in} \\
\end{array}
$$

Division problems, on the other hand, require a unique strategy. The students rewrite the quantity in terms of its lower units before working the problem. For example, in dividing 3 pounds 4 ounces by 2,

we suggest converting 3 pounds 4 ounces to 52 ounces, dividing 52 by 2, which equals 26 ounces, then converting the 26 ounces to 1 pound 10 ounces.

Story Problems

Story problems involving measurement units can be introduced as soon as students have learned to work operations. The strategies are the same as outlined in the problem-solving chapter. Below are examples of story problems:
Division
   a. James has 2 feet of ribbon. He wants to make kites. Each kite needs 4 inches of ribbon. How many kites can James make?
Subtraction
   b. Tania weighed 8 pounds, 4 ounces when she was born. Three months later, she weighed 11 pounds, 7 ounces. How much weight did she gain in those 3 months?
Multi-step
   c. Bill's plant is 4 feet tall. If it grows 3 inches a year for 5 years, how tall will it be?

Teachers should present about five problems daily for at least several weeks. When a new type of story problem appears, the teacher should lead the students through the problems. Division problems such as the one illustrated above will be particularly difficult and should receive extra emphasis. Examples should include a mix of the new problem type and previously introduced types.

Measuring Tools

During the early primary grades, students are taught to read calibrated measuring tools to the nearest unit. In later primary grades, students are taught to read fractional parts of units. We will discuss a procedure for teaching students to read rulers used in the customary system. Once students can read rulers, they should have little difficulty transferring these reading skills to other tools such as scales and measuring cups.

Rulers in the customary system are usually calibrated to allow measurement to the closest sixteenth of an inch. Because the different marks on the rulers tend to confuse students, a systematic approach should be taken in teaching students to measure the various fractional parts of an inch. We recommend preparing a set of rulers. In the first ruler, each inch would be divided into halves. In the second ruler, each inch would be divided into fourths. In the third and fourth rulers, each inch would be divided respectively, into eighths and sixteenths of an inch. Figure 17.5 illustrates the four rulers. A preskill for reading these tools is the ability to read and write mixed fractions.

A ruler in which an inch is divided into a greater number of parts is introduced only after students have demonstrated mastery in using the preceding ruler in the series.

A simple model-test procedure can be used to teach students to read units to the nearest half inch. The teacher points out that since the line between the numbers divides the inch into two equal parts, each line represents a half-inch. The same procedure would be used to introduce rulers divided into fourths. The teacher points out that since there are four parts between each inch, each inch is divided into fourths. The teacher then models and tests, reading the ruler starting at the $\frac{1}{4}$ inch mark: "$\frac{1}{4}$, $\frac{2}{4}$, $\frac{3}{4}$, 1, $1\frac{1}{4}$, $1\frac{2}{4}$, $1\frac{3}{4}$, 2" etc. Note that the teacher would not initially have the students read $\frac{2}{4}$ as $\frac{1}{2}$. The teacher then presents an exercise in which she points to a line on the ruler and has students determine how far it is from the front end of the ruler.

When students can identify the lengths represented by various lines, the teacher can present an exercise to teach that the line that indicates $\frac{2}{4}$ of an inch also is the line that indicates $\frac{1}{2}$ of an inch. The teacher explains that the line is in the middle of the inch and so divides it into halves. The teacher explains further that when using a ruler, the length is always reported with the smallest numerical denominator. Therefore, instead of saying a line is $3\frac{2}{4}$ inches, the line is said to be $3\frac{1}{2}$ inches. A practice exercise in which the teacher has the students find the lines on the ruler that represent various distances would follow the explanation (e.g., "Find the line on the ruler that shows $4\frac{1}{2}$ inches. Find the line that shows $2\frac{1}{4}$ inches," etc.). Practice can be provided in worksheet exercises like the one in Figure 17.6.

Rulers in which each inch is divided into eighths are introduced when students (1) can use rulers in which each inch is divided into fourths and (2) have learned fraction equivalency skills. Students should have had enough practice rewriting $\frac{6}{8}$ as $\frac{3}{4}$, $\frac{4}{8}$ as $\frac{1}{2}$, and $\frac{2}{8}$ as $\frac{1}{4}$ so that they can make these conversions with ease. The teacher introduces the ruler containing eighths by pointing out that since each inch is divided into eight parts, the lines tell about eighths of an inch. The teacher then has students read the lines on the ruler: "$\frac{1}{8}$, $\frac{2}{8}$, $\frac{3}{8}$, $\frac{4}{8}$, $\frac{5}{8}$, $\frac{6}{8}$, $\frac{7}{8}$, 1, $1\frac{1}{8}$," etc.

After several days, the teacher presents exercises teaching students to express $\frac{2}{8}$, $\frac{4}{8}$, and $\frac{6}{8}$ as $\frac{1}{4}$, $\frac{1}{2}$ and $\frac{3}{4}$, respectively. The teacher reminds students that length is always reported with fractions expressed in their simplest, smallest possible terms, and then she models and tests the various equivalencies.

The same basic procedure would be followed for introducing rulers in which each inch is divided into sixteenths. These rulers would not be introduced, however, until students were very fluent in using the ruler divided into eighths. Daily practice over a long period is needed to develop student fluency in these skills.

FIGURE 17.5   Recommended Set of Rulers

a. Marked to the nearest half of an inch

b. Marked to the nearest quarter of an inch

c. Marked to the nearest eighth of an inch

d. Marked to the nearest sixteenth of an inch (standard rulers)

FIGURE 17.6   Worksheet Exercise for Determining Length

Make an X over the line that indicates $3\frac{3}{4}$ inches.
Make an R over the line that indicates $2\frac{1}{2}$ inches.
Make an S over the line that indicates $\frac{5}{8}$ of an inch.
Make a B over the line that indicates $2\frac{3}{8}$ inches.

APPLICATION ITEMS: MEASUREMENT

1. Write a format for introducing the yard unit. Assume students have previously learned inches and feet, ounces and pounds. Include all five steps discussed on page 397. For step 4 write six questions.

2. Below are errors made by students on conversion tasks. For each error, tell the probable cause and specify a remediation procedure.

    Ann
    6 feet = <u>75</u> inches

    $$\begin{array}{r} \overset{1}{12} \\ \times\ 6 \\ \hline 75 \end{array}$$

    Janet
    6 feet = <u>60</u> inches

    $$\begin{array}{r} 10 \\ \times\ 6 \\ \hline 60 \end{array}$$

    Tim
    9 yards = <u>3</u> feet

    $$3\overline{)9}$$

3. A student says the x is over the line that shows 1¾ inches. Specify the wording in the correction made by the teacher.

4. Specify the wording in the correction to be made by the teacher.

    1 foot 7 inches
    +   8 inches
    2 feet 5 inches

5. For each error, tell the probable cause and specify what the teacher says to correct.
    Jim
    148 meters equal _____ km   **148 ÷ 1000 = 1.48**
    Tina
    148 meters equal _____ km   **148 × 1000 = 148,000**

6. Write a structured-worksheet presentation to lead students through working this problem.
    348 centimeters = how many meters?

FORMAT 17.1   Format for Metric Prefixes

PART A: PREFIXES FOR LESS THAN 1

TEACHER   **STUDENTS**

1. *(Write the following prefixes on the board.)*
    milli-   —thousandth of
    centi-   —hundredth of
    deci-   —tenth of
    one whole
    deka-
    hecto-
    kilo-

FORMAT 17.1   (continued)

TEACHER	STUDENTS
2. These are prefixes used in the metric system. They tell us how much of the base unit we have.	
3. *(Point to milli-, centi-, deci-)* These prefixes say there is less than one whole. What do these prefixes tell?	There is less than one whole.
(Point to deka-, hecto-, kilo-) These prefixes say there is more than one whole. What do these prefixes say?	There is more than one whole.
4. *(Point to milli-.)* This says milli. What does it say?	milli
Milli means a thousandth of. What does milli mean?	a thousandth of
(Repeat step 3 with centi-, and deci-.)	
5. Let's read all these prefixes and read what they mean. *(Point to milli-, centi-, deci-.)*	
6. *(Erase the words thousandth of, hundredth of, tenth of.)*	
(Point to milli-.) What is this prefix?	milli
What does milli mean?	a thousandth of
(Point to centi-.) What is this prefix?	centi
What does centi mean?	a hundredth of
(Point to deci-.) What is this prefix?	deci
What does deci mean?	a tenth of
(Point to the three prefixes in random order until students identify all three correctly.)	

PART B: INTRODUCING PREFIXES (MORE THAN ONE WHOLE)

1. *(Write the following prefixes on the board.)* milli- centi- deci- one whole deka- —ten wholes hecto- —one hundred wholes kilo- —one thousand wholes	
2. What does milli- mean?	a thousandth of
What does centi- mean?	a hundredth of
What does deci- mean?	a tenth of
3. Let's read the prefixes that tell about more than a whole. *(Point to deka-.)* This says deka-. What does it say?	deka
What does deka- mean?	10 wholes
(Point to hecto-.) This says hecto-. What does it say?	hecto
What does hecto- mean?	100 wholes
(Point to kilo-.) This says kilo-. What does it say?	kilo
What does kilo- mean?	1,000 wholes
(Erase the words: ten wholes, hundred wholes, thousand wholes.)	

(continued on next page)

FORMAT 17.1   (continued)

TEACHER	STUDENTS
4. *(Point to deka-.)* What does this say?	deka
What does deka- mean?	10 wholes
(Repeat step 3 with hecto- and kilo-.)	
5. Now let's tell what all the prefixes mean. *(Point to milli-.)* What is this prefix? What does it mean? *(Pause, signal. Repeat the question in step 4 for all prefixes, presenting them in random order; give individual turns.)*	

PART C: STRUCTURED BOARD PRESENTATION

1. What does kilo- mean?	1000 wholes
2. Kilo- means 1000 wholes. So kilometer means 1000 meters. What does kilometer mean?	1000 meters
Yes, a kilometer equals 1000 meters. Say that.	A kilometer equals 1000 meters.
(Repeat steps 1 and 2 with millimeter, hectogram, centigram.)	
3. What does deciliter mean? *(Pause.)*	a tenth of a liter

To correct: What does deci mean? *(Repeat step 3.)*

(Repeat step 3 with the following examples.)
dekaliter—10 liters
centigram—a hundredth of a gram
kiloliter—1000 liters
dekagram—10 grams
centiliter—hundredth of a liter

PART D: STRUCTURED WORKSHEET

1. *(Give students a worksheet with problems like the ones below.)*
   a. A kilogram equals
      1,000 grams   .001 gram   100 grams
   b. A millimeter equals
      1,000 meters   .001 meters   .01 meters
   c. A centigram equals
      100 grams   .001 grams   .01 grams
   d. A hectoliter equals
      .01 liters   .1 liters   10 liters   100 liters

2. Look at problem a. You have to circle what a kilogram equals. What does kilo mean?	a thousand wholes
So what does a kilogram equal?	a thousand grams
3. Circle the answer.	

(Repeat steps 1 and 2 with several examples.)

FORMAT 17.2   **Format for Metric Conversions**

PART A: RELATIVE SIZES OF UNITS

TEACHER	**STUDENTS**

1. *(Write the following chart on the board.)*

milligram	centigram	decigram	gram	dekagram	hectogram	kilogram
$\frac{1}{1000}$ gm	$\frac{1}{100}$ gm	$\frac{1}{10}$ gm	1 gm	10 gm	100 gm	1000 gm

2. These are the metric units for measuring weight. Milligram is a thousandth of a gram. It is the smallest unit. What is the smallest unit?

    milligram

    Kilogram is a thousand whole grams. It is the biggest unit. What is the biggest unit?

    kilogram

3. *(Start at gram and point to the left.)* If we move this way, we're changing to a smaller unit.

    (Point to the right.) If we move this way, we're changing to a bigger unit.

4. *(Point to the left.)* Which way am I changing?

    to a smaller unit

    (Point to the right.) Which way am I changing?

    to a bigger unit

5. *(Point to centigram.)* If we have centigrams and we want to change to grams, which way are we changing? *(Pause, signal.)*

    to a bigger unit

    (Repeat step 4 with grams to kilograms, grams to milligrams, hectograms to grams, kilograms to grams, grams to decigrams.)

6. *(Erase the board.)* I want to change centigrams to grams. What does a centigram equal?

    a hundredth of a gram

    When I change centigrams to grams, which way are we changing? *(Pause, signal.)*

    to a bigger unit

    (Repeat step 5 with same examples as in step 4.)

PART B: DETERMINING APPROPRIATE OPERATIONS

1. Here are two important rules: When we change to a bigger unit, we divide. Say that.

    When we change to a bigger unit, we divide.

    When we change to a smaller unit, we multiply. Say that.

    When we change to a smaller unit, we multiply.

2. What do we do when we change to a bigger unit?

    divide

    What do we do when we change to a smaller unit?

    multiply

3. *(Write on board: gram to centigram.)* When we change from grams to centigrams, which way are we changing? *(Pause, signal.)*

    to a smaller unit

    Do we multiply or divide when we change from grams to centigrams? *(Pause, signal.)*

    multiply

    To correct: If we have grams and we change to centigrams, which way are we changing? If we change to a smaller unit, what do we do?

(continued on next page)

FORMAT 17.2 (continued)

(Repeat step 3 with these examples: g to kg, g to mg, hg to g, kg to g, g to dg.)

PART C: STRUCTURED BOARD PRESENTATION

TEACHER	**STUDENTS**
1. *(Write the following problem on the board.)* 350 centigrams = _____ grams	
2. This problem says, 350 centigrams equals how many grams? We're changing centigrams to grams. What are we doing?	changing centigrams to grams
3. Are we changing to a bigger or smaller unit? *(Pause, signal.)*	bigger
4. We're changing to a bigger unit, so do we multiply or divide? Yes, when we change to a bigger unit, we divide.	divide
5. How many centigrams in each gram? So we divide by 100. Let's divide by moving the decimal. When we divide by 100, what do we do to the decimal?	100 Move it to the left 2 places.
6. *(Write 350 next to grams.)* If I move the decimal point two places to the left, where will it be? *(Write on board: 350 centigrams = 3.50 grams)*	between the 3 and 5
7. Read the problem now.	350 cg = 3.50 g

(Repeat steps 1-5 with the problems below.)
314 grams = _____ milligrams
(Move decimal point 3 places to right.)
315 grams = _____ kilograms
(Move decimal point 3 places to left.)
7 centigrams = _____ grams
(Move decimal point 2 places to left.)
18 kilograms = _____ grams
(Move decimal point 3 places to right.)
30 meters = _____ decimeters
(Move decimal point 1 place to right.)

PART D: STRUCTURED WORKSHEET

1. *(Give students a worksheet with problems like the one below.)* a. 232 centiliters equal _____ liters	
2. Read problem a. Are you changing to a bigger or smaller unit? *(Pause, signal.)*	bigger
3. So do you multiply or divide? *(Pause, signal.)*	divide
4. What do you divide by? Which way do you move the decimal point? How many places do you move it?	100 to the left two
5. Write the answer. Read the problem.	Students write 2.32. 232 centiliters equals 2.32 liters.

(Repeat steps 1–4 with remaining problems.)

FORMAT 17.3   **Format for Converting to Mixed Numbers**

PART A: STRUCTURED WORKSHEET

TEACHER	**STUDENTS**
1. *(Write the following problems on the board.)*	
a. 27 inches = _____ feet _____ inches	
b. 32 days = _____ weeks _____ days	
c. 28 eggs = _____ dozen _____ eggs	
d. 7 feet = _____ yards _____ feet	
2. Read problem a.	27 inches = _____ feet _____ inches.
In this problem you have to change 27 inches to feet and inches.	
3. To work this problem, first you find out how many feet are in 27 inches, then you see how many inches are left over.	
4. Are we changing to a bigger or smaller unit? *(Pause, signal.)*	bigger
So do we multiply or divide?	divide
5. How many inches are in 1 foot?	12
So we divide by 12.	
6. 12 goes into 27 how many times? *(Pause, signal.)*	2
There are 2 feet in 27 inches. Write 2 in front of the word feet.	
Do you have some inches left over?	yes
You used 24 inches. Subtract 24 from 27 and see how many you have left. *(Pause.)* How many inches left?	3
Write 3 in front of the word inches. So 27 inches equals what?	2 feet, 3 inches
(Repeat steps 1–5 for remaining problems.)	

FORMAT 17.4   **Format for Converting from Mixed Numbers**

PART A: STRUCTURED WORKSHEET

TEACHER	**STUDENTS**
1. *(Write the following problems on the board.)*	
a. 3 feet 4 inches = _____ inches	
b. 2 weeks 3 days = _____ days	
c. 2 pounds 3 ounces = _____ ounces	
d. 3 gallons 1 quart = _____ quarts	
2. Read problem a. This problem asks us to change 3 feet 4 inches into inches in all. First we'll find how many inches in 3 feet. Then we'll add it to 4 inches.	
(Write in. + over first problem.)	
in.+	
3 feet 4 inches = _____ inches	

(continued on next page)

FORMAT 17.4   (continued)

TEACHER	STUDENTS
What do we do first?	Find how many inches in 3 feet.
Then what do we do?	Add 4 inches.
3. Let's change 3 feet to inches. Are we changing to a bigger or smaller unit?	smaller
So what do we do?	multiply
4. How many inches in a foot?	12
So you'll multiply by 12. Everybody, how many inches in 3 feet?	36
Cross out 3 feet and write 36 above it.	
5. Now what do we do?	Add it to 4 inches.
6. How many inches in all? Write it in front of inches.	Students write 40.
7. Read the problem.	3 feet 4 inches equal 40 inches.

FORMAT 17.5   **Format for Renaming Customary Units**

PART A: DISCRIMINATION PRACTICE

TEACHER	STUDENTS
1. (Write the following problem on the board, with blanks for the ounces.)	

a.   3 lbs _____ oz
  + 2 lbs _____ oz
    _____ oz

TEACHER	STUDENTS
2. First, we add the ounces; then we add the pounds. How many ounces in a pound?	16
That means that if we end up with 16 or more ounces, we have to rename.	
3. I'll write numbers for ounces. Tell me if we have to rename.	
4. (Write 7 and 5 in the blanks.)	
What's the answer for ounces?	12
Do we have to rename 12 ounces as pounds?	no
(Repeat step 3 with 9 + 9, 9 + 5, 8 + 9, 8 + 8, 9 + 6.)	

PART B: STRUCTURED WORKSHEET

1. (Give students a worksheet with 8–10 problems such as the ones below.)

a.   5 lb 9 oz
  + 3 lb 9 oz

b.   4 lb 2 oz
  + 3 lb 11 oz

FORMAT 17.5   (continued)

TEACHER	STUDENTS
2. Touch problem a. Read the problem.	
3. We start by adding ounces.	
4. What is 9 + 9?	18
Write 18 under the line.	
5. How many ounces in a pound?	16
6. Do we rename 18 ounces as pounds?	yes
7. Cross out 18 and write a 1 over the pounds column.	
8. We had 18 ounces. We put a pound in the pounds column. How many ounces did we take from 18 ounces when we renamed?	16
To correct: A pound has 16 ounces.	
9. We had 18 ounces; we moved 16 ounces. How many ounces are left?	2
Write 2 under the ounces.	
10. Now add the pounds. How many pounds?	9
11. Read the whole answer.	9 pounds 2 ounces

FORMAT 17.6   **Format for Subtraction with Renaming**

PART A: STRUCTURED WORKSHEET

TEACHER	STUDENTS

1. *(Write the following problem on the board.)*
   5 lb 2 oz
  − 2 lb 9 oz	

2. Read the problem.	5 lb 2 oz minus 2 lb 9 oz
3. Can you start with 2 ounces and subtract 9 ounces?	no
4. You must rename. Cross out 5 pounds and write 4.	
5. We borrowed a pound. How many ounces in a pound?	16
6. Write 16+ in front of the 2 ounces.	
7. How many ounces do we start with now?	18
8. Cross out 16 + 2 and write 18 above it.	
9. And what does 18 − 9 equal?	9
So how many ounces do you end up with? Write it.	9
10. How many pounds do you end up with? Write it.	2
11. What's the answer?	2 lb 9 oz

CHAPTER 18

Mathematics Study Skills: Graphs, Charts, Maps, and Statistics

An understanding of mathematics is often required to comprehend material from other content areas such as science, social studies, or health. Mathematics in content-area material often appears in the form of graphs, charts, maps, and statistics. For example, a health text might contain graphs illustrating changes in the occurrence of lung cancer and changes in the percentage of women who smoke. Questions at the end of the unit could then ask students to give the percentage of changes in smoking and in the occurrence of lung cancer from 1968 to 1978. Or a chart in a science text might give the size, distance from the sun, mass, etc., for the planets in our solar system. A map in a history book might show the principal towns in colonial America, and a question may require students to determine how far apart they were. Obviously, students who lack specific mathematics study skills would find these items difficult. Therefore, mathematics study skills should be included in any comprehensive mathematics instructional program. Mathematics study skills discussed in this chapter include reading and interpreting graphs, reading charts, interpreting maps, and interpreting and determining statistical figures. The Instructional Sequence and Assessment Chart lists the specific problem types discussed in the chapter.

GRAPHS

A graph is a drawing or picture representation of a relationship between two or more sets of numbers. Figure 18.1 includes examples of the various types of graphs students will encounter in the elementary grades. Note that there are four main types of graphs: pictographs, bar, line, and circle graphs.

Graphs are typically introduced during late third or early fourth grade. The first type of graph introduced is usually the pictograph, followed by bar, line, and circle graph, respectively.

Two major factors determine the difficulty of interpreting line and bar graphs: (1) the amount of information on the graph and (2) the need for inferring or estimating amounts. Graphs become more complex as they show more than one set of relationships. For example, a simple line graph may show the performance of one student on a series of tasks. A more complex line graph would show the performance of several students all on the same graph with separate lines representing each student. In reading a graph with more than one set of information, the student must be able to use the key to determine which line refers to which student. Graphs with two sets of information are illustrated in Figure 18.2.

Graphs also become more complex as students must infer the amount indicated. Figure 18.3 includes

Instructional Sequence and Assessment Chart

Grade Level	Problem Type	Performance Indicator
3a	Interpreting line graphs	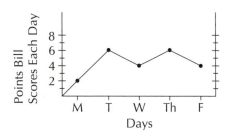 a. How many points did Bill score on Monday? b. On which day did Bill score the least?
3b	Interpreting bar graphs	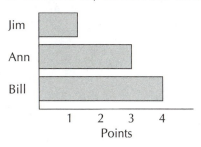 a. How many points did Ann earn? b. How many more points did Ann earn than Jim?
3c	Interpreting pictorial graphs	 How many babies were born in 1978? a. 3 b. 40 c. 30 d. 35 How many more babies were born in 1978 than in 1979?
4a	Determining arithmetic means	Jill plays basketball. She scores 8 points in one game, 2 points the next game, 6 points the next game, and 4 points in the last game. What is her average?
4b	Interpreting map legends (simple application with whole numbers)	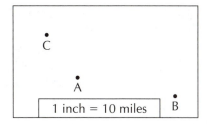 If A is 2 inches from B on the map, how much is the distance in miles between A and B?

(continued on next page)

Instructional Sequence and Assessment Chart (continued)

Grade Level	Problem Type	Performance Indicator
5a	Interpreting complex graphs with one variable—bar graph	

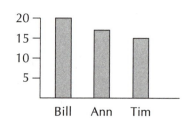

How many points did Ann score?
a. 15   b. 19   c. 17   d. 20

How many points did Bill score?
a. 20   b. 15   c. 19   d. 16

5b   Interpreting complex graphs with one variable—line graph

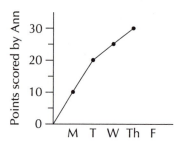

How many points did Ann score on Wednesday?
a. 20   b. 22   c. 28   d. 25

How many points did Ann score on Monday?
a. 15   b. 10   c. 9   d. 12

5c   Interpreting complex graphs with one variable—pictograph

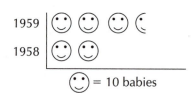

How many babies were born in 1959?
a. 30   b. 3   c. 40   d. 35

5d   Interpreting tables

Players on Taft High School Basketball Team

NAME	BORN	HEIGHT	WEIGHT
Jill Hernandez	1980	5'7"	134
Tammy Smith	1981	5'4"	128
Jackie Wilson	1980	5'2"	140
Tanya Jones	1982	5'8"	132

a. Who is the heaviest player on the team?
b. How much heavier is Tanya than Tammy?
c. How much younger is Tammy than Jill?

Instructional Sequence and Assessment Chart (continued)

Grade Level	Problem Type	Performance Indicator

6a   Reading Timetables

		Bus A	Bus B	Bus C	Bus D
Lv.	downtown	9:09	9:18	9:36	9:47
Ar.	25th St.	9:14	9:23	9:41	9:52
Ar.	34th St.	9:18	9:26	9:44	9:55
Ar.	41st St.	9:21	9:29	9:47	9:58
Ar.	49th St.	9:24	9:32	9:49	10:00
Ar.	62nd St.	9:31	9:39	9:56	10:07

a. When will Bus C arrive at 41st Street?
b. How long does it take Bus B to get from 34th Street to 62nd Street?
c. What time would you leave downtown if you wanted to be at 62nd Street just before ten o'clock?

6b   Interpreting complex graphs with two sets of information—bar graph

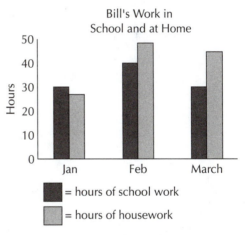

a. How many hours of school work did Bill do in February?
b. In which month did Bill do more school work than housework?

6c   Interpreting complex graphs with two sets of information—line graph

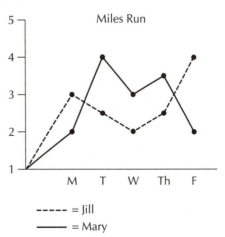

(continued on next page)

Instructional Sequence and Assessment Chart   (continued)

Grade Level	Problem Type	Performance Indicator
		a. On which days did Jill run more than Mary?
		b. How many miles did Jill run on Wednesday?
6d	Calculating statistics (range, median, mode)	Mrs. James gave a test to the 9 students in her class. The marks are written below:

Ann   23   Monica   41
Cathy   18   Naomi   35
David   41   Paul   41
James   23   Sarah   42
                      Tom   38

a. What is the range?
b. What is the median?
c. What is the mode?

6e   Interpreting map legends (complex applications with fractions)

```
┌─────────────────────────────┐
│    •                        │
│    C                        │
│                             │
│            •                │
│            A          •     │
│                       B     │
│  ┌──────────────────┐       │
│  │ 1 inch = 10 miles│       │
│  └──────────────────┘       │
└─────────────────────────────┘
```

a. If city C is 2½ inches from city B on the map, how far apart are cities C and B?

excerpts from four graphs. In examples a and b, the end of the bar is directly across from a mark which has no number next to it. The students must infer the number represented by the mark. In example a, there are five spaces between 20 and 30. Thus, each space represents a quantity of 2. In example b, there are two spaces between 20 and 30; thus, each space must represent 5.

Graphs become even more difficult to read when the end of the bar is not directly across from a mark, as in examples c and d in Figure 18.3. To determine the value, the students must mentally divide the space into equivalent units so that the point corresponds to a unit. In example c, the closest units are 20 and 22. The point is approximately ½ of the unit, so the value of the point is ½ of 2, or 1. Thus, the intersection point is about 21. Example d is significantly more difficult, since there is a greater difference between the numbered spaces, and the intersection does not fall at a halfway mark. To make the estimation, students must mentally divide the space into 10 equivalent units and estimate.

Pictorial graphs become more difficult when (1) each picture stands for a quantity other than one (for example, a pictograph in which each graph represents five units is more difficult than a pictograph in which each picture represents one unit) and (2) when fractional parts of a picture are shown. For example, let's say each smiling face represents 100 students and this picture is shown.

The student must determine the quantity the last picture represents by computing one-half of a hundred. Even more difficult would be an example in which a partial representation greater or less than one-half is shown:

In such an instance, the student must estimate the fraction of the unit shown and then figure out the

Figure 18.1 Simple Graphs

1. Bar Graphs
   a. horizontal

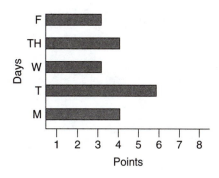

   b. vertical

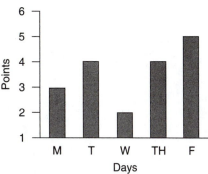

2. Line Graph

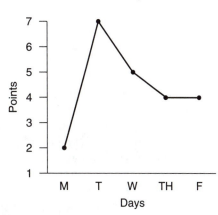

3. Pictograph

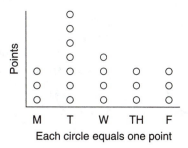

4. Circle Graph

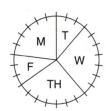

FIGURE 18.2 Complex Graphs

1. Bar Graph (double)

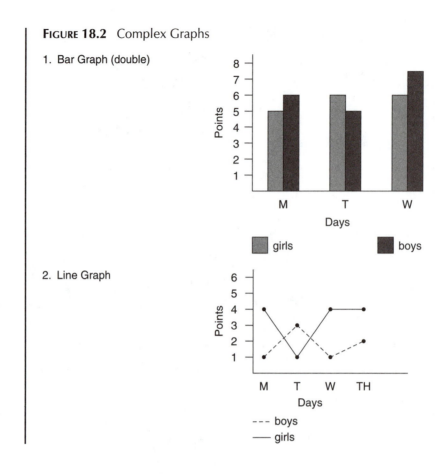

2. Line Graph

quantity it represents. In the above example, about ¼ of the face is shown; ¼ of 100 is 25.

The sequence for introducing various types of graphs should be carefully coordinated with number reading and fraction skills so that students have mastered all component skills before being asked to read graphs. Simple graphs are introduced first. Just one difficulty factor would be introduced at a time as more difficult graphs are taught.

The teaching procedure involves modeling how to find information on the graph, using a given question. For example, students may be given a bar graph that shows the number of points Sarah scored in basketball games during recess each day. An appropriate question is, "How many points did Sarah score on Tuesday?" The teacher first points out what the numbers stand for: "These numbers tell us the points Sarah scored." The teacher next points out what the letters under each bar would stand for: "This M stands for Monday. This T stands for Tuesday. . . ." Finally, the teacher models how to determine how many points Sarah scored on a given day. "To find how many points Sarah scored on Tuesday, I move my finger to the T. Then I move my finger up until the top of the bar. Finally, I move my finger to the numeral across from the top of the bar. It's a 6,

FIGURE 18.3 Graphs Requiring Estimation

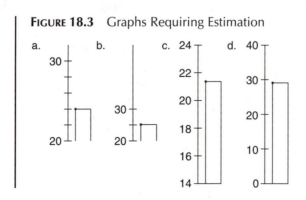

so the graph tells us that Sarah scored 6 points on Tuesday." The same basic procedure is used when more complex graphs are used. The teacher points out the various information shown on the graph and then models how to get information to answer specific questions.

A variety of literal questions should be included in initial examples. Literal questions ask for the amount at a particular time (e.g., "How many points did Sarah score on Monday?") or the particular time on which a specified quantity was given (e.g., "On what day did Sarah score 8 points?"). Questions calling for comparisons should gradually be included and come to represent a greater proportion of the total questions (e.g., "How many more points did Sarah score on Monday than on Tuesday? On which day did she score the most points? On which day did she score the fewest points?").

TABLES OR CHARTS

A table or chart, like a graph, specifies the relationship among sets of numbers. Reading tables and charts is frequently necessary in adult life: time schedules for buses, trains, and airplanes; financial charts dealing with income taxes, loan rates, and eligibility for benefits; instructions for recipes, medicines, and so on.

A preskill for using tables is an understanding of the concepts of row and column. Teachers can explain the terms in this way: "The lines of information going down the page are called columns. The lines of information going across the page are called rows."

The procedure for teaching students to read charts and tables would follow a model-test sequence for the various parts of the table, i.e., title, rows, columns. The teacher first points out the title of the table and discusses its intent. The teacher then points out the heading in each column, discussing the type of information found under each heading. After leading students through interpreting the headings, the teacher would point out how the students read across the row. Lastly, the teacher models the strategy for locating information by looking for the intersection of rows and columns.

The teacher must carefully design questions that require the students to use the table. During the early intermediate grades, these questions should be literal or comparative. A literal question can be answered by simply referring to the chart (e.g., "What time does bus 834 arrive at 145th Street?"). A comparative question, on the other hand, asks the students to tell the difference between two pieces of

information (e.g., "How many minutes between when bus 837 and bus 849 arrive at 135th Street?").

During the late intermediate grades, inferential questions should be introduced. An inferential question is one in which the information on the chart is used in conjunction with other information to answer a question (e.g., "During snowy weather which bus would you take if you wanted to arrive at 125th Street at 5:35 PM?"). The chart would show two buses, one arriving at 5:34 and one arriving at 5:25. The student would have to infer that since buses travel more slowly on snowy days, taking the 5:25 bus would be better.

Format 18.1 gives steps for introducing time schedules. Part A is a structured exercise in which the teacher models and tests how to locate information on the table. To do this, the teacher should put a reproduction of the table on the chalkboard or use an overhead projector to ensure that all students can see. Students should also have a copy of the table so they can practice finding information from the table at their seats. Following Part A, students should be given worksheets containing a table and set of relevant questions to complete under teacher supervision. One or two tables would be presented daily for several weeks.

Note that in the example presented in the format, reading a bus schedule, students must first find the row containing the location of the bus stop, then look across the row for the appropriate time, and finally go up that column to find the bus they must take. Locating a row or column in a bus time schedule differs from locating information in a table where students must locate the intersection of a row and column. For example, in the following table, to find the distance from Springfield to Salem, students would find the row for Springfield, find the column that is headed Salem, and then look for the intersection to find the distance. Students should be given an opportunity to work from a variety of tables.

	Portland	Albany	Salem
Eugene	118	30	62
Springfield	123	35	67
Creswell	132	44	76

MAPS

There are many skills involved in reading a map. However, our discussion addresses only a mathematics skill directly involved in map reading: computing the distance between two points on a map.

The difficulty of computing distances on a map is affected by two factors:

1. The presence of fractional numbers. If the distance between two points is 1¼ inches and the scale says 1 inch equals 20 miles, the student must multiply 1¼ times 20:

$$1\frac{1}{4} \times 20 = \frac{5}{4} \times 20 = \frac{100}{4} = 25$$

or

$$(1 \times 20) + (\frac{1}{4} \times 20)$$

2. The relative size of the numbers. Determining the distance between two points is more difficult when each inch represents 500 miles rather than 5 miles.

The preskills for simple map problems include measuring with a ruler to the nearest inch (or centimeter) and knowing multiplication facts. For more complex map problems, students must also be able to measure to the nearest fractional part of an inch and multiply a whole number and mixed fraction.

The teaching application involves modeling and prompting students in applying these three component skills:

1. locating and reading the scale,
2. measuring the distance between two points on a map, and
3. multiplying the distance by the scale value.

Initially, map problems should involve questions in which no fractional parts of a unit are involved. Fractional parts of a unit should be introduced only after multiplying fractions has been taught.

STATISTICS

The four basic statistical concepts introduced in the elementary grades are range, mean (or average), mode, and median.

The range refers to the difference between the smallest and largest number in a set. For example, the distances that girls in Mr. Adams' class can throw the shotput are: 32 ft., 29 ft., 41 ft., 18 ft., 27 ft., and 42 ft. The range would be computed by subtracting 18 ft., the lowest score, from 42 ft., the highest score: 42 − 18 = 24. The range would be 24 ft.

The mean, the most commonly used statistic, is computed by adding a group of numbers and divid-

ing the sum by the total of numbers added. For example the mean of the numbers 24, 26, 20, and 30 is computed by adding these numbers and then dividing the sum 100, by 4; the mean (100 ÷ 4) is 25.

The median is the middle measurement of a set that has been arranged in order of magnitude. For example, a teacher gives a test to a class of nine students and then lists the marks in order, from lowest to highest: 64, 70, 70, 70, 78, 92, 94, 94, 98. The median would be the score that comes in the middle, 78. Four students scored less than 78, and four scored more than 78. The median is relatively easy to figure with an odd number of scores. If there are 17 scores, the median would be the ninth number: eight numbers would be smaller and eight larger. For 13, the seventh number is the median: six are smaller and six are larger. The median is somewhat difficult to compute for an even number of scores. The teacher must average the middle two numbers. For example, if eight students score 13, 17, 19, 20, 24, 28, 31, 37, the median would be computed by figuring the average of the middle two numbers:

$$\frac{20 + 24}{2} = \frac{44}{2} = 22$$

The median equals 22.

The mode denotes the most frequently occurring value in a collection of values. For example, in looking at the students' scores on the tests in the preceding paragraph, we note that one student scored 84, three scored 70, one scored 78, one scored 92, two scored 94, and one scored 98. The score that occurred most often, 70, is the mode.

Statistical concepts should be introduced cumulatively, beginning with the mean, which is the most common statistic. When students have demonstrated mastery in computing the mean, the teacher can introduce the range, since computing the range is relatively easy and is unlikely to be confused with the mean. The median should be introduced third, and mode last, since it is the least frequently used. The mean is usually introduced in fourth or fifth grade.

Teaching Procedure

A similar teaching procedure can be used to teach mean, median, range, and mode. The teacher defines the term, models how to figure out the particular statistic, and then leads the students through working several problems.

Sets of problems should contain cumulative review. After each new statistical concept is introduced, the teacher should present exercises in which the students apply all the statistical concepts introduced to date. For example, if range and mean had been taught previously and the median had just been introduced, the teacher should present an exercise in which the students are required to compute all three statistics (range, mean, and median).

Since the teaching procedure is similar for all the statistics, we have included a format only for mean, the most difficult and commonly used statistic (see Format 18.2). This format demonstrates the mechanics of determining the mean. The teacher presents two steps: (1) add the numbers and (2) divide the sum by how many numbers were added.

When presenting the format, examples should be prepared initially so that the mean will be a whole number; i.e., the sum of the quantities must be a multiple of the divisor. A problem in which the sum

is 24 and the divisor is 5 would be inappropriate initially, since 24 is not a multiple of 5.

After this format has been presented for several days, a demonstration illustrating the concept of mean with a balance bar may be presented.

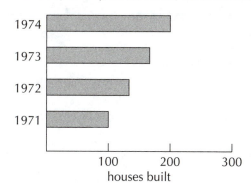

$$2 + 5 + 7 + 10 = 24, 24 \div 4 = 6$$

Next, the teacher places a fulcrum under position 6 and shows that the bar balances. The teacher summarizes by saying that the mean (6) is the center that balances the numbers on both sides.

APPLICATION ITEMS: STUDY SKILLS

1. For each pair of questions below, tell which is more difficult and why.

1974
1973
1972
1971

100   200   300
houses built

Pair one
a. How many houses were built in 1974?
b. How many houses were built in 1972?

Pair two
a. How many more houses were built in 1974 than 1971?
b. How many more houses were built in 1973 than 1972?

2. Below are two errors made by students on the problem specified. Tell the cause of each error. Specify the remediation procedure.
Jill played in 5 basketball games.
She scored 25 points in the first game, 15 points in the second game, 17 points in the third game, 21 points in the fourth game and 22 points in her last game.

(continued on next page)

What was her average?

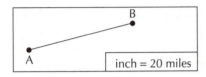

Alex	Jill		Ramon	
25	25	19.8	25	200
15	15	5)99	15	5)100
17	17	5	17	
21	21	49	21	
+22	+22	45	+22	
100	99	40	100	

3. Tell the component skills a student must have mastered to work the following problem. (*Note: A is 1¾ inches from B*)

```
        B
   ┌─────────●──────────┐
   │        /           │
   │       /            │
   │      /   ┌─────────────────┐
   ●      │ inch = 20 miles │
   A      └─────────────────┘
```

FORMAT 18.1   **Format for Reading Time Schedules**

PART A: STRUCTURED WORKSHEET

TEACHER	**STUDENTS**

1. *(Write the following schedule on the board, or use an overhead projector.)*

   Bus Time Schedule

Locations	Bus 287	Bus 124
23rd St.	2:15	3:44
37th St.	2:25	3:54
45th St.	3:05	4:02
64th St.	3:34	4:31
76th St.	3:48	5:06

2. This is part of a bus time schedule. It tells us when buses arrive at different places.

3. Remember: The lines of information going down the page are called columns. Touch the heading for the first column. Read it.

   Under this heading are all the places that the buses stop. They stop at 23rd St., 37th St., 45th St., 64th St., and 76th St. Touch the heading for the next column. Read it.

   That is the number of a bus. Under this heading are all the times bus 287 will arrive at different bus stops. What time does bus 287 stop at 23rd St.? *(Pause, signal.)*

STUDENTS responses:

Locations

Bus 287

2:15

FORMAT 18.1   (continued)

TEACHER	STUDENTS
(Repeat question with remaining locations. Repeat step 2 with bus 124.)	
4. *(Point to the time schedule.)* Let's say that we want to find out what bus stops at 45th Street around 4:00. First, I find 45th Street; then I go across until I find a time close to 4 PM. Last I go up the column to find the bus number. The bus I would take to go to 45th Street at about 4:00 would be bus 124, since it stops at 45th Street at 4:02.	
5. Now it's your turn. Find the bus that stops at 76th Street at about 3:45. First find the row for 76th Street. Now find the time you want—close to 3:45. *(Pause.)* What is the number of the bus?	287
What bus would you take on 76th Street at about 3:45?	Bus 287
(Repeat steps 3 and 4 with several questions.) a. How long does it take to get from 23rd Street to 45th Street on bus 124? b. How long does it take to get from 45th Street to 76th Street on bus 287? c. When does bus 287 arrive at 64th Street? d. When does bus 124 arrive at 45th Street?	

FORMAT 18.2   **Format for Computation Strategy (the Mean)**

PART A: STRUCTURED BOARD PRESENTATION

TEACHER	STUDENTS
1. Listen: Ben got 4 points on Monday, 7 points on Tuesday, 3 points on Wednesday, and 6 points on Thursday. *(Write 4, 7, 3, 6.)* We want to figure the average number of points Ben got each day. What do we want to figure out?	the average number of points Ben got each day
2. Here's how we figure the average. First we add, then divide the sum by how many numbers we added. First we add, then what do we do?	Divide the sum by how many numbers we added.

3. First we add. *(Write the problem on the board.)*
    4
    7
    3
  +6
 ———
What is the sum of 4, 7, 3, and 6? *(Pause.)*
	20

4. The sum is 20. We added. Now we divide by how many numbers we added. *(Point to 4, 7, 3, and 6 as you say.)* We added 1, 2, 3, 4, numbers.	

(continued on next page)

FORMAT 18.2   (continued)

TEACHER	STUDENTS
5. We added 4 numbers, so we divide 4 into 20. What do we divide?	4 into 20
How many times does 4 go into 20?	5
Yes, Ben's average is 5 points each day. What is Ben's average?	5 points each day
Did Ben score exactly 5 points every day?	no
5 points a day is his average.	

(Repeat steps 1–5 with the examples below.)
Jill scored the following points in each game: 6, 8, 9, 5, 0, 10, 4.
Tom ran these numbers of miles each day: 3, 1, 1, 7, 0, 0.

PART B: STRUCTURED WORKSHEET

1. *(Give students worksheets with several problems like the one below.)*
    Jack ran 5 miles on Monday, 2 miles on Tuesday, 4 miles on Wednesday, 0 miles on Thursday, and 9 miles on Friday. What is the average number of miles he ran each day?

    ☐ —————   ————   —————

2. Read the problem. What does the problem ask for?	the average number of miles he ran each day
3. What do we do first to figure the average?	Add the miles.
Add all the miles. *(Pause.)* How many miles did he run altogether?	20
4. What do we do after we find the sum?	Divide by how many numbers we added
5. How many numbers did we add? *(Pause, signal.)*	5
Say the division problem.	5 goes into 20
How many times does 5 go into 20?	4
Write the numeral in the box.	
6. Now we have to write in the words. Read the last sentence.	What is the average number of miles he ran each day?
So the words we put in the answer are miles each day.	
What are the words that go in the answer?	miles each day
What is the answer? Say the whole answer.	4 miles each day
Write the words.	

(Repeat steps 1–5 with remaining problems.)

CHAPTER 19

Geometry

The geometry objectives discussed in this chapter fall into three major categories:

1. Identifying and defining various figures and concepts
2. Measuring a figure, e.g., determining perimeter, area, circumference
3. Constructing figures using an instrument such as a compass or protractor

The specific skills to be taught can be found in the Instructional Sequence and Assessment Chart. Next to each objective in the Instructional Sequence and Assessment Chart are one, two, or three asterisks. These asterisks indicate the teaching procedure required for the specific skill. One asterisk indicates that the objective falls in the category of identifying and defining geometric figures and concepts. Specific teaching procedures for skills for this area appear on pages 427, 431–433. Two asterisks next to an objective indicate that the objective falls in the category of measuring geometric figures. Procedures for measuring geometric figures appear on pages 433–434. Three asterisks next to an objective indicate that the objective falls in the category of constructing geometric figures. Procedures for constructing geometric figures appear on page 434.

IDENTIFYING AND DEFINING GEOMETRIC FIGURES AND CONCEPTS

Table 19.1 lists most figures and relationships taught in the elementary grades. The table shows the relationship between various figures and concepts. It is not intended to imply an order for introducing skills. A suggested order for introducing skills appears in the Instructional Sequence and Assessment Chart.

Teaching students to identify new figures and concepts is simply a form of vocabulary teaching. Three basic methods of vocabulary instruction are used to teach the concepts or vocabulary in this chapter: (1) examples only, (2) synonyms, and (3) definitions. The examples-only method is used to present vocabulary terms and concepts that cannot be readily explained by using a synonym or definition. In teaching vocabulary through examples, the teacher constructs a set of examples, half of which are examples of the concept (positive instances) and half of which are examples of a similar but different concept (noninstances). The set must be carefully designed to show the range of positive instances and rule out possible misinterpretations. For example, when ovals are introduced, a variety of ovals should be presented to demonstrate the range of figures called ovals:

Instructional Sequence and Assessment Chart

Grade Level	Problem Type	Performance Indicator
1a	Identify circle.*	Mark each circle with X.
1b	Identify rectangle.*	Mark each rectangle with X.
1c	Identify triangle.*	Mark each triangle with X.
1d	Identify square.*	Mark each square with X.
1e	Identify interior of closed figure.*	Tell me when I touch the interior of this figure.
1f	Identify exterior of closed figure.*	Tell me when I touch the exterior of this figure.
2a	Identify cube.*	Mark each cube with X.
2b	Identify sphere.*	Mark each sphere with X.
2c	Identify cone.*	Mark each cone with X.
2d	Identify the diameter of a circle.*	What is a diameter? Put X on each line that is the diameter of a circle.

Instructional Sequence and Assessment Chart (continued)

Grade Level	Problem Type	Performance Indicator
2e	Draw a line segment.***	Draw the line segment CD.
3a	Measure perimeter.**	Find the perimeter of this square.
3b	Measure area of rectangle or square .**	Find the area of this rectangle.
3c	Identify pyramid.*	Mark each pyramid with X.
3d	Identify cylinder.*	Mark each cylinder with X.
4a	Define/identify radius.*	What is the radius of a circle? Mark each line that is a radius with X.
4b	Using a compass, construct a circle, when given a radius.***	Draw a circle that has a radius of 2 inches. Use a compass.
4c	Label angles.*	For each example, write the name of the angle.

(continued on next page)

Instructional Sequence and Assessment Chart (continued)

Grade Level	Problem Type	Performance Indicator
4d	Define degree/measure angles, using a protractor.**	Measure each of the following angles.
4e	Construct angles, using a protractor.***	Construct the following angles. 90° _____ 45° _____
4f	Define/identify right angle.*	What is a right angle? Circle each right angle.
4g	Define/identify acute angle.*	What is an acute angle? Circle each acute angle.
4h	Define/identify obtuse angle.*	What is an obtuse angle? Circle each obtuse angle.
4i	Define/identify right triangle.*	What is a right triangle? Circle each right triangle.
4j	Define/identify equilateral triangle.*	What is an equilateral triangle? Circle each equilateral triangle.
4k	Define/identify isosceles triangle.*	What is an isosceles triangle? Circle each isosceles triangle.
4l	Define/identify scalene triangle.*	What is a scalene triangle? Circle each scalene triangle.

Instructional Sequence and Assessment Chart (continued)

Grade Level	Problem Type	Performance Indicator
4m	Identify the following polygons:* pentagon hexagon octagon	Draw a P over the pentagon. Draw an H over the hexagon. Draw an O over the octagon.

Grade Level	Problem Type	Performance Indicator
4n	Measure the volume of a cube.**	What is the volume of a figure that is 5 inches long, 3 inches wide, and 6 inches high?
5a	Identify parallel lines.*	Circle each group of parallel lines.

Grade Level	Problem Type	Performance Indicator
5b	Identify perpendicular lines.*	Circle each group of perpendicular lines.

Grade Level	Problem Type	Performance Indicator
5c	Identify a parallelogram.*	Circle each parallelogram.

Noninstances should include circles, so that the students will not consider circles as ovals. As the examples are presented, the teacher points to each example saying, "This is an oval," or "This is not an oval," and then she tests the students by asking, "Is this an oval?"

The presentation of examples and nonexamples has been shown to be an effective way of teaching geometric concepts. In a study done by Petty and Jansson (1987), students in one group were taught to identify various geometric shapes using a rational sequence of examples and nonexamples, while students in the other group were given definitions of shapes in a traditional basal-style of instruction. Not surprisingly, students who were given the systematic sequence of instruction using examples and nonexamples performed significantly higher on measures of concept attainment than those who experienced the more traditional instruction.

Teaching vocabulary through synonyms involves explaining a new term by using a word or phrase already known to the students. For example, the word *interior* may be explained as meaning "inside". Teaching vocabulary through definitions, on the other hand, involves using a longer explanation. For example, a pentagon may be defined as a closed figure having five straight sides. Following either a synonym or a definition, the teacher presents a set of positive and negative examples asking, "Is this a _____?"

The synonym or definition selected need not meet all the requirements of a formal definition of the concept. A teacher may initially choose a simplified definition that is not technically correct but will help the students master the concept (e.g., "A rectangle has four sides and four square corners."). More sophisticated definitions can be used in later grades.

Table 19.1   Elementary Level Figures and Relationships

1. *Open Figures*
    a. *Line Segment*—the shortest distance between two points (*Note:* A line extends infinitely in space in two directions).
    b. *Ray*—a line beginning at a point and extending infinitely into space
    c. *Angle*—formed by two rays both of which have the same end point, which is called the vertex

         1. *Right angle*—measures 90°

         2. *Acute angle*—measures more than 0° and less than 90°

         3. *Obtuse angle*—measures more than 90° and less than 180°

         4. *Straight angle*—measures 180°

2. *Closed Figures*
    a. *Polygons*—simple (no crossed lines) closed figures bound by line segments
        1. *Triangles*—three-sided figures
            a. Equilateral—all sides measure the same length
            b. Right—contains one right angle
            c. Isosceles—two sides of equal length
            d. Scalene—no two sides are of the same length
        2. *Quadrilaterals*—four-sided figures
            a. Rectangle—four right angles, two pairs of sides with equal lengths
            b. Square—four equal sides, four right angles
            c. Parallelogram—two pairs of parallel lines

            d. Rhombus—parallelogram having two adjacent sides congruent

            e. Trapezoid—no right angles, one pair of nonparallel lines

        3. *Additional Polygons*
            a. Pentagon—five-sided figure
            b. Hexagon—six-sided figure
            c. Septagon—seven-sided figure
            d. Octagon—eight-sided figure
    b. *Curved Figures*
        1. *Ovals*

        2. *Circles*
            a. Center—midpoint of circle
            b. Radius—line segment extending from midpoint to edge
            c. Diameter—line that divides the circle in half

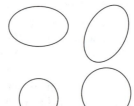

3. *Identification of Dimensional Shapes*
   a. *Cube*
   b. *Pyramid*
   c. *Cone*
   d. *Cylinder*
   e. *Sphere*

4. *Line Relationships*
   a. *Perpendicular lines*—lines that intersect to form a 90° angle
   b. *Parallel lines*—lines that exist beside each other without intersecting
5. *Figure Relationships*
   a. *Similarity*—having the same shape
   b. *Congruence*—having the same shape and size
   c. *Symmetry*—a figure can be folded along a line and the two parts coincide

---

Whether the concept is best taught through examples only, definition, or synonym, the teaching format consists of the same parts. Format 19.1 illustrates the basic identification/definition teaching procedure. In Part A, the teacher first models identifying several examples (if teaching by example only) or models and tests the synonym or definition. The teacher then tests students orally on a set of instances and noninstances of the concept. Part B is a worksheet exercise in which students must use the information they have just learned. For example, after modeling and testing the definition of a parallelogram and testing students on several positive and negative examples of parallelograms, the teacher has students complete a worksheet requiring them to circle all examples of parallelograms.

Worksheets should contain two distinct sections, one section should test application of the new definition and one section should review concepts taught previously. This cumulative review serves two important functions. First, it helps prevent students from forgetting previously taught concepts. Second, it helps provide the discrimination practice needed when similar figures are presented. Note that student performance on the review sections of the worksheets should determine when a new concept can be introduced. Generally, new information should not be introduced until students can demonstrate mastery on previously introduced information. In addition to worksheet review, extra practice should be incorporated into the classroom routine in the form of games and displays.

One way for students to practice identifying figures is to use flash cards. In flash-card practice, the figure is drawn on one side of a flash card and the label of that figure is written on the other side. Students study the cards and then take turns asking each other to identify the terms.

MEASURING A FIGURE

During the elementary grades, students are taught to measure (1) the perimeter of polygons, (2) the radius and diameter of a circle, (3) the area of a rectangle and square, (4) the volume of a cube, and (5) the number of degrees in an angle. Recommendations regarding when to introduce each measurement skill can be found by consulting the Instructional Sequence and Assessment Chart.

The perimeter of a polygon is the sum of the length of each of its sides. The radius of a circle is the distance between the midpoint of the circle and the edge of the circle:

The diameter is a line running from one side of the circle to the opposite side through the midpoint:

In teaching the students to measure the perimeter of a closed figure, the teacher defines *perimeter* and models how to compute it. The same procedure would be used in measuring the radius and diameter of a circle.

Area refers to the relative surface occupied by a plane figure. In teaching students to measure the area of a rectangle or square, the teacher first presents an exercise showing how a rectangle may be divided into square inches by making horizontal and vertical lines at inch intervals:

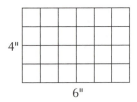

The teacher points out the meaning of the term *square inch.* After presenting several illustrations, the teacher gives a rule for determining the area (i.e., multiply the length times the width) and demonstrates its application, computing the area of several rectangles and squares. The teacher emphasizes the need to express the answer in terms of square units (square inches, square feet, etc.). A final exercise involves the students' having to determine the perimeter and area of a rectangle or square. A sample worksheet exercise appears in Figure 19.1. The purpose of the worksheet exercise is to provide students with the practice needed to discriminate these two similar measurements.

Volume refers to a number indicating the amount of space inside a figure. A procedure similar to that described for teaching the area of a rectangle would be used to teach students to determine the volume of a cube. The teacher first demonstrates how a cube may be divided into inch cubes. The teacher then models and tests finding the volume of a cube, multiplying the length times the width times the height, emphasizing the need to express the answers in terms of cubic inches.

Teaching students to calculate the number of degrees in an angle requires teaching them to use a protractor. The teacher first models how to align (1) the base of the protractor and the base of the angle

and (2) the vertex (point of the angle) with the center of the protractor base.

The next step requires deciding which row of numbers to read. As indicated in Figure 19.2, protractors have two rows of numerals. If the baseline of the angle points to the right:

the lower numbers are read. If the baseline of the angle points to the left, the top numbers are read:

The third step involves determining the number of degrees by noting the places at which the ray and the protractor intersect. In Figure 19.2, the intersection is at 70. Thus, the angle is 70°.

CONSTRUCTING FIGURES

Constructing figures requires the use of tools such as a ruler, compass, and protractor. In order to teach students to use such tools to construct or measure geometric figures, teachers must provide a clear model as well as sufficient, structured practice. The practice gives the teacher an opportunity to give feedback to as many students as possible. In modeling the use of a compass, for example, the teacher should emphasize the need to keep the compass upright when drawing a circle, not letting it slant. The teacher can then demonstrate how circles can be drawn the "wrong way," as well as show how to correctly use the instrument.

FIGURE 19.1   Sample Measuring Worksheet

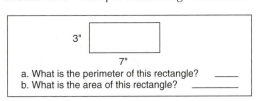

FIGURE 19.2   Using a Protractor

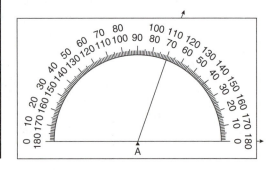

APPLICATION ITEMS

1. Using Format 19.1 as a model, write a teaching format for teaching the concept of parallelogram.

2. Construct a set of examples and nonexamples to use in teaching the concept of right angle.

3. Write a teaching format for teaching students to measure:
   a. the perimeter of a rectangle,
   b. the area of a square, and
   c. the radius of a circle.

4. Outline the steps in teaching students to use a protractor. What examples and nonexamples should teachers be sure to include in their demonstrations?

FORMAT 19.1   Format for Identification/Definition—Triangle

PART A: STRUCTURED BOARD PRESENTATION

TEACHER	**STUDENTS**
1. Listen to this definition: A triangle is a closed figure that has three straight sides. How many sides does a triangle have?	3
2. I'm going to point to some figures, and you tell me if they are triangles. *(Point to △)*	
Is this a triangle?	yes
How do you know?	It has three sides.

(Point to the following figures in the sequence shown.)

PART B: LESS-STRUCTURED WORKSHEET

(Give students a worksheet with problems like the ones below.)
   a. Draw a circle around each triangle.

   b. Write the letter R over each rectangle.
      Write the letter S over each square.
      Write the letter T over each triangle.
      Write the letter C over each circle.

1. Look at problem a on your worksheet. Read the directions.	Draw a circle around each triangle.
2. Touch the first figure. Is that a triangle?	yes
So what are you going to do?	Draw a circle around it.
Do it.	
3. Touch the next figure. Is that a triangle?	no
So what are you going to do?	nothing
4. *(Have students complete the worksheet by themselves.)*	

Direct Instruction Mathematics: A Longitudinal Evaluation of Low-Income Elementary School Students

Russell Gersten and Doug Carnine
UNIVERSITY OF OREGON

The recent National Assessment of Educational Progress (1979) found that at all grade levels, in all components of mathematics (concepts, problem solving, computation), students from disadvantaged urban areas performed at a lower level than their peers in other areas of the country. The National Institute of Education (Cohen, Koehler, Datta, & Timpane 1980, p. 1) concluded, "These differences have not come about recently and have shown little sign of dissipating over time."

The purpose of this paper is to describe an instructional model, the Direct Instruction model, that has been effective in teaching mathematics to disadvantaged students. The first section of the paper describes the methodology and presents an overview of the research conducted. The final section discusses more general implications of the findings for improving classroom practices. Issues to be addressed include training and supervision of teachers, use of paraprofessionals in the classroom, criteria for selection or adaptation of curricula for low-SES students, and methods for assessing student progress.

The Elementary School Journal
Volume 84, Number 4

DIRECT INSTRUCTION MATHEMATICS: AN OVERVIEW

Although in recent years the term "direct instruction" has been used in a multitude of ways, in this paper it refers to a comprehensive educational model involving (a) a specific curriculum, (b) a specific way of teaching (rapidly paced small-group instruction), (c) a specified model of inservice education, and (d) a system for monitoring both student and teacher performance. It is a synthesis of learning theory, behavioral technology, and Engelmann's principles of instructional design (Becker & Carnine 1980; Engelmann & Carnine 1982).

The major principle behind the Direct Instruction model is deceptively simple: Virtually all children can learn mathematics if (a) lessons are designed so that students can readily understand what is being presented, (b) adequate practice with corrective feedback is provided, and (c) progress through the curriculum is assessed regularly.

The Distar materials used with the model were designed for structured small-group teaching situations. The classroom schedule is arranged so that each student receives at least 30 minutes a day of intensive small-group instruction with a teacher or trained paraprofessional aide. A more detailed discussion of materials and instructional strategies appears in Silbert, Carnine, and Stein (1981). There are some similarities with adaptations of basal math series for effective urban education, such as those described by Good and Grouws (1979) and Nagel and McLevie (1981).

Distar Arithmetic I and II and a modified version of III by Engelmann and Carnine (1972, 1975, 1976) *explicitly* teach students rules and strategies for solving problems and performing arithmetic computations. To teach these rules, strategies and concepts efficiently, teachers demonstrate, prompt, and test students on each step of a new skill before expecting the students to work independently. In Direct Instruction, rules for solving word story problems or performing difficult computations (e.g., two-digit divisor problems) are explicitly taught, modeled, and then practiced and reviewed. Nothing is left to chance; children are not asked to infer rules or generalizations. For example, in teaching strategies for solving word story problems, children ask two questions to determine which operation to carry out. In answering the first question, students decide whether the problem entails multiple, equivalent-sized groups. If so, the problem calls for multiplication or division. Problems with unequal-sized groups require addition or subtraction. The second question asks whether the total is given in the problem. When the total is given in problems with equivalent-sized groups, students divide; conversely, when the total is not given, students multiply. A similar strategy is taught for discriminating addition from subtraction problems.

The curriculum also calls for considerable practice with corrective feedback. Teachers and aides are trained to provide immediate corrective feedback to student responses and to model correct problem-solving strategies if a student is confused. Principles of mastery learning are adhered to; groups do not go on to the next lesson until mastery (i.e., 85%–95% accuracy) is reached on the previous one.

An essential component of Direct Instruction is continual assessment both of student progress through the program and of teacher performance. Students are given individually administered criterion-referenced tests (by a tester other than the classroom teacher) on material covered during the preceding two months. Scores on these tests are used to determine whether a child (or group) needs remediation and whether individual students need to be placed in either a more accelerated or slower-paced group. Teachers and aides are observed weekly and given specific feedback. They then follow concrete remediation strategies for improving their teaching techniques (for more details, see Meyer, Gersten, & Gutkin 1983; Morimitsu 1979). The Direct Instruction approach toward teaching mathematics was evaluated in the context of Project Follow Through. The next section describes Follow Through and the results of the mathematics portion of the Follow Through evaluation.

THE NATURE OF FOLLOW THROUGH AND THE QUESTIONS POSED IN THE EVALUATION

Since 1968 the federally funded Follow Through Project has served as a research laboratory for the development and implementation of innovative teaching practices in schools serving low-income students. Over 180 school districts have been involved in Follow Through, ranging from rural areas such as Flippin, Arkansas, to the Rosebud Sioux Indian reservation in South Dakota, to inner-city districts in Philadelphia, New York, and Los Angeles. Each school district was aligned with a sponsor—a university or educational laboratory representing a specific model of education. The range of educational philosophies and models included in Follow Through was as diverse as the children served. They ranged from Piagetian-derived approaches to open classroom models, psychodynamic approaches, and several models based on discovery learning, as well as three approaches with a behavioral orientation.

Two sets of research questions were addressed in the independent evaluation conducted by Abt Associates (Stebbins 1976; Stebbins, St. Pierre, Proper, Anderson, & Cerva 1977), for the U.S. Office of Education (commonly called the Abt Report). The first set are methodologically intricate: Do children involved in the Direct Instruction Follow Through mathematics program for 3 years (first through third grade) or 4 years (Kindergarten through third grade) perform significantly higher on the mathematics subtests of the Metropolitan Achievement Test (Durost, Bixler, Wrightstone, Prescott, & Balow 1971) than *(a)* demographically similar students in local comparison groups and *(b)* children in other Follow Through programs?

In contrast, the second question asked was relatively simple and down to earth: Can low-income students taught with a Direct Instruction math program for 4 years perform at a level comparable to their middle-class peers?

We will also address a few questions supplemental to the Abt evaluation: Are there traces of the effects 2–3 years after the intervention is completed? What effect does the program have on those children entering Kindergarten or first grade with low academic skills, as measured by IQ tests and the Wide Range Achievement Test (Jastak & Jastak 1965)? These questions were explored through a variety of quasi-experimental designs.

Results of the National Follow Through Evaluation

It is important to note that Follow Through was not only one of the largest and most expensive social experiments ever conducted (McDaniels 1975) but also one of the most controversial (see Bereiter & Kurland 1981–82; Haney 1977; House, Glass, McLean, & Walker 1978). The methodological intricacies of the Follow Through evaluation go well beyond the scope of this article. However, some of the issues raised concerning the "fairness" of the measures used in the Follow Through evaluation are unpersuasive when the target is mathematics instruction. Both the affective instruments in the battery (the Coopersmith [1967] Self-Concept Inventory and the Intellectual Achievement Responsibility Scale [IARS] [Crandall, Katkowsky, & Crandall 1965]) and the reading and language subtests of the Metropolitan Achievement Test (Durost et al. 1971) have been criticized as being too narrow in scope (e.g., House et al. 1978; McLean 1978). However, there is considerably less controversy concerning either the content validity or the reliability of the math problem-solving and math computation subtests of the elementary form of the Metropolitan Achievement Test (see Bereiter & Kurland 1981-82; Wolf 1978), even though these tests do not necessarily assess a child's ability to devise unique solutions to complex mathematical problems.

The Abt Report attempted to examine the effectiveness of the nine major Follow Through sponsors by using a longitudinal design with replications across sites and across two cohorts of children. For each of these sponsors, six to 10 representative sites were selected for intensive study.

Since random assignment of children to treatment was deemed politically unfeasible, a quasi-experimental design (Campbell & Stanley 1966) was utilized; for each Follow Through site chosen, a roughly equivalent local "comparison group" was selected by the Stanford Research Institute. Demographic information was collected on all Follow Through and comparison children on the following variables (which were later used as covariates): family income, ethnicity, mother's education, pri-

mary language spoken at home, and academic entry skills.

The nature of math instruction in either the Follow Through or comparison classrooms was *not* measured in a systematic fashion. It is highly unlikely that Direct Instruction methods were used in the comparison classrooms. However, Stallings's (1975) observations of a small sub-sample of schools indicated that Direct Instruction classrooms could be correctly discriminated from comparison classrooms and other Follow Through classrooms over 90% of the time on the basis of observable variables, such as type of questions teachers asked during math lessons, amount of small-group instruction, and how teachers responded to student errors.

OUTCOMES MEASURES. All students in the Follow Through and comparison classrooms were tested upon entry into the program on the arithmetic subtest of the Wide Range Achievement Test (Jastak & Jastak 1965). Children were tested at the end of Grades 1, 2, and 3 on the Metropolitan Achievement Test (MAT). The math problem-solving and math computation sections of the MAT are generally considered reliable (with coefficients over .85) and valid subtests; the validity of the math concepts subtest is more open to question (Bereiter & Kurland 1981–82; Buros 1978; Wolf 1978).

Two affective measures, the Coopersmith Self-Concept Inventory and IARS, were utilized as supplemental measures. The reliabilities of these tests are appreciably lower than the MAT—.69 for Coopersmith, .55 for IARS (House et al. 1978)—though many would argue they are reliable enough to be utilized in evaluations of mean group performance (Cook & Campbell 1979; Wisler, Burns, & Iwamoto 1978). In any case, their role was primarily supplemental.

COMPARISONS WITH LOCAL AND "POOLED" COMPARISON GROUPS. For each site selected for the national longitudinal evaluation sample (Stebbins et al. 1977), an analysis of covariance (with multiple covariates) was conducted on each of the math subtests of the MAT, as well as the total math composite.

An effect was considered significant if the result was statistically significant and the magnitude of the treatment effect was at least .25 SD pooled. (This procedure eliminated the possibility of finding effects that were statistically significant but not large enough to be considered educationally meaningful.)

Using the entire non-Follow Through control sample (with sample sizes of approximately 1,000 depending on the variable) and the entire set of demographic variables, a "predicted" or "expected" score was derived for each site using a multiple regression level. If a site's performance on a subtest significantly deviated from this predicted score, the effect was tallied. (Even if the local comparison group was less disadvantaged than the Follow Through sample, leading to possibly biased results, the estimate based on the large "pooled" non-Follow Through sample was unlikely to be biased.)

The authors of the Abt evaluation presented what is essentially a "box score" for each of the nine major educational models. The performance of Follow Through students was compared with (a) students in a local comparison group and (b) an "expected" score based on the demographic characteristics of the Follow Through students. For each sponsor, a box score or net percentage was derived in the following fashion: Net Percentage of Significant Outcomes = [(Number of Positive Effects − Number of Negative Effects)/Total Number of Effects] × 100.

Percentages of significant outcomes are presented in table 1 for each math subtest—computation, problem solving, concepts, and the total math composite.[1]

The highest incidence of significant positive effects is in math computation, where 66% of the effects are both statistically and educationally significant. On math problem solving, 55% of the effects for Direct Instruction are positive. Thirty-seven percent of the effects for Direct Instruction are positive in math concepts. The results indicate that the Direct Instruction model produced consistently positive effects in both basic skills and higher-order skills in a variety of sites for two cohorts of children. Performance of students in the Direct Instruction model is superior to that of students in the other eight approaches in all domains of mathematics.

NORMATIVE PERFORMANCE. The mean standard score in total math on the elementary level of the Metropolitan Achievement Test for each Follow Through sponsor, converted to a percentile, is reported in Figure 1. The dark horizontal line near the top (at 50) represents national median performance. The shaded horizontal line at the bottom represents mean performance for students in low-income minority schools according to recent Department of Education evaluations (Ozenne et al. 1976) and the study of low-income students in comparison schools (Molitor, Watkin, Napior, & Proper 1977). Each box represents .25 SD. Children in the Direct Instruction Follow Through program are performing within two percentile points of the national median and over 1 SD above the typical level for children in low-income minority schools. These children perform at a significantly higher level than children in the other Follow Through models. Stebbins (1976, pp. 168–69) states, "The Direct Instruction Model is specific in stating that children participating in the Follow Through program are expected to, on the average, perform at the same level as their middle-class peers by the end of third grade. This goal has largely been achieved."

EFFECTS OF DIRECT INSTRUCTION ON SELF-CONCEPT. People unfamiliar with Direct Instruction or behavioral approaches were surprised by the finding that children taught with these procedures reported higher self-concept and more sense of responsibility for their academic successes and failures than children taught with approaches (such as Bank Street and Educational Development Center)

Table 1. Net Percentage of Statistically and Educationally Significant Outcomes Favoring Follow Through Students on the Metropolitan Achievement Test

Approach (and Sponsor)	Math Computation	Math Problem Solving	Math Concepts	Total Math
Direct Instruction (University of Oregon)	+59	+50	+32	+47
Behavior analysis (University of Kansas)	+38	−12	− 4	+ 8
Parent education (University of Florida)	+ 4	0	− 8	0
Bilingual (Southwest Educational Development Lab)	+13	+ 6	+25	+19
Child centered, responsive education (Far West Lab)	+ 6	0	0	0
Child development, psychodynamic (Bank Street)	− 8	− 8	− 8	−17
Language experience (TEEM) (University of Arizona)	+ 7	−13	−20	−20
Piagetian (High Scope Foundation)	− 6	−11	−11	−17
Open education (Educational Development Center)	−20	−10	−15	−20

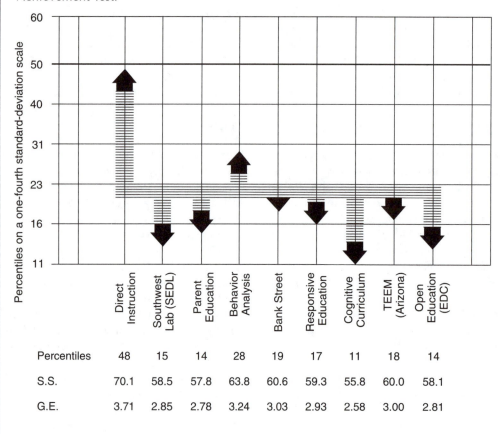

FIGURE 1.   Median standard scores, percentiles, and grade equivalents for the nine major Follow Through sponsors on the total math subtest of the Metropolitan Achievement Test.

	Direct Instruction	Southwest Lab (SEDL)	Parent Education	Behavior Analysis	Bank Street	Responsive Education	Cognitive Curriculum	TEEM (Arizona)	Open Education (EDC)
Percentiles	48	15	14	28	19	17	11	18	14
S.S.	70.1	58.5	57.8	63.8	60.6	59.3	55.8	60.0	58.1
G.E.	3.71	2.85	2.78	3.24	3.03	2.93	2.58	3.00	2.81

Grade equivalent for 50th percentile is 3.75

whose explicit goal was to build up the self-concept of students in the program through psychodynamic methods. The results of the three self-concept measures are presented in Table 2.[2] Direct Instruction is among the three highest-ranked models on all measures. While it is true that the Coopersmith Self-Esteem Inventory and the IARS measures have less than ideal reliability for individual assessment, their reliability is adequate for research involving large samples (Cook & Campbell 1979; Nunnally 1978; Wisler et al. 1978). Trends that are replicated with thousands of children in eight sites over two cohorts of children would appear to be more than a chance finding. Scheirer and Kraut (1979) discuss other replications of this finding.

Results of the University of Oregon Evaluation

REPLICATION ACROSS TIME.   In their recent work on quasi-experiments, Cook and Campbell (1979) indicate that, no matter how well designed, quasi-experiments cannot rule out rival hypotheses; therefore, replication is essential. The nature of Follow Through allowed for extensive replications across time—that is, replications of effects over seven to nine cohorts of children at the same site. For each of the 11 Direct Instruction projects, students were pretested (on entry) on the Wide Range Achievement Test (WRAT) and posttested (at the end of third grade) on both the WRAT and the MAT. These data allowed for an intensive examination of stability of effects across cohorts. The results (Gersten 1981) indicate strong replication of effects over six to eight cohorts of children. For 10 of the 11 projects, mean scores for low-income students on both the MAT and WRAT are consistently at, above, or within .25 SD units of the national norm level. All 11 sites were recently validated by the Joint Dissemination Review Panel of the National Institute of Education and Department of Education as demonstrating consistent, significant evidence of effectiveness in mathematics. As effects are replicated over six to

Table 2.   Net Percentage of Statistically and Educationally Significant Outcomes on Affective Measures

Approach	No. of Sites	Coopersmith Self-Esteem		IARS −		IARS +	
		%	Rank	%	Rank	%	Rank
Direct Instruction	16	+18	3	+21	2	+21	1
Behavior analysis	13	+24	1	+30	1	− 9	6
Parent education	12	+ 5	4.5	+19	3	+14	2
Southwest Lab	8	+21	2	0	4	0	4
Cognitive curriculum	9	0	7	−13	6	0	4
Responsive education	16	+ 4	6	− 8	5	0	4
Bank Street	12	+ 5	4.5	−17	7	−11	7
Open education (EDC)	10	− 6	8	−19	8	−18	8
TEEM (Arizona)	15	−12	9	−23	9	−23	9

eight cohorts of children, with a variety of teachers, supervisors, and consultants, it becomes increasingly clear that the effects are a result of the components of the educational model rather than other factors.

THE LOW-IQ STUDY. This study explored the hypothesis that, with appropriate educational programming, all students—regardless of entry skill level or IQ—can make roughly comparable yearly gains in mathematics achievement. To explore this hypothesis, yearly total math scores on the MAT were analyzed to explore whether there was a significant interaction between the child's IQ at entry (measured by the Slosson Intelligence Test [Slosson 1963]) and yearly growth on the total math subtest of the MAT. A 6 × 3 mixed analysis of variance was performed with one between-subjects factor (IQ level at entry) and one within-subjects factor (year of test) (Gersten, Becker, Heiry, & White, in press). No significant interaction was found between entry IQ and yearly achievement scores, despite the large sample size of 2,100 and consequent high statistical power. Those entering with low IQ scores tended to begin and end with lower MAT scores than their peers, *but they still maintained the same average growth rate of 1.0 grade-equivalent units a year.* These analyses appear to indicate that, when the curriculum is broken down into small steps and students are taught in small groups based on skill level, virtually all children, not just the upper half, can progress at a reasonable rate without the need for special education or remediation services.

LATER EFFECTS OF DIRECT INSTRUCTION. In 1975 and 1976, an attempt was made to ascertain whether the effects of the mathematics program were enduring. Fifth and sixth graders at seven sites

were tested on all subtests of the intermediate level of the MAT. Scores were contrasted with the performance of local comparison children, using analysis of covariance techniques with SES, parent education, rate, and primary home language as covariates. Analyses were performed on math problem solving, concepts, computation, and total math. The results indicated consistent, significant, positive findings in the area of math problem solving, weaker but significant effects in concepts, and null effects in computation. It appears that students retain some of the general problem-solving strategies taught in Distar arithmetic programs and use them in the fifth- and sixth-grade material they encounter. However, once graduated from the program after third grade, they are *not* learning the new computational skills in multiplication, division, measurement, and other new areas that should be taught in the intermediate grades. Details of the study are reported in Becker and Gersten (1982).

CONCLUSIONS AND IMPLICATIONS

The data presented above indicate that low-income primary-grade students who received the full 3- or 4-year Direct Instruction mathematics program tended to perform significantly better in all mathematic subtests of the Metropolitan Achievement Test than students who received other approaches, whether experimental or traditional. Direct Instruction Follow Through students achieved at a level much higher than is typical for students with similar demographic characteristics (see, e.g., NAEP 1979; Ozenne et al. 1976); in fact, their mean performance was at a level comparable to that of their middle-income peers.

What the data do not tell the reader is exactly what implications this study has for improving mathematics instruction in the primary grades. In this section, we will offer our speculations.

The Direct Instruction mathematics program can be broken down into three components. Each is likely to have contributed to the positive effects. The first component is organization of the classroom to maximize the amount of time students are actively engaged in mathematics activities at a high success level. Stallings's (1975) observational study of Follow Through classrooms indicated that students in Direct Instruction classrooms did spend more time engaged in math instruction than students in traditional classrooms and all but one other Follow Through Model (behavior analysis). The second component is the teacher performance variables that are part of the model and the focus of in-service training, such as techniques for procuring high student accuracy rate, systematic use of praise, and strategies for correcting errors that children make. The third component is the principles behind the curriculum developed and used in the program.

The academic learning time component is a recurrent issue in recent teacher effectiveness studies. The amount of time students are observed to be engaged actively in academic activities consistently correlates with student academic gain, both in compensatory education settings (Cooley & Leinhardt 1980; Rosenshine 1976; Stallings 1975) and regular education settings (Fisher, Berliner, Filby, Marliave, Cahen, & Dishaw 1980).

One way academic engaged time was increased in Direct Instruction Follow Through classrooms was to teach math in small groups of six to 10 pupils at all grade levels. In a naturalistic study of six classrooms, Good and Beckerman (1978) found that small-group instruction with a teacher provided the highest percentage of time on task for students—82%. Peterson, Janicki, and Swing (1981) also found that maximal learning in math occurred for low performers when students were taught in small groups.

In many of the Follow Through sites, the math program was taught by trained paraprofessional aides, while the teacher worked on reading and language. The use of paraprofessional aides as teachers (rather than classroom helpers or tutors) is unprecedented. This required extensive in-service training. The scripted Distar lessons facilitated the process. The advantage was that children could be taught math (as well as reading and language) in what appears to be an optimal-size group of five to 10 students at approximately the same current skill level. A long-term benefit of this procedure was that it led some of the paraprofessionals to pursue professional careers in education.

Research on the second component demonstrates that the proper use of various Direct Instruction teaching techniques enhances learner performance in mathematics: academically oriented feedback (Good & Beckerman 1978), appropriate correction of student errors (Carnine 1980; Siegel 1977), rapid pacing of tasks (Carnine 1976), and provision of signals to encourage group participation (Cowart, Carnine, & Becker 1976). Moreover, research indicates that the training of teachers in appropriate procedures for correction of student errors (Siegel 1977) and in cuing and pacing of lessons (Carnine & Fink 1978) is necessary if the techniques are to be used properly. For example, Siegel (1977) reported that, after training, teachers who were initially "low correction" implementers (i.e., rarely used correction procedures) actually surpassed their higher-performing peers who did not receive training. Moreover, students in the classes of the "low correction" teachers who underwent training outperformed students of initially higher-performing teachers who were not trained. A naturalistic study conducted in an urban Direct Instruction Follow Through setting (Gersten, Carnine, & Williams 1982) indicated that classrooms in which teachers (a) corrected student errors at a rate of at least 80%, (b) paced lessons at a rapid rate, and (c) procured mean student accuracy of 80% or higher during lessons, gained more on standardized achievement measures than students whose teachers were not performing at that level. These findings suggest that the Follow Through scores at the end of third grade may have resulted in part from teacher training on Direct Instruction teaching techniques.

The relative importance of the curriculum compared with other variables (degree of teacher implementation, amount of academic engaged time, and use of criterion-referenced assessment systems) has not been rigorously investigated. Yet an interesting perspective on this question emerges if one reexamines the data in Figure 1. It is clear that both the behavior analysis and the Direct Instruction models are effective in teaching skills in math computation, with 55% and 66% of significant outcomes, respectively. In the higher-order conceptual operations, the Direct Instruction model also produces significant gains: 55% for problem solving and 37% for concepts. Behavior analysis, on the other hand, produces negative values of −13% and −5%. Both behavior analysis and Direct Instruction utilize principles of extensive academic engaged time and reinforcement (Stallings 1975) and consistent monitoring of student performance (Becker, Engelmann, Carnine, & Rhine 1981; Ramp & Rhine 1981); yet the behavior analysis model utilizes the mathematics curriculum currently used in the school district, whereas Direct Instruction classrooms use the Distar arithmetic series, which is based on the explicit teaching of general case strategies for cognitive skills. Thus, there is some evidence suggesting that, when amount of engaged time is kept relatively constant, learning higher-order cognitive skills is enhanced by a well-designed curriculum that explicitly tries to teach them.

Darch, Carnine, and Gersten's (1983) research is a first step in this direction. They examined the relative effects of (a) mastery learning and (b) type of curriculum on the achievement of fourth-grade students in solving math word problems. Half the students received instruction using traditional basal curriculum; the other half used a Direct Instruction curriculum. Each sample was further subdivided so that half received a fixed number of lessons on the material, and half received additional practice lessons if they did not reach mastery on the material. They found that the additional practice did nothing to enhance the performance of students taught with traditional materials. Even with up to eight additional "practice" lessons to ensure mastery, their performance was no different than the students who had the fixed number of lessons. (Their mean scores, at the 60% level, were far from mastery, whereas the mean for Direct Instruction groups was in the 90%–95% range.)

The research of Good and Grouws (1979) in fourth-grade mathematics also tends to support the importance of a well-designed curriculum. Teachers were trained to adapt their teaching of traditional basal arithmetic texts by incorporating the following features of Direct Instruction: (a) systematic sequencing of skills and strategies, (b) daily review and practice of previously learned material, and (c) explicit teacher modeling and explanation of problem-solving strategies. Classes taught by teachers trained in these techniques gained significantly more than comparison classes (where the basal texts were taught in a conventional fashion).

The key principles of Direct Instruction curriculum design are (a) making each step in the problem-solving process explicit in the early stages of instruction, (b) beginning instruction in a highly structured context and then systematically moving the learner to unstructured applications, and (c) teaching general case strategies for working a wide range of complex problems. The importance of teaching explicit general case strategies is illustrated in two recent studies, one on teaching a multiplication algorithm (Carnine 1980) and one on teaching fact relations

(Carnine & Stein 1981). Engelmann and Carnine (1982) and Stevenson (1975) give additional research and an elaboration of the instructional design procedures.

The advantages of improved mathematics instructional methods like Direct Instruction or the Good and Grouws (1979) method are numerous. Schools *can* respond to public criticism of current levels of mathematics achievement by providing a foundation in basic mathematical operations and problem-solving strategies for virtually all students. When mathematics foundations are taught more efficiently, time becomes available for intensive work on problem solving and, for students who are interested, topics in higher-level mathematics.

These possibilities must be tempered by caution in generalizing our results to other, less disadvantaged, learners, grades other than the primary grades, and activities other than those covered in standardized achievement tests.[3] However, demonstration of the capability of thousands of low-income minority children to succeed in mathematics gives some basis for optimism in more far-reaching efforts to improve mathematics instruction.

NOTES

The authors wish to thank Paul Williams and Peter Sharpe for their assistance in the data analyses, and Bill White, Harriet Kandelmann, and Craig Darch for feedback on an earlier version of this manuscript.

1. In many of the communities, the comparison (non-Follow Through) students were less disadvantaged than the Follow Through students. To remedy this problem, all comparisons involving noncomparable control groups (differing by more than .5 SD on any demographic covariate) were considered untrustworthy and "grayed out" (deleted from the analysis). This was done because covariance adjustments tend systematically to *under*adjust for the more disadvantaged group (usually the Follow Through children). Because of the underadjustments, truly positive treatment effects may yield nonsignificant F ratios. Our analysis differs from Abt's in that the "gray out" rules have been revised in the following fashion: If there is a discrepancy of over .5 SD units between Follow Through and comparison group on a covariate favoring the comparison group and the analysis of covariance indicates a positive effect for Follow Through, the result is *not* grayed out. Campbell and Erlebacher (1970) clearly indicate that the covariance adjustment should handicap the Follow Through sample; if the Follow Through children—with this handicap—still significantly outperform the comparison children, there is clear evidence of a strong effect. (For further discussion, see Becker [1978].)

2. The Abt results on affective measures differ somewhat from earlier results obtained by Stallings and

Kaskowitz (1974). Stallings and Kaskowitz found that the Direct Instruction and behavior analysis students did well on the IARS−, but not IARS+. However, this finding *was not replicated* in the larger Abt evaluation, as can be seen in Table 2 of this paper. Considering the small sample size in Stallings's third-grade study (often only two or three sites per model) versus the larger Abt sample (usually 10–18 sites per model), we believe the Abt findings to be more reliable.

3. There is some evidence suggesting that Direct Instruction can also be successful with middle-income students. Guthrie (1977) reported that Direct Instruction was the only Follow Through model to have consistent effects for both low- and middle-income children enrolled in Follow Through. On the MAT computation subtest, the mean grade-level performance for the 321 non-low-income students who were enrolled in Direct Instruction classrooms was 4.76, almost a full year ahead of the national norm, corresponding to the 83d percentile. The mean for the concepts subtest was 4.42 (corresponding to the 68th percentile), and 4.26 for problem solving (75th percentile). Since no non-low-income comparison groups were available, the results must be considered merely exploratory. A study by Adamson (1976) with a control group also illustrates the potentiality of Direct Instruction with above-average students. (The students had an average IQ of 111.) The Distar program was compared with Developing Mathematical Processes (DMP), which "relies heavily on perceptual activities, discovery, and open-ended questions with a manipulative approach utilizing measurement" (p. 70). She found that Distar students were able to transfer from a previously taught form of computation, whereas the DMP students were largely unable to do so. She also reported that Distar worked equally well with both cooperative and noncooperative students, whereas DMP tended to work mainly with the cooperative students. "In the Distar program the child is not given the choice not to learn, and therefore he learns" (p. 75).

REFERENCES

Adamson, G. Mathematics achievement between first-grade students using developing mathematical processes and DISTAR arithmetic mathematics instruction (Doctoral dissertation, Brigham Young University, 1975). *Dissertation Abstracts International,* 1976, **36,** 4211A. (University Microfilms No. 76-683).

Becker, W. C. The national evaluation of Follow Through: behavior-theory-based programs came out on top. *Education and Urban Society,* 1978, **10,** 431–458.

Becker, W. C., & Carnine, D. W. Direct Instruction: an effective approach to education intervention with disadvantaged and low-performers. In B. Lahey & A. Kazkin (Eds.), *Advances in child clinical psychology.* Vol. **3.** New York: Plenum, 1980.

Becker, W. C., & Gersten, R. A follow-up of Follow Through: meta-analysis of the later effects of the Direct Instruction model. *American Educational Research Journal,* 1982, **19,** 75–93.

Becker, W. C.; Engelmann, S.; Carnine, D. W.; & Rhine, W. R. The Direct Instruction model. In W. R. Rhine (Ed.), *Encouraging change in America's schools: a decade of experimentation.* New York: Academic Press, 1981.

Bereiter, C., & Kurland, M. Were some Follow Through models more effective than others? *Interchange,* 1981–82, **12,** 1–22.

Buros, O. *Eighth mental measurements yearbook.* Highland Park, N.J.: Gryphon, 1978.

Campbell, D. T., & Erlebacher, A. How regression artifacts in quasi-experimental evaluations in compensatory education tend to underestimate effects. In J. Hellmuth (Ed.), *Disadvantaged child: compensatory education—a national debate.* Vol. **3.** New York: Brunner/Mazel, 1970.

Campbell, D. T., & Stanley, J. *Experimental and quasi-experimental designs for research.* Chicago: Rand McNally, 1966.

Carnine, D. Effects of two teacher presentation rates on off-task behavior, answering correctly, and participation. *Journal of Applied Behavior Analysis,* 1976, **9,** 199–206.

Carnine, D. W. Preteaching versus concurrent teaching of the component skills of a multiplication algorithm. *Journal of Research in Mathematics Education,* 1980, **11,** 375–378.

Carnine, D. W., & Fink, W. T. Increasing the rate of question-asking and use of signals in Direct Instruction trainees. *Journal of Applied Behavior Analysis,* 1978, **11,** 34–56.

Carnine, D., & Stein, M. Organizational strategies and practice procedures for teaching basic facts. *Journal of Research in Mathematics Education,* 1981, **12,** 65–69.

Cohen, M.; Koehler, V.; Datta, L.; & Timpane, M. Instructionally effective schools: research area plan. Unpublished manuscript, National Institute of Education, 1980.

Cook, T. D., & Campbell, D. T. *Quasi-experimentation: design and analysis for field settings.* Chicago: Rand McNally, 1979.

Cooley, W. W., & Leinhardt, G. The instructional dimensions study. *Education Evaluation and Policy Analysis,* 1980, **2,** 7–25.

Coopersmith, S. *The antecedents of self-esteem.* San Francisco: W. H. Freeman, 1967.

Cowart, J. B.; Carnine, D.; & Becker, W. C. The effects of signals on child behaviors during Distar instruction. In *Analysis of achievement data on six cohorts of low-income children from 20 school districts in the University of Oregon Direct Instruction Follow Through model* (Technical Report 76-1, Appendix A). Eugene: University of Oregon, 1976.

Crandall, V. C.; Katkowsky, W.; & Crandall, V. J. Children's beliefs in their own control of reinforcements in intellectual-academic achievement situations. *Child Development,* 1965, **36,** 91–109.

Darch, C.; Carnine, D.; & Gersten, R. Instructional approaches and level of practice in fourth-grade math problem solving. Paper presented at the annual meeting of the American Educational Research Association, Montreal, April 1983.

Durost, W. N.; Bixler, H.; Wrightstone, J.; Prescott, G.; & Balow, I. *Metropolitan Achievement Test.* New York: Harcourt Brace Jovanovich, 1971.

Engelmann, S. E., & Carnine, D. W. *Distar arithmetic III.* Chicago: Science Research Associates, 1972.

Engelmann, S. E., & Carnine, D. W. *Distar arithmetic II* (2d ed.). Chicago: Science Research Associates, 1975.

Engelmann, S. E., & Carnine, D. W. *Distar arithmetic II* (2d ed.). Chicago: Science Research Associates, 1976.

Engelmann, S., & Carnine, D. W. *Theory of instruction.* New York: Irvington, 1982.

Fisher, C. W.; Berliner, D. C.; Filby, N. N.; Marliave, R.; Cahen, L. S.; & Dishaw, M. M. Teaching behaviors, academic learning time, and student achievement: an overview. In C. Denham & A. Lieberman (Eds.), *Time to learn.* Washington, D.C.: USOE/National Institute of Education, 1980.

Gersten, R. Final reports to Joint Dissemination Review Panel, National Institute of Education, for Direct Instruction Follow Through projects. In *Education programs that work: a catalog of exemplary programs approved by the Joint Dissemination Review Panel* (8th ed.). Washington, D.C.: Department of Education, National Diffusion Network Division, 1981.

Gersten, R.; Becker, W. C.; Heiry, T. J.; & White, W. A. Entry IQ and yearly academic growth of children in Direct Instruction programs: a longitudinal study of low SES children. *Educational Evaluation and Policy Analysis,* in press.

Gersten, R.; Carnine, D.; & Williams, P. Measuring implementation of a structural educational approach: an observational approach. *Educational Evaluation and Policy Analysis,* 1982, **4,** 67–79.

Good, T. L., & Beckerman, T. M. Time on task: a naturalistic study in sixth-grade classrooms. *Elementary School Journal,* 1978, **78,** 193–201.

Good, T., & Grouws, D. The Missouri Mathematics Effectiveness Project. *Journal of Educational Psychology.* 1979, **71,** 355–362.

Guthrie, J. T. Research views—Follow Through: a compensatory education experiment. *Reading Teacher,* 1977, **3,** 240–244.

Haney, W. *A technical history of the national Follow Through evaluation.* Cambridge, Mass.: Huron Institute, August 1977.

House, E. R.; Glass, G. V.; McLean, L. D.; & Walker, D. F. No simple answer: critique of the "Follow Through" evaluation. *Harvard Educational Review,* 1978, **28,** 128–160.

Jastak, J. F., & Jastak, S. R. *The Wide Range Achievement Test.* Wilmington, Del.: Guidance Associates of Delaware, 1965.

McDaniels, G. L. The evaluation of Follow Through. *Educational Researcher,* 1975, **4,** 7–11.

McLean, L. D. Evaluation of early childhood education: no simple answer to the right questions. Paper presented at the conference entitled "Nature, Nurture, and School Achievement." York University, Toronto, May 1978.

Meyer, L. A.; Gersten, R. M.; & Gutkin, J. Direct Instruction: a Project Follow Through success story in an inner-city school. *Elementary School Journal,* 1983, **84,** 241–252.

Molitor, J.; Watkin, N.; Napior, D.; & Proper, E. C. *Education as experimentation: the non-Follow Through study.* Cambridge, Mass.: Abt, 1977.

Morimitsu, C. Supervision of Direct Instruction. Unpublished manuscript, University of Oregon, 1979.

Nagel, T., & McLevie, J. *Status Report 1 on the progress of implementing the Achievement Goals Program in San Diego schools.* San Diego: Board of Education, 1981.

National Assessment of Educational Progress. *Mathematical knowledge and skills.* Washington, D.C.: National Institute of Education, August 1979. (ERIC Document Reproduction Service No. ED 176 964)

Nunnally, J. *Psychometric theory* (2d ed.). New York: McGraw-Hill, 1978.

Ozenne, D., et al. *Annual evaluation report on programs administered by the U.S. Office of Education, fiscal year 1975.* Washington, D.C.: Capital Publications, Educational Resources Division, 1976.

Peterson, P. L.; Janicki, T. C.; & Swing, S. R. Ability × treatment interactions effects on children's learning in large-group and small-group approaches. *American Educational Research Journal,* 1981, **18,** 453–473.

Ramp, E. A., & Rhine, W. R. Behavior analysis model. In W. R. Rhine (Ed.), *Encouraging change in America's schools: a decade of experimentation.* New York: Academic Press, 1981.

Rosenshine, B. Classroom instruction. In N. L. Gage (Ed.), *Psychology of teaching. Seventy-seventh yearbook of the National Society for the Study of Education.* Chicago: National Society for the Study of Education, 1976.

Scheirer, M. A., & Kraut, R. E. Increasing educational achievement via self-concept change. *Review of Educational Research,* 1979, **49,** 131–150.

Siegel, M. A. Teacher behavior and curriculum packages: implications for research and teacher education. In L. J. Rubin (Ed.), *Handbook of curriculum.* New York: Allyn & Bacon, 1977.

Silbert, J.; Carnine, D.; & Stein, M. *Direct Instruction mathematics.* Chicago: Merrill, 1981.

Slosson, R. L. *Slosson Intelligence Test.* East Aurora, N.Y.: Slosson Educational Publications, 1963.

Stallings, J. Implementation and child effects of teaching practices in Follow Through classrooms. *Monographs of the Society for Research in Child Development,* 1975, **40**(7–8, Serial No. 163).

Stallings, J., & Kaskowitz, D. *Follow-through classroom observation evaluation, 1972–73.* Menlo Park, Calif.: Stanford Research Institute, 1974.

Stebbins, L. B. (Ed.). *Education as experimentation: a planned variation model.* Vol. **3A.** Cambridge, Mass.: Abt, 1976.

Stebbins, L. B.; St. Pierre, R. G.; Proper, E. C.; Anderson, R. B.; & Cerva, T. R. *Education as experimentation: a planned variation model.* Vols. **4A, 4C.** *An evaluation of Follow Through.* Cambridge, Mass.: Abt, 1977.

Stevenson, H. W. Learning and cognition. In J. N. Payne (Ed.), *Mathematics learning in early childhood.* Reston, Va.: National Council of Teachers in Mathematics, 1975.

Wisler, C.; Burns, J.; & Iwamoto, D. Follow Through: a response to the critique by House, Glass, McLean, and Walker. *Harvard Educational Review,* 1978, **48,** 171–185.

Wolf, R. Review of Metropolitan Achievement Test. In O. K. Buros (Ed.), *The sixth mental measurements yearbook.* Highland Park, N.J.: Gryphon, 1978.

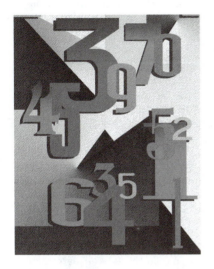

Frequently Asked Questions About Direct Instruction Mathematics

The direct instruction approach has been the target of many queries, controversies, and criticisms since its inception in the 1960s. Therefore, we have included this appendix to answer questions most frequently asked about direct instruction, specifically pertaining to the teaching of mathematics. The appendix is organized into two distinct sections: (1) Instructional Questions and Issues and (2) Issues of Instructional Organization and Management. Although some of the answers to the questions can be found in the research literature, some are questions of common practice. Moreover, many are not questions at all but merely instructional issues that require collective problem solving.

INSTRUCTIONAL QUESTIONS AND ISSUES

A. How does a direct instruction approach to mathematics instruction correspond to the standards put forth by the National Council of Teachers of Mathematics (NCTM)?

The goals of the NCTM standards are:

To value mathematics

To reason mathematically

To communicate mathematics

To solve problems

To develop confidence.

Teachers using a direct instruction approach to mathematics instruction will find that their teaching goals do not differ greatly from those of the NCTM. However, what teachers will find is that the instruction they design to meet those goals will look different from the instruction based on recommendations made by the NCTM. For example, a direct instruction teacher will examine carefully various strategies for teaching a concept or skill and choose to teach a single strategy on the basis of its generalizability and clarity. A teacher following recommendations made by the NCTM might have students generate their own individual strategies and have the students share them with the class. While we think generating strategies to solve problems may be an engaging activity, we know that presenting several strategies to students may confuse them. In addition, we want students to learn relationships among math concepts and, therefore, we design instructional strategies intentionally to highlight those relationships. One danger in relying on student generated strategies is that those strategies may cause misconceptions that go undetected until the time that students are introduced to related concepts. While we endorse the goals of the NCTM, we feel that the methods recommended to reach those goals must be examined carefully.

B. Doesn't direct instruction mathematics result in only rote learning?

Many critics of direct instruction perceive that the approach as rote memorization of basic skills. These critics are often confusing **rote** instruction with **explicit** instruction, and they may be misled due to the appearance of the instruction (e.g., use of scripted formats) rather than the instructional content. Because in a direct instruction approach, teachers are encouraged to write teaching formats prior to actual teaching, and because the formats articulate instruction in a step-by-step fashion some educators confuse the structure of the lesson with the content of the instructional strategy. The more scripted a lesson, the stronger the perception that some form of rote instruction is being delivered.

In reality, no skills or concepts are taught by rote in a direct instruction mathematics approach that can be taught using an explicit strategy. Certainly, direct instruction mathematics includes the teaching of the counting sequence (e.g., 1 2 3 4 5) and symbol identification (6 is "six"), both of which require rote memorization. Notice, however, that the tasks of counting and symbol identification are inherently rote tasks. Programs will always contain some rote instruction, but the decision to teach something by rote is driven by the demands of the task, not the instructional developer.

Direct instruction program designers have designed useful strategies even for the teaching of basic facts. Teachers using a direct instruction approach are encouraged to teach fact number-family strategies that facilitate student understanding of the relationships among fact families and that reduce the number of facts that must be memorized. For example, the introduction to the fact family 4, 3, and 7 facilitates learning the following facts: $4 + 3 = 7$, $3 + 4 = 7$, $7 - 4 = 3$, and $7 - 3 = 4$. Instead of memorizing four isolated facts, students are taught a *strategy* for deriving facts when one of the family members is unknown. For example, they are taught when the *big number* is missing they must add, and when one of the *small numbers* is missing they must subtract. (Note that the language of big and small numbers is used so that the strategy may be applied to multiplication and division, as well as addition and subtraction.)

The point of the above example is that, despite the fact that the instruction *appears* as if it might be rote, when teachers examine the instruction from the perspective of the learner, and look closely at the *content* rather than the *form* of the lesson, they will find generalizable strategies. (See Chapter 1 for a more thorough discussion of strategy instruction and Chapter 6 for instruction on basic facts.) In this text, we provide generalizable strategies for many computation and problem-solving skills. These strategies promote conceptual understanding and develop reasoning skills.

C. How do you know that direct instruction mathematics strategies are effective?

The strategies presented in this book have been field-tested extensively with students of various ages and abilities to ensure that they are viable and useful. The underlying research basis for the design of the strategies was presented in Chapter 3. The research reviewed in Chapter 3 incorporates relevant research from mathematics instruction and the teacher effectiveness literature, as well as research on specific direct instruction mathematics strategies. However, the strategies presented in this text also have been developed with feedback from students and their teachers. The article in Appendix A discusses the results of a large-scale evaluation of direct instruction mathematics with low-income students throughout the United States and provides a research basis for the strategies presented in this text. Many of the teachers involved in that research provided important feedback to those designing mathematics strategies during the development of the instructional materials. In addition, student errors were carefully examined, so that errors caused by a faulty strategy could be identified and the strategy rewritten. The development of effective strategies through feedback from field-testing is an important feature to highlight about direct instruction mathematics because of the notable absence of field-testing in educational publishing. Most commercially available programs are not field-tested with students prior to their publication. (See Appendix A for more detail on the development and evaluation of direct instruction mathematics strategies.)

D. What role do manipulatives play in mathematics instruction using a direct instruction approach?

First, it is important to note that the research literature on the use of manipulatives, or concrete objects, in elementary mathematics is mixed. While some researchers have found minimal support for using manipulatives (Sowell, 1989), others have found that proficiency in using concrete representation was inversely related to proficiency in symbolic representation (Resnick and Omanson, 1987). Manipulatives in and of themselves are neither helpful nor harmful. The *way* in which manipulatives are incorporated into instructional activities will determine their value. Consistent with a direct instruction approach, however, manipulatives would be most useful *after* an algorithm is taught. The concrete objects can be used as a means of demonstrating understanding of the symbolic representation. Many instructional programs do the opposite. That is, their initial instructional activities often require students to use manipulatives to generate or represent an algorithm before the students are taught the algorithm. The danger is that students either fail to learn the algorithm or are unable to transfer the concrete representation to a symbolic one. That is, students can work the problem with manipulatives only and not understand how to compute the answer on paper.

Another potential problem with the use of manipulatives is related to the issue of efficiency. In a study involving subtraction, Evans and Carnine (1990) found that although there were no differences in proficiency levels between groups of students who were taught algorithms and those who were taught with manipulatives, there was a significant difference in the amount of time required by each group to reach a level of proficiency. The authors concluded that no matter what type of representation is used, students can gain a conceptual understanding of the problem. However, instruction takes significantly more time when initial instruction involves concrete representations.

Finally, many teachers feel that, with respect to instruction with young children, using manipulatives makes monitoring individual student performance more difficult. In Chapter 7 of this text, we recommend teaching an early addition algorithm by using line drawing instead of concrete objects. The line drawing provides students with a pictorial representation of the problem. However, even more important, the line drawing strategy allows the teacher to examine individual student performance easily and remedy errors in a timely fashion.

E. Should teachers spend time teaching memorization of math facts?

Chapter 6 in this text provides the reader with a good rationale for teaching students basic facts. Briefly, the reason for teaching math facts is that they are a prerequisite for higher-level computation and problem-solving skills. When a student must stop working a problem to figure out a fact, attention is drawn away from solving the problem and is directed to computing the fact. The continuity required to learn new problem-solving routines is interrupted. Fluent knowledge of math facts not only facilitates the acquisition of higher-level skills, but also facilitates independence and confidence in learning.

While we advocate teaching math facts, we understand that this instruction is time consuming, especially with remedial students. Therefore, we suggest that instruction in math facts be supplemental to the teacher-directed lesson. Also, if the students require remediation, we recommend that they have a reliable alternative, such as a fact chart, on which to depend while they are honing their skills.

F. Should students be allowed to use calculators in math class?

Issues regarding the use of calculators are similar to issues of manipulatives in that it is not *whether* students use calculators but *how* and *when* they use them. Teachers must make conscious decisions about the degree to which they will allow students to rely on calculators for computation. If teachers do allow calculators, they must *teach* students to use them properly.

ISSUES OF INSTRUCTIONAL ORGANIZATION AND MANAGEMENT

A. Is direct instruction only for low-performing students?

Because direct instruction has been effective with low-performing and special education students, educators assume the strategies are appropriate only for those students who are struggling with mathematics. On the contrary, we believe the strategies are effective because they are well-designed, generalizable, and clearly presented. *All* students can benefit from well-designed instruction. The mistake many teachers make when using direct instruction with higher-performing students is that they pace the instruction too slowly. These teachers may be providing more repetition and practice than is necessary for students, or they may be teaching skills students already possess. Careful monitoring of student progress will allow teachers to provide appropriate instruction for a diverse range of student abilities in the classroom.

B. How does a direct instruction approach in mathematics work in inclusive classrooms? with students with disabilities?

Most classrooms reflect a range of student ability that teachers must consider when designing and implementing direct instruction mathematics (or any) instruction. In this text, we refer to students representing the range of student ability as high- and low-performing students. The underlying philosophy of direct instruction is that **all** students can learn if given well-designed instruction and opportunities for practice and that high- and low-performing students differ in their need of each. Two principles, then, guide the implementation of direct instruction with low-performing students and help define a population of students: Low performing students are those students who require 1) well-designed, unambiguous, teacher-directed instruction and 2) *More* practice opportunities.

It is our contention that instructional models that are driven by location (in-class versus pullout) are overlooking critical instructional factors that are directly related to student success. We have observed excellent pullout programs and excellent in-class programs. Therefore, in our opinion, when designing services for low-performing students, including students with disabilities, the design of the instructional strategies and corresponding practice activities must be addressed prior to discussing location.

As mentioned earlier, the direct instruction strategies in this text have been demonstrated to be effective with a range of student ability. But the instruction is just one of three components necessary to ensure student success. The other two components are assessment and service delivery. The assessment component must include provisions for appropriate initial screening and diagnostic testing, in addition to a system for continued progress monitoring. Service delivery in this context refers to the systematic coordination of efforts by general and special education that includes a process of shared responsibility and collaborative problem solving.

Using the guiding principles of well-designed instruction and more practice opportunities, all teachers of students with special needs must discuss the *who, what, where,* and *how* of designing an effective program. *Who* will be responsible for teacher-directed instruction? *What* will be taught? *Where* will the student receive the instruction? *How* will the teachers orchestrate additional practice opportunities? All of the above questions are relevant to the education of low-performing students.

If a school has made a commitment to full inclusion of students with special needs in the general education classroom, the two principles of well-designed instruction and more practice remain within the context of the general education classroom. *What* teacher-directed instruction will the student receive and *how* will increased practice be made available?

Models for service delivery that address the components of assessment, instruction, and service delivery will vary from school to school and include whole-class grouping and small-group instruction; peer, cross-age and classwide tutoring; before- and after-school programs; and instruction delivered by parents, volunteers, and paraprofessionals, in addition to general and special education teachers. The possibilities for designing effective instructional programs for students are numerous.

We fully understand the changes occurring in classrooms throughout the country and appreciate that, currently, many models of service delivery exist. However, we feel strongly that there is no one "right" way to provide services for low-performing students and just as strongly that meeting student needs requires the coordination and collaboration of all teachers.

References

Algozzine, B., O'Shea, D. J., Crews, W. B., & Stoddard, K. (1987). Analysis of mathematics competence of learning disabled adolescents. *The Journal of Special Education, 21*(2), 97–107.

Anderson, R. C., & Faust, G. W. (1973). *Educational Psychology: The Science of Instruction and Learning.* New York: Dodd, Mead & Company.

Ashcraft, M. (1985). Is it farfetched that some of us remember our arithmetic facts? *Journal of Research in Mathematics Education, 16*(2), 99–105.

Ashlock, R. B. (1971). Teaching the basic facts: Three classes of activities. *The Arithmetic Teacher, 18,* 359.

Baroody, J. J., & Ginsburg, H. P. (1983). The effects of instruction on children's understanding of the "equals" sign. *The Elementary School Journal, 84*(2), 199–212.

Barron, B., Bransford, J., Kulewicz, S., & Hasselbring, T. (1989). *Uses of macrocontexts to facilitate mathematical thinking.* Paper presented at the American Educational Research Association conference (March).

Behr, M. J., Wachsmuth, I., & Post, T. R. (1985). Construct a sum: a measure of children's understanding of fraction size. *Journal of Research in Mathematics Education, 16*(2), 120–131.

Bloom, B. S. (1968). Learning for mastery. *Evaluation Comment, 1*(2), UCLA: California.

Brophy, J., & Good, T. (1986). Teacher behavior and student achievement. In M. Wittrock (Ed.), *Third Handbook of Research on Teaching* (pp. 328–375). New York: Macmillan.

Cacha, F. B. (1975). Subtraction: Regrouping with flexibility. *The Arithmetic Teacher, 22,* 402–404.

Carnine, D. (1980). Preteaching versus concurrent teaching of the component skills of a multiplication algorithm. *Journal of Research in Mathematics Education, 11*(5), 375–378.

Carnine, D. W., & Stein, M. (1981). Organizational strategies and practice procedures for teaching basic facts. *Journal of Research in Mathematics Education, 12*(1), 65–69.

Carroll, J. (1963). A model for school learning. *Teacher's College Record, 64,* 723–733.

Case, R., & Bereiter, C. (1984). From behaviorism to cognitive behaviorism to cognitive development: Steps in the evolution of instructional design. *Instructional Science, 13,* 11–158.

Charles, R. I. (1980). Exemplification and characterization moves in the classroom teaching of geometry concepts. *Journal of Research in Mathematics Education, 11*(1), 10–21.

Cooper, G., & Sweller, J. (1987). Effects of schema acquisition and rule automation on mathematical problem-solving transfer. *Journal of Educational Psychology, 79*(4), 347–362.

Darch, C., Carnine, D. C., & Gersten, R. (1989). Explicit instruction in mathematics problem solving. *Journal of Educational Research, 77*(6), 351–358.

Deno, S. L. (1985). Curriculum-based measurement: The emerging alternative. *Exceptional Children, 52*(3), 219–232.

Drucker, H., McBride, S., & Wilbur, C. (1987). Using a computer-based error analysis approach to improve basic subtraction skills in the third grade. *Journal of Educational Research, 80,* 363–365.

Eicholz, R. E., O'Daffer, P., & Fleenor, C. R. (1987). *Addison-Wesley mathematics.* Menlo Park, CA: Addison-Wesley Publishing Co.

Engelmann, S. E. (1969). *Conceptual learning.* San Rafael, CA: Dimensions Publishing.

Engelmann, S. E., & Carnine, D. W. (1975). *Distar Arithmetic I* (2nd ed.). Chicago: Science Research Associates.

Engelmann, S. E., & Carnine, D. W. (1976). *Distar Arithmetic II* (2nd ed.). Chicago: Science Research Associates.

Engelmann, S. E., & Carnine, D. W. (1982). *Cognitive Learning: A Direct Instruction Perspective.* Science Research Association: Chicago, IL.

Evans, D., & Carnine, D. (1990). Manipulatives-The effective way. *ADI News,* 10(4), 48-55.

Fisher, C. W., Berliner, D. C., Filby, N. N., Marliave, R., Cahen, I. S., & Dishaw, M. M. (1980). Teaching behaviors, academic learning time, and student achievement: An overview. In C. Denham & A. Lieverman (Eds.), *Time to Learn,* Washington, D.C.: National Institute of Education.

Fuchs, L. S., Fuchs, D., Hamlett, C. L., and Stecker, P. M. (1990). The role of skills analysis in curriculum-based measurement in math. *School Psychology Review,* 19(1), 6–22.

Gleason, M., Carnine, D., & Boriero, D. (in press). Improving CAI effectiveness with attention to instructional design in teaching story problems to mildly handicapped students. *Journal of Special Education Technology.*

Good, T. L., & Grouws, D. A. (1979). The Missouri mathematics effectiveness project. *Journal of Educational Psychology,* 71, 355–362.

Good, T. L., Grouws, D. A. & Ebmeier, H. (1983). *Active Mathematics Teaching.* New York: Longman.

Hamann, M. S., & Ashcraft, M. H. (1986). Textbook presentations of the basic addition facts. *Cognition and Instruction,* 3(3), 173–192.

Jackson, M. B., & Phillips, E. R. (1983). Vocabulary instruction in ratio and proportion for seventh graders. *Journal of Research in Mathematics Education,* 14(4), 337–343.

Jerman, M. E., & Beardslee, E. (1978). *Elementary mathematics methods.* New York: McGraw-Hill Publishing Co.

Jones, V. F., & Jones, L. S. (1995). *Comprehensive classroom management.* Needham, MA: Allyn & Bacon.

Kameenui, E. J., & Carnine, D. W. (1986). Preteaching versus concurrent teaching of component skills of a subtraction algorithm to skill-deficient second graders: A components analysis of direct instruction. *Exceptional Children,* 33(2), 103–115.

Kameenui, E. J., Carnine, D. W., Darch, D., & Stein, M. L. (1986). Two approaches to the development phase of mathematics instruction. *Elementary School Journal,* 86(5), 633–650.

Kelly, B., Carnine, D., Gersten, R., & Grossen, B. (1986). The effectiveness of videodisc instruction in teaching fractions to learning-disabled and remedial high school students. *Journal of Special Education Technology,* 8(2), 5–17.

Kulik, J., Kulik, C-L., & Bangert-Drowns, R. (1990). Effect of mastery learning programs: A meta-analysis. *Review of Educational Research,* 60, 265–299.

Leinhardt, G., Zaslavsky, O., & Stein, M. K. (1990). Functions, graphs, and graphing: tasks, learning, and teaching. *Review of Educational Research,* 60(1), 1–64.

Leinhardt, Gaea. (1987). Development of an expert explanation: An analysis of a sequence of subtraction lessons. *Cognition and Instruction,* 4(4), 225–282.

Lewis, A. B., & Mayer, R. E. (1987). Students' miscomprehension of relational statements in arithmetic word problems. *Journal of Educational Psychology,* 79(4), 363–371.

Lindvall, C. M., & Ibarra, C. G. (1980). Incorrect procedures used by primary grade pupils in solving open addition and subtraction sentences. *Journal of Research in Mathematics Education,* 11, 50–62.

Lloyd, J. W., & Keller, C. E. (1989). Effective mathematics instruction: Development, instruction, and programs. *Focus on Exceptional Children,* 21(7), 1–10.

Marcucci, R. B. (1980). *Metanalysis of research on methods of teaching mathematical problem solving.* Unpublished doctoral dissertation, University of Iowa.

Markle, S. K., & Tiemann, P. W. (1970). Problems of conceptual learning. *Journal of Educational Technology,* 1, 52–62.

McDaniel, M. A., & Schlager, M. S. (1990). Discovery learning and transfer of problem-solving skills. *Cognition and Instruction,* 7(2), 129–159.

Offner, C. D. (1978). Back-to-basics in mathematics: An educational fraud. *Mathematics Teacher,* 71(3), 211–217.

Paine, S. C., Radicchi, J., Rosellini, L. C., Deutchman, L., Darch, C. B. (1983). *Structuring your classroom for academic success.* Champaign, IL: Research Press.

Paine, S. C., Carnine, D. W., White, W.A.T., & Walters, G. (1982). Effects of fading teacher presentation structure (convertization) on acquisition and maintenance of arithmetic problem-solving skills. *Education and Treatment of Children,* 5(2), 93–107.

Park, O., & Tennyson, R. D. (1980). Adaptive design strategies for selecting number and presentation order of examples in coordinate concept acquisition. *Journal of Educational Psychology,* 72(3), 362–370.

Peck, D. M., & Jenks, S. M. (1981). Conceptual issues in the teaching and learning of fractions. *Journal for Research in Mathematics Education,* 12(5), 339–348.

Pellegrino, J. W., & Goldman, S. R. (1987). Information processing and elementary mathematics. *Journal of Learning Disabilities,* 20(1), 23–32.

Petty, O. S., & Jansson, L. C. (1987). Sequencing examples and nonexamples to facilitate concept attainment. *Journal for Research in Mathematics Education,* 18(2), 112–125.

Porter, Andrew. (1989). A curriculum out of balance: The case of elementary school mathematics. *Educational Researcher,* 18(5), 9–15.

Resnick, L. B. (1986). The development of mathematical intuition. In M. Perlmutter (Ed.), *Perspectives on Intel-*

lectual Development: The Minnesota Symposia on Child Psychology (Vol. 19, pp. 159–194). Hillsdale, NJ: Erlbaum.

Resnick, L. B., Cauzinille-Marmeche, E., & Mathier, J. (1987). Understanding algebra. In J. A. Sloboda & D. Rogers (Eds.), *Cognitive processes in mathematics* (pp. 169–203). Oxford: Clarendon Press.

Resnick, L. B., & Omanson, S. F. (1987). Learning to understand arithmetic. In R. Glaser (Ed.), *Advances in instructional psychology* (pp. 41–95). Hillsdale, NJ: Erlbaum.

Romiszowski, A. J. (1981). *Designing Instructional Systems: Decision Making in Course Planning and Curriculum Design.* London: Kogan Page.

Rosenshine, B., & Stevens, R. (1984). Classroom instruction in reading. In D. Pearson (Ed.), *Handbook of research on teaching* (pp. 745–798). New York: Longman.

Rothman, R. (1988). Student proficiency in math is "dismal," NAEP indicates. *Education Week, 1,* 23–26.

Rucker, W. E., N. Dilley, C. A., & Lowry, D. A. (1987). *Heath mathematics.* Lexington, MA: Heath Publishing.

Schminke, C., Maeterns, N., & Arnold, W. (1978). *Teaching the child mathematics.* New York: Holt Publishing.

Slavin, R. E. (1990). Mastery learning reconsidered. *Review of Educational Research, 57,* 175–213.

Sowell, E. J. (1987). Developmental versus practice lessons in the primary grades. *The Arithmetic Teacher, 34*(7), 6-80.

Sprick, R. S., & Howard, L. M. (1995). *The teacher's encyclopedia of behavior management.* Longmont, CO: Sopris West.

Stallings, J. (1975). *Implementation and child effects of teaching practices in follow through classrooms.* Monographs of the Society for Research in Child Development, *40,* 50–93.

Stebbins, L., St. Pierre, R. G., Proper, E. C., Anderson, R. B., & Cerua, T. R. (1977). *Education as experimentation: A planned variation model,* Vol. IV A. Cambridge, MA: ABT Associates.

Stigler, J. W., & Faranes, R. (1988). Culture and mathematics learning. In E. Z. Rothkopf (Ed.), *Review of Research in Education,* 15.

Swing, S., & Peterson, P. (1988). Elaborative and integrative thought processes in mathematics learning. *Journal of Educational Psychology,* 80(1), 54–66.

Thornton, C. A. (1978). Emphasizing thinking strategies in basic fact instruction. *Journal of Research on Mathematics Education, 9,* 214–227.

Trafton, P. R. (1984). Toward more effective, efficient instruction in mathematics. *The Elementary School Journal, 84*(5), 514–530.

Underhill, R. G. (1981). *Teaching elementary school mathematics* (3rd ed.). Columbus, OH: Merrill Publishing.

Van Patten, J., Chao, C., and Reigeluth, C. M. (1986). A review of strategies for sequencing and synthesizing instruction. *Review of Educational Research, 56*(4), 437–471.

Wheatley, G. H., & McHugh, D. O. (1977). A comparison of two methods of column addition for pupils at three grade levels. *Journal of Research in Mathematics Education, 8*(5), 376–378.

Williams, P. B., & Carnine, D. W. (1981). Relationship between range of examples and of instructions and attention in concept attainment. *Journal of Educational Research, 74*(3), 144–148.

Woodward, J., Carnine, D., & Gersten, R. (1988). Teaching problem solving through computer simulations. *American Educational Research Journal, 25*(1), 72–86.

Zawojewski, J. (1983). Initial decimal concepts: Are they really so easy? *Arithmetic Teacher, 30*(7), 52–56.

Index